LAW AND JUDICIAL DUTY

LAW AND JUDICIAL DUTY

Philip Hamburger

Harvard University Press
Cambridge, Massachusetts, and London, England 2008

Printed in the United States of America

Library of Congress Cataloging-in-Publication Data

Hamburger, Philip, 1957–
Law and judicial duty / Philip Hamburger.
p. cm.
Includes bibliographical references and index.
ISBN-13: 978-0-674-03131-9 (alk. paper)
1. Judicial review—United States—History. 2. Judicial process—United States—History. 3. Constitutional law—United States.
I. Title.
KF4575.H36 2008
347.73'12—dc22 2008007121

In gratitude to my parents,
Joseph and Lotte Hamburger

. . . facturi quod ad justitiam pertinet secundum legem, & consuetudinem Angliæ . . .

Commissions to Judges

[W]e are almost daily called upon to minister justice according to law, whereunto we are bound by our office and our oath.

Opinion of the Judges (1591)

[I]t shall appear from time to time . . . where the King's acts have been indeed against law, the course of law hath run, and the Judges have worthily done their duty.

Francis Bacon (1610)

The duty of the Power I conceive, in all cases, is to decide according to the Laws of the State.

James Iredell (1786)

But it is said, if the Judges have this power, so have the County Courts. I admit it. The County Courts, in the exercise of equal judicial power, must have equal Authority.

James Iredell (1786)

CONTENTS

PREFACE

This book is part of a journey. The physical journey began more than a decade ago, when in the course of reading eighteenth-century newspapers and the correspondence of religious societies I occasionally stumbled across allusions to judicial decisions about constitutional law. These snippets of evidence intrigued me because they came from the first fifteen years following Independence—a period when judicial opinions in America were not regularly published and when there allegedly was little judicial review. Although for years I managed to push this early evidence to the back of my mind, I eventually made the foolhardy decision to edit the early records of constitutional decisions in the states. It struck me that this would involve little more than a brief stroll through materials I already knew with some intimacy. As I wandered through the evidence, however, more came into view, and the short walk became a long, meandering exploration that has repeatedly taken me up and down the eastern coast of the United States, from North Carolina through New England.

The intellectual journey has taken me even further, for in the course of editing the documents, it became apparent that the decisions did not fit within the conventional history of judicial review. There were many decisions; they did not all occur in cases; and they came from a wide range of courts, including mere county courts. Accordingly, the decisions that had once seemed simply curious soon revealed a conceptual framework very different from what I had assumed. By the end of the journey, it became apparent to me that when I began I had not even recognized what I was studying. Indeed, it became clear that "judicial review" is a misnomer and that what Americans in retrospect call "judicial review" was a much broader and more interesting phenomenon.

To explain these conclusions, I began to write a brief introduction to the documents—an introduction that has evolved into this separate and rather lengthy book. I hope—although I cannot be confident—it will one day be followed by two documentary volumes, which will in effect provide reports of constitutional decisions in the states from 1776 through 1791. In the meantime, this independent volume uses the evidence to reconsider what is known as "judicial review."

The Study of Ideals

Despite my intention to study judicial decisions, the evidence has led to a historical inquiry about a pair of ideals. Such an enterprise has risks, but also at least in this instance some advantages.

Among the risks is that this book will seem somewhat whiggish, both for focusing on ideas and for studying them as ideals. Certainly there would be perils in an exaggerated sort of history of ideals, in which the ideals of law and judicial duty were taken to be unchanging or uncontested or in which the ideals were confused with the motivations felt by judges or the reality of how they behaved. The need to avoid such distortions, however, is hardly a reason to avoid a history of ideals, and although no approach to the past is without its costs, the approach pursued here at least has the advantage of allowing one to understand the old ideals of law and judicial duty on their own terms. It will become apparent that "judicial review" is not an old ideal, but rather the sort of illusion that arises from looking into the past and seeing, as if in a mirror, an early reflection of modern assumptions. To escape this kind of history, in which the contemporary is observed in the past, it seems essential to examine the older ideals as they were then understood.

Another advantage of studying ideals is the opportunity to understand how men did what might otherwise seem improbable. An exploration of the "internal" logic of ideas has long been unfashionable. Yet only in a rarified sense can the logic of ideas and especially ideals be considered merely internal. Through their ideas and particularly their ideals, men responded to their circumstances—both to sort out their impressions of the world and to act in it—and although they frequently recalibrated and even adjusted their understandings of their ideals, they tended to do so because they relied on these conceptions of themselves and their conduct to get them through the difficulties they saw ahead. Much therefore about human action can only be understood by studying ideals. To be sure, like all human artifacts, ideals are apt to break down on close examination, and often their distance from reality is a source of weakness. Yet what is predictably a weakness in a mechanical device can at times be a strength in an ideal—as when a limit sets the upper bounds of a curve, which rises up to approach the line, though never quite reaching it. Here, it will be seen that through their ideals, even though not merely because of them, judges could rise above their mundane selves and thereby do what today is sometimes assumed to have been politically or intellectually impossible.[1]

Although scholarship on ideals has sometimes been divorced from social circumstances, this inquiry attempts to understand the ideals of law and judicial duty as responses to failures that seemed to lie at the very foundation of human life. Much has been said in the past century about studying human behavior in the context of material experience, but although detailed accounts of the material texture of experience can be valuable, what matters here is how men adopted their ideals in response to their perceptions of their circumstances and their associated fears and hopes. This book cannot adequately explore the underlying social circumstances of the ideals of law and judicial duty (whether at the national level, the professional, or the personal), but at a minimum it attempts to examine these common law ideals as responses to the problems contemporaries considered significant—as responses to enduring anxieties about human and social fractures. Of course, what today is understood sociologically then tended to be understood more theologically, but whether considered in one way or the other, the underlying difficulties and eventually also the solutions seemed inherent in men and their divided circumstances, and this gave the problems and the intellectual solutions much of their appeal, their strength, and their longevity.

In its attention to the continuity of the ideals of law and judicial duty, this book eventually runs up against the modern emphasis on revolutions and other new beginnings. The expectation of transformative possibilities has been profoundly appealing amid the restlessness of modern life, and it has seemed to confirm the strength of historical studies that concentrate on particular times and places, such as revolutionary America, in which men are assumed to have transcended their past. It is a flattering conception of history, at least for Americans, but the attention to human creativity and revolution can easily be taken so far as to give short shrift to the relative continuities in human development, including some conceptions of legal obligation and duty. An illustration of the hazards can be found in the writing of Gordon Wood, who argues that Americans in the wake of their

[1] Most explicit is Jack Rakove, who suggests that "[j]udicial review could only become possible after" various developments in popular political culture during the late 1770s and the 1780s. Jack N. Rakove, "The Origins of Judicial Review: A Plea for New Contexts," *Stanford Law Review,* 49: 1034 (1997).

revolution had the insight to invent modern constitutions and judicial review. These were part of "a revolutionary clarification in the Americans' understanding of law and of politics," which amounted, he acknowledges, to "a remarkable transformation, taking place as it did in such a relatively short period of time."[2] In a book entitled *The Creation of the American Republic,* such conclusions are apt to seem very satisfying, but in a book that takes a closer look at the American evidence and a broader view of its European context, it seems necessary to consider the possibility that Americans did not so much invent a judicial power as inherit ideals about law and judicial duty.

Ideals often seem unrealistic and unsophisticated, and this is how academically inclined lawyers have long viewed the common law ideals of law and judicial duty. Traditionally, lawyers of an academic bent tended to appreciate the learned law—the academic study of the civil and canon law they often pursued at university—for in this law they could enjoy wide-ranging intellectual inquiry, including an open acknowledgment of the incompleteness and injustice inherent in human law. It seemed to them only realistic to recognize that human law (and especially national custom) could not comprehend the breadth of human experience, and it therefore also seemed only realistic to admit that judges had to look beyond the law of the land. From this perspective, academically minded lawyers were apt to view the common law ideals as unrealistic, unjust, and even crude. The contempt, however, was often mutual, and most common lawyers were almost dogmatically indifferent to the academic vision of reality and justice. Common lawyers often quietly drew upon academic learning, but they persistently rejected the learned challenge to the common law ideals of law and judicial duty. In fact, common law sensibilities have nearly always to some extent conflicted with academic sensibilities—this persistent tension being part of the ancient, invaluable, but decidedly uncomfortable coexistence of national law and academic law. It will be seen that common lawyers typically had to deny or at least minimize the very "realities" that academics expected to see candidly acknowledged, for just as academically inclined men

[2] Gordon S. Wood, *The Creation of the American Republic 1776–1787,* at 305, 462 (Williamsburg: Institute of Early American History and Culture, 1969); Gordon S. Wood, "Judicial Review in the Era of the Founding," in *Is the Supreme Court the Guardian of the Constitution,* 157, ed. Robert A. Licht (Washington, D.C: AEI Press, 1993). All of this would lead to "a more radical reconstruction of their political system than anyone had conceived possible a few years earlier." *The Creation of the American Republic,* 463. See also 260, 292–293, 295, 304, 453–463; "Judicial Review in the Era of the Founding," 153, 157–158; Gordon S. Wood, "The Origins of Judicial Review," *Suffolk University Law Review,* 22: 1293, 1306 (1988).

frequently accentuated what they considered the realities in order to reshape common law ideals, so common lawyers often needed to insist on their blunt ideals to protect against the alleged realities. Academics should therefore be prepared in a study of common law ideals to find much they may initially consider unrefined and unrealistic, and it can only be hoped they will understand that common law sophistication was different from academic sophistication. Certainly, among those who valued common law ideals for their capacity to shape reality, such ideals were anything but unknowing.

Sources

In attempting to recover the ideals of law and judicial duty, this book relies on a wide range of printed and manuscript sources. For England, much important material has gradually been printed, and this study therefore turns to English manuscripts only for salient details—for example, to understand what Coke was really doing in his report of *Bonham's Case* and to illustrate that English judges actually held acts unconstitutional. For America, however, many of the most basic sources are unpublished, and manuscripts therefore take on greater significance. J. H. Baker observes how in England, before the development of adequate printed reports, lawyers frequently relied on manuscript accounts, and his argument about the consequent necessity of studying manuscripts is also applicable to the American states during the first fifteen years after Independence.[3] This book therefore attempts to reconstruct early American decisions and how they were understood by relying on manuscript reports, court records, judges' notebooks, collections of pleadings, legislative and executive files, private correspondence, newspaper commentaries, and student moots.[4] Such sources are plentiful, and many have been used here, but it cannot be overemphasized that numerous others remain to be found.

Quotations are reproduced in a form as close to the originals as permitted by printing conventions and readability. Underlined words are

[3] J. H. Baker, "The Dark Age of English Legal History," in *Legal History Studies,* 1, 5, ed. Dafydd Jenkins (Cardiff: University of Wales Press, 1975).

[4] There have been a few attempts to publish American manuscript reports from this period, including William Hamilton Bryson, *Miscellaneous Virginia Law Reports, 1784–1809: Being the Reports of Charles Lee, John Brown, David Watson & David Yancey* (Dobbs Ferry: Oceana, 1992), and the typescript of the William Cushing reports at Harvard, prepared for publication by John D. Cushing but sadly never published. Cushing also began an edition of the notes taken by Robert Treat Paine. For Charles Cullen's discovery of St. George Tucker's reports and the plans for an edition of these manuscripts, see Charles Hobson, "St. George Tucker's Law Papers," *William and Mary Law Review,* 47: 1250 (2006).

printed in italics. The orthography of quotations is modernized—for example, in printing an initial *ff* as an *F* and in printing the letters *j, s,* and *u* in place of earlier or Latinate variants (the only exception being that in quotations in Latin, the letter *i* is left unchanged). Similarly, for the convenience of readers, the slashes or virgules in early printed volumes appear here as commas, and abbreviations are occasionally expanded within brackets. Colons beneath superscripts are printed as periods. Otherwise, quotations are unmodified. Readers unaccustomed to older forms of spelling should therefore be warned that what appears to be the letter *y* in *ye* and *yt* is often a thorn, which is pronounced *th*—as in *the* and *that.*[5]

Although citations largely follow the usual conventions, some books seem familiar enough to be mentioned in abbreviated form. These include, for example, the standard editions of *The Dictionary of National Biography,* Howell's *State Trials,* and *Statutes of the Realm.* Unless otherwise indicated, citations to English nominate reporters follow either the earliest reliable English editions or the *English Reports.* Similarly, citations to Coke's *Institutes* rely on the second edition of the *First Institute* and the first editions of the others. State archives are cited by their familiar abbreviation—so that, for example, the North Carolina State Archives appears as "NCSA" and the Library of Virginia as "LVA." As for case names, those familiar from the printed reports are repeated without alteration, but otherwise cases are named with the plaintiff first.

Acknowledgments

My acknowledgments are both intellectual and personal. Over the past century, many scholars have carefully examined some of the manuscript sources, and although my argument rests on much unfamiliar material, it also relies on the invaluable work of the scholars who have done so much to document the cases, including John D. Cushing, Henry B. Dawson, Julius Goebel, Jr., Richard M. Lambert, William G. McLoughlin, William O'Brien, Austin Scott, William Michael Treanor, John Charles Waldrup, and Charles Warren. My understanding of the decisions tends to

[5] In a similar spirit of staying as close to the sources as possible, the book often reproduces early English translations of medieval and early modern sources. Particularly when truncated and Anglicized, early translations must be used with caution, but when they express forceful ideas in equally robust prose, they command attention in ways that modern translations sometimes do not, and at the very least they suggest how the English appropriated Continental ideas.

be rather different from theirs, but my debt to them is not therefore less substantial.

Among many colleagues who shared their learning with me, I am particularly grateful to Barbara Black, William Hamilton Bryson, Bradford Clark, Jacob Corré, Marc DeGirolami, Michael Dorf, Charles Gray, Kevin Grove, Michael Hoeflich, Emily Kadens, Harry Kavros, Carol Lee, Renee Lerner, V. Bradley Lewis, James Lindgren, Barbara Oberg, Liam O'Melinn, Kenneth Pennington, David Seipp, Robert Somerville, John Witt, and last but not least Jody Armstrong, Richard Helmholz, Richard Kay, Henry Monaghan, and the three anonymous readers for Harvard University Press, who read the entire manuscript and offered many suggestions as to how it could be improved. It was invaluable, moreover, to be able to use David Seipp's *Abridgement* of the Yearbooks and to study the English manuscripts that Jacob Corré and Charles Gray kindly drew to my attention. When my own efforts flagged, a series of superb research assistants—Robert Bailey, Michael Cabin, Corinne O'Melia, Daniel Hibshoosh, David Levitt, Spencer Marsden, Diana Silverman, Brando Starkey, and Benjamin Vetter—came to my aid, and I am deeply grateful to each of them. In addition, I am indebted to Mary Harney and Lovetta Holmes, who did such careful typing, and the *George Washington Law Review,* which in 2003 published an initial rough sketch of the arguments presented here.[6]

Perhaps most fundamentally, I am obliged to the librarians, archivists, curators, and court clerks whose manuscripts I have examined. Among those who have generously assisted me with collecting materials, I must particularly thank Brigitte Burkett; the clerk of the Supreme Court of Virginia David B. Beach; the clerk of the Strafford Superior Court Julie W. Howard; and above all Margaret Schilt at the University of Chicago Law School and Aslihan Bulut at the Columbia Law School, who helped me obtain innumerable books, microfilms, and photocopies. My experiences in various state archives, historical societies, religious societies, and courthouses has been deeply satisfying, for in these institutions the largely unread records of American law remain to be explored, and they offer riches to anyone who takes the time to read them.

For their kindness in allowing me to quote materials in their possession, I am grateful to many public and private institutions: the British Library; the Library of Congress; the Folger Shakespeare Library; the Huntington Library; the Connecticut State Archives; the Massachusetts State

[6] Philip Hamburger, "Law and Judicial Duty," *George Washington Law Review,* 72: 1 (2003).

Archives; the Massachusetts Historical Society; the American Antiquarian Society; the Phillips Library, Peabody Essex Museum; the Franklin Trask Library, Andover Newton Theological School; the New Hampshire State Archives; the New Hampshire Historical Society; the Strafford County Court, New Hampshire; the New Jersey State Archives; the New Jersey Historical Society; Monmouth County Archives; Princeton University Department of Rare Books and Manuscripts; the New York Historical Society; the North Carolina State Archives; the Friends Historical Collection, Hege Library of Guilford College, Greensboro; Duke University Rare Book, Manuscript, and Special Collections Library; the Southern Historical Collection, University of North Carolina at Chapel Hill; the Pennsylvania Historical Society; the Rhode Island State Archives; the Rhode Island Judicial Archives, Supreme Court Judicial Center; the Rhode Island Historical Society; the Newport Historical Society; the South Carolina Archives; the Library of Virginia; the Virginia Historical Society; the Swem Library, College of William and Mary; the Baltimore Orthodox Friends; the Valentine Museum, Richmond; the Fairfax Circuit Court Archives, Virginia; the Middlesex County Court, Virginia; the Northampton County Court, Virginia; the York County Court, Virginia.

Finally, I owe much to Michael Aronson and everyone else at Harvard University Press who has taken such good care of my manuscript.

Introduction

Almost every day a judge in the United States holds a statute unconstitutional. This is "judicial review," and it often seems the central feature of American constitutional law.

American constitutions, however, are almost silent about judicial review. Even today, they scarcely mention the power of judges to decide constitutional questions. The power of judges to hold statutes unlawful and void is therefore a puzzle. Where does this power come from? And what is its character and scope?

The familiar answer to these questions comes in the form of a history of "judicial review." According to the conventional version of this history, the American people in the 1770s and 1780s discovered the principle of popular power and thereby invented written constitutions. The people, however, apparently did not foresee how their constitutions should be enforced. Fortunately—so the story goes—the judges discerned the possibility of enforcing constitutions in their cases, and they made some fitful experiments in this direction in the 1780s and then more confidently in the 1790s. Although they could draw upon earlier, English and colonial traditions, they had to develop the mechanism of reviewing enactments for their unconstitutionality, and they most decisively settled the authority of this new power in 1803 in *Marbury v. Madison.* Evidently, although the people created their constitutions, the judges had to complete the creation of American government by developing and finally establishing their own most significant power.

Even the most familiar stories, however, can turn out to be misleading, and few stories about America are as misleading as that about judicial review. The history and its implications rest on the fragile assumption that there is little evidence of judicial review from the decade and a half after

1776—this being the basis for concluding that American judges must have created this power. The evidence admittedly is meager if one looks for a concept of judicial review—a concept of a judicial power to hold statutes unconstitutional. Yet if one does not look for something so modern, there is much evidence—not of a power of judicial review, but of a duty of judges to decide in accord with the law of the land. The evidence thus reveals the history of judicial review to be largely an illusion produced by modern assumptions, and in its place the evidence supplies another, much broader history—that of law and judicial duty.

The History of Judicial Review

For more than a century, much scholarship has been done within the framework of what is here called "the history of judicial review." This scholarship tends to be very learned, and it is frequently relied upon here, but the framework itself must be questioned. It will soon be seen that eighteenth-century judges did not understand themselves to have a distinct power of review and that it is therefore misleading to inquire about their conception of such a power. Before reaching this conclusion, however, it is first necessary to linger within the framework provided by the history of judicial review. In particular, it is necessary to understand why scholars study the origins of judicial review and why this sort of history almost inevitably becomes one of judicial self-empowerment.

The problem that gives rise to the history of judicial review is the apparent lack of authority for this power in American constitutions. The various state constitutions said almost nothing about any such power. The U.S. Constitution, moreover, in 1789, directly authorized only a very narrow type of judicial review—that "the judges in every state shall be bound" by federal law notwithstanding contrary state law—but this apparently did not extend to federal judges; nor for that matter to state judges under their state constitutions.[1] It is therefore difficult to avoid the conclusion that the judges themselves developed and established their power of review.

[1] According to Article VI of the U.S. Constitution, "This Constitution, and the Laws of the United States which shall be made in Pursuance thereof; and all Treaties made, or which shall be made, under the Authority of the United States, shall be the supreme Law of the Land; and the Judges in every State shall be bound thereby, any Thing in the Constitution or Laws of any State to the Contrary notwithstanding." Julius Goebel hints that this applied to "all judges," federal as well as state. Julius Goebel, Jr., *History of the Supreme Court of the United States: Antecedents and Beginnings to 1801,* 1: 239 (New York: Macmillan, 1971). This, however, would suggest that the framers meant to exclude judges in the federal district, not to mention the territories, which is, to say the least, improbable.

The most popular version of the history focuses on *Marbury v. Madison.* This version acknowledges that by 1803 state and federal judges had already experimented in holding statutes unconstitutional, and it recognizes that after 1789 they could draw on the Constitution's incomplete hints about judicial power, but it emphasizes that in 1803, in *Marbury,* Chief Justice John Marshall gave judicial review the force of an unimpeachable precedent of the U.S. Supreme Court.[2] Marshall would thus seem to have been the founding father of judicial review, and his opinion in *Marbury* its authorizing text.

Of course, there are less implausible variations on the theme of judicial self-authorization, and some identify earlier origins, but without displacing the suggestion that the judges themselves established their power of review. For example, after examining the debates in Philadelphia during the summer of 1787, Charles Beard and many later scholars suggest that "judicial control" was "the intention of the framers of the Constitution."[3] Certainly the framers recognized that judges would sometimes hold enactments unconstitutional. Yet this makes it all the more puzzling that the Constitution explicitly authorized only a very confined portion of such re-

[2] For the way in which Americans later created this story, see Davison M. Douglas, "The Rhetorical Uses of *Marbury v. Madison:* The Emergence of a 'Great Case,'" *Wake Forest Law Review,* 38: 375 (2003); G. Edward White, "The Constitutional Journey of Marbury v. Madison," ibid., 1463.

[3] Charles A. Beard, *The Supreme Court and the Constitution,* 15–16 (New York: Paisley, 1938). See also Charles A. Beard, "The Supreme Court—Usurper or Grantee," *Political Science Quarterly,* 27: 1 (1912). A recent example is Saikrishna B. Prakash and John C. Yoo, "The Origins of Judicial Review," *University of Chicago Law Review,* 70: 893 (2003).

In support of this point, many scholars of the state cases of the 1780s argue that the framers in Philadelphia knew about some of these decisions. Austin Scott, "Holmes v. Walton: The New Jersey Precedent: A Chapter in the History of Judicial Power and Unconstitutional Legislation," *American Historical Review,* 4: 464, 467–468 (1899); Brinton Coxe, *An Essay on Judicial Power and Unconstitutional Legislation,* 266 (New York: Da Capo, 1970); William Winslow Crosskey, *Politics and the Constitution in the History of the United States,* 2: 970–971, 973 (Chicago: University of Chicago Press, 1953); Gordon S. Wood, "The Origins of Judicial Review," *Suffolk University Law Review,* 22: 1295 (1988); Patrick T. Conley, "Rhode Island's Paper Money Issue and Trevett v. Weedon (1786)," in *Rhode Island History,* 30: 107 (1971).

Jack Rakove suggests that the framers invented judicial review as a means of enforcing federal law against the states—his argument being that what began as an ingenious solution to the problem of federalism was later developed by the judges into a more complete judicial review. Jack N. Rakove, "The Origins of Judicial Review: A Plea for New Contexts," *Stanford Law Review,* 49: 1031, 1064 (1997); Jack N. Rakove, *Original Meanings: Politics and Ideas in the Making of the Constitution,* 175 (New York: Knopf, 1997). If judicial review, however, was a product of concerns about federalism in the summer of 1787, it is puzzling that the Constitution failed to specify that federal judges were bound to review state acts under federal law. Indeed, it will be seen that state judges had already reached decisions about the constitutionality of state legislation under the Articles of Confederation.

view. If the framers understood judicial review but did not directly authorize more than part of it, then there still was work to be done. Evidently, it was the judges in their later cases who more completely established this power.

Rather than accept this focus on 1787 and later cases, another version of the history looks back to a handful of state cases from the 1780s.[4] In this account, most notably expounded by Gordon Wood, judicial review developed during the 1780s, particularly toward the end of the decade, because this allegedly was when Americans came to have respect for their judges and came to view constitutions unambiguously as ordinary law—the sort of law that was subject to ordinary adjudication.[5] Sylvia Snowiss cautions that at first judicial review must have been "an extraordinary political act" rather than part of the judges' "conventional legal responsibility," but she otherwise agrees that judicial review first developed in the 1780s.[6] With this sort of focus on a single decade, some scholars even go so far as to seize on an individual case in the 1780s (or even just a single document relating to such a case) as a distinctively important and influential contribution to the new theory of judicial power. One way or another, the concentration on early state cases pushes the development of judicial review back before the summer 1787, but it necessarily assumes a "massive rethinking . . . in the

4 For example, see Goebel, *History of the Supreme Court of the United States,* at 1: 126, 142; William E. Nelson, "Changing Conceptions of Judicial Review: The Evolution of Constitutional Theory in the States, 1790–1860," *University of Pennsylvania Law Review,* 120: 1166 (1972); Richard M. Lambert, "The 'Ten Pound Act' Cases and the Origins of Judicial Review in New Hampshire," *New Hampshire Bar Journal,* 53 (2002). Treanor notes that there were many decisions prior to *Marbury,* but at the same time, he emphasizes the significance of the decisions after 1791, and for the period up through that date, he focuses on the familiar cases. William Michael Treanor, "Judicial Review Before Marbury," *Stanford Law Review,* 58: 473 (2005).

5 Gordon S. Wood, *The Creation of the American Republic 1776–1787,* at 292, 454 (Williamsburg: Institute of Early American History and Culture, 1969); Gordon S. Wood, "Judicial Review in the Era of the Founding," in *Is the Supreme Court the Guardian of the Constitution,* 153, 157–158, ed. Robert A. Licht (Washington, D.C: AEI Press, 1993).

Notwithstanding the arguments of Wood, respect for the judges and an appreciation of the ideal of independence were different matters, and some elegant and detailed studies reveal that Americans already before Independence were keenly aware of the need for constitutional guarantees of independence. Barbara Aronstein Black, "Massachusetts and the Judges: Judicial Independence in Perspective," *Law and History Review,* 3: 101, 162 (1985); Joseph H. Smith, "An Independent Judiciary: The Colonial Background," *University of Pennsylvania Law Review,* 124: 1104 (1976). Moreover, even at the time of *Bayard v. Singleton*—the 1787 North Carolina case that is most widely accepted as an early instance of judicial review—the state's judges were held in utter contempt by much of the bar.

6 Sylvia Snowiss, *Judicial Review and the Law of the Constitution,* 2 (New Haven: Yale University Press, 1990).

1780s"—even a "quasi-revolutionary process"—and it thus reinforces the conclusion that judicial review was established by the judges.[7]

Seeking yet earlier foundations for judicial review, Mary Bilder and other historians explore the judicial enforcement of English law and charters against colonial and corporate acts. Both English and American courts held colonial and corporate acts contrary to English law, and these decisions are clearly significant for the question of "judicial review."[8] Yet while the early corporate and colonial decisions are suggestive, it is not apparent exactly how they relate to the later decisions about state statutes, unless there was a more general concept of review.[9] Without some such general concept—one broad enough to explain both pre- and post-1776 cases—the early corporate and colonial decisions seem little more than roughly analogous precursors to the later, more ambitious cases that held state and federal statutes unconstitutional. Without some overarching concept, moreover,

[7] Wood, "Judicial Review in the Era of the Founding," 157; Gordon S. Wood, "The Origins of Judicial Review Revisited, or How the Marshall Court Made More Out of Less," *Washington and Lee Law Review,* 56: 796, note 41. As Wood recognizes, this would mean "[i]t was a remarkable transformation, taking place as it did in such a relatively short period of time." "Judicial Review in the Era of the Founding," 157. Rakove agrees that this is a "puzzle" but does not challenge the underlying assumption of "massive rethinking." Rakove, "The Origins of Judicial Review," 1063.

[8] For the Privy Council's review of colonial legislation, see Mary Sarah Bilder, *The Transatlantic Constitution* (Cambridge: Harvard University Press, 2004); Joseph Henry Smith, *Appeals to the Privy Council from the American Plantations* (New York: Columbia University Press, 1950); Elmer Beecher Russell, *The Review of American Colonial Legislation by the King in Council* (New York: Longmans, Green, 1915); Arthur Meier Schlesinger, "Colonial Appeals to the Privy Council," *Political Science Quarterly,* 28: 279 and 433 (1913). For corporate acts, see Mary Sarah Bilder, "The Corporate Origins of Judicial Review," *Yale Law Journal,* 116: 513–535 (2006); Philip Hamburger, "Revolution and Judicial Review: Chief Justice Holt's Opinion in *City of London v. Wood,*" *Columbia Law Review* 94: 2140 (1994); Philip Hamburger, "Law and Judicial Duty," *George Washington Law Review,* 72: 13 (2003); Barbara Aronstein Black, "An Astonishing Political Innovation: The Origins of Judicial Review," *University of Pittsburgh Law Review,* 49: 962–963 (1988); Smith, *Appeals to the Privy Council,* 525.

[9] Wood and those who follow him avoid this problem by suggesting there was a "massive rethinking" or revolution in ideas during the 1780s. From another perspective, it is suggested here (and in a preliminary sketch of this argument) that the relation of the corporate and colonial decisions to the later decisions under American constitutions can be explained by the persistence of general ideals of law and judicial duty. Hamburger, "Law and Judicial Duty," 13. Mary Bilder questions this account of conceptual continuity by emphasizing the practical experience acquired by Americans in the early corporate and colonial decisions—suggesting that judicial review arose from "[e]xperience . . . rather than logic." Bilder, "The Corporate Origins of Judicial Review," 509. The focus on practice and experience, almost below the level of general ideas, offers a sharp contrast to Wood's assumptions about a revolutionary rethinking, but it still leaves open how judges understood their corporate, colonial, and state cases to be connected.

these subsequent cases have continued to seem an innovation—a dramatic contribution to law and politics by the judges of the new world. The innovative character of judicial review becomes almost inescapable when it is recognized as a review of the legislation of sovereign states. This may have been loosely derived from English and colonial antecedents, but it must have been developed and established after 1776 by American judges.

Last, but not least, some commentators associate judicial review with natural law. From this vantage point, in the words of Andrew C. McLaughlin, "[l]imitations arising from natural rights were . . . *legal* limitations," and the judges thus reviewed acts not only under American constitutions but also under natural law.[10] In the version popularized by Edward S. Corwin, constitutions partook of the character of natural law, and these two types of law together formed a vague "higher law."[11] Gordon Wood and others pursue this suggestion of blurred lines between the natural and the positive. Associating express American constitutions with their "source" in natural law, Wood and those who follow him argue that there was a "basic ambiguity"—indeed, "a peculiar confusion in the American mind about the nature of law—and that the depth of this confusion only gradually became evident in the years after Independence."[12] There is much to be said for considering judicial review in the context of higher laws—but not necessarily only natural law, and not in a way that attributes twentieth-century confusion to eighteenth-century Americans. Of course, the historians who think judges could hold statutes void under natural law seize upon such hints as they can find to anchor their account in English law, but their strained understanding of the English sources (including *Bonham's Case*) only reinforces the suspicion that there is little English evidence.[13] Thus, even if judicial review was suggested by English judges, it apparently became a practical phenomenon only in the hands of American judges—occasionally in the colonies, more substantially in the states, and most de-

[10] Andrew C. McLaughlin, *The Courts, The Constitution and Parties,* 75 (Chicago: University of Chicago Press, 1912). See also ibid., 77; Charles G. Haines, *The Revival of Natural Law Concepts,* 80 (Cambridge: Harvard University Press, 1930).

[11] Edward S. Corwin, "The 'Higher Law' Background of American Constitutional Law," *Harvard Law Review,* 42: 149, 152 (1928).

[12] Wood, *The Creation of the American Republic,* at 292–293, 295; Wood, "Judicial Review in the Era of the Founding," 153, 157–158; Rakove, "The Origins of Judicial Review," 1034; Snowiss, *Judicial Review and the Law of the Constitution,* 2–8, 45–59.

[13] See, for example, McLaughlin, *The Courts, The Constitution and Parties,* 75–77; Theodore F. T. Plucknett, "Bonham's Case and Judicial Review," *Harvard Law Review,* 40: 61–68 (1938); Charles G. Haines, *The American Doctrine of Judicial Supremacy,* 61–62 (New York: Da Capo, 1973); Robert Cook, "Judicial Review and Legislative Power," in *South Carolina Legal History,* 86, ed. Herbert A. Johnson (1980); Allen Dillard Boyer, "'Understanding, Au-

cisively in federal courts, culminating in *Marbury* in the U.S. Supreme Court.[14]

Whether in looking back to 1803, 1787, the earlier years of the 1780s, the colonial period, or the eternity of natural law, these different versions of the history of judicial review all leave the impression that American judges established this power for themselves. These judges could draw on past experience, and they therefore did not have to construct judicial review out of whole cloth, but because they had so little direct authority in their constitutions, they evidently had to develop and institute their review of acts for their constitutionality, and they thus appear to have provided the authority for their own greatest power.

The Logic of Judicial Review

The implication of the history—that judicial review has its authority from the judges—troubles some distinguished scholars of constitutional law, who respond that a more grounded sort of authority can be discerned in the logic underlying judicial review. Rather than attempt to give a full historical account, these scholars examine salient points in the history—usually 1803 and 1787—to draw attention to the logical assumptions from which judicial review can be derived. Yet in pursuing the logic that might support a new judicial function, these scholars miss the more traditional and general logic of judicial duty, and in relying on texts from 1787 and 1803, they seem to suggest that the judges still had to elicit and give shape to the inchoate logic. In both ways, the scholarly observations about the logic exacerbate rather than put to rest the history's implication that the judges authorized their own power to hold acts unconstitutional.

The pursuit of the logic underlying judicial review is familiar from the standard approach to teaching *Marbury v. Madison*—an approach that rests on the significance of deciding cases. Marshall argued in *Marbury* that when judges decide cases, they have "to say what the law is," for "[t]hose

---

thority, and Will': Sir Edward Coke and the Elizabethan Origins of Judicial Review," *Boston College Law Review*, 39: 43 (1997). Even the commentators on the Privy Council's review of colonial legislation treat *Bonham's Case* as a foundation for the Council's review. Smith, *Appeals to the Privy Council*, 524–527; Dudley Odell McGovney, "The British Origin of Judicial Review of Legislation," *University of Pennsylvania Law Review*, 93: 8, 40, 41 (1944). From a slightly different perspective, Corwin focuses on Otis's use of *Bonham's Case*. Edward S. Corwin, *The Doctrine of Judicial Review: Its Legal and Historical Basis and Other Essays*, 31 (Gloucester: Peter Smith, 1963).

[14] *Bonham's Case* (C.P. 1610), Coke, *Reports*, 8: 118a. For more on *Bonham's Case*, see Appendix I.

who apply the rule to particular cases, must of necessity expound and interpret that rule," and "if both the law and the constitution apply to a particular case . . . the court must determine which of these conflicting rules governs the case." Generations of law students have been taught from these words to regard judicial review as the logical outcome of cases, and with this approach to *Marbury* lawyers can understand the decision as derived from premises discernible in law. Judicial review thus becomes a conclusion of law—even if one that Marshall had to spell out and establish in a decisive precedent.

Although this pursuit of *Marbury's* logic can locate analytical foundations for judicial review, it does not make much of a dent in the history of judicial review or its implication that the authority for this power came from the judges themselves. One difficulty is that by relying on a case that postdates the Constitution, such analysis suggests that the judges still had to develop and give substance to the logic of judicial review. A deeper problem is that the study of *Marbury's* logic focuses on what is necessary for deciding cases and thus does not adequately explore *Marbury's* allusions to the traditional ideals of law and judicial duty. It is true that, in order to decide their cases, judges must expound the law. Yet while it is important to understand *when* a judge must decide a constitutional question, this does not resolve *how* he should do so or *what* has the obligation of law, and by compressing these profound questions into the reasoning about deciding cases, the scholarly treatment of *Marbury's* logic tends to omit much of the logical and historical depth. Marshall understood the importance of these more basic questions, and although he did not bother with detailed answers, he gave two fleeting hints. As to law, he asked, "[i]f an act of the legislature, repugnant to the constitution, is void . . . does it constitute a rule as operative as if it was a law?" With respect to duty, he said that the court must decide which of the conflicting rules—the law or the constitution—governs a case, and he then explained, "[t]his is of the very essence of judicial duty."[15] Marshall thus briefly alluded to the pair of ideas that occupy so much of this book, but because he could take them for granted, he made no effort to explain them. Not recognizing the depths of what Marshall simply assumed, scholars of judicial review miss the logical and historical foundations provided by the ideals of law and judicial duty, and they therefore end up concentrating on Marshall's more explicit but less fundamental point about deciding cases. The inquiry about *Marbury's* logic thus not only focuses on a case that postdates the Constitution but also largely bypasses the old, foundational ideals that would allow one to understand the degree to which

[15] *Marbury v. Madison* (1803), Cranch, *Reports,* 1: 178–179.

Marshall was engaged in very traditional judicial reasoning. In both ways, rather than displace the suspicion that judicial review derives from the judges, the inquiry about *Marbury's* logic makes Marshall's opinion seem an act of intellectual prowess in which he and his brethren largely established their own power.

Another effort to discern the logic undergirding judicial review focuses on the U.S. Constitution. Scholars ranging from Herbert Wechsler to Bradford Clark explore how judicial review was assumed in various provisions of the Constitution, and they thereby suggest that, at least in this manner, judicial review was authorized in 1787.[16] Their attention to what was taken for granted in 1787 will be seen to be well justified—though not specifically as to a power of judicial review. Yet even if there was such a power and it was implicitly authorized by the Constitution, it remains unexplained how the power came to be taken for granted and why the Constitution only gave direct authorization for part of it. The attempt to locate the logic of judicial review beneath the surface of the Constitution has thus left the impression that the judges in 1787 still had to develop this power of review and make it practical. The judges may have been able to work with some implicit logic, but the work was very much theirs.

The scholarly analysis of the underlying logic thus offers some legitimacy for judicial review, but it has not displaced the history of judicial self-authorization. The reality remains that the U.S. Constitution expressly authorized only a limited range of decisions holding acts unconstitutional, and it is difficult to overcome this apparent lack of authority without assuming that the judges themselves did much to authorize their power of review.

Implications for Judicial Power

The history of how judges developed "judicial review" has consequences for judicial power. By shifting the constitutional authority for judicial review from the Constitution to the judges, the history appears to imply that the judges enjoy control over the scope and exercise of judicial review—thus leaving them power over their own role in enforcing the Constitution.

[16] Herbert Wechsler, "Toward Neutral Principles of Constitutional Law," *Harvard Law Review,* 73: 3 (1959); Bradford Clark, "Unitary Judicial Review," *George Washington Law Review,* 72: 319 (2003); Prakash and Yoo, "The Origins of Judicial Review," 70: 892. When Louis Pollack asked Barbara Black to speak about "this astonishing political innovation" at the bicentenary of the Constitution, she responded that "[w]hat is astonishing is not that they thought of it, but that they did it." Barbara Aronstein Black, "An Astonishing Political Innovation: The Origins of Judicial Review," *University of Pittsburgh Law Review,* 49: 697 (1988).

Initially, the history of judicial review seemed to call into doubt the legitimacy of judicial review, for if the framers "intended the Court to have the power, why did they not provide for it?"[17] On such assumptions, some commentators almost a century ago charged the judges with "usurpation." Fifty years later, many scholars still treated judicial review as "a debatable proposition," and they thereby questioned the authority of judicial expositions of the Constitution, arguing that all branches of government enjoy a power of interpretation.[18] Today, going even further, Larry Kramer suggests that constitutional interpretation rests fundamentally in the people.[19]

Judicial power, however, has come to seem less troubling than it did to earlier generations, and commentators therefore increasingly assume that the judicial creation of judicial review was but a singularly important example of an inevitable judicial discretion over constitutional law.[20] Aban-

[17] Leonard W. Levy, "Judicial Review, History, and Democracy," in *Judicial Review and the Supreme Court,* 2, ed. Leonard W. Levy (New York: Harper Torchbooks, 1967). In the words of William Trickett half a century earlier, "They could have made their intention . . . clear with a line. . . . *Why did not they not write that line?*" in *American Constitutional History: Essays by Edward S. Corwin,* xi, eds. Alpheus T. Mason and Gerald Garvey (New York: Harper Torchbooks, 1964). Similarly, Crosskey argues that the legislative opposition to judicial review in the states would have "enforced upon the men of the Convention the need of stipulating the right of judicial review in the Constitution, and of protecting the Supreme Court in the exercise of it, if they meant that body to have it." Crosskey, *Politics and the Constitution,* 2: 971.

[18] Levy, "Judicial Review, History, and Democracy," 3, quoting Alan F. Westin. Learned Hand wrote that "when the Constitution emerged from the Convention . . . the structure of the proposed government, if one looked to the text, gave no ground for inferring that the decisions of the Supreme Court, and *a fortiori* of the lower courts, were to be authoritative upon the Executive and the Legislature." Learned Hand, *The Bill of Rights,* 15 (1958; New York: Atheneum, 1964). In a rather crotchety version of this position, Crosskey argues that judges exercised their power of judicial review in defense of their own power or independence—that "the judiciary . . . had the right 'to declare the nullity of a law . . .' *only* if the law invaded the prerogatives of the judiciary itself, as these were established by the constitution." Crosskey, *Politics and the Constitution,* 2: 955. Somewhat similarly, another scholar responds to the absence of constitutional authority for judicial review by suggesting that there is only authority for a minimalist version of it—that judges developed judicial review when merely attempting to avoid their own violations of law and that they otherwise could not review legislation. Robert Lowry Clinton, *Marbury v. Madison and Judicial Review,* 1 (Lawrence: University Press of Kansas, 1989). It will be seen, however, that judges conceived of what they were doing in terms of a judicial duty to decide in *accord* with the law of the land, not merely a duty to act *under* such law.

[19] Larry D. Kramer, *The People Themselves: Popular Constitutionalism and Judicial Review,* 11–12, 24, 95, 127, 253 (New York: Oxford University Press, 2004); Larry D. Kramer, "Foreword: We the Court," *Harvard Law Review,* 115: 10, 19, 33, note 115 (2001).

[20] For the development of such thinking since *Marbury,* see Christopher Wolfe, *The Rise of Modern Judicial Review: From Constitutional Interpretation to Judge-Made Law* (New York:

doning the word "usurpation," they propose that even if judicial review lacks much authority in the U.S. Constitution, it has a broad basis in judicial power and American society. Alexander Bickel writes that "the power of judicial review . . . cannot be found" in the constitution and that therefore "the institution of the judiciary needed to be summoned up out of the constitutional vapors, shaped, and maintained;" but "[i]f any social process can be said to have been 'done' at a given time and by a given act, it is Marshall's achievement . . . in the case of *Marbury v. Madison.*"[21] Less confident that the Chief Justice somehow accomplished so much in a single case, other scholars combine judicial creativity and public acquiescence to overcome the absence of authority in the U.S. Constitution. As put by Eugene Rostow, judicial review "stands now, whatever the Founding Fathers may in fact have meant, as an integral feature of the living constitution, long since established as a working part of the democratic political life of the nation."[22] Although perhaps not "the intention of the Founding Fathers," it is "part of the living constitution."[23]

With this attribution of judicial review to the judges, the history of judicial review gives legitimacy to a broad judicial control over the extent and exercise of judicial power. Justice Jackson argues that "[s]ince the power was not disclosed by the instrument, it follows that it was not limited or regulated by it" and concludes that "[w]hen the power should come into play" and "by what caution and safeguards it would be hedged" were matters left to "evolution of what we know as 'Judicial Supremacy.'"[24] In his more academic manner, Bickel writes that "the Framers expected the Supreme Court to exercise a power of judicial review," but that the framers "had no specific

---

Basic Books, 1986). See also Davison M. Douglas, "The Rhetorical Uses of *Marbury v. Madison:* The Emergence of a 'Great Case,'" *Wake Forest Law Review,* 38: 375 (2003).

[21] Alexander M. Bickel, *The Least Dangerous Branch: The Supreme Court at the Bar of Politics,* 1 (1962; New Haven: Yale University Press, 1986). Bickel thus distinguished between what "cannot be found" in the Constitution and what could "be placed in the Constitution." Ibid.

[22] Eugene V. Rostow, "The Supreme Court and the People's Will," *Notre Dame Law Review,* 33: 576 (1958).

[23] Eugene V. Rostow, "The Democratic Character of Judicial Review," in *Judicial Review and the Supreme Court,* 77–78, ed. Leonard W. Levy (1967). Levy writes: "The legitimacy of judicial review does rest on history, but not on the words of the Constitution nor of the framers during the 1787–1789 period." Levy, "Judicial Review, History, and Democracy," 2, 7, 12. According to Nelson, "*Marbury v. Madison* was a truly seminal case, which ultimately has conferred vast power on the Supreme Court," and "[w]hat makes the case even more important is the absence of any clear plan on the part of the Constitution's framers to provide the Court with this power." William E. Nelson, *Marbury v. Madison: The Origins and Legacy of Judicial Review,* 1 (Lawrence: University of Kansas Press, 2000).

[24] Robert H. Jackson, *The Struggle for Judicial Supremacy,* 5 (New York: Knopf, 1941).

intent relating to the nature and range of the power and to the modalities of its exercise," from which Bickel concludes that "judicial review is an issue in the allocation of competences."[25] The weakness of the authority for judicial review under the Constitution thus suggests the strength of judicial power over such review. As Charles Black complains, "the 'usurpation' myth"—the theory that the judges in *Marbury* created their own power—"profoundly colors some fashionable attitudes toward judicial review."[26]

The judicial discretion implied by the history becomes especially clear from the claims that judges can vary their enforcement of constitutional law. Building on Justice Harlan Fiske Stone's suggestion in *Carolene Products* that the judges can adopt different degrees of "judicial scrutiny," Learned Hand argues that "nothing in the United States Constitution . . . gave courts any authority to review the decisions of Congress," and that "since this power is not a logical deduction from the structure of the Constitution but only a practical condition upon its successful operation, it need not be exercised whenever a court sees, or thinks it sees, an invasion of the Constitution. It is always a preliminary question how importunately the occasion demands an answer."[27] In response to this suggestion of different standards of review, Herbert Wechsler famously defended what he called "neutral principles" by arguing that judicial review was "grounded in the language of the Constitution," but his task was not easy, for he lacked a clear conception of judicial duty, and he had to work from the Constitution's apparently incomplete language. He therefore has left the impression that even if judicial review was logically evident in the Constitution, the judges still had to tease out and establish the implications, and if the judges apparently had to do so much of what was necessary to establish their power of review, it is difficult to avoid the conclusion that they can decide when and how to employ it.[28]

The weakness of the constitutional authority has left the judges to analyze their power in terms of political theory. If the U.S. Constitution did not authorize judicial review, "the function must be supported by . . . other reasons," and with this sense that judicial review rests on functional justifications, Bickel concluded that "there will . . . be instances when it seems justifiable to exercise judicial review more vigorously against the states than the federal legislature or executive, and instances calling for less vigor as

25 Bickel, *The Least Dangerous Branch,* 104.
26 Charles L. Black, Jr., *The People and the Court,* 27 (New York: Macmillan, 1960).
27 *United States v. Carolene Products Co.,* 304 U.S. 144, 152, note 4 (1938); Hand, *The Bill of Rights,* 10, 15.
28 Wechsler, "Toward Neutral Principles of Constitutional Law," 3, 10.

well"—the latter being times for prudence and what Bickel called the "passive virtues."[29] The theory invited by the apparently weak constitutional authority for judicial review has thus appeared to suggest that judges should adjust the severity of their review in accord with a wide range of considerations, including the judges' institutional competence, the danger from different levels of government, the importance of different types of rights, and the political circumstances of different social groups. In one version or another, this sort of political theorizing has been the preeminent mode of analyzing judicial review for half a century, and after being intimated by Hand and Bickel, and elaborated by Jesse Choper and John Hart Ely, it has become profoundly influential.[30]

The history of judicial review thus creates an opening for an expansive judicial power. If judges established their power of review on their own authority, they would appear to have control over the character and exercise of

[29] Bickel, *The Least Dangerous Branch,* 33, Chapter 4 (The Passive Virtues). For "prudential judgment," see ibid., 142.

[30] Choper argues that "[w]hen judicial review is unnecessary for the effective preservation of our constitutional scheme," particularly when it is unnecessary "to protect individual rights," the Court "should decline to exercise its authority"—a point he rests on the historical assumption that "the constitutional text provides neither explicit nor firm support for the Court's assumption of authority—at least in respect to invalidating acts of Congress or the President." Jesse H. Choper, *Judicial Review and the National Political Process: A Functional Reconsideration of the Role of the Supreme Court,* 2, 63 (Chicago: University of Chicago Press, 1980), citing Bickel, *The Least Dangerous Branch,* 3–14. For John Hart Ely's theory of "a representation-reinforcing theory of judicial review," see John Hart Ely, *Democracy and Distrust* (Cambridge: Harvard University Press, 1980). For the acceptance of such views by at least four justices of the U.S. Supreme Court, see Bradford Clark, "The Supremacy Clause as a Constraint on Federal Power," *George Washington Law Review,* 71: 97–98 (2003).

The theme that judges should apply different levels of review to different types of decisions has recently received some historical attention. William Treanor argues that almost all early instances of judicial review either involved federal judges reviewing state laws or involved statutes affecting courts and juries, and on this basis he suggests that the early decisions occurred "when legislation affected coordinate constitutional departments that were not part of the political process that had produced the legislation." More generally, he concludes that early American courts took "a structural and process-based approach to judicial review" that allowed the judges to adjust "the standard of review." William Michael Treanor, "Judicial Review Before Marbury," *Stanford Law Review,* 58: 458 (2005). For purposes of evaluating such arguments, however, it would be helpful to have evidence that many or even any eighteenth-century lawyers and judges said that they were taking such an approach. One might add that when one broadens the evidence to include the full range of determinations about the constitutionality of government acts, it becomes apparent that the underlying empirical claim (about a focus on legislation affecting courts and juries) depends on an artificially narrow range of decisions—a selection framed in response to modern conceptions of judicial review of statutes rather than eighteenth-century conceptions of judicial duty. Incidentally, there is also a question as to whether cases that turned on different doctrines, including doctrines not necessarily involving constitutional law, can be relied upon to show the standard of review in a supposed judicial power to hold statutes unconstitutional. See note 36 below.

the power, and this would seem to leave them with an extraordinary discretion over the liberty of their fellow Americans.

The Evidence

The judicial authorization of judicial review and its intimations of judicial power are only plausible because the most significant evidence appears to be missing. Although many cases of judicial review occurred after the adoption of the U.S. Constitution, the evidence of earlier cases seems weak. As Edward Corwin explains, "[t]he capital difficulty consists in the paucity of the evidence."[31]

In fact, the problem is not so much evidentiary as conceptual. The trouble arises from the very notion of judicial review, which is a concept so tightly focused on modern concerns that it renders many of the early decisions almost irrelevant. If judicial review is today considered prototypically a review of legislation, then early decisions about executive and judicial acts do not appear very central.[32] Similarly, if judicial review is associated with cases, then other types of decisions, such as resolutions and advisory opinions, seem anomalous.

The assumption that the historical inquiry must be a search for judicial review further narrows the evidence by reducing it to a matter of precedent. The difficulty of finding evidence of judicial review in the 1780s or earlier has appeared to suggest that the American judges must have subsequently developed this power, and it therefore seems necessary to find the precedents with which they established it. Many scholars therefore largely ignore the judicial determinations that were not cases, and on the assumption that judicial review could only have been established by the highest court of a state or the nation, the scholars even tend to discount state and especially lower court cases.[33] Actually, the determinations of the most

31 Edward S. Corwin, "What Kind of Judicial Review Did the Framers Have in Mind?" in *Corwin's Constitution: Essays and Insights of Edward S. Corwin,* 71, ed. Kenneth D. Crews (New York: Greenwood, 1986). For the extent of the evidence up through the adoption of the Constitution and the Bill of Rights, see Parts IV–VI below and Hamburger, "Law and Judicial Duty," 1. For the extent of the evidence up through *Marbury,* mostly after 1791, see Treanor, "Judicial Review Before Marbury," 455.

32 See, for example, Corwin, *The Doctrine of Judicial Review,* 75; Goebel, *History of the Supreme Court,* 1: 125; Louis B. Boudin, "Precedents for the Judicial Power: Holmes v. Walton and Brattle v. Hinckley," *St. John's Law Review,* 3: 173, 174 (1929); William Montgomery Meigs, "The Relation of the Judiciary to the Constitution," *American University Law Review,* 19: 175 (1885).

33 In this spirit, Julius Goebel writes: "The significance of the early cases as precedents . . . was local." Goebel, *History of the Supreme Court,* 1: 126. See also McLaughlin, *The Courts,*

lowly of courts are the best evidence of what men took for granted, and one of the great pleasures of this study has been to locate some of these humble and therefore all the more revealing decisions. In pursuit of precedent, however, most commentators focus on familiar and elevated sources—on cases, federal courts, and especially the U.S. Supreme Court.

Adding to these evidentiary limitations is a deep suspicion of the early decisions. It is not unreasonable for scholars to distance themselves from celebratory accounts of early state cases, but some scholars examine early decisions so critically that they question well-documented decisions. This skeptical attitude can be illustrated by the title of an article called "The Cases of the Judges: Fact or Fiction"—as if the very existence of the decisions were in doubt.[34] The skepticism is sometimes even candidly conceptual. In an essay devoted to "Critical History," Jack Rakove does not consider the evidence of decisions from prior to 1787 and instead focuses on the Constitutional Convention in Philadelphia—his assumption being that "judicial review" was not intellectually "possible" before then.[35]

These evidentiary and ultimately conceptual constraints leave so few decisions to work with that scholars often lump different types of cases together to assemble evidence of judicial review. It will be seen that although a judge could hold a statute contrary to a constitution, he could also reach other conclusions. For example, he could hold a subordinate law contrary to law and reason, or he could interpret a statute charitably in accord with natural law or occasionally a constitution. Each sort of decision was doctrinally different from the others, and the latter two (regarding subordinate laws and charitable interpretation) usually had nothing to do with constitu-

---

The Constitution and Parties, 48–49; Boudin, "Precedents for the Judicial Power," 173, 176; Corwin, *The Doctrine of Judicial Review,* 71; Smith, *Appeals to the Privy Council,* 634; Crosskey, *Politics and the Constitution,* 2: 970, 974; Levy, "Judicial Review, History, and Democracy," 8, 10.

34 Margaret Nelson, "The Cases of the Judges: Fact or Fiction," *Virginia Law Review,* 31: 243 (1944). An even more aggressive attitude was taken by Louis Boudin and William Crosskey. Louis B. Boudin, "Government by Judiciary," *Political Science Quarterly,* 26: 244 (1911); Crosskey, *Politics and the Constitution,* 2: 943–975. For example, Boudin writes: "The supposed constitutional decisions in both *Holmes v. Walton* and *Brattle v. Hinckley* are the figments of an overheated imagination." Boudin, "Precedents for the Judicial Power," 215. He is correct about *Brattle,* but to compare *Holmes* with it in this way is polemical, at best.

35 Rakove, "The Origins of Judicial Review," 1034. He writes that "before judicial review could become legitimate, Americans first had to accept a concept of judicial independence that they could not have easily formulated, much less endorsed, before the Revolution, and which still encountered substantial resistance in popular political culture." Ibid. Indeed, "[j]udicial review could only become possible after influential segments of the American political community moved away from the belief that juries were competent triers of law and fact alike." Ibid., 1034–1035.

tions. Nonetheless, many scholars treat these diverse decisions together as evidence about a distinct judicial power to hold statutes unconstitutional—apparently on the ground that such cases could have roughly similar practical consequences.[36]

All of these evidentiary problems (including the scarcity of precedents and the difficulty of sorting a limited number of cases) can be avoided here because, although the precedents for judicial review remain difficult to discern, the evidence about law and judicial duty turns out to be abundant. A simple shift in focus from judicial review to judicial duty is all that is necessary to bring the evidence into view. With this conceptual adjustment, what was previously little more than an evocative blur becomes an expansive and well-defined landscape, filled with vivid details. The evidence in such ways thus requires a change in paradigm—a return from the modern notion of judicial review back to the old, forgotten ideal of judicial duty.

The very label "judicial review" is misleading, for it suggests both too little and too much. Judges had an office or duty to decide in accord with the law of the land in all of their decisions, not merely when engaged in "review," and the phrase "judicial review" therefore describes only a fraction of the instances in which judges were bound by their duty and only some of the instances in which judges determined that customs or acts were unlawful. At the same time, the phrase suggests too much, for it alludes to judicial power without reference to judicial duty and thus lends itself to discussion of a power broader than the duty. In fact, although judges understood that in doing their duty, they enjoyed a power to enforce constitutions and protect rights, they ordinarily conceived of this power in terms of their duty and did not understand the power to extend any further.

A concept as familiar as judicial review may be difficult to put aside. Certainly, some readers will attempt to understand the argument here in terms of judicial review—as if the point were simply that judicial review was older and slightly different than usually assumed. The evidence, how-

[36] Corwin, *The Doctrine of Judicial Review,* 32, note 47 (citing *Robin v. Hardaway*); Plucknett, "Bonham's Case and Judicial Review," 62 (citing *Giddings v. Browne* in Massachusetts in 1657); Kramer, *The People Themselves,* 41 (citing state cases holding statutes unconstitutional together with *Bowman v. Middleton*); Prakash and Yoo, "The Origins of Judicial Review," 933 and notes 169 and 171 (similarly citing the *Symsbury Case*); Treanor, "Judicial Review Before Marbury," 455 (2005) (citing *Rutgers v. Waddington,* the *Symsbury Case,* and *Ham v. M'Claws*). William Nelson generalizes about cases in which the "courts effectively invalidated three . . . acts," without clarifying that only one held a statute unconstitutional and that the other two merely involved charitable interpretation. Nelson, "Changing Conceptions of Judicial Review," 1172 (citing *Bayard v. Singleton,* together with *Rutgers v. Waddington* and *Ham v. M'Claws*).

ever, leads away from notions of judicial review, and to understand the history, it is necessary to follow the evidence.

Law and Judicial Duty

The evidence reveals the importance of the common law ideals of law and judicial duty. It shows that these two ideals, taken together, required judges to hold unconstitutional acts unlawful. In pursuing the evidence, therefore, this book cannot focus on a distinct power to hold acts unconstitutional, but rather must more generally study the nature of law and of judicial office as understood by common lawyers.

The initial question concerns the obligation of law and especially constitutions. Long before Americans declared their independence, many English lawyers understood that the law made by the people, their "constitution," was of higher authority and obligation than other human law in their jurisdiction. Not merely the arrangement of government, this sort of constitution was the most fundamental part of the law of the land, and although many men questioned its application to Parliament, many others understood it to limit Parliament and thus to render any unconstitutional government act unlawful and void.

The second question regards judicial office and, in particular, judicial duty. Judges in America did not have to create for themselves a power over constitutional law, for already in England judges had a duty to decide in accord with the law of the land, including the constitution. The judges appreciated the functional benefits of this duty, such as its protection of liberty, but they understood it more basically to be part of their office, to which they were bound by their oaths. Judges therefore assumed they had no choice but to decide in accord with the law of the land. Accordingly, even in England they sometimes had to hold unconstitutional acts unlawful. Although judges faced obstacles in the law itself barring them from holding acts of Parliament unlawful, their duty to decide in accord with the law of the land was general, and thus where not barred by the obstacles relating to Parliament, their duty reached all types of government acts, regardless of whether the acts were executive, judicial, or legislative. As a result, both before and after Independence, judges were bound by their duty to hold unconstitutional American statutes unlawful.

Judicial duty was both more general and more mundane than what has come to be understood as judicial review, and it therefore had greater authority and more balanced implications. If there was a distinctive judicial power of review, it must have come from the judges themselves, and this has led to the conclusion that judicial review is of questionable authority. It has even led to the conclusion that judges, having created the power, can exercise it with either restraint or vigor, as seems to them required by different circumstances. Judicial duty, however, arose from the very office of a judge, and it thereby simultaneously strengthened and confined judicial decisions: It gave strength to judicial decisions about the constitutionality of government acts, and it confined the judges to making such decisions in the same way they made any other decisions—in accord with the law of the land.

Historically, it will be seen that the common law ideals of law and judicial duty developed not merely in reaction to local or transient considerations of policy, but more generally in response to underlying worries about the obligation of law and the role of judges, which in turn rested on deeper anxieties about human nature. It was widely assumed that human law existed within a hierarchy that reached from God down to man and that therefore even human law had a divinely derived obligation. Yet how human law acquired this binding force and how judges should decide about law were matters of profound dispute. Some theologians and academically minded lawyers had a high enough view of human potential that they suggested rulers and judges could partly transcend the rough, earthly texture of human law. Most common lawyers, however, pursued approaches less trusting of their rulers and judges and more grounded in the law of the land, and they thereby developed ideals of law and judicial duty that served the function of limiting government far more effectively than the high-minded ideals elaborated by their academically inclined contemporaries.

In the end, such ideals—whether academic or more narrowly legal—were responses to problems that might not be entirely susceptible of solutions. Men could use their ideals to rise above their worst tendencies, but they could never afford to forget that lurking below even the best of their ideals were problems as enduringly worrisome as men themselves. Their solutions therefore could never be perfect, and even if the common law solution avoided the dangers of the more academic approaches, this is not to say that it could rise above the nature of men.

I

LAW

What was the obligation of the law of the land? And was a constitution made by the people a part of this law? In a book arguing that the judges had a duty to decide in accord with the law of the land, it is necessary to begin with these basic questions about the law.

The depth of the problem of legal obligation tends to get lost in the history of judicial review, because from the vantage point of those who seek the origins of judicial review, the legal obligation of constitutions often seems to have been merely a choice made by Americans in the decade or two after 1776. This obligation of constitutions, however, was not so late, so narrowly American, or so contingent on local circumstance and taste. On the contrary, the development of the modern idea of a constitution—the idea of a constitution as a legally binding enactment by the people—was part of a broader shift in ideals of law and its obligation, a shift that already became widespread in late medieval and early modern Europe and that was inextricably bound up with the formation of modern life.

As will be seen in Chapter One, medieval lawyers tended to think about the obligation of law within their understanding of a hierarchy of law, and within this hierarchy they could optimistically assume that the law made by human rulers participated in the rationality or structure of the universe and thus enjoyed its obligation. In the late Middle Ages, however, as will become apparent in Chapter Two, many observers increasingly found it difficult to believe that men were competent to agree about what was reasonable or just in law, and in response to these fears about human discord and the disorder it was apt to cause, Europeans largely realigned the hierarchy of law along lines of lawmaking authority. Europeans thereby overcame the problem of divergent reasoning among men, but at the cost of concentrating lawmaking authority in rulers. The cure could thus be as dangerous as the disease, and therefore, as will be seen in Chapter Three, many men, particularly Englishmen, carefully embraced the shift toward authority on the assumption that beyond the lawmaking authority of rulers there was a deeper and more diffuse lawgiving authority among the people, whose law was their constitution. From this perspective, the highest human lawmaking authority in any land rested in the people, whose will thus had a legal obligation greater than that of any other law in their land, including any law made by their rulers.

This legal obligation of constitutions made by the people, like the broader shift toward authority, developed as a response to the fractures among men, and it therefore should be no surprise that it became so significant in the modernizing circumstances of European society. Authority was a measure of power or freedom, and although it might often be abused, it offered a mechanism for channeling and thus taming the divisions that increasingly seemed to be opening up in all spheres of human existence. Ideals of authority can thus be understood as both a part of, and a notable response to, the fragmentation so often associated with modernity. Amid this splintering, or at least the perception of it, men pursued different types of authority wherever they could, and thus at roughly the same time that men explored ideals of individual authority in religion, literature, and art, they also pursued ideals of communal authority in law, including ideals about a government's authority to make law and a people's authority to establish law for their government.

1

The Hierarchy of Law

To UNDERSTAND how one law could render another lawless and void, one must begin with the hierarchy of law that once seemed to reach from heaven down to earth. The medieval hierarchy of law is generally familiar, but it is important to examine it more precisely as a hierarchy of legal obligation and to ask about its reception among English lawyers. From within the hierarchy, it seemed that the eternal reason of the universe was evident in human law, thus giving it legal obligation, and that the absence of such reason in other human laws left them devoid of legal obligation, which meant that they were not really law. The hierarchy thus attributed to human law the force of eternal reason, but its apparent rigor in conferring or denying legal obligation troubled many Englishmen, who worried about its implications for their law.

The Hierarchy of Legal Obligation

In the hierarchy of law, human law ordinarily enjoyed an obligation that reached the heights of eternal reason and justice. Today, a strong a sense of hierarchy seems implausible. Having little confidence about a hierarchy of law, truth, or anything else, modern observers tend to assume that law rests on infinitely contingent foundations—that below law, there are turtles all the way down. It once, however, was conventional that there was law all the way up—all the way up to God and the rational order of his universe. By sharing in this heavenly reason, human enactments could be binding as law. Otherwise, they were lawless and void.

This theory had classical origins. The Stoics speculated about a natural law above human law, and Aristotle distinguished natural and conventional justice, but it was Roman moralists who pursued the most elevated implications of natural law.[1] Cicero, for example, argued that "[j]ustice does not exist at all, if it does not exist in Nature." Although Cicero suggested that social virtues "originate in our natural inclination to love our fellow-men, and this is the foundation of Justice," he also looked upward to suggest that natural law was "not a product of human thought . . . but something eternal which rules the whole universe"—"the primal and ultimate mind of God, whose reason directs all things." Natural law was thus "the reason and mind of a wise lawgiver," under whom "human life is subject to the degrees of supreme Law."[2]

In the preeminent medieval version of the hierarchy, natural law was derived from the eternal law, and no one elaborated this more profoundly than the medieval theologian Thomas Aquinas. The eternal law, according to Aquinas, was the reason or just order of the universe. It was "the Divine Reason's conception of things," for "the very Idea of the government of things in . . . the Ruler of the universe has the nature of a law."[3] The eternal law was known to human beings most generally through natural law, which was accessible to human beings through their use of reason, and which was "nothing else than the rational creature's participation of the eternal law." More directly, the eternal law was known through divine law—the law revealed by God in scripture. Most concretely, the eternal law was known through human law, for when human legislators made laws that shared in the accessible reason of natural law, their enactments also participated in the eternal law and so had the strength of its divine obligation. Without this divinely derived reason, the obligation of human law was apt to be contingent on fluctuating calculations of its utility, but with this divine reason, it had the sort of obligation that could be observed in the universe's eternally established order.

Aquinas could enjoy so elevated a vision of legal obligation because he was confident that "all men" had the potential to "agree . . . in that which is natural to them."[4] He understood that most men could only discern the general requirements of natural law, but he thought that at least wise men could accurately understand its practical implications for human law, and he therefore was optimistic enough to believe that "the force of a law de-

[1] Frederick Pollock, "The History of the Law of Nature: A Preliminary Study," *Columbia Law Review,* 1: 11 (1901). At a more practical level, Roman lawyers developed notions of the *ius gentium*—a law of nations that transcended national boundaries.
[2] Cicero, *The Laws* (I.xv) (II.iv) (III.ii), in *De Re Publica, De Legibus,* 345, 381, 461, trans. Clinton Walker Keyes (London: Loeb Classical Library, 1928).
[3] Thomas Aquinas, *Summa Theologica,* 2: 996 (Part 1–2, Q. 91, Art. 1), eds. Fathers of the English Dominican Province (Westminster, Md: Christian Classics, 1981).
[4] Ibid., 3: 1426 (Part 2–2, Q. 57, Art. 3).

pends on the extent of its justice"—on its "being right, according to the rule of reason."[5]

Eventually, the obligation of law would seem to shift from reason to authority, and some men were already heading in this direction, but Aquinas would not go so far. Although he fully recognized the necessity that human law be made by a ruler with human authority, he understood reason to be the source of law's obligation, and he thus described law as "an ordinance of reason for the common good, made by him who has care of the community, and promulgated."[6] Without quite expounding a modern constitution, he sufficiently appreciated authority to observe that "laws are said to be just" only when "they are ordained . . . from their author," which meant that a law could "not exceed the power of the lawgiver."[7] Yet even while thus acknowledging human lawmaking authority and its limits, Aquinas conceived of authority as an element of the justice of law—emphasizing that it was "unjust" when "a man makes a law that goes beyond the power committed to him."[8] In such ways, Aquinas wrapped questions of authority and will within the folds of reason and justice.

This morally rigorous theory had its risks, for if "[l]aws framed by man are either just or unjust," it was not obvious what could be said for laws that were merely useful. On the one hand, if laws were just, "they have the power of binding in conscience, from the eternal law whence they are derived."[9] On the other hand, if they did not participate in the eternal law, they were unjust and not lawful: "Human law has the nature of law in so far as it partakes of right reason; and it is clear that, in this respect, it is derived from the eternal law. But in so far as it deviates from reason, it is called an unjust law, and has the nature, not of law but of violence."[10] Aquinas thus forcefully rejected the lawfulness of unjust human laws, and he might therefore seem to have denied the lawfulness of merely useful human regulations—laws that were willed by human rulers for human reasons but that were not so substantially just as to partake of the eternal reason of the universe.

[5] Ibid., 2: 1019 (Pt. 1–2, Q.96, Art. 4). Note that the focus here is on obligation and that therefore questions of obedience are left aside. The distinction matters, especially in medieval theory, because although the problem of obedience was apt to have reference to that of obligation, it was also apt to involve other questions, which are not immediately relevant in this chapter.

[6] Ibid., 2: 995 (Pt. 1–2, Q.90, Art. 4).

[7] Ibid., 1: 489 (Part 1, Q. 96, Art. 4c); ibid, 2: 1019 (Pt. 1–2, Q.96, Art. 4).

[8] Ibid., 2: 1020 (Pt. 1–2, Q.96, Art. 4).

[9] Ibid., 2: 1019 (Pt. 1–2, Q.96, Art. 4).

[10] Ibid., 2: 1005 (Part 1–2, Q. 93, Art. 3).

Aquinas, however, did not sacrifice the practicability of the legal hierarchy, for he recognized a type of law which was willed but was not itself just, and that even Aquinas had to move so far toward a theory of authority as to deny that all law had to be substantively just is an early clue as to why English lawyers tended to be uncomfortable with any suggestion that natural law was a direct measure of legal obligation. According to Aquinas, a human law that was derived as a conclusion from the premises of natural law had "some force from the natural law." At the same time, he left freedom for human lawmakers to will what was not substantively just by suggesting that some laws were specifications or determinations of natural law where it was merely general—these laws being of "no other force than that of human law." Such laws concerned what Aristotle considered *adiaphora* or "a matter of indifference"; but in classical accounts, laws on *adiaphora* were neither permitted nor forbidden and yet were binding, and this was awkward for the later philosopher, who assumed that the justice of a law gave it obligation.[11] In Aquinas's view, even these exclusively human laws had to be just, and as they concerned matters on which the generality of natural law was indifferent, they could only be just in the less direct sense that "[t]he human will" could "make a thing to be just"—that is, because they were "decreed by the prince who is placed over a people."[12] Aquinas thus left space for law that was exclusively human while still maintaining that "[h]uman law has the nature of law in so far as it partakes of right reason." He did so, however, by relying on the justice of human institutions rather than the justice of the particular laws they promulgated.[13] Aquinas's acceptance of this merely human law, which partook of the eternal by its authority rather than its substance, illustrates the lengths the philosopher had to travel from his primary vision of law, in which human law more substantively participated in the reason or justice of the universe, and it already suggests why men might find satisfaction in another account of obligation—one more directly hospitable to the human laws that did not substantively share in God's eternal reason.

Not only the freedom of human lawmakers but also the limits on them were at risk from the attempt to rest obligation on reason, for reason was a standard that permitted and might even require deference to rulers when they went beyond their bounds. In assuming that law enjoyed its ob-

[11] Ibid., 2: 1014, 1015 (Pt. 1–2, Q.95, Art. 2).
[12] Ibid., 3: 1426 (Pt. 2–2, Q. 57, Art. 2). He wrote: "The human will can, by common agreement, make a thing to be just provided it be not, of itself, contrary to natural justice, and it is in such matters that positive right has its place." Ibid.
[13] Ibid., 2: 1005 (Part 1–2, Q. 93, Art. 3).

ligation from its participation in the eternal, Aquinas acknowledged that an unjust law might have to be binding if this was necessary to preserve the appearance of justice, for "even an unjust law, in so far as its retains some appearance of law, is derived from the eternal law; since all power is from the Lord God."[14] It might also be necessary to accept the obligation of an unjust law "to avoid scandal or disturbance."[15] Reason itself thus often gave obligation to laws that exceeded a ruler's authority. Perhaps not surprisingly, a deference in this style to laws that otherwise lacked the obligation of law would flourish among sophisticated Continental scholars, but it would not always recommend itself to Englishmen.

The hierarchy of law that Aquinas derived from eternal reason became part of the study of common law through *Doctor and Student,* a dialogue between a doctor of divinity and a student of English law published by Christopher St. German in the 1520s and 1530s. Although England had not yet departed from Rome, it was a time when individuals increasingly felt a need to reach their own moral judgments, including moral judgments about law, and in St. German's dialogue they could find an explanation of how to judge English law in conscience. Reassuringly, it suggested that most of English law was in accord with higher law.[16]

St. German's Doctor repeated the conventional medieval hierarchy of law. There were four laws: the "lawe eternall," the "lawe of nature" (which English lawyers called the "lawe of reason"), the "lawe of god" (revealed in scripture), and the "lawe of man." The law eternal was "called the fyrste, for it was byfore all other lawes. And all other lawes be deryvyed of it." In contrast to the eternal law, the others were the "thre[e] maner of wayes almyghte god maketh this lawe eternall knowen to his creatures reasonable": "Fyrste by the lyght of natural reason. Seconde by hevenly revelacyon. Thyrdly by the ordre of a prynce."[17]

The eternal law, as discerned in revelation or the law of nature, was thus the measure of what was binding as human law. Human law was "not . . . obligatorye" if not "consonant to the lawe of god." Nor was human law obligatory if contrary to the law of nature or "reason." Against this law, therefore, neither "prescripcyon statute nor custome" could "prevayle, and

[14] Ibid., 2: 1005 (Pt. 1–2, Q.93, Art. 3).
[15] Ibid., 2: 1019 (Pt. 1–2, Q.96, Art. 4).
[16] He concluded the first dialogue: "Thus I have shewed unto the[e] in this lytle Dyaloge howe the lawe of Englande is grounded upon the lawe of reason, the law of god, the generall customes of the realme . . ." T. F. T. Plucknett and J. L. Barton, eds., *St. German's Doctor and Student,* 174 (London: Selden Society, 1974).
[17] Ibid., 7, 9–11, 12–13.

yf any be brought in agaynst it they be no prescripcyons statutes nore customes, but thyngis voyd & agaynst justyce."[18]

St. German occasionally recognized the alternative view, that a statute could bind "in lawe and conscyence" simply because it was enacted. In the civil law, his Doctor noted, it was sometimes said "a posytive lawe that is lawfully made" could "bynde al[l] that be subgiettes to that lawe accordyng to the mynde of the maker." Such a law was binding not merely in the courts of law but also "in the courte of conscyence." Yet like most civilian commentators, neither St. German's Doctor nor his Student rested with this observation. Instead, they proceeded to elaborate that for "posytive lawe" to be "lawfully made," it had to share in the law of nature and of God.[19]

The awkwardness was that men might disagree as to whether a particular human law participated in the generalities of higher law, and this was especially a problem for the laws of England, which rarely approached academic ideals of reason and justice. St. German acknowledged it was difficult to discern whether a particular human law participated in the eternal law, but being a traditionalist, he denied that the task was unmanageable. Disagreement about what was reasonable was already transforming the hierarchy of law—in ways that would soon lead to modern constitutions—but St. German would not let the underlying difficulties disturb his assumptions about legal obligation. He still assumed that "in every lawe posytyve well made is somwhat of the lawe of reason, and of the lawe of god," and although "to discerne" these laws in "the lawe posytyve is very harde," such inquiry, he thought, was "moche necessary."[20]

English Misgivings

The hierarchy of reason presented so morally rigorous an account of legal obligation that common lawyers limited its place in English law. Historians of judicial review sometimes suggest that generalizations about natural law translated directly into English law, but common lawyers understood that they needed a more complex response. Those who had studied at university probably appreciated the connections between their law and the reasoned order of the universe, and those who had studied carefully probably understood that Aquinas and others who expounded the hierarchy of law were not ordinarily questioning the obligation of human law. Whether or not

[18] Ibid., 9–11, 13, 15, 29.
[19] Ibid., 158.
[20] Ibid., 27.

they had studied at university, however, common lawyers tended to understand the risks posed by the hierarchy. They tended to understand that academic generalizations about natural law were apt to undermine the distinctive features of their worldly law, and their misgivings provide yet another hint as to why they would soon welcome a more modern version of the hierarchy of legal obligation.

Medieval common lawyers were so anxious to avoid the delegitimizing implications of the hierarchy that they usually refrained from even mentioning natural law.[21] The English had already responded to the civil law with a combination of fascination and unease—as when in the twelfth century the English chronicler Ralph Niger praised the virtues of civil law but worried that it was being propounded by men who would use it to displace "communis status arbitria" or the authority of the established community.[22] By the mid-twelfth century the danger was such that King Stephen declared Roman law should have no place or at least no authority in England.[23] During the following centuries, common lawyers took a similar stance toward natural law: They avoided speaking of it and instead alluded to "reason"—apparently finding safety in studied indifference. As observed by an early fourteenth-century gloss on Bracton, "[i]n England less attention is paid to natural law than in any other part of the world."[24] This is sometimes thought by historians to have been merely a sign of English ignorance, but common lawyers so consistently referred to "reason" when others would have spoken of natural law that they could not have been entirely unknowing.[25] Just how far common lawyers took their politic understatement can be illustrated by Chief Justice John Fortescue, who argued from

[21] Common law suspicions are an old theme, and for a particularly valuable discussion, see J. H. Baker, ed., *The Reports of Sir John Spelman,* 2: 24–43 (London: Selden Society, 1977).
[22] "An English Theologian's View of Roman Law: Pepo, Irnerius, Ralph Niger," in Hermann Kantorowicz, *Rechtshistorische Schriften,* 240–241, 243 (Karlsruhe: C. F. Müller, 1970).
[23] Francis de Zulueta and Peter Stein, eds., *The Teaching of Roman Law in England,* xxvi (London: Selden Society, 1990).
[24] Frederick Maitland, ed., *Select Passages from the Works of Bracton and Azo,* 125 (1895) ("in Anglia minus curatur de jure naturali quam in aliqua regione de mundo"), discussed by William Holdsworth, *A History of the Criminal Law,* 2: 602 (London: Sweet & Maxwell, 2003); Morris S. Arnold, "Statutes as Judgments: The Natural Law Theory of Parliamentary Activity in Medieval England," *University of Pennsylvania Law Review,* 126: 330 (1977). The date is conjectural. According to St. German's Doctor, the "lawe of nature" was "called by them that be lernyed in the lawe of Englande the lawe of reason." Plucknett and Barton, eds., *St. German's Doctor and Student,* 7.
[25] Morris Arnold suggests that because discussions of natural law "are simply absent from English law books" in the Middle Ages, it "seems probable that the concepts employed were absent as well from the minds of medieval English lawyers." Arnold, "Statutes as Judgments," 342. This conclusion, however, seems difficult to reconcile with the arguments in the yearbooks about "reason."

natural and eternal law in his political tracts but usually left such law unmentioned when he sat on the bench.[26] Far from ignorance, this was a self-conscious segregation of academic learning.

Even St. German, who candidly discussed natural law, hesitated to conclude that reason or natural law rendered English law legally void. St. German did not put himself in a position in which he would have to challenge English law directly, for in writing a book of cases of conscience—even if with special interest in the chancellor's conscience—he only needed to determine what was binding on a man's conscience within his soul, not what was binding or void in a court of law.[27] Perhaps most tellingly, St. German acknowledged that the chancellor himself could not always meet the standard of reason, for "in some case there is no remedye for suche an equytie by waye of compulsyon, but all the remedye therin muste be commytted to the conscyence of the partye."[28] St. German later rendered this point concrete by enumerating "divers cases and groundes, whereby it apperethe that a man may have ryght in conscyence which he can not cum to by ye common lawe, and . . . yet he shal have no sub pena" in Chancery.[29]

Of course, most common lawyers went much further in questioning claims of higher reason, and none did so more vociferously than an anonymous writer—said to be a serjeant at law—who feared that law students would be seduced by St. German's academic niceties about conscience. In his dialogue with a student, the cantankerous old serjeant urged the youngster to stick to the law:

> Me thinkithe that the lawe aughte not to be lefte for conscience yn no caas; for the lawe commaundith all thing that is good for the commen welthe to bee doon, and prohibitithe all thing that is evill and that is againste the

[26] Sir John Fortescue, *De Laudibus Legum Anglie,* ed. S. B. Chrimes (Westport: Hyperion, 1979).

[27] For his framing of his enterprise as a book of cases of conscience, see Plucknett and Barton, eds., *St. German's Doctor and Student,* 3, 174.

St. German's discussion of whether the law of nature or of God could deprive English law of its obligation in conscience touched upon a version of what would later be called "passive obedience." When St. German's Student asked about "wylfull dysobedyence" to a penal statute, the Doctor suggested that there were some statutes that "byndyth not in conscyence to the payment of the penaltye, tyll it be recoveryd by the lawe," at which point "it doth bynde in conscyence." But "yf a statute be made pryncypally to remedy the hurte of the partye, and for that hurte it gyveth a penaltye to the partye," then "the offendour" was "bounde immedyatlye to restore the damages to the value of the hurte . . . but the penaltye above the hurte he is not bounde to paye tyll Jugement be gyven." Ibid., 158.

[28] Ibid., 103.

[29] "A Little Treatise Concerning Writs of Subpoena," in *Christopher St. German on Chancery and Statute,* 115, ed. J. A. Guy (London: Selden Society, 1985).

> commen welle. Wherfore yf ye observe and kepe the lawe . . . ye shall not nede to studie so moche upon conscience, for the lawe of the realme is a sufficiente rule to ordre you and your conscience.[30]

This was strongly put, and it made no pretense of offering a well-rounded account of either conscience or English law, but it captured the common law attitude—in particular, its defensive edge when under pressure from learned ideals.

The most urbane of lord chancellors, the courtier and royal confidant Sir Christopher Hatton, cautioned against high-minded expectations of reason in law. He had reason to tell common lawyers what they wanted to hear, and in a treatise that he apparently allowed to be circulated under his name, he warned about "some, who hold the Law to be so perfect and so large, as [to think] Reason is in everything and beyond Reason a man cannot go." Against this academic idealism, Hatton observed that "our Laws are not grown to that perfection," nor are "the grounds of Law . . . all so perfect, but that the contraries of some are as reasonable as our Laws." The common law rule of primogeniture epitomized the way in which English law was often unreasonable, and from this example the Chancellor concluded that "the law of *England* and reasonable be not convertible, nor always coincident together." In short, "[r]eason must be bridled and restrained in the course of the Law."[31]

In repudiating complaints that English law should follow reason, Hatton also rejected the related argument that English law was incomplete. Academically inclined common lawyers were sophisticated in recognizing the incompleteness of human law, and by pointing out the reality that no human custom could anticipate all questions of justice, they could suggest that judges had to do what was reasonable where the common law was silent. Most common lawyers, however, at least instinctively defended the limited reach of their law, which even in equity left much to the con-

[30] "The Replication of a Serjeant at the Laws of England," in ibid., 102–105. At stake was both conscience and the jurisdiction of the Chancery. As the serjeant told the student: "I perceyve by your practyse that ye leve the commen lawe of the Realme, and ye presume moche upon your owne mynde, and thinke that your conceyte ys ferre bettre then the commen lawe," and "therupon ye make a bill of your conceyte, and then ye put yt yn to the Chauncery, saying that it is groundede upon conscience." Instead, according to the serjeant, "the lawe" was "to determyn which is conscience, and whiche is no conscience." Ibid., 103, 105.

[31] Christopher Hatton, *A Treatise Concerning Statutes, or Acts of Parliament: And the Exposition Thereof,* 24–26 (London: 1677). Similarly, he worried about the "Opinions, that by circuity of Argument would batter or beat down any good Law of man by colour of contrariety thereof to the Word of God, when the truth in plainness of dealing is otherwise to be discerned." Ibid., 32.

science of each party. Adopting this stance, Hatton acknowledged "that Reason may be called the Mother of the Law" but then hastened to echo St. German that "we are so far from Perfection in our Law, that both our Courts of Law, yea, and our Courts of Conscience . . . must leave of necessity some things that need reformation to the Conscience of the party himself."[32] Rather than aim for comprehensive rules of justice, the common law tended to enunciate relatively formal rules, often more procedural than substantive, within which parties could work out their own justice. The common law was thus not so much incomplete as of limited domain, and although academically minded lawyers might think this unreasonable and unjust, others tended to consider the confined character of the law an essential foundation of their freedom.

Academic ideals about the hierarchy of eternal reason and justice thus seemed to run aground on the shores of England. In reaching from the eternal down to the human, the hierarchy gave divine obligation to most human laws and rendered others merely lawless and void. All hierarchies, however, have their cost, and the moral rigor of this one seemed to threaten England's distinctive system of law. Put more abstractly, amid diverse communities, a hierarchy of law based on strong claims about universalistic morality was apt to endanger the freedom of a people to maintain their own laws within their land. This tension did not by itself change the hierarchy, but it left many common lawyers deeply reluctant to acknowledge the laws that rose above their own. It also, as will now be seen, left them very open to another, less confining version of the hierarchy—one that would legitimize rather than threaten the law of the land.

[32] Ibid., 25–27.

2

The Shift toward Authority

A PROFOUND change gradually occurred in the dominant conception of the hierarchy of law. Whereas the obligation of law once rested on a law's participation in a divinely ordained higher reason, Europeans and especially Englishmen increasingly became skeptical as to whether mere mortals could adequately discern, let alone agree about, what was reasonable, and they thus came to view the obligation of law as resting on the authority of the lawmaker, whose will was binding as law. This was, for many men, little more than a slight shift in weight—as if from one leg to another—but it thoroughly altered the posture of law, for whereas the law had once leaned toward intellect and justice, it now in the late medieval and early modern era began to incline toward authority and will, and from this would follow modern law, including constitutions.

The tilt toward authority and will requires all the more attention because it often gets short shrift in histories of Anglo-American law, especially the history of judicial review. Scholars widely recognize that the candid acknowledgment of human authority reshaped much of modern life, including religion, art, politics, and social relations.[1] Yet the implications for law, particularly Anglo-American law, have not been studied as systematically.[2]

[1] The preeminent work is John Neville Figgis, *Political Thought from Gerson to Grotius* (New York: Harper Torchbooks, 1960). Incidentally, although there will be reference here to the "new" and "old" versions of the hierarchy, these words obviously are not to be taken literally, but rather merely as convenient shorthand allusions to the different understandings of the hierarchy that more or less prevailed, respectively, in the Middle Ages and afterward. So too, the words "modern" and "modernizing" are not always to be taken literally.

[2] For Continental law, there have been valuable studies. See, for example, Brian Tierney, *Religion, Law, and the Growth of Constitutional Thought 1150–1650* (Cambridge: Cambridge University Press, 1982); Brian Tierney, "Hierarchy, Consent, and the 'Western Tradition,'" *Political Theory*, 15: 650 (1987); and, with a particularly sharp focus on the obligation of

Some accounts of judicial review even leave the impression that the transition toward authority and will as the basis of legal obligation occurred only in the last decade of the eighteenth century. This shift, however, took place already in Europe, and it broadly realigned law, including the common law, in a way that would eventually seem to suggest the necessity and obligation of constitutions enacted by the people.

Divine Will

The pressure for human authority came primarily from below—from forebodings about human and social fractures—but the legitimization of authority and of the consequent role of a ruler's will came primarily from above, from disturbing speculations about divine will and the possibility that if God were free, he could have exercised his will in a manner other than he had in establishing the rationality of the universe. These unsettling ideas about God did not by themselves prompt the shift toward authority in human law, but they could be taken to suggest that it was will rather than reason that made any law binding.

The dislocations and disorder of the late medieval and early modern world appear to have stimulated fears that God could will what was contrary to reason. Aquinas acknowledged that human law had to be willed by a human lawmaker, but in his bright vision of the divine order, although human law required will, it was binding because it participated in the reason and justice of the universe. Many other Europeans, however, when they looked around at their turbulent, even shattered circumstances, had grounds to worry that not only on earth but also above, will was not always exercised along merely reasonable lines, and when they speculated about God's freedom, some scholars wrestled with the knotty paradox that if God were of unlimited perfection and power, he always had the capacity to exercise his will differently than he had when he created the universe. Philosophers might hesitate to conclude that God would actually exercise this potential, for if he had ordained the eternal order of the universe, it was difficult to believe that he would contradict himself; but if he had the capacity to exercise his will otherwise than he had, was it plausible that his law was binding because of its reason or justice? It was disturbing to think

law, Kenneth Pennington, *The Prince and the Law, 1200–1600* (Berkeley: University of California Press, 1993). With respect to England, these issues have been pursued most directly by Norman Doe, although in a rather different way than here. Norman Doe, *Fundamental Authority in Late Medieval English Law* (Cambridge: Cambridge University Press, 1990).

that God could will what was naturally unreasonable and unjust—in concrete terms, that he could save Judas and damn Peter. Yet if God was omnipotent and free, he had at least the potential to make a law that led to so perverse a result, and this troubling observation could lead to the conclusion that it was ultimately God's will rather than his reason or justice that gave obligation to his law.[3]

These hints as to how God could have ordered the universe differently may seem little more than philosophical speculation, but they offered a divine model as to how will created obligation, and this was probably significant for the development of ideals of human authority and will. Especially in a hierarchy of law, men were apt to generalize their ideals, and in contemplating whether God gave obligation to his laws through his will, men could come to wonder whether human lawmakers similarly gave obligation to their laws through their will.[4] The divine example was thus suggestive about human authority and will—most obviously as exercised by rulers, but perhaps also by the people.

Human Failings and the Shift toward Human Authority and Will

The shift toward the authority and will of human rulers developed not merely from above but more substantially from below—not simply from the legitimacy conferred by idealized conceptions of the divine being, but from realistic observations and fears about human beings. If men by their very nature were apt to disagree in their reasoning about justice, then perhaps God meant for them to be governed, and thus the fallen character of men seemed to suggest that human rulers, by virtue of their office, enjoyed their lawmaking authority under God's authority. In retrospect, this vision of legal obligation may seem to have been unduly focused on human rulers, but by resting legal obligation on the lawmaking authority and will of such

[3] For God's potential to ordain the law differently and the characterization of this as a sort of "absolute" power, see William J. Courtenay, *Capacity and Volition: A History of the Distinction of Absolute and Ordained Power,* 87 (Bergamo: Pierluigi Lubrina Editore, 1990). For the power to exercise will irregularly, outside ordained law, which came to be called "absolute" power in the context of political and legal debate, see Francis Oakley, *Omnipotence, Covenant, and Order: An Excursion in the History of Ideas from Abelard to Leibniz,* 43, 63 (Ithaca: Cornell University Press, 1984).

[4] Tierney cautions against seeing a logically necessary connection between the obligation of divine will and the obligation of human will, commenting that "the divine will and human wills were incommensurable." Brian Tierney, *The Idea of Natural Rights: Studies of Natural Rights, Natural Law, and Church Law, 1150–1625,* at 197 (Atlanta: Emory University Press, 1997). By the same token, the example of divine will offered an ideal of legal obligation that was not lost on men.

rulers, this perspective would soon open up ideas about the lawmaking authority and will of the people.

Underlying this new version of the hierarchy was the development of European society. It was one thing in the twelfth century to imagine that human law participated in the rationally ordered hierarchy of the universe, but quite another in the following centuries. As the bonds that held men together were loosened and as divisions reached up from ordinary individuals to princes and even popes, men seemed too limited to share in the reasoned order of the heavens. Men seemed so weak in their intellect and so corrupted by their passions that they apparently could not resolve whether their laws participated in the rationality of the universe without quarreling and perhaps even descending into strife. In these circumstances, many Europeans, not least the English, began systematically to develop both the epistemological skepticism and the corresponding anxieties about fragmentation and diversity that would shape the modern world and its law.

This sense that men were too human to reason without disagreement and dispute—in addition to its familiar implications for theology and philosophy—brought about a shift in perceptions about the central problem in law.[5] If men by their very nature could not agree in their moral reasoning about law, it no longer sufficed to ask about the justice revealed by reason. Rather, it first seemed necessary to ask who had authority to decide such a matter—to ask, ultimately, whose will was law. This was the problem that gave rise to the modern version of the hierarchy of law, and although it would eventually lead to constitutions, this is because it more immediately seemed to suggest the divine authority of rulers.

No medieval writer more systematically explored the relationship between human failings and the obligation of a lawmaker's will than Marsilius of Padua in his 1324 treatise, *Defensor Pacis.*[6] An advocate of the holy roman emperor in opposition to the pope, Marsilius explained the lawmaking authority of the secular human ruler.[7] Marsilius feared that men by

[5] For a study of these issues in the learned law, see Tierney, *Religion, Law, and the Growth of Constitutional Thought,* at 45; Pennington, *The Prince and the Law.* For early hints of systematic approaches to the question of authority among twelfth-century civilians at Bologna, see Emily Kadens, "Attitudes Toward Equity and Judicial Discretion in Medieval Roman Law," 6, 11, 12, 28 (unpublished ms.), citing Charles Lefebvre, *Les Pouvoirs du Juge en Droit Canonique* (Paris: Recueil Sirey, 1938). For fourteenth-century philosophers who pursued the implications, see Tierney, "Hierarchy, Consent, and the 'Western Tradition,'" 649–650.

[6] This is not to say, however, that he was entirely original, being preceded in some respects c. 1315 by Hervaeus Natalis and having much in common with "a whole group of early fourteenth-century thinkers who were concerned with the problem of political obligation." Tierney, *Religion, Law, and the Growth of Constitutional Thought,* 48.

[7] Ibid., at 48.

their nature could not agree in their reasoning about justice—that they were of such limited "wytte" and "croked affeccyon" they could not rely on their own reasoning about justice to ascertain what was binding as law—and he therefore argued that they needed to rely on the judgment of their ruler to determine such matters.[8] He thus reversed the arguments of Aquinas, for whereas Aquinas thought that to attain justice, men had to preserve order, Marsilius feared that if men were to avoid "contencyons, bralles and stryffes," then [i]t was necessarie" for them "to ordeyne a rule of Justyce"—indeed, to ordain a ruler "to kepe and execute the sayd Justyce."[9] Even philosophers, when they attempted to identify what was right, were vulnerable to "great dyfference and errour," and this seemed to suggest that things were right "onely by the [civil] lawe, and not by nature." Marsilius himself did not deny the natural difference between right and wrong, but he worried that men could only recognize right and wrong in practical matters by reference to human will—"onely because men wyll so . . . ordayne of them"—and he therefore argued that to achieve the peace and orderly existence necessary for felicitous human life, men needed a law made by the ruler with coercive power.[10] Were this simply a functional point about the benefits of deferring to the will of the powerful, it could not give more than a contingent obligation to human law, but Marsilius hinted that this law enjoyed a stronger obligation by citing scripture and explaining that peace was the natural end of human society.[11] Thus, in contrast to Aquinas, who hoped men could rise above their earthly situation to make law that participated in eternal reason, Marsilius feared men were so mired in their limitations they usually could only agree on human authority, and from this perspective, if peace was the natural end of men, the coercive law made with human authority had an obligation derived from nature.

In pursuit of authority, many Europeans eventually envisioned a systematic hierarchy of will—running from God down to human rulers—and in this way, as hinted in the prior section, ideas about God's will gave heightened legitimacy to the natural law claims for human will. The most prominent exponent of a hierarchy of will was John Calvin. No less than Marsilius, Calvin recognized the importance of the coercive laws of civil

[8] Marsilius of Padua, *The Defence of Peace,* fol. 11[r] (I.i) (London: 1535).
[9] Ibid., fol. 13[v] (I.iv).
[10] Ibid., fol. 32[v] (I.xiv). Alan Gewith observes that "Marsilius does not himself endorse this conventionalist position here." Marsilius of Padua, *The Defender of Peace,* 2: 57, note 7, trans. Alan Gewirth (New York: Columbia University Press, 1956).
[11] He quoted Cicero that men were created "for mennes sake"—that is, to help one another—and therefore "we ought to folowe the gydynge of nature, and to bryng forth co[m]mune utylyties." Marsilius of Padua, *The Defence of Peace,* fol. 10[r] (I.i).

government—although he recast the familiar natural law argument about peace into a religious observation about disobedience to God.[12] Being a Protestant, moreover, Calvin was particularly emphatic that the contentiousness of men arose from their wickedness rather than their lack of knowledge, for although "a discrimination between what is just and unjust" was "imprinted on their hearts," it was not imprinted "on their will," and although men had "a *full* knowledge of the law," there was but little sense of "what is right implanted in their nature." God evidently had not given men the nature to do what was right voluntarily, and Calvin therefore concluded it was the will of the divine magistrate that men should obey the will of their human magistrates.[13] Human lawmakers thus held their authority by divine authority, and "[t]he reason why we ought to be subject to magistrates is, because they are constituted by God's ordination."[14]

The logical conclusion was that human laws were binding, regardless of whether they were just. Although particular human laws on *adiaphora* were neither just nor unjust, they nonetheless had to be obeyed because "we are still held by God's general command, which commends us to the authority of magistrates."[15] Even clearly unjust laws were binding, for he "who is the founder of civil power" appointed magistrates "for the legitimate and just government of the world." Admittedly, "tyrannies and unjust exercise of power" were not the sort of government "ordained" by God, "yet the right of government is ordained by God for the wellbeing of mankind."[16]

[12] John Calvin, *Institutes of the Christian Religion,* 1502 (IV.xx.14), trans. John T. McNeill and Ford Lewis Battles (Philadelphia: Westminster, 1960).

[13] *Commentaries on the Epistle of Paul the Apostle to the Romans by John Calvin,* 97–98, 480 (Romans ii.15 and xiii.3), trans. John Owen (Grand Rapids: Baker Book House, 1984). As Calvin notes, the heart is "to be taken" not "for the seat of affections, but only for the understanding." Ibid., 97–98. More generally, see Calvin, *Institutes of the Christian Religion,* 270–271 (II.ii.12); John T. McNeill, "Natural Law in the Teaching of the Reformers," *Journal of Religion,* 26, no. 3: 181–182 (July 1946).

[14] *Commentaries on the Epistle of Paul the Apostle to the Romans by John Calvin,* 479 (Romans xiii.2). See also Calvin, *Institutes of the Christian Religion,* 1489 (IV.xx.4).

[15] Calvin, *Institutes of the Christian Religion,* 1183–1184 (IV.x.5).

[16] *Commentaries on the Epistle of Paul the Apostle to the Romans by John Calvin,* 479 (Romans xiii.2). Even "good and just laws" were binding because of their source rather than their content. Although these "human laws . . . have to be observed," they "do not of themselves bind the conscience. For all obligation to observe laws looks to the general purpose, but does not consist in the things enjoined." Calvin, *Institutes of the Christian Religion,* 1184 (IV.x.5).

In looking at human nature to understand the divinely ordained authority of rulers, Calvinists obviously were not alone. For example, the Lutheran theologian Philipp Melancthon worried that if men, including scholars, had their reason clouded by sinful desires and selfishness, they would have difficulty discerning natural law or what was just: "Concerning natural laws, I have seen nothing worthily written either by theologians or lawyers." Indeed, "I have not yet seen this done by anyone, and I do not know if it can be done, since human reason is so enslaved and blinded—at least it has been up until now." Accordingly, the

The Calvinist derivation of human authority from divine authority became widely familiar in England, as can be illustrated by the writing of William Ames—a Cambridge academic who argued that "humane Lawes are to bee observed" because "the Law of God, hath constituted this power and order, and hath enjoyned us to yield obedience and subjection to the same." Divine command enjoined submission to human command, and therefore "the contempt of authority" was "by it selfe a sinne against the Law of God." Recognizing the implication of authority for the obligation of human law, Ames did not shy away from asking "[*w*]*hat proportion the Civill Law, holds with the Law of Nature.*" He understood that civil law, "in as much as it is Right," was "derived from the Law of Nature," and that in this sense what was "not just and right" was "not Law." Yet Ames feared that "the Reason of man, can onely imperfectly judge, nay, and is often . . . cozened," and "hence it must needs follow, that all humane Constitutions are of necessity liable to imperfection, errour, and injustice." Thus, "[i]t is impossible, that a reason should bee given of all things," and "it is proved in innumerable cases, that there are many things received in the Civill Law for the publicke good, which are somewhat contrary to a disputative reason."[17]

Of course, this is not to say that Englishmen in the sixteenth and seventeenth centuries stopped worrying about the morality of their law, but they increasingly differentiated questions of authority and morals, thus splitting political and legal inquiry away from the study of morals and legislation. While writers on morals continued to focus on the substantive rules of justice evident in natural law, political theorists examined natural law for hints about the authority of human rulers, and they thereby developed an aspect of this law that had hitherto been left understated. In particular, they established a mode of studying natural law in which the uncertainty of its

---

"methods and shortcuts of our reason" were not to be preferred to "what is prescribed in Holy Scripture. For in general the judgment of human comprehension is fallacious because of our innate blindness, so that even if certain patterns of morals have been engraved on our minds, they can scarcely be apprehended." Philip Melanchthon, *Loci Communes Theologici* (1521), in *Melanchthon and Bucer,* 50, ed. Wilhelm Pauck (Philadelphia: Westminster, 1969). More generally, see McNeill, "Natural Law in the Teaching of the Reformers," 173, 175. On such assumptions, Melanchthon concluded that "[t]he Civill magistrate by Gods aucthoritie, hath ryght to make honest and profitable lawes, in those matters whiche parteyne to the defence of this corporall life and civil societie." Philipp Melanchthon, *Whether it be mortall sinne to transgresse ciuil lawes, which be the commaundementes of ciuill Magistrates,* 11 (London: nd) (2nd ed., STC 10391.5) (citing Proverbs 8).

17 William Ames, *Conscience with the Power and Cases Thereof,* Fourth Book, 166–167, Fifth Book, 105–106 (V.i) (np: 1639). In observing "[t]he imperfection of the best Civill Law," Ames also noted the reality that "it containes not in its compasse the whole Law of Nature, but so much of it, onely, as such or such men have approved and thought appliable to their owne manners." Ibid, 106.

moral injunctions seemed to show the necessity of focusing on its clearer suggestions about human authority. Political theorists could thus rely on natural law to determine the divinely ordained location and extent of lawmaking authority, and then, turning to the implications of natural law for morals, lawmakers could consider how they should legislate. The philosophic danger was that the political theorists would end up justifying human authority by relying on a thin, minimalistic version of natural law, or even mere nature, without explaining how this natural law could be reconciled with the thicker version still recited by moralists.[18] The expectation of the moralists that men could draw detailed substantive moral rules from reason was very much at odds with the assumption of the political theorists that men could not agree on the substantive requirements of reason, and it would therefore not be until the eighteenth century, with a shift in the foundation of moral reasoning to human affections and sentiments, that men more successfully integrated their study of morals and authority.[19]

Like political writers, common lawyers did not forgo their attention to reason, but they were now all the more confident that common law was binding even if it was unreasonable or contrary to natural law. With their ideals of authority, common lawyers could bluntly say that justice was "the end" but law "the meane, whereby we may attaine to the end."[20] From this perspective, although judges could reason about the common law, they could not discern the common law from natural law or "reason" except where the common law was otherwise unclear. In *Slade's Case,* for example, Coke reported that "if none, or no usual presidents are shewn, the Court ought to Judge according to Law and reason," but absent such uncertainty, the "common course makes a law, although . . . perhaps reason willeth the contrary."[21]

[18] One of the difficulties faced by Locke and other liberal theorists of government was that they needed a natural law that established only a limited political authority but could not afford to share with the world an equally limited account of natural law as to morals. It therefore is probably not a coincidence that Locke never published a systematic account of morals based on natural law and that he claimed the middle two books of his *Treatise of Government* were lost.

[19] See, for example, the efforts of Francis Hutcheson and Adam Smith.

[20] Coke, *Institutes,* 2: 56.

[21] *Slade's Case* (K.B. 1602), Coke, *Reports,* 4: 93b–94a. For an early illustration of such analysis, see Theodore F. T. Plucknett, *Statutes and Their Interpretation in the First Half of the Fourteenth Century,* 35 (Cambridge: University Press, 1922).

Chief Justice Fortescue said that if "a form or course be used, and is and has been used contrary to reason, it is not bad to amend this," and according to Alan Cromatie, "[t]he idea of law as rational thus . . . functioned for Fortescue . . . as a licence to amend those rules where they were found unsatisfactory." Y.B. Trinity 36 Henry VI, 25b–26a, at pl. 21; Alan Cromartie, *The Constitutionalist Revolution: An Essay on the History of England, 1450–1642,*

In contrast to Coke and the myriad other common lawyers who tended to speak of reason in place of natural law, there were some common lawyers (usually academically minded men with expansive views of royal power) who went out of their way to emphasize that wherever English law was uncertain, it was to be understood by "resort to the law of nature."[22] In adopting this stance, some were apparently expressing their attachment to the old academic ideal that human law was obligatory because it participated in natural law. Yet even these men tended to recognize that they were swimming against the tide. Sir John Doddridge, for example, still believed that "all Lawes are derived from the law of Nature, and doe concur and agree in the principles of Nature and Reason," but although he thus rejected the ideals of authority, he understood that he had to explain why natural law did not deprive unreasonable English laws of their obligation. One way he avoided any such tension was to declare that the common law came close to the law of nature, claiming that "the Law of this Land hath alwayes followed best and approved Reason." This self-congratulatory line could not have satisfied serious readers, and Doddridge therefore also more elaborately accommodated English law by distinguishing between primary and secondary principles of nature. It was difficult, however, to rest the obligation of the common law directly on "Morall Philosophie," and although

at 20 (Cambridge: Cambridge University Press, 2006). Yet even Fortescue—the medieval English judge with the most clearly demonstrated intellectual attachment to natural law—did not go so far. Rather than simply suggest that common law could be abandoned where it was unreasonable, Fortescue evidently assumed that the custom of the realm was binding because it enjoyed a presumption of rationality, and he therefore framed his argument as an explanation of what was necessary to overcome this presumption. He noted that the reasons underlying many courses and forms of the common law were beyond memory, and he apparently thought that these courses and forms thus had a presumptive rationality, based on what was unknown about their past. He therefore proposed that one could overcome this presumed rationality by showing that the law both "is and has been used contrary to reason."

[22] Sir John Doddridge in Harleian Ms. 5220, as quoted by Cromartie, *The Constitutionalist Revolution,* at 189. Doddridge was quoting the fifteenth-century judge Yelverton, but as Cromartie notes, whereas Yelverton said that we thus "make a positive law"—a most unusual statement—Doddridge merely said we "do adjuge it for law." Ibid., 22, 189. Hans S. Pawlisch quotes not only Doddridge but also Serjeant Ashley in 1604 about how "the ius gentium . . . serves for a supply in the defect of the common law." Hans S. Pawlisch, "Sir John Davies, the Ancient Constitution, and Civil Law," *Historical Journal,* 23: 691 (1980).

Coke could acknowledge that common law sometimes had to be discerned from "nature or the course of nature." Coke, *Institutes,* 1: 11a. The most compelling instance was probably *Calvin's Case,* which involved a claim across national boundaries. Recognizing that this case stretched beyond the distinctive reason of English law, Coke explained that "for want of an expresse text of law . . . and of examples and presidents in like cases (as was objected by some) wee are driven to determine the question by naturall reason." *Calvin's Case* (Ex. Ch. 1608), Coke, *Reports,* 7: 18b.

such an ambition would always appeal to lawyers of an academic bent, it would not become more widely popular among common lawyers.[23] Indeed, when natural law analysis in the eighteenth century openly flourished in the common law, this would not be because men such as Doddridge established faith in the legal obligation of reason, but rather because other lawyers became confident that arguments from reason were no longer apt to be used to threaten human authority or the law to which it gave obligation.

The most substantial challenge to the ideals about authority in English law came from the Anglican adherents of Luther, who echoed his cautions against obeying laws contrary to scripture.[24] Even in this, they did not mean more than what would come to be known as "passive obedience"—a hesitation to obey unscriptural law until one was specifically ordered to do

23 John Doddridge, *The English Lawyer,* 158–159 (London: 1631). The secondary principles of nature were "not so well knowne by the light of Nature, as by other meanes," and like Coke's artificial reason, they were "peculiarly knowne . . . to such onely as professe the study and speculation of Lawes." Moreover, they were merely presumed to be true—either because they enjoyed an irrebuttable "[p]resumption" created by law or because they were "supposed true . . . till the contrary be proved." Because the secondary principles were only of "[*c*]*ontingent verity,*" it "is scarcely possible to make any secondary Rule of Law, but that it shall faile in some particular case," and to cure this, there had to be equitable exceptions. Doddridge in this way relied upon equity to reconcile English law to natural law. Ibid., 194, 206, 209.

Henry Finch similarly reconciled English law with the law of nature by focusing on "the secundarie rules of reason"—known to the English as "the Law of reason," which, even among corrupted human beings, "yet shineth, so that from it all the other Lawes receive their Light." Henry Finch, *Law, or, a Discourse Thereof,* 3–4 (London: 1627). Wrestling with this problem, he wrote that "laws positive" that were "contrarie to the Law of nature" would "lose their force and are no laws at all," but he promptly explained that although his statement was true of the primary law of nature, it was only generally true of the law of reason: "But because the law of reason is knowne onely to such as are able to judge aright, and that but imperfectly . . . therefore here the case is harder, what lawes may be said [to be] agreeable and what repugnant thereunto." Thus, "[o]nely in general . . . is it truly said, . . . that lawes indeed repugnant to the law of reason, are as well void, as those that crosse the law of nature." Ibid., 75–76.

In contrast to these academic perspectives, there were at least some lawyers and judges—particularly during the Commonwealth—who took a distinctly religious vision of how higher law could limit the law of the land. See, for example, Judge Keble's comments that "there is no law in England, but is as really and truly the law of God as any Scripture-phrase that is by consequence from the very texts of Scripture. . . . And whatsoever is not consonant to Scripture in the law of England, is not the law of England." Trial of Christopher Love (1651), *State Trials,* 5: 172.

24 A more radical position was taken by Quakers who questioned the obligation of an individual to obey a law contrary to his conscience. Strong versions of such views, however, came under severe attack, and beginning during the Restoration period the Quakers adopted distinctly defensive versions of these ideas. See, for example, Robert Barclay, *The Anarchy of the Ranters and Other Libertines* ([London]: 1676).

so, this being the point at which disobedience became resistance.[25] It was a narrowly religious remnant of the older ideals of obligation, but even this was incompatible with the new ideals of authority.

From the perspective of Calvinism and increasingly the Crown, any disobedience was rebellion, and therefore any hesitation to obey—even mere passive obedience—soon lost its legitimacy. Although the Bishops had taken the Lutheran line in their *Book of Homilies,* they responded to the Catholic rebellion of 1569 by adding a homily declaring that Christians should "most readily obey their naturall gratious Soveraigne."[26] The heightened royal and Calvinist demands for prompt obedience sharpened the already strong common law tendencies in this direction, and thus not only King James I but also Edward Coke could insist that "to command and to be obeyed, belong to Soveraign and supreme Government."[27]

Passive obedience increasingly became the stance of high church Anglicans who had been pushed aside by the force of English politics, and especially after the Revolution of 1688 it became the distinctive view of the Tories who sought to reconcile themselves to their political exile. William Blackstone, for example, suggested that the obligation of unjust laws extended no further than "submission to the penalty."[28] Like some other dis-

[25] In their *Book of Homilies,* the bishops acknowledged that if kings "woulde commaunde us to do any thing, contrary to gods co[m]maunde[n]ts . . . we must rather obey God then man," but they buried this fleeting allusion to disobedience within Lutheran exhortations against any active resistance and within more English exhortations for loyalty to a king who was "supreme governour of all his realmes . . . by the authoritie of God, and by gods ordinaunces." *Certayn Sermons Appoynted by the Queens Majestie, To Be Declared and Read . . . Every Sonday and Holy Daye, in Their Churches,* sig. Siv[v]-Ti[v] (London: 1559). See Franklin le van Baumer, *The Early Tudor Theory of Kingship,* 140 (New Haven: Yale University Press, 1940); Francis Oakley, "Religion, Civil Government, and the Debate on Constitutions," in J. H. Burns, *The Cambridge History of Political Thought 1450–1700,* at 178, 181 (Cambridge: Cambridge University Press, 1994); Richard L. Greaves, "Concepts of Political Obedience in Late Tudor England: Conflicting Perspectives," *Journal of British Studies,* 22: 23, 27 (1982).

[26] *An Homelie Against Disobedience and Wylfull Rebellion,* sig. Giv[r] (London: 1570).

[27] "Of the King's Ecclesiastical Law," Coke, *Reports,* 346 (Fourth Reports) (London: 1658).

[28] William Blackstone, *Commentaries on the Laws of England,* 1: 57 (Oxford: 1765). Blackstone understood law to be "that rule of action, which is prescribed by some superior, and which the inferior is bound to obey." Ibid., 1: 38. Yet he wrote: "[I]n regard to *natural duties,* and such offences as are *mala in se:* here we are bound in conscience, because we are bound by superior laws, before those human laws were in being, to perform the one and abstain from the other. But in relation to those laws which enjoin only *positive duties,* and forbid only such things as are not *mala in se* but *mala prohibita* merely, annexing a penalty to noncompliance, here I apprehend conscience is no farther concerned, than by directing a submission to the penalty, in case of a breach of those laws." Ibid., 1: 57–58.

From such distinctions, Oliver Wendell Holmes developed his deliberately reductionist tinguished Tory lawyers, he was allowed a place on the bench, but his politics cost him the Regis professorship of civil law at Oxford. In the broader stream of English life, human rulers seemed to have an authority derived from God's natural law, and if their law had an obligation derived from his, it required not mere passive obedience but *"Active Obedience."*[29]

For a while—especially in the seventeenth century—some men argued that not only human law but also natural law was binding because it was willed, thus envisioning a fully consistent hierarchy of will, in which all law had legal obligation because it was commanded or willed by its maker. The possibility that natural law itself enjoyed its obligation from the will of God had already been explored by scholars in the Middle Ages, and it now finally found a broader audience, including English lawyers. For example, the treatise attributed to Chancellor Hatton alluded to "the Law Eternal" but meant by it "the Will of God, known to every man by the light of natural Reason."[30] It was an approach that would become widely familiar in the next century through the work of the Lutheran philosopher Samuel Pufendorf. In response to Hobbes's suggestion that precepts of natural law were really mere theorems about utilitarian ends, Pufendorf supposed that they had their obligation from God's will: "[A]lthough those precepts have manifest utility, still, if they are to have the force of law, it is necessary to presuppose that God exists, and . . . that He had enjoined upon the human race that they observe those dictates of reason, as laws promulgated by

ideas about law and the bad man. For sardonic effect, he generalized about law in terms that Blackstone reserved for *mala prohibita* and collapsed the moral obligation of submission into a mere physical risk of punishment.

29 Benjamin Hoadly, *The Measures of Submission to the Civil Magistrate Consider'd. In a Defense of the Doctrine Delivered in a Sermon Preach'd before the Rt. Hon. the Lord Mayor, Aldermen, and Citizens of London, Sept. 29, 1705,* at 111 (London: 1706). The distinction between "[p]ositive and active" obedience and "[n]egative and passive" obedience harked back to prior centuries. See, for example, note 27 in Chapter One, and [Philip Hunton], *A Treatise of Monarchie,* 8 (London: 1643). Speaking of obedience to God, one observer noted: "Active obedience is the doing of his will . . . upon signification of his pleasure without disputing or debating the matter." Thomas G. Olsen, ed., *The Commonplace Book of Sir John Strangways,* 79 (Tempe: Renaissance English Text Society, 2004). In effect, to insist upon active obedience was to make "no distinction . . . betwixt active and passive obedience." Jonathan Mayhew, *A Discourse Concerning Unlimited Submission and Non-Resistance to the Higher Powers,* 14 (Boston: 1750).

30 Christopher Hatton, *A Treatise Concerning Statutes, or Acts of Parliament: And the Exposition Thereof,* 32 (London: 1677). Ames frequently suggested that the obligation of higher laws generally rested on God's will, as when he wrote that "obedience properly consists in this, that we do simply, and absolutely apply our will to the will of God." Ames, *Conscience with the Power and Cases Thereof,* Third Book, 55. Similarly, he argued that "[t]he Word *Ius,* signifying *Right,* is derived from the Latine Word *Iussus,* because it implies a Power of some Authority, commanding this or that to be done," and that it therefore should be taken for, among other things, "the Law commanding." Ibid., Fifth Book, 9[9].

Himself by means of our natural light. For otherwise they might, to be sure, be observed perhaps, in view of their utility . . . but not as laws."[31] It could be disconcerting to think that natural law was binding because it was willed, but in an era so dominated by ideals of authority and will, it often seemed that natural law could only have the obligation of law if it had been willed by God.

Eventually, in the late seventeenth and early eighteenth centuries, many men reverted to the view that the obligation of natural law arose from its nature, but this erosion of will at the top of the hierarchy did not displace will as the source of obligation below, in human law. In particular, many eighteenth-century Englishmen came to believe that natural law was obligatory because of its nature—no longer usually in the manner of Aquinas because of its eternal reason, but rather because of the nature of man, including his sociable sentiments or affections. Such analysis deprived law-making will of its role as the source of obligation at the top of the hierarchy, but left will in place as the source of obligation at the lower end, for even if men might have sociable natures and thus might hope to govern themselves, this was hardly to say that they were apt to agree about the injunctions of nature—let alone predictably obey them. Thus, even a sociable human nature seemed to reveal the natural authority of human rulers and the obligation of their will.

The way in which natural law continued to be understood to give obligation to human will can be observed in the lectures of Thomas Rutherforth. Although Blackstone taught his students at Oxford that the authority of human law was subject to a remnant of old natural law ideas in the form of passive obedience, Thomas Rutherforth explained in the more Whiggish halls of Cambridge how natural law gave human law an obligation that required active obedience. There was disagreement, he told his students, as to whether natural law acquired its obligation from its rationality, from divine will, or from the natural affections of men. Yet regardless of the source of obligation for natural law, this law gave a divinely derived obligation to "positive laws," which were "those, which mankind are obliged to observe by the immediate will and appointment of a superior."[32] In particular, Rutherforth believed that "the authority of the legislative body" and the

[31] Samuel Pufendorf, *De Officio Hominis et Civis Juxta Legem Naturalem Libri Duo,* 2: 19 (I.iii.x), ed. Frank Gardner Moore (New York: Oxford University Press, 1927). Similarly, see John Locke, *Questions Concerning the Law of Nature,* 159, trans. Robert Horwitz, Jenny Strauss Clay, and Diskin Clay (Ithaca: Cornell University Press, 1990); Samuel Parker, *A Demonstration of the Divine Authority of the Law of Nature and of the Christian Religion,* 23–24 (London: 1681).

[32] Thomas Rutherforth, *Institutes of Natural Law,* 5 (I.i.5) (1754; Baltimore 1832).

obligation of the laws made by it were derived from natural law through the consent of the people, and this allowed Rutherforth to observe that if "obligations, arising from consent, are obligations of the law of nature, it follows that the members of any civil society are obliged by the law of nature to obey the civil laws of it"—this being "the internal obligation of such laws."[33]

In sum, it seemed to be the nature of men to have discordant views of reason and justice, and this left the English with a revised hierarchy of law—one in which natural law gave a divinely derived authority to human rulers and a corresponding obligation to their lawmaking will. This new version of the hierarchy still reached from God down to man, but it now gave a divinely established natural obligation to human lawmaking will, and although it most obviously gave binding force to the law willed by rulers, it could also (as will later become apparent) give obligation to the law willed by the people.

The Altered Relation between Different Levels of Law

The recognition of authority and will as the basis for legal obligation relaxed the relationship between different layers of law in a way that left men all the more freedom in making their law. It was not simply that authority and will, whether popular or governmental, were increasingly understood as the measure of legal obligation. In addition, the shift to these sources of obligation loosened up the relationship among laws and thereby enlarged the space available for the exercise of human authority and will.

When law came to seem binding because it was willed by a body with lawmaking authority, there was no longer any need to conclude that it participated in the eternal reason or any other higher law, and this left men free to make law as long as it did not contradict any law of greater authority and obligation. If law had to participate in the eternal reason, each layer of law was but an aspect of the single, larger order, and each part of it was obligatory because it shared in the reason and justice of the eternal law. If law, however, could stand on the authority and will of its maker, without participation in the eternal law, then each law more clearly stood apart from any

[33] Ibid., 361–362 (II.vi.3). Rutherforth did not think there was "any great necessity for entering into the question concerning the cause of our obligation to observe" the law of nature, but he understood the obligation of the law of nature to come from God, for even if natural law was not as immediately a matter of divine will as scripture, man at least could observe what was "contrary to his nature and constitution" and thus was "contrary to the will of that Being, who made his nature and constitution what they are." Ibid., 5 (I.i.5–6), 7 (I.i.7).

higher laws and had merely negative relations to them. Thus, in the sixteenth and seventeenth centuries, the question of participation in the eternal order of the universe was largely displaced by a simpler question about avoiding contradiction. It was a subtle shift in emphasis, but by freeing each law from having to participate in a higher reason and justice, the newly prominent role of will left each law less completely dependent on the laws that stood above it.

The shrinking role of the eternal law was evident, for example, among English Protestants. Calvin had so doubted the capacity of men to discern the eternal through reason or natural law that he urged men to attend to the "moral law"—the scriptural testimony of natural law, to which God gave obligation through his "eternal and unchangeable will"—and many sixteenth- and seventeenth-century Englishmen eventually went even further in this direction.[34] Although some English Protestants, such as the Anglican apologist Richard Hooker, still accepted that eternal reason could be found in lesser forms of law, others, such as the Puritan moralist William Ames, collapsed the eternal law into natural law—thus in effect truncating the top of the hierarchy. He suggested that the phrase "eternal law" was really just the name for an aspect of natural law: "The *right Naturall,* or *Naturall Law,* is the same, which usually is called the *Eternall Law:* but it is called *Eternall,* in relation to God, as it is from *Eternity* in *Him,*" and "it is called *Naturall,* as it is engraffed and imprinted in the *Nature* of man, by the God of *Nature.*"[35] Chief Justice Edward Coke similarly spoke of the "*Lex eterna,* the Moral Law, called also the Law of Nature," and shortly afterward emphasized that "[t]his Law of Nature . . . indeed is the eternal law of the Creator."[36] These men could afford to reduce the eternal law to the enduring character of natural law, for they did not assume that human law had to participate in the eternal in order to have obligation.

A hint of how this development opened up space for human will can be observed in notions of *adiaphora.* Aquinas viewed all law as just, including that regarding *adiaphora.* As already seen in Calvin, however, many sixteenth- and seventeenth-century commentators increasingly took an-

[34] Calvin, *Institutes of the Christian Religion,* 1503–1504 (IV.xx.15–16).

[35] Ames, *Conscience with the Power and Cases Thereof,* Fourth Book, 100–101. Thus, "the right naturall is alwayes the same, and like it selfe, and for this reason also, it is called the Law eternall." Ibid.

[36] *Calvin's Case* (Ex. Ch. 1608), Coke, *Reports,* 7: 12b–13a. Henry Finch referred to natural law as "that soveraign reason fixed in mans nature" and noted that Cicero "calleth it the high & supream law of all." Henry Finch, *Law, or, a Discourse Thereof,* 3–4 (London: 1627). In the next century, Blackstone thought the "law of nature, being co-eval with mankind and dictated by God himself, is of course superior in obligation to any other." Blackstone, *Commentaries on the Laws of England,* 1: 41 (Introduction, §2).

other view. Assuming that law was obligatory because it was willed rather than because it shared in the rationality of a higher justice, they relied on the classical view of *adiaphora* to defend human laws that were neither just nor unjust.[37] On behalf of the English church, for example, Thomas Starkey observed that there were "[t]hynges indifferent," which were "by goddis worde" or scripture "nother prohibyted nor commaunded, but lefte to wordly polycie, wherof they take their ful authoritie."[38] More broadly, on behalf of the Crown, Starkey noted that things could be indifferent not only within divine law but also within natural law and that the obligation to obey in these indifferent matters was a matter of human authority: "[T]o be obedient to the laws civil, so long as they be not contrary to the law of God nor of nature, is ever virtue and honesty, yet to this law or that law all men are not bounden, but only such as receive them and be under the dominion of them which have authority of making thereof." Thus, while some nations "reputed it a certain virtue" to abstain from eating flesh upon the Friday" and "to marry but one wife," other nations could follow different approaches.[39] So candid a justification of arbitrary laws would once have seemed abhorrent. Now that Englishmen, however, placed the obligation of their laws on the lawmaker's authority and will, they no longer expected their laws to participate in the eternal reason of the universe, and they therefore merely had to consider whether their laws kept within the bounds set by higher laws.

This new relationship among laws, such that a law only had to avoid contravening laws of greater obligation, had even more profound implications outside the realm of *adiaphora.* The English tended to think in terms of *adiaphora* when worrying about church government—*adiaphora* being the matters in which government enjoyed a freedom of religious regulation within the substantive limitations set by divine and natural law. As to civil government, however, the English increasingly asked not so much about particular substantive moral limitations as about the general scope of the ruler's authority to impose his will; and whether the limitations on his authority were to be found in natural law, scriptural law, or human law, the

37 John Finnis, *Aquinas: Moral, Political, and Legal Theory,* 268 (Oxford: Oxford University Press, 1998).

38 Thomas Starkey, *Exhortation to Christian Unity and Obedience,* sigs. 50[v], 6[v] (London: 1536).

39 Thomas Starkey, *A Dialogue Between Reginald Pole and Thomas Lupset,* 33, ed. Kathleen M. Burton (London: Chatto and Windus, 1948). Blackstone later observed that "[t]here is, it is true, a great number of indifferent points, in which both the divine law and the natural leave a man at his own liberty; but which are found necessary for the benefit of society to be restrained within certain limits." Blackstone, *Commentaries on the Laws of England,* 1: 42 (Introduction, §2).

laws delineating his authority were all the more clearly a measure of his freedom when it was recognized that he merely had to avoid contradicting them.[40] Instead of having to make law that participated in the rationality of higher law, a ruler now only had to avoid colliding with the legal boundaries on his authority.

The changing perception of human nature—or at least the perception of such nature in a changed society—thus left Europeans with an altered vision of law, freedom, and government. In circumstances in which it was no longer plausible to expect men to participate in higher law, men merely had to avoid violating law, and this left them more free, at least within their authority under law. Put another way, freedom shifted from a matter of justice to a matter of authority. For the people, their authority under natural law would come to be their liberty to make a constitution; for the ruler, his authority under the constitution would come to be his constitutional power, including his freedom in devising laws; for individuals, their authority under the law of the land would come to be their civil liberty—"[a] Liberty to follow my own Will in all things, where the Rule prescribes not."[41] This liberty to exercise will under law, however, arose from diminished moral expectations about men and their governments. Europeans had once been apt to recite how men, including rulers, could have the intellect and dispassion to exercise their will in a way that participated in the eternal verities of reason and justice. Now, Europeans paid greater attention to their fears about the corrupt character of men. Whether rulers or subjects, men seemed so limited that perhaps they could at best be bounded by law—ideally by natural law, and more certainly by human law.

Intent

It has been seen that in the newer version of the hierarchy, authority gave obligation to the lawmaker's will, and this is as much as to say that authority gave obligation to the lawmaker's intent. Today, intent seems little more than a judicially adopted interpretative method—a path not evident in the

[40] Stephen Gardiner, Bishop of Winchester, for example, took a sufficiently strong view of "the supreme power and authoritie of princes" within their jurisdiction that he said "christ's Vicar" had to obey the laws of princes—"not onely whan thei commaunde thinges indifferent, and easy to be done, but also whan thei commaunde thyngs not indyfferent"—his only substantive limitation on such laws being, "so [long as] they be not wycked." Stephen Gardiner, *De Vera Obediencia,* fols. xxxix[v]–xl[r], [trans. John Bale] (1553). Gardiner in this way still accepted the Lutheran caveat, but with an English emphasis on obedience to rulers who were free to act within their authority.

[41] John Locke, *Two Treatises of Government,* 302 (II.iv.22), ed. Peter Lazlitt (Cambridge: Cambridge University Press, 1960).

nature of law, but apparently laid down by judges and thus perhaps within their discretion. Once, however, intent was understood differently. It was the will of the authoritative lawmaker, which seemed, amid the fractiousness of men, to have been established by God as the origin and measure of legal obligation. Put more sociologically, when men, in response to changes in their society, lost confidence in their capacity to agree upon what was just, they found legal obligation in the will or intent of their lawmaker.[42] Not surprisingly, common lawyers rapidly assimilated the view that intent rather than eternal justice was the measure of legal obligation, but they did so with a distinctive, common law variation. At common law, the formality required for lawmaking was that there be an act of a court of record, and when common lawyers became convinced that intent was the measure of obligation, they ended up focusing not merely on the intent of the lawmaker, but more specifically on the intent of legislative acts.

It was not just any intent or command of a lawmaker that could make law, for rulers sometimes expressed their will irregularly—independently of the law rather than through it. This absolute power increasingly seemed to be of a very different character from the ordinary power to ordain law, and to understand the distinction, it is necessary briefly to step back to the Middle Ages. Already within the old hierarchy of reason, in which intent was not the measure of obligation, intent was a necessary element of human law, and men began to worry whether the intent ordinarily conveyed through human law might sometimes be pursued above it.

If the highest of rulers occasionally exercised his will outside the channel of his laws, then perhaps earthly rulers might also at times have to take extra-legal measures. The possibility of miracles and of divine forgiveness could seem to suggest that God himself sometimes departed from his natural law, and far from being merely an academic question, this was, like equity and pardons, a problem that potentially reached deep into the nature of the universe. It was only to be expected that human language could not adequately capture the complexity of the world and that human rulers might therefore sometimes have to act in a manner that could not be re-

[42] Chrimes observes that "[t]he rule of reference to the intention of the legislators—limiting, as it does, the absolute discretion of the judges but relieving them, as it does, of rigid adherence to the express words of a statute—was certainly established by the second half of the fifteenth century." S. B. Chrimes, *English Constitutional Ideas in the Fifteenth Century,* 293 (Cambridge: Cambridge University Press, 1936). More generally, see Richard S. Kay, Adherence to the Original Intentions in Constitutional Adjudication: Three Objections and Responses," *Northwestern Law University Review,* 82: 226 (1988); Keith Whittington, *Constitutional Interpretation: Textual Meaning, Original Intent, and Judicial Review,* 113–123 (Lawrence: University Press of Kansas, 1999).

duced to the regular generalizations of law, but if God himself sometimes exercised his will absolutely, beyond his law, then perhaps the universe itself was not essentially regular or subject to law. The disturbing implications for law—as for science, philosophy, and literature—would take many centuries to unfold, and it was probably not a coincidence that in both physical and moral inquiries such notions about the fundamentally fractured character of the universe only flourished with the disintegration of communal relations in recent centuries. In the meantime, medieval kings did not have to resolve the profound questions about nature (or even merely sociology) to exercise a human version of the divine power above law. Their learned advisers told them that a power above law was characteristic of sovereigns, divine and human, and the kings were human enough to be persuaded.[43]

Irregular will, however, was not law, and therefore in a country such as England, in which legitimacy was so closely associated with rule through law, the Crown in the Middle Ages tended to avoid making open claims for the king's irregular or absolute will. Although English monarchs asserted prerogatives above the law of the land, they remained cautious enough to avoid generalizing that this was what they were doing—it being safer to leave ambiguous whether such prerogatives were exercised through the law of the land or above it.

In fact, the will that increasingly seemed to be binding in England—whether to make law or to make lesser sorts of legally binding orders—not only had to be regularly ordained but also usually had to come through the formal act of a court. This sort of formality is all too often forgotten, but whereas learned Continental theories of legal obligation required publica-

[43] Although an absolute power in dispensing with the requirements of law was initially claimed by the pope and defended by canon lawyers, it was soon also claimed by the English Crown. In England, an act of Parliament could be considered an act of the king in Parliament, and the king might therefore be able to authorize a departure from his own act—at least, increasingly, when he made his subsequent and contrary intent clear with a *non obstante* clause, stating that notwithstanding the statute, the grantee could do what was thereby prohibited. "The Early Statutes," in H. G. Richardson and G. O. Sayles, eds., *The English Parliament in the Middle Ages,* essay no. xxv, 25–26, 39 (London: Hambledon, 1981); Chrimes, *English Constitutional Ideas in the Fifteenth Century,* 279–283. Popes had issued bulls with *non obstante* clauses, and from the thirteenth century onward, English kings regularly followed this practice in some of their grants. In 1251, the chronicler Matthew Paris complained about the introduction of this "detestable" clause. Matthew Paris, *Chronica Majora,* 5: 210, ed. Henry Richards Luard (Rolls Series, Rerum Britannicacrum Medii Ævi Scriptores, vol. 57). For early scholarship on the introduction of *non obstante* clauses in England, see William Prynne, *Brief animadversions on, amendments of, & additional explanatory records to, the fourth part of the institutes of the lawes of England,* 129–133 (London: 1669); "The Birth and Parentage, Rise and Fall of Nonobstante," in Alexander Luders, *Tracts on Various Subjects in the Law and History of England,* 327 (London: 1810). For the canon law, see Courtenay, *Capacity and Volition.*

tion of a ruler's will, the English tended to accept an act as binding only if it was the act of a court—the underlying assumption being that the court of a community was the place where the community could act. Such a court included a manor court, a corporation's court or board, a colony's general court, and above all Parliament.[44] Summarizing this tradition, Coke observed that even when the king merely commanded that a person be arrested, "the king cannot doe it by any commandement, but by Writ, or by Order, or Rule of some of his Courts of Justice, where the cause dependeth, according to Law." Indeed, there were some acts that the king could only make by act of record in a court of record: "The King being a body politique cannot command but by matter of Record, for *Rex præcipit, & Lex præcipit*"—the *king orders* and the *law orders*—"are all one, for the King must command by matter of Record according to the Law."[45] The king made his lesser acts through his various inferior courts of record, and he made his statutes in Parliament, which was his highest court of record. This enactment of English statutes as acts of record defined their obligation, for "[e]very Record imports a truth in it[self]," and although one could challenge the operation of a record, one could not "aver . . . contrary to the Record."[46] The act of a court of record was thus the formality required if an enactment of legislative will was to have the obligation of law, and already here it should be added that this formality, which seemed essential for the king in Parliament when making statutes, would one day also seem necessary for the people when they enacted express constitutions. Prior to the

44 The English thus departed from learned assumptions that laws obliged only from the time of publication and instead dated acts from the first day of court—whether in dating writs from the first day of term or acts of Parliament from the first day of the session. This came to be justified in terms of consent with the fictional assumption that the entire community was present in court.

45 Coke, *Institutes,* 2: 186–187. Coke's initial point, that when the king commanded that a person be arrested, he had to do it "by Writ, or by Order, or Rule of some of his Courts of Justice," was more general than his second point, concerning acts of record, because most arrest warrants were not acts of record. As Hale later noted, although the warrants "upon appeals and indictments" were "by writ" and thus were understood to "issue upon matter of record," most arrest warrants were not of this nature. Like Coke, however, Hale understood that the issuance of arrest warrants belonged to "courts and persons, that have judicial power by the common law, or by act of parliament for the conservation of the peace." Matthew Hale, *Historia Placitorum Coronæ,* 2: 105 (London: 1736).

46 *Holland & Franlkin's Case* (K.B. 1589), Leonard, *Reports,* 1: 183; *Sir Thomas Howard's Case* (C.P. 1588), Owen, *Reports,* 138–139. Unlike custom, the act of a court of record enjoyed an irrebuttable presumption of validity: "Records are of so high a nature, that for their sublimity they import veracity in themselves; And none shall be received to aver anything against the Record itself." *Floyd v. Barker* (Star Chamber 1607), Coke, *Reports,* 12: 24. See also Coke, *Institutes,* 1: 260a.

widespread adoption of express constitutions, however, the more central question concerned custom.

In a hierarchy that required human law to be willed, even custom might have to be understood, at least in theory, to have received its obligation from the will of the relevant lawmaker, and for the custom of England this meant the will of the people—perhaps even their formal legislative will. Medieval commentators almost uniformly said that longstanding custom shared the same authority and obligation as written law, except that it was made by tacit rather than express consent—*tacitus consensus populi* rather than *expressus consensus populi.*[47] Accordingly, as Baldus explained, "the strength given by time is required not for introducing the custom but for formalizing the consent," and in this sense, "[c]ustom and statute do not differ in their efficient cause and its efficacy, but they . . . differ in their mode and form."[48] Some commentators, not least Marsilius, pursued the logic of authority by lumping custom together with legislation under the old rubric of *lex,* and Marsilius thus concluded that "under this accepcyon or sygnyfycacyon of this worde lex, are comprehended all of the rules of Cyvyle ryghtes and utylyties" made "by ye auctoryte of man, as customes, statutes, ordenunces or actes made by the co[m]mens." All of these, including the customs, were "the Cyvyle actes of men" and were "grounded" on their "autoryte."[49] Of course, in the learned law, custom was no more *lex* than, in English law, common law was statute. The point, however, was that the custom of a land could be considered a sort of legislation willed by the people, and in England this not only required that the common law be willed by the people but also that it be recorded. Exactly how custom could be recorded was something of a mystery, but among the common lawyers

[47] Walter Ullmann, *The Medieval Idea of Law as Represented by Lucas de Penna: A Study in Fourteenth-Century Legal Scholarship,* 63 (New York: Barnes & Noble, 1969); Joseph Canning, *The Political Thought of Baldus de Ubaldis,* 95, 101 (Cambridge: Cambridge University Press, 1987).

[48] Canning, *The Political Thought of Baldus de Ubaldis,* 100–101. Much later, William Salkeld observed that "no law can oblige a people without their consent," to which he added: "Now this *consent* is either *verbis* or *factis;* (i.e.) it is expressed by *writing,* or implied by deeds and actions; and where a law is founded on an implied assent . . . it is either common law or [local] custom." Custom, Salkeld, *Reports,* 112.

[49] Marsilius of Padua, *The Defence of Peace,* fol. 24[r] (I.x). The phrase, the "actes made by the co[m]mens," was a sixteenth-century interpolation. Marsilius von Padua, *Defensor Pacis,* 51, ed. Richard Scholz (Hanover: Hahnsche Burchhandlung, 1932). For earlier versions of Marsilius's sort of analysis—by Salvius Julianus, as recorded in the *Digest,* and by Glanville with regard to common law—see Charles Howard McIlwain, *Constitutionalism Ancient and Modern,* 64 (Ithaca: Great Seal Books, 1947); Brian Tierney, "'The Prince Is Not Bound by the Laws': Accursius and the Origins of the Modern State," *Comparative Studies in Society and History,* 5: 397 (1963).

who pursued this line of thinking, custom was said to be recorded in popular memory. Whereas charters and acts of Parliament "are actes reduced to writting, and are alwayes matter of *Record*," the common law "being onely matter of *fact*, and consisting in use and practice, it can bee recorded and regist[e]red no where but in the memory of the people."[50]

Although both custom and statutes could thus be considered matters of record adopted by an authoritative body, statutes required not merely a conceptual justification in terms of intent, but an actual effort to discern their intent, and this could be difficult. On the assumption that law had its obligation from its maker's will, common lawyers began in the fifteenth century and especially the sixteenth to wrestle with problems such as the hidden character of a lawmaker's mind and the divergent minds of multiple legislators. For example, in theory there could only be a single legislative body, but in a representative system of government, the intent of such a body rested in the minds of many individuals, and there were apt to be as "many wittes" as "heades" and as "many myndes" as "statute makers."[51]

Notwithstanding the vagaries of intent, common lawyers remained confident that intent could be discerned. The conventional academic solution lay in the lawmaker's words, it being familiar among civilians that words were the vehicles, images, or signs of intent.[52] Justinian's *Code*, how-

[50] Sir John Davies, *Reports*, sig. *2[r] (Preface Dedicatory). A later commentator bitterly complained that when legal writers said that custom *"cannot be recorded anywhere but in the memory of the people,"* this was as informative as if they had "directed them to the inhabitants of the world in the moon," for to say that law "is not any where recorded but in the frail memory of the people . . . is only telling us, in effect, that it is not any where to be found at all." *A Plain Argument To Shew, From the Theory and Practice of the Laws of England, That There Is Really No Law At All Subsisting Among Britons, for Security of the Properties*, 17–18 (London: 1761).

[51] Samuel L. Thorne, ed., *A Discourse upon the Exposicion & Understanding of Statutes*, 151–152 (San Marino: Huntington Library, 1942).

This treatise had a more interesting history than Thorne understood, and the history of its rewriting suggests how English views on law and interpretation were shifting. As observed by Thorne, Thomas Egerton owned a copy of the treatise and rewrote it, but Egerton was not alone, for William Fleetwood apparently also rewrote a copy—largely by replacing the front of the treatise. For this new portion, see William Fleetwood, *The Office of a Justice of the Peace, Together with Instructions, How and In What Manner Statutes Shall Be Expounded*, 97–128 (London: 1658). Whereas the treatise originally opened with a statement that "[a]ll that lawe which ys posytyve consisteth either in proclamacions or in actes of Parlyament," it now in Fleetword's hands stated that "Acts of Parliament make Laws Positive." Ibid., 97. More generally, it now included passages on intent that resonated with Plowden and that, in a manner characteristic of Fleetwood, acknowledged the breadth of possible departures from a statute's words. In short, whereas Egerton—later Lord Chancellor Ellesmere—was content with the treatise's old-fashioned account of interpretation and its strident assertion of royal power, Fleetwood felt obliged to correct what he undoubtedly considered errors.

[52] For an illustration of such analysis, see Ullmann, *The Medieval Idea of Law*, 113–114.

ever, had already criticized those who took advantage of the words of a law to depart from its intent, and some civilians and especially common lawyers similarly assumed that it was sometimes necessary to seek the intent beyond the words.[53] An anonymous sixteenth-century treatise explained that because "wordes were but invented to declare the meanynge of men, we muste rather frame the wordes to the meanynge" rather than "the meanynge to the wordes."[54] Departing further from the academic conclusion that words were images of intent, English lawyers often emphasized the necessity of discerning not merely the intent of the words, but the intent of the statute as a whole—as when Serjeant Saunders argued that "the words . . . are not the statute, but only the image of the statute, and the life of the statute rests in the minds of the expositors of the words, who are makers of the stat-

[53] Justinian, *Codex* (I.xiv.5).

In seeking intent, judges ideally had to read old statutes in accord with the old meaning of their words. In 1456, Chief Justice Walter Moyle said that the judges read old statutes not according to the "the letter" but in accord with the "common intendment" and the "intendment with which it was made," and in one case he therefore consulted a grammar teacher. Y. B. Michaelmas 35 Henry VI, pl. 25, fol. 16b. Two centuries later, Chief Justice Vaughan similarly noted that "[t]he meaning of *words* in any Law are to be known, either from their use and *signification,* according to common acceptation before the *Law* [was] made, or from some *Law* or *Institution* declaring their *signification.*" *Hill v. Good* (C.P. 1673), Vaughan, *Reports,* 305. In the mid-eighteenth century, Thomas Rutherforth taught: "Laws operate at a distance of time: those who live many years after the laws were made, are obliged to act upon them; and are, therefore, concerned to know their true meaning. But, in length of time, the meaning of a law may become doubtful, though it was clear and precise when it was first made." Hence the need for "looking back into the contemporary practice." He also noted that "[t]hough the persons, who preside" in courts of judicature "in later times, may have the same authority to interpret a law that their predecessors had; yet what their predecessors have done, who were contemporaries with the legislator, will help to guide them in the use of this authority: because it will show them in what sense the law was understood by those who had the best opportunity of knowing the true sense, either by advising with the legislator himself, or, at least by seeing the situation of things, which led him to make the law." Rutherforth, *Institutes of Natural Law,* 418–419 (II.vii.9).

[54] Thorne, ed., *A Discourse upon the Exposicion & Understanding of Statutes,* 140. See also Fleetwood, *The Office of a Justice of the Peace,* 141. Note the synonymous allusions to the lawmaker's "intent" and "meaning." Referring to contracts, Serjeant Catline said that if the law "would rather apply the intention of the parties to the order and form of the words, than the words to the intention of the parties, such law would be more full of form than of substance." *Browning v. Beston* (K.B. 1555), Plowden, *Reports,* 1: 140 (1816). In *Eyston v. Studd,* counsel for the defendant "and the whole Court" took the view that "the Intent of Statutes is more to be regarded and pursued than the precise Letter of them, for oftentimes Things, which are within the Words of Statutes, are out of the Purview of them, which Purview extends no further than the Intent of the Makes of the Act, and the best Way to construe an Act of Parliament is according to the Intent rather than to the Words." *Eyston v. Studd* (C.B. 1574), ibid., 464. William Fleetwood sardonically observed that "the wordes of an act of Parliament are not ever [i.e., always] to bee followed, for that sometyme the construccion is meere contrary to what is written . . . and some statutes are wincked at by non observacion or otherwise, soe that they seeme to bee noe lawes." Fleetwood's Speech (April 19, 1571), Anonymous Journal, in *Proceedings in the Parliaments of Elizabeth I,* 1: 236.

ute."[55] Words might in theory be signs or images of intent, but at common law it was often necessary to revert more directly to the intent—indeed, not merely the lawmaker's intent or meaning in the words, but in the statute or the act of record, for this is what created legislative obligation.

Common lawyers ended up with a two-tier approach, in which they were initially to discern intent from the words but were to pursue the intent more generally when the words were "ambiguous" or "obscure."[56] Although these two levels of inquiry were often described in a sort of shorthand as a choice between following either the "words" or the "intent," both approaches were merely the means of understanding the intent—one being an initial presumption that the intent could be discerned from the words, and the other being a recognition that when the words remained unclear it was necessary to inquire more broadly about the act's intent. This distinction between the words and the underlying intent often found expression in the Christian trope of the letter and the spirit, and it was therefore commonplace for early modern English lawyers to argue from the spirit of the law against the letter, and for opposing counsel to respond that the letter was clear or that the letter and the spirit were in accord—all of this being a debate about the intent.

When pursuing the intent of an act, men sometimes had to adopt an equitable interpretation. In particular, where legislators did not make their intent clear, it could be presumed that they intended what was lawful, and for acts of Parliament this at least meant what was just or equitable according to natural law. The *locus classicus* of such ideas was Aristotle's discussion of *epieikeia*—the equity that corrected the unjust generalizations of human law. For Aristotle, this justice that "goes beyond the written law" was only "partly" intended by legislators, because although it was intended "where they find themselves unable to define things exactly," it was "not intended, where they have noticed no defect in the law."[57] Common lawyers of the

55 Plowden, *Reports,* 1: 82. This was reiterated by Fleetwood, *The Office of a Justice of the Peace,* 98.

56 Fleetwood, *The Office of a Justice of the Peace,* 98. In the late fifteenth century, it was said that "every statute made must be taken according to the intent of those that made it, when its words are doubtful or ambiguous, and according to its preamble." Y.B., Pascal, 4 Edward IV, pl. 4 (1465), as quoted by Chrimes, *English Constitutional Ideas in the Fifteenth Century,* 294. Fleetwood recited that "[t]he intent of the makers of the Statutes is to be enquired, and the exposition of the ambiguous words in such Statutes, and the Letter shall be aided by the Intent." Moreover, "if the Termes and the Letters of any Statute are obscure and difficult to be perceived . . . you ought to understand the sense of the Letter." Fleetwood, *The Office of a Justice of the Peace,* 98.

57 Nicomachean Ethics, 1137b (V.x); Rhetoric, 1374a (I.xiii), in *The Complete Works of Aristotle,* 2: 1795–1796, 2188, ed. Jonathan Barnes (Princeton: Princeton University Press,

sixteenth century who were old-fashioned could still follow Aristotle's tradition and so could discuss the equitable understanding of statutes as a matter of directly avoiding injustice.[58] Increasingly, however, common lawyers followed ideals of authority and therefore said that injustice was avoided in the interpretation of statutes through the charitable supposition that the injustice had not been intended. The underlying logic was the view, as stated already in the late fifteenth century, that "in every statute one must construe it in accord with the intent of those who made the statute."[59] On this assumption, drawn from ideals of authority, judges at least by the sixteenth century came to recognize that they could pursue charitable suppositions about a statute's intent only when its intent was otherwise unclear.[60]

In justifying their equitable interpretation of uncertain statutes, some judges said that an Act of Parliament "made against natural equity . . . is void," but this cannot be taken out of context.[61] Rather than suggest that they could actually hold an inequitable act of Parliament void of legal obligation, these judges apparently meant that such an act was void of moral obligation. More exactly, they probably meant it was void in the court of conscience—this being a foundation for their equitable interpretation of the statute in a court of law. If a statute was contrary to natural law or equity and thus without obligation in conscience, this did not by itself render the statute void in a court of law, for the obligation of the statute rested on

1985). Moreover, according to the *Digest,* "Statutes ought to be given the more favorable interpretation, whereby their intendment is saved." Alan Watson, ed., *The Digest of Justinian* (I.iii.18) (Philadelphia: University of Pennsylvania Press, 1998).

58 In a very traditional manner, the *Discourse upon the Exposicion & Understanding of Statutes* stated that one situation in which "an estatute shalbe taken against the wordes is *ut euitetur iniquum*"—in order that injustice be avoided—"for statutes come to stablyshe lawes, & yf anie iniquitye shulde be gathered out of them they doe not so muche as deserve the name of lawes." *A Discourse upon the Exposicion & Understanding of Statutes,* 162. St. German's Student viewed reason and intent as distinct grounds for charitable interpretation, saying that "it apperyth that somtyme a man maye be exceptyd . . . fro the rygoure of a statute by the lawe of reason, and sometyme by the intent of the makers of the statute," but this was on the assumption that exception by the law of reason was only to be had in Chancery. T. F. T. Plucknett and J. L. Barton, eds., *St. German's Doctor and Student,* 103 (London: Selden Society, 1974).

59 *Coste v. An Undersheriff,* Y.B. 21 Henry VII, Hil. pl. 28, cited by Chrimes, *English Constitutional Ideas in the Fifteenth Century,* 295 ("Et en chescun statut on covient de construir l'entent de eux que fesoient le statut").

60 Chrimes, *English Constitutional Ideas in the Fifteenth Century,* 294; "The Equity of a Statute and Heydon's Case," in Samuel E. Thorne, *Essays in English Legal History,* 160 (London: Hambledon, 1985).

61 *Day v. Savage,* Hobart, *Reports,* 87 (K.B. 1614); *Hutchins v. Player,* O. Bridgman, *Reports,* 300 (C.P. 1663). Similar statements apparently were made already in the early sixteenth century in Gray's Inn. John Baker, *The Oxford History of English Law,* 6: 80 (Oxford: Oxford University Press, 2003).

the intent and authority of its maker. Where the intent of the statute was uncertain, however, a judge could not presume the maker had intended an injustice, and therefore the judgment that a statute was void in the interior court of conscience required the judge in his exterior court to interpret the statute to avoid this conclusion.[62] Thus, although it sounded bold to say that an act of Parliament was void, this was merely an attempt to build upon the presumption of just intent in the narrow space left by ideals of authority and will.

The equitable pursuit of intent could be necessary when statutes were drafted either too broadly or too narrowly. Where a statute was casually drafted so generally that it worked injustice in particular cases, "it shall be taken that it was the intent of the makers of the statute to except such cases." In contrast, where the statute was drafted too narrowly, "the intent of a statute shall be taken ferther than the expresse letter stretchyth." The intent, however, could "not . . . be taken agaynst the expresse wordes of the statute."[63] Summarizing these two types of charitable interpretation, Chancellor Hatton observed that whereas "some Statutes are general in Words, and particular in Intent; some are particular in words, and general in intent," but for both, "when the intent is proved, that must be followed."[64]

In all of this there was a risk that for many a judge "the bare letter of a lawe for him maks no conscienc[e] to wrest a lawe, contrary to the meaning of the makers of that lawe," but this was a reason to be cautious rather than to abandon the pursuit of intent.[65] Under the guise of resolving uncertainty, there was always room for judges to make moral adjustments in the law, and exactly where the pursuit of intent became manipulation could be difficult to discern. Nonetheless, it was the lawmaker's intent or will that both justified and limited equitable interpretation. "For when the words express not the intent of the Makers," it was necessary to interpret "further . . . than the bare words; but ever it must be thought" that this was "the meaning of the Maker."[66] Two centuries later, Lord Mansfield repeated: "There can be

[62] For further details, see Appendix I.

[63] Plucknett and Barton, eds., *St. German's Doctor and Student,* 101, 166. In other words, the judges "may many tymes Juge after the mynde of the makers as farre as the lettre maye suffre." Ibid., 101.

[64] Hatton, *A Treatise Concerning Statutes,* 13–14. Such matters were also discussed by Plowden, Doddridge, and Coke. More recently they have been analyzed by John Manning, "Textualism and the Equity of the Statute," *Columbia Law Review,* 101: 1 (2001), and William N. Eskridge, Jr., "All About Words: Early Understandings of the 'Judicial Power' in Statutory Interpretation, 1776–1806," *Columbia Law Review,* 101: 990 (2001).

[65] Speech on bill for ban on printing certain books (Feb. 10?, 1585), in Hartley, ed., *Proceedings in the Parliaments of Elizabeth I,* 2: 41.

[66] Hatton, *A Treatise Concerning Statutes,* 28–29. He also said that "whensoever there is de-

no doubt but Acts of Parliament are to be expounded by equity: that is, have a sound construction put upon them, according to the meaning of the Legislature, who cannot include every particular case, nor set forth all the exceptions," but "the *Equity* of an Act can be carried no further than to what was within the *View and Intention* of the Legislature, and the *Mischief* meant to be prevented."[67]

Ultimately, as already suggested, legislative obligation in England rested on the intent associated with an act of record. Whereas in Continental theory legislative intent had to be promulgated, at common law it had to be enacted by a court and enrolled in its record, and whether as to a corporate by-law or a statute adopted by Parliament, the two elements of legislative obligation—intent and an act of record—had to be combined. The standard solution was to speak of the intent of the act. Today, it is commonplace to draw a sharp distinction between the intent of individuals and the meaning of words, to worry about reconciling the actual intentions of multiple legislators, and to despair of drawing meaning from even a single legislator's intent. Yet the two elements that created legal obligation—as succinctly summarized in the phrase "intent of the act"—once required lawyers to ask what the legislature intended or meant in its enactment, and this was not a narrowly literal inquiry, either about intent or about words, but rather a more abstract investigation, which might draw upon the words and upon the intent of individual legislators, but which sought the intent, sense, or meaning of the act attributable to its maker, which in England was Parliament.[68] In the two-tier analysis, one began narrowly with "the words," but when these were obscure one had to move to a more general examination of "intent," and as Edmund Plowden explained in his account of equitable interpretation, this required one to follow the "sense of the act," which

---

parture from the words to the intent, that must be well proved that there is such meaning." Ibid., 14–15. For Ellesmere's bold departure from this position and the context in which it must be understood, see the discussion of the *Earl of Oxford's Case* in Appendix I.

[67] *King v. Williams* (K.B. 1757), Kenyon, *Reports,* 2: 74; Burrow, *Reports,* 1: 407 (K.B. 1757). Mansfield may have been up to his own mischief, for he may have been attempting to suggest that mischief was a separate standard rather than a means of understanding intent. In fact, the question of mischief had been understood as a matter of intent. See, for example, Fleetwood, *The Office of a Justice of the Peace,* 106, 109, 115, 128, 143, 145, 146. See also *The Case of the Master and Fellows of Magdalen College* (K.B. 1615), Coke, *Reports,* 11: 73b. For the way in which "[o]ccasionally, Mansfield's awareness of the legislative intent prevented him from reaching what he regarded as the just result," see James Oldham, *The Mansfield Manuscripts and the Growth of English Law in the Eighteenth Century,* 1: 105 (Chapel Hill: University of North Carolina Press, 1992).

[68] Baker, *The Oxford History of English Law,* 6: 79. Some aspects of these points are recognized from a nonhistorical perspective by Gary Lawson and Guy Seidman, "Originalism as a Legal Enterprise," *Constitutional Commentary,* 23: 47 (2006).

he also described as "the intent of the law and the pleasure of the lawmakers."[69] Plowden was anything but naive, and through his close juxtaposition of such different characterizations of intent, this greatest of early reporters evidently hoped to convey what he meant. In less elaborate versions of this approach, common lawyers spoke ambidextrously about "the intention of the makers of the act" and "the intention of the said Act," and precisely because it was at least superficially incoherent to speak of the intent of an act, lawyers could rely on this shorthand expression to avoid a shallow literalism and suggest the depth of what they meant.[70] Of course, they did not thereby escape all of the difficulties of discussing intent, but they at least avoided the obstacles that today so often arise from a narrow literalism.

One way or another, intent had to be discerned, for it was the source and measure of the obligation of law. As summarized by the Cambridge professor Thomas Rutherforth, "the obligations . . . produced by the civil laws of our country, arise from the intention of the legislature," and thus the obligation of such law could only be ascertained by "collect[ing] the meaning and intention of the . . . lawmaker, from some outward signs," which was "called interpretation." Of course, in pursuing the intent of a law, one would sooner or later reach a point at which no further intent could be discerned, and beyond that point the law lacked obligation: "A voluntary law can oblige no farther than the law-maker intended that it should oblige: because all the authority that it has, is derived only from his will and intention: so that, wherever this will or intention stops, the obligation of the law must stop with it." Although today this breadth and limit of legal obligation seems elusive and artificial, it once seemed natural. The authority of a human lawmaker and the obligation of his will appeared to be derived from natural law or at least human nature as established by God, and therefore "the intention of the legislator" was "the natural measure of the extent of the law."[71]

[69] *Eyston v. Studd* (C.B. 1574), Plowden, *Reports,* 2: fol. 466[r] ("le sense del act," "le sense del parolles del act," "lentent del Institutors del ley," "parols del ley," and "lentent del ley, & plest bien les Institutors del ley").

[70] Note on Justice in Wales (1608), Coke, *Reports,* 12: 48. Rutherforth later spoke interchangeably of "the intention of the legislator," "the design of the legislator," "the meaning of the law," "the meaning of the legislator," and "the design of the law." Rutherforth, *Institutes of Natural Law,* 433 (II.vii.13). He explained that intent created obligation "not merely as this intention is an act of the mind, but as it is declared or expressed by some outward sign or mark, which makes it known to us." Ibid., 404 (II.vii.1).

[71] Rutherforth, *Institutes of Natural Law,* 8 (I.i.9), 404 (II.vii.1), 433 (II.vii.13). More generally, "the way to ascertain our claims, as they arise from promises, contracts or wills, and our obligations, as they arise from instituted laws, is to collect the meaning and intention of the

Jurisdiction

The assumptions that underlay the lawmaker's authority and the obligation of his will also implied a unity of jurisdiction—thus making his law, the law of the land, supreme across the land. This supremacy of the law of the land initially heightened the danger arising from ideals about a ruler's authority and will. Yet having thus sharpened the problem of authority, the supremacy of the law of the land soon also gave strength to the solution that would be found in the highest part of this law.

Claims of authority had long been framed in terms of jurisdiction, but jurisdiction in the Middle Ages did not typically extend to an undivided human authority over temporal matters within a territory. On the contrary, medieval jurisdictions were as irregular as their origins, and they often intersected and even overlapped within a territory. Although there was much friction between the jurisdictions of the two cities—most dramatically between the popes and the holy roman emperors—the division typically led to cooperation, even if with much jostling at the boundaries.[72] Thus, in an actual city, London, the jurisdictions of the Crown and the city coexisted with a host of local religious jurisdictions, such as Whitefriars and the Minories, which offered sanctuary from arrest.[73] Even more than the abstract division between church and state, this fragmentation of authority into a hodgepodge of lesser jurisdictions illustrates the tolerance for complexly divided jurisdictions that flourished within the old hierarchy—a system in which law enjoyed its obligation from its participation in the eternal reason and thus could be enunciated by different bodies in a single realm.

Ideals of authority, however, increasingly led men to expect a single authoritative lawmaker with a unified civil jurisdiction. If the discordant views of men about natural law revealed it to be God's will for the ruler of each land to have authority to make coercive, binding law, then a ruler presumably enjoyed this lawmaking authority throughout his jurisdiction. For the sake of order, in other words, God apparently gave lawmaking authority to only one lawmaker in any one place, and this indivisible temporal

---

promisor, contractor, testator, or lawmaker, from some outward signs or marks." This was the "collecting of a man's intention" that was "called interpretation." Ibid., 404.

72 Richard Helmholz, "Canonists and Standards of Impartiality for Papal Judges Delegate," in *Canon Law and the Law of England,* 76 (London: Hambledon, 1987); Richard Helmholz, "The Writ of Prohibition to Court Christian Before 1500," in ibid., 98–99; Richard Helmholz, "Conflicts Between Religious and Secular Law: Common Themes in the English Experience, 1250–1640," *Cardozo Law Review,* 12: 727–728 (1991).

73 For the law of sanctuary in England, see Richard Helmholz, *The ius commune in England: Four Studies,* Chapter 1 (Oxford: Oxford University Press, 2001).

jurisdiction, in which the government's law enjoyed supremacy, became the jurisdiction of the modern state. Marsilius (to take a prominent example) concluded in his *Defensor Pacis* that "it is necessary" that there be "but one prynce, kynge, or heed governoure in a cyvyule co[m]munytie, unto whome all other heddes and offycers must be obedyent and subjects."[74]

This was a powerful argument against the Church, and English monarchs seized upon it in ways that elevated their lawmaking authority and the jurisdiction of their law.[75] Medieval kings and their Parliaments had occasionally asserted their jurisdiction against that of the pope. Now, going even further, Henry VIII rejected appeals to Rome by having Parliament declare that he was "institute[d]" by "Almyghtie god with plenarie hoole and intiere power p[re]emynence autoritie p[re]rogatyve and jurisdiction to rendre and yelde Justice and finall det[er]mynacion to all . . . within this his realme."[76] Put more generally by William Tyndale, the king "ought not . . . suffer" clerics "to have a severall lawe by them selves," for "one kynge, one lawe, is Gods ordinau[n]ce in every realme."[77]

Yet having resisted the pope by claiming the exclusive obligation of the king's law within his realm, the Crown in the sixteenth century had to worry that its ideal of unified jurisdiction would interfere with its own prerogative. Although English kings had rarely been satisfied to act merely through their law, they had usually understood the advantages of leaving it ambiguous whether in the exercise of their prerogatives they acted entirely

[74] Marsilius of Padua, *The Defence of Peace,* fol. 37[v] (I.xvii). Harry Stout concludes that "the *Defensor Pacis* shifted theories of church and state away from a Galasian dualism to a monistic theory of the state in which the government was the supreme authority." Harry S. Stout, "Marsilius of Padua and the Henrician Reformation," *Church History,* 43: 318 (1974). More generally, see Figgis, *Political Thought from Gerson to Grotius,* 91.

[75] According to Marsilius, civil jurisdiction similarly reached all civil objects, including Jesus himself, for "chryste shewed . . . that hym selfe is under the coactyve jurysdyccyon of ye seculer pri[n]ce as touchyng reall, or te[m]porall substau[n]ce"—that is, "his p[er]son & bodye." This was a "personal jurysdyccion," and "it is not possyble for any prynce to have greatter jurysdyccyon." Marsilius of Padua, *The Defence of Peace,* fols. 14[r] (I.iv), 53[r] (II.iv). For the English reception of Marsilius, see F. Le von Baumer, "Thomas Starkey and Marsilius of Padua," *Politica,* 2: 188–205 (1936); Stout, "Marsilius of Padua and the Henrician Reformation," 43: 308–318; Paul O'Grady, *Henry VIII and the Conforming Catholics,* Chapter 3 (Collegeville: Liturgical Press, 1990).

[76] An Acte that the Appeles in suche Cases as have ben used to be pursued to the See of Rome shall not be from henseforth had ne used but wythin this Realme, 24 Henry VIII, cap. 12 (1534). Later claims of such jurisdiction appeared in the Proclamation of Edward VI (July 31, 1547), in Paul L. Hughes and James F. Larkin, eds., *Tudor Royal Proclamations,* 1: 393–394 (New Haven: Yale University Press, 1964); An Act restoring to the Crowne th[e] au[n]cyent Jurisdiction over the State Ecclesiasticall and Sp[irit]uall, and abolyshing all Forreine Power repugnaunt to the same, 1 Elizabeth I, c.1 (1558–1559).

[77] [William Tyndale], *The obedie[n]ce of a Christen man and how Christe[n] rulers ought to governe,* fol. lxxiii[v]–lxxix[r] ([1548]).

through or above the law. The awkwardness was that after they opposed papal power on the theory that their lawmaking authority was exclusive in their jurisdiction, they had to explain why their own prerogatives were not fully subject to their law. It was one thing for the king to ride the horse of authority against the pope, but quite another to be taken for a ride, and Crown lawyers in the sixteenth century therefore made increasingly open claims that the king had absolute powers. Citing civilian commentators, they defended the parts of the king's prerogative that had not been clearly a matter of law by making explicit that although the king exercised some "ordinary" prerogatives through and under his law, he exercised other, "absolute" prerogatives above the law.

Common lawyers, however, tended to welcome the Crown's claim for its exclusive lawmaking authority throughout its jurisdiction, for this seemed to confirm, what most common lawyers were glad to believe, that the king enjoyed authority only through or at least under his law. In pushing back against the open claims for an absolute power, these common lawyers undoubtedly pursued the jurisdiction of the common law beyond its medieval sphere, and modern scholars therefore tend to view Edward Coke and his fellow common lawyers as opportunistic and aggressive, but this ignores the shift toward authority and the degree to which the English assumed that authority should be exercised through or under the law of the land. Against the pope, both the Crown and the common lawyers had insisted that royal law—the law of the land—had the highest authority and obligation in the land, and common lawyers, as might be expected, took such professions as confirmation that no exercise of power (ecclesiastical or secular, ordinary or extraordinary) could have authority and obligation in the realm unless through the law of the land or at least under it. From this perspective, common lawyers looked back on the variety of coordinate jurisdictions that had once flourished in England and assumed that they had existed merely at the sufferance of the king's law. The Crown might protest that the king could exercise authority either through his law or above it, but according to the common lawyers, if the king's law was the source of all other authority in the land, nothing could have legal obligation within the land except through or under his law.

The ideal of royal authority thus eventually seemed to establish the unified jurisdiction of the king and especially of his law—the law of the land. The common law doctrine that only the law of the land and what it authorized had obligation in England has long been familiar. Not merely a doctrine, however, this was an expression of the broader ideal that the lawmaker had authority throughout his jurisdiction, and although conventionally the king in Parliament was the lawmaker with supreme authority and unified jurisdiction, there would soon come a time when the people came to be understood as the fundamental maker of English law.

The unified jurisdiction of the law of the land was most bold in its implication that even natural law and divine law were part of the law of England. Like Fortescue and St. German, Coke acknowledged that "the law of nature was before any judicial or municipal law in the world" and that it "is immutable, and cannot be changed," but rather than suggest that English law participated in higher laws, he subordinated obligation of natural law to English jurisdiction with the arresting statement that the "law of nature is part of the laws of England."[78] In the same manner, Chief Justice Matthew Hale said that "*Christianity* is parcel of the *Laws of England*."[79]

The unqualified obligation of English law across its jurisdiction denied independent obligation not only to higher laws but also to what today would be considered international law. Unless adopted in the law of England, treaties and the law of nations were not legally binding in England.[80] Nor, it will be seen, were declarations of international bodies.

In denying obligation to external sources of law, English lawyers saved

[78] *Calvin's Case* (Ex. Ch. 1608), Coke, *Reports,* 7: 4b. See also ibid., 12b.

[79] *Taylor's Case* (K.B. 1676), Ventris, *Reports,* 1: 293, discussed by Stuart Banner, "When Christianity Was Part of the Common Law," *Law and History Review,* 16: 29–30 (1998). Although often taken to be an expression of the establishment of Christianity, Hale's statement was only one of many assertions about the authority of the law of the land over "foreign" law.

English lawyers occasionally relied on scripture in their arguments about law, but even this could be viewed with suspicion, as when in 1610 James Whitlocke responded to such arguments in favor of a royal power of impositions by reciting how little success Cardinal Wolsey had when relying upon scripture to justify a non-Parliamentary imposition: "And if any Churchmen will endeavour by application of the text of Scripture, to overthrow the ancient lawes, and liberties of the Kingdome, I would advise them to be admonished by the ill success of the Cardinall." [James Whitlocke], *A Learned and Necessary Argument To Prove that Each Subject Hath a Propriety in His Goods,* 13 (London: 1641). Later, in 1684, while John Holt was still practicing law, he defended the lawfulness of the East India Company's charter by arguing that "ye Christ^{n} Relig^{n} . . . is ye main end of ye Governm^{t}," and that thus "if any Law be made ag^{t} any point of ye Christ^{n} Relig^{n}, y^{t} Law is ipso facto void." Even this rather extravagant claim, however, was based on human, constitutional law—Holt's argument being that the law would be void "because it is made ag^{t} ye origin^{l} of Governm^{t}." *Governor and Company of Merchants Trading to the East Indies v. Thomas Sandys* (K.B. 1683), Volume of Miscellaneous Reports, 122, Folger Library, Ms. V.a. 203. The case was apparently decided in 1684. Shower, *Reports,* 2: 366.

[80] The implications of the common law assumptions for the law of nations were spelled out with clarity by Matthew Tindal, who had been educated in civil law but had a decidedly common law attitude: "The several Legislative Powers of Nations never enacted such Laws [of nations]; nor have all other Nations Authority to oblige any Sovereign Independent State," and thus "the Law of Nations and Nature, is in effect the same," except that the one was the law of nature "as it respects the duty of single Persons to one another," and the other, "as it respects Men collectively as they are Bodies Politick." Moreover, the law of nations could not be binding as custom, because "[i]n a Civil Society, Customs grow into Laws, be-

their sharpest admonitions for those who would threaten the authority and jurisdiction of English law with the academic learning of the civil and canon laws. This "foreign" learning came as close to academic speculation as common lawyers knew, and although it frequently shaped how they perceived legal problems, it thereby posed an especially serious challenge to the authority and jurisdiction of their domestic law. English lawyers were therefore particularly emphatic that the civil and canon laws could not have obligation in England, except as incorporated within the law of the land. English law permitted the direct application of civil law in the Court of Admiralty to the extent maritime law had been "allowed by the lawes of the Realme."[81] English law also allowed canon law in the ecclesiastical courts. Otherwise, Hale noted, "it is most plain, That neither the Canon Law nor the Civil Law have any Obligation as Laws within this Kingdom . . . for the King of England does not recognize any Foreign Authority as superior or equal to him in this Kingdom." Thus, "their Authority is founded merely on their being admitted and received by us, which alone gives 'em their Authoritative Essence, and qualifies their obligation."[82] Chief Justice Holt was relatively open-minded when he explained that "thô . . . some Use is made of the Civil Law . . . it is quoted not to be relyed upon as authority but only for Information and Illustrac[i]on to open and Explain the nature and reason of things." Common lawyers could learn from such law, but by itself "the Civil Law never had force in England, Because nothing can give it any force, but it's being received and [there being] an immemorial Usage thereupon."[83]

---

cause it is the Will of the Supreme Powers, they should. Customs are their presumed or unwritten Will, which they by their express Will may alter as they please. But amongst different Nations, there is no Common Legislative Power; but every Nation is at liberty to act as it pleases. . . . A Nation, it is true, ought not lightly to change what they have generally practiced, . . . but if they do, they break no Law." Much was "a Matter of Decency" but not "a part of the voluntary Law of Nations, more than wearing of Clothes, or twenty other things Mankind generally do, either out of Necessity, or Conveniency, or for other reasons." In this manner, "the Laws of different Countries, when they happen to be the same," were often mistaken for the law of nations, "yet they have not their Force and Authority from any tacit Compact, but because the supream Powers in each Society have made them Laws, which any one of them may alter without any Violation of the Laws of Nations." Matthew Tindall, *An Essay Concerning the Laws of Nations, and the Rights of Soveraigns,* 2–7 (London: 1694).

[81] Coke, *Institutes,* 2: 51. So too, the proceedings of the Constable and the Marshal. Ibid. Coke also wrote that "forrein precedents are not to be objected against us, because we are not subject to forrein lawes." Ibid., 98. See also ibid., 365, 488.

[82] Matthew Hale, *The History of the Common Law of England,* 19–20, ed. Charles M. Gray (Chicago: University of Chicago Press, 1971).

[83] *Blackbourn v. Davis* (K.B., 1701), British Library, Holt's Opinions, Add. Ms. 35980, fol. 26[v]. In another case, when alluding to Roman law to suggest the reason of the common law, he carefully explained that "I do not quote this as an Authority; for if I should be so un-

This individual authority and obligation of the law of the land within its jurisdiction laid out what would become the path of constitutional authority in England, for when the authority of the ruler became such a problem that it required a solution in the authority of the people, their law would enjoy the supreme obligation and indivisible jurisdiction of the law of the land. In the meantime, however, the unqualified obligation of the law across its jurisdiction could make the lawmaking authority of the ruler seem all the more worrisome.

Extreme Claims of Authority

The ideal of authority, accentuated by the notion of unified jurisdiction, tempted men in the sixteenth and seventeenth centuries to make extreme claims about the power of rulers. The ideal of authority was an appealing response to social and intellectual divisions, but it elevated a potentially all-or-nothing vision of what a ruler could do, and it thus stimulated restless ambitions and fears. It was in the context of these aspirations and anxieties about authority that the notion of a constitution would come to seem so valuable.

The all-or-nothing effect of ideals of authority can be observed in the changing role of divine and natural law. Although these higher laws had once been measures of the obligation of particular human laws, they now became measures of a general allegiance—or resistance—to government as a whole.

The leading Protestant Reformers nicely illustrate the transition. Martin Luther still echoed old ideals about obligation, for he viewed scripture as a measure of the obligation of particular human laws and so held that individuals could not actively obey an unscriptural law. He began, however, to explore the question of allegiance, and although he long denied any right of resistance, he seems eventually to have contemplated some communal resistance against especially unjust rulers.[84] Calvin moved more emphatically toward treating natural and divine law as measures of allegiance rather than of obedience, for he rejected any individual disobedience to particular laws, however unjust, and he thereby left men to escape oppression only through communal resistance to the magistrate—to be precise, only through the divinely authorized opposition undertaken by inferior magis-

---

derstood, it might raise an Accusation, that I presume to Judge the people of England by the rules of Civil Law." *Lane v. Cotton & Frankland* (K.B. 1701), British Library, Holt's Opinions, Add. Ms. 35981, fol. 96[r].

[84] Quentin Skinner, *The Foundations of Political Thought,* 2: 199–202 (Cambridge: Cambridge University Press, 2000).

trates. Calvin thus joined those who brought questions of justice completely within those of authority, and in thus closing off any individual duty or right to disobey an unjust law, he placed all hope of relief on the possibility of a communal uprising against the ruler.

This transition from decisions about the obligation of particular laws to all-or-nothing communal decisions about allegiance seemed to follow inexorably from the fallen condition of man and the consequent elevation of the ruler's authority. On account of the inability of men to agree on what law would be reasonable or just, God had apparently ordained civil rulers so that they might ordain laws for their subjects, and if all human laws made with authority thus had a divinely derived obligation, individuals could not escape the obligation of a particular law simply because they thought it unreasonable or unjust. Instead, a people could only refuse to obey when they (or, according to Calvin, their inferior magistrates) had divine authority to throw off their ruler altogether. The pursuit of authority thus transformed the effect of natural and divine law. It deprived these higher laws of their role as measures of individual obedience to particular human laws and simultaneously established these higher laws as measures of communal allegiance or resistance to entire regimes. Of course, each human government necessarily had its injustices, but men now squarely had to reject their government altogether or had to submit to the obligation of all its laws.

So stark a choice would be painful enough under a representative government, but under a royal government, it was ominous. Ideals of authority had simultaneously given rulers an elevated justification for the imposition of their will and had largely deprived individuals of any justification for disobedience—except through the cataclysm of communal rebellion against the government as whole.

Making matters worse, some scholars raised the stakes by expanding upon old ideals of absolute power. Late medieval civilian commentators generally viewed the civil law as a concrete explication of God's eternal rationality, and from this idealized, academic perspective it often seemed that human law had to be a reasonable command and that when the will of the ruler deviated from justice or reason, it was not really law.[85] The civilian commentators, however, combined this high idealism with a keen apprecia-

[85] Ullmann, *The Medieval Idea of Law,* 4, 16, 38, 44, 54–55. For Baldus and others, see Canning, *The Political Thought of Baldus de Ubaldis,* 76–77; Manlio Bellomo, *The Common Legal Past of Europe 1100–1800,* at 153, 165, 180, 199 (Washington: Catholic University of America Press, 1995). For similar observations about canon law, see "Only the Truth Has Authority": The Problem of 'Reception' in the Decretists and in Johannes de Turrecremata," in Brian Tierney, *Church Law and Constitutional Thought in the Middle Ages,* 257 (London: Variorum Reprints, 1979).

tion of princely authority and patronage. It was an appreciation of a ruler's will that they refined through their reading of Roman Imperial texts, and because their high-minded vision of legal obligation did not leave sufficient scope for a worldly, let alone Imperial, exercise of will through law, civilians tended to find space for such will outside of law. In other words, if law was expected to participate in the eternal verities, it was simply not plausible that a ruler could always govern through his law, and it therefore seemed necessary for him to act on occasion with absolute power—to exercise his will independently of his regularly ordained law.[86] Civilian commentators could be pleased that they thereby made room for the will of rulers while preserving the ideal that civil law participated in the eternal reason, and their dual conception of power—both through law and above law—could seem in princely circles to reveal their acumen in statecraft. Yet their open acceptance of human authority outside human law widened a narrow fissure of lawlessness into a gaping breach, and this would be of profound consequence.

This tear in the fabric of regular lawmaking authority left sixteenth-century Continental Europeans with a more ominous understanding of authority than the English, and it would soon license men to rend state authority apart, until they held lawful governance in one hand and simple state power in the other. Recognizing the injury from their candid acknowledgment of absolutism, most civilian commentators sought to bind it up with at least theoretical restraints. For example, many commentators denied that the ruler could exercise absolute power to take property without cause, and many presumed that the ruler could have not intended to act "supra ius et contra ius, et extra ius" unless he did so expressly—unless, that is, he adopted a *non obstante* clause, which, indeed, became the requirement for the dispensing power in England.[87] More broadly, the civilian commentators recognized the power above human law to be exceptional—the or-

[86] Canning, *The Political Thought of Baldus de Ubaldis,* 74–75; Pennington, *The Prince and the Law,* Chapters 2 and 3. They also tended to adopt the Roman law notion that a ruler was *legibus solutus*—not bound by laws—and this gave rise to an ambiguity. A ruler who was *legibus solutus* was above his law in one sense, but when he exercised power absolutely—that is, independently of his regularly ordained law—he acted above his law in another sense. Put succinctly, there was a difference between a ruler's merely being above his law and his exercising power above his law, and the latter was the point that now became so significant. Ibid., 58, 60, 74, 117. See note 3 above.

[87] For the requirement of a *non obstante* clause, see R. W. Carlyle and A. J. Carlyle, *A History of Medæval Political Theory in the West,* 6: 149 (New York: Barnes & Noble, nd); Ullmann, *The Medieval Idea of Law,* 104, note 3. More generally, for the efforts of Continental lawyers to tame the dangers of absolutism, see Pennington, *The Prince and the Law,* Chapters 3 and 4, who also observes, however, that their limitations "did not offer robust protection from the prince's arbitrary authority." Ibid., 120.

dained law being the ordinary law, and the absolute power being extraordinary.[88] Nonetheless, the breach in expectations of lawfulness—not only for popes but also increasingly for civil rulers—had been sanctified by scholarship, and learned men would soon take it further. English lawyers had traditionally hesitated to generalize that the king had absolute power, and when in the sixteenth century they acknowledged that such a power existed in the monarch, they not only treated it as exceptional but also often took care to confine it within the safety of particular prerogatives that were acknowledged by law. In contrast, learned civilians tended to consider the ruler's absolute authority a general, transcendent power, and as already suggested, most of their limitations on it were more intellectually satisfying than effectual. Jean Bodin was the most systematic of those who seized upon this opening. Candidly theorizing—what had long been apparent—that the exception was in fact central, he declared that absolute power was the defining feature of sovereignty.[89]

The shift toward authority had drawn men toward this extreme. The difficulty of agreeing on what was reasonable had led men to appreciate the ideal of a single coercive authority in each realm, and this affected how kings thought about their power. It was not simply that a king could now

[88] See, for example, Canning, *The Political Thought of Baldus de Ubaldis,* 74–75.

[89] Pennington, *The Prince and the Law,* at 276–283. For the traditional English focus on particular prerogatives and the way in which this was threatened in the sixteenth century, see W. S. Holdsworth, "The Prerogative in the Sixteenth Century," *Columbia Law Review,* 21: 561 (1921).

Bodin proudly declared that his was a theory that "neither lawyer nor politicall philosopher hath yet defined," but as Pennington makes clear, Bodin was elevating civilian ideas into theory. Jean Bodin was a French lawyer trained in Roman law, and he defined "Majestie or Soveraigntie" as "the most high, absolute, and perpetuall power over the citizens and subjects in a Commonwealth"—"that is to say, The greatest power to command." He thus not merely attributed lawmaking authority to the ruler but more broadly claimed that sovereignty was necessarily absolute—that "unto Majestie, or Soveraigntie belongeth an absolute power, not subject to any law"—a "perpetuall power . . . to dispose of the goods and lives, and of all the state at his pleasure." Such a ruler could deign to act through his ordinary laws, but he could not thereby limit himself if he was to remain sovereign or absolute. J. Bodin, *The Six Books of a Commonweale,* 73, 84, 88, 92, trans. Richard Knolles (London: 1606). Of course, as Pennington emphasizes, even this was not a freedom from "the lawes of God and nature," for "all princes and people of the world are unto them subject," even if only "before the tribunall seat of almightie God." Ibid., 92, 104.

Although Bodin began his definition of sovereignty in terms of absolute power, he then introduced the old doctrine of *legibus solutus*—that a ruler is not bound by laws—explaining that rather than "be bound unto the lawes and ordinances he maketh himselfe," a sovereign "is not subject to his lawes." Ibid., [91]–92. This addition was necessary to preserve the absolute power of the sovereign. While the sovereign acted above his law, he was not subject to it. Yet if he acted through his law, he might be thought to subject himself to its limits, and against this possibility, Bodin had to add that the ruler was not bound by his law.

openly idealize an unlimited authority; in addition, he had to worry that if such authority did not rest entirely in him, it would end up elsewhere. Just as subjects now faced an all-or-nothing choice of submission or resistance, so too rulers had to fear that there might be no middle ground—that if they did not preserve all authority for themselves, they would not really be sovereign and so might lose what authority they had. Such was the anxiety that gave force to Bodin's theory. It was also the sort of mental precipice occupied by James VI of Scotland. Widely read in Continental theories, James had high expectations of his authority—not only to make law but also to act above it—and he tended to fear that legal checks on royal authority would inevitably pull away the ground beneath his throne.[90] This high sense of authority boded ill for a man who in 1603 would become James I of England.

Even merely as to the power exercised under law, England was a place increasingly fraught with conflicting anxieties about royal authority. At the end of Elizabeth's reign, when members of the House of Commons protested against monopolies, the Queen's trusted adviser Robert Cecil warned the Commons that "the Queene meanes not to be swepte out of her prerogatyve." His fears, however, extended beyond Parliament, for he understood that the prerogative was "subjecte to a publique expectacion." He exclaimed to the House:

> Whie, Parleamente matters are ordinarye talke in the streetes. I have hearde my selfe, being in my coache, these wordes spoaken alowde: 'God prosper those that further the overthrowe of these monopolies. God send the prerogative touche not our libertie.' . . . I thincke those persones would be glad all soveraignitye were converted into popularitye.[91]

The conversion of sovereignty into popularity was the basic question of political authority, and whether in Parliament or on the street, it all too often seemed to leave little space for a middle ground.

The notion of authority thus solved one set of problems and exacerbated another. Sociologically, it overcame the fractures in society, but only

[90] Scottish kings, he argued, had existed prior to Scottish Parliaments, and therefore "the kings were the authors and makers of the Lawes, and not the Lawes of the kings." Taking this a step further, he held that "the King is above the law, as both the author and giver of strength thereto." Therefore, "although . . . a good king will frame all his action to be according to the Law; yet hee is not bound thereto but of his good will, and for good example-giving to his subjects." *The Trew Law of Free Monarchies* (1598), in *The Political Works of James I,* 62–63, ed. Charles Howard McIlwain (Cambridge: Harvard University Press, 1918).

[91] Robert Cecil's Speech (Nov. 25, 1601), in *Proceedings in the Parliaments of Elizabeth I,* 3: 398.

by concentrating authority in the state. Theologically, it responded to the fallen character of men, and yet left them peculiarly subject to the failings of their ruler. The difficulty was that human will has never been an unmixed blessing, and although the ideal of authority allowed men to overcome their discordant reasoning about justice, it left them dangerously exposed to the will of their ruler.

3

Constitutions

In response to their fears about the authority and will of rulers, Europeans and especially the English developed their ideas about constitutions. When rulers claimed an expansive lawmaking authority, let alone an authority above their law, many other men responded with claims about a higher human authority—a lawmaking authority diffused among the people. From this perspective, a constitution willed by the people was law, and being of the highest authority among the laws of the land, it was of the highest obligation.

According to the history of judicial review, a constitution was not considered binding law until the very late eighteenth century. Until then, according to much of the history, a constitution was an ambiguous mixture of natural and human law, and even to the extent it was made by men, it was more of an arrangement than a law.[1] It is true that the constitution of a government, in the sense of its arrangement, was not necessarily a law; but a constitution that was understood to have been willed by the people was another matter. This sort of constitution was a human enactment, and it

[1] Gordon S. Wood, *The Creation of the American Republic 1776–1787,* at 261 (Williamsburg: Institute of Early American History and Culture, 1969). Writing of the 1760s, Bernard Bailyn explains that "[t]he dominant view of the constitution" was "still the traditional one" of "the whole complex of existing laws and public institutions"—the arrangement of government. Bernard Bailyn, *The Ideological Origins of the American Revolution,* 178–179 (Cambridge: Belknap, 1968).

Underlying some of the confusion has been the tendency to refer to all limitations on government as constitutional, regardless of their character. Many limitations served constitutional functions, and at times, as in 1215 and 1258, these limitations were drawn up in writing. G. O. Sayles, *The Functions of the Medieval Parliament of England,* 65 (London: Hambleton, 1988); C. R. Cheney, "The 'Paper Constitution' preserved by Matthew Paris," *English Historical Review,* 65: 213 (1950). The ideal of a constitution enacted by the people, however, developed in the wake of ideals of lawmaking authority.

could overcome the king's lawmaking authority (and even the authority he exercised above his law) precisely because it was a law—a law made with the higher lawmaking authority of the people. Such a constitution was "the *origo* or first production of Civill Authority," and it thus was the limit of all such authority.[2]

The English Interpretation of the Lex Regia

Some early hints of what would become the nature of constitutional law can be observed in the English interpretation of the *Lex Regia.* It is notorious that the English were deeply attached to ideals of lawful government, but some medieval English lawyers went much further. In response to the Roman *Lex Regia,* they theorized about laws made by the people to authorize and limit their rulers.

The most prominent limit on English kings—their coronation oath—was not a law, but a promise about the law. Edward II, for example, "confirm[ed] to the people of England" their prior "laws and customs" and granted that "the just laws and customs" determined by "the community of your realm" would be "held and observed." Although this royal commitment concerned the law, it was merely a "promise" and perhaps, it will be seen, a condition.[3]

The law itself, however, could also bind the Crown—as already evident in Bracton. This thirteenth-century English judge is often cited to illustrate English ideals of governance through and under law, but he went considerably beyond this, for he hinted that a law made by the people might bind the ruler. The notion of *legibus solutus*—of a lawmaker unbound by laws—appealed to many rulers and to the academics who sought their patronage. A more measured ideal, however, recommended itself to other scholars, including Gratian, who wrote that "princes are to be bound by their own enactments" and that this "in itself prohibits them from infringing the ordinances they have imposed on their own subjects."[4] Bracton similarly emphasized that what a king forbade to others, "he ought not to do himself." The king was thus to "temper his power by law, which is the bridle of power, that he may live according to the laws"—to which Bracton

[2] [Henry Parker], *Jus Populi,* 2 (London: 1644).

[3] Coronation Oath of Edward II (1308), in *Sources of English Constitutional History,* 192, eds. Carl Stephenson and Frederick George Marcham (New York: Harper and Brothers, 1937).

[4] Gratian, *The Treatise on Laws with the Ordinary Gloss,* 29 (Distinction Nine, cap. 2), trans. Augustine Thompson and James Gordley (Washington, D.C.: Catholic University of America Press, 1993).

suggestively added: "for the law of mankind has decreed that his own laws bind the lawgiver."[5]

The notion that "the law of mankind" might "bind the lawgiver" was the English interpretation of the *lex regia.* Imperial Roman sources described the *lex regia* as the grant of legislative power from the people to the emperor: "A pronouncement of the emperor . . . has legislative force because, by the Regal Act *(lex regia)* relating to his sovereign power, the people conferred on him its whole sovereignty and authority."[6] This was a disturbing text, for it appeared to be an irrevocable and complete grant of power by which "the control of the state is transferred for all time to the emperors"—such that "when a prince is constituted he is given the right that whatever he decrees shall hold good." Continental medieval commentators therefore had reason to explore different interpretations of the *lex regia,* and although many took the conventional view that "all power was transferred to the prince by the people, who were thereby stripped of every vestige of sovereignty," others toyed with an alternative perspective, "that power was conferred on the prince in order that he might freely legislate, but in such a way that neither the power of the people nor the force of plebiscita and senatus consulta, old or new, should be diminished."[7] This new reading apparently departed from old, Imperial ideas, and a scholar might therefore hesitate bluntly to endorse it. Nonetheless it enjoyed considerable appeal as a counterpoint to the dominant Roman line on the *lex regia.*

[5] Bracton, *On the Laws and Customs of England,* 2: 305, ed. Samuel E. Thorne (Cambridge: Belknap, 1968). See Kenneth Pennington, *The Prince and the Law, 1200–1600,* at 92 (Berkeley: University of California Press, 1963).

[6] *Justinian's Institutes,* 37 (I.ii), trans. Peter Birks and Grant McLeod (Ithaca: Cornell University Press, 1987). There were different accounts of the *lex regia.* For example, according to the *Digest,* "[a] decision given by the emperor has the force of a statute. This is because the populace commits to him and into him its own entire authority and power; doing this by the *lex regia* which is passed anent his authority." *The Digest of Justinian* (I.iv.1), trans. Alan Watson (Philadelphia: University of Pennsylvania Press, 1998).

[7] Joannis Seldeni, *Ad Fletam Dissertatio,* 27, 31–33, trans. David Ogg (Cambridge: Cambridge University Press, 1925). The different interpretations of the *lex regia* are also discussed by Walter Ullmann, *The Medieval Idea of Law as Represented by Lucas de Penna: A Study in Fourteenth-Century Legal Scholarship,* 48–49 (1946; New York: Barnes & Noble, 1969); Brian Tierney, *Religion, Law, and the Growth of Constitutional Thought 1150–1650,* at 56–58 (Cambridge: Cambridge University Press, 1982); Brian Tierney, "'The Prince Is Not Bound by the Laws': Accursius and the Origins of the Modern State," *Comparative Studies in Society and History,* 5: 378 (1963); Joseph Canning, *The Political Thought of Baldus de Ubaldis,* 55–56 (Cambridge: Cambridge University Press, 1987); Kenneth Pennington, *The Prince and the Law, 1200–1600,* at 85 (Berkeley: University of California Press, 1993). McIlwain echoes Selden's views but muddies the question when he says that "Bracton's seems to be a clear assertion of constitutionalism." Charles Howard McIlwain, *Constitutionalism Ancient and Modern,* 71 (Ithaca: Great Seal, 1947).

Bracton and other English legal writers elevated this underlying tune to be their dominant melody, "interpreting the maxim to mean that the royal will has the force of law only so far as consistent with the Lex Regia and acquiring its authority thereby."[8] In Bracton's words, "the king must not be under man but under God and under the law, because the law makes the king." Thus, "there is no *rex* where will rules rather than *lex*." Far from being a sort of subservience, the king's obedience was appropriate, for "[n]othing is more fitting for a sovereign than to live by the laws, nor is there any greater sovereignty than to govern according to law."[9] None of this was the "correct interpretation" of the *lex regia*, but as John Selden later observed, it became the English interpretation.[10]

Contractual Consent and Lawmaking Will

What was generally considered consent could take many particular forms, including contractual consent and lawmaking will. Although the people's consent could be understood to create contractual obligation, another type of consent, their will, could create legal obligation, and it was this sort of volition—the lawmaking will of the people—that would become particularly important for constitutions. Scholars often casually find "constitutional" developments in generic early European discussions of consent, and they thereby tend to lose sight of the degree to which constitutions were conceived more specifically to be laws—to be expressions of legislative will, with legal obligation. In fact, even before Europeans widely discussed "constitutions" made by the people, they sometimes went beyond vague assumptions about a generic popular consent to analyze not only contractual consent but also lawmaking will. As already glimpsed in the debates about the *lex regia*, they contemplated the possibility that rulers enjoyed the force of their lawmaking will from the underlying lawmaking will of the people.

Popular consent found its most concise expression in the line *Vox populi, vox Dei*. This was already a familiar and powerful maxim in the time of Charlemagne, when the English scholar Alcuin wrote to the Emperor to dissuade him from deferring to it: "Nor are those to be listened to who are accustomed to say, 'The voice of the people is the voice of God.' For the clamor of the crowd is very close to madness." The saying probably became current through controversies over the election of bishops, and medi-

8 Seldeni, *Ad Fletam Dissertatio*, 31.
9 Bracton, *On the Laws and Customs of England*, 2: 33, 306.
10 Seldeni, *Ad Fletam Dissertatio*, 39.

eval writers often justified it by referring to God's admonition (in Samuel 1:8.7), "Listen to the voice of the people."[11] The secular implications of the phrase can be observed in the events of 1327, when Parliament pressed Edward II to abdicate. Edward had alienated his countrymen through his military failures and his domestic oppression, and after he quarreled with his wife and his son, their Continental allies invaded England in 1326. Edward fled westward, until he eventually was captured, and during this crisis, summons went out for a meeting of Parliament, including commoners. At the meeting of this high court early in 1327, Archbishop of Canterbury Walter Reynolds brought charges against the king, and Parliament voted to replace Edward with his son Prince Edward. The men present then swore homage to the prince, and Archbishop Reynolds—the son of a baker—"preached on the text *Vox populi, vox dei.*" About a week later, Reynolds more formally proposed Edward II's deposition with the same text—leading to the king's abdication and his son's becoming Edward III.[12] Evidently, the throne changed hands on the assumption that rulers exercised an authority held from God but voiced by the people.

On the Continent, churchmen developed ideas of communal consent into more elaborate, academic theories. When different men claimed to be pope, many Christians eventually saw no other solution to the controversy than to convene church councils to decide the matter on behalf of the Church, and defenders of this consiliar power theorized that although the pope's authority came from above, it was communicated to him from below, by the community.[13] As put by Nicholas of

[11] George Boas, *Vox Populi: Essays in the History of an Idea,* 9 (Baltimore: Johns Hopkins Press, 1969); S. A. Gallacher, "Vox Populi, Vox Dei," *Philological Quarterly,* 24: 14 (1945).

[12] M. V. Clarke, *Medieval Representation and Consent,* 179, 184 (London: Longmans, 1936); J. R. S. Phillips, "Edward II," DNB. It was a time of enlarged public participation. The year 1327 "saw the presentation of the first full set of commons' petitions; the first comprehensive statute to derive from such petitions; the first known request from the commons for the publication of the king's concessions in the provinces; and the first instance of the circulation of an unofficial version of parliamentary proceedings." J. R. Maddicott, "Parliament and the Constituencies, 1272–1377," in R. G. Davies and J. H. Denton, eds., *The English Parliament in the Middle Ages,* 86 (Manchester: Manchester University Press, 1981). For the development of the House of Commons in the ensuing years, see D. Pasquet, *An Essay on the Origins of the House of Commons,* 226–227, trans. R. G. D. Laffan (Hamden: Archon, 1964).

[13] Much of the scholarship on consiliarism emphasizes the degree to which political ideas developed within the church and then migrated into political theory, and even the preeminent challenge to this theory takes issue with it in order to give pride of place to canon law. For example, John Neville Figgis and Julian H. Franklin find the basis of representative and constitutional ideas in consiliar thought, and Brian Tierney and Francis Oakley point in turn to the foundations of consiliar thought in canon law. John Neville Figgis, *Political Thought from Gerson to Grotius,* xiii, 41–70 (New York: Harper Torchbooks, 1960);

Cusa, "[r]ulership is from God through men and councils, by elective consent."[14]

Although the consent thus given by communal bodies could serve many purposes, it did not always amount to legislation done by the community or even by its representative body. Roman texts, such as Justinian's *Institutes,* had stated that the ruler exercised lawmaking authority, and consistent with this perspective, acts of Parliament were usually understood to be acts willed by the king, to which Parliament merely gave its assent. The Roman model, however, could seem to depart from old English assumptions about consultation and the binding effect of acts of courts, and Bracton therefore cautioned that "despite the statement [in the *Institutes*] that the will of the prince has the force of law," the king was not to do "anything rashly put forward of his own will, but what has been rightly decided with the counsel of his magnates"—this being the English foundation for Bracton to conclude in more Roman style that the king had the role of "giving it *auctoritas.*"[15] Chief Justice Fortescue similarly maintained that the king was the authoritative lawmaker while admonishing that "in the kingdom of England the kings make not laws . . . without the consent of the Three Estates of the Realm."[16] Already, however, there were occasional hints of a shared lawmaking authority, and by the mid-sixteenth century acts of Parliament no longer regularly recited that they were made by the king with the assent of the Lords and Commons; instead, such acts increasingly made

---

Julian H. Franklin, "Constitutionalism in the Sixteenth Century: The Protestant Monarchomachs," in *Political Thought and Social Change,* 120, ed. David Spitz (New York: Atherton, 1967); Brian Tierney, *Religion, Law, and the Growth of Constitutional Thought 1150–1650* (Cambridge: Cambridge University Press, 1982); Francis Oakley, "Figgis, Constance, and the Divines of Paris," *American Historical Review,* 75: 368 (1969); Francis Oakley, "On the Road from Constance to 1688: The Political Thought of John Major and George Buchanan," *Journal of British Studies,* 1: 1 (1962). All of this scholarship takes evident pleasure in suggesting that secular constitutionalism has its origins in religious thought—that the ecclesiastical preceded the secular. Yet as suggested by earlier communal limits on royal ambition, in England or elsewhere, there is a risk of overstatement in suggesting pride of place for consiliar or canon law thought—just as there would be in claiming the "honor" for secular ideas. Even if one looks for theoretical understandings rather than merely practical limitations, the earlier English experience is at least suggestive, as illustrated by the 1327 sermons in Parliament on *Vox populi, vox Dei.* Such ideas were neither peculiarly religious nor secular but rather pervasive, finding expression across European life, whether in Parliaments at Westminster or at the council at Constance.

14 Nicholas of Cusa, *De Concordantia Catholica,* 293 (II.34), as quoted by Arthur P. Monahan, *From Personal Duties Towards Personal Rights,* 102 (Montreal: McGill-Queen's University Press, 1994).

15 Bracton, *On the Laws and Customs of England,* 2: 305, alluding to *Institutes* (1.2.6); *Digest* (1.4.1.pr).

16 *De Natura Legis Naturæ* (I.xvi), in *The Works of Sir John Fortescue,* 1: 205, ed. Thomas Fortescue (London: 1869).

explicit that they were made by the authority of Parliament or by the authority of the monarch, Lords, and Commons assembled in Parliament.[17] Rather than mere consent, this was finally a systematic assertion of a lawmaking authority residing in Parliament.

Underlying all lawmaking—whether by the people or their government—would develop deeper questions about the consent of individuals. Early hints as to how individual agreement would seem to sustain lawmaking authority arose amid the dislocations of late medieval Europe, when Nicholas of Cusa speculated about the condition of men in nature—in the absence of government. In this situation, individuals were not yet subject to one another and were equally free, and "if by nature men are equally powerful and equally free, the valid and ordained authority of one man naturally equal in power with the others cannot be established except by the choice and consent of the others." Thus, "by nature all are free," and from this individualistic assumption, it seemed evident that "every government" as a matter of nature "is based on agreement alone and the consent of the subjects." On such foundations, Nicholas of Cusa and eventually many others concluded that "the binding force of all statutes consists in agreement and consent, tacit or explicit."[18]

This atomistic sense that governmental authority had to rest on consent became popular in England when the English became self-conscious about their fragmentation—in particular, when they had to make explicit that communal consent implied individual consent. By the late fifteenth century, it was argued that an act of Parliament was obligatory without promulgation because "everyone is party and privy to such an act, and it shall bind everyone."[19] Similarly, St. German insisted that "every statute there made ys of as stronge effecte in the lawe as yf all the comons were there

[17] [John Brydall], *Jura Corona. His Majesties Royal Rights and Prerogatives Asserted,* 47 (1680); *Statutes of the Realm,* vol. 4 (part 1). See, however, note 17 in Chapter Nineteen.

[18] Nicholas of Cusa, *De Condordantia Catholica* (II.xiv–xv), in *Medieval Political Ideas,* 1: 192, 2: 418, ed. Ewart Lewis (London: Routledge and Kegan Paul, 1954). Such ideas became familiar among common lawyers long before Locke adopted them. Chief Justice Hobart noted that "by law of nature . . . all men are free, and cannot be brought under the dominion of any." *Moore v. Hussey et al.* (C.P. 1609), Hobart, *Reports,* 99. Hale even introduced his work on the prerogative with this sort of analysis. Matthew Hale, *The Prerogatives of the King,* 1, ed. D. E. C. Yale (London: Selden Society, 1976).

[19] "Arguments of Cases in the Inner Temple in the time of Edward IV and Henry VII," in *Readings and Moots at the Inns of Court in the Fifteenth Century,* 2: 139, Case No. 25, eds. Samuel E. Thorne and J. H. Baker (London: Selden Society, 1990). For such assumptions in the year books, see S. B. Chrimes, *English Constitutional Ideas in the Fifteenth Century,* 78–80 (Cambridge: Cambridge University Press, 1936). See also Pecock as quoted by Norman Doe, *Fundamental Authority in Late Medieval English Law,* 18 (Cambridge: Cambridge University Press, 1990).

present personallye at the makyng thereof."[20] Writing about Parliament, Sir Thomas Smith explained, "everie Englishman is entended to be there present, either in person or by procuration and attornies, of what preheminence, state, dignitie, or qualitie soever be he, from the Prince . . . to the lowest person of Englande," and therefore "the consent of the Parliament is taken to be everie mans consent."[21] At a time when individual authority was beginning to break up communal religion and politics, this sort of argument used an ideal of individual consent to fortify Parliament's claims of communal authority.

What would matter more for constitutions, however, than this consent of individuals to particular laws was the will of the people in forming their government and the potential of their will to create not merely communal assent, nor even contract, but law—a point pressed home by Marsilius. He argued, as already seen, that the authority to make human law rested with the body that had the coercive power to enforce it. This could have led to Hobbesian conclusions, but not for Marsilius. When he asked who could ensure that laws would be "observed," he concluded that "such is onely the hoole multytude: ergo to the hole multytude onely, belongeth the actoryte of instytutynge or makynge lawes."[22] Thus, even if the people "com[m]ytted" legislative power "to some persone or persons, to be done of hym or them," such "persone or persons are not, neyther maye be utterly and holly and generally the maker of the lawe: but they are onely [the lawmaker] after a certayne maner" and "by the auctoryte of the pryncypall lawe maker"—that is, by the authority of the people. Marsilius therefore inquired into "the maners of the instytucyon of governours done by the wyl of man."[23] Marsilius thought the best government to be one in

[20] T. F. T. Plucknett and J. L. Barton, eds., *St. German's Doctor and Student,* 279 (London: Selden Society, 1974).

[21] Thomas Smith, *De Republica Anglorum,* 35 (London: 1583). The underlying assumption was that the entire community attended its courts. The English adopted the fiction that every individual was presumed to be present in Parliament in order to explain why acts of Parliament were binding from the first day of Parliament and thus without promulgation. The civilian rule, drawn from the Novels (Const. No. 66), was that laws had to be promulgated before they had obligation. In England, however, acts of Parliament were binding from the first day of the session, just as the writs of any other court were dated from the opening day of its sessions. See, for example, Y. B. Pascal 39 Edward III, pl. 3, fol. 7, in Chrimes, *English Constitutional Ideas in the Fifteenth Century,* 76; Plucknett and Barton, eds., *St. German's Doctor and Student,* 279; [Christopher St. German], *An Answere to a Letter,* sig. Gvi[r–v] (London: [1535]).

[22] Marsilius of Padua, *The Defence of Peace,* fol. 28[v] (I.xii) (London: 1535). Nicholas of Cusa later wrote of how "the coercive power of a prince or a law" was "constituted by the approval of the subjects, by their common consent thereto, whether tacit or explicit." Nicholas of Cusa, *De Condordantia Catholica* (II.xxxiv), in *Medieval Political Ideas,* 2: 421.

[23] Marsilius of Padua, *The Defence of Peace,* fols. 20[v] (I.ix), 28[r] (I.xii).

which a king was "instytuted by the eleccyon of the inhabytau[n]tes" (or in which the king otherwise rightfully acquired the throne), and Marsilius contemplated that the king could be "instytuted governoure" with various limitations on his succession, on the duration of his office, and even on his exercise of office. For example, he could be "instytuted eyther to exercise all maner [of] Judycyall offyce: or els to exercyse but onely one." The people were thus "the lawe gyver" or efficient "cause" of the law, and "in suche thynges, as are determyned by the lawe, the prynce or governoure ought to folowe the determynacyon of the lawe."[24] This was very nearly the notion of a constitution.

On account of the lawmaking authority of the people, their rulers eventually came to seem bound by two layers of legal authority superior to their own. God's authority constrained the ruler through natural and divine law, and as has been seen, these higher laws were coming to be a measure of allegiance or resistance. In addition, the people's authority constrained their ruler through their contractual conditions and their law. Thus, the power of magistrates "is not absolute, but carries a double limitation, one from the will of God," and "[a]nother from that will of man, which is included in those conditions and Lawes, in which the power of rule is founded."[25]

No one wrote more audaciously about the potential for the people to subject their rulers both to contractual conditions and to law than the learned George Buchanan. He was the tutor to the young James VI of Scotland, and he wrote his *De Jure Regni* in the late 1560s to justify the removal of Queen Mary and the consequent succession of the youthful king. In 1579, however, Buchanan published his tract with a prefatory letter to the then thirteen-year-old monarch, explaining that the book would serve to protect him from "flattery, which is the nurse of Tyranny."[26] Buchanan began with the usual ideas about equal liberty—that by the "law of Nature . . . equals neither can, nor ought to usurpe dominion" over each other, "for by nature . . . amongst these that are equal in all other things, their course of ruling and obeying should be alike." Thus, "unless we have a King chosen by suffrages, I am afraid we shall have no lawfull King at all."[27]

The consent of the people was in part a matter of contract and condition. The people "are indeed bound" to their monarch, but kings "do first

[24] Ibid., fol. 21[v]–23[r] (I.ix–x), 33[r] (I.xiv).
[25] William Ames, *Conscience with the Power and Cases Thereof,* Fourth Book, 164 (np: 1639).
[26] George Buchanan, *De Jure Regni Apud Scotos,* sig. A5[v] (Epistle) (np: 1680).
[27] Ibid., 19, 21.

promise that they shall rule in equity and justice," and "[t]here is, then, a mutuall paction betwixt the King and his subjects." Accordingly, if the king were to "break the contract and covenant," the "bond" that held "fast the King with the people" would be "loosed," and then any individual "with whom the Covenant was made becometh as free as ever he was before the stipulation"—free even to conduct "a just and Lawfull war" against the king and "to kill that enemy."[28]

The people, however, did not only make a contract, for at the same time they also willed their law. In an imaginary colloquy, Buchanan quizzed his young neighbor Thomas Maitland in the didactic tone that must have been all too familiar to his students, and one of Buchanan's points was that all of society was subject to law. Aristotle had written that "he who is unable to live in society, or who has no need because he is sufficient for himself, must either be a beast or a god," and Buchanan now played upon this theme:

> *Buchanan:* Within what limites do you circumscribe humane society[?]
> *Maitland:* Within . . . the hedge of lawes. Which whosoever transgress . . . I see them publickly punished . . . because they transgressed the limites of humane society.
> *Buchanan:* What say you of those, who would never once enter within these hedges?
> *Maitland:* I think they should be accounted enemies to God and men, and reckoned amongst wolves, or some other kind of noisome beasts, rather than amongst men . . . & whosoever killeth them, doth not only good to himself, but to all others . . .

Later, after eliciting from Maitland that the king had "authority . . . from the Law," Buchanan pressed for the source of this law that simultaneously authorized the king and hedged him in:

> *Buchanan:* . . . Is not the voice of the people and the Law the same?
> *Maitland:* The very same.
> *Buchanan:* Which of the two is most powerfull, the people or the Law?
> *Maitland:* I think, the whole people.
> *Buchanan:* Why do you think so?
> *Maitland:* Because the people is as it were the parent of the Law, cer-

[28] Ibid., 126–127.

tainly the Author thereof, they being able to make or abrogate it, as they please.

Thus, "in receiving of Lawes," kings were accountable to "the People, who are the Lawgivers," and "the faults of Lawes being found out, they may be amended or abrogat[ed] by the Lawgivers." Indeed, it was "in the peoples power, who gave" the king "authority over themselves, to prescribe to him a modell of his government."[29]

A law in which the people prescribed a model of government had implications for ordinary judges, and although Buchanan justified resistance, he paused to consider a better possibility, saying to Maitland, "let us come to the ordinary Judges." This judicial enforcement (as will be seen in Part II) was already a reality in England, but Maitland was a character in a dialogue on political theory, and he therefore protested that the king could not be brought "[b]efore them over whom he hath the supream power to judge." Rather than be put off, Buchanan answered that there was a "greater power than that of kings," and "this power is in the people." To be precise, the people had the authority to make law, and Buchanan therefore asked "whether the judge" had his authority "from the Law, or the Law from the judge?"

Maitland: The judge from the Law.
Buchanan: The strength of the sentence is then from the Law, and pronunciation of the words of the Law is alone the judges.
Maitland: It seemes so.
Buchanan: Yea, there is nothing more certain.

[29] Ibid., 39, 71–72, 87, 113–114. For Aristotle, see his *Politics,* 1253a (I.ii), in *The Complete Works of Aristotle,* 2: 1988, ed. Jonathan Barnes (Princeton: Princeton University Press, 1985).

Buchanan was not alone. According to *Vindiciæ Contra Tyrannos,* "the King receives the Laws from the people," and "if the Laws be superior to the King," and if "the King be tyed in the same respect of obedience to the Lawes, as the Servant is to his Master[,] who will be so senslesse, that will not rather obey the Law, then the King?" Thus, "the King is not Lord over the Lawes." *Vindiciæ Contra Tyrannos,* 63, 66 [sic] (sigs. K2[r], K[3v]) (London: 1648). Francois Hotman noted that "the kings of France have not been granted unmeasured and unlimited power by their countrymen and cannot be considered absolute," for "they are bound by definite laws and compacts"—the laws being *"leges regias,"* which came from the people. Francois Hotman, *Francogallia,* in *Constitutionalism and Resistance in the Sixteenth Century: Three Treatises by Hotman, Beza, and Mornay,* 90, 92, ed. Julian H. Franklin (New York: Pegasus, 1969). This was from Chapter XXV, which Hotman added in the third, 1586 edition to emphasize that the French king "does not have unlimited dominion in his kingdom but is circumscribed by settled and specific law." Ibid., 90.

Buchanan concluded: "Whilst then the King is condemned by a Judge, he seemes to be condemned by the Law."[30] It was a hint of what might follow if the people were the lawgivers.

Constitutions

The law by which a people simultaneously authorized their government and limited it was coming to be known as a "constitution." Rather than merely the arrangement of government, a constitution of this sort was also an enactment by the people establishing their government, and it thus was the most fundamental sort of human law.

Although the modern use of the label "constitution" became popular only after the development of the concept to which it referred, the name had a clarifying effect, for it evolved through the merger of two related usages, which together aptly captured what was becoming the modern ideal of a constitution. Underlying both usages was the verb *constituere,* which meant to cause to stand, to set up, or to establish. In one variant, when the word was used as a noun, it could mean an established arrangement: Augustine, for example, often alluded to the *constitutione mundi*—the constitution, structure, or arrangement of the world—and men would eventually refer to the constitution of government in this sense. In another, even more familiar variant, however, the word alluded to an act of setting up or establishing—especially a statute, ordinance, decree, or other legislative act. Since Roman times, a *constitutio* thus was legislation—initially the legislation of the people and eventually that of the emperor.[31] Men recognized that the derivation of the word did not necessarily imply a writing, and they therefore sometimes had to spell this out, as when Gratian explained that "lex is a written constitution."[32] Legislative acts, however, were often written, and constitutions therefore tended to be associated with written

[30] Buchanan, *De Jure Regni Apud Scotos,* 116–117, 122–123.

[31] Alan Watson, ed., *The Digest of Justinian,* xxx (I.iv.1) (Philadelphia: University of Pennsylvania Press, 1998). Albericus de Rosate quoted the *Decretum* for the proposition that "[t]he law is the constitution of the people in which the greater by birth together with the common people ratify something." Alberici de Rosate, *Dictionarium Iuris tam Civilis, quàm Cononici,* 423 (Venice: 1573). Although the derivation from Roman law is noted by McIlwain, he mistakenly suggests, on what he concedes to be limited reading, that this notion "is apparently never used in our modern sense, to denote the whole legal framework of the state . . . before the opening of the seventeenth century." McIlwain, *Constitutionalism Ancient and Modern,* 24. For similar treatment, see Federigo Bambi, "I nomi delle 'leggi fondamentali,'" *Studi di lessicografia Italiana,* 11: 177 (1991).

[32] Gratian, *Decretum* (Distinction I, cap. 3).

enactments. Drawing on the Roman heritage, secular and ecclesiastical rulers on the Continent called their enactments "constitutions," but the English entitled their enactments "constitutions" only when these specially concerned or were made by the Church—as when Henry II and his council joined with the English bishops to adopt the Constitutions of Clarendon.[33] Otherwise in England a "constitution" was a generic label for either an arrangement or a legislative act.

The two conceptions of a constitution gradually blurred together to refer to a third understanding of a constitution—the constitution of government. This constitution could be understood ambidextrously as the legislative act by which a people constituted government and as the arrangement of government they thus established. Many Europeans were accustomed to assuming that the arrangement of their government had once been decreed or legislated in some way, and if the people somehow exercised will in the formation of their government, they could be understood to have a constitution in both of the traditional senses—an enactment and the consequent arrangement.[34] In this way, what long remained merely an indistinct implication of its parts increasingly became the modern conception of a constitution.

A constitution of this sort, which drew its obligation from human will, could run up against the ideal that law enjoyed its obligation from its participation in the eternal and natural law, and this worried Chief Justice Fortescue. An advocate of the Lancasterian claims to the succession, Fortes-

[33] McIlwain, *Constitutionalism Ancient and Modern,* 23. When writing about human law in general rather than merely in England, Fortescue observed that statutes "are also called constitutions." Sir John Fortescue, *De Laudibus Legum Anglie,* 37 (xv), ed. S. B. Chrimes (Westport: Hyperion, 1979) ("statuta que et constitutiones appellantur").

[34] Although Calvin apparently did not use the word "constitution" in the modern sense, his writings illustrate the capacity of the word to refer to the arrangement of government and to suggest the enactment of this arrangement. At times, Calvin used the word "constitution" to mean an arrangement of government, as when he wrote of "the true and lawful constitution of the church." John Calvin, *Institutes of the Christian Religion,* 1052 (IV.ii.12), trans. John T. McNeill and Ford Lewis Battles (Philadelphia: Westminster, 1960) (de vera & legitima Ecclesiae constitutione). He also, however, understood constitutions of government to have been created or constituted. Where Paul (in Ephesians 4.12) wrote about renewing or perfecting of the saints, Calvin used the word *"constitutio"* because this suggested the act of constituting: "But as Paul intended to express here a just and orderly arrangement, I prefer the word constitution *(constitutio),* taking it in that sense in which a commonwealth, or kingdom, or province, is said to be constituted *(constitui),* when confusion gives place to the regular administration of law." John Calvin, *Commentary on the Epistles of Paul to the Galatians and Ephesians,* 281 (Ephesians 4:12), trans. William Pringle (Grand Rapids: Baker Book House, 1984) (printed here with minor modifications) (Sed quoniam hic Paulus statum bene & ordine compositum indicare voluit, mihi magis probatur Constitutio. Nam dicunt proprie Latini, constitui Remp. aut regnum, aut provinciam, quum ex dissipatione omnia in rectum & legitimum statum restitui contingit.)

cue discounted the claims of the House of Gloucester, which ran through a female descendant of Edward III—Fortescue's position being that, on account of the natural inferiority of women, natural law barred any claim for a daughter or her heirs. An enactment or custom might seem to allow a daughter to succeed to the throne, but Fortescue followed Aquinas in believing that "the law of nature . . . so partakes of the eternal law as to be itself . . . nothing else but a participation of that law" and that therefore any human laws that "degenerate from" natural law "deserve not to be called laws." Such reasoning allowed Fortescue to deny that a constitution or custom about the succession—such as one allowing succession through a daughter—could "have any force" against natural law. Aquinas had acknowledged that the constitutions or enactments made by princes sometimes departed from natural law without losing their obligation, but in Fortescue's opinion, "the constitutions of princes *(constitutiones principum),* which only bind subjects, were not capable of constituting the kingly height, which knows no superior." In contrast, men could make constitutions establishing kings, but according to Fortescue, these "ordinances of men, by which some of them are raised into kings," do not "deserve to be called constitutions *(constitutiones merenter dici),* but rather acts of the law of nature." Fortescue justified his different treatment of the constitutions made *by* princes and those *about* princes by suggesting that the law of nature "alone established the first beginnings of kingly elevation" and that the enactments establishing princes therefore could not deviate from the law of nature. Similarly, he concluded that "if any custom hath grown into use, which for the possession of kings superadds anything to the law of nature," it was to be adjudged "annulled" if it was "repugnant in any respect to the law of nature," and that it was "not to be called a custom, but a corruption."[35] Fortescue evidently understood that kings were elevated by "ordinances of men" called "constitutions" and that in England kings were also elevated in this manner by custom, but he denied that such laws could depart from the heavenly ideals enunciated by Aquinas.

To be sure, Fortescue and his contemporaries were not using the word

35 *De Natura Legis Naturæ, The Works of Sir John Fortescue,* I: 189 (Introduction), 200 (I.x), 240 (I.xlii). For the sort of "ordinances of men" that could seem to allow succession through a woman, see Craig Taylor, "Sir John Fortescue and the French Polemical Treatises of the Hundred Years War," *English Historical Review,* 114: 114 (1999); Michael Bennett, "Edward III's Entail and the Succession to the Crown, 1376–1471," ibid., 113: 581 (1998). Alan Cromartie translates *constitututiones* as "decrees," which is not inaccurate, but which misses the significance of the word. Alan Cromartie, *The Constitutionalist Revolution: An Essay on the History of England, 1450–1642,* at 22 (Cambridge: Cambridge University Press, 2006).

constitutiones as a name specifically for the enactments that established rulers. But this is to be expected. The word "constitution" long kept its generic meaning, and therefore not only in the fifteenth century but also much later, it remained necessary to indicate when one meant the constitution that elevated rulers—or, as put in later centuries, when one meant the constitution that was made by the people and that established government. In fact, it was the generic character of the term that gave this application of it such significance. From Fortescue's era until relatively recently, educated men could assume that, as in Rome, what were generically called "constitutions" were enacted laws that took their obligation from the authority of their maker. Hence, the power of referring to a constitution elevating rulers, establishing government, or made by the people. Hence also Fortescue's objection. Believing that the enactments establishing rulers took their obligation from the law of nature and could not vary from it, Fortescue protested that they did not "deserve to be called constitutions."

Under Elizabeth, the English revived their disputes about the succession and thus also about the nature of England's constitution, and no commentator in these controversies more caustically recognized that constitutions were human artifacts than Cardinal William Allen. Toward the end of his life, after failing to overthrow Queen Elizabeth and restore Catholicism to England, he wrote a final plea for a Catholic succession, and one of his arguments was that constitutions were merely human law and thus changeable. The royal succession was determined "not by law of nature or divine, but only by humane and positive lawes of every particular common wealth," and consequently the succession could "be altered by the same." One could not therefore claim authority for an individual prince directly from natural law—"as though any Prince had his particuler government or interest to succeed by institutio[n] of nature." This was "rediculous," because "nature giveth it not." On the contrary, the succession came from "the particuler constitution of every co[m]monwealth with-in it selfe."[36]

[36] [William Allen], *A Conference About the Next Succession to the Crown of Ingland,* 1, 14 (np: 1594).

Earlier, another Catholic—the ever scheming John Leslie—argued that Queen Mary's claim as heir to the English throne rested on natural law as adopted in the English constitution, but he could not and carefully did not dispute that constitutions were by consent rather than nature. He was a scholar of civil and canon law who had served as Mary's chief adviser, and he assumed that the injunctions of the divine and natural laws had been adopted in English customs dating back to the first constitution of the realm. As he explained, his "arguments and proufes" were "gathered and grownded upon the lawes of God and nature, and not onlie receaved in the civill pollicies of other nations, but also in the olde lawes and customes of our owne contrey, by reason approved, and by use and longe . . . continewance of time observed, from the first constitution of this realme in politicall order

Although Englishmen drew upon the notion of a constitution in these disputes about the succession, they gave the English constitution far greater prominence in their controversies over the prerogative. Against royal claims of prerogative—whether that exercised through the law or above it—the most decisive response was to assert the superior authority and obligation of the constitution that established the king and his government. The constitution therefore seemed to offer a singularly powerful defense against the full range of royal power.

King James recognized the formidable strength of constitutional arguments. Already while only king of Scotland, he conceded that there were human laws more fundamental than those made by government, but at the same time he attempted to fend off the implications by insisting that at least in Scotland the fundamental laws had royal origins. He defended his power with arguments from "the Scriptures . . . from the fundamental Lawes of our owne Kingdome . . . [and] thirdly, from the law of Nature," and when arguing on the basis of "the fundamentall and civill Lawe, especially of this contrey," he took his stand on "the first maner of establishing the Lawes and forme of government among us"—it being his contention that the kings of Scotland rather than the people had established the laws and form of his government.[37]

This was not, however, the prevailing assumption about constitutions, and it would not help James against the Englishmen who distrusted

---

unto this present daye." John Leslie, *A Defence of the Honour of the Right Highe, Mightye and Noble Princesse Marie Quene of Scotlande and Dowager of France,* fol. 55[v] (London [i.e., Rheims]: 1569).

From a very different religious perspective, John Hales had written that "the devec[i]on [i.e., division] of kyngdomes and States, ordinance[s] of citties and commonweales, and ye liberties & freedoms thereof is not by nature, but cometh by the consent of man & mans Lawes." A motion of Succession in the Parliam^t^ . Anno xiii [sic] Elizabethe Rne, British Library, Cotton Ms. Julius, F.6, at fol. 440[r]. See also A Discours Uppon certaen pointes touchinge the Enheritaunce of the Crowne, British Library, Harleian Ms. 555, fol. 6[r]. Although the tract is usually said to date from 1563, Anthony à Wood says with great specificity that it was written by Hales "in his house in Channel-row within the city of Westminister, in Oct. 1560." Anthony à Wood, *Athenæ Oxonienses,* 1: 404–405 (London: 1813).

Questions about constitutional or fundamental law also arose in the dispute as to whether ecclesiastical courts could lawfully require men to answer upon oath. For example, in defense of the ecclesiastical courts, Richard Cosin wrote that "albeit the matter in some degree, happen to be criminall," this did not mean that such oaths were "contrary to the fundamentall lawes." [Richard Cosin], An Apologie for Sundrie Proceedings by Jurisdiction Ecclesiasticall, 3: 53 ([1593]).

37 *The Trew Law of Free Monarchies* (1598), in *The Political Works of James I,* 54, 61, ed. Charles Howard McIlwain (Cambridge: Harvard University Press, 1918). Similarly, he viewed his coronation oath as "the clearest, civill, and fundamentall Law, whereby the Kings office is properly defined." Ibid., 55.

his expansive understanding of his prerogative. In his early years as king of England, James sought to raise money through duties or "impositions," and many men in the House of Commons, including the lawyer James Whitlocke, questioned whether the king by himself "without assent of parliament" was "lawfully entitled to . . . alter the property of his subjects' goods." In denying any such power in the king to tax without consent, Whitlocke distinguished the constitution from other laws: An imposition without parliamentary consent "is against the naturall [i.e., native] frame and constitution of the policie of this kingdome . . . and so subverteth the fundamentall Law of the Realme, and induceth a new forme of state and government." Revealingly, Whitlocke distinguished this constitutional "ground" from his other, less elevated arguments—namely, that impositions were "against the municipall Law of the Land," that they were "against Divers statutes made to restraine our King," and that they were "against the practice and action of our Common wealth."[38]

The conventional assumption about the human, popular manufacture of constitutions was perhaps most systematically elaborated by Henry Parker. A brilliant pamphleteer, he justified the cause of Parliament during the opening years of the Civil War with the incisive argument that because constitutions were of human construction, royalists could not claim that the king's rights had been defined by God. "The Royalists take a great deal of superfluous pains," Parker wrote, "to prove *that all powers are from God,*" and yet "tis not by us questioned whether powers are from God or no; but whether they are so extraordinarily from God, as that they have not dependence upon humane consent." According to Parker, *"Princes were created by the people, for the peoples sake, and so limited by expresse Laws as that they might not violate the peoples liberty."* But as to how the people did this, "God had left the choice indifferent, and arbitrarie, and therefore there was no scandall or trespasse in the choice."[39]

Put in terms of order, although the obligation of law came from

[38] [James Whitlocke], *A Learned and Necessary Argument To Prove that Each Subject Hath a Propriety in His Goods,* 8 (London: 1641). Shortly afterward in the same argument, Whitlocke spoke of "the original right of the Kingdome, and the very naturall constitution of our State and policy," but once again, this was natural not in the sense of natural law but in the sense that "it is *jus indigena* an old homeborne right." Ibid., 11. For the sixteenth- and seventeenth-century use of "natural" to refer to what was innate or native to a country, see the *Oxford English Dictionary.*

[39] [Henry Parker], *Jus Populi,* 2, 5. Thus, "the founding or new erecting of authorities at first, and the circumstances the same after by consent, is so farre from being Gods sole immediate act, that it is, as far as any act can be mans proper and intire act: for except we allow that God has left it indifferent to man to form government as he thinks most for his behoof, we must condemne all forms except one, as unlawfull." Ibid., 7. More generally, see Michael Mendle, *Henry Parker and the English Civil War: The Political Thought of the Public's "Privado"* (New York: Cambridge University Press, 1995).

above, the choice of how order was to be established by law came from below. The need for order was a matter of natural law and had "God as its Author," but the divine requirement of order "conveys nothing speciall to Kings, inasmuch as the benefit of it is generall, and extends to families, as well as to States, and popular States as well as Monarchies." The decision about the means of order thus belonged to men in their formation of "[t]he constitution or ordinance of Jurisdiction."[40]

Harking back to aspects of the reasoning that had given rise to the ideal of authority, Parker observed that men had to create their constitutions because "the Lawes of God and Nature" were not enough "to cement us, and to hold us fast together." Parker acknowledged:

> Bounds are set, by God and Nature, to the greatest and most absolute Monarchs, as well as to the least, and most conditionate: but those Bounds seem but as imaginary Lines, or as meer stones, not reall Trenches, or Fortifications: They serve only to discover to the Subject what his Right is, but they have no strength at all to protect him from wrong.

Nor could one rely on shared, transnational customs—"the common consent of Mankinde (that which we now call, *Jus Gentium*)"—for this "was too slack and loose a bond, to keep the World from dissipation."[41] Hence the need for men to create "particular constitutions."

The liberty of the people therefore depended most immediately on human law. Englishmen had long said that their law protected both the prerogatives of the Crown and the liberties of its subjects, and they now could say the same more specifically of their constitution—or as Judge David Jenkins preferred to say, their "constitutions."[42] By order of Parliament,

[40] Ibid., 4. Parker thus emphasized both the "humanitie" and "the divinitie of the English constitution." Ibid. As he put it elsewhere: "Power is originally inherent in the people, and it is nothing else but that might and vigour which such or such a societie of men containes in its selfe, and when by such or such a Law of common consent and agreement it is derived into such and such hands, God confirms that Law: and so man is the free and voluntary Author, the Law is the Instrument, and God is the establisher of both." [Henry Parker], *Observations Upon Some of His Majesties Late Answers and Expresses,* 1 ([London: 1642]). Of course, the argument was a commonplace, but Parker stated it with unusual detail and clarity. Later in the century, when considering whether there was "one Form of Government, established by God," Algernon Sidney went so far as to argue that "having given to all Men in some degree a capacity of judging what is good for themselves, he hath granted to all likewise a liberty of inventing such Forms as please them best, without favouring one more than another." Algernon Sidney, *Discourses Concerning Government,* 14 (i.6) (London: 1698). For earlier suggestions that the *lex regia* "was promulgated at divine command," see Canning, *The Political Thought of Baldus de Ubaldis,* 26.

[41] [Henry Parker], *Jus Populi,* 43, 51.

[42] Historically, the English constitution seemed evident from multiple sources in various past enactments or customs, and Jenkins was therefore not alone in alluding to a plurality of English constitutions. For example, see William Prynne, *The Soveraigne Power of Parliaments*

Jenkins spent fifteen years in the Tower, where he had a clear view of Parliament's tyranny and plenty of time to protest. Thus, while men in Parliament still complained about the king, Jenkins denounced the legislature. As was recited beneath his portrait,

> *Here* JENKINS *stands, who thundering from the* TOWER
> *Shook the bold Senates* Legislative Power.[43]

From this perspective, all liberties—not only those held against the Crown but also those held against Parliament—rested on constitutional law: "[T]he safety and security of the *English* People, their Lives, their Liberties, and peculiar Proprieties, are as it were entrusted to the Guardianship, and deposited in the keeping and defence of Laws and Constitutions of their own framing."[44]

The constitution made by the people could protect their liberty because it was the law of highest authority and obligation within the law of the land, and in this sense it was fundamental. The word "fundamental" was a generic label for what was essential or basic, and it could therefore apply to either natural law or constitutional law—a breadth of application that has led generations of scholars to believe that natural and human law blended together in a single fundamental law. To say something was fundamental, however, was relative—natural law being fundamental as to all hu-

---

and Kingdomes: Divided into Foure Parts, (First Part) 41 (London: 1643); John Cooke, *The Vindication of the Professors and Profession of the Law,* sig. [A4r] (Epistle Dedicatory) (London: 1646).

43 *Jenkinsius Redivivus: or the Works of that Grave, Learned, Truly-Loyal, and Courageous Judge Jenkins, Whilst A Prisoner in the Town, and Newgate* (London: 1681). Incidentally, something like an express constitution—the *Agreement of the People*—was proposed and widely discussed in 1647 and again in 1649.

44 [David Jenkins], *The King's Prerogative and the Subject's Priviledges Asserted,* 49 (London: 1684). Jenkins explained that the laws and constitutions framed by the people were "[n]ot of yesterday, but deriv'd from the provisions of distinct Legislators and Princes, from the most ancient to these present times"—meaning that the constitutions of the people had to be discerned from such provisions. He understood, however, that each country overall had a single constitution, and when discussing constitutions in the abstract, he could speculate about "a well constituted Nation" and its "Humane Constitution." Ibid., 2, 49, 123. Thus, although England had many particular constitutions, it had a single "law of *Royal-Government,*" which "is a *Law-Fundamental*" composed of common law *"Custom," "Judicial Records,"* and *"Acts of Parliament."* [David Jenkins], *The King's Prerogative and the Subjects Privileges Asserted According to Law and Reason,* 1 (London: 1680). Less systematically, one of his editors wrote in both the plural and the singular about England's constitution. He claimed that "the Constitutions of her Government are the best in the World" and two pages later wrote of "the excellency of our Constitution." [Jenkins], *The King's Prerogative and the Subject's Priviledges Asserted,* fol. A2[v], [A3v] (1684).

man laws, and a constitution being fundamental only as to the human laws of its society.[45] These different usages coexisted, but not with equal prominence. Whereas men in the Middle Ages were apt to focus on the fundamental character of natural law—saying "Ratio est fundamentum legis" or that reason is the fundamental law—they tended by the late sixteenth century to focus on the fundamental character of human law.[46] From this perspective, a constitution made by the people was fundamental not because it was confused with natural law, but rather because it had the strongest possible human authority and obligation, and thus when men in the seventeenth century wrote about the fundamental character of natural law, they had to struggle against the more common allusions to fundamental human law. This was the burden borne by John Milton when he explained that "the Law of Nature" was "the only Law of Laws truly and properly to all Mankind fundamental; the beginning and the end of all Government."[47] He had to insist that natural law was "truly and properly" fundamental to all mankind because it was more familiar that, among the human laws of any one society, a constitution was fundamental.

Of course, there were different possible ideals of a constitution and much disagreement, but the ideal of a constitution as a popularly enacted law was particularly forceful, and it therefore shaped much of the English debate. For example, it was in opposition to the conception of the English constitution as a law adopted by the people that some commentators preferred to suggest the constitution was merely an arrangement of govern-

[45] Human laws, moreover, could be fundamental in different ways. For example, William Perkins adapted the word "fundamental" to refer to the laws for which the ruler sought obedience: "Statutes are of two sorts. Some are principall or fundamentall, which serve to maintaine the state of that bodie or Corporation. Others less principall, or mixt, that serve for order or decencie. In the statutes principall, the lawmaker intends obedience simply; and therefore they are necessary to be kept. But in the less principall, he exacts not obedience simply, but either obedience, or the penaltie." William Perkins, *The Whole Treatise of the Case of Conscience,* 398 (II.13) (Cambridge: 1606). Obviously, the form of his argument, although not the exact point, followed the distinction between *malum in se* and *malum prohibitum.*

[46] Ullmann, *The Medieval Idea of Law,* 45. Although the concept of fundamental human law flourished in France in the sixteenth century, it was soon also noted in England—for example in a memorandum of royalist tendency that alluded to "Leges fundamentales galliae, lex salica et alia." "Leges Fundamentales," British Library, Cotton Vespasian CXIV, vol. II, fol. 16[v].

[47] *The Ready and Easy Way to Establish a Free Commonwealth* (1660), in *Milton's Prose,* 448, ed. Malcolm W. Wallace (London: Oxford University Press, 1931). Tindal later wrote that "none can have a Right inconsistent with the *Publick Good,* which *is the only Fundamental Law of all Societies:* contrary to which, no Law (and consequently no Legal Right, which is built upon Law) can be valid." [Matthew Tindal], *An Essay Concerning Obedience to the Supreme Powers, and the Duty of Subjects in all Revolutions,* 19 (London: 1694).

ment. By the same token, there were observers who acknowledged the English constitution to be a law but who proposed that it arose, not from the authoritative will of the people, but instead from a more amorphous communal consent. These alternative views are interesting, but of particular significance here, they tended to arise in response to the ideal of a legally binding enactment by the people, and they thus are suggestive about the strength of this increasingly central ideal. Although it was not the only conception of a constitution, a constitution enacted by the people seemed to have obligation as the most fundamental part of the law of the land, and as recognized by those who sought to avoid the implications, this high authority and obligation gave the ideal its potency in disputes with the Crown and eventually with Parliament.

Constitution and Custom

The customary character of the common law posed a problem for Englishmen who sought to establish that their constitution was enacted by the people. A constitution might be an enactment willed by the people, but the substratum of English law was the common law, which was a type of custom, and therefore to find an enacted constitution within inherited English law could be difficult.

Seventeenth-century English lawyers often sidestepped the issue by focusing on labels other than "constitution." Like their colleagues on the Continent, English lawyers often understood custom to arise from tacit consent, and they therefore could speak of the people's "consent" to their customary limitations on their rulers. Even when the English needed to emphasize that they were arguing from a *law* made by the people, they could avoid any awkwardness by speaking of "fundamental law," which did not necessarily imply something expressly enacted.

The English ran into difficulties, however, when they spoke about their "constitution," for this word clearly suggested an express enactment, thus making a customary constitution nearly a paradox. Among those who feared that England's largely customary constraints on government might suffer from the expectation of an express enactment was Algernon Sidney. He was the sort of man who even on the scaffold declared that "the Right and Power of Magistrates in every Country, was that which the Laws of that Country made it to be."[48] He knew that "every People may govern, or con-

[48] *The Very Copy of a Paper Delivered to the Sheriffs, Upon the Scaffold on Tower-hill . . . By Algernon Sidney,* 2 (London: 1683).

stitute and chuse one or more Governors" and "may divide the Powers between the several men, or ranks of men, allotting to every one so much as they please, or retaining so much as they think fit," and that thus "[t]he Laws of every place show what the Power of the respective Magistrate is." Nonetheless, he worried lest "any doubts do hereupon arise," and anxious that England's merely tacit contractual or legal constraints on government might seem mere fantasies, he insisted that "they are not dreams, but real things, and perpetually obliging."[49]

Unwilling to concede that their constitution was illusory, lawyers who assumed they had a constitution limiting royal power seized upon one hypothesis after another that might confirm its substance in common law—their primary stance being that they had inherited an ancient, original constitution so deeply lost in the past that it survived only in later custom and statutes. The original enactment was long gone, but it arguably remained discernible in the common law handed down over the generations. It was similarly said to be preserved in later reenactments, as when Chief Justice Coke explained that Magna Charta "was for the most part declaratory of the principall grounds of the fundamentall Laws of *England*" and "was no new declaration."[50] Coke's pedantic falsehood provoked learned contempt already in the seventeenth century, but Coke had good company in attempting to discern the original constitution from what apparently survived in existing law. Matthew Hale wrote that "inasmuch as the original of that pact or constitution of our government appears not, we must . . . examine and measure it by those sound and authentical evidences of the laws and allowed customs and usages."[51]

A less artificial solution was to abandon any expectation of an original constitution, in the sense of an enactment by the people, and to view custom as the means by which the people tacitly consented to their constitution over time. For centuries, as already noted, learned lawyers had said that custom had the same authority as communal legislation, even if based on

[49] Sidney, *Discourses upon Government,* 248 (ii.32). As if to prove this, he observed that "Judges are in many places appointed to decide the Contests arising from the breach of these Contracts." Ibid., 248.

[50] Coke, *Institutes,* 2: sig. [A4v] (Proeme). At least Coke was self-conscious about what he was doing, as when he candidly explained about the antiquity of the law that "(to speake what we think), we would derive from the Conqueror as little as we could." Coke, *Institutes,* 3: Proeme. More generally, see J. G. A. Pocock, *The Ancient Constitution and the Feudal Law: A Study of English Historical Thought in the Seventeenth Century* (Cambridge: Cambridge University Press, 1987).

[51] Hale, *The Prerogatives of the King,* 10. In this theory, "implied consent" was only "a presumption of the concurrence of all necessary requisites to the establishing of it for a law in the original." Ibid., 169.

tacit rather than express consent.[52] From this perspective, custom was not mere evidence of an earlier compact but was itself the mechanism of consent. Matthew Hale suggested in this manner that custom was "the implied consent which long admission evidenceth." If custom was "constant and immemorial," it was like an enactment in having "a kind of introductive or institutive power."[53] A political commentator similarly asked: *"By whom was this government framed in this sort? or who is to be accounted the Immediate Efficient of the Constitution thereof?"* His answer: "The Experience and Wisdom of your Ancestors hath so moulded this." At least in this sense, "the Immediate Originall of it was from the People."[54]

Such a constitution, however, which was adopted gradually by experience and tacit consent, was vulnerable. One problem was that the constitution might continue to change, and this opened up the danger that popular acquiescence would legitimize threats to liberty. Although tacit consent had apparently once enlarged popular freedom, it was well understood in the seventeenth century that tacit consent was now apt to diminish this freedom, for the Crown might wrest power from the people and call this acquiescence.[55] No less seriously, if the obligation of custom rested on its being ancient and continuous, an acknowledgment of evolving, tacit consent could undermine a custom's obligation as law.

Many English lawyers therefore fell back upon the safe but improbable claims about the ancient, original constitution, which, even though lost in the mists of time, had survived in statutes and common law without significant alteration. Such a constitution had all the force of ancient customary law. And if it was imagined to be recorded in the memory of the people, it could be considered an act of record, which could not be defeated by evidence of contrary custom or practice, such as an evolving acquiescence to power. Thus, both as to the common law and more particularly as to their constitution, English lawyers tended to take a defensive posture. They oc-

[52] See Chapter Two.
[53] Hale, *The Prerogatives of the King,* 7, 169. Similarly, see "Sir Matthew Hale's Criticisms on Hobbes's Dialogue of the Common Laws," in William Holdsworth, *A History of English Law,* 5: 507 (London: Sweet & Maxwell, 2003). For a discussion of the distinction between the evidentiary and institutive roles of custom, see Gerald J. Postema, "Classical Common Law Jurisprudence (Part II)," *Oxford University Commonwealth Law Journal,* 3: 23–24 (2003).
[54] *A Political Catechism,* 2, 3 (London: 1643).
[55] For a notable English account of how in the past "silent allowance, famously notified through custome," led to the moderation of forceful governments, see *Of Ecclesiastical Polity, The Works of Mr. Richard Hooker,* 446 (VIII.iii.3) (London: 1682) (citing Aristotle's *Politics*). Other writers, however, soon became sufficiently worried as to argue that "no such prescription nor prævarication can justly prejudice the right of the people." *Vindiciæ Contra Tyrannos,* 63 (sig. I[1r]) (London: 1648).

casionally conceded that their law had been "refined and perfected," but they denied that there had been more substantial change, and on this basis they insisted that they retained their original constitution.[56]

Some of the most distinguished English lawyers so feared that the Crown would take advantage of any acknowledgment of common law change that they discussed legal development in metaphors, unpublished manuscripts, and scholarly Latin. In his *Iani Anglorum facies altera,* John Selden examined the Janus-faced character of the common law in the safety of a learned language.[57] Hale carefully left most of his legal writings in manuscript, and when he summed up the development of English law, he did so in the story of the Argonauts' ship, which "was the same when it returned home, as it was when it went out, tho' in that long Voyage it had successive Amendments, and scarce came back with any of its former Materials."[58] Not merely poetical, this sort of metaphor allowed Hale to discuss

[56] Sir John Davies, for example, described how custom "taketh beginning and groweth to perfection." John Davies, *Les Reports Des Cases & Matters en Ley, Resolves & Adjudges en les Courts del Roy en Ireland,* (Dedication) (1615; London 1674). More cautiously, Coke urged that at least "[f]or any fundamentall point of the ancient Common laws and customes of the Realme, it is a Maxime in pollicie, and triall by experience, that the alteratio[n] of any of them is most dangerous," for having "beene refined and perfected by all the wised men in former succession of ages, and prooved and approved by continuall experience to be good & profitable for the common wealth," it "cannot without great hazard and daunger" be "altered or chaunged." Coke, *Reports,* 4: sig. B2[v] (London: 1604). Matthew Hale wrote that custom was "a law, that hath abidden the test of time," that had survived the "varieties and complications" that "experience hath in all that process of time discovered," and that had "applied suitable remedies and cures for these various emergencies." Matthew Hale, "Considerations Touching the Amendment or Alteration of Lawes," in *Collectanea Juridica,* 2: 254, ed. Francis Hargrave (London: 1792).

[57] John Selden, *Iani Anglorum facies altera* (1610).

[58] Matthew Hale, *The History of the Common Law of England,* 40, ed. Charles M. Gray (Chicago: University of Chicago Press, 1971). He also wrote that "Titius is the same Man he was 40 Years since, tho' Physicians tells us, That in a Tract of seven Years, the Body has scarce any of the same Material Substance it had before." Ibid. Both of these metaphors were familiar among civilians, and it may be presumed that Hale had seen them paired together in Richard Zouch, *Cases and Questions Resolved in the Civil-Law,* 140 [misprinted as 180] (Oxford: 1652).

Although Hale discussed common law more directly in his *History of the Common Law,* this was a manuscript he self-consciously did not publish. Hale, *The History of the Common Law of England,* 41. Similarly, the Marquis of Halifax wrote about legal change in his manuscripts, for although not a lawyer, he understood the risks. "Political Thoughts and Reflections," in George Savile, Marquis of Halifax, *A Character of King Charles the Second: and Political, Moral and Miscellaneous Thoughts and Reflections,* 68–69 ("Of Fundamentals") (London: 1750). The preservation of popular liberty evidently could require men to be discreet about legal change, and not surprisingly, the man who published the most emphatic account of how the law evolved was the Tory doctor Robert Brady, who hoped to show that the monarchy was not subject to constitutional limitations. Robert Brady, *An Introduction to the Old English History* (London: 1684).

the mutability of law in a manner both politic and honest. The common law thus had both a public face and a more introspective, scholarly aspect—the one looking out toward the ideal of unaltered, ancient common law, and the other looking inward to the more complex reality. The interior musings about change through tacit consent have always been more intellectually satisfying, but the outward ideal of an ancient, original constitution was essential for the preservation of liberty.

In this public ideal, even the power of Parliament had to rest on the ancient, original constitution, and the lengths to which a judge might go to place parliamentary power on the original constitution rather than mere tacit consent can be observed in Chief Justice Holt's opinion in *Brewster v. Kidgell.* The case arose in 1698 from an agreement to pay a rent charge or annuity without deducting amounts for statutory land taxes. In the course of giving his opinion, Holt conceded that "Parliamentary taxes" were not among the original methods of raising money in England. Yet rather than suggest they had become constitutional over time, he explained that they had a basis in a more general requirement of the original constitution. Even "thô not only" or exclusively established "by the Original Frame and Constitution of the Governm^{t}.," parliamentary taxes were constitutional, because by the original constitution—a constitution "repeated and Confirmed by . . . Acts of Parliament"—these taxes "must be by an Act made by the whole Legislative Authority." Holt therefore concluded that "they are such things as have[,] thô not Actually or formerly[,] yet they have Fundamentally and Virtually an Existence in the Constitution and are not to be looked upon as things of a Meer Forreign and Strange Nature." In other words, parliamentary taxes as such were not part of the "Original Frame and Constitution," but because the mechanism for adopting enactments was part of the original constitution, "there was some kind of being of those Taxes in the Constitution of the Government."[59]

[59] *Brewster v. Kidgell* (K.B. 1698), British Library, Holt's Opinions, Add. Ms. 35979, fol. 109[v]–110[r]. See also Comberbach, *Reports,* 466. Holt returned to the constitutional authority of Parliament—in particular, the House of Commons—when in *Ashby v. White* he said "for sure the Constitution of England is not derived from the House of Commons, but the House of Commons is a part of it." *Ashby v. White* (K.B. 1702), in *The Judgements delivered by the Lord Chief Justice Holt in the Case of Ashby v. White and Others, and in the Case of John Paty and Others,* 23 (London: 1837).

There was a long tradition of resting parliamentary power and practices on ancient common law—a tradition that was buttressed by suggesting that the absence of a written law created a presumption of ancient custom. Whitlocke asked in 1610: "Can any man give me a reason, why the King can only in Parliament make lawes? No man ever read any law, whereby it was so ordained; and yet no man ever read that any King practised the contrary: Therefore it is the original right of the Kingdome, and the very naturall [i.e., native] constitution of our State and policy, being one of the highest rights of soveraigne power." Thus, "it

In the eighteenth century, notwithstanding the reality of constitutional change, lawyers continued to rely on ideals about the ancient custom of the realm, including the constitution. After the Revolution of 1688, many Whig political observers boldly argued that the Revolution had established England's modern constitution, and they thereby created political space for an open acknowledgment of constitutional evolution, but lawyers, as might be expected, tended to be more cautious, for they were more concerned about the force of law than political or historical truth. Looking back at the end of the century, Edmund Burke noted that "[a]ll the reformations we have hitherto made, have proceeded upon the principle of reference to antiquity." This was hardly to say that the constitution did not change, but rather that common law writers, from Coke to Blackstone, tended to idealize an unchanged ancient law, and if the reality of change was different, this only confirmed the significance of the vision held out by the lawyers: "In the matter of fact, for the greater part, these authors appear to be in the right, perhaps not always: but if the lawyers mistake in some particulars, it proves my position still the more strongly; because it demonstrates the powerful prepossession towards antiquity, with which the minds of all our lawyers and legislators . . . have been always filled."[60] Custom had to be ancient, and a constitution that was binding as law—indeed, binding upon all parts of the government—had to be in some sense enacted by the people, and although it was increasingly evident to historians that the English did not actually have a constitution that met these standards, many English lawyers were therefore all the more adamant that they had an ancient, original constitution.

Contract and Law

A constitution, as already apparent, could be considered not only a contract but also a law—a law of higher authority and obligation than the rest of the law of the land—and a constitution therefore offered a range of different remedies for breach. Both as a contract and as a law, a constitution could allow the people to take matters into their own hands. As a law, however, it

is *jus indigena* an old homeborne right." [Whitlocke], *A Learned and Necessary Argument To Prove that Each Subject Hath a Propriety in His Goods,* 11. As was more candidly argued in the 1670s, "we must not be governed by historians in matters of law; and therefore . . . we must presume that the House of Commons, and elections of knights of the shire, as ancient as the common law, and have been time immemorial; because we find no written law that does first begin any such institution." *Samuel Barnardiston v. William Soame* (K.B. 1674), *State Trials,* 6: 1085.

[60] Edmund Burke, *Reflections on the Revolution in France,* 45 (2nd ed.; London: 1790).

also determined the obligation of other laws, and this, it will soon be seen, left decisions about the lawfulness of the other laws in the hands of the judges.

The contractual conception of a constitution suggested contractual remedies. Europeans often argued that a people formed a contract with their ruler, subject to conditions that released the people from their allegiance upon his breach of the agreement. For example, if the people consented to a monarch on conditions stated in his coronation oath or various laws, then their allegiance could be considered conditional on his adherence to these conditions, and as already observed in the writings of Buchanan, a breach of the constitutional contract thus justified resistance.[61]

The ideal of the constitution as an enacted law similarly justified resistance, but it also suggested other, less violent mechanisms by which the people could preserve their liberty. If the constitution was enacted by the people, they could alter it without having to wait for a breach or even the king's consent, and if the king was conceived to be their servant or agent, it was especially clear that they could alter their constitution at their pleasure.[62] Common lawyers, as it happened, tended to avoid focusing on the possibility of a popular amendment of their customary constitution, lest the Crown take the occasion to question the antiquity of the constitution or to claim popular acquiescence in a loss of liberty. The underlying conception of popular lawmaking authority, however, left little doubt that amendment was possible. As Buchanan had said, "the faults of Lawes being found out, they may be amended or abrogat[ed] by the Lawgivers," who were "the People."[63]

[61] See also, for example, *Vindiciae, Contra Tyrannos* (Edinburgh: 1579).

[62] On the assumption that the constitution was the law by which the people authorized their servant, the English could avoid the old conundrum that if the people and the king were parties to any dispute about his power, neither could be the judge. Algernon Sidney expostulated: "It were the most absurd Folly, to say, that a man might not put away . . . an Unlawful Servant, because he is a Party and Judge." *The Arraignment, Tryal & Condemnation of Algernon Sidney, Esq; for High Treason,* 23 (London: 1684). Instead, "[h]e that institutes, may also abrogate," and "[i]f the Multitude therefore do institute, the Multitude may abrogate." Thus, only the people could be "fit Judges of the performance of the Ends of the Institution." The people in forming their society had "the liberty of framing it according to our own Wills, for our good," and "we our selves are Judges how far 'tis good for us to recede from our natural liberty." Algernon Sidney, *Discourses Concerning Government,* 15 (i.6), 23 (i.10). Of course, it would be otherwise "where other Rules are agreed upon, and a Superior-Judge constituted," but there was "none such between King and People," and therefore the "People must needs be the Judg of things happening between Them." *The Arraignment, Tryal & Condemnation of Algernon Sidney,* 23.

[63] Buchanan, *De Jure Regni Apud Scotos,* 86–87. The reasoning permitting popular amendment can be observed in greater detail in the pamphlets of William Ball, who argued that the power of the people was not merely original but also continual. Rather than be "consti-

The advantage of considering a constitution a law, however, was not only the possibility of popular amendment but also the effect of the constitution's legal obligation. When a sovereign bound himself by contract, then, as Bodin was quick to suggest, he could escape its provisions, for although he might make his contract under oath, he could depart from his agreement "if the equitie thereof ceased"—indeed, he could perhaps do so "of himself without consent of his subjects."[64] Even when the sovereign more firmly bound himself to obey his own law, he still could claim a separate power to act above his law, this being an approach increasingly taken by English kings in the early seventeenth century. Yet whether a ruler acted through his law or above it, he could not claim any authority or create any obligation against a law of higher authority and obligation, and this made a constitution a singularly important limitation on all governmental acts. If

---

tuted, or determined . . . by some other instrumentall cause," a free people "in general constitute or determine themselves," and it therefore was "destructive to the very Essence of their Freedome not to be able to determine themselves to that which they conceive to be *Bonum commune.*" Indeed, "this they must not be able to do sometimes only, and *originally,* but *perpetually,*" for "otherwise . . . they cease to speak truly, to be free, and are onely free in Denomination." According to Ball, "if a people can *Originally* dispose or determine themselves, and cannot afterwards *Actually* do it, their Original power, or form of disposing, or determining themselves ceases to be." William Ball, *Constitutio Liberi Populi. Or, the Rule of a Free-born People,* 4–5 (London: 1646).

What this meant for amendment became clear in the mid-1650s, when Ball quarreled with the Catholic defender of Cromwell, Thomas White. On the assumption of *salus populi*—that the good of the people was the end of government—White held that a "high or supream Magistrate" who was "tyed, bound, or concluded by the *Peoples Limitations*" nonetheless had discretion to violate such limitations. In particular, "[w]hen some great fault discovers itselfe in the limitations, and the end of Government is prejudiced by such a defect," the magistrate still should be able to act. White admitted "it is no doubt but 'tis the intention of the people or the Trustees of the people to binde their Magistrate to such conditions." Precisely for this reason, however, White asked "[w]hether, in such a case," the magistrate "be bound to his orders . . . or whether the duty of a wise and good man doth enfranchise him to doe what is truely best for the people, though it be against their wills?" Thomas White, *The Grounds of Obedience and Government,* 83–84 (London: 1655).

To this suggestion of a power above constitutions because of their imperfection, William Ball answered that the people could amend their limits on government. Such limits were "matters generally well prepondered and debated by the most prudent of the People, or their Trustees," and if they proved defective, there was no "difficulty":

> [I]f *any great fault discover it self in any Limitations* . . . the high Magistrate may in convenient time convene the Trustees of the People, to whom he may propound, with whom he may debate, and by whom he may reform, *such fault in the Limitations* (if any such be) and no doubt but some of them will be as quick sighted as himself, and as willing to reform any fault for the Peoples good.

Both before and after this "reform," however, the magistrate was "strictly tied to the observation of his Orders and Oath." William Ball, State Maxims, 12–13 (London: 1655).

64 J. Bodin, *The Six Books of a Commonweale,* 92–93, trans. Richard Knolles (London: 1606).

natural law left the initial human lawmaking authority in the people, then the obligation of their lawmaking will in their constitution could never be defeated by the obligation of any lawmaking or other will expressed by the king. This insurmountable legal obligation was the distinctive strength of a constitution enacted by the people, and although such a law initially appealed to the English against the threat from the Crown, it obviously had the potential to limit all parts of government—not least in a court of law.

Rather than choose between the contractual and legal aspects of their constitution, English lawyers tended to conjoin the contract and the law—as may be observed in the pamphlets of the irrepressible William Prynne. Having learned about lawless government at the hands of the Star Chamber (which in 1637 had his ears cut off), he vehemently opposed the Crown on the basis of what he called both "the Fundamentall Law, and originall compact."[65]

While the English continued to make crude arguments of this sort, Continental academics came to prefer a more careful theory of three stages in the formation of constitutions. According to this theory, individuals in the state of nature first agreed to form themselves into a people, community, or society; second, a form of government was decreed or stipulated; third, the people and their ruler agreed to the form of government—the ruler taking an oath of office or otherwise promising to adhere to the form of government, and the people promising obedience. Thus, as laid out by Samuel Pufendorf, "for a state to coalesce regularly, two compacts and one decree are necessary." In contrast to the first and third steps, which clearly involved contracts, the second—the decree about the form of government—was a law. As put by a seventeenth-century English translation of Pufendorf, "there are requir'd Two *Covenants*, and One Decree or *Constitution*."[66]

This elaborate tripartite theory could not flourish in England's popular politics, and most English political commentators therefore persisted in speaking about law and contract as different aspects of one act of consent. In his lectures at Cambridge, Thomas Rutherforth explained:

[65] William Prynne, *The Soveraigne Power of Parliaments and Kingdomes: Divided into Foure Parts*, Fourth Part, 22 (London 1643). On other occasions, however, Prynne simply alluded to the constitution as law, as when he wrote about the "things specially provided for by our Fundamental Laws, and the original Constitution of our Government." William Prynne, *A Summary Collection of the Principal Fundamental Rights, Liberties, Properties of all English Freemen*, 22 (London: 1656) (32-page ed.; Wing P4094).

[66] Samuel Pufendorf, *De Officio Hominis et Civis Juxta Legem Naturalem Libri Duo*, 2: 107 (II.vi.7), ed. Frank Gardner Moore (New York: Oxford University Press, 1927); Samuel Pufendorf, *The Whole Duty of Man According to the Law of Nature*, 253 (II.vi.7) (London: 1698).

> Sometimes we consider this act of joint consent as a law, and call it the law of the civil constitution. Sometimes we consider it as a compact. . . . There is some reason for calling it by these different names; because in respect of what passes between the collective body [of the people] and the several members, it is a law; and in respect of what passes between the same collective body and the particular persons who are called to the office of civil legislation, and established into a legislative body, it is a compact.[67]

The English in this way rejected the academic distinctions among different contracts and a decree and continued, instead, to assume a single act of consent that was both contract and law. The first contract posited by Continental academics—that of society—could be taken for granted by a people who already considered themselves part of a community; and as for the second and third acts of consent, the English had little incentive to separate the law willed by the people and the contract by which a ruler bound himself, for English law more clearly bound the monarch than any distinct coronation oath or other agreement. The English therefore tended to view all these distinctions as aspects of a single constitution, which they were fortunate enough to have received as ancient custom. When holding a ruler or the people to account outside the legal system, the English sometimes focused on the contractual aspects of the constitution, which rested on the people's consent. When holding a ruler responsible within the legal system, however, they needed to consider the constitution a binding law that rested ultimately on the people's will.

Thus, a constitution willed by the people was law, and this would be essential for judicial enforcement. Such a constitution was not merely an arrangement of government; nor (as imagined by some scholars) was it a confused combination of positive and natural law; rather, it was an enactment by the people. Of course, many Englishmen refused to concede that there had ever been such an enactment, but at least among some Englishmen, including many lawyers, there was a deep attachment to the view

[67] Thomas Rutherforth, *Institutes of Natural Law,* 360 (II.vi.2) (1754–56; Baltimore: 1832). He added: "The law, therefore, which introduces and establishes the form of the legislative body, must be the joint act of the collective body. And this act, when we consider it in respect of the several members, may rather be called a law than a compact; because it obliges even those who immediately and directly dissent from it, at the time of making it; and this obligation arises from that remote and indirect consent which they gave to the future acts of the society, by making themselves parties to the social compact. But this act of the collective body, though it binds the several members of the society as a law, can be binding upon the collective body itself only as a compact; nothing but the immediate or direct consent of the collective body of a civil society, can take from such body the legislative power which it has by means of civil union, and lodge this power exclusively in some particular government." Ibid., 360–361. For the civil union and its formation of "the collective body of the people," see ibid., 314.

that the constitution, even if known only through ancient custom, had originally been popularly enacted. From this perspective, the people had an authority—perhaps even a divinely derived authority evident from natural law—to make a constitution establishing and limiting the authority of their government, and because the obligation of their legislative act seemed to limit the obligation of the acts of their government, this understanding of the constitution laid a foundation in the law of the land for judicial decisions holding a wide range of government acts unlawful.

II

JUDICIAL DUTY

Having considered thus far the obligation of law, including constitutions, this book can now examine the duty of judges. The duty of common law judges was to decide in accord with the law of the land, and because the constitution was the highest part of this law, the judges in the course of doing their duty had to hold unconstitutional customs and acts unlawful and void. Today, it is difficult to talk about such matters without using the phrase "judicial review." Once, however, not all that long ago, the judges typically conceived of what they did rather differently—in terms of the duty inherent in their office.

Chapter Four introduces the distinctive common law office or duty of a judge to decide in accord with the law of the land. More generally, in Chapter Five, it will be seen that the office of a judge was one of independent judgment—an exercise of intellect or understanding free from any intrusion of will. With their resulting duty to exercise independent judgment in accord with the law of the land, the judges, as will become apparent in Chapter Six, regularly held government acts unlawful—even those of the Crown. In holding such acts unlawful, the judges expounded the law, and Chapter Seven shows that when the judges expounded the law, including the constitution, in the course of doing their duty in cases, they could speak with the authority of their office.

Upon reflection, judicial duty may seem so basic as to be obvious. Remnants of the duty remain vaguely familiar, particularly to the extent it can be discerned from the logic of *Marbury v. Madison.* The duty, however, tends to get lost in Marshall's reasoning about the necessity of deciding cases, which was only a narrow slice of the duty of judges. This thin portion of the duty, moreover, is today characterized as "judicial review"—thus allowing the duty to be understood as a sort of power. As a result, judicial review largely obscures any substantial recognition of the traditional judicial duty. It is therefore necessary to put aside the modern assumptions about *Marbury* and about judicial power if one is to understand the judges' duty and how it required them to hold unconstitutional acts void.

The need to disregard modern assumptions will become especially apparent when it is observed that the ideal of judicial office or duty could have its consequences for unlawful acts because it united worldly law with sacred obligation. The judges bound themselves by oath to a duty that grounded their decisions in the law of the land, and they thereby acquired a divine obligation to decide in accord with human law. With this combination of the heavenly and the worldly, they could rise above the king's will and even above their own to decide in accord with their country's law, including its constitution.

4

Judicial Duty

A COMMON law judge had a duty to decide in accord with the law of the land. Any judge generally had to exercise judgment, but a common law judge more specifically had to exercise his judgment in accord with the law of the realm, and this distinctive duty of common law judges was of profound consequence for English law, including, it will eventually be seen, the enforcement of the English constitution.

Although the common law ideal of judicial duty was taken for granted by most common lawyers, it was continually under pressure from Englishmen who were attracted to competing, academic visions of judicial duty. Such men developed their alternative conceptions of judging from the cosmopolitan ideals of the learned law—the scholarly enterprise that encompassed both the civil and the canon law—and with this academic inspiration, they argued that judges had to look beyond the narrow confines of the common law. Far from being merely academic, their sophisticated vision of judging offered the Crown a means of escaping or at least relaxing the law of the land, and therefore when anxieties about royal authority reached their height in the seventeenth century, the learned challenge to the common law conception of judicial duty became particularly significant.[1]

The common law judges, however, defended their ideals—primarily by insisting on their duty and sharpening their understanding of what it required. They did not always adhere to their duty, and they often made use of academic learning; but against the threat to their duty from learned sen-

[1] The importance of this period for the development of the English judiciary is noted by W. J. Jones, "The Crown and the Courts in England, 1603–1625," in *Law, Liberty, and Parliament: Selected Essays on the Writings of Sir Edward Coke,* 282–283, ed. Allen D. Boyer (Indianapolis: Liberty Fund, 2004).

sibilities, they usually stood on their office and their oaths—on their identity as judges and their obligation to God.[2]

Judicial Duty

The duty of English judges to decide in accord with the law of the land was not the only duty of their office, but it was the most distinctive and prominent. It identified the law they had to follow in their decisions, and it thereby delineated some aspects of the law itself.

This duty to decide in *accord* with the law differed from the duty to act *under* the law. All men in England had a duty to obey the law of the land, but the judges had the additional duty to decide in accord with the law, and this mattered because most cases centered on the application of the law to the parties rather than the judges. It therefore could not be said that the judges in deciding such cases were merely acting under the applicable law or that they reached their decisions because they were bound by the law they applied. Instead, the judges followed the law of the land in their decisions because they had a duty as judges to decide in accord with it.

Their duty seemed to derive from their office. An office was traditionally a duty, but increasingly since late Roman times it was also the position of one who had specialized duties. The classic account of general offices or duties was Cicero's *De Officiis,* and although he also discussed specialized positions, he did not describe them as offices. Other Roman authors, however, combined his conception of office with a narrower notion of office as a position in government, and this dual sense of office as both a duty and the position of a particular officer was commonplace among English lawyers of the sixteenth and seventeenth centuries.[3] As Henry Finch observed, "[o]ffice is a dutie of attendance upon a charge."[4] Similarly, Coke explained that "Offices are duties, so called, to put the Officer in minde of his duty."[5] The modern conception of office as a specialized "charge" or "function, by

[2] There has been much important scholarship on the role of the learned laws in England, and here it should suffice to note that even while English lawyers drew upon civil and canon law for their understanding of particular substantive problems, they tended to fear learned sensibilities about legal obligation and judicial duty, including learned expectations about the domain of law and about the role of judges in extending it.

[3] For the other Roman authors, see David Johnston, "The General Influence of Roman Institutions of State and Public Law," in *The Civilian Tradition and Scots Law,* 92, eds. D. L. Carey Miller and R. Zimmerman (Berlin: Duncker and Humblot, 1997).

[4] Henry Finch, *Law, or, a Discourse Thereof,* 162 (London: 1627).

[5] Coke, *Institutes,* 3: 185. In his notes, Richard Hutton of Common Pleas wrote: "What are the highest places, but obligations of the greatest dewties?" *The Diary of Richard Hutton 1614–1639,* at 122, ed. W. R. Prest (London: Selden Society, 1991).

vertue whereof a man hath some imploiment in the affaires of another, as of the King," was becoming ever more prominent, but conjoined with this was still the underlying duty.[6] Thus, even in the eighteenth century, "the Word *Officium* principally implies a Duty, and in the next Place the Charge of such Duty."[7]

Within his office, an English judge had a duty to decide in accord with English law. It had long been understood that judges should decide *secundum legem* or at least *secundum ius*—the latter being particularly open-ended in referring to either right or law.[8] The generic requirement, however, that the judges decide in accord with the law soon came to seem inadequate—probably because it left room for civil or other "foreign" law—and therefore already at an early date in the history of the common law the king's commissions to his judges specified their duty with the clause *"facturi quod ad iustitiam pertinet secundum legem, & consuetudinem Angliæ."* In other words, they were to do that which pertains to justice according to the law and custom of England.[9] As Coke explained, the law of the land "is the

[6] John Cowell, *The Interpreter,* sig. Zz2[r] (Cambridge: 1607).
[7] Matthew Bacon, *A New Abridgment of the Law,* 3: 718 (London: 1778). Thus, "every Man is a Public Officer, who hath any Duty concerning the Public; and he is not the less a Public Officer, where his Authority is confined to narrow Limits; because it is the Duty of his Office, and the Nature of that Duty, which makes him a Public Officer, and not the Extent of his Authority." Ibid., 3: 719.

The duty associated with judicial office was not so much a professional duty as a duty that was inherent in the office of a judge, and in fact many of those commissioned as judges—for example, those commissioned to sit on assize—were not professional judges. Later, it will be seen that some American judges were not even lawyers. Nonetheless, the early development of a small, professional judiciary, serving for long periods, must have been very significant. Paul Brand, "Edward I and the Transformation of the English Judiciary," in *The Making of the Common Law,* 135, 141–144 (London: Hambledon, 1992).
[8] The word *ius* could notoriously be used in different ways with different meanings: "Ius pluribus modis dicitur, hoc est, multa significat." *Lexicon Iuridicum: Hoc est, Iuris Civilis Et Canonici in Schola Atque Foro usitatarum vocum Penus,* 520 (np: 1607).

There was an ancient tradition of describing the judicial role rather generally. According to Justinian's *Code,* "judges in former times could not accept the judicial office unless they had previously made oath that they would on all occasions decide according to the truth, and in compliance with the law." Codex (III.i.12), *The Civil Law,* 12: 264, trans. Samuel Parsons Scott (Cincinnati: Central Trust, 1932). Similarly, as Selden notes, John of Salisbury had written about Henry II's reign that "'[t]he judges are bound to the laws by an oath so that they must always give judgment in accordance with truth and with obedience to the law.'" Joannis Seldeni, *Ad Fletam Dissertatio,* 173, trans. David Ogg (Cambridge: Cambridge University Press, 1925). A further hint of the general way in which judicial decisions could be discussed comes from early academic lectures in which it was propounded that a judge was "to conduct the proceedings according to the decrees of the laws." Francis de Zuleta and Peter Stein, eds., *The Teaching of Roman Law in England Around 1200,* at 135 (London: Selden Society, 1990).
[9] Coke, *Institutes,* 2: 51. For a minor variation in a commission of Henry IV to justices for taking the assize, see *A Formula Book of English Official Historical Documents,* 2: 218, ed.

right line, where by Justice distributive is guided, and directed," and "therefore all the Commissions of *Oier,* and *Terminer,* of goale delivery, of the peace *&c.* have this clause . . . to doe Justice and Right, according to the rule of the law and custome of England."[10] A century later, the more pedestrian commentator Giles Jacob similarly observed that "all the Commissions of *Judges* are bounded with this Limitation" and that "*Judges* have not Power to *judge* according to that which they think fit; but that which by Law they know to be right."[11]

Judicial Oaths

Judges were bound to their duty by their oaths and thus by an obligation that reached from the law of the land all the way up to heaven. A judge who somehow acquired his office without taking his oath might, perhaps, have felt obliged by the office itself.[12] A judge, however, could only enter his of-

Hubert Hall (New York: Burt Franklin, 1969). For related language in a commission to the justices on eyre from the time of Edward I, see ibid., 2: 194. Incidentally, early medieval scribes or notaries on the Continent might purport to follow the customs of the laws of Rome—*secundum consuetudines legum Romanorum*—but this had rather different connotations. Manlio Bellomo, *The Common Legal Past of Europe 1100–1800,* at 46 (Washington: Catholic University of America Press, 1995).

Anxious that kings might try to pervert the office of the judges by adjusting their commissions, Coke emphasized that the Crown could not change the customary wording without an act of Parliament: "For it is a rule in law, that ancient offices must be granted in such forms and in such manner, as they have used to be, unlesse the alteration were by Authority of Parliament." Coke, *Institutes,* 4: 75. Similarly, in the wake of disputes about the power of the High Commission to administer oaths, Coke more generally emphasized that oaths required the allowance of law. "A new Oath cannot be imposed upon any Judge, Commissioner, or any other subject without authority of Parliament . . . but the giving of every Oath must be warranted by Act of Parliament, or by the Common Law time out of mind." Coke, *Institutes,* 2: 479. See also Coke, *Institutes,* 3: 165.

10 Coke, *Institutes,* 2: 56.

11 Giles Jacob, *Law Dictionary,* sig. Fff2[v] ("Judge") (London: 1732).

One consequence was that the judges could not enter consent decrees they knew to be contrary to law: "The court will not give a Judgment which they know would be against the Law, altho' the Plaintiff and Defendant do agree to have such a Judgment given. . . . For the Judges are to do equal Justice according to their best Skill, and not to err wilfully, and against their Knowledge, to please the Parties." John Lilly, *The Practical Register,* 2: 98 (London: 1735) (citing a King's Bench case of 1671). Similarly, when an ecclesiastical court pressured one party to give a bond to the other party, Lord Keeper Wright refused to enforce the bond on the ground that it had not been "given freely and voluntarily." Even if not so much "compulsion . . . as to make it *per dures,* it ought to be set aside, or at least not carried into execution," for "[a] judge may fairly mediate an accommodation; but not put terms upon pronouncing sentence, or giving judgment." *Attorney General, ad relationem Cossart & Dutrie v. Sothon et Ux* (Ch. 1705), Vernon, *Reports,* 2: 497.

12 In this respect, office differed from status. If an individual was already of a status to which

fice by taking the oath, and in this way he bound himself to his office before the highest of judges.

The sanctity of this obligation became manifest in ceremony. When the king chose a new judge, the chancellor brought the letters patent into court and had the letters read aloud. The keeper of the rolls then read the oath, and the new judge swore to it "upon the Holy Gospels of God." At this point, the chancellor gave him his letters patent, and the chief justice of the court assigned him his place on the bench, where he took his seat.[13]

Before the judge took his oath, the chancellor or lord keeper would speak about judicial office, and the appointee would modestly speak about his imperfections and his desire to do his office diligently. When Anthony Fitzherbert became a justice of Common Pleas, Lord Chancellor Wolsey "expounded the office of a judge, and [said] that it belongs to him to administer justice indifferently, as well to the poor as to the rich, and that he should not have a faint heart, but fortitude in all his judgments"—after

---

the law attributed a duty, the oath made no difference in his duty. For example, subjects owed allegiance, regardless of whether they took the oath of allegiance, and therefore, although prelates, abbots, and peers were excused from appearing at the tourn and leet, they "yet are all Subjects . . . as firmly bounden to their allegiance, as if they had taken the oath, because it is written by the finger of the Law in every one of their hearts, and the taking of the corporall oath, is but an outward declaration of the same." Coke, *Institutes,* 2: 121.

Judges, in contrast, entered their office only by taking their oath of office, and therefore little was said about what their duties might be in the absence of an oath. One exception occurred when it was suggested in *Calvin's Case* in 1608 that an opinion of the judges in a prior case, heard by Parliament, was not binding because the judges gave their opinion outside their court and thus not under the obligation of their oaths. In response, Chancellor Ellesmere said: "The reverence, and worthiness of the men is such, as is not to bee quarrelled and doubted of, if there were not Oathe at all: for, if men of so great and eminent places feare not God and his Judgements, even out of a religious conscience . . . it may be doubted that the externall ceremonie of adding a Booke will little availe." *Speech in the Exchequer Chamber, Touching the Post-Nati* (1608), in *Law and Politics in Jacobean England: The Tracts of Lord Chancellor Ellesmere,* 209–210, ed. Louis A. Knafla (Cambridge: Cambridge University Press, 1977).

The judges of the period clearly felt bound by their oaths even when not giving judgment in their own court, which Ellesmere handily pointed out: "This Exception may serve against the Judges, as well in Cases when they sit and give Judgement, as Justices of Assises, *Nisi prius, Oyer* and *Terminer,* and Gaole Delivery, as in this Case of Parliament: for, there they have none other Oath but their generall Oath." Ibid.

13 Sir John Fortescue, *De Laudibus Legum Anglie,* 127 (li), ed. S. B. Chrimes (Westport: Hyperion, 1979). In later centuries, the judge would take the oaths of supremacy and allegiance before taking his oath of office, and the chancellor might show him to his seat, but the basic form of the ceremony remained unchanged. It should be noted, moreover, that the appointment of a chief justice of King's Bench was by writ rather than letters patent. Sir John Sainty, *The Judges of England 1272–1990,* xvii (London: Selden Society, 1993). Until a relatively late date the keeper of the rolls read the oath from the roll of oaths. John Bruce, ed., *Liber Famelicus of Sir James Whitelocke,* 81 (London: Camden Society, 1858).

which Fitzherbert came to the bar and was sworn.[14] A century later, Lord Keeper Thomas Coventry had occasion to speak to many new judges, but he usually assumed that judicial duty was too obvious to require much discussion. In 1626, for example, he told the new Chief Justice of Common Pleas, Sir Thomas Richardson, that "[t]o speak to you of the dewties of a judge, and with what vertues a judge should be indowed withall is a matter needlesse."[15] As it happens, Richardson might have benefited from such instruction, but not because the duties and virtues were unfamiliar.

The incentives for a judge to do his duty are known in particular detail from a speech Coventry gave to Sir John Finch upon his becoming Chief Justice of Common Pleas. One reason was that "by the oath that you are to take, you submyt yourselfe to the Kinge, if you doe unjustly, to forfeite lands and goods and all you have." This worldly threat, however, was not among the primary motives, for judges were also obliged to God, and as suggested by Psalm 82, they sat in God's place—as gods among men:

> Ther are three things [that] may move you to be carefull to performe this duty of doeinge justice. First, it is a duty you owe to God. Second, in *respectu loci,* the place is the throne of God. Third, in *respectu judicii,* the judgement is Gods, if it be just and he doeth assist you. Psalm 82: God is in the congregation of princes, he is judge amonge the gods, and the judgment when it is just is Gods judgment not yours. When you come to sett uppon your quishon lett theis things be remembered, and that wilbe a principall motive to be carefull and watchfull in all your judgments and proceedings.

After listening to this, Finch spoke of his gratitude to the king, to God, and to his fallen patron, Francis Bacon, for whose encouragement in earlier years he "was exceedingly beholden." Finch then took his oath and shook the hands of his new colleagues.[16]

These ceremonies are suggestive about how social pressures were brought to bear in support of the obligation owed to God. Men cannot live on ideals alone, and as evident from the ceremonies, the judges in doing their duty could draw courage from the expectations of the bench and the bar, not to mention the broader populace. At the same time, these social pressures cannot be understood in a narrowly materialistic manner. Judges could occasionally find solace in the expectations of their contemporaries, but such reinforcement was unreliable, and the judges therefore often had to take refuge in what they took to be the more predictable expectations of

[14] J. H. Baker, ed., *The Reports of Sir John Spelman,* 1: 159 (London: Selden Society, 1977). The transcription of the word "faint" is conjectural.
[15] *The Diary of Richard Hutton 1614–1639,* at 67.
[16] Ibid., 100–102 (1634).

their predecessors on the bench—"the ancient Judges and Sages of the Law."[17] When much buffeted by the opinions of their contemporaries, they could also take comfort in the opinion of a higher judge. As Coke reminded his brethren, "though some may maligne you, yet God will give you his blessing" and "will defend you as with a shield: *For thou Lord wilt give a blessing unto the righteous, and with thy favourable kindnesse wilt thou defend him, as with a shield.*"[18] At least in this sense, a judge did not have to consider himself entirely alone.

Nonetheless, a judge had a lonely task, for by virtue of his oath, the obligation of judicial office rested on him as an individual. Not the judiciary, nor even a particular court, but each judge took the oath of office. As Lord Chancellor Ellesmere explained, "[a]n oathe must be sworne by a naturall bodie . . . a politike body cannot doe it."[19] The judges thus had a personal obligation to God to serve in their office, and this was true whether they acted as part of their court in giving judgment or more individually—for example, when giving advisory opinions.[20] With regard to all such matters, each judge was bound to judge the law for himself in his own conscience.[21] This obligation to God to reach an individual decision could weigh heavily on the judges. They were expected, whenever possible, to join a majority opinion for the sake of unanimity, but having individual obligations under oath, they also sometimes anxiously insisted on their personal judgment and decided against their brethren.[22]

[17] Coke, *Institutes,* 1: fol. 379b.

[18] Ibid., 4: [365–366] (Epilogue), citing Psalm 5.

[19] *Speech in the Exchequer Chamber,* in *Law and Politics in Jacobean England,* 246. Ellesmere made this observation when discussing allegiance, but the point was more general.

[20] Ellesmere noted that according to the judges' oath, "they shall counsell the King truely in his business," and on this basis he suggested that "the grave Resolution of the Judges in Parliament, which (although some may tearme & accompt as bare opinions) I must alwayes valew, and esteeme as a reall and absolute Judgement." Ibid., 209–210, 213. In contrast, common lawyers assumed that judges were bound by their oaths and duty when giving advisory opinions, but increasingly also assumed that such opinions lacked authority precisely because they were not given on judgments.

[21] As put by the regicide John Cooke, "every Judge must proceed according to his owne judgement and conscience." John Cooke, *The Vindication of the Professors and Profession of the Law,* 85 (London: 1646).

[22] This happened most notoriously in the *Shipmoney Case.* When Charles I sought an advisory opinion from the judges in support of his shipmoney writs, Sir George Croke and some of the other dissenting judges were "pressed" by their brethren to subscribe on the ground that this was "usual in cases of difference," whether in court or in conference. Croke recognized that "in our court, if three judges agree in opinion against one, or two where there are five judges, judgment is to be entered *per curiam,* if the major part agree, and the other are to submit to it." Other judges confirmed the "continual practice" in conferences among the judges of the different courts for dissenters to "submit their opinions" to the majority (al-

Rather than specify every duty inherent in judicial office, the oaths of the different types of judges tended to spell out their duties only to the extent explicit reminders seemed necessary. For example, the barons of the exchequer, who historically had faced financial temptations, swore nothing specific about deciding in accord with the law of the land, but they did have to swear to an aspect of the more basic duty, which they shared with every subject, that they themselves would not act contrary to the law. In particular, they swore that they would not release the king's right or release or disturb anyone else's right contrary to law.[23]

Revealingly, the judges who expressly swore to decide "after" or in accord with English law were not the common law judges, but rather the judges who might be especially apt to make decisions that did not conform to the law of the land. The most prominent such judge was the lord chancellor or lord keeper, who had to recite that he "shall doe right to all man-

though it is probable that this was a generalization about cases in which the dissenters viewed the question as doubtful). The majority added that "it was not fit, especially in a case of this nature so much concerning the service of the king, for some to subscribe, and some to forbear." On these arguments, Croke and the other dissenters finally signed the advisory opinion, but only on the express assumption that "although we did subscribe, it did not bind us," and that "in point of judgment, if the case came in question judicially before us, we should give our judgments as we should see cause after the arguments on both sides."

The next year when shipmoney was challenged in court, Croke was one of those who dissented and held the writ unlawful. He declared that because the advisory opinion had been "before arguments heard on either side, or any precedents seen, I hold that none is bound by that opinion." Moreover, having now heard arguments and examined the precedents, he stated, "I am now of an absolute opinion that this writ is illegal." Argument of Sir George Croke in the Case of Shipmoney, *State Trials,* 3: 1146–1147. Rather than defer to his brethren or King Charles, Croke declared himself accountable to a higher sovereign: "I have considered maturely of what hath beine delivered by my brothers; uppon hearing of their grave judgments I endeavoured as much as in mee lay to conforme my own opinion to theirs, much suspecting that my owne judgement was not guided aright when I heard them all judicially uppon their oathes give their judgement against my single opinion. Yet, because every one hath a private conscience to satisfie and give accoumpt of to God, I cannott be swayed by anything that hath beine yet saide to give my judgement with the multitude; but in my opinion judgement ought to be given for the defendant." He concluded that the writ of shipmoney "is not agreable to the common law." "Notes of the Judgment Delivered by Sir George Croke in the Case of Ship-Money," in *Camden Miscellany,* 7: 1–2, ed. Samuel Rawson Gardiner (London: Camden Society, 1875).

Incidentally, although many contemporaries praised Croke for not adhering to the advisory opinion, one later commentator complained that Croke and Hutton were willing to sign it in compliance with the other judges, "[w]hich in my humble opinion is so far from being an Apology that it is an Aggravation of their Crime," for "[t]hey were then upon their Oaths to Counsel the King according to Law, and they confess'd they broke those Oaths by doing the Contrary knowingly." [Peter Hughes], *Georgicum: or, A Supplement to the Mirror of Justices,* 17 (np: 1716).

23 A baron swore not to "let the Kings right. . . . Nor none other persons right he shall disturbe, let or respite contrary to the lawes of the land." Coke, *Institutes,* 4: 109. See also *The Book of Oaths and the Several Forms Thereof, both Ancient and Modern,* 119 (London: 1689). See also the oath of justices on eyre. Ibid., 131.

ner of people, poore and rich, after the lawes and usages of the Realm."[24] The other judges who swore to do right "after" the law of the land were mere justices of the peace. They might need an extra reminder to attend to their statutory duties, and they therefore were asked to swear that "you shall do equal right to the Poor and the Rich after your cunning, wit, and power, and after the Laws and Customs of the Realm, and Statutes thereof made."[25] At their different extremes of the legal system, Chancellors might be considered partly above the jurisdiction of the common law, and justices of the peace might be considered partly below it, and they therefore had to make explicit that they would do right in accord with the laws of the realm.

An administrative version of judicial duty was shared by the attorney general and other Crown lawyers. Serjeants at law were the lawyers admitted to plead before the Court of Common Pleas, and they swore that "ye shall truly counsel them, that ye shall be retained with after your cunning." Some serjeants, however, were elevated to serve the king, and on becoming king's serjeants, they swore: "ye shall duly and truly Administer the *Kings* matters, after the course of the Law, after your cunning."[26] With these words, the king's serjeants acknowledged that they had a more substantial duty than most lawyers; and the attorney general, the solicitor general, and other government lawyers thus came to share an administrative version of the duty to decide in accord with the law.

It was unnecessary, however, for the common law judges to recite such a duty, for it was inherent in their office, and they needed no reminder of this. The common law judges began their oath with the general declaration "[t]hat well and truly ye shall serve our Sovereign Lord, the *king* and his People in the Office of Justice." They then recited more specific duties: that they would preserve the king's rights, not take bribes, and not give council in matters touching the king, and that they would "do equal Law and Execution of Right, to all the *Kings* Subjects Rich and Poor, without having regard to any person."[27] Yet it was nothing so specific that committed the

[24] Coke, *Institutes,* 4: 88; John Brydall, *Jus Sigilli,* 14 (London: 1673). See also *The Book of Oaths and the Several Forms Thereof,* 118. Employing a similar usage, the recorder of London swore: "ye shall well and continually, keep and rule the *Kings Majesties* Courts, in the Chamber, and in the Hustings, after the Custome of this City." Ibid., 241. See also the oath of justices in eyre. Ibid., 131. The words about deciding in accord with the law of the realm apparently appeared in the oaths of councilors and at least some judges by the mid-thirteenth century. Paul Brand, "Ethical Standards for Royal Justices in England, c. 1175–1307," *Roundtable,* 8: 240–244 (2001).

[25] Ibid., 175.

[26] Ibid., 138–139. More generally, for the history of the office of attorney general, see Baker, ed., *The Reports of Sir John Spelman,* 2: 385.

[27] *The Book of Oaths and the Several Forms Thereof,* 120–121 (translating oath enrolled and printed with 20 Edward III, c. 1 [1346]); Bracton, *On the Laws and Customs of England,* 2: 309, ed. Samuel E. Thorne (Cambridge: Belknap, 1968). According to Richard Hutton, the

common law judges to the law of the land, for they understood as well as anyone that this was part of their office. Their opening words about serving in "the Office of Justice" were therefore sufficient to establish that they were "sworn to execute Justice according to [the] Law and custome of England."[28]

The Function of the Duty

The duty of the judges gave them their constitutional role. Today, it often is said that judges should adapt their decisions to their function of enforcing the constitution and protecting liberty. Traditionally, however, it was understood that the judges served their function of enforcing law and preserving liberty by adhering to their duty.

Seventeenth-century Englishmen, especially those who distrusted the Crown, recognized that the judges in doing their duty preserved property and freedom. When Nicholas Fuller in 1607 argued that proceedings by *ex officio* oaths and thus by self-incrimination were "voyd," he flattered the judges that they "are me[n] of courage, fearing god," whose "Courtes are the principall preservers of this high inheritance of the law" for both the king and his subjects.[29] Later, when Parliament impeached the *Shipmoney* judges, Lord Falkland declared: "The Constitution of this commonwealth hath established, or rather endeavoured to establish to us the security of our goods, and the security of those laws which would secure to us and our goods, by appointing for us Judges, so settled, so sworn, that there can be no oppression"—although, as the impeachment proceedings revealed, this security depended on the independence of the judges.[30] Similarly, after reciting the statutory provisions for judicial oaths and other limits on the judges, the antiquary Roger Twisden concluded: "I doe not know that ever

oath of office taken by Thomas Richardson in 1626 was that "appointed per le statute d'18 E. 3, cap. 1"—meaning that now associated with 20 Edward III. *The Diary of Sir Richard Hutton 1614–1639,* at 68.

28 *Prohibitions del Roy,* Coke, *Reports,* 12: 64.

29 *The Argument of Master Nicholas Fuller, in the Case of Thomas Lad, and Richard Maunsell, his Clients,* 15, 32 (London: 1607). For the relation of this pamphlet to Fuller's arguments in court, see Roland G. Usher, *The Reconstruction of the English Church,* 2: 151 (New York: D. Appleton, 1910).

30 Speech of Lord Falkland, in *State Trials,* 3: 1260. He observed that there could be no oppression "but they of necessity must be accessory; since if they neither deny nor delay us justice . . . the greatest person in this kingdom cannot continue the least violence on the meanest." As it happened, they had done the opposite: "But this security hath been almost our ruin; for it hath been turned, or rather turned itself into a battery against us: and those persons who should have been as dogs to defend the sheep, have been as wolves to worry them." Ibid.

any kingdome did take more just and honorable waies for limiting monarchy then this, by tying the instruments it was to act by." He too, however, worried that the judges first needed independence and therefore declared, "set Westminster Hall right, that is, let the judges deale justly, uprightly, and honestly," and then "it is not possible for the king of England to injure his people."[31] As Gilbert Burnet summed up, "[h]e that holds the high Office of *Justiciary*" in King's Bench was "the Ch[ie]f Trustee, and Assertor of the Liberties of his Countrey."[32]

Judicial office and oaths thus allowed common law judges to serve functions that tended to elude judges in the learned law or in political theory. A common law judge, being obliged to decide in accord with the law of the land, had no choice but to hold some of the king's acts contrary to the king's own law. It could be difficult, however, for judges to decide against their king if they could take into account the law or right that reached beyond the law of the land. This had been the problem traditionally faced by civilian and canon law judges, who had been expected to frame, elucidate, and in a sense realign national law within their academic models of reason and justice, and the problem had perhaps been particularly severe for canon law judges, who had sometimes been said to have the power to hold temporal laws contrary to the law of the Church. Because these learned judges, both civilians and canonists, ideally could pursue various laws that stood above the law of any one country, they theoretically enjoyed more power to interfere with human law than their common law colleagues, but because their discernment of such elevated concerns involved much discretion, they in practice had to bear an unsustainable political burden. The civil and canon law visions of judging were in this way more ambitious and less practical than the common law vision: These learned perspectives were more open to law above that of the land, but they thereby also left judges without the safety of always standing firmly on the concrete requirements of the law

[31] Roger Twysden, *Certaine Considerations upon the Government of England,* 109, 111–112 (London: Camden Society, 1849). Writing of the judges, he explained: "[I]n short, they were to bee guided by the lawes made for the government of the commonwealth; to deal plainly with the prince when he went against them; . . . to countenance no man in wronging another, the king having no prerogative to protect any in doing injury, of which all ages are full of examples, wherein severall of his graunts have beene made voyed, and such as have illegally put them in execution punisht; it beeing most just, 'de facto,' to hinder the injustice which under pretence of the prince's power an instrument of his would lay upon any particular, by bringing his actions to the tryall of law, and himselfe to condign punishment, for doing what is not warrantable by it." Ibid.

[32] Gilbert Burnett, *The Life and Death of Sir Matthew Hale,* 91 (London: 1681). Shortly before, it was said in Parliament that "[t]he Judges are but the great Trustees betwixt the King and his People." Speech of Sir Francis Winnington (Nov. 23, 1680), in Anichitell Gray, *Debates of the House of Commons,* 8: 56 (London: 1768).

of the land. It is therefore not surprising that although Continental jurists and judges frequently held customs unlawful, they rarely overturned the acts of a ruler.[33] Instead, they more deferentially used sophisticated interpretative techniques to bring the ruler's enactments into conformity with their ideals about what was reasonable or simply accepted that the ruler was the final judge of his own acts.

English political theorists even more bluntly rejected the common law vision, for they were interested in the functional question of who could enforce limitations on royal government, and they doubted whether the king's judges would be sufficiently independent. John Locke, for example, was so skeptical as to whether an aggrieved people would find an indifferent judge on earth that he thought they might have to judge for themselves—or, failing that, would have to make an appeal to heaven.[34] Common law judges, however, could serve the function of enforcing the law of the land against the Crown simply by doing their duty. Being bound to God to decide in accord with English law, the judges had reason to think that they should neither rise above this law nor stoop below it, and they therefore often felt little choice but to do what usually seemed improbable among learned lawyers and political theorists.

Just how far the common law ideal of judicial duty stood from a functional analysis of political power is apparent from the reach of the duty down to justices of the peace. On account of their local status and limited training, justices of the peace were unlikely candidates for enforcers of law against government—even when they sat together as a court at their county's quarter sessions. Nonetheless, they received commissions authoriz-

[33] The Freiburg legal scholar Ulric Zasius briefly alluded to having heard a judgment given against a German prince in his consistory. R. W. Carlyle and A. J. Carlyle, *A History of Medæval Political Theory in the West,* 6: 320 and note 2 (New York: Barnes & Noble, nd). According to Ewart Lewis, "[c]anonists and civilists were quick to disallow mere custom on the grounds of irrationality, but as time went on they increasingly argued that enacted law could be a[n]nulled only by a regular magistrate, or perhaps only by the pope or emperor himself. . . . This position did not necessarily involve a full conception of sovereignty, but when the maker of law was presented as its only competent judge, the practical result might be indistinguishable." Ewart Lewis, *Medieval Political Ideas,* 1: 30 (London: Routledge and Kegan Paul, 1954). For a decision of the Roman Rota holding an English practice unlawful, see Walter Ullmann, "A Decision of the Rota Romana on the Benefit of Clergy in England," in *Collectanea Stephan Kuttner,* III, *Studia Gratiana,* 13: 457 (1967).

[34] John Locke, *Two Treatises of Government,* 445 (II.xix.242), ed. Peter Laslett (Cambridge: Cambridge University Press, 1963). Locke understood that the English judges regularly decided upon the lawfulness of government acts, and he therefore confined his conclusions to "Cases where the Prince hath a Trust reposed in him, and is dispensed from the common ordinary Rules of the Law"—that is, where he enjoyed an absolute power under the constitution and so, traditionally, was not subject to judicial decisions holding his acts unlawful. Ibid.

ing any two or more of them to hear and try indictments and "[t]o determine thereof, by giving judgement . . . according to the Lawes and Statutes," and as has been seen, they swore to do equal right "after the lawes and customes of the realme, and statutes thereof made."[35] Their office and their oaths thus gave them the same duty as any other judge to decide in accord with the law of the land.

Not being defined in functional terms, judicial duty could be rigidly inefficient, but this could not justify the judges in departing from their office—as they made clear in the controversy over prohibitions. In the post-medieval era, the Chancery, Common Pleas, and King's Bench could each issue writs of prohibition to bar proceedings in church courts—for example when litigants complained that the church courts had strayed into common law territory—and the consequent interference with ecclesiastical proceedings troubled Archbishop Richard Bancroft.[36] He therefore asked the Regis Professor of Civil Law at Cambridge, John Cowell, to prepare arguments against the issuance of writs of prohibition by the common law courts. With Cowell's assistance, Bancroft in 1605 presented the Privy Council with a list of "abuses," one of which was that the common law courts could independently issue writs of prohibition in the same case, thus "pester[ing]" the church courts with uncoordinated and often "needlesse" prohibitions. On this basis, Bancroft demanded centralization of the issuance of prohibitions, and to achieve this "great benefit and conveniency," he proposed that prohibitions no longer issue from King's Bench or Common Pleas and instead come *"out of the Chancery onely."*

What was a matter of "conveniency" for Bancroft seemed dangerous to the common law judges. These judges and the barons of the exchequer responded that they could not centralize decisions about prohibitions because each court was bound to decide in accord with the law. They expostulated: "A strange presumption in the Ecclesiastical Judges, to require that the kings Courts should not doe that which by law they ought to doe, and alwayes have done and which by oath they are bound to doe!" The remedy for any inconvenience lay elsewhere: "And if this [issuing of prohibitions] shall be holden inconvenient, and they can in discharge of us obtaine some Act of Parliament to take it from all other Courts th[a]n the Chancery, they shall doe unto us a great ease: but the law of the Realme cannot be changed,

[35] Michael Dalton, *The Country Justice, Containing the Practice of the Iustices of the Peace out of their Sessions,* 10–11, 17 (London: 1619).

[36] For the writ and when it would be granted, see Charles M. Gray, *The Writ of Prohibition: Jurisdiction in Early Modern English Law* (2004), electronic copy in D'Angelo Law Library, University of Chicago Law School.

but by Parliament." The judges then darkly added that "what reliefe . . . such an Act may work to the Subject, wise men will soone find out."[37]

Bancroft's proposals shocked the common law judges. He well understood that these judges "doe oftentimes insist upon . . . their oath, for doing of justice in Temporal causes." Nonetheless, he asked them to forbear from deciding in accord with what they understood to be the law. This astonished the judges and prompted them to declare that their "doing but what they ought, and by their oaths are bound to doe . . . is not to be called in question."[38]

Competing Visions of the Judicial Role

The duty that the judges thought beyond question was in fact frequently challenged. In a practical sense, the judges themselves almost every day undermined the ideal of their duty through their mundane compromises, hypocrisy, and other merely human failures. The greater threat, however, was conceptual, and it came from men (including some prominent common lawyers) who in varying degrees took an academic perspective on law.

The common law vision of judicial duty often troubled Englishmen whose university education in civil and canon law had left them with a low view of national custom and high expectations for reframing it within academic generalizations. The common law, like other national customs, seemed to them necessarily incomplete, uncertain, unjust, and thus in need of learned explication.[39] Of course, these men with academic visions of law denied that judges should decide on the basis of their personal views, but they tended to doubt whether any judge could decide merely in accord with national custom, and they therefore expected even the common law judges to engage in a sort of moral and politic discernment of verities beyond the law of the land—an exercise of judgment by which the judges would render English law more complete and rational.[40] This academic

[37] Coke, *Institutes,* 2: 609. For a history of the Articuli Cleri, see Usher, *The Reconstruction of the English Church,* 2: 74–88.

[38] Coke, *Institutes,* 2: 617–618.

[39] Baker notes the distaste of learned men for what they considered common law barbarism. Baker, ed., *The Reports of John Spelman,* 2: 29. According to Kirshner, "jurists were acutely aware of practicing their profession in a world of bounded rationality, open textures, and ethical uncertainties." Julius Kirshner, "*Consilia* as Authority in Late Medieval Italy: The Case of Florence," in *Legal Consulting in the Civil Law Tradition,* 121, eds. Mario Ascheri, Ingrid Baumgärtner, and Julius Kirshner (Berkeley: Robbins Collection, 1999).

[40] Looking back on this understanding of the learned tradition, the common law writer Giles Jacob crudely summarized, although not without insight, that in the civil law, "[t]he Duty of a Judge is to administer Justice to all that ask it, according to Equity, not according

ideal of judging was not exactly the same as that of Continental commentators, and it was usually only based on a smattering of knowledge in the civil and canon laws, but it still posed a sophisticated and politically dangerous challenge to the common law ideal of judicial office.[41] Not surprisingly, it appealed to intellectuals whose experience with the rigidities of the common law made them eager for approaches that "le[ft] the wit of man more free to turne and tosse."[42] It especially attracted those whose cosmopolitan appreciation of an expansive judicial role coincided with their ambitions for royal patronage, for these men understood that if judges necessarily had to exercise a discernment that rose above the law of the land, then perhaps the king would not be so limited by this mundane law.[43]

The competing academic and common law visions of judicial office drew upon the conflicting theories of legal obligation. Civilians and canonists in the late Middle Ages usually accepted the authority and obligation of a ruler's lawmaking will, but only within the broader theory that legal obligation still rested ultimately on reason and justice. Building upon this old conception of the hierarchy of law, these men understood the learned law to be a human embodiment of eternal reason and justice and thus a model within which national custom could at least be framed and adjusted.[44]

Most common lawyers, by contrast, could increasingly find support for their conception of judicial duty in the perspective adumbrated by Marsilius. English lawyers ordinarily discussed the common law version of judicial duty without generalizing about it, but when they needed theoreti-

---

to strict Law." Giles Jacob, *A Treatise of Laws: Or, A General Introduction to the Common, Civil, and Canon Law,* 329 (London: 1721). Elements of the learned conceptions can be discerned among Continental and English moralists. Henrie Bullinger, *Fifty Godlie and Learned Sermons, Divided into Five Decades,* 191, 193 (2nd decade, 8th sermon) (London: 1587); William Ames, *Conscience with the Power and Cases Thereof,* Fourth Book, 283 (V.liv.24) (np: 1639).

41 For hints of how the English often worked with limited knowledge of the learned law, see R. H. Helmholz, "Thomas More and the Canon Law," in *Medieval Church Law and the Origins of the Western Legal Tradition,* 375, eds. Wolfgang P. Müller and Mary E. Sommar (Washington, D.C: Catholic University of America Press, 2006).

42 Francis Bacon, *The Elements of the Common Lawes of England,* sig. B3[r] (Preface) (London: 1630). Bacon wrote this in justification of "delivering of knowledge in distinct and disjoyned Aphorismes" rather than in "a certaine method or order," ibid., as discussed by Daniel R. Coquillette, *Francis Bacon,* 38 (Stanford: Stanford University Press, 1992).

43 In these ways, the royal threat from the learned law often concerned the basis of legal obligation and the role of judges. As J. H. Baker notes about the introduction of civil law in Germany, "the change was more in technique than in content"—although perhaps "technique" understates what was at stake. Baker, ed., *The Reports of John Spelman,* 2: 27.

44 As Canning observes, "the Commentators universally define jurisprudence as a subdivision of moral philosophy." Joseph Canning, *The Political Thought of Baldus de Ubaldis,* 76–79, 163 (Cambridge: Cambridge University Press, 1987).

cal support, they turned to the assumptions about human nature that underlay the ideal of lawmaking authority. The limited competence of men had already seemed to Aristotle to suggest that law should leave judges as little discretion as possible, and late medieval accounts of authority had gone even further in pursuing fears about human nature. If judges were as weak-minded and strong-willed as other men, they could not be relied upon to adjust law in accord with learned models of reasonableness and justice, for this would invite all the difficulties that men had sought to avoid by establishing an authoritative lawmaker. As put by Marsilius, "the croked wronge & lewde affeccyon of the judge," such "as hatred, love or covetousness," usually "p[er]verteth ye desyre of the judge," and it was therefore necessary that the judge "be appoynted or assygned to gyve jugements, accordynge to the lawes," which for Marsilius meant human laws. Thus, "no maner [of] judgement (as moche as possyble is) oughte to be co[m]mytted and put all togyther to the arbrytrement or will & pleasure of the Judge, But oughte to be determyned by the lawe, and sentence or judgement to be pronounced and gyven of them, accordynge to the same lawe."[45] Those who adopted this mode of reasoning could emphasize either the judges' frail intellect or their distorted will, but either way, the fears about human nature seemed as applicable to the judges as anyone else. Many Englishmen, therefore, like Marsilius, concluded not only that the law made with authority had obligation but also that the judges had to decide in accord with such law.

Private Judicial Knowledge

Nothing offered a better test of the two visions of judicial office than the conundrum of private judicial knowledge. The question had been familiar since Roman times, but it attracted intense interest among medieval scholars, who often relied on arguments about a judge's private knowledge as a proxy for arguments about a judge's moral objections. It was an uphill

[45] Marsilius of Padua, *The Defence of Peace,* 24[v] (I.xi) (London: 1535). Of course, Marsilius cited Aristotle, who in "his Poytykes" aimed to determine "whether it is better for a co[m]mon wele to be governed of the beste man without any lawe, or elles of the best lawe," and Marsilius followed the philosopher in concluding that "of all thynges it is moste necessarye that no thynge be lefte to the arbytryment or pleasure of the judge, to be judged without a lawe . . . for the judgement of the lawe maker (that is to saye the lawe) is not made for any pertyculer person, but it is of thynges to come and of generall thynges, but the offycer and the judge syttynge in judgement do judge of thyngs present & of determynate or p[er]tyculer thyngs." Ibid. See *Politics* (III.xv), in *The Complete Works of Aristotle,* 2: 2040, ed. Jonathan Barnes (Princeton: Princeton University Press, 1985); *Rhetoric,* 1354a–b (I.i), ibid., 2: 2153.

struggle to argue that a judge could acquit a man because of the judge's moral objection to the lawmaker's view of what was just, for this would only confirm the fears about human disputatiousness and about the necessity of deferring to the will of the lawmaker. Yet if the judge himself had factual knowledge about the innocence of a defendant—knowledge about a defendant whom the law otherwise condemned—then perhaps the judge had to spare him. This hypothetical illustrated why a judge could not always conform to human law, and although on its face it only concerned factual knowledge, its strength in suggesting the necessity of judicial departures from law made it a familiar opening wedge for arguments on behalf of a judge's moral objections.[46]

The prevailing range of positions taken by Continental scholars on this point can be illustrated by Thomas Aquinas and Lucas de Penna. Aquinas had a profound regard for human authority, at least within the realm of reason, and in keeping with this general perspective, he largely put aside the problem of judicial knowledge by drawing a distinction between the judge's public and personal roles: "In matters touching his own person, a man must form his conscience from his own knowledge, but in matters concerning the public authority, he must form his conscience in accordance with the knowledge attainable in the public judicial procedure."[47] Yet being attached to an ideal of obligation that did not rest with human authority, Aquinas elsewhere added a qualification for cases of murder: If a man is convicted of murder by false witnesses and the judge knows him to be innocent, the judge must "examine the witnesses with great care, so as to find a motive for acquitting the innocent" or, failing this, "should remit him for judgment by a higher tribunal"—although "[i]f even this is impossible, he does not sin if he pronounce sentence in accordance with the evidence, for

[46] The long history of the problem is outlined by Max Radin, "The Conscience of the Court," *Law Quarterly Review*, 192: 506 (1932), although without full attention to its place amid ideals of authority. For the question of private knowledge and the tendency of some scholars to overstate the degree to which medieval commentators barred judicial reliance on private knowledge, see James Q. Whitman, *The Origins of Reasonable Doubt: The Theological Roots of the Criminal Trial*, 108–111, 146–149 (New Haven: Yale University Press, 2008).

On the whole, there seem to have been at least two strands in the debates about private judicial knowledge. One question, not pursued here, concerned a guilty defendant: If there was insufficient proof in court to convict a defendant, but the judge privately knew him to be guilty, the judge might still have to free him—this being an illustration of the need for formal proof and process in court. A second question, more central to this book, concerned an innocent defendant: If a defendant faced conviction on the formal allegations in court, but the judge privately knew him to be innocent, the judge might have to save him, and as argued above, this illustrated some very broad theoretical concerns.

[47] Thomas Aquinas, *Summa Theologica*, 3: 1478 (Q. 67, Art. 2), eds. Fathers of the English Dominican Province (Westminster, Md: Christian Classics, 1981).

it is not he that puts the innocent man to death, but they who stated him to be guilty."[48] This narrow path for a judge's private knowledge did not go far enough for many jurists, including Lucas de Penna—the fourteenth-century Neopolitan civilian—who answered that each man had but one conscience and that on the last day a judge would be personally accountable for his official conduct. This was not to say that a judge could convict simply on the basis of his conscience, but nor could he convict on the basis of legal proceedings if he knew the accused to be innocent.[49]

St. German took up this question about private knowledge in one of his discussions of the Court of Chancery, and of course, like his predecessors, he had an eye on moral as well as factual knowledge. "[I]f the chauncellor gyve Jugemente according to the proves, thoughe they be untrewe, that it suffiseth for his discharge oonles he knowethe the contrary of his owne knowlege. For he hath followede thordre of the *tryall that is appoyntyd* by ye lawe *in that case.*" This sounded deferential to the law of the land, but it allowed St. German to preserve a conscientious objection based on the chancellor's personal factual knowledge or even his moral knowledge, for "the Chauncellor shall never be bounde to gyve Jugement againste his owne knowlege, nor againste" that which "apperethe evidentlie to stande againste conscience."[50]

In contrast, to decide in accord with the law of the land, the common law judges had to decide in accord with their judicial knowledge, without regard to what they knew privately. Already in the *Year Books* English judges had rejected any acquittal based on private knowledge—even in cases of murder.[51] St. German, however, predictably resisted this conclusion. Although he had to concede that, unlike the chancellor, the common law judges could generally "gyve Jugemente againste theyre owne knowlege, and also againste the trouthe," he held on to a crude version of the exception for murder—suggesting that the typical approach of the common law judges was applicable "yn all tryalles excepte dethe of man, where they may not gyve Jugemente againste theyre own knowlege."[52] Edward Saunders—soon to join the bench—owned the manuscript in which St. German had

48 Ibid., 3: 1464 (Q. 64, Art. 6).

49 Ullmann, *The Medieval Idea of Law,* 127–129. In a variant of this sort of argument, de Penna added that a judge entrusted with the execution of a judgment could not carry out a judgment he knew to be based on false testimony. Ibid., 129.

50 "A Little Treatise Concerning Writs of Subpoena," in *Christopher St. German on Chancery and Statute,* 120, 124, ed. J. A. Guy (London: Selden Society, 1985).

51 Y.B., Paschal 7 Henry IV, pl. 5, page 41. See also William Holdsworth, *A History of English Law,* 9: 136–137 (London: Sweet & Maxwell: 2003).

52 "A Little Treatise Concerning Writs of Subpoena," 124.

St. German was more qualified when examining the question in his dialogues between Salem and Bizance—Jerusalem and Byzantium—the one having a slightly more academic vi-expounded how common law judges should take their private knowledge into account in cases of murder, but when Saunders had occasion to argue about private judicial knowledge, he cited the *Year Books* to show that, whether or not in a case of murder, a judge could make no use of such knowledge, except to recommend a pardon. Arguing to Common Pleas, Saunders summarized that a judge "could not acquit" a man "and give judgment of his own private knowledge," for "you judges have a private knowledge, and a judicial knowledge, and of your private knowledge you cannot judge."[53] As was said in the House of Commons, "a judge is to judge *secundum allegata et probata,* yea though himselfe knew the contrary."[54]

---

sion of judging than the other. Salem began by reciting, rather generally, that "truth ruleth in conscience, what soo ever the order of the lawe be." Yet rather than simply conclude that a judge therefore had to depart from the law of the land, Salem suggested that the judge might have to give up his position: "[I]f the appelle[e], in an appele of morder be founde gyltie, & the judge of his owne knowledge knewe that he is not gyltie, he may not gyve jugeme[n]t agaynste hym, but must rather resygne his office." Bizance assented, but being a more worldly observer, he added that if the judge acquired his knowledge through an examination not authorized by law, he had to remain on the bench and simply put aside the knowledge: "I agree well there, but I put case, that the appelle[e] in thy case be founde gyltie by false verdite, & the juge by examination of wytnesse, and by confessio[n] of the same jury also come to perfyt knowledge, that the appelle is not gilty, he may never the les in ye case geve jugement, and is bounde to do it, for he toke the examination against the order of the law, & therfore he must remove that knowledge, bicause he is com to it of his owne wronge, & ageinst the order of the lawe." Salem would not go so far as to say that the judge had to remain on the bench, but he too recognized that the judge in his judicial conduct should "remove" his private knowledge, for the judge "dyd ageynst the lawe, to examyn new witnes." He sat as a judge of this law, and as "the verdite is of recorde in the same court, and it is given by auctorite of the same lawe, that he sitteth as judge to juge upon," and as "it is also tried after the order of the same law," therefore "I agre wel that he ought not to have take[n] ther any newe examination." [Christopher St. German], *The Addicions of Salem and Bizance,* fols. 43[v]–44[r] (London: 1534).

A century later, Ames also took a view that straddled the learned and the common law—being attentive to conscience but with the suggestion that the judge should abstain from judgment rather than strain the law to save the innocent defendant: "The Judge ought not to passe sentence against the things alleaged and proved, whatsoever there be in his private knowledge." On the contrary, "hee must judge either according to publique knowledge which ariseth out of the things alleaged, and proved, or else wholy abstaine from judgement." Ames, *Conscience with the Power and Cases Thereof,* Fifth Book, 281–282.

53 *Patridge v. Strange & Croker* (C.P. 1553), Plowden, *Reports,* 1: 83 (Dublin: 1792). Similarly, see *Caudry's Case* (1595), "Of the King's Ecclesiastical Law," Coke, *Reports,* 343–344 (Fourth Reports) (London: 1658).

54 Francis Alford's Speech (June 25, 1572), Thomas Cromwell's Journal, in *Proceedings in the Parliaments of Elizabeth I,* 1: 407, ed. T. E. Hartley (Leicester: Leicester University Press, 1981–1995). Oliver St. John later argued, citing Cajetan, that "Man ought not to be judge as God"—that is, "out of his own private knowledge"—but rather "as God would have him to judge: that is *secundum Allegata & probata,* and by a publike not a private knowledge." *Mr. St. Johns Speech or Argument in Parliament; Shewing, Whether a Man May Be a Judge, and a Witnesse in the Same Cause,* 3 ([London]: 1641).

Chancery

Learned opposition to the common law ideal of judicial duty was strongest in the Court of Chancery, where chancellors aspired to offer a justice not available under the rough generalizations of the law. Even in Chancery, however, the common law ideal largely prevailed.

Thomas More got to the heart of the dispute during a memorable afterdinner conversation. When he was chancellor, More issued injunctions that were "misliked" by some of the common law judges, and being told of their views, he "invited all the Judges to dyne with him in the councell chamber at westminster"—this being not merely a social gathering but a familiar way of bringing the judges together on questions of moment. Following dinner, More explained to the judges why he had issued each of his injunctions, and he got the judges "to confes that they in like case, could have done no other wise themselfes." Had he been content with this, More might have assuaged their fears, but he was no less persistent about justice than he would be about religion, and he asked the judges to imitate his correction of law. He explained that they were the judges "unto whome the reformacion of the rigour of the lawe, by reason of their office most especially appertained." Accordingly, if they "wold uppon resonable considerations, by their owne discretions (as they were, as he thought, in conscience bound) mitigate and reforme the rigour of the lawe themselves, there should from thenceforth by him no more Injunctions be graunted." The judges, of course, "refused to condiscend." More took this as a vindication of his injunctions, but the judges surely had very different sentiments about the suggestion that they rely "uppon resonable considerations" in "their owne discretions" to depart from "the rigour" of the law.[55]

[55] William Roper, *The Lyfe of Sir Thomas Moore, knighte,* 44–45, ed. Elsie Vaughan Hitchcock (London: Early English Text Society, 1935).

When pressed to defend his conception of judging, More sometimes fell back on professional standards: "[I]t ys in a judge as yt ys in a physycyon, to whom there be many good bokys wryten, able to gyve good lyght and instruccyon. And yet who wold so precysely bynde hym to his boke, y^{t} he shold nothyng use the dyscressyon of hys brayne, he shold somtyme do full evyll service." *A Dyaloge of Syr Thomas More Knyghte . . . Wheryn Be Treatyd Dyvers Maters* (1530), in *The Complete Works of St. Thomas More,* 6 (Part 1): 261–262 (New Haven: Yale University Press, 1981). Similarly, he quoted Chief Justice Fineaux that whoever "takenth from a justyce the order of hys dyscrecyon, taketh surely frome hym more thanne halfe hys offyce"—although whether the Chancellor really rested on the same understanding of discretion as the Chief Justice is doubtful. *The Debellacyon of Salem and Bizance* (1533), in *The Complete Works of St. Thomas More,* 10, 164 (New Haven: Yale University Press, 1987), discussed by Baker in *The Reports of Sir John Spelman,* 2: 41.

In the end—at least More's end—he still maintained his expansive vision of a judicial duty in conscience to decide in accord with higher laws. After opposing Henry VIII's stance

Divergent Chancery and common law sensibilities about judging became apparent at a more prosaic level when the anonymous serjeant at law criticized St. German's dialogues. The serjeant objected to writs of subpoena—the writs issued by Chancery prohibiting parties from proceeding at common law and requiring them to answer before the chancellor. These writs, the serjeant feared, rendered "the lawe of the realme . . . voyde" and "of non effecte," for they left Englishmen to be "ordrede by the discrecion of the Chauncellor" rather than by law. After observing that "the kinges Juges of this realme" were "sworen to mynystre his lawes," the serjeant asked, "and so is not the Chauncellor?" A chancellor, however, decided in accord with conscience, and "for asmoche as conscience is a thinge of great uncerteyntie," a chancellor might proceed "regarding no lawe, but trusting to his owne wyt and wisdom," thus giving "Jugemente as it pleasith hym self." In short, "divers men, divers conscience"—leading the serjeant to conclude that "the lawe aughte not to be lefte for conscience yn no caas."[56]

St. German answered in a manner unlikely to satisfy common lawyers, for like some other sixteenth-century common lawyers who were academically attracted to the canon law, he suggested that the chancellor could not decide in accord with the law of the land where it was contrary to divine and natural law. St. German believed that although the chancellor "be not bounde to do Justice by his othe, yet he is bound therto yn conscience, and

against Rome and spending time in the Tower, this former lord chancellor was indicted under a statute penalizing anyone who denied the king's supremacy over the English church. After More was found guilty by his jury, the new lord chancellor, Thomas Audley—the chief member of the commission—began to give judgment. More interjected, however, that it was customary before condemning a prisoner to ask him "why Judgment should not be geven agaynste him." The new chancellor therefore stayed his judgment and asked More "what he was able to say to the contrary." More answered that "this Indictment is grounded uppon an acte of parlamente directly repugnant to the lawes of god and his holy churche" and that "it was contrary to . . . the lawes and statutes of our owne Land." When the Chancellor responded that Parliament (including the bishops and the representatives of the universities) had agreed to the statute and that therefore "[i]t was muche [to be] mervayled" that More "alone against them all would so stiffly stick," the old chancellor rested on conscience, observing that he was "not bounde . . . to conforme my consciense to the Councell of one Realme against the generall Councell of Christendome." Faced with this argument from conscience, the new chancellor paused and turned to Chief Justice Fitzjames, who resolutely answered, "if th[e] act of parliament be not unlawfull, then is not the Indictment in my conscience insufficient." Whereupon the Chancellor gave judgment. Roper, *The Lyfe of Sir Thomas Moore,* 92–95.

56 "The Replication of a Serjeant at the Laws of England," in Guy, ed., *Christopher St. German on Chancery and Statute,* 100–101. See also D. E. C. Yale, "St. German's *Little Treatise Concerning Writs of Subpoena,*" *Irish Jurist,* 10: 324 (New Series) (1975). Guy argues that St. German wrote the "Replication," but another conclusion seems to follow from the manuscript's prose style, its content, and the inadequacy of St. German's response.

that more depelie than the Juges bee, for he muste forme his Jugementes according to the lawe of God, or to the lawe of reason, or to the law of the realme." So high-minded a response left St. German all the more vulnerable to the objections about men being "put from the lawe of the rea[l]me" and being "compellede to be orderede by the discretion and conscience of oon man." At this juncture, however, St. German could do no better than to insist that "an erroniouse conscience" was not the conscience that "the Chauncellor or any other is bounde to followe." Unable to satisfy those who feared that even a chancellor might err in his conscience, St. German only could persist in saying that the chancellor was "bound to followe" the "conscience which is groundede upon the lawe of God, and the lawe of reason, and upon the lawe of the realme" to the extent it was "not contrary to the saide lawes of God nor to ye lawe of reason." This was hardly reassuring, and St. German prudently left his argument in manuscript.[57]

The conflict between equitable and legal visions of judicial duty reached its depths during the chancellorship of the irascible Lord Ellesmere. Lacking More's saintly sense of superiority, Ellesmere at the beginning of the seventeenth century often simply taunted the common law judges for hypocritically claiming a duty to which they could not reasonably adhere. He resented the disdain of common lawyers toward "the Court of starre chamber, and all Courtes of equitye, which they termed Courtes of arbitrary Discrecion," and he replied that they were calling the kettle black: "The Judges of th[e] Kinges bench and Commen place have of late yeares taken upon theym as Chancellors to mak[e] orders in Equitye, according to theyr owne discrecions, not regarding nor standing upon, the stricte rules of Lawe, (wherunto they use to saye they are sworne)."[58] Ellesmere had a point, for common law judges did sometimes quietly moderate the law of the land, thus doing equity while speaking about law. Ellesmere, however, systematically "laboured to derogate from the common law and the judges," and although this seemed to confirm that he was "sowre, severe and implacable," it might also portend much worse.[59] Since the fifteenth century, there had been suggestions that equity was a sort of absolute

[57] "A Little Treatise Concerning Writs of Subpoena," 122–123. He apparently did not even circulate the manuscript, for it survives only in his own copy and later copies that were made from it long after his death. Ibid., 60.
[58] "Speciall Observacions Touching All the Sessions of the Last Parliament Anno 7 Regis & Etc." (1611), in *Law and Politics in Jacobean England,* 259; "Memorialles for Judicature. Pro Bono Publico" (1609), ibid., 280–281. See also his similar complaint in *Earl of Oxford's Case* (Ch. 1615), *Chancery Reports,* 1: 12.
[59] For the quotations, see J. H. Baker, "The Common Lawyers and the Chancery: 1616," in *Law, Liberty, and Parliament,* 259–260.

power, which the chancellor exercised above the law, and Ellesmere pressed the point, declaring that he had "an absolute and uncontrolable Power"—in contrast to common law judges, who "are to judge according to a strict and ordinary (or limited) Power."[60] Absolute power had always been a bold conception of the chancellor's role, and by the early seventeenth century, a chancellor could not espouse such a vision of equity without seeming to imply a royal power that might reach far beyond the ordinary exercise of equitable jurisdiction.

After Ellesmere's death in 1617, chancellors wisely abandoned their antagonism toward the law. They were already familiar with the notion that equity followed the law, but they now took this notion to heart and used it to harmonize the two jurisdictions. It was not merely that political winds were shifting. More fundamentally, it was becoming increasingly evident to lawyers that the law was the source and measure of all royal authority. Chancellors therefore had to worry that if equity conflicted with the law, it might not enjoy the authority and obligation of law. Certainly, inasmuch the Crown exercised its authority through its law, it was not in the interest of the Crown to have chancellors exercise equity in conflict with the law. Recognizing the threat to his authority, King James asked Ellesmere's successor, Francis Bacon, to keep the jurisdiction of Chancery within its "true and due limits." Accordingly, as soon as Bacon became chancellor, he met with the judges to assure them that "the former discords and differences between the Chancery and other courts" were at an end.[61] Going further in enunciating the principle on which peace would be established, Bacon's successor, Lord Keeper John Williams, declared at his appointment that "I will never make any Decree, That shall Cross the Grounds of the Common or Statute Laws."[62] To be sure, the grounds of the laws were not quite the laws themselves, but the message was clear enough, and after listening to the new lord keeper, Justice Richard Hutton of Common Pleas recorded with satisfaction in his diary that Willliams said "[h]e would not doe anything against fundamental points of the comon lawe."[63]

Chancellors, moreover, increasingly sought to reduce equity itself to a rule—indeed, a rule within the law of the land. In the mid-sixteenth century, learned men still disagreed as to whether the chancellor should adopt

[60] *Earl of Oxford's Case* (Ch. 1615), *Chancery Reports,* 1: 14–15.

[61] The Effect of that which was Spoken by the Lord Keeper (1617), in *The Letters and the Life of Francis Bacon,* 6: 184, ed. James Spedding (London: 1869); Account of Council Business (1617), ibid., 198, quoted by Baker, "The Common Lawyers and the Chancery," 278.

[62] John Hacket, *Scrinia Reserata,* 73 (Part 1) (London: 1693), quoted by Baker, "The Common Lawyers and the Chancery," 279.

[63] *The Diary of Richard Hutton 1614–1639,* at 40.

"certaine *Rules* and *Limits* of *Equity*"—some thinking it a "hard thing to prescribe to *Equity* any certaine bounds," and others saying that "if it bee not knowne before hand in what cases the Chancellour will reach forth his helpe, and where not," the subject would not know "how, or when he may possesse his owne in peace."[64] As Ellesmere had revealed, however, the vision of equity as something distinct from rules was apt to become an instrument of a broader lawlessness, and by the middle of the seventeenth century, judges and chancellors largely agreed that equity was not so much an Aristotelian pursuit of exceptions from rules as another set of rules within the law. Matthew Hale "look[ed] upon Equity as a part of the Common-Law, and one of the Grounds of it; and therefore as near as he could, he did always reduce it to certain Rules and Principles, that men might Study it as a Science, and not think that the Administration of it had any thing arbitrary in it."[65] This shift soon came to be embraced by chancellors and was of profound importance, for although a chancellor could not defer to all the rules of the law, this mattered less now that equity itself had become another set of rules within the law. Chancellors often formulated their rules as vague, abstract principles, but they generally acknowledged that they had to decide in accord with rules of equity and that their rules, being part of the law of the land, had to respect its rules.

[64] William Lambard, *Archion, or, A Commentary upon the High Courts of Justice in England,* 84 (London: 1634), discussed in *Lord Nottingham's Chancery Cases,* 1: xli, ed. D. E. C. Yale (London: Selden Society, 1957). More generally, see *St. German's Doctor and Student,* 105, eds., T. F. T. Plucknett and J. L. Barton (London: Selden Society, 1974); William S. Holdsworth, *A History of English Law,* 5: 336–338 (London: Sweet & Maxwell, 2003); J. H. Baker, *An Introduction to English Legal History,* 110 (London: Butterworths, 2002).

[65] Gilbert Burnett, *The Life and Death of Sir Matthew Hale,* 177 (London: 1681). Hale's point was taken up by the less charming but equally analytic Lord Chancellor Nottingham, who held that "[m]any things are against inward and natural conscience, which cannot be reformed by the regular and political administration of equity," because "if equity be tied to no rule, all other laws are dissolved, and everything becomes arbitrary." D. E. C. Yale, ed., *Lord Nottingham's 'Manual of Chancery Practice' and 'Prolegomena of Chancery and Equity',* 194 (Cambridge: Cambridge University Press, 1965). See also *Lord Nottingham's Chancery Cases,* 1: xlvi. Nottingham explained in 1676: "With such a conscience which is only *naturalis et interna* this Court hath nothing to do; the conscience by which I am to proceed is merely *civilis et politica,* and tied to certain measures." *Cook v. Fountain* (Ch. 1676), ibid., 1: 371. Indeed, as Charles Gray suggests, the notion that equity follows law was merely the generality with which chancellors assuaged fears across the full range of equitable jurisdiction, and in some areas, such as land law, the chancellors very specifically had to adhere to the law. Charles M. Gray, "The Boundaries of the Equitable Function," *American Journal of Legal History,* 20: 203, 217 (1976). See also David Lieberman, *The Province of Legislation Determined: Legal Theory in Eighteenth-Century Britain,* 85 (Cambridge: Cambridge University Press, 1989). In the eighteenth century, a theoretically inclined writer on equity (who was the uncle of "Junius") outlined some of the "inviolable Rules of Equity" by "collecting the Rules and Grounds, dispersed throughout the Body of the same Laws." Richard Francis, *Maxims of Equity,* "To the Reader" (London: 1727).

Change

Associated with the conflict between the academic and the common law visions of judging were different attitudes toward legal change. Whereas academically minded common lawyers tended to acknowledge the reality that judges at times had to modify the law, most common lawyers assumed that the duty to decide in accord with the law of the land required judges to discern rather than alter the law. In fact, as will be seen, there was plenty of room within judicial duty for various sorts of change, and many common law judges surely understood that in some respects their law had evolved. The duty of the judges, however, seemed to leave little space for deliberate change, and this limitation on judicial power was of profound significance for the freedom enjoyed under law.

The judges often took questions of policy into consideration, but at least ideally they did so not to alter the law but to understand it. For example, judges in the Middle Ages repeatedly said they would not alter their decisions to avoid a "mischief" in a particular case, and when judges in the sixteenth century took a broader view of "mischief"—as the problem against which a statute was directed—they apparently aimed to discern the statute's intent. Similarly, when judges examined "inconvenience" in their efforts to ascertain the common law, they were speaking not about what was inconvenient in any particular case, but rather about the inconvenience of alternative rules or of not adhering to the existing rule, and they repeatedly made clear that there was no greater inconvenience than to change the law. As summarized in *Slade's Case,* "we cannot change the law now, for that would be inconvenient."[66]

---

[66] *Slade's Case* (K.B. 1602), Coke, *Reports,* 4: 93b. On the limited meaning of inconvenience, see Charles Gray, "Bonham's Case Reviewed," in *Proceedings of the American Philosophical Society,* 116: 47 (Feb. 1972); Gerald J. Postema, "Classical Common Law Jurisprudence (Part I)," *Oxford University Commonwealth Law Journal,* 2: 178 (2002); Norman Doe, *Fundamental Authority in Late Medieval English Law,* 155–174 (Cambridge: Cambridge University Press, 1990); Ralph V. Turner, Review of Norman Doe, *Fundamental Authority in Late Medieval English Law, American Journal of Legal History,* 36: 381 (1992); Baker, *The Oxford History of English Law,* 6: 47.

A challenge to the conventional understanding of inconvenience can be observed in *Annesley v. Dixon*—an early eighteenth-century case concerning the proceedings of the commissioners for confiscated estates in Ireland. Chief Justice Holt was always very candid about the practical consequences of judicial decisions, but when Justice Powis (whose intellectual limitations were a source of ridicule) argued from the inconvenience of unraveling the commissioners' sales of land, Holt tartly responded by pointing to the inconvenience of departing from rules of law. He observed: "Brother Powis's Objection is, That it will be a great Mischief and Inconvenience to Ravell into these Sales. And therefore these Sales thô without Title must be good, because it is very Convenient it should be so." To this, Holt responded:

In explaining that neither kings nor judges had power over law, Coke noted the imperfection of human reason—especially as compared to the wisdom of the ancient law. It was a theme that allowed him to use biblical images, which rendered even his grim prose almost poetic:

> [W]e are but of yesterdaie (and therefore had need of the wisedome of those that were before us) and had beene ignorant (if we had not received light and knowledge from our forefathers) and our daies upon the earth are but as a shadow, in respect of the old auncient daies and times past, wherein the lawes have beene by the wisedom of the most excellent men, in many successions of ages, by long and continuall experience (the triall of right and truth) fined and refined, which no one man (beeing of so short a time) albeit hee had in his head the wisedom of all the men in the world, in any one Age could ever have effected or attayned unto. And therefore . . . no man ought to take upon him to be wiser than the lawes.[67]

"1st Suppose some Inconvenience. It is not fit for us to Supply the defect of the Law by Judgment. [I]t is beyond that Trust which is reposed in us, for that would be not to Execute a Judicial power, but would be an Incroachment upon the Legislature." He then added, as so often, an explanation of how the doctrine was no more inconvenient than in other instances: "2d There is no Inconvenience, for these purchasors must purchase at the same hazard that all persons do that purchase forfeited Estates. They must Enquire what Title the Forfeiting Person had; And if he mistakes the Title, it is at his peril that Purchaseth." The greater inconvenience, moreover, was the departure from law: "3: The Inconvenience would be greater and most pernicious to the whole Kingdom of Ireland if they should be dispossessed of their own Estates and be Subject to the final Determinac[i]on of the Commrs, thô those Estates were not forfeited," for "[t]his would be to Overthrow Magna Charta to Allow a Man to be turned out of his Freehold sine Judicio Parium suorum . . ."—that is, without the judgment of his peers. *Annesley v. Dixon* (K.B. 1707), in British Library, Holt's Opinions, Add. Ms. 35980, fols. 92[r]–92[v]. As might be expected, Powis dissented alone. For Powis, see Edward Foss, *Biographica Juridica,* 533 (London: 1870).

[67] *Calvin's Case* (Ex. Ch. 1608), Coke, *Reports,* 7: 3b–4a. Similarly, see Coke, *Reports,* 4: sig. Bii[v] (To the Reader) (London: 1604).

Arguments that human failings required governance by more than one were commonplace. Calvin wrote that "men's fault or failing causes it to be safer and more bearable for a number to exercise government, so that they may help one another, teach and admonish one another; and, if one asserts himself unfairly, there may be a number of censors and masters to restrain his willfulness." Calvin, *Institutes of the Christian Religion,* 1493–1494 (IV.xx.8), trans. John T. McNeill and Ford Lewis Battles (Philadelphia: Westminster, 1960). Putting this sort of point in colloquial terms, Thomas Starkey noted that "it is commonly said: 'Many eyes see better than one.'" Thomas Starkey, *A Dialogue Between Reginald Pole & Thomas Lupset,* 101, ed. Kathleen M. Burton (London: Chatto and Windus, 1948).

The claim for the common law, however, went further, for it placed the law on the experience of men across the ages. The argument could be understood to hark back to Aristotle, at least as understood by men such as Marsilius. The latter not only cited Aristotle but also explained: "that, whiche one man alone fyndeth out or may knowe by hym selfe alone" is "very lytell or els no thynge," and "that, which the men of one age or tyme can observe or marke is but an unperfyghte thynge, in comparyson of that thynge, whiche is observed or marked of men of many dyvers ages or tymes." Marsilius of Padua, *The Defence of Peace,* fol. 25[r] (I.xi). In fact, Marsilius may have read the passage in Cicero's *Republic* that attributed re-

Thomas Hedley echoed Coke to criticize the decision of the judges in *Bates Case,* saying that "the Comon lawe [was] tryed by tyme, which is wiser than all the Judges in the land." In other words, rather than depend on the human mind and its limitations, the law was to be tried "[b]y tyme out of mynde."[68] The common law thus seemed a lesson in modesty, for it had an authority that rose above the reason accessible to any king, judges, or other men at any one time.

Coke elaborated this point by distinguishing the reason of English law from natural reason, let alone private reason. Cicero had said, *lex est ratio summa, insita in natura*—"law is the highest reason, implanted in nature"—but Coke described the common law as "an artificial perfection of reason, gotten by long study, observation, and experience, and not by every mans naturall reason." Emphasizing his departure from Cicero, he explained that it was not the natural reason discerned by a single man, but rather the artificial, "legall reason" that was "summa ratio," and this brought him back to his argument about the imperfection of human reason: "And therefore if all the reason that is dispersed into so many severall heads were united into one, yet could he not make such a law as the Law of England is, because by many succession of ages it hath beene fined and refined by an infinite number of grave and learned men, and by long experience growne to such a perfection, for the government of this Realme." Accordingly, "No man (out of his private reason) ought to be wiser than the Law, which is the perfection of reason."[69] From this perspective, the law it-

---

markably similar ideas to Cato, but it is not yet clear whether the relevant portion of Cicero's text remained familiar until the Vatican manuscript was rediscovered in the early nineteenth century. Cicero, *Republic* (II.i).

68 Speech of Thomas Hedley (June 23–28, 1610), *Parliamentary Debates in 1610,* at 73, ed. Samuel Rawson Gardiner (Westminster: Camden Society, 1862). When Thomas Hedley in 1610 asked "What is the comon law of England?" he simply answered: "It is not what the Judge will, nor more then [one would] say that is the truth which the Jury will." Ibid., 81: 72.

69 Cicero, *De Legibus* (I.vi.18); Coke, *Institutes,* 1: fol. 97b. Doddridge celebrated the natural foundations of common law, but even he cautioned that although the law "is called reason . . . it is artificiall reason." John Doddridge, *The English Lawyer,* 242 (1631).

For an earlier attempt to dampen expectations raised by reading Cicero, see Christopher Hatton, *A Treatise Concerning Statutes, or Acts of Parliament: And the Exposition Thereof,* 26 (London: 1677). The Ciceronian context, even if not how Coke distinguished common law, is discussed by Allen D. Boyer, "Sir Edward Coke, Ciceronianus: Classical Rhetoric and the Common Law Tradition," in Boyer, *Law, Liberty, and Parliament,* 224, 249. A seventeenth-century commentator explained: "*Cicero* defineth the Law to be a certain reason flowing from the Divine mind, which doth persuade what is right, and prohibit the contrary. . . . But whilst the Law is defined by the Divine mind, it seemeth (as one saith) . . . to be defined by that which is more remote and general, than subject to common capacities." The author would only concede that "these definitions" are "in some sort true, being rather re-self could be considered the judge, and judges merely took "cognizance" of the "the artificiall reason and judgment of Law."[70]

This rejection of self-conscious change in law found a more sociological expression in the writing of another great seventeenth-century judge, Matthew Hale. Chief Justice Hale recognized in his manuscripts how "in Process of Time" the earliest law had been "changed, altered or antiquated," but rather than say that judges could deliberately alter the law, he suggested that laws developed "insensibly" in course of being "accommodated to the Conditions, Exigencies and Conveniencies of the People." He thus depicted change as more of a sociological process than a decision within the self-conscious discretion of a judge.[71]

Lord Nottingham, being a chancellor, more openly acknowledged the judicial alteration of the law in disputed matters, but he feared that any greater judicial power to change it was dangerous. Judicial "change in the law is not to be objected [to] in points controverted, wherein the opinion of one age may differ from another," but it was another matter "in points where the law was never doubted but universally received, and yet hath been changed by the succeeding judges." In such instances, even "though the change hath been for the better, without which the presumption would never be endured, yet the example of it is so much the worse, because it is

---

ferred to the eternal Law, than to the positive and humane Laws." *Enchiridion Legum,* 3 (1673).

[70] *Prohibition del Roy* (1608), Coke, *Reports,* 12: 65.

[71] Hale, *The History of the Common Law of England,* 39, 42. He also suggested that "the mutations" have "not been so much in the Law, as in the Subject Matter of it." Henry Rolle, *Un Abridgment des Plusieurs Cases et Resolutions del Common Ley,* sig. [a2v] (Hale's Preface) (London: 1668).

That the duty of judges barred them from relying upon their reason to alter the law was made painfully clear to Justice Robert Berkeley of King's Bench when he was impeached in 1641 for his opinion in the *Shipmoney Case.* William Pierrepont complained in the House of Commons that this judge had abandoned his duty for the pursuit of his own ideas of reason: "This judge will have the law to be what to him seems reason," but "the reason limited to him to judge of, is what the common law saith is so" or "what a statute hath so enacted." Thus, "[f]or him to judge this or that is law, else a mischief shall follow" or to say that "because the law in such a thing is imperfect, therefore he will make a law to supply it" was to substitute his reason for the law, and it "then must follow" that "as often as a judge's reason changes, or judges change, our laws change also." This mattered because "[o]ur liberties are in our laws, which a subject may read, or hear read"—as in, "this is his" or "this he may do and be safe"—and thus only when the judge decided in accord with the laws could the subject be free. Of course, Pierrepont recognized that the law had to be adapted, for "[u]nlimited power must be in some to make and repeal laws, to fit the dispositions of times and persons." Yet "[n]ature placeth this in common consent," and as the English could not all "conveniently meet" to make new laws, they exercised "their consents . . . in parliament." The power to alter the law thus lay in Parliament, not the judges. Speech of William Pierrepoint, *State Trials,* 3: 1293–1294.

the ready way to introduce, though insensibly, an arbitrary power in the judges to change the law without Parliament, and to make it depend on their resolutions." The ultimate consequence of this arbitrary power was even more worrisome—namely, "that whensoever there shall be a King disposed to extend his power beyond the limits of his laws, he that hath the making of the judges, will have the making of the law too."[72]

All of this repudiation of judicial power may seem to have been incompatible with the reality of legal change in England, but the tension was not as great as may be supposed, as there were opportunities for legal development that did not threaten the ideals of law or judicial duty. If judges were to adhere to their duty, judicial change had to be a matter of discerning the law, and the common law was therefore open to development as long it occurred in this indirect way. For example, litigants repeatedly pressed new facts into old forms, and if they thereby eventually stretched an old writ into a new type of claim, the judges might have little choice but to acknowledge a new form of action. Although the causes of action that developed in this way would come to be regarded in the nineteenth century as legal fictions, they were a valuable product of the sort of unplanned legal development that could be safely attributed to the ingenuity of lawyers rather than the power of judges.[73] Similarly, change could occur when lawyers sought minor exceptions from rules, for some such exceptions might eventually coalesce into a generalization, which the judges might feel bound to accept. It was their duty to decide in accord with the law, and if the change had already occurred, they might be obliged to recognize it. Of course, more candid innovations had once taken place in equity, but less so after it was brought within the law of the land. The most open and substantial change took place through legislation, and it is no coincidence that

[72] *Lord Nottingham's 'Manual of Chancery Practice,'* 353. Even considerations of humanity, according to Nottingham, would not justify the judges in altering law and thus displacing the power of Parliament. He recalled a resolution of medieval judges sparing a man outlawed for felony "from the peril" of being "killed by any man that met him," and although he agreed with Coke's sense of "the humanity of the resolution," he added: "But who can excuse the presumption of it, to mend the Common Law without Parliament?" Nottingham preferred the approach taken by later judges who had faced a similar question. Being "much more wise and more modest," they "suffered the inhumanity of the law to continue until there was an express Act of Parliament to alter it." Ibid., 354. Nottingham also observed that there is "[n]o relief in equity against Act of Parliament" and that "no case can be found where any relief hath been given against Act of Parliament, be the circumstances never so pitiable." Ibid., 330, 351.

[73] The somewhat fortuitous character of the doctrinal obstacles to legal change was itself a significant barrier to exertions of power. See Philip Hamburger, "The Development of the Nineteenth-Century Consensus Theory of Contract," *Law and History Review,* 7: 244 (1989).

when the common law was reformed in the nineteenth century, this had to be done by statute, for straightforward change within the common law would have violated the ideals of law and judicial duty. The law evolved in many ways, but when change occurred within the common law, it usually had to come at oblique angles that did not threaten the aspirations about the obligation of the law and the duty of the judges.

More generally, although it may be thought in retrospect that the ideal of judicial duty was more rigid than an evolving society could bear, it was in fact well suited to a system of law that allocated authority in a manner permissive of social change. Whereas the civil law recited high moral ambitions that soared far above lived realities, the common law typically aimed for limited ends, such as keeping the peace; and whereas the civil law offered justice through elaborate substantive rules, the common law often did little more than allocate authority among men, thus leaving them to enjoy the sort of justice they could make for themselves. The English judges were therefore bound to decide in accord with a law that left many questions of justice undetermined by law, and this combination of a relatively limited domain for law and a very constrained vision of judging allowed the English to enjoy both social flexibility and political freedom. If the common law had had a more ambitious reach, and if it had acknowledged a judicial power to make calculated changes, the judges and the kings who appointed them would probably have exploited this power in ways incompatible with freedom. The circumscribed province of the common law, however, allowed it to remain relatively stable even as it left space for flexibility in social arrangements, and in these circumstances, the ideal of judicial duty could simultaneously limit judicial power and leave freedom for vigorous social development.

The ideal of judicial duty thus permitted some judicial change, but only of the sort that could occur while judges decided in accord with the law of the land. It was a limitation on judicial change that could have significant costs. It at least, however, had the advantage of preserving the freedom enjoyed under law from any blunt exercise of judicial power—let alone the royal power that was apt to lurk not far behind.

Discretion

The common law vision of judicial duty limited not only judicial change but also more generally judicial discretion. Although judges perhaps inevitably exercised discretion in the sense of wisdom or judgment when discerning the law of the land or its application, it was typically expected that they should not exercise their own discretion—in the sense of their will, power, or choice.[74] This may seem today, as it often seemed to academically inclined English lawyers in the past, an illusory distinction, which obscures the reality of human will or power. To most common lawyers, however, the boundary between the discretion that was discernment and the discretion that went further was the boundary between judgment and lawmaking will.

The sincerity with which judges ideally were to avoid deciding in accord with their willful discretion was recognized by Martin Bucer. A German Reformer dislocated by the defeat of German Protestants, Bucer in 1549 accepted a position at Cambridge, only to find himself so ill he sometimes could scarcely write. He had all of the insight and misunderstanding of a foreign visitor, and before his death in 1551, he collected enough information about England to address Edward VI in *De Regno Christo*—an idealized vision of an England in which Edward would achieve the "restitution of the Kingdom of Christ." The judges in this kingdom would have a duty to decide in accord with the law, and this would require that "they judge sincerely according to the laws, that is, according to the meaning germane to the laws, and not permit themselves to relax any part of the laws in any case." Bucer hoped the laws would leave "as little as possible . . . to the judges to decide or modify," for "what profit is it to make excellent laws if it is conceded to the judges that they may depart from them according to their good pleasure in making judgments, or even that they interpret laws fraudulently?"

Notwithstanding his understanding of English judicial duty, Bucer went further than his hosts when he imagined that good-faith performance of this duty could ordinarily be enforced with legal penalties. Noting that judges "take an oath that they will judge according to the laws," he thought that "this must be demanded of them with utmost severity, and those who have manifestly not acted in very good faith should be most severely punished."[75] Some medieval judges—most notoriously Chief Justices Thorp

[74] For more on this point, see Baker, *An Introduction to English Legal History,* 143–144, 151.

[75] Heinrich Bucer, *De Regno Christi,* in *Melanchthon and Bucer,* 358, 376, ed. Wilhelm Pauck (Philadelphia: Westminster, 1981), but printed here with minor modification based on Martini Buceri, *Scripta Anglicana,* 160 (Basel: 1577). Like so many who wrote about judges, Bucer self-consciously drew upon Aristotle.

Both the Crown and those who were suspicious of it had occasion to worry that they depended on judges to exercise their office with sincerity or good faith. In *Calvin's Case,* Ellesmere said of the king: "Hee ruleth by his Lawe, and commaundeth his Judges to minister to all his Subjects Law and Justice sincerely and truely." *Speech in the Exchequer Chamber,* 214. Later in the century, Sidney wrote that the power of the judges was "to be executed *bone fide.*" Algernon Sidney, *Discourses Concerning Government,* 371 (iii.26) (London: 1698).

and Tresilian—had been condemned for their departures from duty, but these were dubious precedents.[76] Perhaps in an England restored to the Kingdom of Christ, judges would sincerely do their duty for fear of worldly punishment, but in England as it actually existed, a lack of good faith in judging was not normally punishable by law—it being more conventional for judges to worry about damnation or dismissal. In Coke's words, the judges were "to make an account to God and the King."[77]

Although a judge could suggest—in the manner of a modern legal realist—that the law was what he said it was, he took this position at the risk of public opprobrium. In 1571, the House of Commons considered whether to repeal a statute of Henry VIII that gave "discretion" to the archbishop of Canterbury to grant licenses, dispensations, faculties, and rescripts, and when arguing in favor of the repeal William Fleetwood spoke "pleasantly" but "learnedly" about "this word *discretion.*" Known for his "marvellous, merry, and pleasant conceit," Fleetwood was a scholarly lawyer who would soon serve with distinction as recorder of London. He understood that judges had to exercise discretion in the sense of wisdom, but he worried about the sort of discretion that amounted to a freedom or power over law. He explained that he had often read the word "discretion" and that "hee had beene troubled with it"—as when he read that "'the Queene is sworne to [ad]minister justice with mercy and discretion.' What mercy is . . . hee knewe, but what discretion was hee would gladly learne." After playing on the different meanings, Fleetwood concluded by "discipher[ing]" the conduct of a judge who openly said to him, "'Mr. Fleetwood, you are a lawyer but I am a judge.'" Against this suggestion that a judge had more discretion, in the sense of power, than a lawyer, Fleetwood caustically remarked that this man "might have witt, but hee nether had lawe, wisdome or discretion, other than in his owne judgment." He did not name the judge, but "whom hee ment many did guesse."[78]

[76] Hale observes that Chief Justice Thorp was attainted for bribery in 1350 and "sentenced to death, before special commissioners assigned *ad judicandum secundum voluntatem regis,* in respect of the oath he had made to the king and broken." He was not executed, however, and although Parliament affirmed the judgment against him, it did so with a "caution for the future to prevent such an arbitrary course of proceedings" and a proviso that "this should not be drawn into precedent." Matthew Hale, *Historia Placitorum Coronæ,* 1: 263 (London: 1736). For Tresilian, see ibid., 1: 266. As might be expected, when Cardinal Wolsey was accused, Crown lawyers justified criminal prosecutions of judges. Letter from Stephen Gardiner to Protector Somerset (Oct. 14, 1547), in *The Letters of Stephen Gardiner,* 390, ed. James Arthur Miller (Cambridge: Cambridge University Press, 1933).

[77] *Floyd v. Barker* (Star Chamber 1607), Coke, *Reports,* 12: 25.

[78] Fleetwood's Speech (April 14, 1571), Anonymous Journal, in *Proceedings in the Parliaments of Elizabeth I,* 1: 223. Fleetwood observed that "for rescriptes or faculties what they

Coke similarly distinguished between "each mans discretion, which commonly rather deserveth the name of affection and selfe-will" and the discretion "that ariseth upon the right discerning, and due consideration of the true and necessary circumstances of the matter." Coke in this way acknowledged the value of discretion but carefully understood it as a discernment of the nature of circumstances. More generally, he thought it was "very necessary, that the Law and discretion should bee Concomitant"— "the one to be an accident inseparable to the other"—so that there would be "neither Law without discretion, least it should incline to rigour, nor discretion without Law, least confusion should follow." Concerned that this statement might be misunderstood, Coke emphasized that "my meaning hereby, is not to allow of every mans discretion that sitteth on the seate of Justice (for that would bring forth confusion)." And "in associating discretion so neare to Law, it is not meant to preferre it to that [of] society." Instead, Coke's goal was to explain the sort of discretion that was concomitant with law, and this was the discretion that "grave and reverend men" had "used in such cases before" or that arose from "the circumstances of the matter."[79]

Coke recognized that English law sometimes appeared to leave judges to do as they pleased, but he explained that they had to bring their discretion within the law—even if only the law discernible from reason. He made this point as to the Commission of Sewers, which was appointed to repair the banks of the Thames. Their commission gave them "authority . . . to doe according to their discretions." Nonetheless, "their proceedings ought to be limited and bound with the rule of reason and Law. For discretion is a science or understanding to discern between falsity and truth, between right and wrong, between shadows and substance, between equity and colourable glosses and pretences, and not to doe according to their wills and private affections."[80] "Law and reason" was an old common law ap-

bee in all the world hee knewe not." Ibid. For his learning and merry character, see Anthony à Wood, *Athenæ Oxonienses,* 1: 598 (London: 1813). Obviously, Fleetwood was not the first to reprimand a judge in this manner. When Judge Hillary suggested that the law "is the will of the justices," Chief Justice Stonore promptly corrected him: "No, the law is that which is right." Y.B. Hillary 19 Edward III, 375, pl. 3 (1345) ("ley est resoun"). See note 68 above.

79 Edward Coke, *A Little Treatise of Baile and Maineprize,* 30–31 (London: 1635). Similarly, see Doddridge, *The English Lawyer,* 211. The notion that discretion was a discernment of circumstances was by no means exclusive to the common law. See, for example, Joachim Mynsinger, *Singvlarivm observationvm Imper. camerae centuriae VI,* 366 (VI.97) (Lugduni: 1608). It acquired new significance, however, within the common law and the duty of its judges to decide in accord with the law of the land.

80 *Rooke's Case* (C.P. 1598), Coke, *Reports,* 5: 100a. Cromartie suggests that Robert Callis in his 1622 Reading at Gray's Inn took the opposite view. Cromartie, "The Constitutionalist

proach for understanding what otherwise might be obscure in common law and for testing the acts of subordinate bodies, and Coke recited it to suggest that even when commissioners found themselves upon a broad river of discretion, with little more to rely on than their discernment of right and wrong, they were not to enter dangerous currents of discretionary will, but instead were to steer a course that followed the law of the land. Returning to this theme, Coke later emphasized, "Discretion ought to be thus described[:] *Discretio est discernere per legem quid fit justum*"—discretion is to discern by law what does justice.[81] He understood that even within its domain, English law was incompletely elaborated, and that it therefore at times had to be ascertained from other considerations, but he also recognized that the law of the land was the measure of legal justice and judicial duty, and on this account he viewed the discernment of circumstances and the pursuit of reason as but the means of discerning the law of the land.

Lawyers of a learned inclination recognized that when common lawyers rejected willful discretion, they were often repudiating what they feared in academic ideals of judging. For example, on behalf of the ecclesiastical courts, Thomas Ridley defensively observed that their decisions were not discretionary but *secundum ius*—that ecclesiastical judges had "authoritie . . . not to judge according as him best liketh, but according as the right of the cause doth require."[82] Other men more aggressively threw the accusa-

---

Revolution," 91. There is a risk, however, of overstating their differences. Whereas Coke strained to assimilate all discretion to a legal discretion, Callis acknowledged the legal discretion that was done according to law and then openly propounded another discretion, which "is the absolute Judge of the Cause, and gives the rule." Yet even in thus departing from Coke's analysis in *Rooke's Case,* Callis relied upon Coke to suggest how such discretion was to be exercised in a law-like manner, and he even added that "I had rather trust to the worst certain Law, then to give too much way to the uncertain discretion of the Commissioners." *The Reading of That Famous and Learned Gentleman, Robert Callis Esq; Sergeant at Law, Upon the Statute of 23 H. 8. Cap. 5. of Sewers: As it was Delivered by Him at Grays-Inn, in August, 1622,* at 86 (London: 1647). Baker observes that Coke's attitude toward discretion persisted into the eighteenth century. Baker, *An Introduction to English Legal History,* 151.

81 Coke, *Institutes,* 4: 41, Even John Cooke, who hoped to rely on "right reason," wrote that "the Law must be the rule of all justice, and that Law which is most certaine and leaves least to the Judges arbitrary discretion is ever the best." Cooke, *The Vindication of the Professors and Profession of the Law,* 49. Sidney was more forthcoming about the failings of human law, but he did not give up on English ideals about law and judges. For example, he wrote: "I Confess that no Law can be so perfect, *to provide exactly for every case that may fall out, so as to leave nothing to the discretion of the Judges,* who in some measure are to interpret them: But *that Laws or Customs are ever few, or that the paucity is the reason that they cannot give special rules, or that Judges do resort to those principles or Common Law Axioms, whereupon former judgments in cases something alike have bin given by former Judges, who all receive their Authority from the King in his right to give Sentence,* I utterly deny." Sidney, *Discourses Concerning Government,* 369 (iii.26).

82 Thomas Ridley, *A View of the Civile and Ecclesiastical Law,* 209 (London: 1607). Follow-

tion of discretion back at the common lawyers.[83] Chancellor Ellesmere, for example, derided common lawyers for failing to acknowledge that because all law inevitably was incomplete, it required judicial discretion:

> No lawe ever was, or ever can be made that can provide remedie for all future cases; or comprehend all circumstances of humane actions which Judges are to determine: Therefore, when such happen, and complaint is made; what shall Judges doe? Shall they give no remedie to the partie grieved? Shall they stay for a Parliament?

Assuming that the judges had to "follow *Dictamen rationis*"—the dictate of reason—and so "give speedie justice," Ellesmere claimed that they therefore "in many matters of materiall circumstances" had to "guide themselves by discretion." Common lawyers would "[*o*]*bject*"—saying "[t]hat if this be thus, then the common Lawe of England is uncerten" and "the rule of Justice, by which the people are governed, is too pliable, and too weake." Yet this was precisely Ellesmere's point: *"That the common Lawe is uncerten"*—

---

ing Ulpian, he defined "what Right or Law is in generall" as "the knowledge of Civile, and humane things, the understanding of those things which are just and unjust." Ibid., 1. That Ridley was simply picking up a familiar trope is evident from Bullinger's complaint about the men who, he said, defended judicial departures from written laws. They "would have every man that is a magistrate to give judgement as he himself thinketh best." In their defense, they would say, "But wee will . . . have them give judgement according to the equitie of natures lawe, and not after the lust of their corrupt affection"—to which Bullinger responded: "Mine aunswere is to that, that they will give judgement as affection leadeth them without controlement, and say that they judged by natural equitie." Henrie Bullinger, *Fifty Godlie and Learned Sermons, Divided into Five Decades,* 189 (2nd decade, 7th sermon) (London: 1587).

83 When Thomas Starkey in the 1530s wrote his *Dialogue Between Reginald Pole and Thomas Lupset,* he had Pole argue: "There is no stable ground in our common law to lean unto. . . . The judges are not bounden, as I understand, to follow them a rule, but after their own liberty they have authority to judge according as they are instructed by the sergeants, and as the circumstances of the cause doth them move," which allowed Pole to urge that "we . . . have the civil law of the Romans to be the common law here of England." Starkey, *A Dialogue Between Reginald Pole and Thomas Lupset,* 173–174, 175. Knafla notes that "[t]he uncertainty of the common law was a subject which the K[ing] was delighted to expose." Ibid., 274, note 2. Similarly, it was said that men inspired by civil law objected to English law on the ground that "the Judges opinion (which may be extended according to humane affection) doth make or alter the Law" and that "the Judges private opinions do usually alter the Laws, and so leave it alwayes in uncertainty"—a position that provoked a long response in *Enchiridion Legum,* 57, 71 (1673). Coke responded to this sort of opinion when he wrote about the uncertainty of the civil law and the certainty of the common law. Coke, *Institutes,* 2: (Preface) (London: 1642).

As for the realities of the learned law, Richard Helmholz carefully traces instances in which "the judges actively exercised the discretion the *ius commune* vested in them," including in cases of inquisition and torture. Richard Helmholz, *The ius commune in England: Four Studies,* 106, 116–17, 121 (Oxford: Oxford University Press, 2001); see also ibid., 99–101, 125, 131.

as, in fact, "all the Lawes of all nations are uncerten"—and therefore judges had to exercise discretion in accord with reason.[84]

Although Ellesmere displayed a sort of realism in saying that all nations' laws were uncertain, it was increasingly unrealistic for chancellors to assault common law ideals. The difficulty, it should be recalled, was not merely political but also legal, for the common law was the law of the land, and when the Chancery positioned itself as a prerogative court dispensing justice above the law of the land, equity could seem to lack the obligation of such law. It was therefore no accident that subsequent chancellors had neither the power nor the desire to echo Ellesmere's tirades on behalf of discretionary reasoning.

Rather than scorn the ideal of deciding in accord with the law of the land, succeeding chancellors and lord keepers repeatedly cautioned new common law judges against following their own will, and although this was an old theme, there was now perhaps special reason to emphasize it. When Sir William Jones in 1621 took his oath in Common Pleas, Lord Keeper John Williams warned him to avoid "quiddities of witt to pervert law, which some tymes may be tollerable in an advocate, but in a judge it is letle better than corruptions. For judges are in their places faithfully and sincerely *interpretare non facere legem*."[85] Similarly, in 1630, Lord Keeper Thomas Coventry addressed Sir Humphrey Davenport in Common Pleas:

> That you stand uppon the old lawes of the kingdome, which are the birth rights of the subjects, and that you beware of yealdinge to any new inventions, for this age is full of witt and much given to novelties and new inventions, and every man can now devise out of wytt somewhat that he may seme to have some shewe of good, but beware of such, and give not any eare or consent to these.[86]

The judges of equity in this manner emphatically told the common law judges that "you stand upon the ancient fundamentall lawes of the kingdome, and not upon conceite of wytt."[87]

[84] *Speech in the Exchequer Chamber*, 225–226. He applied this to *Calvin's Case* by arguing that "his case is rare and new" and so "[t]here is no direct Law for him in precise and expresse tearmes." Ibid., 227. Later, Ellesmere slightly softened his position, arguing that "the Judges of the Common law themselves doe almost every day, extend theire discretion to stay and mitigate the right and strictnes of the common law; And in soe doinge they doe well notwithstandinge the strict wordes of theire Oathes." "A Breviate or Direccion for the Kinges Learned Councell Collected by the Lord Chancellor Ellesmere" (1615), ibid., 321.

[85] *The Diary of Richard Hutton 1614–1639*, at 41. In his speech to Richardson, Coventry urged that "your judgment may be upright, sincere and sound." Ibid., 67 (Michaelmas Term 1626).

[86] Ibid., 80.

[87] Coventry's speech to Sir George Vernon on his transfer from the Exchequer to Common

Coke remained the preeminent critic of judicial discretion, and although his prose was usually crabbed, on this subject he waxed poetic. He explained that "all causes" were "to be measured by the golden and straight metwand of the law, and not . . . the incertain and crooked cord of discretion." Indeed, "the Laws are the Judges guides, or leaders," and with this metaphor, Coke imagined the law itself holding office—"an office of guiding of travellors through dangerous and unknown wayes." Thus, "it appeareth, that the Laws of the Realm hath this office to guide the Judges in all causes that come before them in the wayes of right Justice, who never yet misguided any man, that certainly knew them, and truly followed them."[88]

Although Edward Coke is often depicted in caricature, few common law judges were more careful in noting the difficulty of discerning law at its edges. Looking back on the evidence recited here, the reader will recall that where the law provided little guidance, Ellesmere expected the judges to exercise discretion in accord with reason—a relatively abstract, learned sort of reason—but that Coke insisted upon the common law's artificial reason and urged the judges to exercise discretion in accord with precedent and a discernment of circumstances. He acknowledged that the judges sometimes had to ascertain the law through a more direct inquiry about reason, but he insisted that even this use of reason was a means of discerning the law rather than an independent basis of judgment. Coke clearly understood that the fixities of human law eventually came to an end, but whereas Ellesmere thought judges should exercise discretion beyond this point, Coke assumed that what could not be discerned was not within either the law or judicial duty. The Chief Justice thus recognized the realities that were more openly acknowledged by the Chancellor, but in a very different

Pleas (1631), ibid., 85. Similarly, see Coventry's speech to Sir John Finch on his becoming Chief Justice of Common Pleas (1634), ibid., 101. For "inventions of wytt," see Coventry's speech on appointment of Sir Thomas Heath as Lord Chief Justice of Common Pleas (1631), ibid., 89. In 1632, Coventry told Francis Crawley on his appointment to Common Pleas: "And consider that you doe judge accordinge to the lawes of the realme, they are not your lawes, but Gods lawes and the Kings lawes, and you must not stryve by any streine of wytt to invent tricks or new wayes, but to judge according to the presidents and cases before tymes reported and judged." Ibid., 93.

88 Coke, *Institutes,* 4: 41; ibid., 2: 526. Even Chancellor Ellesmere—at least in 1604—rejected judicial discretion or will, although not so much because of judicial duty as because of "[t]hat absolute prerogative which according to the Kings pleasure is reavealled by his lawes." In writing on the subject, he concluded: "[I]n appearaunce it is easy to him whoe knoweth noe lawe nor Justice to rule as he listeth, his will never wanting a power to itselfe. But it is safe and blamelesse both for the Judge and people, That Judges be appointed whoe know the lawe; and that they be lymited to governe according to the law, is a thing of necessitie and of extraordinary Care." "Discourse Concerning the Royall Prerogative" (c. 1604), in *Law and Politics in Jacobean England,* 197, 201.

manner. Far more than is usually supposed, the narrow path of the common law ran alongside the broad avenue of academic learning. Yet men of a common law mind and those of a more academic bent were headed in opposite directions; even as they covered much of the same ground, they remained at cross purposes.

It may be imagined that Coke stood alone in such controversies, but the common law posture was ancient, and it continued to unite the common law judges. Just how much the judges agreed on the basic common law ideals is apparent from their response to Bancroft that their "doing but what they ought, and by their oaths are bound to doe . . . is not to be called in question."[89] Even a judge such as Sir John Doddridge—who had none of Coke's insular sensibilities, and who openly explored civilian learning—believed that "everie Law doth stand upon permanent Rules, as of Iron not to be bent or broken upon this or that occasion, or to be infringed upon this or that occurrence," for "else there need no Court of Law, but all should be one with the Court of Conscience, and have their proceedings framed according to the Arbitrary conceipt of the Judge." As hinted by his allusion to a court of conscience, Doddridge acknowledged an exception for equity, but this was to be "used in such cases only as are of extremity."[90] Thus, almost as much as Coke, Doddridge saw a choice between iron rules and arbitrary conceit.

If the common law notion of judicial duty sometimes differed from the realities, this was because it was an ideal. Coke himself often failed to live up to his duty—as two colleagues had the satisfaction of telling him when they "very roundly let the Lord Coke knowe their minde, that he was not such a maister of the lawe as hee did take on him, to deliver what he list for lawe, and to dispise all other."[91] Coke and other common lawyers, how-

[89] Coke, *Institutes,* 2: 618.

[90] Doddridge, *The English Lawyer,* 211–212, 214. In his *Treatise Concerning a Judge,* perhaps never completed, Judge Doddridge planned to explain that a judge should "*be Religious, according to the Counsell of* Jethro *unto* Moses, *Provide men fearing God*"; second, that "*they ought to bee men of Courage*"; third, that "[t]hey ought to be men of Integrity" (including that "*they be free from passions and perturbations of the minde, as anger, favour, desire of revenge, &c.*"); fourth, that "[*j*]*udges ought to be wise, men able to discern circumstances, and to foreknow the mischiefes and inconveniences that may ensue of inconsiderate Judgements*"—for all of which he provided biblical citations. Ibid., sig. [A4r] (London: 1631). Sir Edward Bulstrode simply stated that "*the best Law . . . gives least liberty to the arbitrage of the Judge . . . and he is the best Judge, that takes the least liberty.*" Bulstrode, *Reports,* sig. A[2r] (Dedication) (1688).

[91] Letter from Archbishop Abbot of Canterbury to Chancellor Ellesmere (Jan. 22, 1611), in *The Egerton Papers,* 448, ed. James Arthur Miller (London: Camden Society, 1840). Ellesmere wrote that Coke, "forgetting his owne prescript, he hath strawed more novelties then old Corne in theis feilds of his." "Observations on Ye Lord Cookes Reportes" (1615), in *Law and Politics in Jacobean England,* 316.

ever, understood that they drew their ideals in sharper lines than could always be attained in life, and the disparity only gave these lawyers greater cause to delineate their ideals with force. It was an attitude that has led many historians to complain that common lawyers were unsophisticated. More accurately, they were sophisticated in a different manner from men who looked upon judges and law in an academic light.

The Eighteenth Century

By the eighteenth century, the political threat to the common law had largely receded, and as the academic perspective came to seem less dangerous, it could openly flourish within the common law. The long-standing tension between common law and learned ideals had for centuries deprived common lawyers of opportunities to engage in candidly academic analysis, and a reconciliation was therefore of great satisfaction to many Englishmen. Common lawyers, however, tended to welcome the learned reasoning only while it was employed in a manner compatible with their ideals of law and judicial duty, and therefore at the same time that they now unabashedly integrated academic analysis within the common law, they also still tended to repudiate the use of such analysis in ways that challenged the law of the land or the duty of judges to decide in accord with it.

What opened the way for the acceptance of academic ideals within the common law was the collapse of the political threat to the common law ideals. It will be recalled that English lawyers had traditionally hesitated to acknowledge natural law and had rejected the authority of the learned law, lest these other layers of law subvert the obligation of the common law. Nonetheless, since early times, common lawyers had at least furtively drawn their understanding of many legal issues from the insights of learned civilians and canonists. Sophisticated common lawyers had assumed that both the common law and the learned law often echoed the principles of natural law, and they had therefore quietly been able to discern what was understated in their own law by examining the academic reasoning, which seemed more fully to elaborate the implications of natural law. Now, however, they could pursue such reasoning without subterfuge. By the end of the seventeenth century, particularly after the Revolution of 1688, the political challenge to the authority of the law of the land and the duty of judges had been thoroughly put to rest, and common lawyers could therefore finally integrate the academic analysis within the common law without fear for their institutions or their freedom. This candid pursuit of academic reasoning about the law of the land was what would increasingly be understood as common law "jurisprudence," and whereas it once made sense to distinguish common law ideals from academic ideals, it was now possible more moderately to distinguish different perspectives about academic learning within the common law.[92]

No longer fearful that academic law would threaten their law and the liberty enjoyed under it, common lawyers brought their desires for systematization to the surface of their legal discussions. Ambitious to expound English law scientifically in terms of natural law, common lawyers began to write urbane treaties and even judicial opinions that situated the common law within the breadth of the civilian-derived jurisprudence. In this spirit, Sir William Blackstone wrote his *Commentaries on the Laws of England* and Lord Mansfield brought academic learning to bear on commercial law. Moving away from the narrowly civilian tradition toward an empirical approach, Sir William Jones analyzed the natural foundations of bailments by examining not only English and Roman law but also Hebrew, Athenian, and Hindu law.

Such analysis flourished, however, precisely because of the assumptions that it should not be used to threaten the ideals about the authority of the law of the land or the duty of the judges, and when men occasionally pressed the academic approach beyond these bounds, they could encounter a sharp rebuff. These conflicts were particularly apt to occur, as might be expected, in the purviews of the courts of equity. A scholarly writer on equity, Henry Ballow, bluntly exposed the weakness of the common law by explaining that "the Rules of municipal Law are finite, and the Subject of it infinite," so that "there will often fall out Cases, which cannot be determin'd by them." In the view of a conventional English lawyer, some such incompleteness might be cured by reference to natural law, but only because this was a means of discerning the common law, for genuine incompleteness stood beyond the domain of law and judicial duty. In contrast, to Ballow's academic mind, incompleteness suggested the "[n]ecessity of having Recourse to natural Principles," and he therefore took this so far as to conclude that "every particular Case stands upon its own particular Circumstances" and that Chancery could "decree against the general Rule of Law."[93] Certainly, equitable discretion was a discernment of circumstances, and thus, like legal discretion of this sort, it might often be largely beyond

[92] For the integration of a generalized version of civilian learning as jurisprudence, see Hamburger, "The Development of the Nineteenth-Century Consensus Theory of Contract," 256–265, 266.

[93] [Henry Ballow], *A Treatise of Equity*, 2–3 (London: 1737). See also Richard Francis, *Maxims of Equity*, "To the Reader" (London: 1727).

reconsideration on error, but this was not to say it was necessarily beyond rules of either equity or law. Sir Joseph Jekyll—the distinguished master of the rolls—cautioned: "[T]hough Proceedings in Equity are said to be *secundum discretionem boni viri*"—according to the discretion of good men—"yet when it is asked, *Vir bonus est quis?* The Answer is, *Qui consulta patrum qui leges juraque servat.*" This was an echo of Horace: "Who is the good man? He who takes the advice of the fathers, who serves the laws and justice." Jekyll then quoted Coke on the Commission of Sewers and concluded that "the Discretion which is executed here, is to be governed by the Rules of Law and Equity," and "in no Case does it contradict, or over-turn the Grounds or Principles" of the law, "as has been sometimes ignorantly imputed to this Court. That is a discretionary Power, which neither this nor any other Court . . . is by the Constitution intrusted with."[94] It was a calculated affront to say that learned challenges to common law were ignorant, but Jekyll was laying down the constitutional limits on the pursuit of jurisprudential truths beyond the law of the land. At the end of the century, the commentator John Fonblanque summarized that the elevation of equity above the rules of law was "neither sanctioned by principle nor authority." Nor "does it any where appear, that . . . courts of equity are invested with a larger or more liberal discretion than courts of law."[95]

Similarly, at law, learned analysis could thrive, but only to the extent compatible with law and judicial duty—as can be illustrated by two notable chief justices. Sir John Holt, who served at the beginning of the century, was second to none in his sense of the duty to decide in accord with the law of the land, not least the constitution, but at the same time, he was open to academic-style analysis as a means of elucidating common law. Most famously in 1703 in *Coggs v. Barnard,* he relied on civilian doctrine to confirm the rightness of English law on bailments—to show that it "is the Law

[94] *Cowper v. Cowper* (Ch. 1734), Peere Williams, *Reports,* 2: 753–754 (Dublin: 1741). A careful study of Hardwicke's decisions concludes that he "usually relied upon general rules of equity to a greater or lesser extent" and that "rules and principles were pre-eminent and the cases . . . were merely evidence of them.' Clyde Croft, "Lord Hardwicke's Use of Precedent in Equity," in *Legal Record and Historical Reality,* 154–155, ed. Thomas G. Watkin (London: Hambledon, 1989). For the relatively well ascertained rules in property cases and the difficulty of establishing invariable rules as to fraud, see ibid., 129.

[95] *A Treatise of Equity with the Marginal References and Notes by John Fonblanque,* 1: 20, note (g); 22, note (h) (Dublin: 1793). A mid-eighteenth-century chancellor summarized why there could only be a limited role for natural law reasoning when he noted that the "Law of Nature is perfect, Immutable, & eternal" and then contrasted "[t]he Civil Law," which "is a law instituted by a particular set of people & peculiar to them." It "is not in all things Consonant to ye Law of Nature & Nations, nor is it opposite to them. It is mutable being chang'd by disuse [of] ye Laws[,] Consent of the People, or by a Publick Act of Repeal." Robert Henley's Commonplace Book, British Library, Add. 26060, fols. 14v–15r.

of the World" and "common and natural Justice." He even used civilian ideas to elaborate details that, to put it generously, the common law had left understated, and he thereby laid the foundation for the approach taken by Jones in his essay on bailments.[96]

What Holt did without controversy, however, came under fire when employed by Lord Mansfield in ways that did not so clearly remain within the line of judicial duty. This later chief justice came from a family of Tory and even Jacobite leanings, and having acquired at Oxford an elevated taste for academic rationality in law, he often looked with disdain upon common law technicalities.[97] Mansfield usually kept up the appearance of remaining within his duty, for he ostensibly used natural law principles to discern the common law where it was indeterminate, but he tended to find such lacunae in places they had not been found before. He expected that "the law must adapt itself to the various situations of mankind," and to this end he actively enlarged openings in the law and self-consciously developed exceptions into new general rules, which displaced the old.[98] In an area such as commercial law, which came before the judges as the subordinate custom of merchants, the common law itself left much room for development in ac-

[96] *Coggs v. Barnard* (K.B. 1703), British Library, Holt's Opinions, Add. Ms. 35981, fol. 126[v]. In considering the liability of a man who accepted goods that were "[b]ailed to be kept for the Use of the Owner," Holt held that "such a Bailee . . . is not Answerable if the Goods be Stolen from him," for in civil law, this "is a Deposite," and relying on this doctrine to fill in what Englishmen and their law left inexplicit, Holt explained: "Acceptance to keep is no Express understanding to keep ag^{t} wrong Doers," and "[t]herefore the Person trusted hath not Obliged himself thereunto," unless the "[t]he Law" obliged him, and "that the Law doth Oblige him must be made out either by Constant Usage or Custom or by the Rules of natural reason or Justice." As it happened, neither "laid such a Charge upon the Bailee." Ibid., fols. 124[r]–124[v].

[97] Holdsworth observed: "Though he was widely and accurately read in the technical doctrines and technical history of the common law, his knowledge of other systems of law, and his desire to bring the common law into conformity with the needs of his day sometimes led him to lay down rules which were demonstrably not rules of English law." William Holdsworth, *A History of English Law,* 8: 29 (London: Sweet & Maxwell: 1992).

[98] For both of these techniques, see Lieberman, *The Province of Legislation Determined,* 126–127, quoting *Barwell v. Brooks,* Douglas, *Reports,* 3: 371–373 (1784). Prest notes Mansfield's "flexible" mind. Wilfred Prest, "Law Reform in Eighteenth-Century England," in Peter Birks, ed., *The Life of the Law,* 148 (London: Hambledon, 1993). For the common law's treatment of subordinate customs, see Chapter Six.

James Oldham and David Lieberman observe that Mansfield paved the way for modern ideals of lawmaking. James Oldham, *English Common Law in the Age of Mansfield,* 364–370 (Chapel Hill: University of North Carolina Press, 2004); Lieberman, *The Province of Legislation Determined,* Chapter 5. As Mansfield worked within the academic perspective, it might also more generally be observed that this perspective eventually opened up the way for the nineteenth-century reforms. Bentham did not appreciate the irony, but the success of the civilian jurisprudence and its claims for natural law made possible the reception of the utilitarian jurisprudence.

cord with reason and the public interest, and Mansfield's techniques could therefore enjoy considerable admiration. The law of the land, however, set bounds to subordinate customs, and when Mansfield departed from the law of the land, he provoked some of the preeminent reversals of modern law. Most notoriously, in 1765, in *Pillans v. Van Mierop,* Mansfield concluded that "[i]n commercial cases amongst merchants, the want of consideration is not an objection"—only to have this novelty repudiated in 1778 in *Rann v. Hughes.*[99] On behalf of the judges, Chief Baron Skinner pointedly began his opinion in *Rann* by distinguishing the law of the land from the law of nature: "It is undoubtedly true that every man is by the law of nature, bound to fulfil his engagements," but "[i]t is equally true that the law of this country supplies no means, nor affords any remedy, to compel the performance of an agreement made without sufficient consideration."[100] Notwithstanding the law of nature, the judges had a duty to decide in accord with the law of their country.

The way in which Mansfield's learned vision of the judicial role provoked a defense of common law ideals can also be observed in Lord Camden's opinion in *Doe v. Kersey.* Mansfield had sought in an earlier case to escape the requirement of the Statute of Frauds that wills be subscribed, in the presence of the devisor, by three credible witnesses. From Mansfield's academic vantage point, this statutory rule was a mere formality, which stood in the way of enforcing wills that were not fraudulent. In *Doe,* however, Chief Justice Charles Pratt of Common Pleas—Lord Camden—adhered to the Statute's requirement and bluntly responded to Mansfield that "it is not my Business to decide Cases by my own Rule of Justice, but to declare the Law as I find it laid down," and "if the Statute of Frauds has enjoined this Determination, it is not my Opinion but the Judgment of the Legislature." Camden voiced the deep distrust of many common lawyers, especially those of a Whiggish persuasion, about the use of academic analysis to elevate judges above the law. Camden understood that "positive law" was often over- or under-inclusive and that in this case it caused an injustice, but "it is better to leave the Rule inflexible than permit it to be bent by the Discretion of the Judge." With Mansfield in mind, Camden declared: "The discretion of a Judge is the Law of Tyrants; it is always unknown; it is different in different Men; it is casual, and depends upon Constitution, Temper, and Passion. In the best it is often-

[99] *Pillans v. Van Mierop,* Burroughs, *Reports,* 3: 1663 (B.R. 1765).

[100] *Rann v. Hughes, Term Reports,* 7: 350 note a (H.L. 1778), discussed by Holdsworth, *A History of English Law,* 8: 36.

TIMES CAPRICE, IN THE WORST IT IS EVERY VICE, FOLLY, AND PASSION TO WHICH HUMAN NATURE IS LIABLE."[101]

Although Mansfield became the model of ingenuity in law, his anonymous critic Junius captured the spirit of the constitutional objections to his excesses. Junius complained to Mansfield: "Instead of those certain, positive rules, by which the judgment of a court of law should invariably be determined, you have fondly introduced your own unsettled notions of equity and substantial justice," until "the court of King's Bench becomes a court of equity, and the judge, instead of consulting strictly the law of the land, refers only to the wisdom of the court, and the purity of his own conscience."[102] Echoing Coke, Junius declared that "[t]he discretion of an English judge is not of mere will and pleasure," and he called upon Lord Camden "to stand forth in defence of the law"—to which Junius added that he did not know a judge or lawyer "of any note in Westminister-hall, who shall be daring enough to affirm that, according to the true intendment of the laws of England . . . the discretion of an English judge is merely arbitrary, and not governed by rules of law."[103] Of course, Mansfield did not think he was exercising a merely arbitrary discretion, but he pursued the academic vision of judging beyond the law and his duty, and he thereby provoked both judicial reversal and popular complaint.

Common law judges would continue to employ academic learning, but on account of their office, they had to decide in accord with the law of the land. They were bound to their office by their oaths, and they thus had the most elevated of obligations to fulfill the most grounded of duties. This

101 *Doe v. Kersey* (C.P. 1765), *Lord Camden's Argument in Doe on the Demise of Hindson, & Ux. & al. v. Kersey,* 15, 53 (London: 1766).

As for new cases, when these required more than a discernment of the applicable law of the land, Camden rejected Mansfield's approach: "But who has a right to decide these new cases, if there is no other rule to measure by but moral fitness and equitable right? Not the judges of the common law, I am sure. Their business is to tell the suitor how the law stands, not how it ought to be; otherwise each judge would have a distinct tribunal in his own breast, the decisions of which would be irregular and uncertain, and various, as the minds and tempers of mankind. As it is, we find they do not always agree: but what would it be, where private opinion of the judge, as to the moral fitness and convenience of the claim? Caprice, self-interest, vanity, would by turns hold the scale of justice, and the law of property be indeed most vague and arbitrary." *Donaldson v. Becket* (H.L. 1774), *The Parliamentary History of England,* 17: 998 (London: 1813), discussed by James Oldham, *The Mansfield Manuscripts and the Growth of English Law in the Eighteenth Century,* 1: 108 (Chapel Hill: University of North Carolina Press, 1992). For such disputes and the toll they took on Mansfield, see ibid., 2: 1253–1357.

102 Letter from Junius to Lord Mansfield (Nov. 14, 1770), *The Letters of Junius,* 2: 50 (New York: 1821).

103 Letter from Junius to Lord Mansfield (Jan. 21, 1772), ibid., 2: 185; Letter from Junius to Lord Camden (nd), ibid., 2: 210.

combination of high obligation and mere human law would never fully satisfy academic ambitions for justice. Nonetheless, it would serve to protect the sort of liberty that could be obtained under human law and to advance the sort of justice that could be achieved through such liberty—perhaps especially, it will be seen, in the decisions in which the judges held government acts unlawful.

5

Independent Judgment

IN DOING their duty, judges had to exercise independent judgment. Although in England a judge's office specifically required him to decide in accord with the law of the land, judicial office more generally required the exercise of judgment, and this by its nature meant judgment independent of will.

Judicial independence tends to be understood as legal protection from external threats—in England, parliamentary protection from royal interference—and it is therefore easy to assume that independence is centrally a matter of legal prohibitions protecting the power of one part of government from the power of another. The judges, however, had long been recognized to have an office of judgment, which was considered an exercise of intellect or understanding—an exercise of a faculty of the soul that was distinguished from the faculty of will. Judges thus had an office that required them to exercise judgment, meaning a judgment independent of not merely external, royal will, but most centrally their own, internal will. With this ideal of judgment, they often managed to put aside their fears, and in this way their ideal of judgment—a judgment free from will—was a large part of what allowed them to hold government acts void.

External Threats

Part of what the judges in the exercise of their office had to avoid was any externally imposed will. Late in the day, Parliament guaranteed judicial tenure and salaries, and the independence of the judges therefore appears in retrospect to consist of legal limitations on the institutional power of the Crown.[1] These legal barriers, however, were merely outward fortifications

[1] The English experience is elegantly discussed by Joseph H. Smith, "An Independent Judiciary: The Colonial Background," *University of Pennsylvania Law Review,* 124: 1104 (1976).

for the office of judgment—an office centrally defined by the old ideal of judgment undisturbed by will—and even before Parliament added its protections, this ideal of independent judgment had often given the judges the resilience they needed to hold off royal demands.

The royal will from which the judges needed independence was the king's private, informal will. Obviously, the judges had a duty to decide in accord with the king's will when it had been adopted in an act of Parliament—a formal act of the highest court of record.[2] The king's private or personal will, however, was another matter. His private will could perhaps be considered an exercise of absolute power to which the judges had to defer, but it was ordinarily without any obligation under the law of the land, and a judge might therefore think he had to remain independent of the king's private will if he was to exercise judgment and decide in accord with the law of the land.

Medieval judges already understood that they could not delay justice—not even at the behest of the king. The king himself had the duty to see justice done to his people, and he had once sat in judgment with his judges. He soon, however, had to leave them to sit by themselves, and when he no longer regularly sat with them, he lost his direct influence on their decisions. It appears that he therefore increasingly resorted to sending them written missives, and if he sought only to delay their proceedings, he might think he was not asking them to depart from their duty. The judges, however, could take another view, as became apparent during an eyre in Kent. Upon learning that the judges had decided to hang a leading baron for robbery, Edward II wrote to put a hold on the proceedings, but "though letters were brought from the King bidding the Justices stay their hands, they would not for such reason give way."[3] Letters of this sort eventually led Parliament to clarify the extent of judicial duty, thus giving the judges a firm basis on which to resist the king's importunities. King John had promised

---

For hints of what can be found in theology and the learned law, see "Canonists and Standards of Impartiality for Papal Judges Delegate," in Richard Helmholz, *Canon Law and the Law of England,* 76 (London: Hambledon, 1987).

[2] Civilians had long distinguished between a lawmaker's legislative will and his less formal will. For example, where the *Institutes* stated, "What has pleased the Prince has the force of law," the glossator Accursius noted that in the *Codex* it was said, "Not every statement of the judge is a sentence. So too not every statement of the Prince is a law." Brian Tierney, "'The Prince is not Bound by the Laws': Accursius and the Origins of the Modern State," *Comparative Studies in Society and History,* 5: 378, 397 (1963).

[3] William Craddock Bolland, ed., *Year Books of Edward II,* 12: 17 (the volume for 5 Edward II, 1312) (London: Selden Society, 1916). As observed by Holdsworth, there were other instances in which the judges do not seem to have been so independent, but at least some of them are easily distinguishable. William Holdsworth, *A History of English Law,* 2: 561–564 (London: Sweet & Maxwell, 2002).

in Magna Charta that "to no one will we deny or delay right or justice," and Parliament in 1346 required the judges to swear:

> [T]hat ye shall not delay any person of Common Right, for the Letters of the *King,* or of any other person, nor for any other cause; And in case that any Letters come to you contrary to the Law, that ye shall nothing do for such Letters, but ye thereof shall certifie the *King;* And ye shall proceed to do the Law, the same Letters notwithstanding.[4]

Of course, kings could ignore this commitment, and the judges might lack the personal strength to adhere to it, but the judges now had the highest possible obligation not to give way on this contested element of their duty.[5] As Chief Justice Fortescue summarized, "the judges . . . are all bound by their oaths not to render judgment against the laws of the land, although they should have the commands of the sovereign to the contrary."[6]

The question of judicial independence became a central political is-

[4] J. C. Holt, *Magna Charta,* 461 (Cambridge: Cambridge University Press, 1992); *The Book of Oaths and the Several Forms Thereof, both Ancient and Modern,* 121–122 (London: 1689) (translating oath enrolled and printed with 20 Edward III, c. 1 [1346]). Although the oath was often in later centuries associated with 18 Edward III, this point is corrected in *Statutes of the Realm,* 1: 306. More interestingly, with an echo of Magna Charta, the word "delairez" has often been printed as "deny" or as "deny or delay."

An earlier statute had not gone so far. According to the Statute of Northampton, no command was to be made to disturb or delay common right, and the justices were to do right notwithstanding such command, but this was not very effective. 2 Edward III, cap. 8 (1328); Theodore F. T. Plucknett, *Statutes & Their Interpretation in the First Half of the Fourteenth Century,* 142–143 (Cambridge: Cambridge University Press, 1922).

[5] The tension between the ideal and the realities is evident from the petition of the Commons "that neither the lords spiritual or temporal, nor the justices should in future be permitted to excuse themselves by saying that they did not dare to do or proclaim the law, or their opinions, for fear of death; or that they are not free in themselves. Because they are more properly obliged to keep their oath than to fear death or any forfeiture." Petition, 1 Henry IV, number 97 (1399), in Chris Given-Wilson, ed., *The Parliament Rolls of Medieval England* (National Archives, CD). Also revealing is that there was need for the writ *de procedende ad judiciam,* with which a party fearing a command from the king could obtain a writ commanding the judges to proceed nonetheless. Fitzherbert observed that it would not be necessary "to sue forth such Writ, if the Justices do consider their Oath, and their duty to God and the King; but because some Justices are fearful, and will not do a thing which may turn to their displeasure, that Writ was ordained." Anthony Fitzherbert, *The New Natura Brevium,* 599 (London: 1652).

[6] *De Natura Legis Naturæ* (I.xvi), in *The Works of Sir John Fortesque,* 1: 205, ed. Thomas Fortescue (London: 1869). For even stronger suggestions that they enjoyed considerable independence, see the rather whiggish Thomas Pitt Taswell-Langmead and Theodore F. T. Plunknett, *English Constitutional History,* 519 (Boston: Houghton Mifflin, 1946). In *Calvin's Case,* Coke rejected "fears founded on no just cause" and closed by making clear that "no commandement or message by word or writing was sent or delivered from any whatsoever to any of the Judges, to cause them to incline to any in this case, which I remember, for that it is honourable for the State, and consonant to the Laws and Statutes of this Realm." *Calvin's Case* (Ex. Ch. 1608), Coke, *Reports,* 7: 28a.

sue in the wake of pressing questions about authority. Queen Elizabeth's "continuall charge to her Justices" was that "for no commaundement under the great or privie Seale, writtes or letters, [should] common right be disturbed or delayed. And if any such commaundement (upon untrue surmises) should come, that the Justices of her Lawes should not therefore cease to doe right in any point."[7] Thus, when Speaker Christopher Wray in the 1570s extolled Queen Elizabeth's "absolute" power in "spiritual or ecclesiastical" matters, he also commended her for "not sendinge or requiringe the stay of justice by her letters or privie seales, as heretofore sometyme hath bene [done] by her progenitors."[8] Lord Keeper Nicholas Bacon, however—a Crown officer more dependent on royal patronage than Wray—insisted that "the prince by his prerogative hath a power to order causes otherwise then the lawe is," and although Nicholas could not establish this power, his son Francis would one day come close.[9] Nicholas's claim preceded the more open conflict of the seventeenth century, but it already hints at how men with narrow ambitions and broad ideals of royal authority could stimulate fears for judicial independence.

One of the most effective ways in which monarchs pressured the judges was by seeking advisory opinions. Although the judges began their oaths by agreeing that "well and truly ye shall serve our Soveraign Lord, the *King* and his People in the Office Justice," they then swore that "ye shall counsel, our Soveraign Lord the *King* in his needs."[10] The judges thus had a specific duty to advise the king, and kings regularly requested the judges'

[7] Coke, *Reports,* 2: sig. 5[r] (To the Reader), discussed by Richard Helgerson, "Writing the Law," in *Law, Liberty, and Parliament: Selected Essays on the Writings of Sir Edward Coke,* 52, ed. Allen D. Boyer (Indianapolis: Liberty Fund, 2004). Coke recalled: "When I was the Queens Attorney, she said unto me, I understand that my Counsel will strongly urge, *Prærogativa Reginæ,* but my will is, that they stand, *pro domina veritate* rather then *pro domina Regina,* unless that *domina Regina* hath *veritatem* on her side." *Harris v. Austin* (1615), Bulstrode, *Reports,* 3: 44.

[8] Christopher Wray (April 4, 1571), in *Proceedings in the Parliaments of Elizabeth I,* 1: 198–199, ed. T. E. Hartley (Leicester: Leicester University Press, 1981).

[9] Nicholas Bacon, Speech on Lord Cromwell's Case (June 1572), ibid., 1: 265. Bacon said this in defense of the Court of Chancery, but it nonetheless is revealing.

[10] *The Book of Oaths and the Several Forms Thereof,* 120 (translating oath associated and enrolled with 20 Edward III, c.1 [1346]). The judges even acted as agents of the Crown for limited purposes, as when, for example, before judgment in a criminal case, the judges compounded on behalf of the Crown with the defendant for a penalty or forfeiture. Coke, *Institutes,* 3: 187. In giving advice, however, the judges had to decide as judges, in accord with the law of the land, as can be illustrated by their opinion of 1355 that the king could not seize the temporalities of the Bishop of Ely, because this would violate the statute of 1340 barring the seizure of temporalities without due process of law. H. G. Richardson and G. O. Sayles, "The Early Statutes," *The English Parliament in the Middle Ages,* XXV, 32 (London: Hambledon, 1981).

advice on a wide range of decisions. The danger was that kings could manipulate this specific duty so as to interfere with the judges' general duty to decide in accord with the law. In particular, a monarch could solicit an advisory opinion to precommit the judges on a question, thus undermining their independence in subsequent cases on the issue.[11]

Although royal abuse of advisory opinions was not new, it became more serious in a period of expansive hopes and anxieties about royal authority. Amid fractures that reached from the top to the bottom of European society, questions of authority had come to seem of central importance, and they were already beginning to have sweeping consequences: for individuals in relation to God; for Parliament with respect to the Crown; for the people as to the entirety of their government; for judges as to kings. Monarchs, in pursuing their own authority, increasingly pressed their will upon the judges, and the judges became correspondingly sensitive about the threat to their office of judgment—an office that necessarily had to be independent of will. Being consumed with his own authority, James I was especially indifferent to the nature of judicial office, and although he systematically used advisory opinions to make the judges accountable to him, he thereby led many Englishmen to conclude that he was interfering with the freedom of the judges to decide in accord with the law.

This was the threat to judicial duty that Chief Justice Edward Coke observed in 1615 in *Peacham's Case.* Edmund Peacham was an obscure clergyman of Puritan leanings who persisted in preaching against King James I, until he went so far as to write a sermon predicting the king's death.[12] James

[11] For example, in 1486, after Henry VII prevailed against Richard III at Bosworth Field, he sought the prosecution of one of Richard's adherents for treason, only to find that the defendant, Humphrey Stafford, had sought sanctuary. Henry asked the judges for their advice, but when they discussed the matter, they asked, "how shall we judges argue this matter when it is a question . . . that . . . will soon come before us? It is not seemly to argue the matter and give our opinions before it comes before us in a judicial way." Chief Justice William Hussey subsequently "went to the King and desired his Grace that he would not ask their opinions," noting that Stafford "was to come before the judges in the King's Bench judicially" and that "they would then do that which of right they ought to do." M. Hemmant, ed., *Select Cases in the Exchequer Chamber,* xliii–xliv, 117 (London: Selden Society, 1948); *King v. Humphrey Stafford* (Ex. Ch. 1486), Y. B. Trin. 1 Henry VII, plea 1, at 26a (largely as translated by Hemmant, with some emendations). Brooke summarized that the justices "ought not give nor express their opinions beforehand, but only when it comes before them by due original in due form of law." Robert Brooke, *La Graunde Abridgment,* "Judgment," pl. 157 ([London]: 1573).

The general problem of precommitment was familiar from the learned law and derivative theological and moral writings, which reminded Englishmen that "[j]udgement before the matter be decided, is utterly excluded, because it carieth away the minde of the Judge before the matter is knowen." Henrie Bullinger, *Fifty Godlie and Learned Sermons, Divided into Five Decades,* 193 (2nd decade, 8th sermon) (London: 1587).

[12] For details about Peacham, see Roger N. McDermott, "Edmund Peacham," DNB. To Peacham's misfortune, Attorney General Francis Bacon and other men of civilian sensibili-

and his advisers sought to charge Peacham with treason, but before commencing so serious a prosecution on such slim evidence, they sought the judges' opinions. Not content to learn whether the Crown could proceed against Peacham, James hoped to influence the judges. Attorney General Francis Bacon and his fellow Crown lawyers therefore talked to the judges not "jointly" but "severally" and in "secrecy"—even though, as Bacon understood, "the ordinary course was to assemble them."[13] Chief Justice Coke hesitated to cooperate, his reasons being "that Judges were not to give opinion by fractions, but entirely according to the vote whereupon they should settle upon conference; and that this auricular taking of opinions, single and apart, was new and dangerous."[14] Coke understood that he could not stop the king from seeking such opinions in *Peacham's Case,* but when after delaying he gave his views, he concluded against the Crown.[15]

James was so importunate in his attempts to secure opinions in private, when the judges were most vulnerable, that Coke eventually could no longer attend dinner at the king's court, lest he find himself alone with the monarch. As Coke explained, "whilest he stood by the king at dynner," James "wolde be ever asking of him questions of that nature that he had as li[e]fe be out of the roome."[16]

---

ties took an interest in his case and insisted that he be tortured to learn whether he was a member of a broader plot, but even after he was subjected to agony, the only evidence against him was the manuscript of his sermon. Upon observing the torture of Peacham, Bacon and others reported that "Peacham this day was examined before torture, in torture, between tortures, and after torture. Notwithstanding, nothing could be drawn from him." Interrogatories Whereupon Peacham is to be Examined, in *The Letters and the Life of Francis Bacon,* 5: 94, ed. James Spedding (London: 1869). In his *Essays,* Bacon had written that "there is no worse torture then the torture of Lawes: specially in case of Lawes penall," and after witnessing Peacham's torture, Bacon repeated this view, saying, for example, "it is truly said by a civilian, *Tortura legum pessima,* the torture of laws is worse than the torture of men." Francis Bacon, *The Essaies,* sig. H8[v] Of Judicature (No. 36) (London: 1613); "The Charge given by Sir Francis Bacon . . . against I.S. [Oliver St. John] for scandalizing and traducing in the Public Sessions Letters sent from the Lords in Council touching the Benevolence" (1615), ibid., 5: 141. Spedding attempts to excuse Bacon, noting that the common law neither authorized nor prevented torture. Ibid., 93, note 2. Perhaps more accurately, as Bacon understood, the common law did not allow torture as evidence, but the common law courts had difficulty controlling the king in his prerogative.

13 Letter from Francis Bacon to James I (Jan. 27, 1614), in *The Letters and the Life of Francis Bacon,* 5: 100–101.

14 Letter from Francis Bacon to James I (Jan. 31, 1614), ibid., 5: 107.

15 For the delay, see Letter from Francis Bacon to James I (Feb. 11, 1614), ibid., 5: 120.

16 John Bruce, ed., *Liber Famelicus of Sir James Whitelocke,* 48 (Sept. 3, 1615) (London: Camden Society, 1858). When presenting the charges against St. John in the Star Chamber, Bacon said, apparently without irony: "Neither was there ever King . . . that did consult so oft with his Judges, as my Lords that sit here know well." "The Charge given by Sir Francis Bacon . . . against I.S. [Oliver St. John] for scandalizing and traducing in the Public Sessions Letters sent from the Lords in Council touching the Benevolence" (1615), in *The Letters and the Life of Francis Bacon,* 5: 143.

These royal demands eventually made it clear to Coke that at least in criminal cases, advisory opinions were not compatible with judicial office. "To the end that the triall may be the more indifferent, seeing that the safety of the prisoner consisteth in the indifferency of the Court, the Judges ought not to deliver their opinions before-hand of any criminall case, that may come before them judicially." This mattered "especially in cases of high nature, and which deserve so fatall and extreme punishment. For how can they be indifferent, who have delivered their opinions before-hand without hearing of the party, when a small addition, or subtraction" of evidence or argument "may alter the case?" Revealingly, Coke concluded by asking: "And how standeth it with their Oath, who are sworn, That they should well and lawfully serve our Lord the king and his people in the office of a Justice?"[17] It was but one illustration of how royal demands could focus the attention of the judges on the nature of their office.

Deeply conscious that he held an office of independent judgment, Coke repeatedly resisted royal pressures—sometimes standing squarely within his office but occasionally stepping beyond it—and James I responded by reminding judges that whatever their ideal of office, he could simply remove them. The Crown almost always had the power to remove its judges, for the monarch typically gave them their office with the limitation that they held it "during our good pleasure"—*durante bene placito nostro.* The Crown could use this caveat to take back what it gave, and although it had rarely before used this power, it now saw the question as a matter of its authority. Coke had seemed to resist royal authority, and therefore, under Bacon's influence, James in 1616 dismissed Coke from the bench.[18]

[17] Coke, *Institutes,* 3: 29.

[18] Ibid., 4: 75. Coke was first suspended, then censured, and finally replaced. Francis Hargrave, *Collectanea Juridica,* 1: 4 (London: 1791). Coke bound up "the writt of discharge of mine office [of] Cheife Justice" in a volume of manuscripts that began with a "booke intitled liber sacramentorium," containing the "oathes of Judges and great officers," and that also included a "commission against lawe to examine the acts of Judges." W. O. Hassall, ed., *A Catalogue of the Library of Sir Edward Coke,* 25 (No. 324) ([New Haven]: Yale Law Library, 1950).

There was some suggestion later in the century that the chief justice of King's Bench was not removable at pleasure. The chief justice of King's Bench was appointed by writ and apparently had been since the time of Edward I. The other justices, however, continued to be appointed by letters patent. Coke, *Institutes,* 4: 74–75. Coke suggested in his discussion of the associate justices of King's Bench that they "ought not to be removed without just cause," but he did not specify that this was a matter of law, and he did not suggest that the appointment of the chief justice by writ gave him greater independence. Indeed, he generally observed that "both the Chief Justice, and the rest of the Judges may be discharged by Writ under the Great Seal." Ibid., 75. Nonetheless, at least one subsequent chief justice, Sir John Kelyng, seems to have thought he enjoyed a greater security. Accordingly, when his

The judicial subservience desired by James and his attorney general found its most enduring expression in a metaphor. Without denying the commonplace that judges were to be courageous, Bacon regretted the sort of courage with which Coke resisted the king's will, and therefore when, after Coke's removal, Bacon became lord chancellor, he explained to a new justice of Common Pleas what kind of courage was acceptable to the Crown. The most philosophically and politically ambitious of chancellors declared:

> [I]t is proper for you by all means with your wisdom and fortitude to maintain the laws of the realm: wherein nevertheless, I would not have you headstrong, but heart-strong; and to weigh and remember with yourself, that the twelve Judges of the realm are as the twelve lions under Solomon's throne: they must be lions, but yet lions under the throne: they must shew their stoutness in elevating and bearing up the throne.[19]

This metaphor vividly recalled both the throne of Solomon and the carved animals that supported the English throne, and it thereby suggested a subservience and a weight of royal pressure that might interfere with the duty of the judges when deciding between the Crown and the people. Recognizing the power of this image to shape public opinion, Bacon later added it to his *Essays:* "Let *Judges* also remember, that *Salomons Throne,* was supported by Lions, on both Sides; Let them be Lions, but yet Lions under the Throne; Being circumspect, that they do not checke, or oppose any Points of *Sovereigntie.*"[20] Bacon thus idealized the duress he had helped to bring to bear against the judges.[21]

---

successor Matthew Hale resigned, he did so by way of a deed, which he wrote in his own hand, sealed, and then had enrolled—his purpose being to make two points: "the one was to shew the World his own *free Concurrence* to his Removal: Another was to obviate an Objection heretofore made, *that a Chief Justice being placed by Writ, was not removable at pleasure, as Judges by Patent were;* Which opinion, as he said, was once held by his Predecessor the *Lord Chief Justice Keyling,* and though he himself were always of another opinion, yet he thought it reasonable to prevent such a Scruple." Gilbert Burnett, *The Life and Death of Sir Matthew Hale,* 102 (London: 1681).

19 The Lord Keeper's Speech in the Common-Pleas, to Justice Hutton (1617), in *The Letters and the Life of Francis Bacon,* 6: 201–202 (London: Longmans, Green, Reader, & Dyer, 1872).

20 "Of Judicature," Francis Bacon, *Essayes or Counsels, Civill and Morall,* 324 (No. LVI) (London: 1625). Bacon made the double meaning explicit in the speech he prepared to give as attorney general in *Brownlow v. Mitchell:* "For *the court,* it is our strength. . . . The judges of the land as they are the principal instruments of obedience towards the king in others, so have they ever been principal examples of obedience to the king in themselves. The twelve judges may be compared to the twelve lions." Hargrave, *Collectanea Juridica,* 1: 169.

21 In contrast to Bacon, Coke later wrote that the judges were "presumed to be indifferent between the king and the Subject" and that this independence was essential for the preservation of law and liberty. Coke, *Institutes,* 3: 187; ibid., 3: 29; ibid., 2: 419.

It was an era, however, in which the judges and many other Englishmen were becoming more self-conscious about the difference between lawmaking and judicial office, and in which, therefore, the Crown's attempts to impose its will clarified the ideal of judgment independent of will. All sorts of pressures upon the judges, whether small gifts from private litigants or casual prodding from the Crown, had long been part of the reality of judicial life, and a judge could traditionally reassure himself that such things were "hard . . . for any man to avoyd" who "meaneth not to be at difference or war with all the world." Although a judge might "seeme to lend his outward care to those importunities," he could be satisfied that "his heart is upright" and that "he doth and will doe according to the exigencie of his oath and office." Amid ever sharper ideals of authority, however, this complacent "affabilitie" about gifts, let alone royal pressures, was giving way to anxiety.[22] The shifting character of European society made the issues of lawmaking authority and the consequent worries almost inescapable, and the tensions were all the greater because whereas some men feared limitations on the authority and office of kings, others feared intrusions on the authority of judges. Most Tudor and Stuart monarchs understood the ideal of lawmaking authority to imply that they could subject their judges to their will, including not only their regular lawmaking will but also to some degree their personal, irregular will. Lawyers, however, increasingly understood the monarch to enjoy authority only within the law of the land, and in contemplating the office of lawmaking authority and will, which they increasingly thought belonged to the king only in Parliament, they solidified their understanding of the different character of the office of judgment. Conflict between the Crown and the judges was therefore becoming difficult to avoid, for at the same time that English kings were growing confident that they had the authority to impose their personal will on the judges, the judges and other lawyers were hardening their conception of judicial office as necessarily free from such will.

Although the Crown continued during much of the seventeenth century to threaten recalcitrant judges—often successfully—it repeatedly ran up against judges who stood on their duty and their oaths and adhered to the ideal of independent judgment, and the Crown therefore repeatedly had to resort to dismissals. Even when most of the judges took a broad view of the prerogative, they still at least repudiated royal demands in the clearest cases. For example, when Charles I in 1630 went beyond his father's

[22] W[illiam] L[ambard], *The Courts of Justice Corrected and Amended,* 11–12 (London: 1642). Lambarde was discussing gifts and other private rewards, but the problem was more general.

lawlessness by requesting the judges "to proceed no farther" in a cause, the judges responded that "they conceived such a message not to stand with their oaths," for it "commanded an indefinite stay of a cause between party and party, that might stop the course of justice so long as the king would."[23] When push came to shove, the Crown could dismiss uncooperative judges—as it did on forced loans and later as to seditious libels—but the fact that it sometimes had to go so far reveals that it occasionally could not otherwise get its way.[24]

The threat of dismissal eventually came to an end when the English in the wake of the Revolution of 1688 confined the Crown to lawful governance. In his Declaration of Reasons for invading England, William of Orange—soon to become William III of England—brought Englishmen to his side by protesting, among other things, that James II's councillors "have studied to discover before hand, the Opinions of the Judges; and have turned out such, as they found would not conform themselves to their intentions: and have put others in their places, of whom they were more assured" and "whom they will have to submit in all things, to their own will, and pleasure."[25] Shortly afterward, in a draft of the Declaration of Rights in February 1689, Parliament briefly considered the proposal: "Judges Commissions to be made *Quam dieu se bene gesserint*"—that is, upon good behavior—"and their Salleries to be ascertained and established to be paid out of the publick Revenue only, and not to be removed or suspended from Execution of their Office, but by due Course of Law."[26] Although this provi-

[23] *Huntley v. Barker*, et al. (1630). Huntly was a minister in Kent who had been imprisoned by the Court of High Commission and who then brought an action of false imprisonment against the keeper of the prison and some of the members of the Commission. Ibid. For examples of at least mild judicial resistance in 1628 and 1629, see W. J. Jones, *Politics and the Bench: The Judges and the Origins of the English Civil War*, 166–169 (London: Allen and Unwin, 1971).

[24] For example, when the judges in the mid-1620s twice refused to give an advisory opinion legitimizing forced loans, the king responded by dismissing Chief Justice Randolph Crewe. Wilfred Prest, "Randolph Crewe," DNB; *The Diary of Richard Hutton 1614–1639*, at 66, ed. W. R. Prest (Nov. 10, 1626) (London: Selden Society, 1991). Much later, after three judges in 1679 refused to sign an advisory opinion against seditious libels, Charles II dismissed two of them, and the third, perhaps not coincidentally, then signed an even more severe opinion in favor of royal licensing of books. Philip Hamburger, "The Development of the Law of Seditious Libel and the Control of the Press," *Stanford Law Review*, 37: 685–686 (1985).

[25] *The Declaration of His Highnes William Henry, By the Grace of God Prince of Orange, &c. Of the Reasons Inducing Him, To Appear in Armes in the Kingdome of England, for preserving of the Protestant religion, and for restoring the lawes and liberties of England, Scotland and Ireland*, 2 (The Hague: 1688); James C. Corson, "Judges and Statutory Tenure in England in the Seventeenth Century," *Juridical Review*, 42: 142 (1930).

[26] *The Publick Grievances of the Nation; Adjudged Necessary, by the Honorable the House of Commons, To be Redressed*, 2 (item No. 18) (1689).

sion could not be understood to declare an inherited freedom and therefore had to be dropped from the Declaration of Rights, it suggests the degree to which many Englishmen entered the Revolution with hopes for judicial independence, and in this spirit William III gave the judges commissions that assured them of their office during their good behavior.[27]

Parliament finally gave the judges statutory protection a decade later, when the Whigs began to worry that future monarchs might fail to recognize the Revolution Settlement. In particular, Whigs worried that William's successors might not follow his example of granting commissions on good behavior. When judges depended upon the Crown, there was reason to fear that "their judgments were not free," and Parliament therefore enacted that all commissions for judges were to "be made Quam diu se bene Gesserint and their Salaries ascertained and established." The only limitation was that "upon the Address of both Houses of Parliament it may be lawfull to remove them."[28]

Parliament thus fortified the judges in their office with a narrow statutory barrier against the imposition of royal will, but otherwise the judges continued to stand on their own—on their ideal of their office. In the struggle over questions of authority, it had become apparent that the judges might need legal protection against particularly severe external threats, such as dismissal and a reduction of salary. The imposition of will, however, might still come in many other forms, including a wide range of financial, political, and social blandishments, and against these external dangers it

[27] By 1692, some Tories, such as Sir Bartholomew Shower, supported parliamentary protection. [Bartholomew Shower], *Reasons for a New Bill of Rights,* 3–4 (London: 1692). Once the tables had turned, however, William and the Whigs surrounding him became hesitant. They feared the Crown might one day need the option of not granting life tenure and also may have worried about who would pay the judges. Wilfred Prest, "Law Reform in Eighteenth-Century England," in *The Life of the Law,* 130–131, ed. Peter Birks (London: Hambledon, 1993); Dennis Rubini, *Court and Country 1688–1702,* 120 (London: Rupert Hart-Davis, 1967); Joseph H. Smith, "An Independent Judiciary: The Colonial Background," *University of Pennsylvania Law Review,* 124: 1109 (1976).

Notwithstanding that the history of parliamentary protections is largely familiar, the earlier development of royal policy in granting commissions under similar terms regrettably remains unexplored—although John Sainty, *The Judges of England 1272–1990* (London: Selden Society, 1993), has prepared the way by identifying the different types of commissions and patents given to judges at different times. In effect, the Crown's occasional grant of property rights to the judges could serve to protect at least aspects of their independence, and the Act of Settlement took advantage of this device. Max Radin, "The Doctrine of the Separation of Powers in Seventeenth-Century Controversies," *University of Pennsylvania Law Review,* 86: 859 (1938).

[28] D. W. Hayton, ed., *The Parliamentary Diary of Sir Richard Cocks, 1698–1702,* at 72 (March 5, 1701) (Oxford: Clarendon, 1996); "An Act for the further limitation of the Crown and better securing the Rights and Liberties of the Subject," 12 & 13 William III, cap. 2, §III (1701).

seemed enough to leave the judges to rely upon the ideal of their office—an office of judgment free from will.

Internal Independence

Valuable as was the ideal of independent judgment against external threats from the Crown, the ideal at its core was an ideal of judgment free from the judge's own, internal will. Royal temptations and threats had only been effective to the extent the judges yielded to their own desires and fears, and thus the underlying problem had always been the judges' internal freedom. With or without institutional protection against external dangers, a judge had to be vigilant lest his own will or passion interfere with his judgment, and in this solitary inward struggle each judge had to look into his soul and wrestle with his most human tendencies.

According to a prominent philosophic tradition—familiar from Aquinas and many others—intellect and will were different faculties of the soul, and after the intellect or understanding reached its judgment, the will followed. As in God, so in men, it was said that the will could prompt the exercise of understanding or intellect; the intellect discerned or judged what was reasonable to the best of its limited abilities; then the will naturally sought the most recent conclusion of the intellect. From this perspective, human immorality was always at its foundation a failure of intellect—a failure of intellect or understanding and thus of judgment.[29]

Although it was understood that intellect and will were not severable in the human soul, this was less clear in the office of a judge. Writing about the soul, scholars observed that whereas the ordinary exercise of intellect in judgment was passive, the will was blind, and it therefore was desirable for the two faculties to function together, the will being thus the active pursuit of the good, based on the truth apprehended by the intellect's judgment.[30] Nonetheless, will and judgment were located in different faculties of the soul, and in government, they were different offices. The will that created legal obligation belonged to a different office from the judgment that de-

[29] Anthony Levi, *French Moralists: The Theory of the Passions 1585–1649,* at 32 (Oxford: Clarendon, 1964); Norman S. Fiering, "Will and Intellect in the New England Mind," *William and Mary Quarterly,* 29: 523 (Series 3) (1972); Thomas E. Davitt, *The Nature of Law* (St. Louis: B. Herder, 1951). Ames began his book on conscience by observing: "I call Conscience *Judgement,* First, to shew that it belongs to the Understanding, not to the Will"—although, of course, he added that "the Will by some act or inclination can both command the Understanding to judge, and also follow that judgement." William Ames, *Conscience with the Power and Cases Thereof,* First Book, 1 (I.i.1) (np: 1639).

[30] Norman Fiering, *Moral Philosophy at Seventeenth-Century Harvard,* 108 (Chapel Hill: Institute of Early American History and Culture, 1981).

cided cases, and although the lawmaker was to exercise judgment, including moral judgment, in deciding what should become law, he made laws and gave them obligation through his will. The judge, in contrast, was to exercise will only in the most peripheral way—in commanding his understanding to judge, but not in following his judgment, except so far as to state it. Essentially, therefore, the office of a judge required him to exercise only judgment, not will. The awkwardness was whether anyone human could do this.

Such doubts arose from fears about the rebelliousness of human will. Long before Aquinas held that the will naturally followed the intellect, Augustine observed that the will often seemed to take its own path—even in rebellion against the intellect. Augustine therefore suggested that the will was little different from love or the passions, which were not necessarily susceptible to guidance by the judgment of intellect or understanding. Instead, the will or the passions seemed to be directed toward good or ill by the heart's disposition and thus ultimately by the grace of God.[31]

Protestants enlarged upon this theory of the will. If all men since the fall—since Adam and Eve tasted the apple—had been corrupted by their passion or will, and if they therefore could not fully elevate themselves above their will any more than they could rise above their human condition, then men could at most attempt to repress and redirect their base or willful character. As Melanchthon explained, "[m]orall vertue" required men "as it were with a bridle" to "drawe backe the furious mind into the right way"—this being a not a full repression of the passions, but the means by which men reoriented their moderated desires toward virtue. Unable entirely to divest themselves of their will, love, or passion, men could only hope to channel these tendencies into a desire for higher satisfactions; and from this point of view, the human capacity for morality was merely "that facilitie of the mynde, or equabilitie, moderation, and stay, wherwith it can restraigne it self, untyl . . . it be well advised of the matter, to do that which is most ryght, with a certayne pleasure."[32] Protestant theology thus acknowledged the inevitability of human desire, sentiment, and unreason—this being part of a broader acceptance of human will that eventually would unfold in philosophy, literature, and politics in ways as dark as they sometimes were light.[33] In conceptions of judicial office, however, human will

[31] Fiering, "Will and Intellect in the New England Mind," 529; Dan D. Crawford, "Intellect and Will in Augustine's Confessions," *Religious Studies,* 24: 300 (1988).

[32] Philipp Melanchthon, *Whether it be Mortall Sinne to Transgresse Civil Lawes, Which Be the Commaundementes of Civill Magistrates,* 3–4 (London: nd) (2nd ed., STC 10391.5).

[33] Fiering, *Moral Philosophy at Seventeenth-Century Harvard,* 121–123; Richard Strier,

was slow to acquire legitimacy, for will seemed the essence of legislation and the opposite of judgment or understanding.

The result was a disjuncture between judicial and human identity. In the old, enduring conception of their office, judges necessarily put aside their will to exercise judgment. In Protestant theology, however, all men, by virtue of their humanity, were fallen creatures and thus irrepressibly subject to their will.

Pious Protestant judges therefore had reason for anxiety that their office required them to do what no mortal could. Commentators had long analogized human judgment to divine judgment, which excluded all will, without much doubt that at least some men could achieve this divine freedom from will, but the Reformation message that men were inescapably sinful because they could not put aside their willfulness gave new intensity to the office of a judge by implying that judges were being asked to achieve what was beyond human capacity. Protestants continued to recite the old ideals of judicial office, saying that "the affection of the Judge ought not to encline to any side" and that "[a] Judge undergoeth the person of God, who is free from all passion."[34] Yet if willfulness was an inescapable feature of humanity, judges had to worry whether any man could actually live up to the ideal.

Chief Justice Coke cursorily recognized the problem but was too self-confident to feel much tension between his human condition and his judicial office. Bracton had already complained about judges "who decide cases according to their own will rather than by the authority of the laws."[35] Coke similarly declared that "neither have Judges power to judge according to that which they think to be fit, but that which out of the laws they know to be right and consonant to law."[36] Being a Protestant, however, Coke assumed that judges would be subject to their will. Although their will might not always follow their intellect or understanding, this was merely reason for them to take care to suppress their corrupt will and pursue their better will. At one point Coke generalized that "Princes, Nobles, Judges, and Magistrates" had the "custody" and "due execution" of the laws and that they therefore all needed a combination of "*Understanding, Authoritie,* and *Will.*" Of course, rather than any will, this was a "[*w*]*ill,* prompt and readie

"Against the Rule of Reason: Praise of Passion from Petrarch to Luther to Shakespeare to Herbert," in *Reading the Early Modern Passions,* 29, eds. Mary Floyd-Wilson, Karen Rowe, and Gail Kern Paster (Philadelphia: University of Pennsylvania Press, 2004).

34 Ames, *Conscience with the Power and Cases Thereof,* Fourth Book, 283–284.

35 Bracton, *On the Laws and Customs of England,* 2: 19, ed. Samuel E. Thorne (Cambridge: Belknap, 1968).

36 *Calvin's Case* (Ex. Ch. 1608), Coke, *Reports,* 7: 27a.

duely, sincerely, and truely to execute the Lawe." Indeed, Coke urged in Protestant fashion that a judge had to be ever careful to protect "this good and ready will" from the inevitable "assault" of his corrupt will, which would lead him astray. "[T]he greatest losse a Judge or Magistrate can have" was "to give himselfe over to passion and his owne corrupt will" and thereby "to loose the way of righteousnes."[37]

This expectation that a judge need only steel himself against his corrupt will probably served Coke well in facing down so many threats from the Crown. Recognizing that a judge's internal passion or depraved will could become an avenue for the external imposition of another person's will, Coke distinguished between "secret" and "open" attacks on an uncorrupted will and cautioned judges to defend this better will with "*Fortitude* and *Constancie*" against its "two open Enemies"—"the terror of Mallice, and fear of danger."[38] Thus protected, a judge's better will would direct him toward the law. In his dealings with James I, Coke always had to be on guard against his fears, for there were times when even he was reduced to trembling, but this only further stimulated him to prepare himself internally against these external assaults and to admonish his fellow judges, as he did at the close of his *Institutes:* "[F]ear not to do right to all, and to deliver your opinions justly according to the Laws."[39]

Not all Protestants, however, were so confident that they could defeat their corrupt will or even that this would suffice. Regardless of whether they could secure protection from the external will of the Crown, the judges still needed an internal freedom from their own will that their theology denied them as men, and although this did not much trouble Coke, it could seem daunting to men of more introspective tendencies. Whereas Coke robustly faced up to the external questions of his age, others would more anxiously pursue the troubling internal problem—that judicial office

37 Coke, *Reports,* 4: sig. B[4r] (To the Reader) (London: 1604).

38 Ibid.

39 Coke addressed "you honourable and reverend Judges and Justices, that do or shall sit in the high Tribunals and Courts or Seats of Justice":

> [F]eare not to do right to all, and to deliver your opinions justly according to the Laws: for feare is nothing but a betraying of the succours that reason should afford. And if you shall sincerely execute justice, be assured of three things: First, though some may maligne you, yet God will give you his blessing. Secondly, that though thereby you may offend great men and Favourites, yet you shall have the favourable kindnesse of the Almighty, and be his Favourites. And lastly, that in so doing, against all scandalous complaints and pragmaticall devices against you, God will defend you as with a shield: *For thou Lord wilt give a blessing unto the righteous, and with thy favourable kindnesse wilt thou defend him, as with a shield.*

Coke, Institutes, 4: [365–366] (Epilogue), citing Psalm 5.

seemed to require judges to free themselves from an inescapable trait of their humanity.

This conundrum would eventually provide the opening for men to question the ideal of judgment independent of will, and where this would lead can be observed in some modern attitudes about judicial decisions, including decisions on the lawfulness of government acts. Today, when it is commonly assumed that no one can entirely escape his prejudices, it is often taken for granted that a judge cannot help but understand the law in light of his predispositions—whether lurking prejudices or noble passions—and it therefore seems odd that men were once so unrealistic as to imagine they could rise above their will or desire. Such, however, was the ideal of judicial office, and thoughtful men therefore worried about how it could be reconciled with a judge's willful humanity.

Jeremy Taylor

An exploration of the tension between judicial office and human will survives in the introspective musings of Jeremy Taylor. An Anglican divine of latitudinarian sensibilities, Taylor hoped to assist his fellow Englishmen to pursue godly lives by providing them with a Protestant book on cases of conscience, and he therefore pondered whether a judge should decide in accord with a human law if it was contrary to his conscience. Taylor, like so many of his predecessors, began with conscientious objections based on the judge's factual knowledge and moved to those arising from his moral knowledge.[40] On the Protestant assumption that human conscience was inevitably informed by human will, Taylor concluded that a judge might ultimately have to follow his will rather than the law, and this clergyman thus ended up taking a position that even the most pious of English judges would reject. In his scholastic, dialectical style, however, Taylor preserved two views of judgment—one aligned with the common law and the other with Protestant piety—and he wrestled with these perspectives in a way that already revealed glimpses as to how Protestant notions of irrepressible human will would one day more substantially undermine traditional ideals of judgment.

Conventionally, as recounted by Taylor, "a Judge . . . is oblig'd to proceed according to the process of Law, and not to his own private Conscience." From this point of view—associated with Aquinas—"there is a

[40] Jeremy Taylor, *Ductor Dubitantium, or the Rule of Conscience In All Her General Measures,* 1: 82 (I.ii.Rule 8.5) (London: 1660).

double person or capacity in a judge." As a "private person," he "must proceed upon the notices and perswasions of his Conscience. . . . But as he is a *Judge,* he is to doe the office of a *Judge,* and to receive information by *witnesses* and *solemnities of Law,* and is not to bring his own private conscience to become the publick measure." Such a "Judge does not goe against his conscience, because by oath he is bound to goe according to Law."[41]

The alternative, Taylor understood, might be to unravel the law with private claims of conscience and thus, perhaps, personal will. If a judge were to acquit "him whom the Law condemnes, upon the account of private knowledge," it would be "like speaking oracles against publick authority from a private spirit," and "the whole order and frame of Judicatures would be altered, and a door opened for a private and an arbitrary proceeding." Shifting from the question of factual knowledge to that of moral knowledge, he argued that the case "would be the same" if a "confident and opinionative" judge thought himself "to be as sure of his own reason, as of his own sense," for then "his conscience might be as effectively determined by his argument as by his eyes; and . . . he might think himself bound to judge against the sentence of the Law according to his own perswasion." Rather than accept this moral vanity, it was generally assumed that "the Judge lays aside the *affections* of a man, when he goes to the seat of judgement"—this being a place where he divests himself of "*his own reason,* and submits to the reason of the Law." He thus sacrificed "*his own will,* relinquishing that to satisfy the Law."[42]

In more general terms, Taylor acknowledged that "the publick order must be kept" and that epistemological problems required deference to the conventions of men. On such assumptions, it was said: "[L]et no man . . . pretend to a zeal for truth and righteousness . . . since in Judicatures, *legal* or *seeming truth* is all that can be secured." Taylor then pointed to the implications for moral truth by quoting St. Ambrose: "A good judge does nothing of his own will, or . . . of his private choice, but pronounces according to Laws and publick right" and "obeys the sanctions of the Law, giving no way to his own will."[43]

Taylor, however, had his mind on another world, and he therefore resisted the arguments about societal danger and epistemological difficulties. Convinced that a judge "may not doe any publick act against his private conscience," Taylor adopted the view he attributed to "the Canon Law,"

41 Ibid., 1: 82 (I.ii.Rule 8.7).
42 Ibid., 1: 82–83 (I.ii.Rule 8.7).
43 Ibid., 1: 83 (I.ii.Rule 8.7), quoting St. Ambrose on Psalm 118.

which "expressly enjoyns that a Judge should give sentence according to his own conscience." Indeed, Taylor eventually concluded that this duty to decide according to conscience might require the judge to decide in accord with his will.[44]

Concerned that his ideas not be confused with religious fanaticism, he emphasized that he opposed any abuse of claims of conscience. He explained he was speaking of exceptional instances and that he did not assume that judges would ordinarily place their opinions of natural or divine law above human law.[45] After decades of civil and religious conflict, many Anglicans viewed claims of conscience against human law as the effect of human passion and will, not to mention less elevated, bodily motions, and Taylor therefore reiterated that "a confident and opinionative Judge . . . may not preferre his private opinion before the sentence of the Law, and bring it into open judgement," for the judge "himself may be deceived in his opinion, and his confidence is no argument that he is not deceived." He also elaborated the epistemological point:

> In matters of prudence and civil government there is no demonstration of reason, but the Legislative power may determine for the publick interest as is presently apprehended, and may refuse the better counsel, and yet doe well enough; for that which is simply the better is not in these cases necessary; and in such things a mans reason ought not be so confident, as he is of *what he sees,* or what is *matter of faith.*[46]

These cautions, however, were but a preface to his acknowledgment of judicial will.

Taylor wrote to provide a spiritual guide for souls—to explain "what God requires of us"—rather than to preserve any particular society's sense of justice, and he therefore so worried about the moral purity of judges that he ultimately upheld conscience against law. In the end, the judge could not escape his conscience as a man, and "if a Judges conscience were effectively determin'd against a Law, and that he did beleeve it to be unjust and unlawful, he ought to follow his conscience," for he otherwise "makes himself a partner in the injustice by minist[e]ring to an unjust Law against his conscience." This was not to say, however, that the judge should decide the case in accord with his conscience. With scant patience for fanaticism, Taylor merely concluded that when judicial duty conflicted with conscience,

[44] Ibid., 1: 84 (I.ii.Rule 8.9), 88 (I.ii.Rule 8.19).
[45] He pointed out that St. Ambrose "speaks of a Judges office regularly and usually, not what he is to doe in cases extraordinary." Ibid., 1: 94 (I.ii. Rule 8.33).
[46] Ibid., 1: 90 (I.ii.Rule 8.23), 1: 92 (I.ii.Rule 8.29).

the judge had to resign: "[E]ither the Judge must lay aside his *opinion* or his *office,* for his conscience must not be laid aside."[47]

Recognizing that even so moderate a form of noncooperation was not clearly compatible with the conception of judicial office taken by "the other side," Taylor fell back upon Protestant theology and assumed that judges, being human, could not escape their will. On the one hand, "the Judge must lay aside *his affections* and *his will,* and *his opinion* when he sits upon the seat of judgement, because these are no good measure of Judicature, nor ought to have immediate influence upon the sentence." On the other hand, the judge's conscience was binding even if informed by his erroneous will or passion, and "if he lay aside his *conscience* he will make but an ill Judge." At best, he could hope to develop and follow his just will, and therefore "the Judge must lay aside his affections and his will never but when they tempt him to injustice."[48] This Protestant view that men, even judges, could not entirely escape their will would one day, especially in the nineteenth and twentieth centuries, become a popular vision of how judges, juries, and perhaps anyone might passionately, as obliged by conscience, depart from human law to do justice—thus making individual human will the instrument of higher law.[49] Even in those later centuries, however, such ideas would

[47] Ibid., 1: 92–93 (I.ii.Rule 8.29). For an earlier English discussion of resignation along these lines, see note 52 in Chapter Four.

[48] Ibid., 1: 90 (I.ii.Rule 8.23), 1: 93–94 (I.ii.Rule 8.32), 27 (I.i.Rule 3.2). Put generally, he thought that "a Right and Sure Conscience" required "*a formal judgement,* that is, a deliberation of the understanding, and a choice of the will, *that* being instructed, and *this* inclined by *the grace of God.*" Ibid., 1: 64 (I.ii.Rule 4.7). Like the medieval canon lawyers he studied, Taylor was confident that men could discern justice (even if, as he explained, this was only by determining one course of action to be more or less just than another), and to this he added a Protestant sense of the authority of conscience. Like a king who had authority and whose law thus was binding even if not always just, conscience enjoyed an authority that was obligatory even when it was informed by passion or will:

> Conscience is like a King whose power and authority is regular, whatsoever counsel he follows. And though he may command fond things, being abused by flatterers, or mis-information, yet the commandement issues from a just authority, and therefore equally passes into a Law; so it is in Conscience. If error, or passion dictates, the King is mis-informed, but the inferiors are bound to obey; and we may no more disobey our Conscience commanding of civil things, than we may disobey our King injoyning things imprudent and inconvenient.

Ibid., 1: 27 (I.i.Rule 3.2).

[49] Although these later developments are beyond the scope of this inquiry, it should be noted that some twentieth-century scholars almost literally repeat the notion that a judge, being unable to put aside his will, must try to will what is right, and although some of these scholars ride the high road of conscience above the law, others take the low road of legal realism. Bickel quotes Chafee: "No doubt, as the late Zechariah Chafee, Jr., wrote, 'the man himself is a part of what he decides.' But, as he concluded, if 'law is the will of the Justices,' it is 'the will of the Justices trying to do that which is right.'" Alexander Bickel, *The Least*

only slowly become conventional among common lawyers, and in the meantime, the lawyers and many others still expected judges to put aside their will and judge in accord with the law of the land.

Human Judges in a Divine Office

Rather than follow Taylor in adjusting judicial office to human nature, Englishmen more typically accepted the divine ideal of judicial office as free from will, and English judges therefore faced the difficult task of bringing their humanity (or at least their Protestant conception of it) in line with their God-like office. It has been seen that Coke was confident enough to think that a judge could repress his corrupt will or passion and direct his better will toward judging in accord with the law of the land. A more introspective judge, however, might remain worried, for as already hinted, even if a human judge could direct his will toward the law, he could not escape exercising will in judgment, and although this might be enough in moral, scientific, and most other worldly judgments, it seemed presumptuous in an office exercised in imitation of God.

At about the same time that Taylor subordinated judgment to will, another minister, the Rev. Thomas Gilbert, preached the confident version of the common law vision—the perspective already observed in Coke—that even though judges were human and thus willful, they could be expected to direct their will toward judging in accord with the law. Gilbert was a learned Anglican who drifted toward Puritanism and then became an Independent.[50] Like Taylor, he apparently assumed that judges, as much as other men, were subject to their will and thus in need of grace so that they could at least put aside their corrupt will or "lust," but unlike Taylor, Gilbert adhered to common law assumptions and preached to the judges sitting on assize in Shropshire that they were to judge, in imitation of the divine judge, in accord with the law.

The danger was that men might be judged by a rule of decision different from the law they were bound to obey. The heavenly judge, Gilbert explained, judged men according to the law, and this was the model for human judges, who in the familiar words of Psalm 82 were "the gods on Earth." As a "Law-giver," God gave laws to men, and as judge, he held them accountable in accord with these laws, and thus "the same Law of God is the rule of mans obedience and Gods Judgment." From this Gilbert

Dangerous Branch: The Supreme Court at the Bar of Politics, 236 (1962; New Haven: Yale University Press, 1986).

50 Anthony à Wood, *Athenæ Oxonienses,* 4: 406 (London: 1820).

concluded: "Let it be so with the gods on Earth too: *Let the same Law of man be the Rule of mens Civil Obedience, and the Civil Magistrates Judgment.*" In particular, "Let not men be required obedience according to Law, and proceeded with in Judgment according to will . . . and against Law." Pursuing the practical implications, Gilbert quoted Deuteronomy (16:19) that *"Thou shalt not wrest Judgment"*—a line popular among commentators on judges—and explained that this meant not "*retching* or *stretching* of a thing into another posture than it was in."[51] As for the judges who "pretend to carry all in civil affaires according to the Law of the Land" but "do the contrary," Gilbert declared that "*God will require a severe account of it.* . . . God will judg those according to his rule of Judgment, *His Law,* that judg others contrary to their Rule of Judgment, the *Law of the Land.*"[52]

Yet the problem that judges were "Gods by name, but men by nature" defied simple answers—at least when examined by more inwardly inclined men. The superficial solution—as seen here from Coke and the more obscure Rev. Gilbert—was for judges to suppress their corrupt will or lust so as to direct their better will or desire toward the law of the land. To be a judge, however, a man might have to put aside all of his will or desire, not merely that which was profane. If judgment belonged to a faculty of the soul distinct from will, and if judges were really to be God-like—if they were really "to do his work, and in his way"—then a thoughtful judge had reason to fear that human nature was fundamentally at odds with judicial office.[53]

[51] Thomas Gilbert, *An Assize Sermon, Preached before the Right Honorable the Lord Chief Justice Glyn, and Mr Serjeant Earle Judges of Assize at Bridgnorth in Shropshire, July the 2d 1657,* at 14, 19, 20–22 (London: 1657).

[52] Ibid., 23. In support of this, he argued that "[*i*]*f Judges do not according to the Law as a rule of Judgment, 'tis to be fear'd, people will not long Do according to the Law as a rule of obedience*"—"[p]artly because of their example." Ibid., 23–24. Of course, Gilbert also ran through the usual more detailed requirements for judges. They were, for example, to be *"well Skil'd in the Laws"*; they were to "[*b*]*eware of Partiality*" and to "[*m*]*ake your Law* as God his *a Law of Liberty, and* judg according to *Yours, as God to his, freely and without respect of Persons*"; they were to remember that "in the *case of judicature* there's not any Respect to be had to any Person . . . *by Considerations of Rich, or Poor, High, or Low, Small, or Great, Mean, or Mighty, nor* indeed *Godly, or Ungodly; But* onely according to the *intrinsecall Merits of the Cause.*" Not least, they were to "[*t*]*ake heed of passion.*" Ibid., 24, 26, 27. In addition to this rather conventional account of judging in terms of theology, Gilbert wrote a rather more idiosyncratic account of theology in terms of law: [Thomas Gilbert], *A Learned and Accurate Discourse Concerning the Guilt of Sin, Pardon of that Guilt, and Prayer for that Pardon* (London: 1695).

[53] Henry Symons, *A Beautifull Swan with Two Black Feet. Or Magistrates Deity, Attended with Mortality & Misery, Affirmed & Confirmed Before the Learned and Religious Judge Hales at the Assize Holden at Maidstone, July 7. 1657. For the County of Kent,* 11, 17 (London: 1658). Like so many commentators on judicial office, Symons began with Psalm 82, which "may fitly be stiled and titled, *The Judges Charge,*" and he explained, "[i]t would be profit-

No judge worried about this question with greater anguish than Matthew Hale, and he thereby came to exemplify the common law ideal of repressed will or passion. He was "himself *naturally passionate,*" and he was therefore all the more anxious to "overcome his own Inclinations."[54] To this end, he prepared for himself a list of *"Things Necessary to be Continually had in Remembrance,"* such as *"[t]hat in the Execution of Justice, I carefully lay aside my own Passions, and not give way to them, however provoked"* and *"[t]hat I never engage my self in the beginning of any Cause, but reserve my self unprejudiced till the whole be heard."* Although the judges' oaths elaborated their office of independent judgment by enjoining that they "shall do equal Law and Execution of Right, to all the *kings* Subjects Rich and Poor, without having regard to any person," Hale further specified *"[t]hat I be not biassed with Compassion to the Poor, or favour to the Rich, in point of Justice."* It was an era in which the power of the people was displacing that of the Crown, and fearing his own weaknesses, Hale distanced himself from both sources of authority, hoping *"[t]hat Popular, or Court Applause, or Distaste, have no Influence into anything I do in point of Distribution of Justice."*[55]

---

able to the Judges to have this *Psalm* sung before them alwaies, before they go to their Judicatories." He elaborated this theme in three "[p]ropositions": *"That Judges, Rulers, Magistrates, are Gods on earth"; "Though they are Gods on earth, yet they are but Gods of earth"; "That if Gods on earth, and of earth, neglect to do their duty, they shall be damned among Devils in hell."* With these ideals, Symons reminded judges to "Judge as Gods," and that "God judgeth" from "an innate principle of affection to justice," and "so ought Judges to execute justice and judgment, from an inward principle of love to them: The wheels of affection within, should cause the hand of execution to go without." Ibid., 1, 2, 4, 17.

[54] Burnett, *The Life and Death of Sir Matthew Hale,* 158.

[55] Ibid., 58–59. Similarly he added, *"Not to be sollicitous what Men will say or think, so long as I keep my self exactly according to the Rule of Justice."* Ibid., 59. For the oath, see *The Book of Oaths and the Several Forms Thereof,* 120–121.

More generally, Hale raised the standard of integrity in relation to private suitors. He "would never receive *private Addresses* or *Recommendations* from the greatest Persons in any matter, in which *Justice* was Concerned," and he insisted on paying for the customary provisions given by local notables to the judges on assize. Burnett, *The Life and Death of Sir Matthew Hale,* 60, 62–63. Similarly, see the suggestion that the judges take oaths once a year that they "have not received, nor will receive any gift or reward." *Enchiridion Legum,* 117 (London: 1673).

In the sixteenth century, William Lambarde had cautioned against men who abused their acquaintance with judges. For example, he complained about the *"Counsellor"* who "insinuated himselfe . . . with the Judge by the benefit of kindred, alliance [or] recommendations of great persons, former education and acquaintance, or by his owne obsequie" and then took advantage of his relationship to ensure that he would be "followed with a cloud of Clients." Of course, "[t]he Remedie of all which evil is so easie, that the same is . . . in the very hand and power of the judge himselfe: For if he be willing to maintaine the authoritie and coutenance of his call," he could prevent this "unadvised tampering with him in matter of his judiciall and sworne dutie." Lambarde concluded: "As for the Judge himselfe, let him not feare to la[u]nch his boat into the deep, where is Sea-roome sufficient, and let him rest upon

Hale's anxiety about his passions arose from his understanding of himself as a judge, which conflicted with his Protestant vision of himself as man. Earlier, Coke agonized about holding off the king's will but boldly assumed he could combat the corrupt element of his own will. Hale, however, worried whether he could really defeat his own corrupt will or passion, and more fundamentally he feared it was insufficient for a judge merely to conquer his will.

In one of his theological treatises, Hale described the necessity of *"putting off the Old Man."* The Old Man was "nothing but that Ataxy, Disorder, and Corruption, which by sin did fall upon our Nature," and this "Corruption and Disorder is so universal" that the soul "hath no supplies of its own to rescue it self." Having described this corruption of the Old Man, Hale then considered *"How he is to be put off."* Hale concluded in the standard Protestant manner that men could not escape their affections and passions and that they therefore had to try to pursue them moderately and for good. Thus, "Lawful Pleasures, natural Relations, Conveniences in the World, [and] a Man's own self, may be Objects of a moderate and subordinate Love: But when they take up the whole compass of our Love, our Love becomes our Sin." Similarly, one must "learn to carry a Watch over thy Will" and, orienting one's will toward God, must "[l]earn . . . to make his Will the Rule of thine."[56] The affections, passions, or will could at best be tamed and well directed.

Of course, the problem of willful judgment occurred in all walks of life, ranging from the mundane pursuit of moral conduct to the extraordinary paths opened up by science. As explained by a notable member of the Royal Society, science required "such a free, sedate, and intent minde, as it may be is no where to be found but among the *Platonical Ideas,*" for "[d]o what we can, Prejudices will creep in, and hinder our Intellectual Perfection."[57] Among most men, including scientists, this was reason to redouble one's effort at unbiased judgment. Among judges, however, the limitations

---

God (whose image he is) and stir up those Divines [sic] Talents which he hath received, merely forbearing to saile neere the Shallow . . . of this most dangerous Sollicitation." L[ambard], *The Courts of Justice Corrected and Amended,* 10–13.

[56] Matthew Hale, *A Discourse of the Knowledge of God, and of Our Selves,* 276, 288, 334, 335, 364 (London: 1688). His attitude can be further illustrated by his acceptance of anger: "Be angry, but sin not, . . . keep it not too long, nor act it too far." Incidentally, on moral judgments, he wrote: "Suspect thy Judgment of Partiality; put thy self in the others Condition before thou judgest." Ibid., 336–337.

[57] Joseph Glanvill, *The Vanity of Dogmatizing: Or Confidence in Opinions Manifested in a Discourse of the Shortness and Uncertainty of Our Knowledge,* 74 (London: 1661), defending Descartes' method or *"Skepticism"* as "the only way to *Science.*" Ibid. An apostrophe before the "s" in *"Ideas'"* has been omitted here.

of human nature were more worrisome, because judges were traditionally thought to exercise judgment entirely without will and even to "act as almighty God's substitute."[58]

Hale therefore worried how he or any other man could be a judge. One might strive to put off the corrupt will of the Old Man, but could any mortal appointed to judicial office be so God-like as put off will itself? Hale did not even think he could put off his corrupt will. He laid out his fears in his diary: "The office of a judge, it is true, is a necessary office," but "most certainly . . . it is a wonder that any man in his right judgment should desire it"—one reason being that it "requires an entire absence of affection and passion," which otherwise "will easily occasion a wresting of judgment." In practical terms, this meant a judge needed to maintain "a temperate body, with great abstinence and moderation in eating and drinking," and more substantively it required "a temperate mind totally abandoning all manner of passion, affection, and perturbation that so he may come to the business with clearness of understanding and judgment." These worldly precautions, however, were not sufficient, for although there had to be a worldly judge, it was "impossible to find any person in the world but he has his sins and corruptions." Against this danger of corrupt will and sin, Hale thought his position "requires a mind constantly awed with the fear of almighty God and [a] sense of His presence" and that "the want or any intermission of the very exercise of this fear will endanger a treading awry sometime or other in judgment."[59] Hale surely knew of Justinian's direction that the judges keep the scriptures before them in court to remind them that "they must not judge others in any other way than they themselves are being judged," and it was a familiar echo of Psalm 36, in both canon and English law, that a judge should have God before his eyes.[60] Anxious that he

[58] Sir Matthew Hale's Diary, in Maija Jansson, "Matthew Hale on Judges and Judging," *American Journal of Legal History*, 9: 206–207 (1989). These entries appear to be from c. 1668.

[59] Ibid., 205, 207, 210.

[60] In canon law, it was grounds for disqualification of a judge if he "has not God before his eyes." Richard Helmholz, "Canonists and Standards of Impartiality for Papal Judges Delegate," *Traditio*, 25: 398 (1969). Although not the basis for disqualification in English law, this vision of accountability to God was sometimes held out as an ideal for English judges. For example, when after the death of Henry VIII the Council sent new commissions to justices of the peace, it commanded them to assemble with the others named in their commissions and instructed them: "You shall first cry and call to God to give you grace to execute this charge committed unto you with all truth and uprightness, according to your oaths, which you shall endeavour your selves to do in all things appertaining to your office accordingly: in such sort as all private malice, sloth, negligence, displeasure, disdain, corruption, and sinister affections set apart, it may appear that you have God, and the preservation of your sovereign lord, and natural country before your eyes." The Council's Letter to the Jus-

was too human for his office, Hale similarly believed that a judge had "to be careful to set almighty God before him" and even "to have the fear of his great name and presence actually sitting upon the seat."[61]

In the end, no man could succeed in "totally abandoning all manner of passion," and not having a solution to this impediment, Hale painfully acknowledged that he was presumptuously serving as a judge while subject to human passion and sin. He recognized that "[i]t is true I am not a murderer, an adulterer, [or] a thief," and "[y]et Have I never had revenge, lust, lawlessness, immoderate causeless anger? Was there never any . . . partiality in my heart?" This was evident of "the most righteous judge or man on earth," and therefore "I stand in need of mercy from my great Lord and judge of the whole world." Being too human for his office, even the most pious "earthly judge" had to fear the punishment that would be meted out by the heavenly judge and had "[t]o call upon the name of that great God whom he thus fears, imploring His direction, guidance, assistance, wisdom, [and] strength in the exercise of that employment."[62]

The exercise of judicial office by mere mortals thus created a strange

---

tices of the Peace of Norfolk (Feb. 12, 1547) (Document No. 3; Cotton Library, Titus.b.2), Gilbert Burnet, *The History of the Reformation of England,* 2 (part 2): 134 (Oxford: University Press, 1829).

61 Sir Matthew Hale's Diary, 205, 207; Codex (III.i.12), *The Civil Law,* 12: 264, trans. Samuel Parsons Scott (Cincinnati: Central Trust, 1932).

62 Sir Matthew Hale's Diary, 206–207, 210–211. Elsewhere, he wrote that if judgment belonged to God, then "[w]hen a Man takes up the Office of his Judge, he injures both the Judge and Party." Hale, *A Discourse of the Knowledge of God,* 337. Naturally, Aquinas had earlier discussed this problem with considerably less anxiety. Thomas Aquinas, *Summa Theologica,* 3: 1441 (Part 2–2, Q. 60, Art. 2), eds. Fathers of the English Dominican Province (Westminster, Md: Christian Classics, 1981).

Among Hale's contemporaries who took up the theme that judges would be judged was the Rev. Thomas Lodington. He contrasted "[t]he high *Honour,* great *Authority* and *Power* of the *Magistrates*" and "[t]heir *infirmity* and *low condition,* in respect of their nature," for "[t]hough they are *Gods* by *office,* yet they remain *men* still by *nature,*" and "[t]heir advancement to the *name* and *office* of God, doth not divest them of the *nature* of man." Like Hale, he therefore observed: "Their sitting upon an *Earthly Tribunal,* to give sentence upon *men,* and their causes, doth not priviledge them from standing at a *Higher Tribunal* to receive a sentence from God upon *themselves.*" Thomas Lodington, *The Honor of the Magistrate Asserted. In a Sermon Preached At the Assizes Holden at Lincoln on Monday, March the 23, 1673/4,* at 3 (London: 1674).

A half-century later, Dr. Nicholls paraphrased the first line of Psalm 82: "O All ye Princes and Magistrates, whom God has raised to a particular eminency above your Brethren, and advanced to be a sort of Inferior Gods, as being commission'd by his Authority, and acting as his Proxies; do you consider, that God exercises a superior Judicature over you, he minds what you do amiss in our Courts, and will bring you to a severe Reckoning, for any Prevarication in your Acts of Justice." His paraphrase of the fifth line included the suggestion that "our whole National Constitution is like to be subverted, when those who ought to maintain the Laws, do offer the greatest Violence to them." William Nicholls, *A Comment on the Book of Common-Prayer,* sig. Yyyy [2r–v] (Psalm 82) (London: 1710).

bird—a combination of the "Magistrates Deity" with "Mortality & Misery." It was, in the metaphor adopted by an assize sermon, "A Beautifull Swan with Two Black Feet."[63] Men were too human to support the divine office of a judge, but even while acknowledging their frailty, they struggled to uphold the heavenly ideal, and they thereby sustained a vision of independent judgment that would serve them well in cases that aroused human passion, including cases in which they had to hold government acts unlawful.

Internal Independence from Political Prejudice

Even more than the external will of the Crown, the internal will of the judges could undermine their judgment, and therefore when seventeenth-century English kings systematically appointed judges prejudiced in favor of royal interests, the English gradually became self-conscious about political leanings as a threat to independent judgment. It was hardly new that judges had to exercise judgment free from their own will, including their predispositions, but the English increasingly became aware of the political version of this threat.

Already in the *Shipmoney Case* there were hints as to how the judges' internal attitudes could skew judgments about the lawfulness of royal acts —although contemporaries still tended to view such situations in terms of personal fears rather than political inclinations. Charles I needed to raise a professional, standing navy at a time when the peril was not obvious and Parliament was unsympathetic. He therefore relied on the medieval right of the Crown in times of danger to demand the use of private ships from coastal towns. Charles, however, employed the old precedents concerning actual ships to justify requests for annual financial contributions, even from inland counties. To precommit the judges, Charles asked them for an advisory opinion, and when in 1638 the legality of shipmoney came before the common law judges and the barons of the exchequer, seven of the twelve held for the Crown. Far from putting the matter to rest, this decision only exacerbated the issue, for after decades of royal interference with the judiciary, it seemed only reasonable to wonder whether the judges had bowed to royal pressures. Soon, moreover, an even more disturbing conclusion came to mind—that the judges had merely given way to their own trepidations. When Parliament later impeached the judges who supported shipmoney, some members observed that the underlying problem was not so

[63] Symons, *A Beautifull Swan with Two Black Feet,* 11, 17.

much the king's attempt to influence the judges as their lack of fortitude. Edward Hyde recalled Francis Bacon's conceit "that the twelve Judges were like the twelve lions under the throne of Solomon," and playing upon this metaphor, the future historian and Earl of Clarendon complained that the judges who favored shipmoney "were no lions," for "upon vulgar fears" they "delivered up the precious forts they were trusted with, almost without assault."[64] This voluntary surrender suggested to Lord Falkland an entirely internal danger. Earlier, judges had succumbed to external threats, but "in the present business there is none of all this; it came from within; there is no outward force."[65]

Anxieties about the independence of the judges from their political prejudices came more clearly to the forefront of English politics in response to one of the men who followed Matthew Hale in Westminster Hall, Chief Justice William Scroggs. After appointing such a judge, the king had no need to impose his will, for Scroggs's own will was irrepressible. When Scroggs became a judge in 1676, he recited that "Integrity" is "part of a Judge's Duty," but he protested too much about the temper required of a judge, who was to avoid "impetuous haste," the "Imperiousness" of a "Proud Man," and an unbecoming "Harshness." This sounded much like Scroggs himself, and whereas Hale sought to avoid both popular and royal approval, Scroggs declared that he would be "no Seeker" of "the Applause of the Multitude," but would "earnestly covet" men "heartily affected to the Government."[66]

Scroggs made little effort to suppress his passion against the government's opponents. In one case, he allegedly berated the defendants "with most severe menaces, and scurrilous threatenings and clinching his Fist at

[64] Speech of Edward Hyde, *State Trials,* 3: 1282.

[65] Speech of Lord Falkland, *State Trials,* 3: 1260, 1279.

[66] *A Speech Made by Sir William Scroggs, One of his Majesties Sergeants at Law, To the Right Honourable the Lord High Chancellor of England, At his Admission to the Place of One of His Majesties Justices of the Court of Common-Pleas,* 4–7 (London: 1676). When his own affection for the government earned him the position of lord chief justice in 1681, he declared that he would *"rouse"* himself to the "more busie and stirring Court" of King's Bench and hastily explained: "I would not be mis-understood herein, as if by rouzing, I thought that to be a Judge in this Court, a Man must be a Lion, fierce and furious: He should have the Lion's Courage to support the Throne, but not the savage to worry a Lamb." He told the assembled lawyers: "The Preservation of Government, is more immediately the Duty and Business of our Profession, than all mens else whatsoever," to which he added that "by the Government, I mean, *The Government as it is established with all its Rights, not as a Current of Law only to serve Common . . . Estates.*" Indeed, "though Justice must be done unto all, the Favour that is extended to the Robe, shall be measured to them by their Loyalty; and he shall be first heard, that best moves for the King." *The Lord Chief Justice Scroggs His Speech to the Lord Chancellor,* 1–2 ([London: 1681]).

them," saying that "he would shew them no mercy" and that "he would fill all the Goals with them, and pile them up like Faggots."[67] In another case, he allegedly "Roared, Ranted, and Blustered more like an *Hector,* than a *Judg.*"[68]

Scroggs's conduct eventually provoked an attempt at impeachment, but more substantially, it stimulated public condemnation of judicial prejudice, passion, and will.[69] According to one commentator, the problem arose from judges who "lean rather to the one side, than the other." The oaths of the judges "bind them to the *due Administration of Justice to the Subject, according to the Laws,*" and if some medieval judges who allowed themselves to be *"threatened from their Duty"* were not excused "from the *Rope* . . . how much more then do they deserve it who shall presume to do as bad things or *worse,* without any *Menaces* at all but willfully and presumptuously, purely out of their own base inclinations." Judges thus had to steady themselves not merely against the king's will, but their own: "[B]y this their *Oath, Judges* are to proceed according to *Law;* their Business is *Jus Dicere,* to Declare and Administer the Laws Establish't; not *Jus Dare,* to Impose their own Whimsical, Arbitrary, *Peevish,* or Self-designing Opinions, for *Law;* or to Usurp a *Legislative* Power, so as to deliver that to be Law, which in truth is not so."[70]

Against Scroggs, men sanctified Hale as the model of a judge. The "ever Famous" Hale was celebrated as "that grand Example of *Uprightness,*" whose "whole Life was one continuous Thred of *Sincere, and Understanding Justice.*" A man who pursued "his constant Road of *Integrity,*" he was "[a]n exact *Standard* whereby *Future Princes* may measure the Qualifications of their *Judges.*"[71] The Whig clergyman Gilbert Burnet wrote a hagiography of

[67] *A New-Years-Gift for the Lord Chief Justice Sc[rog]gs. Being Some Remarks on his Speech Made the First Day of Michaelmas Term, 1679,* at 3 ([London: 1680]).

[68] *Another New-Years-Gift for Arbitrary Judges: or, Some Sober Reflections on Injustice,* 1 (London: 1681).

[69] One pamphleteer imagined how Scroggs responded to news that Parliament would meet and impeach him: "What a damn'd Fool was I, that I did not run away in time? . . . A dull Beast! to stay thus to be Nooz'd.: I was often told of a *Parliament,* but by the *Popes Toe,* I never believed that the King would call one." *The Bellowings of a Wild-Bull: or Scroggs's Roaring Lamentation for Being Impeached of High-Treason,* 1 ([London?: 1681]).

[70] *The Triumphs of Justice over Unjust Judges. . . . Humbly Dedicated to the Lord Chief Justice Scroggs,* 1, 9, 12, 32 (London: 1681). The pamphlet, as it happens, echoed some of the speeches given in 1640 during the impeachment of the judges who upheld shipmoney. By the next decade even a Tory, Sir Bartholomew Shower, recalled that under prior monarchs, "the Humour of the Man, and not his Knowledge in the Law, was the most considerable in the Election of a Judge: that Complaisance to Prerogative was a much better Quality than that of a judicious and crabbed, if stubborn Lawyer." [Shower], *Reasons for a New Bill of Rights,* 4.

[71] *The Triumphs of Justice over Unjust Judges,* 35.

Hale because *"he was a great example while he lived"* and because Burnet wanted his account of Hale's life to *"have its due influence"* upon *"Posterity"*—a message Burnet declared in capitals: "THAT HE WAS ONE OF THE GREATEST PATTERNS THIS AGE HAS AFFORDED."[72] In fact, lawyers have ever since looked upon Hale as a saintly exemplar of how a judge could rise above his passions.

The ideal of judicial dispassion as to politics became entrenched in the mind of the public through the legendary misconduct of Chief Justice Jeffreys and the self-conscious rectitude of one who eventually followed in his place, Chief Justice Holt. George Jeffreys was not as loathsome as depicted in popular mythology, but after his almost prosecutorial vigor in trials for treason, he was castigated as "L[ord] Chief-hangman *Jeffreys*."[73] In contrast, after the Revolution of 1688, the bench as a whole finally began to rise above partisan political passions, and no judge did more to set this tone than Sir John Holt. He emphasized the traditional understanding that the law of the land, including now the constitution, protected both the power of the government and the rights of the people, and he took pains to make clear that he would rule either for or against the government as required by his duty and the law. A contemporary who reported Holt's opinions summarized that "his Integrity would not suffer him to deviate from Judgment and Truth in Complaisance to his Prince, or to either House of Parliament: And they all paid that Regard to Justice, in the Person of Lord Holt, as not to be offended at his Decisions."[74]

The English in the eighteenth century put to rest their most intense anxieties about judicial independence, both external and internal. The Revolution of 1688 and the introduction of a new bench, including Holt, ended the most obvious royal threats to independent judgment, and the English therefore did not have to wait for the statutory guarantees of 1701 to recognize that the matter was largely settled. More broadly, the government itself now upheld the ideal of independent judgment. Rather than demand deference to royal will, the government merely expected the judges to

[72] Burnett, *The Life and Death of Sir Matthew Hale,* sig. [b2r] (Preface), 218.
[73] *A New Martyrology: Or, the Bloody Assizes,* 80 (second pagination series) (3rd edition; London: 1689).
[74] *A Report of all the Cases Determined by Sir John Holt, Knt. from 1688 to 1710,* ii (Preface) (London: 1738). In their controversy with the Commons over the imprisonment of Paty and the other Aylesbury men, the Lords said of Holt that his "learning and Judgment is well-known, and as Universally esteemed as his Integrity." "Some of the Arguments that were made use of by the Lords in their Debates, and at the Free Conference," *The Humble Representation and Address, of the Right Honourable the Lords Spiritual and Temporal In Parliament Assembled, Presented to Her Majesty The Fourteenth Day of March, 1704,* at 20 (London: 1704).

support the constitution as settled by the Revolution, and the Crown as established by the constitution; and at least outside Jacobite circles, this general attachment to the legally constituted system of government seemed compatible with the ideal of independent judgment. Most profoundly, the opening up of space for judicial independence was possible because a deep shift in English attitudes, including an easing of both political pressures and more personal fears. It was a period when political alarms about royal authority gave way to widespread confidence in Parliament, and when Calvinist anxieties about corrupt will or passion were softening into a calmer sentimentalism, and in these circumstances, it seemed only natural that judges could put aside their worst inclinations and follow their virtuous sentiments in adhering to their duty.

Fears about departures from independent judgment thus lost their edge. Although some judges socialized with the king's ministers and engaged in politics, it was widely assumed that they could leave their political attachments behind when they sat on the bench. As summarized in the urbane prose of the *Gentleman's Magazine,* "a Judge should be a Person of singular Integrity of Mind, as well as remarkable Steadiness of Behaviour," and "[u]pon the Bench, he should certainly act as if he had neither Acquaintance, Friends, nor Relations existing." It was almost as an afterthought that the essayist bothered to add: "I need not, I presume, take Notice that he must be entirely free from, or (if I may use the Expression) untainted with the Prejudices of Party, for wherever that Malignity infects the Mind of a Judge, it proves a Source of perpetual Injustice."[75]

Only when Lord Mansfield seemed to mix politics and judging did independence again become the focus of widespread political agitation, and as might be expected, his conduct deepened the consciousness of the English about their ideal of independent judgment. Although Mansfield was

[75] "Qualifications of a Judge" (from *Common-Sense,* Nov. 18, No. 94), *Gentleman's Magazine,* 8: 590 (1738). Personal traits were important in the selection of judges, for although "[t]he Virtues and Vices of one who has never acted in a publick Station cannot, perhaps, be generally understood, or known . . . Men are apt to discover their Passions in little Things," and "Who is Tyrant in his own Family, or among his Neighbours, will be a Tyrant on the Bench." The essayist was particularly concerned about men who were too forward in seeking judicial office:

> I am sensible, Men in Power have pretended, that it is extremely difficult for a Minister to defend himself against the Importunities of bold and forward Men; and I am not insensible, that they are sometimes tried with the Solicitations of Creatures without Shame. But I will beg Leave to say, that where this happens it is their own Faults; for if they sought out Merit, and prefer'd it when they found it, those Men of Front would despair.

Ibid.

widely admired for finding justice amid the technicalities of the common law, his academic vision of judging and his decisions in some constitutional cases stirred up fears that he was influenced by his political inclinations and even at one point by his receipt of an extra salary as Speaker of the House of Lords. Particularly when he took positions against John Wilkes, many men feared the worst. For example, although William Eden still recited the familiar point that "the present independence of our Judges is the best safeguard of our constitutional liberties," he now felt compelled to wonder whether the judges' salaries might be too meager "amidst the general opulence of the kingdom."[76] It was not possible, however, to support most judges at Mansfield's level of opulence, and because of fears that he maintained his wealth through his politics, Mansfield became the model of the social ostentation and political engagement judges were to avoid.[77] It was an example that only sharpened perceptions of the ideal. As Edmund Burke later told the Commons, "[t]he judges are, or ought to be, of a *reserved* and retired character, and wholly unconnected with the political world."[78]

Judges, in sum, held an office that by its nature was one of independent judgment, and with this high ideal of their office, they could overcome the obstacles to doing their duty. Parliament eventually provided some legal protection against the external imposition of will, but this was only an outward, institutional protection for the ideal of independent judgment, and both before and after Parliament created this institutional barrier, the judges most centrally depended on the ideal. At its core, the ideal of independent judgment required a judge to remain divinely free from his own will, and this was a source of great strength against external threats. Although the judges lacked the political power to challenge government acts, they had a divine model of their office—a model that centered on the freedom they maintained in their own mind—and with this ideal, to which they were bound by their oaths, many judges found that they could rise to the occasion when they encountered unlawful government acts.

[76] William Eden, *Principles of Penal Legislation,* 176–177, note o (London: 1771).
[77] In an otherwise almost uncritical biography, Fifoot notes that Mansfield's "political associations were a source of embarrassment." C. H. S. Fifoot, *Lord Mansfield,* 41 (Oxford: Clarendon, 1936).
[78] Speech of Edmund Burke, Esq. Member of Parliament for Bristol, On Presenting to the House of Commons (On the 11th of February, 1780) A Plan for the Better Security of the Independence of Parliament, 83 ("A New Edition"; London: 1780).

6

Judicial Decisions

GUIDED by their duty, and sustained by their office of independent judgment, the judges regularly held customs and government acts unlawful. They even, it will be seen, sometimes held government acts unconstitutional. It may come as a surprise that English judges held government acts unconstitutional or otherwise unlawful, but once it becomes apparent that this was an ordinary part of their duty, much that seems extraordinary in later, American law will begin to fall into place.

The English decisions about the lawfulness of customs and government acts scarcely make an appearance in the history of judicial review because decisions that did not concern acts of Parliament have come to seem irrelevant. Judicial review is understood essentially as a power to review sovereign legislation, and from this perspective only the precedents holding sovereign statutes unlawful are really of much significance, and the judicial decisions about other types of acts, let alone about customs, are at best peripheral. Accordingly, the English decisions, which did not include cases holding acts of Parliament unlawful, seem to be distractions—the only exception supposedly being *Bonham's Case,* which briefly alluded to the notion that an act of Parliament could be void.[1] The study of judicial review thus systematically excludes most of the English evidence—reducing it to little more than a distant prehistory, a dimly lit background in which there are inchoate intimations of judicial review but nothing directly connected to later developments.

The later, American decisions holding sovereign legislation unlawful,

[1] For this case and what Coke meant in his report of it, see Appendix I. For scholarship recognizing some of the significance of the broader range of English cases, see Charles H. McIlwain, "The Fundamental Law behind the Constitution of the United States," *Constitutionalism and the Changing World,* 244 (Cambridge: University Press, 1939).

however, must be considered as part of the expansive array of judicial decisions holding various customs and government acts unlawful, and when it is recognized that all such decisions were within judicial duty, it should become evident that the full range of English decisions about the lawfulness of customs and government acts are directly relevant. Thus, a wide range of decisions that are traditionally part of English constitutional history but not part of the history of judicial review must be examined afresh for what they reveal about judicial duty.

Subordinate Acts and Customs

The common law judges frequently had to determine the lawfulness of various subordinate laws, including local customs and corporate by-laws. Such decisions over the centuries left the judges familiar with the evaluation of both customary law and legislation, and mundane as such decisions were in England, they would soon acquire broader significance in the colonies, where subordinate legislation was almost sovereign.[2]

The common law requirement for the lawfulness of a subordinate law, whether a corporate by-law or a local custom, was a test of law and reason. The requirement of reason may once have derived from concerns about natural law unameliorated by questions of authority, but it had come to be merely a requirement of English law. As Hale summarized with respect to local customs, "[t]he Common Law does determine what of those Customs are good and reasonable, and what are unreasonable and void" and "gives to those Customs, that it adjudges reasonable, the Force and Efficacy of their Obligation."[3]

[2] On corporate by-laws, see Mary Sarah Bilder, "The Corporate Origins of Judicial Review," *Yale Law Journal,* 116: 513–535 (2006); Philip Hamburger, "Law and Judicial Duty," *George Washington Law Review,* 72: 13 (2003); Philip Hamburger, "Revolution and Judicial Review: Chief Justice Holt's Opinion in *City of London v. Wood,*" *Columbia Law Review* 94: 2140 (1994); Barbara Aronstein Black, "An Astonishing Political Innovation: The Origins of Judicial Review," *University of Pittsburgh Law Review,* 49: 962–963 (1988); Joseph Henry Smith, *Appeals to the Privy Council from the American Plantations,* 525 (New York: Columbia University Press, 1950).

[3] Matthew Hale, *The History of the Common Law of England,* 18, ed. Charles M. Gray (Chicago: University of Chicago Press, 1971). For the degree to which this was a matter of English law, see the discussion of various "foreign" legal systems in Chapter Two. Indeed, Parliament occasionally adjusted the standard applicable to some types of corporate acts. See text below.

For the application of the law-and-reason test to corporate acts, see *The Chamberlain of London's Case* (K.B. 1590), Coke, *Reports,* 5: 63a. Many corporate charters stipulated that corporate by-laws contrary to the law of the realm were void, but this was an unnecessary precaution. As Chief Justice Hobart of Common Pleas said in 1616 in *Norris v. Staps,* the

The use of "law and reason" as a test of subordinate laws stood in contrast to another use of the law-and-reason measure: to discern such common law as was otherwise uncertain. In this more general use of the standard, the judges relied on the element of reason to understand the common law rather than to test its lawfulness, and in fact the judges never held common law doctrines void but rather merely declared them, for the common law was the custom entrusted to the royal courts at Westminster. These common law courts could hold the custom of a local court void for being contrary to law and reason, but just as a local court declared its local custom, so the common law courts declared the common law—the custom of the realm. Noting the parallel, Chief Justice Hobart explained of local courts, "the Judges of every place are supposed to have knowledge of the laws of the place whereby they do Judge," and they "therefore in suits in their own Courts do determine them, as the Judges at the Common Law do in the Kings Courts" when they "judge the general customs of the whole Kingdom, being the Common Law."[4] The custom of the realm was declared by the courts of the realm, and thus although the judges of such courts would occasionally misstate the common law, they would then correct their earlier statement rather than consider any part of the common law void.[5] Hence the different uses of the law-and-reason standard as to local law and common law. The common law judges used "law and reason" to test subordinate acts and customs and thus to determine whether these lesser laws were void, but with regard to common law, they merely used this standard to discern and declare the law where it was uncertain.

Especially when used as a test of subordinate law, the word "reason,"

laws of corporate bodies "must ever be subject to the general law of the Realm as subordinate to it. And therefore though there be no Proviso for that purpose, the law supplies it." *Norris v. Staps* (C.P. 1616), Hobart, *Reports,* 211. Similarly, William Sheppard noted the superfluity of these provisions: "The Clause of addition, that they may not make Ordinances repugnant to the Lawes, &c. is idle, and to no purpose. For the Law doth understand that, and it is included, and such By-lawes made by a Corporation, are void by the very Common-Law." William Shepheard, *Of Corporations, Fraternities, and Guilds,* 83 (London: 1659).

[4] *Day v. Savage,* Hobart, *Reports,* 86–87 (K.B. 1614).

[5] Blackstone explained: "But even in such cases the subsequent judges do not pretend to make a new law, but to vindicate the old one from misrepresentation. For if it be found that the former decision is manifestly absurd or unjust, it is declared, not that such a sentence was *bad law,* but that it was *not law;* that is, that it is not the established custom of the realm, as has been erroneously determined. And hence it is that our lawyers are with justice so copious in their encomiums on the reason of the common law; that they tell us, that the law is the perfection of reason, that it always intends to conform thereto, and that what is not reason is not law." William Blackstone, *Commentaries on the Laws of England,* 1: 70 (Oxford: 1765). Thus, "*the law,* and the *opinion of the judge* are not always convertible terms." Ibid., 71.

as might be expected, did not refer to an open-ended, abstract measure of reason or natural law. Most tangibly, the test of law and reason was said to bar subordinate laws from violating either the shared liberties of the people or the distinct rights of particular persons (such as the king or a franchisee), but this much would have been accomplished by a test of law alone. A hint of what was added by the element of reason is apparent from suggestions that the test concerned the public interest.[6] It must wait to be seen what underlay the test, but although described broadly in terms of law and reason, it evidently had a more precise significance.[7]

A specialized version of the law-and-reason test left extra space for local customs. All sorts of traditional customs had come to seem peculiar and even arbitrary, and therefore many of them could not even satisfy common law expectations of reasonableness.[8] The problem was inherent in the notion of ancient, immemorial custom, which was the foundation of property rights across England, but which was apt to include much that had come to seem irrational. The common law avoided this difficulty by moderating the requirement that subordinate law be reasonable. Under common law, local custom only had to be reasonable in its origin, and the common law acknowledged that "the Reason of every Custom cannot be assign'd."[9] Local customs thus enjoyed at least an initial presumption that they had once had

[6] For example, it was said that "liberties which are prejudicial to the common wealth are void." Edmund Dudley's First Lecture (1486–1489), in *John Spelman's Reading on Quo Warranto,* 56, Appendix 1 (E), ed. J. H. Baker (London: Selden Society, 1997). Similarly, two centuries later, Chief Justice Holt recited: "Every corporation hath a Power to make By Laws for the Advantage & better Government of the place which is the true Touchstone by wch the Goodness of all By Laws & Ordinances are to be Tryed. . . . it's enough if they Tend to the public Benefit or profit of the place within the Limits of the Corporation." *Mayor & Commonalty of the City of London v. John Vanhacker* (K.B. 1699), British Library, Holt's Opinions, Add. Ms. 35981, fol. 63[v].

[7] For the later discussion, see Chapter Nine. Postema observes that "'reason' was understood in a special way. This was not 'natural' reason . . . the reason of broad, universal principles external to ordinary sources of law, accessible to individual rational minds . . . but reason *in* the law," and "for a custom, practice, rule or judgment to be 'against reason' (or often 'inconvenient') was for it to be inconsistent with the law as whole, to fail to fit coherently into the common law." Gerald J. Postema, "Classical Common Law Jurisprudence (Part I)," *Oxford University Commonwealth Law Journal,* 2: 178 (2002).

[8] Thomas Blount, *Fragmenta Antiquitatis. Antient Tenures of Land, and Jocular Customs of Some Mannors. Made Publick for the Diversion of Some, and Instruction of Others* (London: 1679).

[9] Thomas Wood, *An Institute of the Laws of England,* 1: 11 (Introduction) (London: 1720). In the early seventeenth century, "Walter of the Inner Temple" explained that "such a custom as is reasonable or which could have had a good commencement will by presumption, by the usage thereof from time &c., be taken as a good custom." *Gittins v. Cooper* (K.B. 1610) (citing Y.B. Mich. 35 Henry VI, pl. 25), Add. Ms. 25,208, fol. 96[v]–97[r], as translated by Charles Gray in his mimeographed teaching materials. According to Sir John Davies, "custom . . . ought to have a reasonable commencement." *The Case of Tanistry,* in

a reasonable commencement. Corporate acts, in contrast, which had been created within memory and which could easily be changed, did not enjoy this sort of accommodation.

Although most decisions about subordinate, corporate enactments were fully judicial decisions, it is necessary to distinguish the judges' administrative decisions giving prior approval to such laws. To prevent overreaching corporate legislation, Parliament in the 1430s enacted that if a guild, fraternity, or incorporated company made laws interfering with the "King's franchises" or "the common Profit of the People," it had to get prior approval from either the local mayor or the justices of the peace. If these officials did not find the by-law "good and reasonable," it would be considered "revoked and repealed."[10] Even though based on the common law test of law and reason, such revocation was not exactly a judicial decision, and this became all the more clear under a statute of 1504. By this date, the initial statute had expired, and some corporate bodies were again taking excessive advantage of their lawmaking powers. Parliament therefore forbade guilds or fraternities from making by-laws that diminished the prerogative of the king or other persons or that were "ageynste the comen p[ro]fite of the people," unless these acts were "examyned & approved" by various officials, primarily the judges.[11] These administrative decisions, which might license what the law otherwise forbade, could not be assumed to amount to judicial decisions in accord with the law of the land, and it therefore came to be acknowledged that the judges still could hold a by-law unlawful after it had been allowed. As decided by King's Bench, the 1504 statute "doth not strengthen any of the Ordinances made by any Corporation" even if they were "allowed and approved as the Statute speaketh," but rather "leaveth them to be affirmed as good, or disaffirmed as unlawful by the Law."[12] Thus, whereas the judges could hold corporate by-laws lawful or

---

John Davies, *A Report of Cases and Matters of Law, Resolved and Adjudged in the King's Courts in Ireland,* 87 (Dublin: 1762). See also Reading on Magna Charta, c. 9 (probably c. 1500), in *John Spelman's Reading on Quo Warranto,* 11, Appendix 1 (A); *Farmer v. Brooke,* (K.B. 1590) & *Higges v. Gardener* (K.B. 1613), in Henry Rolle, *Un Abridgment,* 1: 559 (London: 1668); Custom, Salkeld, *Reports,* 112; Blackstone, *Commentaries on the Law of England,* 1: 77. In contrast, in canon law and the civil law, custom did not have to be immemorial but did have to be reasonable. For the ten- and forty-year rules of civil and canon law, see Thomas Wood, *A New Institute of the Imperial or Civil Law,* 9 (London: 1704). See also R. H. Helmholz, *The ius commune in England, Four Studies,* 154, 184 (Oxford: Oxford University Press, 2001).

[10] 15 Henry VI, cap. 6 (1436–1437).

[11] D[e] privatis & illicitis statutis non faciend., 19 Henry VII, cap. 7 (1503–1504).

[12] *Case of the Taylors, &c. of Ipswich* (K.B. 1614), Coke, *Reports,* 11: 54b. See also *Master, Wardens, Assistants, and Community of Stationers in the City of London v. Salisbury* (K.B. 1693), Comberbach, *Reports,* 221; Shepheard, *Of Corporations,* 91. "[T]he onely benefit

unlawful under the test of law and reason, their administrative allowance of these corporate acts could not even create a presumption in their favor.

The judicial decisions about corporate by-laws were decisions about local legislation, which seemed to be adopted in the same manner as the legislation of states, but which were subject to the law-and-reason test. Just as the king and the three estates in Parliament "are the great Corporation or Body politick of the kingdome," so the Court of Common Council of the corporation of London "hath some resemblance of the High Court of Parliament."[13] Indeed, all municipal corporations were "[i]n their Nature . . . Communitys Politic and Civil Societys Invested with a Legislative Authority that shall bind all the Members & all others Inhabiting or maintaining any commerce within the Limits of their City or Town," and if their legislation was "just and reasonable . . . the Obligation then is absolute, and the party hath no way to Avoid it, but is bound as much to Submit to it as if Imposed by the Legislative Authority of the Kingdom."[14]

In explaining why local enactments, like local customs, were subject to the requirement of law and reason, judges observed that corporate acts were subordinate to the law of the land—that they "must ever be subject to the general law of the Realm as subordinate to it."[15] This amounted to a distinction between the acts of bodies with sovereign power and the acts of bodies without it. Chief Justice Holt observed that the mayor and aldermen of the City of London "have not a Sovereign power" and that therefore their by-laws "are so far valid as they are Agreeable to Law and right reason, and if contrary to either they are ipso facto void." The test of law and reason was in this way the common law's measure of when bodies without sovereignty remained within "those Matters . . . they are to perform with . . . Subordination to the Government of the Kingdom or State of which they are Members"—this subordination being the condition on which they could "Act as a State or Com[m]on Wealth."[16]

Later, it will be seen that whereas the common law evaluated subordi-

---

which the Incorporation getteth by such allowance is, That they shall not incur the penalty of forty pound[s] mentioned in the Act, if they put in use any Ordinances which are against the Kings' Prerogative, or the common profit of the people." Ibid. Ellesmere worried that Coke's report of *The Taylors of Ipswich* would encourage challenges to the authority of those who controlled corporations. Revealingly, however, he did not question the accuracy of Coke's report; nor did he support his assertion that the "true meaning" of the statute was different. "Observations on Ye Lord Cookes Reportes" (1615), in *Law and Politics in Jacobean England: The Tracts of Lord Chancellor Ellesmere,* 308, ed. Louis A. Knafla (Cambridge: Cambridge University Press, 1977).

[13] Coke, *Institutes,* 4: 2, 249.

[14] *City of London v. Wood* (1702), British Library, Add. Ms. 35980, fols. 2[r], 12[v].

[15] *Norris v. Staps* (C.P. 1616), Hobart, *Reports,* 211.

[16] *City of London v. Wood* (1702), British Library, Add Ms. 35980, fol. 13[r].

nate acts in accord with law and reason, it measured sovereign acts merely against the law. It will also become apparent that the absence of a test of reason for sovereign acts was an essential element of sovereignty. For now, however, it should suffice to note that under the law-and-reason test, judges often held subordinate acts and customs unlawful.

By-Laws under Corporate Charters

Charters added a layer of law between by-laws and the common law, and the judges therefore had to decide the lawfulness of by-laws and other corporate acts in accord with these corporate constitutions. Long before Americans created their constitutions, English judges thus held local legislation contrary to local charters or constitutions, and what is more, they fully understood the analogy between these local constitutions and the national one.

The judges decided the lawfulness of local legislation in accord with corporate charters because these constitutions usually came from the king with his authority under the law of the land. Being *"Bodies-Politique,"* corporations could enact laws "according to their Charter of Constitution."[17] Yet whereas in the constitutions of states the people granted and limited the sovereign legislative power, in corporate constitutions the Crown granted and limited the legislative power of subordinate governments. For example, on a *quo warranto* against the Mayor of Weymouth, who also served as an alderman, he pleaded a town by-law allowing a burgess of the town to hold both executive and legislative office—a by-law "by which any of the burgesses" could "be put in nomination for the mayoralty, though they were aldermen." The Crown objected that "the by-law is void in itself, being inconsistent with the charter, and creating a new constitution," for it gave "a power of electing the mayor out of the aldermen, which the charter never intended." The judges agreed—holding that the by-law was "entirely out of the case" because it gave the aldermen "a new power" that "the charter did not intend."[18]

The only serious doubt as to the obligation of corporate charters or constitutions concerned their provisions on representation, and when this issue eventually came to have implications for the constitution of the nation, the judges would have to wrestle with it. Municipal charters typically stated that the mayor and other leaders of a town were to be elected by its commonalty or burgesses, but over time it had become the practice in

[17] Shepheard, *Of Corporations,* title and 87.
[18] *King v. Mayor of Weymouth* (K.B. 1740), *Modern Reports,* 7: 373–374.

many towns for suffrage to be confined to "certain selected number of the principal of the Comminality, or Burgesses." Most dramatically, suffrage might be confined to those who sat in the common council. These practices or customs that narrowed suffrage ensured stability in municipal government and therefore seemed attractive to the Crown and its officers. Many burgesses, however, resented that they were excluded by these customary arrangements and therefore turned to their charters—particularly the clauses stating that elections were to be by the commonalty or by the burgesses, which seemed "as much [as] to say" that the elections were to be "by all the Commons, and all the Burgesses" or at least "by so many of them as would come to the election." Men thus relied on their written charters to demand "popular elections," and when this sort of demand for popular suffrage occurred in Ipswich and Doncaster, Elizabeth and her council became nervous about the implications. The council therefore in 1598 sought an opinion from the judges that the customary reduction of electorates was "good in Law."

The judges upheld the narrowing of suffrage, but only by straining the theory that ancient custom revealed consent. According to Coke's report of what he called the *Case of Corporations,* the judges began by resolving that corporate by-laws reducing suffrage could be "agreeable with the law and their charters"—at least if such enactments were by "common assent" and if they kept suffrage within some of the commonalty or burgesses. Of course, few if any of the relevant towns had passed any such by-law, but their ancient custom could be taken as evidence that there had once been such a by-law, and therefore "although now such . . . ordinance cannot be shewed, yet it shall be presumed and intended" from the "special manner of ancient and continual election." Thus far, the analysis of custom remained within a mode of reasoning that was familiar at common law. The practice of narrowing suffrage, however, was not really beyond the memory of man, and this forced the judges to stretch their notions of ancient custom. On the assumption that a narrowing of suffrage "could not begin without common consent," the judges had implied such consent from what was said to be ancient custom, but because in reality the custom was often recent, the judges ended up finding consent in "ancient and continual allowance and usage, although it began within time of memory."[19] With this less than satisfying account of consent through custom, the judges permitted local suffrage to

[19] *The Case of Corporations* (Serjeant's Inn 1598), Coke, *Reports,* 4: 77b–78. That the case arose from the situation in Ipswich and Doncaster is stated in a report of *Darcy v. Allen* (K.B. 1603), King's Bench Reports, British Library, Add. Ms. 25203, fol. 586[v], also printed in Charles Gray's mimeographed teaching materials. For the controversy in Ipswich, see Catherine F. Patterson, *Urban Patronage in Early Modern England*, 107–110 (Stanford: Stanford University Press, 1999).

depart from the requirements of municipal charters, and although at the time, when the government was worried about the stability of the country, they persuaded themselves that their permissive approach was justified by law, their argument was not very persuasive.

The judges soon recognized the broader implications of their laxity, and they therefore—especially in times of constitutional unease—tightened up their approach to charter guarantees of representation. In 1615, Coke and the rest of King's Bench emphasized that suffrage could only be reduced "by and with the general assent of the whole town."[20] The concerns persisted, however, and a century and a half later, during the Stamp Act controversy, some judges further hedged in the *Case of Corporations.* In 1766 in *Rex v. Spencer,* King's Bench had to consider a recent by-law of the town of Maidstone that had gone so far as reduce the electorate to the common council and other elected men, plus some former town officers. Although the lawyers for the defendant, a common council member, justified the restriction on the ground that suffrage "still rests virtually in the body of the commonalty, though restrained as to the particular persons," the judges responded that members of the common council were not part of the commonalty and that the by-law thus had taken the power of election out of the commonalty, contrary to the charter.[21]

One of the judges was particularly emphatic that a municipality's by-laws could never violate its charter or "constitution." In Coke's report of the *Case of Corporations,* it was not clear whether a commonalty's consent to the narrowing of their suffrage somehow defeated the obligation of their charter or whether their consent was simply assumed to be consistent with the charter. This was now a pressing question, and in *Rex v. Spencer* Justice Joseph Yates spelled out that "Corporations cannot make bye-laws contrary to their constitution. If they do, they act without authority."[22] Two years later, after Maidstone passed a new by-law slightly extending suffrage (to sixty elderly members of the commonalty), King's Bench also held this by-law "manifestly contrary to the intention of the charter," and Yates distinguished the *Case of Corporations* by explaining that "the by-law which was

[20] *The Corporation of Colchester* (K.B. 1615), Bulstrode, *Reports,* 3: 71.

[21] *Rex v. Spencer* (K.B. 1766), Burrow, *Reports,* 3: 1831, 1837.

[22] Ibid., 1839. The character of Justice Yates was such that Junius declared to Mansfield: "The name of Mr. Justice Yates will naturally revive in your mind some of those emotions of fear and detestation with which you always beheld him. That great lawyer, that honest man, saw your whole conduct in the light that I do. After years of ineffectual resistance to the pernicious principles introduced by your lordship, and uniformly supported by your *humble friends* upon the bench, he determined to quit a court, whose proceedings and decisions he could neither assent to with honour, nor oppose with success." Letter from Junius to Lord Mansfield (Nov. 14, 1770), *The Letters of Junius,* 2: 50 (New York: 1821).

put in question" in that early case "did not vary the constitution." He added that "where a corporation is by charter, and the common-council is created by the charter, they ought (as being the creature of the charter) to be restrained from making any by-laws inconsistent with it, or counteracting the end intention and directions of it."[23]

This unwillingness to permit any legislative violation of a corporate constitution became even more prominent in 1772 in the House of Lords. The charter of Helston in Cornwall gave the commonalty, aldermen, and mayor the power to elect freemen or burgesses, but a supposed by-law allegedly confined suffrage to the mayor and aldermen, thus depriving the commonalty of their right to vote. Although King's Bench gave judgment against the burgesses for usurpation of office, they brought a writ of error in Parliament, where their counsel relied on the *Case of Corporations.* When one of the judges objected that the by-law was "inconsistent with the constitution given by the charter," counsel for the burgesses claimed that the act of incorporation had not "expressly enjoined an indispensable adherence to the rules prescribed to the charter." The lawyers for the Crown answered "that the supposed bye-law" was "illegal, and void in its creation," for "all the bye-laws made by corporations, must be consistent with and subordinate to their constitution, under their charter." In support of this position, the Crown lawyers added that if a corporation "could make laws to alter their own constitution, the King's prerogative would be taken away." Chief Baron Thomas Parker then delivered the unanimous opinion of the judges that the by-law was not good—upon which the Lords affirmed the judgment of King's Bench.[24]

The by-laws concerning suffrage were only local legislation, and the charters or constitutions limiting these by-laws came from the Crown rather than the people. No one, however, misunderstood what it meant to say that a body's enactments had to be consistent with its constitution.

Review

At this point, it is worth pausing to consider a question of language. The judges could be said to engage in "review" whenever they decided the lawfulness of an act or custom of another body—whether a custom of a local manor, an act of a lower court or a corporation, or an act of the king him-

[23] *Rex v. Robert Cutbush* (K.B. 1768), Burrow, *Reports,* 4: 2207–2208.
[24] *John Hoblyn, and Others v. the King* (H.L. 1772), Brown, *Reports,* 6: 518–519.

self. Indeed, the judges themselves occasionally said they would "review" a custom or an act. Yet they used the word only rarely, and this was not a coincidence.

The English spoke of "review" in various contexts, both moral and more narrowly legal. For example, when alluding to the mental evaluation of an action under natural or divine law, the Puritan moralist William Ames described this as "the application of the Law by Conscience to the person, upon the Reviewing of the Action."[25] More concretely, English lawyers were familiar with bills of review in Chancery and commissions of review to hear ecclesiastical appeals.

Occasionally, a few common law judges mentioned their "review" of subordinate courts and laws. In the mid-seventeenth century, Chief Justice Matthew Hale discussed the power of King's Bench over the proceedings of all "subordinate" courts or jurisdictions—in particular, the Court's power "to review and examine their proceedings upon a writ of error."[26] Similarly, as has been seen, when Chief Justice Holt summarized the common law doctrine on by-laws, he explained that the acts or by-laws of London's Common Council "are Subject to the Review of the Kings Courts."[27]

The word "review," however, was not typically a label for any broader judicial role, for it was too narrow. As a practical matter, it did not adequately describe what the judges were doing: The word aptly described what judges did when examining the customs or acts of other bodies, but it could not so easily be used to refer to the further instances in which judges examined the lawfulness of laws—for example, when giving advisory opinions or adopting resolutions. Nor did the word adequately capture what the judges understood themselves to be doing, for rather than think that they had a distinct power of reviewing or otherwise determining lawfulness, they conceived themselves to have a duty to decide in accord with the law of the land. Both practically and conceptually, this was much broader—if also less ambitious—than any power of "review."[28] Accordingly, rather than use the label of "review," judges tended to speak of the office, duty, and oaths that required them to decide in accord with the law of the land.

[25] William Ames, *Conscience with the Power and Cases Thereof,* First Book, 28 (1639). See also ibid., 26ff.

[26] Matthew Hale, *The Prerogatives of the King,* 184, ed. D. E. C. Yale (London: Selden Society, 1976).

[27] *City of London v. Wood* (1702), in British Library, Holt's Opinions, Add. Ms. 35980, fol. 13[r].

[28] Coke, *Institutes,* 2: 51.

Judicial Acts

Although judges frequently held other judges to have erred, they only rarely held the act of another judge unlawful. Mere error—a judge's failure to decide in accord with the law—was not necessarily a failure to remain under law, and even when judges acted unlawfully, there was not often an occasion to hold their acts unlawful. Judicial decisions holding judicial acts unlawful were therefore very uncommon.

The judges of a court of record could not ordinarily be held legally accountable for their errors, because the record of their court was in the king's name. In this sense, the judges of a court of record made their decisions on the king's behalf, and their errors were his responsibility. This was evident from writs of error, which were issued in the king's name, and which called for the correction of errors done in his courts.[29] Even when a judge not merely committed error but also thereby violated a law that applied to him, he was acting in the king's name, and on such assumptions, it had been clear since the Middle Ages that a judge of a court of record could not be held liable for his judicial acts.[30]

Outside their jurisdiction, however, judges did not really act as judges, and their acts could therefore be held unlawful. As Chief Justice Bryan of Common Pleas explained in the 1490s, "[t]here is a difference between" an "erroneous" decision and one that was "void." Ordinarily, "all is . . . error and not void." Yet when a court went beyond its jurisdiction—for example, when Common Pleas heard a plea on an appeal—"all is void and not error," for "in the Common Bench we have no power to hold plea upon an ap-

[29] As James Whitlocke explained in 1610, "[s]o you see the Appeale is from the King . . . to the King" and "the writ is in his name" and thus "the rectifying and correcting [of] the errours is by him." [James Whitlocke], *A Learned and Necessary Argument To Prove that Each Subject Hath a Propriety in His Goods,* 10 (London: 1641).

[30] Holdsworth attributes this to the "sanctity of the records of courts of record." William Holdsworth, *A History of English Law,* 6: 235 (London: Sweet & Maxwell, 2003). To this, however, it must be added that in some courts there was no writ of error in the king's name, and the judges could be fined. For example, as Coke explained, "the Mayor and Jurats of the severall cinque Ports have power to hold pleas, &c. and upon their judgement no writ of errour out of the Chancery doth lye returnable in the kings Bench, nor writ of false judgement returnable into the court of common Pleas: but by the franchise and custome of the cinque Ports such an erroneous judgement shall be by bill, in the nature of a writ of errour, . . . And if the judgement be erroneous, it shall be reversed by the Warden of the cinque Ports, and the Mayor and Jurats shall be fined, and the Mayor removed from his place, and yet the court is a court of Record." Coke, *Institutes,* 2: 557. See also ibid., 4: 223. For the history of the notion of a court of record, see S. E. Thorne, "Courts of Record and Sir Edward Coke," in *Essays in English Legal History,* 243 (London: Hambledon, 1985). More generally, on judicial immunity, see the work of the late J. Randolph Block, "*Stump v. Sparkman* and the History of Judicial Immunity," *Duke Law Journal,* 879 (1980).

peal," and "in that case we who are justices . . . are punishable."[31] In other words, if the judges' "patent does not give them power and authority, then it is *coram non judice*."[32] Such was the conclusion in the *Case of the Marchalsea,* in which the judges of the Court of Marchalsea heard an action beyond their jurisdiction. Upon examining their judgment in 1612, King's Bench held the judges of the Marchalsea to be liable, for "when the Court has not jurisdiction of the cause, there the whole proceeding is *coram non judice,* and actions lie against them."[33]

The unlawfulness of the judges' acts outside their jurisdiction had come before the judges the year before in a more personal way when they were asked to sit on the Court of High Commission. In 1611 Coke and his brethren were requested to take oaths and sit as judges under a commission for ecclesiastical causes, but they refused because the commission "contained divers points against the Laws and Statutes of *England*." Even when "commanded to sit by force of the said Commission," Coke refused, and "all the time that the long Commission was in reading, the Oath in taking, and the Oration made, I stood and would not sit, as I was requested," and "so by my example did all the rest of the Justices."[34] They thereby refused a commission that, in their opinion, would require them to act without lawful jurisdiction.

The jurisdictional limit delineated when there could be a *judgment* against a judge for unlawful acts, but it left the judges little reason to distinguish in their *holdings* when a judge acted unlawfully. Sometimes a judge could err in a manner that was also contrary to law, and in this way he could violate both his duty as a judge to decide in accord with the law and his duty as a subject to act under law. Yet this distinction between what was erroneous and unlawful tended to get lost in the jurisdictional question. Regardless of whether a judge decided erroneously, he was vulnerable to a judgment against him if he acted outside his jurisdiction. Similarly, whether he acted lawfully or unlawfully in his decision, his erroneous judgments would merely be reversed if he remained within his jurisdiction. The

[31] Anon. (C.P. 1492 or 1493), in *Reports of Cases by John Caryll,* 1: 119, ed. J. H. Baker (London: Selden Society, 1999). For the very different civilian view, which exposed judges to liability, see Walter Ullmann, *The Medieval Idea of Law as Represented by Lucas de Penna: A Study in Fourteenth-Century Legal Scholarship,* 136 (1946; New York: Barnes & Noble, 1969); Julius Kirshner, "*Consilia* as Authority in Late Medieval Italy: The Case of Florence," in *Legal Consulting in the Civil Law Tradition,* 123–125, eds. Mario Ascheri, Ingrid Baumgärtner, and Julius Kirshner (Berkeley: Robbins Collection, 1999).

[32] Y.B. Michaelmas 22 Edward IV, pl.11, at 33b (1482), discussed by Holdsworth, *History of English Law,* 6: 236.

[33] *Case of the Marchalsea* (K.B. 1612), Coke, *Reports,* 10: 76a.

[34] Coke, *Reports,* 12: 88–89 (Lambeth Palace 1611).

cases therefore tended to focus on jurisdiction and error and did not ordinarily bother to clarify whether a judge went so far as to act contrary to law.

Bushell's Case can illustrate how even the most egregious judicial violations of law tended to get subsumed within the jurisdictional issue. Judges occasionally abused and even punished juries for failing to convict, and although it was said that these practices were "contrarie to the libertie and custome of the realme," some judges continued to penalize recalcitrant juries, thus leaving the matter open to question.[35] In the seventeenth century, however, it increasingly seemed difficult to examine any legal problem without getting down to the problem of authority, and jurors and judges thus became almost as self-conscious of their different spheres of authority as the Crown and Parliament. It therefore should be no surprise that the judges finally began systematically to analyze their relation to juries in terms of authority—the preeminent occasion being the case brought by Edward Bushell in 1670 before Common Pleas.

Bushell had the misfortune to be a juryman in the trial of two notable Quakers, William Penn and William Mead, who were prosecuted at the Old Bailey for an unlawful assembly—nothing more dangerous, in fact, than an unlicensed religious meeting on the aptly named Gracious Street. At trial, four jurors, including Edward Bushell, refused to convict the defendants, and the judges, especially the Recorder of London, Sir John Howell, therefore "used many unworthy threats" to persuade the recalcitrant jurors to reconsider, badgering and menacing them and repeatedly sending them back to reconsider their verdict. When the threats failed, Howell told the jurors, "I am sorry, Gentlemen, you have followed your own judgments and Opinions, rather than the good and wholsome advice, which was given you"—after which he fined each of them forty marks and imprisoned them until they paid. The trial thus ended with both the jurors and the defendants going to Newgate.[36]

The unrepentant Bushell challenged his imprisonment on a writ of habeas corpus. The sheriffs of London returned the writ with the explanation "[t]hat the Jury acquitted those indicted against the direction of the

[35] Thomas Smith, *De Republica Anglorum,* 89 (III.i) (London: 1583).

[36] [William Penn], *The Peoples Ancient and Just Liberties Asserted in the Tryal of William Penn, and William Mead,* 16–23, 61 ([London]: 1670). Penn added: "All the various kinds or models of Government, that are in the World, stand either upon *Will* and *Power,* or *Condition* and *Contract,* the first, rule by men, the second, by Laws." Of course, "[t]here is not any Country, that has more constantly exprest her care and deep solicitude, to the preservation of her fundamental Laws, then the *English* Nation," but the actions of the judges in the trial of the two Quakers "deprive us of our Lives and Liberties" and "rob us of (our Birthright) the Fundamental Laws of *England.*" Ibid., 31.

Court in matter of Law," but the judges of Common Pleas unanimously declared this return insufficient and discharged Bushell and his fellow jurors. The judges below and the jurors had disagreed about the facts, and as with the old problem of divergent reasoning about law, it was no longer enough to ask about the truth—to ask who was right. Instead, it seemed necessary to ask the preliminary question of who had authority to decide, and once the matter was considered in this way, it was difficult to avoid the conclusion that the decision belonged to the jurors.[37] Such was the holding of the judges of Common Pleas, and if they went this far, it might be thought that they would have also held that the Recorder and his colleagues had acted unlawfully. Yet the legal point was merely the insufficiency of the return, not a departure from jurisdiction, and the judges of Common Pleas therefore had no occasion to hold the action of the lower court judges contrary to law.

That judges could not ordinarily hold judicial acts unlawful became particularly clear when one of Bushell's fellow jurors pressed the matter. Rather than be content to go free, the persistent juror, John Hammond, brought an action of false imprisonment against the Recorder, John Howell. Hammond's lawyer began by saying that "it must be admitted that the imprisonment of the jury" for failing to pay its fine "was unlawful," and in support of this, he cited Magna Charta and the Petition of Right. Common Pleas, however, unanimously declared that "the bringing of this action was a "greater offence" than the judicial acts complained of. Just because the judges were "mistaken in such judgments, must that needs be against Magna Charta, the petition of right, and the liberties of the subject?"[38] It was undisputed that the Recorder in the trial of Penn and Mead had not merely failed to decide in accord with law but had also acted contrary to law; as Chief Justice Holt later recalled, Common Pleas had "discharged [Bushell] because he was Committed for a Fine illegally Imposed." The

[37] *Bushell's Case* (K.B. 1670), Vaughan, *Reports,* 137, 145. Langbein suggests that "the essential ground" of Chief Justice Vaughan's opinion was the knowledge of the jurors. John H. Langbein, "The Criminal Trial Before the Lawyers," *University of Chicago Law Review,* 45: 298, note 105 (1978). Certainly Vaughan discussed this at length. He made clear, however, that his conclusion turned on the old arguments about the divergent reasoning or judgments of men. He asked "whether any thing be more common, than for two men[,] Students, Barristers, or Judges, to deduce contrary and opposite Conclusions out of the same Case in Law?" And noting the possibility that similarly "two men should infer distinct conclusions from the same Testimony," he observed that "this often is the Case of the *Judge* and *Jury.*" Vaughan then said: "I conclude therefore, That this Retorn . . is no cause of Fine or Imprisonment." Vaughan, *Reports,* 141–142. More generally, see Thomas Andrew Green, *Verdict According to Conscience: Perspectives on the English Criminal Trial Jury 1200–1800,* Chapter 6 (Chicago: University of Chicago Press, 1985).

[38] *Hamond v. Howell* (C.P. 1677), *Modern Reports,* 2: 220.

judges, however, could not usually hold illegal judicial acts contrary to law, and in Hammond's case they only "held that no Action of false Imprisonment did lye." The judges in the trial of Penn and Mead had heard "a Matter within the Limits of their Jurisdiction," and therefore "thô they had proceeded illegally, Yet Acting as Judges they were not Accountable for it or lyable to any Action of the Party."[39] Within the judges' jurisdiction—the realm in which they merely erred—their unlawful acts were not likely to be held unlawful.

Royal Acts

The judges far more regularly held royal acts unlawful, and in these decisions the judges applied the law of the land to the apex of civil power. Many such decisions are discussed in English constitutional history, but as already observed, they have not been treated as part of the history of judicial review because they did not concern acts of Parliament. These decisions about acts of the Crown, however, reveal the strength of the judges' duty, for even in the medieval and early modern eras, when the monarch was still the dominant power in England, the judges frequently held his acts unlawful.

Few types of royal acts led to more decisions holding them void than the royal grants or charters that gave to one subject what had already been given to another. In 1519, for example, King's Bench held that "where the king, by his letters patent . . . grants me an office," and "then by other letters patent" he "grants the same thing to a stranger, these second letters patent are absolutely void."[40] This point was commonplace. As later put by William Sheppard—the author of a widely respected book on conveyancing—the king "cannot by any such Grant, take from any Subject any Jurisdiction or Franchise, that he hath well settled in him by former Grants of Kings, or Prescription," and "if he grant any thing . . . that he himself hath not, it is void."[41]

The judges could hold a grant unlawful not only for infringing the particular property right of an individual but also for violating the general

[39] *Hamon[d] v. Howell* (C.P. 1677), recited in *Grvanralt v. Burwall et al. Censors de le Coll de Physitians & Cose their Servant* (K.B. 1700), British Library, Holt's Opinions, Add. Ms. 35980, fol. 123[v]–124[r]. Incidentally, Holt later said that "the Authority of Bushels Case is beyond all these which upon the Debate were Considered and the practice of them Condemned & so that point rests in peace, never again to be questioned so long as there is Law & Liberty in England." *Carlton v. Mortagh* (K.B. 1704), ibid., fol. 55v.

[40] *Rex v. Savage* (K.B. 1519), in *Reports of Cases by John Caryll,* 2: 704.

[41] Shepheard, *Of Corporations,* 68, 79. For example, "[a] new Charter doth not merge or extinguish any of the ancient Privileges of the old Charter." Giles Jacob, *Law Dictionary,* Corporation, sig. Aa2,4[v] (London: 1732).

liberty or common right of the subject.[42] Such was the issue in a 1561 decision concerning the sweet Greek wine known as Malmsey. King Philip and Queen Mary had granted letters patent to the mayor, bailiffs, and burgesses of Southampton that no Malmsey wine was to be imported except at Southampton, and that anyone who imported such wine elsewhere was to pay treble the ordinary custom to the Crown. Nonetheless, Anthony Donate, Thomas Frederico, and other Venetian merchants imported Malmsey to Kent and then transported it by water to London. The Attorney General brought an information against them on behalf of Queen Elizabeth for the treble custom, and the case eventually came before all the judges in the Exchequer Chamber, where they held that "the law was against the queen." According to the judges, "the letters patent were against the laws, customs and statutes of this realm" both "in respect of the principal matter, concerning the restraint in the landing of malmseys at the pleasure and liberty of the denizens and aliens, and also in the assessment of the penalty of the treble custom," which was "utterly against the law."[43]

Many of the grants that restrained the liberty of the subject could be understood as grants of monopoly. The preeminent seventeenth-century case was *Darcy v. Allen* or *The Case of Monopolies,* in which the judges concluded that Queen Elizabeth's grant of the exclusive right to manufacture, import, and sell playing cards "was utterly void." The judges, as shown by Jacob Corré, were so divided in their reasoning that they did not publically deliver opinions, but they apparently agreed that the patent was void because "it is a monopoly, and against the common law"—in particular, because in restraining trade, it violated "the benefit and liberty of the subject."[44]

42 It was conventional to distinguish between "particular privileges" and the more "general liberties of the people," even if the particular rights ultimately rested upon the general liberties. *Norris v. Staps* (C.P. 1616), Hobart, *Reports,* 211.

43 *Attorney General. v. Donatt* (Ex. Ch. 1561), in *Reports from the Lost Notebooks of Sir James Dyer,* 1: 49–50, ed. J. H. Baker (London: Selden Society, 1994). Similarly, when Common Pleas in 1600 considered a grant from Henry VI to the Corporation of Dyers in London—that they have a "power to search, &c. and if they found any cloth died with logwood, that the cloth should be forfeited"—the judges held that "by the patent no forfeiture can be imposed on the goods of a subject." *Waltham v. Austin* (C.P. 1599), as discussed in *Case of London,* Coke, *Reports,* 8: 125a. See also the 1605 resolution about alnage discussed by Coke, *Institutes,* 2: 62.

44 *Case of Monopolies* (K.B. 1603), Coke, *Reports,* 11: 86a. In his learned study of *Darcy v. Allen,* Jacob I. Corré shows that the judges did not deliver opinions in court on the question of the monopoly, and that the conclusions reported by Coke must be taken with skepticism, but he concludes that "[b]oth sides acknowledged that the playing card patent had been found void as a restraint of trade." Jacob I. Corré, "The Argument, Decision, and Reports of *Darcy v. Allen,*" *Emory Law Review,* 45: 1324 (1996).

The Crown's own financial claims came into tension with the liberties of the people on the question of purveyance. The king's purveyor "had power to take provisions of all kinds for the king" and his household "at reasonable prices," but in requisitioning victuals and other provisions, the purveyor at times attempted to take more, including gravel and trees still growing on the land.[45] Magna Charta, however, barred the Crown from taking wood without the consent of the owner, and when the question of trees came before the judges in 1604, they resolved that "the kings Purveyor could take no Timber, growing upon the inheritance of the Subject, because it was parcell of the inheritance" as much as "the inheritance it selfe."[46]

By the same token, when the Crown had a more plausible financial demand, it could use a favorable judicial decision to show that it was acting lawfully—this being what the Crown did in *Bates's Case.* Parliament had enacted duties on imports, but James I demanded further impositions, including an imposition on currants equal to the amount already authorized by Parliament. An English merchant, John Bates, refused to pay this additional duty, arguing that it was "against the lawes of the land," but all the barons of the exchequer in 1606 upheld it as within the king's prerogative.[47]

Incidentally, the danger that a grant would be held void for infringing the rights of individuals or the general liberties of the subject was what induced Crown lawyers to specify in letters patent that the grant was for an invention or for a product or method new to England. Unaware of this legal point, some scholars assume that the Crown concerned itself with such matters because of a concerted policy to encourage inventions and imports, and some even assume that ideas about invention were still so novel as to be associated with imports. In fact, the Crown all too often granted monopolies to raise revenue or offer patronage, and Crown lawyers developed patents for inventions and imports to avoid running up against problems of property and freedom—the preexisting particular rights of individuals and the general liberties of the people.

45 Hale, *The Prerogatives of the King,* 274.

46 Coke, *Institutes,* 2: 35. James I eventually had to publicize that he would comply. He proclaimed that "some inferiour ministers have presumed to goe so farre beyond their Commission, as they have adventured not onely to take timber trees growing (which being parcell of our Subjects inheritance were never intended by us to be taken) without the good will and full contentment of the Owners, but have accustomed also to take up farre greater quantities of provisions . . . then ever came or were needfull for our use." James declared that he therefore "did particularly direct our Attorney generall to informe against them on our behalfe in our Court of Starre-chamber, where some of them upon their confession, have already received . . . condigne punishment by fine, imprisonment, pillorie, and loosing of their eares." Proclamation for Prevention of Future Abuses in Purveyance (April 23, 1606), *A Booke of Proclamations,* 124 (London: 1609).

47 *Case of Impositions* (Ex. 1606), *State Trials,* 2: 382; Coke, *Reports,* 12: 33–34. Tanner notes that "even the Parliamentarian Hakewill admitted afterwards that at the time, when he was listening to the judgments which the Exchequer Barons gave in favour of the Crown [in *Bates's Case*], he had been perfectly satisfied with their arguments." J. R. Tanner, *English Constitutional Conflicts of the Seventeenth Century 1603–1689,* at 43 (Cambridge: Cambridge

This decision disturbed members of the next Parliament, who worried that on a matter of such importance, the judges might have simply deferred to the Crown, and Solicitor General Francis Bacon therefore reminded the House of Commons that the judges had done their duty against the Crown in matters of equal consequence:

> And if any man shall think it was too high a point to question by law before the Judges, or that there should want fortitude in them to aid the subject; no, it shall appear from time to time in cases of equal reach, where the King's acts have been indeed against law, the course of law hath run, and the Judges have worthily done their duty.

The judges decided according to law, and thus if the Crown's acts were lawful, as Bacon suggested about *Bates's Case,* the remedy lay beyond the courts:

> The King's acts that grieve the subject are either against law and so void, or according to strictness of law and yet grievous; and according to these several natures of grievance there be several remedies. Be they against law? Overthrow them by judgment. Be they too strait and extreme, though legal? Propound them in Parliament.[48]

The judges, in Bacon's view, had done their duty in upholding the impositions in *Bates's Case,* and these royal acts that were merely "too strait and extreme" had to await a remedy in the legislature.

Not only discretionary impositions but also discretionary imprisonments came before the judges. When in 1591 Lord Chancellor Hatton and Lord Treasurer Cecil asked the judges for an advisory opinion about the power of the Queen or her privy councilors to commit persons to prison, the judges gave the requested opinion but simultaneously urged that Hatton and Cecil take action to prevent individuals from being imprisoned "by commandment of any nobleman or counsellor against the laws of the realm." The judges then listed some current abuses and concluded with the observation that "for remedy" of such imprisonments, the judges were "almost daily called upon to minister justice according to law, whereunto we are bound by our office and our oath."[49]

University Press, 1966). Whereas in *Donatt's Case,* concerning Malmsey wine, a penalty three times the imposition was held unlawful, *Bates's Case* only concerned an increase in the imposition itself.

[48] Argument of the King's Solicitor (June 28, 1610), in *The Works of Francis Bacon,* 11: 192, eds. James Spedding et al. (London: 1868).

[49] Declaration of Judges on Unlawful Imprisonments (June 9, 1591), in Holdsworth, *A History of English Law,* 5: 495–96. The 1591 opinion survived in two versions. Ibid., 5: 496–497; *State Trials,* 3: 76–77; J. A. Guy, "Origins of the Petition of Right Reconsidered," in

Beyond questions about the powers of government and the rights of subjects, the judges resolved what today would be considered structural questions within the government—such as when Queen Mary challenged the right of judges to appoint their clerks. The office in dispute was that of the exigenter of London, one of the four exigenters of the Court of Common Pleas, who prepared writs called "exigents." (These asked the sheriff of a county to make public proclamation for the appearance of defendants who eluded ordinary means of serving process.) In 1558, the exigenter of London, Thomas Hemming, died, and shortly afterward Chief Justice Richard Brooke of Common Pleas died without having yet appointed a new exigenter. Queen Mary could not resist the opportunity to fill both offices, and on the same day that she appointed Anthony Browne the new chief justice, she also granted the place of exigenter to Robert Coleshill, who had previously been "a man of war and a soldier." Browne, however, appointed his nephew Alexander Scroggs. The two recipients then disputed the matter at law, and they thereby brought into question whether the monarch could displace the right of the chief justice to fill the place. The judges of Common Pleas obviously had to step aside, but the judges of Queen's Bench and others present held "that the title of Coleshil was null, and that the gift of the said office by no means and at no time belongs or can belong to our lady the queen." On the contrary, "by reason of prescription and usage," the office "is only in the disposal of the Chief Justice for the time being, as an inseparable incident belonging to the person of the said Chief."[50]

Law, Liberty, and Parliament: Selected Essays on the Writings of Sir Edward Coke, 328, ed. Allen D. Boyer (Indianapolis: Liberty Fund, 2004). In 1605, in a very different context, the judges defended their issuing of writs of prohibition against ecclesiastical courts by explaining that "if we see not a just cause of the parties imprisonment by them, then we ought, and are bound by oath to deliver him." Coke, *Institutes,* 2: 616. Baker traces the history of judicial decisions on imprisonments and in this connection observes that the "independent spirit" of the Tudor judiciary enabled them "to react to autocratic tendencies in government by encouraging the development of habeas corpus into a remedy whereby the humblest subject could challenge the greatest ministers of the crown in the courts." J. H. Baker, "Personal Liberty under the Common Law, 1200–1600," in *The Common Law Tradition: Lawyers, Books and the Law,* 321 (London: Hambledon, 2000).

[50] *Scroggs v. Coleshill* (1559), Dyer, *Reports,* 2: 175b; *Reports from the Lost Notebooks of Sir James Dyer,* 1: 24; *The Reports of Sir John Spelman,* 2: 380. There was an attempt to have the dispute decided by a special commission, but the judges apparently held the commission void. Baker, "Personal Liberty under the Common Law," 343–344. Another such dispute in 1558 concerned the so-called Clerk of Hell. *Reports from the Lost Notebooks of Sir James Dyer,* 1: 23. According to Coke, "it appeareth that the Justices of Courts did ever appoint their Clerks, some of which after by prescription grew to be Officers of their Courts." Coke, *Institutes,* 2: 425. Finch noted that the statute 5 Edward VI, cap. 16 against the sale of office "extendeth not . . . to any offices to be given by the chief Justices of the Kings bench, or

With similar reasoning, the judges decided against the power of the king to delegate his personal power. The monarch had a prerogative power to dispense with the law, but if the power was inherent in him, he could not delegate it. Nonetheless, Queen Elizabeth had done precisely this. In her desperation to raise money, she made "a grant . . . of the penalty and benefit of a penal statute, with power to dispense with the said statute, and to make a warrant to the Lord Chancellor, or Keeper of the Great Seal, to make as many dispensations, and to whom he pleased." It was one thing to sell the right to receive fines collected under a statute, but it was another to sell the right to dispense with the act. In 1604, under Elizabeth's successor James I, the judges were asked to consider "the validity" of this grant. All of the judges resolved that the grant was "utterly against Law":

> [W]hen a statute is made *pro bono publico,* and the King (as the head of the commonwealth, and the fountain of justice and mercy,) is by the whole realm trusted with it; this confidence and trust is so inseparably joined and annexed to the Royal person of the King in so high a point of sovereignty, that he cannot transfer it to the disposition or power of any private person, or to any private use: for it was committed to the King by all his subjects for the good of the commonwealth.

Thus, "the King cannot commit the sword of his justice, or the oil of his mercy, concerning any penal statute to any subject." These powers "cannot by law be transferred."[51]

The king's power to make law came before the judges in 1610 in two advisory opinions on proclamations. Tudor kings had assumed that in responding to exigencies they needed a power to regulate without the consent of Parliament, and with a broad sense of their authority, they issued numerous proclamations. These edicts, like the administrative regulations of later centuries, sometimes merely imposed duties on government officers, but they often drifted into imposing new duties on the people.[52] The awkward-

Co[m]monplace, or by any Justices of Assize." Henry Finch, *Law, or, a Discourse Thereof,* 164 (London: 1627).

[51] *Penal Statutes* (1605), Coke, *Reports,* 7: 36b–37a. The Statute of Monopolies in its preamble rejected this sort of delegation. As Coke summarized, "[i]t appeareth by the Preamble of this Act that all Grants of the benefit of any penall law, or of power to dispence with the law, or to compound for the forfeiture, are contrary to the ancient fundamental lawes of this Realm." Coke, *Institutes,* 3: 186.

Similarly, judicial office was inalienable. William Marshall's First Lecture (1516), in *John Spelman's Reading on Quo Warranto,* 61 Appendix 1 (E); Brooke, *Abridgment,* "Office & Off." pl. 39 (citing 9 Edward IV, 31); Viner, *Abridgment,* 14: 581.

[52] This sort of drift can be observed in federal regulations during the nineteenth century. As for sixteenth-century England, although Crown lawyers took care, as much as possible, that any command in a proclamation was "not stated as a new limitation on the subject's liberty,"

ness was that proclamations thereby became an exercise of absolute power.[53] Particularly after Tudor monarchs resisted papal claims by asserting the supremacy of royal law, including acts of Parliament, it became difficult to gloss over the problem that the king's use of proclamations to "co[erce] offenders" was a power exercised not through "ordynarie lawe" but above it.[54]

This question of royal authority came to a head when in 1610 James I and Parliament were struggling over the king's power of impositions. At a time when Parliament was disputing the king's power to impose duties on imports, James hoped to use proclamations in ways that would allow him to raise money outside of Parliament.[55] In these circumstances, an earlier monarch might have tactfully left some ambiguity about the potential of his proclamations to become an avenue for absolute power, but like so many of his contemporaries, James was more anxious than prudent about questions of authority, and he was not discreet about his view that he enjoyed an "irregular" power of issuing proclamations outside of ordinary or regular law—and not only "in Cases of Necessity."[56] The result is well

---

proclamations frequently had this effect. Paul L. Hughes and James F. Larkin, eds., *Tudor Royal Proclamations,* 1: xxvii (New Haven: Yale University Press, 1964). Another scholar draws "[t]he striking revelation" from his statistical analysis "that early Tudor proclamations seldom made new law." R. W. Heinze, *The Proclamations of the Tudor Kings,* 59 (Cambridge: Cambridge University Press, 1976).

53 The underlying theory is suggested by the famous exchange in which Thomas Cromwell, citing civil law, encouraged Henry VIII to believe that "his will and pleasure" was "regarded for a lawe." The Bishop of Winchester, Stephen Gardiner, answered the king that "the forme of his reigne, to make the lawes his wil, was more sure and quiet. 'And by thys forme of government ye be established.'" Letter from Stephen Gardiner to Protector Somerset (Oct. 14, 1547), in *The Letters of Stephen Gardiner,* 399, ed. James Arthur Miller (Cambridge: University Press, 1933).

54 An Acte that P[ro]clamac[i]ons made by the King shall be obeyed, 31 Henry VIII, c. 8 (1539). The Statute of Proclamations temporarily avoided the difficulties by stating that Henry VIII and his council could use proclamations to impose such "penalties and paynes" as they thought "necessarie and requisite"—as long as the statute was not thereby used to deprive persons of their legal rights or to permit existing law to be infringed, broken, or subverted. Ibid. What is significant here is that the Statute of Proclamations candidly acknowledges the need to place proclamations—not least, those made in "cases of necessitie"—on the footing of "an ordynarie lawe."

55 His proclamations would at least have allowed him to collect fines from offenders. Some proclamations, such as that against making starch, could also be tied to the sale of monopolies to engage in the forbidden activities. According to Esther Cope, the question of proclamations arose from a complaint from the Commons in July 1610, and Edward Alford declared in November that "we stand upon impositions and proclamations." Esther S. Cope, "Sir Edward Coke and Proclamations, 1610," *American Journal of Legal History,* 15: 216–217 (1971).

56 A Proclamation Signifying his Majesties Pleasure Touching Some Former Proclamations (Sept. 24, 1610), *A Booke of Proclamations,* 236 (London: 1609); James I, Answer to both Houses concerning the Grievances complained of by the Commons (July 23, 1610), *Journal of the House of Lords* 2: 659 (London: 1802).

known. As recorded by Chief Justice Coke, "I was sent for to attend" Lord Chancellor Ellesmere and others, including the Lord Treasurer, who asked Coke whether "the King by his Proclamation may prohibit new Buildings in and around *London*" and similarly whether he "may prohibit the making of Starch of Wheat." Coke protested that "I did not heare of these questions until this morning, at nine of the Clock," and asked for time to confer with his brethren so he could "make an advised answer according to law and reason." Lord Chancellor Ellesmere responded that "he would advise the Judges to maintaine the power and Prerogative of the king" and even suggested that "in cases in which there is no authority and President," the judges should "leave it to the king to order it according to his wisdome"—a hint, as will be seen, about a royal power to interpret legislatively in the interstices of law. Coke responded with an impromptu advisory opinion that "the King cannot change any part of the Common Law, nor create any Offence by his Proclamation, which was not an Offence before, without Parliament."[57]

Rather than concede this point, James soon issued yet another proclamation, which attempted to place his absolute power on a constitutional footing. He proclaimed his intent to publish all of his proclamations in a book—as if they were like statutes—and he defended his power of proclamation in absolutist terms, it being a power "to apply speedy, proper, and convenient remedies . . . in matters so variable and irregular in their nature, as are not provided for by Law, nor can fitly fall under the certaine rule of a Law." He understood that his claim might seem to threaten the law of the land and the power of Parliament, and he therefore took care to acknowledge that "by the constitution of the frame and policie of this Kingdome, Royall Proclamations and Ordinances are not of equall force, nor in the like degrees with our Laws."[58] Yet even in thus conceding that his power of proclamation did not reach above the law of the land, he simultaneously, in

[57] *Case of Proclamations* (Sept. 8, 1610), Coke, *Reports,* 12: 76. Coke's point was commonplace. For example, Yelverton in 1571 said in the Commons that "[t]he prince . . . could not of her selfe make lawes, nether might shee by the same reason breake laws." *Proceedings in the Parliaments of Elizabeth I,* 1: 239 (April 20, 1571), ed. T. E. Hartley (London: Leicester University Press, 1981–1995). In 1587, Peter Wentworth had asked: "Whether there be anie councell which cann make, adde to, or diminishe from, the lawes of this realme but onelie this councell of Parliament." Ibid., 2: 328. Incidentally, although Coke said he was consulted about the two proclamations in September 1610, James signed a proclamation against the making of starch a month beforehand. Perhaps significantly, a separate publication of this proclamation apparently does not survive.

[58] A Proclamation Signifying his Majesties Pleasure Touching Some Former Proclamations, *A Booke of Proclamations,* 236. James already had alluded to the constitutional argument in his speech of July 23.

his backhanded way, was asserting that he had constitutional authority to act outside the law in creating new offenses.

The king's council was more cautious and insisted on receiving a formal opinion from the judges, who declared that the king "by the laws of this realm cannot by his proclamation create any thing to be an offense which was not an offense before against the laws of this realm."[59] Coke added in his report that "the King by his Proclamation, or other waies, cannot change any part of the Common Law, or Statute," and that there were "divers Presidents of Proclamations which are utterly against Law and reason, and for that void."[60] Looking back from mid-century, Matthew Hale summarized that the king's lack of any "legislative power" outside of Parliament was settled "by the constitution of this realm."[61]

These decisions holding royal acts unlawful are not unfamiliar as part of English constitutional history. They also need to be recognized, however, as instances in which, as Bacon said, "the Judges have worthily done their duty."

The Supremacy of the Law of the Land over All Royal Acts

It is necessary to take a brief detour away from the decisions about royal acts to understand how the king's acts of absolute power came to be viewed as under law and thus within the hands of the judges. While English kings could plausibly claim that some of their power was absolute—that it was above the law—the authority of the judges to do their duty with respect to the full range of royal acts remained in doubt. Once it became clear, however, in the seventeenth century, that even the king's absolute power was under the law of the land—most fundamentally, under the constitution—the judges confidently did their duty as to all acts of the king.

The capacity of the judges to do their duty with respect to all royal acts became a matter of open dispute after Crown lawyers in the last half of the sixteenth century systematically made it explicit that part of the royal prerogative was absolute. Crown lawyers had traditionally left this understated, but they now frequently spelled out that whereas some royal power was regularly ordained through law, other royal power was irregular, absolute, or above the law of the land.[62]

[59] Certain Resolutions Concerning Proclamations (Oct. 26, 1610), in Cope, "Sir Edward Coke and Proclamations, 1610," 221.

[60] *Case of Proclamations* (1610), Coke, *Reports* 12: 76. Coke attributed the October resolution to the two Chief Justices, the Chief Baron, and Baron Altham. Ibid.

[61] Hale, *The Prerogatives of the King,* 141. See also ibid., 172.

[62] Only very late did it became conventional for common lawyers openly to discuss the distinction between absolute and ordinary power. It "appeared in the Year Book for 1469 . . .

The Crown in this period had to assert its claim of absolute power to overcome the strength of its own ideals of lawmaking authority. Against the pope, Henry VIII and later monarchs claimed an exclusive lawmaking authority within their realm, at least when sitting in Parliament, and concomitantly they insisted upon the exclusive jurisdiction of their courts. They thereby, however, as has been seen, elevated ideals of lawmaking authority and unified jurisdiction that seemed to confine them to acting solely through the law of the land. Crown lawyers therefore drew on civilian learning to argue that kings could assert their authority both through and above law. The king, they argued, had an exclusive lawmaking authority in Parliament, but in addition he had an authority above the law—at least in matters inherent in the king's person or essential for the preservation of the realm.

Of course, if the king could exercise his will above the law, he could not be questioned for it under law, and he alone was therefore the final judge. As Henry Yelverton said about the king's prerogative in impositions, "Wee are where the common lawe cannot judge." Impositions were a matter of "reason of government," and therefore "[t]hoe the imposition be excessive, yet none can judge it but the King."[63] Similarly, James assembled the judges in 1616 to tell them that "the absolute Prerogative of the Crown" was "no subject for the tongue of a lawyer, nor is it lawful to be disputed."[64] The king, in other words, had "a double prerogative," and although "the one was ordinary and had relation to his private interest, which might be, and was every day, disputed in Westminster-Hall; the other was of an higher nature, referring to his supreme and imperial power and sovereignty, which ought not to be disputed or handled in vulgar argument."[65] The one prerogative was ordained through or at least under law and so was subject to judicial determinations; the other was so sovereign that the king considered it altogether above both the law and the courts.

being applied there, however, to the difference between the legal powers wielded by the Court of Chancery and those wielded by the Common Law Courts." Francis Oakley, "Jacobean Political Theology: The Absolute and Ordinary Powers of the King," *Journal of the History of Ideas,* 29: 324 (1968). At about the same time, in his treatises, Chief Justice Fortescue alluded to the king's power through law and above it, but in terms of the somewhat different distinction between political and royal regimes and a mixed regime such as that of England. S. B. Chrimes, *English Constitutional Ideas in the Fifteenth Century,* 174 (Cambridge: Cambridge University Press, 1936). Finally, in the sixteenth century, allusions to absolute power begin to turn up regularly not only among importunate courtiers but also among common lawyers.

63 Speech of Henry Yelverton (June 29, 1610), in *Parliamentary Debates in 1610,* at 87–88, ed. Samuel Rawson Gardiner (Westminster: Camden Society, 1862).

64 *The Letters and the Life of Francis Bacon,* 5: 384, ed. James Spedding (London: 1869).

65 Act of Council Concerning Commendams (June 6, 1616), ibid., 5: 363.

Underlying these royal claims to an absolute prerogative were deeper assumptions about the capacity of men to live fully under law. If human law could not fully anticipate the exigencies that might threaten a government or its people, all rulers needed a power unconstrained by law—a power above law and of which only they could judge. Baron Weston asked in the *Shipmoney Case:* What if an act of Parliament required the king alone to pay for "the defence of the kingdom" but "there was a greater power at sea, than the king was able to make defence against"? Then "should this not give way to the present necessity," lest "the kingdom . . . be lost?" On such reasoning, even "acts of parliament should give way to necessity."[66] Justice Berkeley similarly generalized that "there was a *Rule of Law,* and a *Rule of Government,*" and "many things which might not be done by the Rule of Law might be done by the Rule of Government."[67]

That human beings were not capable of establishing government entirely under human law was an interesting proposition for academic dispute, but it was sobering to hear this declared from the bench in cases involving men's liberty, for if the judges themselves acknowledged that kings had a power above the law in matters of necessity, then there could be no legal limit on the abuse of such power. As Benjamin Rudyard recognized in 1628 in the debates on the Petition of Right, the basic problem was that "it lies not in the wit of man to devise such a law as should be able to comprehend all particulars, [and] all accidents," and "yet must the law be general, for otherwise admissions and exceptions will fret, and eat out the law to nothing."[68] "Necessity," the poet Edmund Waller observed, had the effect of "dissolving all Law."[69]

Against this danger, some argued that if God himself chose to govern in accord with his law, the king should govern in accord with his. Indeed, because Calvin had imagined that God exercised his will without resorting to absolute power, and because some Calvinists even assumed that God had

[66] *State Trials,* 3: 1075. In contrast, Sir George Croke relied on his duty, which was recited in the mittimus, and he noted that this left no room for considerations of convenience or reason of state: "The mittimus is that the barrons shall proceed secundum legem et consuetudines Regni Anglie; so wee are not to judge here according to conveniency or state policy, but according to the common law and custome of England we are to judge." "Notes of the Judgment Delivered by Sir George Croke in the Case of Ship-Money," in *Camden Miscellany,* 7: 1–2, ed. Samuel Rawson Gardiner (London: Camden Society, 1875).

[67] *Richard Chambers v. Lord Mayor of London Edward Bromfeild* (K.B. 1636), in *Historical Collections,* 2: 323, ed. John Rushworth (London: 1721). This was an action, brought by a merchant who refused to pay shipmoney, against the Lord Mayor for trespass and false imprisonment. Berkeley's words came back to haunt him when he was impeached. Ibid., 2: 609.

[68] Speech of Benjamin Rudyard (April 28, 1628), *State Trials* 3: 173.

[69] Speech of Edmund Waller on Shipmoney (1640), in *Historical Collections,* 3: 1339.

willed his natural law, what had once been merely an analogy from the divine model of lawfulness now came close to an argument about divine authority.[70] Believing that God had ordained the office of magistrate, perhaps even through his natural law, Calvinists of Edward Coke's generation could envision a breadth of rule through law or at least under it that equally included all rulers, divine and human, and Englishmen in this way acquired a profound sense of lawful governance, reaching from the planets created by God (and increasingly observed through science) down to the little worlds, the governments, created by men. Advocates for the Crown could still claim that the king enjoyed an absolute power in imitation of God, but many other men easily relied on a combination of Calvinism and the common law to answer that throughout the universe, power was exercised under law and even through it.[71]

Not content with theological argument, those mistrustful of royal ambition increasingly insisted that the king enjoyed discretion in the exercise of his absolute prerogative, but only within the limits of the law of the land—this being the argument that would bring the absolute prerogative before the judges. If the king's law had a divinely derived obligation, and if no other law could be binding within the realm, except as allowed by the king's law, then there seemed no room for any power, even royal power, that was not subject to the law. Richard Martyn summarized this point in 1610 in the House of Commons when he argued against impositions that "[t]he comon lawe extends as farre [as] the power of the Kinge extends" and that "[t]he King of England is the most absolute Kinge in his Parliament; but, of hymself, his power is lymited by lawe."[72] Looking back on abuses of the

[70] Such questions are elegantly discussed by Francis Oakley, *Omnipotence, Covenant, and Order: An Excursion in the History of Ideas from Abelard to Leibniz,* 109 (Ithaca: Cornell University Press, 1984). For Calvin's reluctance to distinguish absolute power, see Francis Oakley, "The Absolute and Ordained Power of God in Sixteenth- and Seventeenth-Century Theology," *Journal of the History of Ideas,* 59: 457 (1998).

[71] The religious analogy for lawful governance was used not only against the absolute power of the Crown but also eventually against that of Parliament—for example, by Captain John Streater. He fought for Parliament against the king at Newbury and Edgehill, but in 1653, when Parliament now asserted an absolute power, this erstwhile supporter of Parliament protested that "neither Princes nor Parliaments are . . . absolute in their power," and eventually his publications earned him imprisonment without trial. Streater, however, obtained a habeas corpus and argued to the judges that Parliament was no more above English law than God was above his: "God himself bindeth himself by his laws: he is as well bound, as he bindeth those several beings he gives laws unto, let them be eternal, moral or natural. If he maketh a promise, he performeth it: he must not, he doth not but perform it." Thus, "Law is supreme; none ought to command contrary to law." *Trial of John Streater* (K.B. 1653), *State Trials,* 5: 374. Although Streater took an unusually confined view of what was possible for God, it was a familiar Calvinist point that God did not act absolutely.

[72] Speech of Richard Martyn (June 29, 1610), in *Parliamentary Debates in 1610,* at 89. An-

prerogative, Coke explained to the Commons in 1628 that "the king's Prerogative is a part of the law of this kingdom, and a supreme part . . . yet it hath bounds set unto it by the laws of England."[73]

This dispute over the king's absolute prerogative almost inevitably expanded into a quarrel over the jurisdiction of the different courts. In the Middle Ages, the different courts in England had decided in accord with different systems of law—whether the common law, the canon law, or the civil law. The Crown in the sixteenth century had sought to preserve its absolute power from the common law judges by keeping much of its prerogative within the jurisdiction of the non-common-law courts, and to this end, it increasingly asserted the independence of these "prerogative" courts from

---

other member similarly observed: "The wall betwixt the King and his subjects are his lawes. Now to what purpose are lawes, if his Majestie or his ministers will leape over or breake down this wall." Speech of Thomas Beaumont (Nov. 6, 1610), ibid., 129.

The ideal of lawful governance in England was such that even James I and his advisers found it necessary to place the absolute prerogative on a legal foundation. Chancellor Ellesmere, for example, explained that the king had an "absolute prerogative" that was "revealed by his lawes." Discourse concerning the Royall Prerogative (c.1604), in *Law and Politics in Jacobean England,* 197. Although W. J. Jones takes such statements by Ellesmere to mean that he agreed with Coke, it must be questioned whether a power revealed by law was necessarily a power limited by law. See, e.g., W. J. Jones, "The Crown and the Courts in England, 1603–1625," in *Law, Liberty, and Parliament: Selected Essays on the Writings of Sir Edward Coke,* 284.

73 Speech of Edward Coke (March 24, 1628), *State Trials,* 3: 68. As Coke explained in his *Institutes,* "the kings prerogative is part of the Law of England, and comprehended within the same." Coke, *Institutes,* 2: 496. Parker wrote: "I allow the King to be supreme, and consequently sole Judge in all cases whatsoever, as to the right, and as to the diffusion of Judgement; but as to the exercise and restraint of judgement, he is not, nor ought to be accounted sole Judge. In matters of Law the King must create Judges, and sweare them to judge uprightly and impartially, and for the subject against himselfe, if Law so require, yea, though he be of contrary judgement himselfe." Henry Parker, *The Case of Shipmoney Briefly Discoursed,* 20 ([London]: 1640). Matthew Hale observed that "[i]t is regularly true that the king is bound by his own laws . . . because he hath not a sole or at least an absolute power of making or altering laws, but a qualified [power], requiring the consent of others to concur." Hale, *The Prerogatives of the King,* 176.

The oaths of the judges specifically required them to "not assent to things that may turn to" the king's "damage or disinheritance," including, presumably, his prerogative, but if the prerogative was subject to law, this requirement was not incompatible with the duty to decide in accord with law. *The Book of Oaths,* 6 (London: 1689). For example, when Justice George Croke dissented in the *Shipmoney Case* and questioned the issuance of the writ of shipmoney to inland counties, he said: "I do not conceive there is any such prerogative; for if it were a prerogative, I should not offer to speak against it: for it is part of our oaths, that are judges, to maintain the king's prerogative to the best of our skill, and not to suffer the same to be diminished." The prerogative, however, was limited by law: "But if it be as I have argued, That is against the common law, and against so many statutes, that the subjects should be inforced to sustain, or to contribute to any charge, without the special consent, or common assent in parliament, then there is no such prerogative." Crooke's Opinion in the Shipmoney Case (1638), *State Trials,* 3: 1161.

any supervisory jurisdiction by the courts of the common law. The jurisdiction of the courts thus became the focus of the Crown's attempt to keep its absolute power unconstrained by the common law and its judges, and not coincidentally, this struggle happened at a time when attitudes about divided jurisdiction had largely changed. Although it would once have seemed conventional to have jurisdiction divided among different courts that decided in accord with different systems of law, this now took on a more ominous significance, for amid the ideals of lawmaking authority and unified jurisdiction that English monarchs had relied upon against the pope, the independence of the non-common-law courts seemed nothing less than a threat to the supremacy of the law of the land.[74] Coke in particular could not avoid looking down into the chasm of lawlessness that seemed to lie only just below the surface of the jurisdictional conflict. Assuming that there could be no government power above the law of the land and that the judges had a duty to decide in accord with this law, he defended the supremacy of both the law of the land and its courts.[75] *Bonham's Case* was part of this struggle, for when Coke wrote that the common law controlled acts of Parliament, he was asserting the supremacy of the common law and its courts in interpreting acts of Parliament.[76] In the end, in 1641, Parliament settled the underlying question of absolute power by abolishing

[74] Shortly before the Act of Appeals, St. Germain examined the claims for the supervisory jurisdiction of the common law courts in his dialogue between Salem and Byzance. Salem argued that jurisdiction could be transferred to the king's courts from that of the ordinaries or ecclesiastical judges "if it shoulde happen to appere by experience, that it were as good or better to the kynges subjectes, to have su[ch]e matters determined in his courtes, as in the ordinaries," and he explained that he said this merely to clarify the authority of English law. "Nevertheles I speke not this to thentent, that I wolde that such suites shulde be broughte to the kynges courte, but that hit maye appere, that prelates holde plee therof by the custome of the realme, and by the sufferaunce of the kynge and of his lawes: and not by the imediate auctoritie of the lawe of god." St. German's other character, Byzance, was puzzled: "If they may holde plee of suche thynges, it is all to one effecte, whether it be by the lawe of god, or by the lawe of man"—prompting Salem to explain: "Nay for if they have it only by custome, it may with a cause be taken fro theym, and that maye happely cause them to take the better hede, how they order theym selfe in hit. And yf it were by the lawe of god: then it might in no wyse be altered." More generally, Salem hoped that in temporal matters, in which spiritual courts held pleas only on sufferance of English law, that "they wyll judge therin after the law of the realme as they are bounde to do." [Christopher St. German], *The Addicions of Salem and Bizance,* fols. 14[v]–15[r], 35[v]–36[v] (London: 1534).

[75] Predictably, Chancellor Ellesmere took another point of view. He complained about "the desire of the Reporter [Coke] to intrude upon other mens profession and to weaken the power of the Ecclesiasticall Court, as if they were not absolute in themselves in Jurisdiccions naturally belonging to them, but Subordinate [to] the Judges of the Common Law to be Controlled in thinges that fall not within ye Levall of the Common Lawe." "Observations on Ye Lord Cookes Reportes" (1615), in *Law and Politics in Jacobean England,* 297.

[76] See Appendix I.

the Star Chamber and High Commission, which had been the most threatening of the prerogative jurisdictions.

All sovereign power, even the most absolute, thus came to be bounded by the common law and exercised through its courts, and this meant it was within the reach of the judges in doing their duty. As Hale explained, the law "will determine what rights the prince hath absolutely" and "what qualified." Accordingly,

> *Potestas imperii* or *regalis* in England hath two qualifications: (1) That it is not absolute or unlimited, but bounded by rule and law. (2) It is not simple but mixed with jurisdiction, for the contempt or disobedience to his command ought to receive his punishment by that jurisdiction which the king is intrusted with, *viz.* in his courts of justice.[77]

The sovereign's power—even that which had been absolute—could now only be exercised under the law of the land and through its courts, and it thus was subject to the decisions of the judges who were bound to decide in accord with this law.

Absolute Power as Sovereignty: Discretion over Reason and under Law

Inasmuch as the judges after midcentury clearly had jurisdiction over the king's absolute prerogative, it may be thought that this chapter could finally turn to judicial decisions based on the constitution. One further delay is necessary, however, for the law treated acts within the king's sovereign power differently from subordinate acts, and it is essential to consider this distinction before returning at last to the decisions that held government acts unlawful and even, it will be seen, unconstitutional.

The essence of sovereignty was an exercise of discretionary will—an exercise of will in which the sovereign had the final judgment as to what was reasonable. Accordingly, even once the king's absolute power came to be recognized as unquestionably under the law, this power remained the sphere in which the sovereign had the final judgment about the reasonableness of his acts. Whereas subordinate acts were measured by the old test of law and reason, sovereign acts were measured simply by law.

The monarch had "absolute" or "sovereign" power both in various per-

[77] Hale, *The Prerogatives of the King,* 7, 269. Holt observed that "the Court of the King's Bench hath the Supreme Intendancy over all Jurisdictions and Authoritys in England that are either Ancient or New Erected by any Act of Parliament." *Grvanralt v. Burwall et al. Censors de le Coll de Physitians & Cose their Servant* (K.B. 1700), British Library, Holt's Opinions, Add. Ms. 35980, fol. 122[r].

sonal prerogatives and more generally in Parliament. His absolute personal prerogatives were those inherent in him and those that he needed for the preservation of the realm. In addition, the king exercised a general sovereign power in Parliament—this being "the kynges most hyghe and soverayne courte" and "[t]he most high and absolute power of the realme of Englande."[78]

That sovereign acts stood above judicial second-guessing about their reasonableness was clear enough from acts of Parliament. There were legal obstacles to judicial decisions holding acts of Parliament unlawful, and it might be disputed whether Parliament was subject to the law of the land, but in addition it was apparent that although Parliament was subject to natural law, it had absolute discretion in judging whether its own acts accorded with natural law. Natural law or reason, it will be recalled, had come to be widely understood as a measure of allegiance to government rather than of the obligation of its particular laws, and judges recognized that (regardless of whether the law of the land was a measure of the lawfulness of an act of Parliament) the reasonableness of such an act belonged to the sovereign judgment of Parliament and ultimately the people.

This was the conclusion of Chief Justice Holt in 1702 in *City of London v. Wood.* Coke's report of *Bonham's Case* had sometimes been misread to suggest that a judge could hold an act of Parliament unlawful for being unreasonable—as if it were the act of a subordinate body—and now in *City of London v. Wood* Holt suggested a more plausible remedy by noting the difference between the acts of a body with "Sovereign power" and the acts of bodies with subordinate power. The acts of towns or other corporations "are Subject to the review of the Kings Courts" and "are so far valid as they are Agreeable to Law and right reason, & if contrary to either they are ipso facto void," but "an Act of parliament . . . binds Absolutely without any dispute to be made of its Justice or Equity." In short, there were not merely impediments to any judicial decision holding an act of Parliament unconstitutional or otherwise unlawful, but also the law itself left the reasonableness of a statute to Parliament.[79]

The people, however, could decide what the judges could not. If Parliament were to make a man judge in his own case, its enactment would escape a decision of the judges, but it would violate natural law, and as Holt noted, this had revolutionary consequences:

78 Lord Chancellor Russell, Bishop of London, "Draft Sermon Prepared for the Intended Parliament of Edward V," in Chrimes, *English Constitutional Ideas in the Fifteenth Century,* 174; Thomas Smith, *De Republica Anglorum,* 34 (London: 1583).

79 *City of London v. Wood* (1702), British Library, Add. Ms. 35980, fols. 2[v], 13[r].

> [A] Judge and a party are in their Nature & Institution different and distinct, for the being of the One doth necessarily Exclude the other, [and] Therefore an Act of Parliament that should make a Man to be a Judge in his own Case would be an Absolute Contradiction[.]

This was not to say that there could not be such an act, but it would "leave a Man at Liberty to do what he will" and would "[e]xempt him from any Judicature" and would thus "return him to a State of Nature. For by the Law of Nature before the Foundac[i]on of Statutes and Erection of Tribunals[,] every Man that was Injured by another might Seek his own Satisfaction . . . with that Caution that he kept himself within the Bounds of Reason." In other words, if Parliament were to "make a man Judge in his Own Cause," government would be dissolved: "[I]t is repugnant to [natural] Law, and if a man should be allowed by Act of parliament to do what should Seem good in his own Eyes, the Government would be dissolved and the man or those who have that Liberty are returned to a State of Nature."[80] The Chief Justice, while sitting on the bench, thus justified revolution. Questions about the reason or justice of acts of Parliament under natural law belonged to the sovereign discretion of Parliament, and although this meant that such acts were "[a]bsolutely" binding in a court of law, they still could be judged by the people.

The assumption that sovereign discretion could not be reconsidered in the courts for its reasonableness was equally evident as to royal sovereignty. The king's personal absolute prerogatives, like his more general absolute power in Parliament, were part of his sovereignty, within which he judged the reasonableness of his acts—the qualification being that, as seen above, these personal prerogatives were now clearly under the constitution, as judged in the common law courts. For example, the king had absolute discretion or power in signing bills, in making war and peace, in appointing judges and ambassadors, in choosing his councillors, and in issuing money, but only within the bounds of the constitution—limits that American constitutions would tighten even further. Blackstone summarized:

80 Ibid., fol. 16[r]. He added: "It would be such a Law that should Intitle one Man to Invade the Life or property of another." Ibid., fols. 16[r]–[v]. He used all of this to elucidate English law, his point being that "[t]he Laws of the Kingdom or Community are, that there should be One or more Judges; otherwise the Government would be dissolved." By way of example, he observed that if "a Judge of a Court where there be other Judges of the Court besides himself Sues or be Sued in that Court, he as to that Cause ceases to be a Judge." Ibid., 16[v]. For Holt's derivation of his arguments from Locke and, to some extent, Pufendorf, see Philip Hamburger, "Revolution and Judicial Review: Chief Justice Holt's Opinion in *City of London v. Wood*," *Columbia Law Review* 94: 2091 (1994).

> [I]n the exertion of the lawful prerogative, the king is and ought to be absolute; that is, so far absolute, that there is no legal authority that can either delay or resist him. He may reject what bills, may make what treaties, may coin what money, may create what peers, may pardon what offences he pleases: unless where the constitution hath expressly, or by evident consequence, laid down some exception or boundary; declaring, that thus far the prerogative shall go and no farther. For otherwise the power of the crown would indeed be but a name and a shadow, insufficient for the ends of government.

Absolute power was thus brought under the constitution without being deprived of its value. It was one thing for the constitution to delineate the outer boundaries of the king's absolute power; it was quite another for it to invite judicial second-guessing about the reasonableness of his sovereign decisions. Within "the exertion therefore of those prerogatives, which the law has given him, the king is irresistible and absolute," but only "according to the forms of the constitution."[81]

This conception of the king's sovereign power—as under the constitution but absolutely beyond reconsideration for its reasonableness—had especially sweeping implications because it was accompanied by an erosion of the idea of ordinary prerogative. When the king's absolute prerogative had been claimed to be above law, it had been essential to maintain a distinct notion of an ordinary prerogative, which was exercised through law. In the mid-seventeenth century, however, when the king's absolute power came to be unequivocally under the law, the distinction between the absolute and the ordinary got lost in the broader distinction between the sovereign and the subordinate. Sovereign power had already seemed absolute, and now that it was absolute under the constitution, there was little room for a separate notion of an ordinary prerogative, lest this imply that the absolute prerogative could rise above the law or that there was a lesser type of sovereign power that could be reconsidered for its reasonableness. Writers on the prerogative therefore largely abandoned the notion of ordinary power, and all sovereign power, whether exercised by the king alone or in Parliament, came to seem absolute—meaning absolutely discretionary but always within the limits set by the constitution.[82]

[81] Blackstone, *Commentaries on the Laws of England,* 1: 243–244.

[82] Thus, for example, when Matthew Hale in the mid-seventeenth century wrote his *Prerogatives of the King,* he said about the local enactments that could be permitted with custom and consent: "[T]hese being particular and depending upon particular customs, and still subject to be examined and rejected if unreasonable, I spare to mention [them]." See also Hale, *The Prerogatives of the King,* 176. What varied with judicial determinations of reasonableness was not relevant in a treatise on the prerogative.

This new character of absolute or sovereign power—still within royal discretion but now unquestionably under the constitution—brought the exterior contours of the absolute prerogatives before the judges. Although the reasonableness of sovereign power had to remain within the judgment of the sovereign—it being a power that seemed by its very nature discretionary—the lawful extent of the power was at last clearly within the scope of the constitution, and from the late seventeenth century onward, this can be observed in judicial decisions.

Constitutional Cases

The judges now regularly rested their decisions on the constitution. It was not simply that they retrospectively associated earlier cases with the constitution. They also relied on it themselves—as can be illustrated from the manuscript opinions of Chief Justice Holt.

In 1695 in the *Bankers' Case,* Holt evaluated the constitutionality of a prerogative act: King Charles II's alienation of his hereditary revenues. Although Charles had died a decade earlier, his debts notoriously survived him. He had avoided dependence on Parliament only by borrowing from London bankers, and like many other debtors, he soon found himself so short of cash he had to stop payments. He eventually reassured his creditors by allowing them a security interest in the revenues from his hereditary excise, but Parliament later used the excise to secure other government borrowing, thus taking what Charles had given. The unhappy bankers therefore initiated litigation that lasted throughout the 1690s. In response to their claim upon the hereditary revenues, the Crown's lawyers answered that Charles's attempt to mortgage these revenues had not been lawful. They argued more specifically that the king held such revenues in trust, and in support of this point, they suggested that a royal power to alienate the revenue would be subject to abuse.

Chief Justice Holt held that the constitution necessarily gave the king a power he could misuse—this being the nature of prerogatives that were left to the king's discretion or wisdom. "No human Constitution can be so exactly Framed but there may be some Inconvenience," and although the king could abuse his power, "the Law doth not in the Constitution of this Government Suppose such a Dishonourable thing of the King." Under the constitution, "the King is Invested with Great Powers and large Prerogatives which the Law doth Suppose he will Use and exert in Wisdom and Justice for the Benefit of his Subjects," and therefore "[i]t's no Argument to Say he hath them not because they may be abused." Indeed, "the Disabling of the King from Aliening the Crown Revenues is Repugnant to and Inconsistent with the Constitution of the Government and must produce many Mischiefs and Inconveniences," for all governments needed some discretionary power under law, even though they might misuse it:

> [I]n every Government there ought to be a Constant and Standing Power to defend and Secure the State ag^{t} all Accidents: I meant such as is legal, for a natural Strength may be wanting, but that is accidental and is not the fault of the Constitution. Now suppose that the Nation should be in great danger and the Occasion should be pressing, yet the King wanted a Supply of Money to Enable him to Encounter with it. If he could not borrow Money the Danger wo^{d} be Inevitable. And if the King cannot give Security he cannot have Credit to Borrow; For when Men do Lend Money for the Public Service, they Expect Security.[83]

In discerning how the constitution had been framed, Holt reasoned that there had to be a standing power under law to protect the state, and although a king might abuse this power, this was no argument against it.

If the law of the land, especially the constitution, was the measure of legal obligation in England, then not only the king's prerogative but also foreign claims of authority had to be measured against this law, and Holt in the same case therefore denied that the declarations of international bodies had any independent legal obligation in England. The lawyers for the Crown argued that "by the Ancient Law . . . the Inheritance and Revenue of the Crown could not be Aliened," and in support of this position, they cited an international congress mentioned by the medieval treatise *Fleta*—so called because it allegedly had been written in the Fleet Prison. According to *Fleta,* a meeting of "all Christian kings" at Montpellier in the mid-1270s declared that royal properties were inalienable—that "[t]he property of the Crown consists of the king's ancient manors, homages, franchises and the like," which, "if alienated," he was "bound to resume." Chief Justice Holt acidly observed: "It seems that Author would have that Determination of the Christian Princes at the Congress held at Montpellier . . . to be a Declarac[i]on of the Law of all Kingdoms and States and therefore thô he were a Com[m]on Lawyer he Uses it as an Authority in England." In contrast, Holt took the modern common law view that nothing had legal

[83] *Rex v. Horneby, Williamson, Snow, & Smith,* a.k.a *The Bankers Case* (Ex. Ch. 1695), British Library, Holt's Opinions, Add. Ms. 35979, fols. 29[r]–30[r]. See also Skinner, *Reports,* 601–602. The bankers prevailed in 1691 in the Exchequer, suffered a reversal in 1696 from Lord Keeper Somers in the Exchequer Chamber—notwithstanding the contrary opinions of almost all the judges—and finally prevailed in 1700 in the House of Lords. For details, see J. Keith Horsefield, "The 'Stop of the Exchequer' Revisited," *Economic History Review,* 35: 518–522 (1982); Bruce G. Carruthers, "Politics, Popery, and Property: A Comment on North and Weingast," *Journal of Economic History,* 50: 694–695 (1990).

obligation in England, except under the law of the land. Assuming that this requirement was established by the constitution, Holt said of *Fleta:*

> If he means that the Resolution should be Obligatory in England without any Sanction from the Law or Statutes of the Realm[,] that is contrary to the Fundamental Constitution of our Government and therefore can be no proof of this matter. If he means it as a Declaration of the Law that will be as vain and as much against the Constitution as any other.[84]

The resolution of the congress of princes could not constitutionally be obligatory without the sanction of English law; nor could it constitutionally declare English law.

Holt not only sustained acts of the Crown under the constitution, but also upheld acts of Parliament—as already seen in his opinion in *Brewster v. Kidgell.* This was the 1698 case in which Holt said that although "Parliamentary taxes" were not part of the "the Original Frame and Constitution of the Governmt.," they had "Fundamentally and Virtually an Existence in the Constitution," because they were made by an act of "the whole Legislative Authority."[85]

In addition to sustaining government acts under the constitution, Holt could also hold them unlawful. In 1694, on a writ of error, Holt opined that a judgment for treason should be reversed because it omitted part of the legal punishment and thus lessened it—this being "a Defect in the Judgment itself." Ordinarily, a traitor would be sentenced to a series of painful indignities, including having his bowels cut out and burned in front of him while he was still alive. In the case of Thomas Walcott, however, the judgment omitted the words *ipsoque vivente comburentur,* and Holt and his colleagues held that "when the Law of *England* appoints a particular Judgment for an Offence . . . it is not in the Power of the Judges to alter it, either by any Addition or Diminution." In particular, "[t]he giving of Judgment against Malefactors is Part of the Constitution of Government, and therefore it cannot be discretionary, which is but a softer word for arbitrary." Were the law otherwise, "then the Courts . . . might make new Punishments, as they should think more suitable to the Crimes; for they might pronounce a *Turkish* Judgment, *viz.* that the Offender should be strangled; or a *Jewish* Judgment, that he should be stoned to Death; or a *French* Judgment, that he should be broke on the Wheel; all which are contrary to the

[84] *Rex v. Horneby* (1695), British Library, Holt's Opinions, Add. Ms. 35979, fols. 36[r]–37[v]. For the meeting of kings, see *Fleta,* 3: 12 (III.vi), eds. H. G. Richardson and G. O. Sayles (London: Selden Society, 1972).

[85] *Brewster v. Kidgell* (K.B. 1698), British Library, Holt's Opinions, Add. Ms. 35979, fols. 109[v]–110[r]. For further details, see Chapter Three.

known Laws of the Realm." Accordingly, the judgment was void, and although this was only a matter of judicial error, it offers an initial hint of the sort of reasoning with which the judges could hold acts contrary to the constitution.[86]

Although Holt could not hold an act of Parliament unconstitutional, he did not hesitate to reach such a conclusion about the act of a single house of Parliament. The question arose when John Paty and several other men from Aylesbury brought an action against the town's constables for preventing the plaintiffs from voting in a parliamentary election. The House of Commons viewed the case as a challenge to its privilege of deciding contested elections, and it therefore committed the plaintiffs to Newgate prison for a breach of privilege. On a habeas corpus in 1705, three judges of Queen's Bench held that the commitment by the Commons was a matter of legislative privilege, of which the Court could not take cognizance, but Chief Justice Holt opined for the prisoners. He understood that "every Englishman must be very fearful of giving any offence to so great and venerable a body" as the Commons, but he explained that "there is one thing that doth overrule me, which I do fear more than all the evils and calamities that can befall me in this world, which is my own conscience." He had bound himself in conscience to decide in accord with the law of the land, and he therefore proceeded to give what became one of the most famous dissents in English history. The House of Commons had no power "to restrain and diminish that liberty of the subject which is secured to every one by the fundamental laws and constitution of the kingdom," and thus the proceeding of the House of Commons to imprison the prisoners "is not according to the Constitution of this Kingdom, which admits no such power or authority to be exercised and administered but by the whole

[86] *Walcott's Case* (K.B. 1694) Holt (KB), *Reports,* 680. See also *Modern Reports,* 4: 401. Walcott's counsel argued that "the Constitution of this Kingdom hath prescribed and fixed Rules and Forms, which the Executive Power is obliged and bound to follow; that as Nothing can be made or construed to be an Offence at the Pleasure of the Court, so no judgment can be given for any known Offence at Pleasure. But the Law, either Statute or Common, hath established what is an Offence, and what is its Punishment; and there is nothing of Arbitrary Power allowed in respect of either," upon which the judgment of reversal was affirmed. Shower, *Reports,* 136–137.

In another case, Holt may have held the acts of government commissioners unconstitutional, but he more probably alluded to the constitution for purposes of interpretation. After James II abdicated and the Revolution of 1688 brought William III to the throne, Parliament declared that the Irish land once held by James or received from him was forfeited and vested in named trustees or commissioners, who were to collect and sell these properties. An Act for granting an Aid to His Majesty by Sale of the forfeited and other Estates and Interests in Ireland and by a Land Tax in England, 11 William III, c.2 (1698–1699). The commissioners, however, found themselves in a quandary, for although they hesitated to go to

Legislature."[87] Although the judges voted that the plaintiffs could have a writ of error to the House of Lords, the imprisonment soon came to an end with the dissolution of Parliament, thus leaving the constitutional question unresolved. There was no question, however, about the duty of the judges to hold unconstitutional acts unlawful and void, and at least Chief Justice Holt was clear that this duty even reached acts of the House of Commons.

In the ensuing century, the judges most famously held an act of the Crown unconstitutional after the Crown issued a general warrant against John Wilkes. This brilliant demagogue excoriated the government in 1763 in his newspaper, the *North Briton.* When the government sought to prosecute him for the notorious issue number forty-five, Secretary of State Halifax issued a warrant "in his majesty's name" to apprehend and seize the author, printers, and publishers of issue forty-five, together with their private papers. It had been the practice of secretaries of state to sign warrants for seizing the producers of alleged seditious libels and their papers without specifying such persons by name, and the long-standing practice of issuing these general warrants could be considered a precedent.[88] On such grounds—that it was "the course of office" and that this sort of precedent had been "approved of by the crown-lawyers"—Lord Halifax signed the

---

Irish juries to resolve title, they equally were reluctant to try to sell the land without any prior determination of title. They therefore ventured by themselves to adjudicate title to the lands. Eventually, in 1707, in *Annesley v. Dixon,* King's Bench held that the commissioners had acted beyond their authority—partly on the ground that they could not deprive landowners of their right to a jury trial on the question of title. As a matter of policy, it might be "very Convenient" to accept the commissioners' sales, but Holt rejected such arguments, for it was a matter that "is Tryed and Determined according to the Ancient & Fundamental Constitution of the Kingdom by a Jury." *Annesley v. Dixon* (K.B. 1707), British Library, Holt's Opinions, Add. Ms. 35980, fols. 92[r], 94[r]. The holding that the proceedings and decrees of the commissioners in the case were void and *coram non judice* may have been a conclusion about the unconstitutionality of the act of the commissioners, but the holding was more probably based on an interpretation of the statute in accord with the constitution. *A Report of All the Cases Determined by Sir John Holt,* 393.

In another Irish case, it was argued that "to have the ultimate Judgment, is that which the King cannot grant; for such a Grant would (if allowed) alter the fundamental Constitution of the Realm." *Governor of Ulster v. Bishop of Derby* (H.L. 1698), Shower, *Reports,* 79–80.

87 *Case of Paty et al.* (Q.B. 1705), *The Judgements delivered by the Lord Chief Justice Holt in the Case of Ashby v. White and Others, and in the Case of John Paty and Others,* 43, 61 (London: 1837). He also explained that the Commons' vote "is an extra-judicial proceeding and an assumption of a jurisdiction, superior to that Parliamentary jurisdiction, which is legally exercised and administered in the House of Lords," and "that is the dernier resort appointed by the law and Constitution of England, which the subjects, parties thereunto, are obliged and concluded." Ibid., 47.

88 [Philip Carteret Webb], *Copies Taken from the Records . . . Of Warrants Issued by Secretaries of State for Seizing Persons Suspected of Being Guilty of Various Crimes, Particularly, of Being the Authors, Printers, and Publishers of Libels, from the Restoration to the Present Time* (London: 1763).

warrant.[89] Wilkes, however, was unimpressed by the course of executive practice, and in an action for damages against the arresting officer, he challenged the constitutionality of the warrant. After a trial in Common Pleas, Chief Justice Pratt instructed the jury: "It is my opinion the office precedents, which had been produced . . . are no justification of a practice itself illegal, and contrary to the fundamental principles of the constitution."[90] He therefore concluded: "This warrant is unconstitutional, illegal, and absolutely void."[91]

Thus, not merely in post-1776 America, but already in England, judges held government acts unconstitutional. When an imagined power of judicial review is put aside and it is recognized that the judges had a duty to decide in accord with the law of the land, then the full range of English decisions about the lawfulness of acts and customs becomes relevant, and this evidence reveals that judges regularly did their duty by holding customs and government acts contrary to the law of the land and even the constitution.

89 *State Trials,* 19: 1415.
90 *Wilkes v. Wood* (C.P. 1763), *State Trials,* 19: 1167. At the same time, "its having been the constant practice of the office, might fairly be pleaded in mitigation of damages." Ibid.
91 *The Annual Register, or a View of the History, Politicks, and Literature 1763,* at 145 (London: 1764).

7

Authority to Expound Law

The exposition of law, unlike the making of it, was a matter of judgment, and thus when, in the course of doing their duty, the judges had to explain their decisions, their expositions of law, including the constitution, enjoyed the authority of their office. It is tempting to discuss such matters in familiar terms of "precedent" or "*stare decisis,*" without much attention to the underlying issue of judicial authority, but even if such terms now have a reassuring familiarity, it is not obvious why judicial precedent has the effect of *stare decisis* and why it nonetheless sometimes does not. Such questions are difficult, but they once were not quite so puzzling, for they were understood to rest on more basic assumptions about the office and authority of a judge. Put simply, the exposition of law belonged to the office of judgment rather than of will, and whether as to the constitution or other law, the opinions of the judges in the exercise of their judgment had the authority of their office.

Although the nature of judicial office and its authority was old, it was clarified and refined in response to ideals of lawmaking office and authority. Medieval judges would sometimes cite a prior *ensaumple* or worry whether its position "was laid down as law," but only in the fifteenth and especially the sixteenth century did judges and reporters (as shown by J. H. Baker) become more self-conscious about the authority of holdings in cases.[1] Nor

[1] J. H. Baker, *The Law's Two Bodies: Some Evidential Problems in English Legal History,* 81 (Oxford: Oxford University Press, 2001). When discussing the late medieval period, Baker emphasizes the importance of common erudition but at the same time recognizes the degree to which medieval judges alluded back to *ensaumples,* for although they discussed their understanding of the law mostly prior to judgment and even before the pleading, they did not therefore consider their discussions to be without authority. Ibid., 77; J. H. Baker, ed., *The Reports of Sir John Spelman,* 2: 155, 161, 163 (London: Selden Society, 1977). For what "was laid down as law," see *Lavington v. Seymark* (1317), in *Year Books of Edward II, 11 Edward*

was this a coincidence, for it was a time when the English increasingly pursued ideals of lawmaking authority. The ancient distinction between the making of general laws and the adjudication of particular cases had not always been maintained with much clarity in medieval England, where Parliament was a type of court, but in response to ideals of lawmaking authority, the judges tightened their conception of their rather different office and authority. Especially when seventeenth-century kings systematically attempted to impose their will on the judges, the latter honed their conception of judging, both narrowing their ideal of judicial office and sharpening the authority it gave their opinions.[2]

An Imperial Challenge

Nothing better illustrates how claims of lawmaking authority focused the attention of the judges on the different character of their own authority than the attempt of King James I to establish an imperial power of interpretation. James sought to interpret statutes in an imperial manner that amounted to a power of making law. The judges, however, took a stand on the distinctive feature of their office—their adjudication of cases—and they thereby defended both the law and their authority to expound it.

At common law, when judges explained their judgments, they rea-

II. A.D. *1317–1318,* at 157, ed. John P. Collas (London: Selden Society, 1942). In a case of 1335, it was observed that "[a]fterwards, Stonore CJCP said, when the party wished willingly to accept the averment, the court would well allow it, but one could not take this as a precedent (ensaumple) for law, because he was not driven to this by the court." Y.B. Mich. 9 Edward III, pl. 26, fols. 31a–31b (Seipp's translation). In a late-fifteenth-century case, Chief Justice Hussey said, "I do not see how that can be right, although if the precedents are that way we will respect them." *Anon.* (K.B. 1490), in J. H. Baker, ed., *Reports of Cases by John Caryll,* 1: 38 (London: Selden Society, 1999). Similarly, Chief Justice Bryan warned counsel that the judges would not "overturn all our old precedents." *Hulcote v. Ingleton* (C.P. 1493), in ibid., 1: 141.

[2] Of course, there also were other factors, such as a distaste for civil law. In response to those who condemned the uncertainty of the common law, Coke wrote:

> Upon the Text of the Civill Law, there be so many glosses and interpretations, and again upon those so many Commentaries, and all these written by Doctors of equal degree and authority, and therein so many diversities of opinions, as they do rather increase then resolve doubts, and incertainties, and the professors of that noble Science say, That it is like a Sea full of waves.

These "glosses and Commentaries," being "written by Doctors" who were "Advocates," seemed to Coke "in a manner private interpretations." In contrast, "our Expositions or Commentaries upon *Magna Charta,* and other Statutes, are resolutions of Judges in Courts of Justice in judiciall courses of proceeding," and these "being collected together, shall (as we conceive) produce certainty, the Mother and Nurse of repose and quietnesse." Coke, *Institutes,* 2: [6v] (Proeme).

soned or exercised judgment with the authority of their office. It was well known that in a case, "the judgment byndes betweene the same parties." Beyond the parties, however, what mattered was the reasoning underlying the court's judgment, and "[s]o the reasons, not the judgments, are to be pressed."[3] Put another way, the reasons that judges gave for the judgments of their court had authority, and this rankled King James.

An older, competing vision of judicial authority was familiar to James from the example of Roman law, in which interpretation had sometimes been considered a form of legislation and thus beyond the authority of a judge. According to Justinian's *Digest,* "whenever a new contingency arises," it was the "the imperial function" to "correct and settle it," or as Julian had written, "if anything defective be found, the want should be supplied by imperial legislation."[4] From this imperial perspective, much of what common lawyers would consider the exposition of law was actually lawmaking, and although the *Codex* allowed that judges could decide cases according to their understanding of the law, it precluded any authoritative exposition of the law—cautioning, in the words of Constantine, "It is part of Our duty, and is lawful for Us alone to interpret questions involving equity and law."[5]

When Chancellor Christopher Hatton attempted to explain why this Roman tradition of legislative interpretation did not prevail in England, he pointed to the elective character of Parliament. Although this body was the lawmaker in England, and although it could therefore alter the law with a new statute, the periodic need for reelection of its lower house deprived it of the continuing power to interpret once claimed by Roman emperors. In England, it was "an absurd thing to make an exposition go further than either the words, or the intention" by asking the legislators for their subsequent interpretation, for when "the Assembly of Parliament" was "ended," then "their Authority is returned to the Electors." So clearly was their authority returned, "that if they were altogether assembled again for interpre-

[3] Speech of Thomas Hedley (June 23–28, 1610), in *Parliamentary Debates in 1610,* at 72, ed. Samuel Rawson Gardiner (Westminster: Camden Society, 1862).

[4] *The Digest of Justinian,* lix–lx (The Confirmation of the Digest), ed. Alan Watson (Philadelphia: University of Pennsylvania Press, 1998).

[5] Codex (I.xiv.1), *The Civil Law,* 12: 85, trans. Samuel Parsons Scott (Cincinnati: Central Trust, 1932). See also Codex (I.xiv.11).

On the basis of this learned tradition, the word "interpretation" sometimes had connotations of lawmaking. St. German's Student, for example, emphasized that "there maye not entent be taken agaynst the expresse wordes of the statute, for that shuld be rather an interpretacyon of the statute than an exposition." T. F. T. Plucknett and J. L. Barton, eds., *St. German's Doctor and Student,* 166 (London: Selden Society, 1974).

tation by a voluntary meeting, *Eorum non esset interpretari*"—not one of the statutes should be interpreted by them. Accordingly, the only interpretation that remained possible in England was the more modest sort done by judges when discerning "the intent of the Maker." This was "the interpretation" that the common law judges had "in their hands, and their Authority no man taketh in hand to control."[6]

At the beginning of the next century, however, James I would claim the imperial power of interpretation for himself. James surely studied some such ideas while he was a teenage king in Scotland, and he certainly could not have forgotten the sharp admonition of his learned tutor George Buchanan:

> I shall tell you . . . plainly, that you may understand it. When you grant the interpretation of Lawes to a King, you grant him such a licence, as the Law doth not tell what the Lawgiver meaneth, or what is good and equal for all persons in generall, but what may make for the Interpreters benefit.

This royal interpretation would make law "useless," for if it were admitted, "it will be to no purpose to make good Lawes for teaching a good prince his duty; and hemme in an ill King. Yea, let me tell you more plainly, it would be better to have no Lawes at all."[7] James respected his tutor, but what he thought of this plain speaking can only be imagined.

Shortly after James became king of England, some English civilians

[6] Christopher Hatton, *A Treatise Concerning Statutes, or Acts of Parliament: And the Exposition Thereof,* 28–30 (London: 1677). Hatton was not alone in such reasoning. Fleetwood noted that "although the makers of the Statutes are dispersed, so that their mindes cannot be known, yet those who approach nearest to their minds ought to construe their words: and those are the Sages of the Law, whose wits are exercised in the study of such matters." William Fleetwood, *The Office of a Justice of the Peace, Together with Instructions, How and In What Manner Statutes Shall Be Expounded,* 98 (London: 1658).

The practice of referring questions of interpretation to the lawmaker was familiar to medieval English lawyers, probably from the Roman tradition, and the English occasionally adopted this mechanism. For example, the judges might ask the parties to petition the king to explain what he meant by his charters. *The Abbot of Battle v. Atterbregge and others* (1312), in *Year Books of Edward II,* 12: 17 (the volume for 5 Edward II., 1312), ed. William Craddock Bolland (London: Selden Society, 1916). As for Parliament, the 1352 treason statute recognized that there might be cases of treason it did not specify, and it therefore directed the judges in such a case to delay judgment until they had consulted the king and Parliament as to whether the case ought to be judged treason or felony—this being only one of the ways in which the statute borrowed from Continental law. 25 Edward III, stat. 5, cap. 2 (1352). Looking back, Coke in 1604 wrote that "[t]he *Expounding* of Lawes doth ordinarily belong to the reverende Judges, and Sages of the Realme: And in case of greatest difficultie and importance to the high Court of Parliament," but by the early seventeenth century this must have seemed distinctly out of date. Coke, *Reports,* 4: sig. Bii[r] (To the Reader) (London: 1604).

[7] George Buchanan, *De Jure Regni Apud Scotos,* 44 (np: 1680).

encouraged him to engage in imperial-style legislative interpretation. Dr. Thomas Ridley—a learned scholar of civil law—argued in 1607 that the judges exercised a delegated lawmaking authority when they expounded law and that "his Majestie by communicating his authoritie to his Judges to expound his Lawes, doth not thereby [so completely] abdicate the same from himselfe, but that he may assume it againe . . . as often as him pleaseth." In the Roman manner, Ridley even argued that only the king's interpretation was generally authoritative and that his interpretation was binding as law—that "his Judges interpretation maketh right only to them betwéene whom the cause is, but his highnesse['s] exposition is a Law unto all, from which it is not lawfull for any subject to recéed."[8] English judges recognized that they did justice in the name of the king, but they might doubt whether the king enjoyed a power of exposition, let alone whether exposition was ever a law unto anyone. Nonetheless, according to Ridley, the king had delegated an almost lawmaking power of exposition to the judges, and he could therefore reclaim it.

In 1608 in *Calvin's Case,* Chancellor Ellesmere took up this civilian line. The case concerned the right of Scotsmen to own land in England after the union of the two kingdoms, and Ellesmere suggested that the judges faced a question that "neither direct law, nor Examples and Precedents, nor application of like Cases, nor discourse of reason, nor the opinion of the . . . Judges can resolve." This was, of course, the preliminary to offering a solution—one in which Ellesmere confessed to "being led a little from the Common Law to the Civile Lawe." He proposed that the case ought to be decided "by [the] sentence of the most religious, learned, and judicious king that ever this kingdome or Iland had."[9]

[8] Thomas Ridley, *A View of the Civile and Ecclesiastical Law,* 211, 212 (London: 1607). In the same year the Cambridge academic John Cowell suggested that the power of interpreting royal charters belonged exclusively to the Crown, for "the supream power wheresoever it rest, is above the Lawes for that it may grant priviledges at pleasure, as to single persons, as to Corporations and Colledges, provided they become not injurious to a third person," and "if any dou[b]ts arise, some say it self alone hath sole power of interpreting." Although he acknowledged that "others ascribe this power also unto the Judges, that such Charters may receive construction according to the rules of law," he left the impression that the judges held only a coterminous power of interpretation—perhaps, indeed, only by sufferance. John Cowell, *The Institutes of the Lawes of England,* 5 (London: 1651) (citations and insertions omitted).

[9] *Speech in the Exchequer Chamber, Touching the Post-Nati* (1608), in *Law and Politics in Jacobean England: The Tracts of Lord Chancellor Ellesmere,* 248–249, ed. Louis A. Knafla (Cambridge: Cambridge University Press, 1977). Ellesmere hastened to add: "but I speake only of interpretation of the Lawe in new questions and doubts, as now in this present case: neither doe I meane hereby to derogate any thing from the high court of Parliament; (farre be it from my thought)." Ibid.

That this was no longer merely an academic point became inescapably clear in a series of meetings of the Privy Council. Unceasing in his opposition to writs of prohibition against ecclesiastical courts, Archbishop Bancroft informed James that in anything ecclesiastical "or in any other case in which there is not expresse Authority in Law, the king himselfe may decide it in his Royall person." Bancroft thus seized upon an exaggerated view of uncertainty in English law to open up space for imperial interpretation—an interpretation that was candidly a matter of legislative will rather than judgment. This emphasis on the uncertainty of English law was, for both Ellesmere and Bancroft, a familiar academic move, derived from learned assumptions about the inadequacy of national laws, and as by now should be expected, Bancroft also echoed the standard justification of imperial-style interpretation, that "the Judges are but the Delegates of the king, and that the king may take what causes he shall please . . . from . . . the Judges, and may determine them himselfe."[10] Encouraged by such arguments, James memorably complained: "If the Judges interprete the lawes themselves and suffer none else to interprete, then they may easily make of the laws shipmens hose." Unwilling to accept this risk, James asserted that he was "the supreme judge"; that "inferior judges" were "his shadows and ministers"; even that "the King may, if he please, sit and judge in Westminster Hall in any Court there," for "[t]he King being the author of the Lawe is the interpreter of the Lawe."[11]

These claims of lawmaking authority in interpretation concentrated the minds of the judges on their own office and authority. Coke answered for the barons of the exchequer and all the justices that "the King in his own person cannot adjudge any case . . . but this ought to be determined and adjudged in some Court of Justice, according to the Law and Custome of England." James protested that "the Law was founded upon reason, and that he and others had reason, as well as the Judges," which made sense if the judges' interpretation of statutes was really a delegated exercise of a royal lawmaking power, for lawmaking required the use of natural reason to determine a just policy prior to the exercise of legislative will enacting it. Coke answered, however, that cases "are not to be decided by naturall rea-

[10] *Prohibition del Roy* (1608), Coke, *Reports,* 12: 63.

[11] Julius Caesar's Notes, Lansdowne Ms. 160, as printed in Roland G. Usher, "James I and Sir Edward Coke," *English Historical Review,* 18: 669, 673 (1903). It was in the context of this dispute over the king's legislative power in interpretation that Coke and the other judges emphasized that the king had delegated to them his judicial power: "The King himself is *De jure,* to deliver Justice to all his Subjects: And for this, that he himself cannot do it to all persons, he delegates his power to his Judgs, who have the Custody and Guard of the King's Oath." *Floyd v. Barker,* Coke, *Reports,* 12: 25 (Star Chamber 1608).

son, but by artificiall reason and judgment of Law, which Law is an act which requires long study and experience, before . . . a man can attain to the cognizance of it."[12] Natural reason might be adequate for the exercise of legislative will, but not for judgments in cases about the law of the land, and in this way the judges rejected an imperial power of legislative interpretation by distinguishing judicial office and interpretation.

James's aspirations for imperial interpretation had similar consequences in the controversy over proclamations. This dispute of 1610 is usually thought simply to have concerned royal legislative power, but it will be recalled that when James attempted to use his proclamations to create criminal offenses, Ellesmere urged that the judges should "leave it to the king to order it according to his wisdome" where "there is no authority and President." Like some modern justifications of administrative regulations, this was a more subtle point than a blunt claim of legislative power, and it provoked Coke's retort that "when authority and Precedent is wanting, there is need of great considerations, before any thing of novelty shall be established, and to provide that this be not against the Law of the Land." Coke then punctured Ellesmere's inflated view of proclamations as instruments of legislative interpretation by observing that the king outside Parliament could not create any new offense or otherwise "change the Law."[13]

The Crown eventually shifted tack. Rather than claim that judicial interpretation was a sort of lawmaking that the king could claim for himself, James in 1616 took the apparently more moderate view that the judges should consult with the king about their interpretations. James still said that the king "onlely deputes subalterne Judges," but he now conceded that "their office is to interprete Law, and administer Justice." In thus giving up the claim that judicial interpretation was a form of legislation belonging ultimately to the king, James recognized that judges had to state the law rather than make it: "[R]emember you are no makers of Law, but Interpretours of Law, according to the trew sense thereof: for your Office is *Jus decere,* and not *Jus dare*"—the catch being that "your interpretations must be alwayes subject to common sense and reason" and that "I will never trust any Interpretation, that agreeth not with my common sense and reason."[14]

[12] *Prohibition del Roy* (1608), Coke, *Reports,* 12: 63–65. Usher observes that Coke's account probably conflates a series of discussions at the council table. Usher, "James I and Sir Edward Coke," 669 (1903). For more on Coke's understanding of artificial reasoning, see Chapter Four. Coke's views on artificial reason have been much discussed, but the imperial context and significance of the positions taken by James and Coke apparently have gone unnoticed.
[13] *Case of Proclamations,* Coke, *Reports,* 2: 74–75 (1610).
[14] "A Speach in the Starre-Chamber" (1616), in *The Works of James I,* at 550–551, 555–556 (London: 1620). Richard Hutton—soon to be elevated to the bench—heard James's conces-

At least, however, James now abandoned his fantasy that the judges exercised a delegated lawmaking power.

When confronted with James's hopes for a royal power of lawmaking interpretation, the judges not only clarified that lawmaking will rested in Parliament but also sharpened their understanding of the almost opposite character of their own office and authority. Recalling the threat from James and other monarchs, a popular *Abridgment* later summarized: "The Judges are bound by Oath to determine according to the known Laws and antient Customs of the Realm; and their Rule herein must be the Judicial Decisions and Resolutions of great Numbers of learned, wise and upright Judges, upon Variety of particular Facts and Cases, and not their own arbitrary Will and Pleasure, or that of their Prince's."[15] Theirs was an office of judgment rather than will, and especially in their cases, this seemed to give authority to their exposition of law.

Cases and the Authority of Judicial Expositions of Law

The response to James's assertion of an imperial power of interpretation was only part of a broader shift in judicial office and authority, which had begun much earlier, and which became increasingly pronounced during the centuries after the Middle Ages. Rather than merely a reaction to the pres-

---

sion with evident relief and said nothing of the king's claims to be consulted. *The Diary of Richard Hutton 1614–1639,* xv, 12 (June 19, 1616), ed. W. R. Prest (London: Selden Society, 1991).

An early intimation of James's views may be discerned in Bacon's essay *Of Judicature.* Francis Bacon, *The Essaies,* Of Judicature (No. 36) (London: 1613). As repeated in the more polished 1625 edition, "*Judges* ought to remember, that their Office is *Jus dicere,* and not *Jus dare; to Interpret Law,* and not to *Make Law,* or *Give Law.*" What he meant by this became clear when he wrote, "it is an Happie Thing in a *State,* when *Kings* and *States* doe often Consult with *Judges;* And againe, when *Judges* doe often Consult with the *King* and *State:* The one, when there is Matter of Law, intervenient in Businesse of State; The other, when there is some Consideration of State, intervenient in Matter of Law." Francis Bacon, *Essayes or Counsels, Civill and Morall,* 316, 323, Of Judicature (No. LVI) (London: 1625). Following Bacon, Ellesmere urged that "in doubtfull cases and espetially in construccion of statutes," the judges should "conferr with the Kinges privie councell." "A Breviate or Direccion for the Kinges Learned Councell Collected by the Lord Chancellor Ellesmere" (1615), in *Law and Politics in Jacobean England,* 319.

15 Matthew Bacon, *A New Abridgment of the Law,* 1: 555 (London: 1778). The rejection of imperial notions of interpretation is also apparent in moral writings. Jeremy Taylor argued that an emperor's power of interpretation "obliges the Conscience as much as the law," but that "the case is otherwise in Judges," for "the interpretation of laws made by Judges is matter of fidelity and wise dispensation, but nothing of Empire and power," and thus although the emperor's interpretation "is a good probable warranty of Conscience," it "cannot of itself be a resolution of conscience." Jeremy Taylor, *Ductor Dubitantium, or the Rule of Conscience In All Her General Measures,* 2: 406, 410 (III.vi.Rule 2) (London: 1660).

sures imposed by James and other monarchs, the evolving conception of judicial office and authority was what might be expected in an era dominated by claims about lawmaking authority. In reaction to the claims of sovereign bodies (monarchical or parliamentary) to make law through their exercise of will, lawyers could not help but pay closer attention to the distinctive nature of the judges' office and their exposition of law. It was not simply that the exposition of law was an exercise of judgment, which was an office belonging to the judges. In addition, the office of a judge was increasingly understood to concern cases. Defined in contrast to lawmaking, which was an exercise of will in imposing general rules, the office of judging seemed at its core to involve the exercise of judgment in particular cases, and these therefore became the circumstances in which judges could expound the law, including the constitution, with the authority of their office.

Judges traditionally could expound law not only in cases but also more generally in consultation with other judges. The judges of the common law courts sometimes assembled to consult about advisory opinions or simply to discuss and resolve particularly knotty problems. Edward Coke still revered the authority of the judges at these discussions and claimed that their "answers and resolutions, although they were not enacted by authority of Parliament . . . yet, being resolved unanimously by all the Judges of England, and Barons of the Exchequer, are for matters in law of highest authority next unto the Court of Parliament."[16] The judges, however,

[16] Coke, *Institutes,* 2: 618. Coke often elevated "off-the-cuff remarks with which he agreed" to the status of "resolutions." W. J. Jones, *Politics and the Bench: The Judges and the Origins of the English Civil War,* 51 (London: Allen and Unwin, 1971).

Taking cases as the model for authoritative exposition of law, judges became increasingly attentive to old doubts as to whether resolutions could have any authority if the questions were not fully disputed. In an incident in 1614, the Lords asked the judges to give their opinions on impositions, and the judges therefore retired to the lord chancellor's lodging for consultation. After about half an hour, they emerged and Chief Justice Coke told the Lords: "[A]s we are sworne to deliver our opinions in matters juditiall comeing before us, betwixt party and party, soe are we in matters betwixt the Kinge and the subject. But, my L[ord]s, in this matter as yet we canne deliver noe opinion." Coke was "not yet . . . satisfied" on the question of impositions and therefore "till we have h[e]ard and understood we cannot tell your Lo[rdshi]ps our opinions." Coke explained that "[f]or my part I will not argue the case, it beinge against our othe soe to doe," but "[i]f . . . your Lo[rdshi]ps will undertake to dispute the mat[t]er, we will upon the heareinge of it argued on both sides if it be your pleasures to deliver our opinions." Proceedings in the House of Lords (May 23, 1614), Historical Manuscripts Commission, *Report* [*No. 78*] *on the Manuscripts of the Late Reginald Rawdon Hastings,* 4: 256–257, ed. Francis Bickley (London: His Majesty's Stationery Office, 1947), quoted in Jones, *Politics and the Bench,* 151–152. A later author explained that Coke was particularly reluctant to proceed with an opinion because the Lords had devoted themselves to developing arguments against the king's power and the king had no counsel present to present his side of the matter. *The Original Institution, Power and Jurisdiction of Parlia-*

would soon question whether they could have any authority in such resolutions.

Royal demands were among the immediate pressures that prompted the judges to take a narrower view of their office and authority—as can be illustrated by their response when Charles I asked them to give an advisory opinion about the Petition of Right. In 1628, after Parliament drafted the Petition, Charles worried that it would limit his power to imprison without stating a cause, and he therefore asked the judges about the scope of his power. They answered his first two questions—about the king's existing power—but balked at a third question as to how his power would be altered by the Petition. To this they answered: "Every law, after it is made, hath its exposition, and so this petition and answer must have an exposition as the case in the nature thereof shall require to stand with justice; which is to be left to the courts of justice to determine, which cannot particularly be discovered until such case shall happen."[17] The judges thus held off the demand for an exposition of a prospective enactment by insisting that they could only expound it in a case. Their answer suggests how the judges were withdrawing to a conception of their office that centered on cases, and although they were trying to avoid giving any exposition of a law not yet in effect, they thereby also narrowed the sphere in which they could expound the law with authority.

---

ments, 90 (London: 1707). Similarly, when in 1638 in the *Shipmoney Case* it was "urged that the King in this case . . . treades onely in the stepps of his auncestors," George Croke responded that "the records and presidents" that had been presented were "not judiciall or setled uppon debate of judges, but onely things acted and pased over in silence without dispute," and "by such recordes the judges ought not to be much swayed." "Notes of the Judgment Delivered by Sir George Croke in the Case of Ship-Money," in *Camden Miscellany,* 7: 11, ed. S. R. Gardiner (London: Camden Society, 1875). See also Coke's comments about precedents that "passed without challenge of the party, or debate of the Justices." *Slade's Case* (K.B. 1602), Coke, *Reports,* 4: 93b–94a.

[17] Hargrave Ms. xxxii, 97, as quoted by Henry Hallam, *The Constitutional History of England from the Accession of Henry VII. to the Death of George II.,* 1: 391 (London: 1850). The king's third question was "Whether, if the king grant the commons' petition, he doth not thereby exclude himself from committing or restraining a subject for any time or cause whatsoever without showing a cause?" The judges responded with the opinion in the text above, adding for good measure: "And although the petition be granted, there is no fear of conclusion as is intimated in the question." Ibid. This equivocal final sentence was designed to assuage the king's anxieties, but it hardly had this effect. For further details, see Jones, *Politics and the Bench,* 164. In *Ashby v. White,* Holt observed that it was "a fundamental principle of law, that the Queen's Courts are the original expounders of Acts of Parliament, and . . . they can never have an opportunity of exercising this authority unless it be upon an action depending in the Court." *Ashby v. White* (K.B. 1702), *The Judgements delivered by the Lord Chief Justice Holt in the Case of Ashby v. White and Others, and in the Case of John Paty and Others,* 23–24 (London: 1837).

Within the tightened circle of their office, however, they could be secure in their authority to expound. In the great contest between Crown and Parliament, common lawyers reacted to the threat from the Crown by defending Parliament's authority to make law, but they also became self-conscious about the judges' very different authority, within their office, to expound the law. Lawyers soon became so confident of this judicial authority that they could recite it in constitutional terms—as when a lawyer argued without dispute in King's Bench (in a case involving statutory interpretation) that "a power is implicitly given to this Court by the fundamental constitution, which makes the Judges expositors of Acts of Parliament."[18] Although the constitution might give Parliament the power to make law, it gave the judges the power to expound it.

If judges enjoyed this authority, however, only because of their office of judgment in cases, then outside this office, judicial opinion was without authority. When Justice John Finch in 1640 faced impeachment charges for his advisory opinion on shipmoney, he protested: "I know very well, that extra-judicial Opinions of Judges ought not to be binding."[19] Justice Vaughan later explained in calmer circumstances: "An *extra-judicial* Opinion given in, or out of *Court,* is no more than the *Prolatum* or saying of him who gives it, nor can be taken for his *Opinion,* unless every thing spoken at pleasure, must pass as the speakers Opinion." Indeed, "[a]n Opinion given in *Court,* if not necessary to the *Judgment* given of *Record* . . . is no *Judicial Opinion,* nor more than a *gratis dictum.*"[20]

Not being itself a law—nor even the mere judgment in a case—a judicial opinion seemed no more than evidence of the law. Hale explained that "tho' by Virtue of the Laws of this Realm" the "Decisions of Courts of Justice . . . do bind, as a Law between the Parties thereto, as to the particular Case in Question," they "do not make a Law properly so called, (for that

[18] *Earl of Shaftesbury's Case* (K.B. 1677), *Modern Reports,* 1: 148. After this was argued by Wallop on behalf of Shaftesbury, the Attorney General conceded, "that which is said of the Judges power to expound statutes cannot be denied." Ibid., 154.

[19] Proceedings against John Finch (1640), *State Trials,* 4: 5.

[20] *Bole v. Horton* (C.P. 1673), Vaughan, *Reports,* 382. Chief Justice Orlando Bridgman expressed the increasingly systematic distrust of extrajudicial expositions of law when in 1662 he observed about a judicial resolution of eighty years earlier that "it was an extrajudicial opinion; and though I must give reverence to the opinions of the Judges, yet I make a difference between cases adjudged upon debate and having counsel on both sides, and resolution upon a case reported or referred to them." Accordingly, unlike their "resolution" on "the principal matter," their "other resolutions were but *obiter* and *ex abundanti.*" *Beckman v. Maplesden* (C.P. 1662), Orlando Bridgeman, *Reports,* 79.

only the King and Parliament can do)." Nonetheless, such decisions had an authority:

> [Y]et they have a Weight and Authority in Expounding, Declaring, and Publishing what the Law of this Kingdom is, especially when such Decisions hold a Consonancy and Congruity with Resolutions of former Times; and tho' such Decisions are less than a Law, yet they are a greater Evidence thereof than the Opinion of any private Persons, as such, whatsoever.[21]

Chancellor Nottingham put it more bluntly: "[P]recedents do not make law; they are only evidences of it. . . . For if precedents make law and one Court may make precedents, there's a new way found out to change all our laws and supersede the legislative power."[22]

[21] Matthew Hale, *The History of the Common Law of England,* 45, ed. Charles M. Gray (Chicago: University of Chicago, 1971). Holt even said in one dissent that he hesitated to give dicta on a question not thoroughly argued by the parties: "That being not the Case in the Question I have no Authority to Meddle with it but shall leave it as I found it, for much may be said on both sides, For the Disquisition thereof doth require a more particular Considerac[i]on & Debate Abstracted from the present Point in Question than what hath yet been had, of which if I should give any Opinion it would be Extrajudicial and therefore without the Limits of my Authority." *Lane v. Cotton & Frankland* (K.B. 1701), in British Library, Holt's Opinions, Add. Ms. 35981, fol. 92r.

[22] *Lord Nottingham's Chancery Cases,* 1: xlix, ed. D. E. C. Yale (London: Selden Society, 1957). For an elegant discussion of these sources—although more narrowly in terms of precedent—see Gerald J. Postema, "Classical Common Law Jurisprudence (Part II)," *Oxford University Commonwealth Law Journal,* 3: 12–15 (2003). For concerns about not following incorrect precedents, see, for example, *Slade's Case* (K.B. 1602), Coke, *Reports,* 4: 93b–94a, and for the particular worry about this in constitutional matters, see *Walcott's Case* (K.B. 1694), *Modern Reports,* 4: 401; Shower, *Reports,* 136.

On some questions, new precedents could be best. When, for example, the late fifteenth-century lawyer Kebell cited a precedent, his opponent Jay countered that it was "an aged precedent" and demanded, "Show us such a case adjudged in modern reports." Kebell answered: "No one could do that, because the case has simply not arisen in recent times. However, I have shown you a judgment given when such things were more commonly in use." *Abbot of Hyde v. Benger* (C.P. 1493), in *Reports of Cases by John Caryll,* 1: 180.

For questions with constitutional overtones, however, antiquity was valuable, lest judicial acquiescence to power alter the law. Perhaps the most amusing example occurred in 1628. Appalled by the king's imprisonment of men who refused to give him forced loans, Edward Coke and other members of the House of Commons examined the legality of this practice and eventually responded by drafting the Petition of Right. A Crown lawyer, who was eager to deflate Coke's sanctimoniousness, recounted that less than ten years earlier, when Coke was still on the bench, he and two other judges had upheld a return, on a warrant from the king and his council, that did not state the reason for the commitment. Coke promptly answered: "This report moves not me at all; that report is not yet 21 years old, but under age." Speech of Edward Coke (1628), *State Trials,* 3: 82. The precedent was from 13 James I—or 1615–1616. Similarly, in a later seventeenth-century case, when it was argued that Crown officers "by usage" had the right to collect duties of tunnage and poundage from wrecks, Justice Vaughan noted: "We desired to see ancient *Presidents* of that usage, but could see but

The authority of the judges, moreover, did not extend beyond their court and its jurisdiction. Although a court might to some degree be bound by its erroneous decisions, another court, Vaughan emphasized, was not bound: "[I]f a Court give *Judgment* judicially, another *Court* is not bound to give like *Judgment,* unless it think that *Judgment* first given was according to Law," for otherwise "*Errors in Judgment* would not be admitted, nor a Reversal of them." Accordingly, "if a *Judge* conceives a *Judgment* given in another *Court* to be erroneous, he being sworn to judge according to *Law,*" he "ought not to give the like Judgment, for that were to wrong every man having a like cause, because another was wrong'd before."[23]

Even within his own court, a judge was to defer to precedents only on questions that were otherwise uncertain. Such at least was Hale's view. For example, in one case, he initially opined for the plaintiff with the tepid comment that his incomplete pleading "was well enough," but after Judge Twisden "said he had known many *Judgments* reversed for the same Cause," Hale agreed that the judgment should be reversed in accord with precedent, "for he said it was his *Rule Stare decisis.*"[24] In another case, Hale similarly said he "doubted, but its best *stare decisis.*"[25] These were instances in which Hale was skeptical about the precedents but considered the question of law sufficiently uncertain that he felt obliged to follow them. As Hale explained elsewhere, "I know there is no intrinsical difference in cases by precedents"

---

one in the time of *King James,* and some in the time of the *last King,* which are so new that they are not considerable." *Sheppard v. Gosnold* (C.P. 1672), Vaughan, *Reports,* 169. See also [Lord Camden], "A Discourse against the Jurisdiction of the King's-Bench over Wales by Process of Latitat," in *A Collection of Tracts Relative to the Law of England,* 1: 420, ed. Francis Hargrave (London: 1787).

When judges strained to explain their authority to expound, they sometimes rested on their oaths, which bound them to their office. Hale explained why judicial decisions had "Authority" by reciting that the judges were men chosen for their "Learning, Knowledge, and Experience"; that "they are upon their Oaths to judge according to the Laws of the Kingdom"; that they have "the best Helps to inform their Judgments"; that "their Judgments are strengthen'd and upheld by the Laws of this Kingdom." Hale, *The History of the Common Law of England,* 45. Justice Vaughan similarly alluded to the judges' oath when explaining that "an Opinion, though *Erroneous,* concluding to the Judgment, is a *Judicial Opinion,* because delivered under the Sanction of the *Judges Oath,* upon deliberation, which assures it is, or was, when delivered, the Opinion of the *Deliverer.*" *Bole v. Horton* (C.P. 1673), Vaughan, *Reports,* 382.

23 *Bole et al. v. Horton* (C.P. 1673), Vaughan, *Reports,* 383. Baker suggests that Hale "first promoted" the principle of *stare decisis,* which Baker contrasts with the older principle *Judicandum est legibus non exemplis.* Baker, *The Law's Two Bodies,* 85. Hale, however, probably did not think himself to have so stark a choice, for as will be seen below, he shared with many of his contemporaries an understanding that law and an authoritative exposition of it were different matters.

24 *Hanslap v. Cater* (K.B. 1673), Ventris, *Reports,* 1: 243.

25 *Kirkbright v. Curwin* (K.B. 1676), Keble, *Reports,* 3: 611.

and cases not decided by precedents, "but there is a great difference in a case wherein a man is to make, and where a man sees (and is to follow) a precedent. For if a man be in doubt, *in equilibrio,* concerning a case . . . in prudence he will determine according as the precedents have been, especially if they had been made by men of good authority for learning, &c. and have been continued and pursued."[26]

As for the mere government practices that were often called "precedents," they were of even less authority, particularly on constitutional or more generally fundamental points of law. Acknowledging that the original constitution had to be discerned from custom, Hale suggested that "if the original of government appears not, then we must have recourse to the common custom and usage of the kingdom" for evidence, but he hastened to add:

> And here by custom and usage I mean not those exorbitances on either side which the practice of former times hath shown to the world. For as on the one side we find sometimes practices of treasons and rebellions against princes, and on the other side sometimes practices of oppression and tyranny by them . . . yet such a usage doth not give them credit or make them lawful. But I mean such customs as have been allowed by the known laws of the kingdom. . . . And these . . . are the best evidences of both *facti* and *juris* of the nature and extent of government.[27]

Vaughan observed that "[p]recedents of Process issued" by a court "without a *Judicial* decision upon an Argument" were "of no moment," for "*Presidents* are useful to decide questions, but in such Cases as these which de-

[26] *Fry v. Porter* (Ch. 1669), *Modern Reports,* 1: 309. From a slightly different point of view, Blackstone later wrote: "For it is an established rule to abide by former precedents, where the same points come again in litigation"—among other reasons, "because what before was uncertain, and perhaps indifferent, is now become a permanent rule, which it is not in the breast of any subsequent judge to alter or vary from, according to his private sentiments: he being sworn to determine, not according to his own private judgment, but according to the known laws and customs of the land; not delegated to pronounce a new law, but to maintain and expound the old one. Yet this rule admits of exception, where the former determination is most evidently contrary to reason; much more if it be contrary to the divine law." William Blackstone, *Commentaries on the Laws of England,* 1: 69–70 (Oxford: 1765). This exception for what was evidently or manifestly contrary to reason must be understood in light of Blackstone's academic taste, and his emphasis on what was contrary to divine law must be considered in the context of his Tory passive obedience.

[27] Matthew Hale, *The Prerogatives of the King,* 7, ed. D. E. C. Yale (London: Selden Society, 1976). When Charles I relied on the practices of earlier kings to justify his imprisonment of members of Parliament, a lawyer for one of them distinguished between "*via juris,* and *via facti*" and insisted: "Precedents are not good directions, unless they be judicial." Argument of Calthorpe for Valentine, in Proceedings Against Elliot, Hollis, and Valentine (K.B. 1629), *State Trials,* 3: 303.

pend upon fundamental Principles, from which Demonstrations may be drawn, millions of *Presidents* are to no purpose."[28]

On account of the greater deference they were apt to receive, judicial precedents seemed to pose a particularly serious constitutional danger. Perhaps no precedent could be more than evidence of the law, but if judicial holdings in cases were of greater authority than other precedents, then at least within the scope of uncertainty, judges might well fear that their errors would become permanent. When the Aylesbury voters imprisoned by the House of Commons sought their habeas corpus, Chief Justice Holt distinguished between judicial and extrajudicial precedents. The "extra-judicial" act of the Commons in confining the voters was "not according to the Constitution of the Kingdom," and "the freemen of England are not to be bound by the precedent of such an imprisonment." The decision of the judges on the habeas, however, was another matter. Holt understood that "[t]he judges in the Queen's Courts are judges of the law, but have no power to make a law." At the same time, he worried that "if this commitment in the case of these men shall be determined [by the judges] to be warranted by the laws and customs of this realm, it will be a rule in all other cases."[29]

Whig fears of mistaken precedent—both judicial and nonjudicial—reached their height during the Wilkes affair. The initial question concerned the authority of the nonjudicial precedents for the warrant used against Wilkes, and it will be recalled that Chief Justice Pratt held that "office precedents . . . are no justification of a practice itself illegal, and contrary to the fundamental principles of the constitution."[30] Although Pratt announced this prominently enough, few points of law became more notorious, for Junius declared it to multitudes on both sides of the Atlantic. He observed about the use of precedents against Wilkes: "*General warrants,* it is true, had been often issued; but they had never been regularly questioned or resisted, until the case of Mr. Wilkes. He brought them to trial; and the

[28] *Process into Wales,* Vaughan, *Reports,* 419. For a similar assumption about "the records [that] pass in silence, and without exception of the parties," see *Slade's Case* (K.B. 1602), Coke, *Reports,* 4: 94a.

[29] *Case of Paty et al.* (Q.B. 1705), *The Judgements delivered by the Lord Chief Justice Holt in the Case of Ashby v. White and Others,* 43, 47, 50.

[30] *Wilkes v. Wood* (C.P. 1763), *State Trials,* 19: 1167. At a lower level, when a city's charter left questions open or uncertain, the city could make a by-law to clarify the matter, but it could not thereby displace judicial authority. For example, on a quo warranto against a mayor who also was an alderman, King's Bench determined his holding of the two offices to be in violation of the town charter, and in rejecting a defense based on a by-law, Chief Justice Lee said for the court, "nor can a by-law explain a charter, for that must be done by the Judges." *King v. Mayor of Weymouth* (K.B., 1740), *Modern Reports,* 7: 373.

moment they were tried, they were declared *illegal.*"[31] On these facts, Junius entreated his readers:

> [L]et me exhort and conjure you, never to suffer an invasion of your political constitution, however minute the instance may appear, to pass by, without a determined persevering resistance. One precedent creates another. They soon accumulate, and constitute law. What yesterday was fact, to-day is doctrine. Examples are supposed to justify the most dangerous measures; and where they do not suit exactly, the defect is supplied by analogy. Be assured, that the laws, which protect us in our civil rights, grow out of the constitution, and they must fall or flourish with it.[32]

The constitution was the source of the laws that protected civil rights, and government practices that violated the constitution could therefore not be allowed to become law.

When William Pitt the Elder—the Earl of Chatham—joined the parliamentary debates about Wilkes, he focused on judicial precedents contrary to the constitution. Wilkes had repeatedly won election to the House of Commons, but this body had each time expelled him or refused to seat him, and when Lord Mansfield spoke in the House of Lords in 1770 to defend the Commons, Chatham responded. Far more than office precedents, judicial precedents were evidence of law, but Mansfield's manipulative decisions seemed to many Whigs to illustrate the danger of accepting the authority of judicial precedents beyond the law. Chatham therefore took aim at Mansfield by declaring that if the House of Commons was a type of court, it could not act above the law, for "no Court of Justice can have a power inconsistent with, or paramount to the known laws of the land." Extending this line of argument to questions of authority, Chatham applied it not only to the House of Commons but also to King's Bench. Chatham surely looked toward the chief justice of that court when he asked:

> What security would [the people] have for their rights, if once they admitted, that a Court of Judicature might determine every question that came before it, not by any known, positive law, but by the vague indeterminate, arbitrary rule, of what the noble Lord is pleased to call *the wisdom of the court?* With respect to the decision of the Courts of Justice, I am far from denying them their due weight and authority; yet, placing them in the most respectable view, I still consider them, not as law, but as an evidence of the law; and before they can arrive even at that degree of authority, it must appear, that they are founded in, and confirmed by, reason; that they are supported by prece-

[31] Letter from Philo Junius to an Advocate in the Course of the People (Oct. 18, 1771), *The Letters of Junius,* 2: 168 (New York: 1821).
[32] Ibid., 1: vi (Dedication).

> dents taken from good and moderate times; that they do not contradict any positive law; that they are submitted to without reluctance by the people; that they are unquestioned by the Legislature, (which is equivalent to a tacit confirmation); and, what, in my judgment, is by far the most important, that they do not violate the spirit of the Constitution.

In this Whig vision, an opinion contrary to the spirit of the constitution was without authority, and Chatham taunted Mansfield by reminding the Lords that even "school-boys" knew the underlying principle: "that *Legem f*[*a*]*cere* and *Legem dicere* were powers clearly distinguished from each other in the nature of things, and wisely separated by the wisdom of the English Constitution."[33] The office of judgment was different from that of making law, and although this distinction sharpened the authority of the judges to expound law in their cases, it seemed to cut off their authority when they went beyond their cases or mere exposition.

In sum, already in England it is possible to discern in judicial duty what has come to be called "judicial review." The office of a judge was one of independent judgment, and while at an abstract level it was a judge's duty to exercise independent judgment in accord with law in general, in England it was more specifically his duty to exercise such judgment in accord with the law of the land. By binding themselves to this office with their oaths, the English judges acquired a divine obligation to decide in accord with the law of their country, and with this religious obligation as to worldly law, they could often find the fortitude to do their duty—even when it required them to hold acts of the king unlawful. Finally, as has been seen in this chapter, to the extent the judges in deciding cases had to explain what the law was, they expounded the law with the authority of their office. This judicial authority was hardly new, for it had long been understood that the exposition of law was part of the office of judgment, but in response to claims of lawmaking authority, the judges became newly attentive to their office and its focus on cases, and they thereby strengthened the authority of the expositions of law they gave within their office, including their expositions of the constitution and what it rendered unlawful.

[33] Speech in House of Lords (Jan. 9, 1770), *Anecdotes of the Life of the Right Hon. William Pitt, Earl of Chatham,* 2: 15–17 (London: 1792). If Chatham's speech seems consistent with the writings of Junius, this should not be thought a coincidence, for Junius was probably Sir Philip Francis, who wrote the speech for Chatham. Leslie Stephen, "Chatham, Francis, and Junius," *English Historical Review,* 3: 233 (1888).

III

JUDICIAL DUTY AS TO LEGISLATIVE ACTS

It has been seen in Part I that the English constitution was part of the law of the land, and in Part II that the judges had a duty to decide in accord with this law. Part III therefore must now examine the application of this duty to legislation.

Contrary to what may be expected, it was well understood that judges generally could hold legislation unlawful, but at the same time there were legal and political obstacles to decisions about some significant types of legislation. On the one hand, as will be seen in Chapter Eight, the law itself precluded judicial decisions holding acts of Parliament unlawful, and this raised doubts as to whether Parliament was subject to law—in particular, whether it was the subject to the constitution. On the other hand, as will be observed in Chapter Nine, although there were no legal barriers to holding nonparliamentary legislation unlawful, there were political dangers in overturning colonial enactments, and therefore the judges who specialized in dealing with colonial law—colonial judges and members of the Privy Council—often strained against their duty. Whereas the law preserved acts of Parliament from the adverse effect of judicial duty, it was the judges' politic departure from duty that frequently spared colonial statutes.

This distinction is significant for what has been called "judicial review." If one were merely to examine decisions about acts of Parliament, judicial duty would not seem to explain later American decisions holding statutes unconstitutional. When one examines decisions about other legislative acts, however, including corporate by-laws and, here, colonial statutes, it becomes evident that American legislation had always been subject to judicial decisions holding it unlawful. In practice, few colonial judges or members of the Privy Council were willing to hold colonial statutes unlawful, but at least in the ideals of the common law this was often their duty. Indeed, the reluctance of some of the judges to do in practice what was required of them by their ideals actually confirms the importance of the ideals, for it suggests how much it was the common law ideals rather than the colonial practice that would matter for American judges after 1776.

8

No Appeal from Parliament

Although judges could hold most types of legislation unlawful, the common law barred judges from reaching this conclusion about acts of Parliament. It has been seen that the judges could hold local legislation and even royal acts unlawful. Acts of Parliament, however, were another matter. In a realm governed by a customary constitution, the court of the realm, Parliament, could declare the constitution; as the highest court, moreover, it stood above appeal; and in both ways the common law itself precluded judicial decisions holding acts of Parliament unlawful.

These legal obstacles to holding acts of Parliament unlawful left an opportunity for oppression, but the danger lay not merely in the restrictions on the judges, but more substantially in Parliament's drift toward absolute power. A supreme court, being beyond appeal, can easily come to consider itself above the law, and Parliament increasingly took such a view of its authority. Its absolutist perspective, however, was not unquestioned. A substantial minority of Englishmen assumed that Parliament, like the Crown, was under the law of the land, particularly the constitution. In their view, all government authority—whether executive, judicial, or legislative—depended upon the law made by the people, thus leaving no power above the law in any part of government.

The High Court and the Customary Constitution

Two legal impediments barred judges from holding acts of Parliament unlawful: The English constitution was customary, and Parliament was the highest court in the land. There were undoubtedly other obstacles to decisions overturning acts of Parliament, but these legal hurdles were insurmountable.

Although the legal obstacles are not unfamiliar, the history of judicial review gives them little attention, apparently on the assumption that there were more substantial barriers. For example, it has been widely assumed that the development of judicial review was impeded by Parliament's sheer political dominance over other government institutions. This conventional emphasis on parliamentary power is certainly very satisfying in its suggestion that American judges who later tamed legislative power must have been very bold. It will be seen, however, that English judges declined to hold acts of Parliament unlawful long before this body acquired political preeminence, and it therefore becomes necessary to consider the possibility that Parliament's power rested on preexisting features of English law—on ideals that already barred judges from holding acts of Parliament void.

It has also been thought, along similar lines, that the objection to holding acts of Parliament unlawful was really an unwillingness to hold sovereign acts unlawful. Yet as already observed, English judges were well aware of the distinction between sovereign and subordinate acts, and they did not refrain from judicial decisions about the unlawfulness of either. Instead, as notably elaborated by Chief Justice Holt, they used the distinction to explain the standards applicable to the different types of acts—sovereign acts being examined simply against the law, and subordinate acts being measured against the common law test of law and reason. It therefore seems necessary to move beyond the arguments about sovereignty, let alone the even vaguer claims about political power, and to examine how the common law itself stood in the way of decisions holding acts of Parliament unlawful.

The judges at the very least could not hold an act of Parliament *unconstitutional,* for the constitution was part of the common law and thus was customary. England's constitution developed as an element of the custom of the realm—the common law—which was declared by the court of the realm. Just as a manor court was the body in which a manorial community met and decided about their customs, so Parliament was the court in which the entire realm was presumed to be present to declare or alter their custom, including what came to be considered England's constitution.[1] Thus,

[1] It was commonly assumed that statutes either made new laws, which altered common law, or declared common law. Coke, *Institutes,* 3: Proeme (London: 1644); Matthew Hale, *The Prerogatives of the King,* 141, ed. D. E. C. Yale (London: Selden Society, 1976). From his rather caustic point of view, Halifax wrote: "If the Common Law is Supream, then those are so who judge what is the Common Law; and if none but the Parliament can judge so, there is an end to the Controversy; there is no *Fundamental;* for the Parliament may judge as they please." "Political Thoughts and Reflections," in George Savile, Marquis of Halifax, *A Character of King Charles the Second: and Political, Moral and Miscellaneous Thoughts and Reflections,* 75–76 ("Of Fundamentals") (London: 1750).

when it came to be widely assumed that the English had a constitution within the common law, Parliament appeared to be the court with the authority to judge any constitutional questions about its acts. Parliament's decisions about the customary constitution were thus determinative, and its enactments amounted to decisions upholding their constitutionality.

More broadly, the judges could not hold acts of Parliament *unlawful,* because Parliament was the highest of English courts.[2] Some of the king's courts were specifically judicial, such as King's Bench and Common Pleas. In other, more general courts, however, the king acted in ways that were not only judicial but also executive or legislative—as in his Privy Council and, above all, his great council of Parliament. Although Parliament soon became primarily a legislative body, it retained its judicial forms of proceeding and its status as "the highest court of all other courts," and these other courts remained "each of them inferior to this high court."[3] Thus, King's Bench was only "the highest Court of ordinary Justice," and like the other courts that were inferior to Parliament, it could not question the acts of what was often called the "supreme court."[4] During the seventeenth cen-

[2] For the implications of Parliament's being the high court, see Thomas Smith, *De Republica Anglorum,* xxviii–xxxiii, ed. Leonard Alston (Cambridge: University Press, 1906); J. W. Gough, *Fundamental Law in English Constitutional History,* 8, 42–43 (Oxford: Clarendon, 1955). McIlwain discusses what he calls Parliament's "old 'judicial' supremacy," but he does so to disparage its significance in the seventeenth and eighteenth centuries. He argues that the English did not clearly distinguish the "spheres of legislation and judicature" until very late, and he thus assumes that parliamentary supremacy arose from the political strife of the seventeenth century—such that "the conditions antedate the theory." Charles Howard McIlwain, *The High Court of Parliament,* 312, note 1, 355, 374 (New Haven: Yale University Press, 1910).

[3] Speech of Speaker (Feb. 18, 1589), in Simonds D'Ewes, *The Journals of all the Parliaments During the Reign of Queen Elizabeth,* 434 (1682), quoted in G. R. Elton, *The Tudor Constitution: Documents and Commentary,* 229, 233 (Cambridge: Cambridge University Press, 1968).

[4] Coke, *Institutes:* 3: 219.

The judicial character of Parliament is the subject of some academic enthusiasm. McIlwain so strongly emphasizes Parliament's judicial status as to say that "in the Tudor and even in a large part of the Stuart period, men had not yet reached" a "clear distinction" between the "spheres of legislation and judicature." McIlwain, *The High Court of Parliament,* 134. G. R. Elton writes that prior to the 1530s, statutes were understood as "judicial pronouncements" and that "[a]s late as 1550 a chief justice of Common Pleas could call it 'nothing but a court.'" G. R. Elton, ed., *The Tudor Constitution: Documents and Commentary,* 229, 233 (Cambridge: Cambridge University Press, 1968).

In fact, the combined judicial and legislative character of Parliament was well understood both much earlier and much later. For example, in the Middle Ages, as shown by Morris Arnold, courts distinguished between what today would be called Parliament's private and public acts, treating the former as judgments between private parties and the later as acts known to all and generally binding. Morris S. Arnold, "Statutes as Judgments: The Natural Law Theory of Parliamentary Activity in Medieval England," *University of Pennsylvania Law Review,* 126: 335–340 (1977). Similarly, Matthew Hale noted that "[t]he supreme jurisdiction of parliament acts either *deliberative* where it makes laws or *judicative* when it gives tury, this legal bar to judicial decisions about the lawfulness of statutes acquired something close to physical force on account of Parliament's growing political supremacy, but even before the development of this additional, political impediment, the inferior courts could not hear appeals from the high court or otherwise overturn its acts.[5]

A case of 1327 illustrates how medieval courts already deferred to the judgments of Parliament. Early in the year, Archbishop of Canterbury Walter Reynolds helped to depose Edward II and bring his son Edward III to the throne, but Reynold's great competitor, Archbishop of York William Melton, was slow to shift his loyalties, and Melton apparently took advantage of this situation to secure Parliament's attention to what he undoubtedly considered an old injustice. Although earlier archbishops of York had held the right of "prise" or customs duties on wine transported through the port of Hull, Edward I's butler had seized this franchise and imposed duties on behalf of the king. Now, shortly after Edward III's coronation, the archbishop's right to the duties came before Parliament, which heard evidence and reached a "judgement" that the right had belonged from time immemorial to the archbishop. Edward therefore ordered his butler, Richard de la Pole, to stop collecting the duties. The collection of the duties, however, must have been lucrative for the butler as well as his master, and Richard refused to give way. Edward therefore repeatedly had to command his butler to comply with the judgment, and Edward eventually issued a writ ordering the butler to come to King's Bench "to show why you have scorned our orders." In these proceedings, when the butler questioned the substance of

judgment." Hale, *The Prerogatives of the King,* 181. Yet as Arnold recognizes, this is hardly to say that the acts of Parliament were not the acts of a court, and thus even the legislative acts of Parliament were the acts of the highest court in the realm. Indeed, England was a society in which from early times commands of law ordinarily had obligation as laws only to the extent they came from a court—whether a local manor or Parliament—and accordingly there was no necessary tension between Parliament's role as court and as a legislature.

[5] Another explanation was that Parliament was governed by its own laws and customs, but this had the same weaknesses as the king's claims of a prerogative independent of the law of the land. Less attentive to this problem than perhaps he should have been, Coke wrote: "And as every Court of Justice hath laws and custom for its direction, some by the Common law, some by the the Civill and Canon law, some by peculiar lawes and customes, &c. So the High Court of Parliament *Suis propiis legibus & consuetudinibus subsistit.* It is lex & consuetudo Parliamenti, that all weighty matters in any Parliament moved concerning the Peers of the Realm, or Commons in Parliament assembled, ought to be determined, adjudged, and discussed by the course of the Parliament, and not by the Civill law, nor yet by the Common laws of this Realm used in more inferior Courts . . . and every member of the Parliament hath a judicial place, and can be no witnesse. And this is the reason that Judges ought not to give any opinion of a matter of Parliament, because it is not to be decided by the common laws, but *secundum legem ad consuetudinem Parliamenti.*" Coke, *Institutes,* 4: 15.

the judgment given by Parliament, the Archbishop of York answered that "the aforesaid judgement had been made in so solemn a place as the parliament" and that "judgement cannot be revoked elsewhere than in parliament." King's Bench was inclined to agree, saying that it was "doubtful whether further proceedings could be held in this court on that business," and probably to remove any doubt, the king instructed the chancellor "to convene the whole of the king's council in chancery," including the justices—leading to a decision that "because the judgement was made in the aforesaid parliament . . . execution in accordance with the form of the judgement made in parliament should not be stayed." In short, the case had been "awarded and adjudged in parliament, which is the highest and most solemn judgement in the land."[6]

Parliament's status as a court similarly prevented judicial reconsideration of its acts of attainder, which more clearly than most statutes were simultaneously legislative and judicial acts. The primary illustration of this was a question pressed by Henry VIII and his chief minister, Thomas Cromwell. The king asked the judges whether Parliament could pass an act of attainder against a man for high treason without giving him a chance to answer the charges against him, even if he were available. One of the judges who was consulted, the "grave and reverend" Thomas Gawdy, recalled that the judges initially were evasive, saying:

> [T]hat it was a dangerous question, and that the high court of parliament ought to give examples to inferior courts for proceeding according to Justice, and no inferior court could do the like; and they thought that the high court of parliament would never do it.

The king, however, at Cromwell's urging, insisted on "a direct answer," and the judges therefore said that if a man were attainted by Parliament, "it could not come in question afterwards, whether he was called or not called to answer," for "the act of attainder being passed by parliament, did bind." Ironically, Cromwell himself was the first to suffer under the judges' opinion. Gawdy told this story to his young kinsman by marriage, Edward Coke, who understood both the deference owed to the highest court and the danger. Coke observed that "although I question not the power of the

[6] *Archbishop of York v. Richard de la Pole* (K.B. 1327), in G. O. Sayles, *The Functions of the Medieval Parliament of England,* 382 (London: Hambledon, 1988); Writ (June 4, 1327), in G. O. Sayles, ed., *Select Cases in the Court of King's Bench under Edward III,* 5: 10 (London: Selden Society, 1958). For subsequent proceedings and the chronology of the 1327 proceedings, see Y.B. Michaelmas 5 Edward III, pl. 113, fol. 65b; Y.B. Hillary 6 Edward III, pl. 15, fols. 5a–6b; Y.B. Hillary 6 Edward III, pl. 28, fols. 10b–11a. For other details, see *The Original Institution, Power and Jurisdiction of Parliaments,* 84–85 (London: 1707).

parliament, for without question the attainder standeth of force in law: yet . . . the more high and absolute the jurisdiction of the court is, the more just and honourable it ought to be in the proceeding."[7]

In fact, all acts of Parliament—not merely attainders—were "judgments" of the court of Parliament and thus beyond reversal in any other court. In the early seventeenth century, Henry Finch explained: "The Parliament is a Court . . . having an absolute power in all causes," whether "to make Lawes, to adjudge matters in Law, to trie causes of life and death," or "to reverse errors in the Kings Bench," and "all their Decrees are as Judgements." Accordingly, "if the Parliament it selfe doe erre (as it may) it can no where be reversed but in Parliament."[8] A treatise attributed to Matthew Hale similarly noted that Parliament was "the highest and greatest court, over which none other can have Jurisdiction in the Kingdom," and therefore "[i]f by any means a Misgovernment should any ways fall upon it, the Subjects of this Kingdome are left without all manner of Remedy.[9] Far from being abstruse, this point was repeated in widely read legal publications. Giles Jacob's *Law Dictionary* called Parliament "this supreme Court" and echoed Finch that "though the *Parliament* err, it is not reversible in any other Court." William Blackstone simply quoted the treatise supposedly written by Hale, that because Parliament was "the highest and greatest court . . . the subjects of this kingdom are left without all manner of remedy."[10]

Parliament's Absolute Power

A court that was above judgment might eventually come to be above the law, and being a supreme court that could claim to speak for the people, Parliament's final judgment eventually became its absolute power. At the

[7] Coke, *Institutes,* 4: 37–38; *The Original Institution, Power and Jurisdiction of Parliaments,* 48.
[8] Henry Finch, *Law, or, a Discourse Thereof,* 233 (London: 1627). Of course, Finch understood that although Parliament was one of the "Courts of Record," it was without "ordinary jurisdiction." Ibid.
[9] *The Original Institution, Power and Jurisdiction of Parliaments,* 49. This was also, incidentally, why Parliament could not bind itself into the future. As Serjeant John Cottesmore explained, "Parliament is the highest court, in which he will have a good remedy, and it has been said that Parliament can reverse an act in Parliament, because there is no higher court in which he will have remedy." Y.B. Pasc. 7 Henry VI, plea 22, fol. 29a (K.B. 1429) (as translated by Seipp) ("le Parlement est plus haut *Court,* en quel il aura bon remedy: & ad este dit que le Parlement peut reverser fait en le Parlement, & la cause est, pur ceo que il n'ad plus haut *Court,* en que il aura remedie").
[10] Giles Jacob, *Law Dictionary,* "Parliament" (London, 1732); William Blackstone, *Commentaries on the Law of England,* 1: 157 (I.2) (London: 1765) (citing Hale).

beginning of the seventeenth century, the peril of absolute power still seemed to come from the Crown. By the end of the century, however, the English subdued the lawless power of their kings only by relying on the same sort of power in Parliament. It was a sobering enterprise to defeat absolutism in one part of government by elevating it in another, and it suggested the grim possibility that in all human government there might have to be a power above human law. Perhaps, in other words, government under law was not possible.

It was obvious enough that the deference owed to a higher court could easily become the deference paid to a power that stood above law. Already in the fifteenth century, it was said that "parliament has complete power."[11] In 1532, several years before Henry VIII confiscated the monasteries, St. German ominously observed: "It is holden by them that be lerned in the lawe of this royalme, that the parlyamente hath an absolute power, as to the possession of all temporall thynges within this realme, in whose handes so ever they be, spyrytualle or temporalle, to take them fro oone manne, and gyve theym to an nother."[12] To take property from one man and give it to another was an old example used by civilian commentators to illustrate absolute power, and Sir Thomas Smith, who had studied civil law at Padua, repeated the line that Parliament had the power of "chang[ing] rights, and possessions of private men," this being an example of how Parliament had "[t]he most high and absolute power of the realme of Englande."[13] More amusingly, at the end of the century, the issue arose at a conference between the Commons and the Lords on a bill allowing the Crown to recover from grantees of land if the grantor later fraudulently became indebted to the Crown—presumably on misrepresentations about the extent of his prop-

[11] Third Lecture on Westminster II, c. 1, in Samuel E. Thorne, ed., *Readings and Moots at the Inns of Court in the Fifteenth Century,* 181 (London: Selden Society, 1954).

[12] [Christopher St. German], *A Treatise Concernyinge the Division Between the Spiritualtie and Temporaltie,* fol. 24[r] (London: [1532]).

[13] Thomas Smith, *De Republica Anglorum,* 34–35 (London: 1583). For the commentators, see Walter Ullmann, *The Medieval Idea of Law as Represented by Lucas de Penna: A Study in Fourteenth-Century Legal Scholarship,* 101–103 (1946; New York: Barnes & Noble, 1969). The feeble restraint imposed on such transfers by the civilian commentators was that the ruler had to act with just cause, but some did not even go so far. For example, Cynus distinguished between what was possible *de facto* and *de jure,* and Albericus and Lucas suggested that if a ruler transferred property without just cause he was accountable only to God. Ibid., 101–102; Kenneth Pennington, *The Prince and the Law, 1200–1600,* at 115 (Berkeley: University of California Press, 1963). St. German's Doctor echoed this sort of view: "And yf yt were ordeynyd by statute that one man sholde have a nother mannes lande and noo cause ys expressyed why he sholde have yt, in that case thoughe he myght holde the lande by force of that statute, yet he coulde not holde yt in conscyence without there were a cause why he sholde have yt." T. F. T. Plucknett and J. L. Barton, eds., *St. German's Doctor and Student,* 287 (London: Selden Society, 1974).

erty. When a member of the Commons complained that the bill would take property from an innocent purchaser as if he were a malfeasor, Lord Treasurer William Cecil quipped with Attorney General Edward Coke about what Parliament could do:

> *Cecil:* Whie, you see what the parlement can doe, even make a man a woman.
> *Coke:* Noe, and please your Lordshipp, that is impossible.
> *Cecil:* It is as if the parliament should make an infant a man.
> *Coke:* Ne[i]ther this, but the parliament maie make an infant of full age.
> *Cecil:* I, but, if I saie soe[,] you shall saie the like by your leave, and if the lawe be so[,] you shall doe the like whether you will or noe.[14]

James I later recalled of Cecil: "[T]hat old wise man" was "wont to say, Hee knew not what an Acte of Parliament could not doe in *England*."[15] The highest court in the land was above human adjudication, and Englishmen could thus easily drift into believing it was above the law.

This absolute power of Parliament could cut short the absolute power asserted by kings. After James I claimed a prerogative to levy impositions by "absolute authoritye of the Kinges Majestie, wythout assent of parlement," some lawyers responded with a bill in which they proposed that it "be Inacted as a certen and absolute lawe, That all Imposicions paste . . . wythout assent of Parlement, shall be adjudged in lawe to be voyde."[16] The members of Parliament who in 1628 drafted the Petition of Right similarly claimed an absolute power over the king's absolute power. The Petition was a statute in the form of a petition, and the Lords attempted to add a savings clause stating that although Parliament was attempting to preserve the people's liberties, it was doing so "with a due regard to leave intire that Sovereign Power wherewith your Majesty is trusted for the Protection, Safety, and Happiness of the People."[17] The notion of sovereign power was at this date more familiar from Bodin than the common law, and many members

[14] Townshend's Journal (Jan. 24, 1599), in *Proceedings in the Parliaments of Elizabeth I,* 3: 236 , ed. T. E. Hartley (London: Leicester University Press, 1981–1995). Words attributing these words to the speakers have been omitted here without ellipses so as to present the quotation in the form of a dialogue. Incidentally, compare *Bonham's Case.*

[15] *Speech in Star Chamber* (1616), in *The Political Works of James I,* 329, ed. Charles Howard McIlwain (Cambridge: Harvard University Press, 1918).

[16] *"Speciall Observacions Touching All the Sessions of the Last Parliament Anno 7 Regis & Etc.,"* (1611), in *Law and Politics in Jacobean England: The Tracts of Lord Chancellor Ellesmere,* 260, ed. Louis A. Knafla (Cambridge: Cambridge University Press, 1977).

[17] *Historical Collections,* 1: 561, ed. John Rushworth (London: 1721).

of the Commons were shocked. They regarded the savings clause as a concession that the king had an absolute prerogative above acts of Parliament, and they therefore countered that such acts themselves were absolute. John Glanville asked: "What were this but to admit a Sovereign Power in the King above the Laws and Statutes of the Kingdom?" Glanville's father had been a judge, and he now observed that although a trust was placed in the kings of England, "that trust is regulated by law," including Magna Charta, which was "an absolute law in its self." Edward Coke, who now sat in the Commons, explained: "I know the prerogative is part of the law, but 'sovereign power' is no parliamentary word in my opinion. It weakens Magna Charta and other Statutes, for they are absolute without any saving of sovereign power."[18]

The vision of Parliament as absolute reached its zenith when Parliament in the mid-seventeenth century fought the king and attempted to establish itself as an absolute sovereign, and few men went further on behalf of Parliament's absolute power than William Prynne. One of the Crown's prerogative courts had branded him and lopped off his ears, and when at the beginning of the Civil War Parliament began to legislate without the king, Prynne extolled the prerogative of Parliament in opposition to the "pretended Prerogative, which . . . fantasies onely (not the Law) have unduely attributed unto Kings." Prynne assumed that *"[t]he Court or person to whom the last appeale is to be made, is the Supreamest power,"* and from this perspective, Parliament *"is the most high and absolute power, the supreamest and most ancient Court of the Realme of England"* and *"is above the Law it selfe."* Whereas the king "and his Prerogative" were "subordinate to the Lawes of the Realme," Parliament was so far above them it could imprison men without regard to Magna Charta or habeas corpus, for it had "an absolute Soveraignty over the Laws themselves (yea, over *Magna Charta,* and all other objected Acts)."[19]

18 Glanville (May 23, 1628), in *Commons Debates 1628,* at 565, 569, eds. Robert C. Johnson et al. (New Haven: Yale University Press, 1977); Coke (May 20, 1628), ibid., 495. Edward Alford, a leading proponent of the Petition, asked: "What is 'Sovereign Power'? *Bodin* says it is that that is free from any condition." Accordingly, "[b]y this we shall acknowledge a regal as well as a legal power. Let us give that to the King that the law gives him, and no more." Alford (May 20, 1628), ibid., 494.

19 William Prynne, *The Soveraigne Power of Parliaments and Kingdomes: Divided into Foure Parts,* First Part, 46, 93, 103; Fourth Part, 15 (London: 1643). According to Prynne, "the Parliament is not within . . . any . . . Law against imprisonments," and because Parliament was "the supreamest *Judicature, paramount* [to] all other Courts, their commitments cannot be Legally questioned, determined, nor their prisoners released by *Habeas Corpus,* in or by any other inferior Court or Judicature whatsoever." Even if prisoners were to "bring an *Habeas Corpus*" to end "their perpetuall imprisonment," claiming that Parliament's laws were

To give Parliament's absolute power at least a hint of legality, parliamentarians such as Henry Parker suggested that such power was required by the natural law principles of self-preservation, necessity, and *salus populi.* No human law could anticipate all exigencies, and therefore natural law presumably gave each society a power of necessity or self-preservation above human law. Kings had claimed this as a justification for their absolute power, but because they had asserted communal necessities when they were not clearly apparent, Parker and many others thought that if there had to be a power above law, it could "no where rest more safely than in Parliament."[20]

Parker understood the possibility of a constitutional solution but doubted whether any such law could be enforced, let alone adequately drafted. "'Twas not difficult to invent Lawes, for the limitting of supreme governors, but to invent how those Lawes should be executed or by whom interpreted, was almost impossible." Like so many English theorists, he assumed there could be no indifferent judge between the king and the people, and "what a livelesse fond thing would Law be, without any judge to determine it, or power to enforce it." There were, moreover, deeper problems, for "besides, if it be agreed upon, that limits should be prefixed to Princes, and judges appointed to decree according to those limits, yet an other great inconvenience will presently affront us": the risk that "we cannot restraine Princes too far, but we shall disable them from some good, as well as inhibit them from some evill."

This lack of confidence that human law could define an adequate but safe degree of power left Parker and many fellow Englishmen to place their trust in absolute power—only that of Parliament rather than the prince. In order "[t]hat Princes may not be now beyond all limits and Lawes, nor yet left to be tryed upon those limits and Lawes by any private parties," the

---

"against *Magna Charta,* they shall notwithstanding be remanded and remain prisoners all their dayes." Ibid., Fourth Part, 26–27.

Rather than differentiate the people's original legislative power and Parliament's consequent sovereign power, Prynne conveniently argued that "the originall, prime, Legislative power of making Lawes to bind the Subjects" rested "in the Kingdome, and Parliament, which represents it." Ibid., First Part, 47. He understood that the people reserved a power in themselves, but he attributed this reserved power not only to the kingdom but also to Parliament and thus self-consciously blended the two bodies together to suggest that "the Soveraignest power and Jurisdiction of all others, resides in the whole Kingdom and Parliament." Ibid., First Part, 101.

20 [Henry Parker], *Observations Upon Some of His Majesties Late Answers and Expresses,* 45 ([London: 1642]). More generally, see Michael Mendle, *Henry Parker and the English Civil War: The Political Thought of the Public's "Privado"* (New York: Cambridge University Press, 1995).

"whole community" had to act through its representatives in the "Court which is called a Parliament," where the community would exercise the very power Parker condemned in the king—the power a nation enjoyed under the principle that "*salus Populi* is *suprema Lex.*"[21]

Such arguments avoided the absolute power of the king by placing the same power in Parliament and thus simply shifted the danger of tyranny from one place to another. Prynne and Parker each strained to suggest that the people themselves met as a community in the high court of Parliament to secure their safety—a fiction that conveniently allowed Parliament to exercise what was more conventionally understood to be the power of the people. Parliamentary rule above law, however, would soon come to seem as arbitrary as earlier, royal governance of this sort. It was an eye-opening experience, and many Englishmen thereby learned, even more than in the past, to distinguish between Parliament and the people and to question the safety of attributing absolute power to any part of government.

Parliament Subject to the Constitution

It was one thing to say that the highest court was beyond appeal, but quite another to say that it therefore had a power above law, and some Englishmen repudiated Parliament's claim of absolute power by insisting that the only human power above human law belonged to the people. Rather than substitute the absolute power of the legislature for that of the monarch, these Englishmen argued that all parts of government were subject to the constitution and that even if Parliament lay beyond judicial remedies, it was not beyond the law of the land.[22] Such a distinction could be difficult to maintain, and it would one day frustrate many Americans, but already in England, when sovereignty shifted from the king to the legislature, there were men who insisted that sovereignty could not exist above the lawmaking power of the people.

That such ideas about *"the Fundamental Constitution"* were sufficiently mundane to require no inspiration of genius can be illustrated by the writings of William Ball—a relatively obscure resident of Berkshire who wrote on constitutional questions beginning in the 1640s. Ball rejected unlimited power in either king or Parliament, because both were under the fundamental law. The king had claimed a "*Terra Australis Incognita* of Prerogative

[21] Ibid., 13–15; [Henry Parker], *Jus Populi,* 2, 43 (London: 1644).
[22] Jeffrey Goldsworthy, *The Sovereignty of Parliament: History and Philosophy,* 192 (Oxford: Oxford University Press, 1999).

power," and Parliament had asserted its *"Great Sea of Juridicall power,"* but neither was "so unlimited or boundlesse."[23] With an unfortunate interest in technical-sounding vocabulary, Ball acknowledged that "the Parliament is the highest *Court extensive* (*viz.* to conserve Rule, Order, &c.) but the People in generall (*viz.* the Counties, Cities, and Towns corporate) are the highest, or greatest *Power Intensive,* in that they are the efficient, and finall cause under god, of the Parliament." Accordingly, their power limited Parliament's power:

> Parliament can never deprive the Counties, Cities, and Towns Corporate, by any Act, or Ordinance whatsoever, of their innate, and inseparable Right and Power of Electing, or creating Knights, Citizens, and Burgesses . . . [N]o more can the Parliament deprive the free People, or Nation of *England,* of their *Generall Liberty, and propriety,* for in these things the Sphear of the Parliaments Activity is circumscribed by the Nations large Bulke of *Primitive, or intensive Power.*

It was therefore a "mistake" to say, *"It is impossible that the supreame Court in any Kingdome should be limited."* For example, if Parliament were to "make a Law, or Ordinance that the Knights, Citizens, and Burgesses" should "be appointed or denominated by themselves," this would be to "alter the frame and constitution of this Nation."[24]

Although questions about "the necessity of the Kingdome" belonged to Parliament, "of which Necessity they are the Judges," this did not mean that Parliament was unlimited, for "a Power . . . may bee supream to some things, yet not to all."[25] The king's prerogative—his *ius regnandi*—"comprehends a power ordinary, and extraordinary; both limited, and qualified, neither absolute," and by the same token Parliament's power also was qualified. Together, "the King and Parliament are the *Legislative power* in England . . . in things *disputable* . . . but not in things *indisputable,* such as . . . the generall and fundamental liberty and propriety of the Subject grounded upon the Law of Nature." In these matters, in which "the Kingdome would be wholly damnified, and enslaved, and deprived of its *naturall right,*" it might be claimed for the King and Parliament that they had a right to "dispose of all mens estates *ad placitum,*" but in such things the people "make them no Judges."[26] As Ball later summarized, "the People of *England* were

[23] William Ball, *De Jure Regnandi, & Regni: or, The Sphere of Government,* 2 (1645).
[24] William Ball, *Constitutio Liberi Populi. Or, the Rule of a Free-born People,* 12–13, 16 (London: 1646).
[25] Ibid., 8, 16.
[26] Ball, *De Jure Regnandi,* 5, 14–15. He later sought to "distinguish between *Disposing at Pleasure, and Determining of Right,*" these "being things of a different *species.*" Parliament could dispose of property rights "but onely to determine of them *ad Rectum.*" Ball, *Constitutio Liberi Populi,* 10, 14.

the *primary Power of Laws,* or *of Law-making,*" and the king and Parliament were "onely *secundarily,*" and thus the "supream Magistrate," whether king or Parliament, was "tyed, bound, or concluded by the *Peoples Limitations.*"[27]

Far from assuming that parliamentary power was above the law of the land, the judges themselves recognized some limits on Parliament's power—the most notable instance being when acts of Parliament trenched upon the king's power to pardon offenders. This was an old absolute prerogative that seemed inherent in the king, and unlike some other prerogatives, such as the dispensing power, this one was not restricted in 1689 by the Bill of Rights. Thus, although the judges could not hold an act of Parliament unlawful and void, nor could they enforce an act of Parliament that declared pardons void. As Coke explained, "the Royal power to pardon treasons, murders, rapes, &c. is a prerogative incident solely and inseparably to the person of the King," and thus if an act of Parliament were "to make the pardon of the King void, and restrain the King" from "dispens[ing] with this by *non obstante,*" it "shall not bind the King but that he may dispense with it."[28] Even after Parliament abolished the dispensing power, Chief Justice Holt said that "[t]he power of pardoning all offences is an inseparable incident to the Crown and its Royal Power," and the leading eighteenth-century treatise on criminal law summarized, "let there be never

[27] William Ball, *State Maxims,* 12, 27 (London: 1655). Ball elaborated how the fundamental law protected natural liberty from Parliament when he responded to the imprisoned royalist judge David Jenkins. This judge espoused a royalist version of Parliament's absolute power, arguing that Parliament enjoyed an unlimited power, but only when the king was present, and to Ball's horror, "*Jenkins* saith, *The Law and Custome of this Land, is, that a Parliament hath Power over my life, liberty, lands, and goods, and over every other subject, &c.*" Ball interjected, "good Master *Jenkins,* not so fast"! He then asked, "what doth Master *Jenkins* meane by the word, *Power?*" Surely not a power to take property at will:

> If he meane by the word, *Power,* that the Parliament hath power to protect the lives, liberties, &c. of the People, I grant it him; or if he mean by the word, *Power,* that the Parliament hath power *applicare in necessitatem Regni,* [i.e., a power in necessities of state to use] the Properties of the People, I also grant it him; but if Master *Jenkins* meane by the word, *Power,* that the Parliament (including the *King*) hath an absolute Power to dispose of the Peoples Estates *merè ad Placitum* [i.e., merely at pleasure], I absolutely deny it.

In "things . . . tending to the fundamentall Rights and Lawes of the People, the Parliament cannot, nor ought not any way to violate the People, or Nation," and if Parliament were to violate their rights, although it could not be held to account in the courts, it would "fall and faile from the protection of the People." William Ball, *The Power of Kings Discussed: Or, An Examen of the Fundamental Constitution of the Free-borne People of England,* 12–13 (London: 1649). Incidentally, among the other rights were that "the Parliament cannot . . . deliver over the Free People of *England* to a foraine Government, or to Lawes imposed by Forainers . . . nor can the Parliament by any Ordinance, or Act whatsoever, deprive the Free people of *England* of their innate Right of electing Knights, Citizens, and Burgesses for Parliament." Ball, *State Maxims,* 26.

[28] Coke, *Reports,* 12: 18.

so good Reasons for the making a new Law for the Restraint of the Prerogative [of pardoning] . . . yet it is not in the Power of the Legislature to make such a Law."[29] The doctrine on pardons puzzles the whiggish historians of later centuries, who assume that Parliament was absolute and that constitutional rights were exclusively popular, not royal.[30] In the seventeenth and eighteenth centuries, however, although the judges could not hold acts of Parliament unlawful, they nonetheless recognized that in some instances, such as pardons, the law left power in the discretion of the king rather than Parliament.[31]

Of course, many late seventeenth-century Whigs embraced unlimited parliamentary power and therefore drew no distinction between the status of a high court above judicial reconsideration and the power of such a court above the law. John Somers, for example, thought that "[t]here must be a supreme uncontroulable power lodged somewhere," and this could hardly be found "in *England,* if not in the King, Lords and Commons in Parliament."[32] Other Whigs, however, such as Somers' friend John Locke, argued

[29] *King v. Parsons* (K.B. 1691), Shower (K.B.), *Reports,* 1: 284; William Hawkins, *A Treatise of the Pleas of the Crown,* 2: 390 (II.xxxvii.29) (London: 1721). Nottingham earlier stated: "There is . . . nothing in law that can restrain the King's power of pardoning, either for the matter, or the manner of it." Heneage, Earl of Nottingham, *A Treatise on the King's Power of Granting Pardons in Cases of Impeachment,* 25 (London: 1791).

[30] Unable to reconcile the doctrine on pardons with his nineteenth-century conception of parliamentary power, Hallam explains that Coke expressed his opinion "before he had learned the bolder tone of his declining years" and, moreover, disparages Holt's views, saying that "[t]his savours a little of old tory times." Henry Hallam, *The Constitutional History of England from the Accession of Henry VII. to the Death of George II.,* 2: 269, note (London: 1850).

[31] Another sort of limit on Parliament arose from the need to discern whether a purported act of Parliament was really an act of the high court—for example, if only one house of Parliament passed the act. See *Pilkington's Case,* Y.B. 33 Henry VI, Pas. pl. 8; S. B. Chrimes, *English Constitutional Ideas in the Fifteenth Century,* 231–233, 362 (Cambridge: Cambridge University Press, 1936). In the seventeenth century, some judges were unequivocal. Judge Jones said that "we are Judges of all acts of parliament" and that an "ordinance made by the king and commons is not good." Proceedings Against Elliot, Hollis, and Valentine (K.B. 1629), *State Trials,* 3: 307. The judges faced a similar problem when they had reason to doubt whether a meeting of Parliament constituted one of its sessions. This awkward question arose in 1623 when the justices were asked to meet at Serjeant's Inn to discuss the fate of the nation's temporary statutes, which Parliament had failed to re-enact. Hutton, *Reports,* 61–62; W. J. Jones, *Politics and the Bench: The Judges and the Origins of the English Civil War,* 80–83, 157–158 (London: Allen and Unwin, 1971). Although the judges refrained from unnecessarily unraveling all temporary statutes, they apparently agreed they could decide the question. Once again, Judge Jones put it most succinctly, observing that "we are judges what shall be a session of parliament." *State Trials,* 3: 307.

[32] [John Somers], *A Brief History of the Succession,* 15 ([London: 1681]). He disparaged those who "object, That the Fundamental Laws of the Land against which no Act of Parliament can be of force, have so establisht the Succession that the course of it cannot be alter'd. This is surely a new discovery." Ibid., 16. See the discussion of Somers by Goldsworthy, *The Sovereignty of Parliament,* 155.

that the constitution confined the legislative as well as the executive power. The "Legislative" (in England, the king in Parliament) was "but a delegated Power from the People." Indeed, "[t]he power of the *Legislative*" was "derived from the People by a positive voluntary Grant and Institution," for "[t]he People alone can appoint the Form of the Commonwealth . . . by Constituting the Legislative, and appointing in whose hands that shall be." By this means, "the People have said, We will submit to rules, and be govern'd by *Laws* made by such Men, in such Forms." Although Locke did not expect the judges would have the independence to hold acts of Parliament unconstitutional, he was confident that the people could judge, and with this in mind, he explained that "the Constitution of the Legislative" was "the original and supream act of the Society, antecedent to all positive Laws in it, and depending wholly on the People."[33]

In the eighteenth century, whereas Whigs made the boldest assertions on behalf of the constitution, it was a Tory, William Blackstone, who made the most notorious claim for Parliament.[34] Many Tories felt the necessity of the absolute power claimed by seventeenth-century kings, and being reluctant to acknowledge such a power in the people, these Tories often joined

[33] John Locke, *Two Treatises of Government,* 380–381, 391 (II.xi.141; II.xiii.157) (Cambridge: Cambridge University Press, 1960). He added that therefore "no inferiour Power can alter it." Ibid.

[34] For a while, primarily in response to the Septennial Act, some Tories asserted constitutional limitations on the legislative power—even to the point of quoting Locke. The 1694 Triennial Act had required that Parliament meet and have new elections at least every three years, but in 1716 Parliament passed the Septennial Act, which abandoned triennial elections and thereby extended the duration of the existing Parliament, thus giving members of Parliament—mostly Whigs—longer terms than those for which they were elected. Tories therefore complained that Parliament had assumed a power that belonged to the people. In the House of Commons, the steadfast Tory William Shippen conceded that Parliament was supreme, but "tho' . . . the supream Legislature cannot be bound; yet . . . it is restrain'd from subverting the Foundations on which it stands." Accordingly, "it ought not . . . to touch or alter those Laws, which are so far admitted into the Constitution, as to become essential Parts of It." *The Historical Register,* 370–371 (London: 1717). Shippen was not alone. John Snell, also a Tory, quoted John Locke to show that "the Purpose of this Bill . . . is not within the Compass of the Trust repos'd in us by the People." Reciting Locke's familiar assumption that "*[t]he Power of the Legislative*" was "*deriv'd from the People by a positive voluntary Grant and Institution,*" Snell further quoted that the Legislative "*can be no other than what that positive Grant convey'd*" and that "*the Legislative can have no Power of transfering their Authority of making Laws, and placing it in other Hands.*" Accordingly, the Septennial Act was "an open Violation of the Peoples Liberties, or, to speak most mildly of it, a Breach of our Trust." *The Historical Register,* 368–370, sigs. [Ddd3][v]–[Ddd4][v] (London: 1717) (the page numbers are misprinted). See also the speech of Sir Robert Raymond—a lawyer of moderately Tory sympathies who would become chief justice of Kings Bench within a decade. Ibid., 396. For the passages quoted by Snell, see Locke, *Two Treatises of Government,* 408–409 (II.xi.141), 477 (II. xix.243). Notwithstanding these arguments, the bill passed "in Subversion of so essential a Part of our Constitution." Protest (April 14, 1716), *A Complete Collection of All the Protests Made in the House of Lords,* 178 ([London]: 1748).

Whigs such as Somers in embracing the absolute power of Parliament. In this spirit, Blackstone taught that Parliament enjoyed a power above law, including a power to "change and create afresh even the constitution of the kingdom and of parliaments themselves." Blackstone did not question that England enjoyed a constitution—the "constitutional custom" of the realm. Nonetheless, he suggested that an "absolute" power was necessary in all "forms of government," and he paraphrased Somers to the effect that Parliament was "the place where that absolute despotic power . . . is entrusted by the constitution of these kingdoms."[35]

Although Whigs, being usually a majority, were apt to agree with Blackstone about Parliament's absolute power, other, more radical Whigs continued to insist that there were constitutional limitations on Parliament, even if enforceable only outside the courts. In contrast to what Blackstone taught at Oxford, Thomas Rutherforth lectured at Cambridge that Parliament was obliged to adhere to the constitution: The laws that "determine the form of the legislative body, and give one part of the society an exclusive right or power of legislation, cannot well be understood to have been derived, originally, from the legislative body itself." To be sure, in England the constitution was part of the custom of the realm, which was often declared in acts of Parliament. Nonetheless:

> Laws of this sort, are usually understood to bind the legislative body itself, and not to be alterable by its authority. And for this reason, when a legislative body, after it is established, declares any law of its own making, to be a fundamental law, or a law of the constitution, the meaning of this declaration is, that the legislative body looks upon itself to be bound by this law.[36]

Outside the halls of the universities, men were more blunt. Colonel Barré, who had lost an eye at Quebec, boldly defended Americans during the Stamp Act crisis, declaring that "[t]he supreme power is uncontrollable, but it should control itself." Henry Goodricke observed of Parliament that "its acts can not be controlled or annulled by any other *authority*," but "[t]his does not preclude in the least its being limited, as to the extent of its power, either by the laws of Nature, or by rules and principles of the Constitution."[37] In the words of Junius, "[t]here cannot be a doctrine more fatal to

[35] Blackstone, *Commentaries on the Law of England,* 1: 48–49, 84, 184. For his unacknowledged borrowing from Somers, ibid., 1: 188.

[36] Thomas Rutherforth, *Institutes of Natural Law,* 399 (II.vi.20) (Baltimore: 1832). He also taught that "the notion of a fundamental law of any civil constitution does not consist in its being unalterable by any human power whatsoever, but in its being unalterable by the constitutional legislative body, where this body is only a part of the whole society." Ibid., 401 (II.vi.21).

[37] Col. Barré, in House of Commons (Feb. 3, 1766), in *Proceedings and Debates of the British Parliaments respecting North America 1754–1783,* 144, eds. R. C. Simmons and P. D. G.

the liberty and property we are contending for, than that which confounds the idea of a supreme and an arbitrary legislature."[38]

No Whig argued more passionately that Parliament was supreme over other courts but subordinate to the constitution than Willoughby Bertie, Earl of Abingdon. A nobleman who embraced the American cause, he appreciated Edmund Burke's endorsement of the American Revolution but regretted Burke's failure to make clear that Parliament was subject to constitutional constraints. When Burke in 1777 defended the rights of Americans but spoke of the "supremacy of Parliament," Abingdon protested that "*Supremacy of Parliament* is a combination of terms unknown to the English polity."[39] Abingdon explained three years later:

> When we say that the Legislature is supreme, we mean that it is the highest Power known to the Constitution;—that it is the highest in Comparison with the other subordinate Powers established by the Laws. In this Sense the Word Supreme is relative not absolute. The Power of the Legislature is *limited,* not only by the general Rules of natural Justice, and the Welfare of the Community, but by the *Forms and Principles* of our particular Constitution.[40]

Admittedly, being the supreme court, Parliament was beyond a judicial remedy, but this was all the more reason for Parliament to decide in accord with the constitution. "That the Parliament is *supreme,* I admit. It is the *supreme court,* or *curia magna* of the Constitution." Yet because it was the supreme court, Parliament "is bound by the rules of the Constitution."[41]

Thomas (New York: 1982); Henry Goodricke, *Observations on Dr. Price's Theory and Principles of Civil Liberty and Government,* 43–44 (York: 1776)—both quoted by John Philip Reid, *Constitutional History of the American Revolution: Authority to Legislate,* 43, 83, 127 (Madison: University of Wisconsin Press, 1991); Goldsworthy, *The Sovereignty of Parliament,* 192. Reid and Goldsworthy assemble much evidence that many Englishmen distinguished between Parliament's "power" and its "right." For the biographical detail, see Peter D. G. Thomas, "Isaac Barré," DNB.

38 Letter from Junius to John Wilkes (Sept. 7, 1771), in *The Letters of Junius,* 2: 213 (New York: 1821).

39 Willoughby Bertie, Earl of Abingdon, *Thoughts on the Letter of Edmund Burke, Esq; to the Sheriffs of Bristol, on the Affairs of America,* 15 (Oxford: [1777]).

40 Willoughby Bertie, Earl of Abingdon, *Dedication to the Collective Body of the People of England,* xxxviii (Oxford: 1780).

41 Bertie, *Thoughts on the Letter of Edmund Burke, Esq; to the Sheriffs of Bristol,* 43. Similarly, he wrote: "Precedents . . . of acts of parliament, repugnant to the fundamental principles of the constitution, are no proofs of the supremacy or omnipotency of parliament, but instances only of the abuse of parliament." Ibid., 22. For discussion of Abingdon, see Reid, *Constitutional History of the American Revolution,* 82.

His remarks were widely noticed, not least by persons who litigated or adjudicated such claims in America, including the Virginia judges in the *Prisoners' Case* and William Hooper and James Iredell in North Carolina. Upon learning news of Abingdon from Iredell, Hooper wrote back: "I thank you for the information of publick matters which your Letter so pleasingly afforded me. The Character of Lord Abingdon is a Singular one. Such boldness and unaffected Patriotism opposed to the Court; to the source from which with his talents to

The radical Whig view—that all of government, including legislative power, was subject to the constitution—had great appeal in the American colonies, and at least a hint of this can be observed already here. The southern clergyman John Joachim Zubly saw the choice with clarity: "The Parliament of *Great-Britain* is the supreme legislature in the *British* empire . . . either absolutely or agreeable to the constitution." On the one hand, if it exercised its legislative power absolutely, "it is not bound by the constitution, nor any thing else." On the other hand, if its power was "agreeable to the constitution, then it can no more make laws, which are against the constitution, or unalterable privileges of *British* subjects, than it can alter the constitution itself." Zubly emphatically took the latter perspective. He of course recognized that it was not the judges but Parliament and ultimately "the nation" that had the power to decide whether Parliament's acts were constitutional. At the same time, "Parliament . . . has its bounds assigned by the constitution," for "the measure of power and of obedience in every country must be determined by the standard of its constitution."[42]

Thus, although the law itself elevated the high court of Parliament above judicial decisions holding its acts unconstitutional, this was not to say that Parliament was necessarily above the law. Many Englishmen celebrated Parliament's absolute power, but others vowed that all government power was subject to the constitution—to which they sometimes added the mordant observation that they had not fought absolute power in the king only to submit to it in the legislature.[43] This view of legislative power was, perhaps, a losing proposition in England, but it would one day have greater success in America.

Serve it he might always command preferment and honours are truly extraordinary." Letter of William Hooper to James Iredell (July 15, 1778), in *The Papers of James Iredell,* 2: 41, ed. Don Higgenbotham (Raleigh, N.C.: Division of Archives and History, Department of Cultural Resources, 1976). Pierce Butler also "admire[d] the character of Lord Abbinton." Letter of Pierce Butler to James Iredell (July 31, 1782), ibid., 2: 349.

42 "A Freeholder of South-Carolina" [John Joachim Zubly], *An Humble Enquiry into the Nature of the Dependency of the American Colonies upon the Parliament of Great-Britain,* 5, 11, 12 ([Charleston]: 1769).

43 Chatham declared in the House of Lords: "[W]hen our kings were obliged to confess that their title to the crown, and the rule of their government, had no other foundation than the known laws of the land, I never expected to hear a divine right, or a divine infallibility, attributed to any other branch of the legislature. . . . Power without right is the most odious and detestable object that can be offered to the human imagination." Speech in House of Lords (Jan. 9, 1770), *Anecdotes of the Life of the Right Hon. William Pitt, Earl of Chatham,* 2: 14–15 (London: 1792).

9

Colonial Departures

JUDGES often departed from their duty when it required them to hold colonial legislation unlawful. Whereas the common law barred judges from holding acts of Parliament unlawful, there was no such obstacle to their reaching such a conclusion about the act of a colonial legislature. The judges who most frequently had to examine colonial statutes, however, were not the regular judges who sat in Westminster Hall, but rather were Privy Councillors and colonial judges, who had specialized jurisdictions and who were politically accountable. As might be expected, they were sensitive to imperial responsibilities on one side of the Atlantic and to colonial resentments on the other, and under the weight of these considerations, they often hesitated to do their duty when it required them to condemn American statutes.

The relatively few, rather sporadic instances in which these judges held colonial statutes unlawful are usually understood as the experiments and evolving experience that would eventually, after the Revolution, become a more substantial pursuit of judicial review. From this perspective, judicial review offers yet another account, so satisfying to Americans, of how their distinctive experiences, more than any inherited ideas, gave rise to a significant innovation in government. The history of the ideal of judicial duty, however, places the practices of the Privy Council and the colonial judges in a different light. When illuminated by this duty, which required judges to hold unlawful colonial acts void, the erratic imperial and colonial adjudications about American statutes are revealed to have been something decidedly less exciting than exploratory steps toward a new judicial power. They turn out instead to have been the wavering efforts of men whose political anxieties tore them away from their traditional duty.

These failures to adhere to the ideal of judicial duty are an apt conclusion to Part III's examination of the duty of judges in decisions about legislation, for they hint at the distinctive importance of common law ideals in America after Independence. The cases on colonial statutes may have provided American judges with some experience in holding enactments unlawful, but the early decisions were so scattered and irregular that when post-Revolutionary judges across the nation held state statutes unconstitutional, they cannot have relied very much on either their personal experience or their discernment of patterns in the earlier decisions about American statutes. Rather than suggest the evolving path of American experience, the irregular judicial practices in the Privy Council and the colonies left judges in the states singularly dependent on the old ideal of judicial duty.

Ambiguity

The tensions between colonial legislation and English law centered on an ambiguity—an ambiguity as to when colonial and other subordinate law could contradict the law of the land and nonetheless be considered lawful. Already in England, local law often had to depart from the law of the land, and the common law openly acknowledged and resolved this problem by treating some local variations as reasonable. In America, however, the local departures were more substantial than could be accommodated in this manner. Parliament eventually attempted to settle the status of wayward colonial enactments by reducing the problem to one of repugnancy, but it did not thereby address the underlying difficulty. The obligation of nonconforming colonial statutes therefore remained deeply ambiguous, and as Mary Bilder has observed, although this ambiguity allowed Americans to defend their departures from English law, it simultaneously opened up space for bitter transatlantic misunderstandings.[1]

[1] Mary Sarah Bilder, *The Transatlantic Constitution,* 6–7, 40, 193–196 (Cambridge: Harvard University Press, 2004); Mary Sarah Bilder, "The Corporate Origins of Judicial Review," *Yale Law Journal,* 116: 502 (2006). Bilder notes that there was much ambiguity as to when American enactments violated English law, and she makes the important point that the ambiguity allowed a substantial degree of local legislative freedom. In addition, it is worth focusing more closely on the sources of the ambiguity. Although there is almost always apt to be some ambiguity about the contradiction or repugnancy between two laws, and although it is no surprise that men on both sides of the Atlantic took advantage of this sort of uncertainty, the ambiguity at stake in the decisions about corporate and colonial laws was usually of a more substantial sort, for it arose from the unlimited jurisdiction of English law, which would have barred almost all subordinate law, unless English law itself acknowledged that subordinate acts and customs could sometimes lawfully contradict the law of the realm. The common law did this through the law-and-reason test, under which an otherwise unlawful custom or enactment could be deemed reasonable and thus not really in violation of English law. This use of the element of "reason" came to define the space left for subordi-

A mild version of the problem was familiar in England from the overlap between local and royal jurisdiction. Domestic municipalities and other subordinate bodies frequently adopted their own rules on matters otherwise covered by the law of the realm, and because the law of the land had complete jurisdiction, it ordinarily might be expected to defeat local legislation that did not simply echo English law. In this context, if there was to be space for local and other subordinate laws, there had to be some recognition that they could sometimes contradict the law of the land and still be accepted as lawful. The difficulty was to discern when a contradiction or repugnancy was permissible.

The general doctrine with which the judges sorted out the lawfulness of local deviations from English law was the requirement of reason in the familiar test of "law and reason." Although the requirement of reason had probably developed as a domesticated version of natural law, it came to be something else when applied to subordinate acts and customs. It became a measure of when a local or other departure from English law was nonetheless lawful, and it thus offered an essential means of accommodating local diversity. To be precise, a subordinate custom or act that contradicted the law of the realm but was "reasonable" was not considered unlawful. As Bacon's *Abridgement* summarized about local customs, "such Customs as are against the Rules of the Common Law, yet, not being unreasonable in themselves, are good, and, from the Conveniency of them, bind in particular places."[2]

---

nate law to depart from sovereign law, but it still left much ambiguity about the status of subordinate laws, and this ambiguity became almost intractable in the colonies, which often had to depart from English law in ways that could not be accommodated by the law-and-reason test. Although Parliament in 1696 imposed a more severe standard, that of repugnancy, this simply subsumed the difficulties within the definition of repugnancy.

Against this background, by the way, it is difficult to conclude, as Bilder does, that the ambiguity in the relation between English law and colonial law, let alone the standard of repugnancy, established a model for how Americans later understood the relation between federal and state law. The federal government was of limited jurisdiction, and it therefore did not have to permit state laws that otherwise contradicted federal law. The American states, moreover, were not municipal corporations, colonies, or other types of subordinate bodies. Instead the federal government and each state claimed to enjoy its authority from its people, and at least in this basic sense each such government was sovereign. As a result, the boundary between federal and state law was emphatically demarcated by federal law without any of the ambiguities of accommodating subordinate law, whether done though the law-and-reason test or the definition of repugnancy. Of course, the use of the common law test of law and reason as a measure of noncontradictory differences persisted in America after 1776, but within decisions about local customs, by-laws, and old, colonial statutes, not decisions about the constitutionality of state laws.

2 Bacon, *A New Abridgment of the Law,* 1: 671. Similarly, a lawyer in an American case recognized that "a good custom" could "be contrary to the common law or against the interest

The application of this test in England was particularly manageable because English local customs and by-laws tended to fall within a narrow range of stereotyped categories, in which the judges developed relatively clear understandings as to when a subordinate departure from English law was reasonable.[3] Some requirements of English law, moreover, were so fundamental that the judge assumed any contradiction would render a subordinate law void, without regard to its reasonableness. Although this was not necessarily a question of what was constitutional, it could come close, as when "a custom in an Inferior Court to try an issue by six jurymen, was held void" on the ground that "no custom of an Inferior Court shall be allowed of, which breaks in upon the fundamental rules of proceeding in the superior jurisdiction."[4]

Colonial statures, however, departed from English law in ways that were apt to exceed what was permitted. The colonies necessarily legislated on a much broader range of matters than domestic corporations, and they thus ran up against English law on questions already subject to detailed common law rules—even on issues (such as land law) that to English judges seemed almost constitutional. These colonial violations of English law were of a sort that could not easily be justified as reasonable, and because they regularly went beyond the common law solution, they boded ill for Anglo-American relations.

The Crown occasionally attempted to ameliorate the problem through its drafting of charters. Although in many domestic and colonial charters the Crown prohibited acts "contrary" or "repugnant" to "the laws of En-

---

of an individual—yet it shall be valid." *Frary et al. v. Cook et al.* (Hampshire County Superior Court, April term 1779), in *Notes of Cases Decided in the Superior and Supreme Judicial Court of Massachusetts from 1772 to 1789—Taken by the Honble William Cushing,* fol. 15[v], Harvard Law School, Ms. 4083. Earlier, when Coke was attorney general, he argued in the *Case of Monopolies* that "it has been resolved that a corporation which has authority by charter to make by-laws may make an ordinance by which the subject may be restrained, so long as this ordinance tended to the execution of the law or the benefit of the commonwealth." *Darcy v. Allen* (K.B. 1603), King's Bench Reports, British Library, Add. Ms. 25203, fol. 586[v], as translated by Charles Gray in his mimeographed teaching materials. The law-and-reason test, as it happens, was the source from which the rule of reason was developed in American antitrust cases.

[3] For example, Bacon's *Abridgment* divided by-laws among those relating to "the appointing and electing Members of a Corporation," those "made in Restraint of Trade," those "made to prevent Nuisances," those that "affect Strangers," and those that "in the Frame and Make of them are void, by ordaining a Method of inforcing Obedience to them contrary to Law." Matthew Bacon, *A New Abridgment of the Law,* 3: 337 (London: 1778).

[4] *Ball & Knight* (K.B. 1732), Barnardiston (K.B.), *Reports,* 2: 164. In other words, in a case such as this, which concerned a matter that was fundamental, the act or custom was presumptively unreasonable and was thus in effect only tested against law.

gland," in some colonial charters it more loosely required that the colonies make law "as near as may be agreeable" to the laws of England.[5] The Crown thus created extra space for colonial legislation but without making clear how much.

The question became more pressing when Chief Justice Holt appeared to imply that all the laws of England were in force on the mainland of America. This point arose in 1693 in *Blankard v. Galdy,* an action on a debt incurred in Jamaica. Although the defendant claimed that his debt was unenforceable under English law, Holt held English law irrelevant because Jamaica was a conquered colony. Whereas English law was in force in uninhabited countries newly discovered by Englishmen, it did not take force in conquered colonies "until declared by the conqueror." This decision about Jamaica would ordinarily have been of little significance for the mainland colonies, but Holt stated the rule as to newly discovered colonies rather strongly, saying not merely that English law was generally in effect in such places, but that "all laws in force in England are in force there." Thus, in the course of applying half the rule to Jamaica, Holt overstated the other half, and he thereby seemed to suggest that all English laws were binding on the American continent.[6]

Perhaps to allay concerns arising from Holt's overstatement, Parliament in 1696 confined the relevant contradictions to those between colonial law and such English law as "relate[d]" to the colonies. Parliament thus narrowed the set of English laws against which colonial laws would be measured, but it simultaneously required that colonial laws not contradict such English laws in any way. Although a contradiction and a repugnancy were not typically distinguished, a repugnancy could be understood more broadly, and probably out of an abundance of caution the 1696 statute used this word to bar any conflict between colonial laws and the English laws concerning the colonies:

> That all Lawes By-laws Usages or Customes att this tyme or which hereafter shall bee in practice or endeavored or pretended to bee in force or practice in any of the said Plantations which are in any wise repugnant to the before mentioned Lawes or any of them, soe far as they doe relate to the said Plantations or any of them or which are [any] wayes repugnant to this present Act, or to any other Law hereafter to bee made in this Kingdome soe farr as such

[5] Joseph Henry Smith, *Appeals to the Privy Council from the American Plantations,* 529 (New York: Columbia University Press, 1950).

[6] *Blankard v. Galdy* (K.B. 1693), Holt K.B., 341; Salkeld, *Reports,* 2: 411; 4 *Modern Reports,* 215; Comberbach, *Reports,* 228.

> Law shall relate to and mention the said Plantations are illegall[,] null and void to all Intents and Purposes whatsoever.[7]

No longer would a colonial statute be measured against the full range of English laws, but if a colonial act was "in any wise repugnant" to such English law as "relate[d]" to the colonies, it was "illegal, null and void." Evidently the 1696 act attempted to prohibit all repugnancies—even those that were reasonable.

Yet rather than resolve the ambiguity about colonial legislation, the statute simply collapsed it into a debate about what constituted a repugnancy. Confronted by an English law that rendered all local repugnancies unlawful, the colonists responded by "distinguish[ing] between what is *different* from the laws of England and what is *repugnant* thereto." They lived with the reality that the "differing circumstances of a new plantation may make it necessary in many cases to make differing laws," and they therefore protested that "if every difference be esteemed a repugnancy and contradiction . . . or violation, of the laws of England, it were in effect to say that we

---

[7] An Act for preventing Frauds and regulating Abuses in the Plantation Trade, 7 & 8 William III, c.22, §8 (1696). Smith proposes that in *City of London v. Wood,* Holt endorsed judicial review as established in *Bonham's Case,* and that the 1696 act took a similar approach, perhaps at Holt's suggestion. Smith, *Appeals to the Privy Council from the American Plantations,* 527. Neither case, however, supports such a conclusion. Incidentally, section 8 seems to have been hastily inserted in a preexisting bill; certainly its words about "the before mentioned Lawes or any of them" do not have a clear antecedent—it apparently being assumed that they referred to the laws of England rather than the enactments recited in the statute's preface.

The word "repugnancy" was another way of referring to contradiction, except that it was sometimes used to hint at a slightly broader degree of incompatibility, and Parliament therefore sometimes took the safe route of using the word "repugnant." When expounding an Henrician statute that alluded to both contradiction and repugnancy, the sophisticated English canonist Richard Cosin explained: "The word *Repugnant* in the saide statute . . . is put after *Contrariant,* as of a greater force and efficacie: and therefore is to be understoode, according to the common course of our speach, (albeit the *Logicians* doe not use that worde) for the *contradictorie opposition;* consisting of an *universal affirmative* and a *particular negative;* or of an *universall negative* and *particular affirmative.* And these be so opposite *ex diametro,* and doe always so directly thwart one another; that in every subject matter whatsoever, the one of them being true, the other must needs be false: *& è converso.*" He then recited examples to show how, notwithstanding their different levels of generality, such repugnancies could amount to what was "flat[ly] *Contradictorie.*" [Richard Cosin], *An Apologie for Sundrie Proceedings by Jurisdiction Ecclesiasticall,* 2: 68 ([1593]).

Observing the emphasis on "repugnancy" in decisions about colonial acts under English law, Mary Bilder suggests that this standard left space for a "departure for local circumstances." Bilder, *The Transatlantic Constitution,* 2–3, 7. Repugnancy, however, appears to have been a version of contradiction that limited rather than enlarged the space for local difference. Thus, for example, in its 1696 statute regulating colonial legislation, Parliament used the word "repugnant," rather than "contrary" or "inconsistent," precisely because it hoped to reduce the opportunities for local departures from English law.

must make no law at all."[8] Accordingly, whereas Englishmen tended to see repugnancy, Americans tended to see only difference—a necessary local difference. The transatlantic ambiguity thus persisted. Although it now lurked under the notion of repugnancy rather than appearing openly in the law-and-reason test, it continued to leave room for controversies of a sort that the Privy Council could not afford.

Decisions in the Privy Council

The Privy Council served as a judicial court to hear appeals from colonial courts, but it also oversaw the Empire, and the pressures of this administrative task distorted its performance of its judicial role. The Council needed to avoid antagonizing the colonies, and therefore rather than hold unlawful colonial legislation void, it more typically went out of its way to prevent such cases from arising.[9]

In its executive functions, the Privy Council could disallow the enactments of some colonies. Other judges could traditionally disallow the by-laws of certain types of corporations under the 1504 act of Parliament. Similarly, under the charters of various colonies, the Crown reserved authority to disallow or in effect repeal colonial statutes—though sometimes with the qualification that the Crown had to repudiate a statute within three years of its adoption.[10] The king in his Privy Council thus enjoyed an administrative freedom promptly to reject many colonial enactments on grounds not confined to law.

In contrast, when the Privy Council in its judicial capacity heard appeals from colonial courts, its members, like other judges, were confined to their judicial duty. Most members of the Council were politicians rather

---

[8] Letter from the Rev. Benjamin Coleman to Francis Wilks [?] (Nov. 12, 1735), as quoted by Smith, *Appeals to the Privy Council,* 529–530, note 26. The letter concerned *Philips v. Savage.* Other examples are plentiful, a famous one being Jeremiah Dummer, *A Defence of the New-England Charters* (London: 1721). In another instance, the Pennsylvania General Assembly in 1716 defended an enactment that relieved Quakers of various legal disabilities by arguing that it could not be considered "contrary" to an act of Parliament that relieved them from only one of these disabilities. "[T]hese two differ 'tis true," but it had been "expected" at the time when the colony was chartered "that our acts might in some measure differ from those in England." Representation of General Assembly to Governor (Nov. 1716), as quoted by Smith, *Appeals to the Privy Council,* 529, note 26.

[9] Dudley Odell McGovney, "The British Origin of Judicial Review of Legislation," *University of Pennsylvania Law Review,* 93: 40 (1944).

[10] As with the judges' allowance of domestic by-laws, the Privy Council's allowance of colonial statutes could not cure an act if it was void under English law. See 1758 and 1772 opinions by Richard Jackson, counsel to the Board of Trade, discussed by Smith, *Appeals to the Privy Council,* 636.

than lawyers, let alone judges, and they usually referred their decisions to a committee, which tended to consult with the Board of Trade and its attorney and sometimes even the chief law officers of the Crown. Thus, the Council always had lawyers nearby to remind them that it was "a necessary qualification" of colonial laws that they be judged against the old common law test of law and reason: Statutes made in the colonies had to be "reasonable in themselves and not contrary to the laws of England; and if any laws have been there made repugnant to the laws of England they are absolutely null and void."[11]

The Privy Council, however, could not easily run an empire through its judicial decisions—one problem being that before it could reach such a decision, it had to wait for an appeal. The Privy Council in some instances simply declared a colonial enactment null and void under English law without waiting for a case, but this sort of preemptory declaration lacked the authority of a judicial exposition of law and could therefore be effective only when the Council could count on cooperation with its pronouncement.[12] In contrast, if the Council needed an authoritative statement of the law, it had to wait for an appeal, and this could take decades.[13] For a body that shared with the Board of Trade the responsibility for preserving the empire, such delays were worrisome, for they could put the Privy Coun-

[11] Opinion of Philip Yorke and Charles Talbot on *Winthrop v. Lechmere* (Aug. 1, 1730), in *Calendar of State Papers, Colonial Series, America and West Indies, 1730,* at 226 (No. 363) (London: His Majesty's Stationery Office, 1937); discussed by Smith, *Appeals to the Privy Council,* 558.

At least a judicial decision holding an enactment void had the advantage of severability. For the severability of acts of Parliament as discussed in cases on pleading, see *Hutchins v. Player,* O. Bridgman, *Reports,* 315–316 (C.P. 1663). For the severability of by-laws, in contrast to customs, see *Fazakerley v. Wiltshire* (K.B. 1721), Strange, *Reports,* 1: 464, 469. For the severability of colonial legislation, see Smith, *Appeals to the Privy Council,* 628.

[12] Smith, *Appeals to the Privy Council,* 592.

[13] The frustrations that arose from such delays became explicit when in 1732 some Anglican clergymen from Massachusetts petitioned the Privy Council against some old colonial statutes that they considered "contrary and repugnant to the Laws of England," not "warranted by their Charter," and prejudicial to the Church of England. As these enactments were long past the three-year period for disallowance, the clergymen asked the Privy Council simply "to annull and repeal" them. Faced with these complaints, Yorke and Talbot explained that any question about the Massachusetts statutes being "void" was not before the Council judicially, and even "[i]f they were really void . . . yet no Extrajudicial Declaration that they are so would be conclusive, but the only Method of bringing that Matter to a Determination would be by some Judicial Proceeding." Opinion of Messrs. Yorke & Talbot (Aug. 16, 1732), in William Stevens Perry, *Historical Collections Relating to the American Colonial Church,* 3: 283, 285, 287 (np: 1873), discussed by McGovney, "The British Origin of Judicial Review of Legislation," 33. Smith records that there was "substantial opinion that an act could be declared null and void *ab initio* without judicial proceedings" but that "[t]he Committee, itself, resolutely adhered to the necessity of judicial proceedings." Smith, *Appeals to the Privy Council,* 634–635.

cil in the invidious position of repudiating colonial legislation long after Americans had relied on it.[14]

An early administrative disallowance was therefore preferable to a later judicial determination that an act was void, and nothing made this policy seem more necessary than the Privy Council's experience in 1728 in *Winthrop v. Lechmere.* In contrast to the common law rule of primogeniture, a Connecticut statute distributed both real and personal property in intestate estates equally among any children—the only exception being a double share for the eldest.[15] Connecticut adopted this intestacy statute in 1699, and because the colony's charter reserved no royal power of disallowance, the lawfulness of the statute did not come before the Privy Council until an appeal almost three decades later. At stake in the case was not merely the inheritance claimed by the parties, but Connecticut's system of inheritance and more broadly the ability of colonists to adopt the intestacy laws they considered necessary for their circumstances.[16] The Privy Council's committee for appeals from the colonies was not yet adequately attuned to these political considerations and took a narrow view of how far colonial law could deviate from English law—explaining that the Connecticut statute "should be declared null and void" because it was "contrary to the laws of England, in regard it makes lands of inheritance distributable as personal estates, and is not warranted by the Charter of that Colony." The consequent decision of the Privy Council holding the act "null and void" caused memorable disquiet in Connecticut.[17] The colony feared the case would unsettle title to lands inherited by intestacy, and although the colony avoided this disaster, its response to the decision seems to have reminded the Privy Council about the anxiety it could provoke by holding an old colonial act unlawful. In fact, when a very similar Massachusetts statute came up on appeal a decade later, the Privy Council was surely glad to be told that the prior, Connecticut case could be distinguished. Although the Council did not say as much, it abandoned its Connecticut precedent and

[14] Even brief delays between enactment and disallowance created problems, for the law would be in effect until disallowed. The Crown attempted to avoid this awkwardness by asking governors to include clauses in statutes suspending their effect until the Privy Council had ruled on them, but colonial legislatures did not always cooperate.

[15] An Act for preventing of Fraud in concealing any part of the Estate of any Deceased Person (1699), in *Public Records of the Colony of Connecticut,* 4: 307, ed. Charles J. Hoadly (Hartford: Case, Lockwood and Brainard, 1868).

[16] Thomas Hutchinson, *The History of the Province of Massachusetts-Bay,* 2: 66 (London: 1768), writing about the intestacy rule as adopted in an earlier, 1692 statute.

[17] Record of Report and Order in *Winthrop v. Lechmere* (Feb. 15, 1728), *Collections of the Massachusetts Historical Society,* 5: 507 (Sixth Series) (Boston: Massachusetts Historical Society, 1892).

upheld the Massachusetts act.[18] The Council could not risk unnecessary strains on the empire, and it therefore learned to disallow statutes with vigor and decide appeals with caution.[19]

This reluctance of the Privy Council to reach judicial decisions holding colonial statutes unlawful offers an early clue about the American reception of the ideal of judicial duty. It has been all too easy to conclude that

18 *Philips v. Savage* (P.C. 1738), discussed by McGovney, "The British Origin of Judicial Review of Legislation," 21; Smith, *Appeals to the Privy Council,* 562–572. For the artificial attempt to distinguish *Winthrop,* see ibid., 568–570. In 1774, Richard Jackson, counsel to the Board of Trade, opined about *Winthrop* that he did "not think it to be relied on, as the act on which it decided is yet the law of the colony and universally submitted to." Ibid., 653.

As late as 1768, imperial administrators were still struggling to get something like a power of disallowance over Connecticut's statutes, for only this would allow them to avoid the political catastrophe of holding its statutes void years after they went into effect. The policy desired by the administrators can be illustrated by a conversation in 1768 between the Earl of Hillsborough, the secretary of state for the American colonies, and Connecticut's English agent William Samuel Johnson, who recorded the details in a subsequent letter. Hillsborough "yield[ed]" to Johnson that under the colony's charter, there was no "necessity of any royal approbation as requisite to the validity of our laws." Nonetheless, Hillsborough "insisted that . . . they ought to be regularly transmitted for the inspection of the Privy Council, and for *disapprobation,* if found within the saving of the charter, *repugnant to the laws of England.*" He reasoned that the Connecticut Charter provided that English law was a "limitation of their legislative powers" and that this "alone . . . render[ed] it necessary that their laws should be transmitted and inspected here." Johnson reminded the minister of English law:

> I begged leave to observe to his Lordship, that the Colony did not apprehend that any extrajudicial opinion of his Majesty's Ministers, or even of the King's Privy Council, could determine whether any particular act was within that proviso or not; that this could only be decided by a court of law.

Moreover, unlike when the Privy Council disallowed a colonial statute, such an act was void because it was repugnant to law rather than because of any authority in the Crown:

> [I]f the General Assembly should make a law *repugnant* to a *statute* of Great Britain, (not in the sense of *diverse f[ro]m,* but *flatly,* and in *terms contradictory* to it,) such law, by the *saving in the charter, might* be void, yet a *declaration* of the *King in Council* would still make it neither more nor less so, but be as *void* as the *law itself;* because its being void or not depended merely upon the *restraining clause* in the charter, not upon any *authority reserved to the Crown,* or the Privy Council, to *decide* about it.

Thus, "the only method which could be taken in such case must be for the persons aggrieved by such act to bring their action at law, in such manner as to bring in question the validity of such act of Assembly," and then "the court before whom the trial should be, could fairly and legally determine upon it." In Connecticut, "the interposition . . . must be in the judicial only, not by any means in the official way." Letter from William Samuel Johnson to Governor William Pitkin (Feb. 13, 1768), in Trumbull Papers, *Collections of the Massachusetts Historical Society,* 9: 259–260 (fifth series) (Boston: 1885), discussed by McGovney, "The British Origin of Judicial Review of Legislation," 36–37; Smith, *Appeals to the Privy Council,* 652.

19 According to Smith, there was only one adjudication holding a colonial act void, in *Winthrop v. Lechmere,* and two declarations of nullity. Smith, *Appeals to the Privy Council,* 634.

the Council made experiments in holding colonial legislation unlawful and thus contributed to the practical evolution of a power of judicial review. The common law ideal of judicial duty, however, was ancient and familiar—as was its application to subordinate legislation—and therefore rather than reveal practical experimentation and development, the scarcity of decisions by the Privy Council holding colonial statutes unlawful leaves the impression that Privy Councillors allowed their duty as imperial administrators to pull them away from their duty as judges. Of course, the theoretical applicability of judicial duty to colonial enactments would later seem suggestive about the application of judicial duty to state legislation. Yet the practical experience of Americans with the decisions of the Privy Council could not have offered state judges after 1776 much of a model as to how they should hold acts unlawful, and state judges therefore must have been rather dependent on the common law ideal of their duty.

Decisions in the Colonial Courts

Even more than Privy Councillors, many colonial judges strained against their duty as judges. They had none of the councillors' administrative freedom to escape their judicial duty by means of a disallowance, and they had far more immediate, local reasons to avoid holding colonial statutes unlawful. They therefore frequently wrestled with their duty, all too often bending it out of shape in order to preserve local statutes.

A series of cases in South Carolina reveals with unusual clarity both what judges felt obliged to do under their duty and how they became profoundly reluctant to do it. In the late seventeenth century, the South Carolina judges apparently felt little compunction about questioning the lawfulness of acts adopted by the assembly, and the Commons House of Assembly therefore listed as a grievance "Inferio^r^ Courts takeing upon them to try ajudge & Determine the power of assembly for ye Validity of acts made by them."[20] By referring to inferior courts, the Assembly asserted its pretensions of being a high court, but the judges of the judicial courts evidently recognized their duty.

[20] *Journals of the Commons House of Assembly of South Carolina for the Four Sessions of 1693,* at 17 (Jan. 18, 1693), ed. A. S. Salley (Columbia: Historical Commission of South Carolina, 1907). The Commons continued: "or of such matters and things as are acted by o^r^ Relateing to ye House of Commons all which we humbly Conceive is only inquireable into and Determinable by ye Next Succeeding General assembly." For interpretations of this in terms of *Bonham's Case,* see McGovney, "The British Origin of Judicial Review of Legislation," 8; Robert Cook, "Judicial Review and Legislative Power," in *South Carolina Legal History,* 86, ed. Herbert A. Johnson (Spartanburg: Reprint Company, 1980).

The South Carolina judges continued through the 1730s to do their duty in occasionally holding their colony's statutes unlawful—the most dramatic example being *Rex v. Thomas Mellichamp.*[21] The defendant was a member of a Georgia crime family who was indicted and eventually in 1736 convicted by a South Carolina jury for counterfeiting the colony's bills of credit—in particular, for engraving a copper plate in imitation of a one-pound bill. The indictment, however, was under a South Carolina statute against counterfeiting that imposed the death penalty without benefit of clergy—that is, without the old right of first-time offenders to avoid the death penalty. Mellichamp's lawyers therefore moved in arrest of judgment that the statute conflicted with the English statute of 25 Edward III, "which allows Clergy in all Felonies at common Law, where it's not expressly taken away by some Statute"—meaning a statute passed by Parliament.[22]

Chief Justice Robert Wright began his opinion by observing that "it's requisite that we consider our own Constitution"—the British constitution—which was "founded on Reason and the Law of Nature" and was "framed and settled by the Wisdom of our Ancestors." According to this constitution, British subjects were bound by "no Laws but those of our own making, that is by King, Lords and Commons in Parliament assembled,"

[21] This case is examined in detail by Robert Cook, albeit with rather strong statements as to Lamboll's ideology and how "[i]t was Coke and *Bonham* . . . in command." Cook, "Judicial Review and Legislative Power," 86, 88.

Another case was *Thomas Saunders v. The Ludlow Galley,* which was heard in 1717 by the South Carolina Vice-Admiralty Court. Saunders sailed with the Ludlow Galley on its return voyage from Guinea with a cargo of slaves. He and the rest of the crew were promised to be paid in the currency of the colony in which they landed, which they thought would be Virginia. The ship, however, arrived in South Carolina, where the owner offered to pay the crew in the colony's paper money, which consisted of depreciated bills of credit. Saunders and others of the crew therefore sued in the Vice-Admiralty Court, where Judge Nicholas Trott relied on a recent act of Parliament setting rates of exchange to give redress, explaining that "the several acts of Assembly made in this province for stamping bills of credit"—in other words, its tender laws—"are very repugnant and contrary to said statute." *Thomas Saunders, et al. v. the Ludlow Galley* (South Carolina Vice-Admiralty Court, May 1717), as quoted by Smith, *Appeals to the Privy Council,* 536. See An Act for ascertaining the Rates of Foreign Coins in Her Majesties Plantations in America, 6 Anne cap. 57 (1708). This is chapter 30 in eighteenth-century editions of the statutes.

[22] One indictment was for felony in counterfeiting bills of credit of the province; a second was for felony in counterfeiting one-pound bills of credit; a third for a misdemeanor. Letter from Timothy Telltruth to Printer (July 20, 1735), *South-Carolina Gazette* (July 26–Aug. 2, 1735); Correspondence (Charlestown, Mar. 13), ibid. (Mar. 13–20, 1736); Correspondence (Charlestown, Mar. 23), ibid. (March 20–27, 1736). For the conviction on the second indictment, and for the Crown's abandonment of the other indictments on account of errors, see Correspondence (Charlestown, Mar. 23), ibid. (Mar. 20–27, 1736). Among the reasons for the delay was his dramatic escape from jail. Ibid. (Oct. 4–11, 1736).

and this was significant because it was necessary to "consider the Prisoner at the Bar as a British Subject . . . who claims the Benefit of all the Laws of his Country." Wright explained that under his commission, he was sworn to decide whether the colonial statute was in accord with British law:

> Far be it from me, to impeach or question the Validity of any Law of this Province, or the Authority by which it is made; but by my Commission I am required and sworn to judge between the King and his People, according to the Laws and Statutes of *Great Britain* and the Laws of this Province, [and] therefore must inquire by what Authority they are made, and whether this Law be agre[e]able to the Laws of *Great Britain,* or can operate to supersede any Law of *Britain.*

Emphasizing his duty to decide in accord with the English constitution, Wright further noted that the king had instructed governors "to preserve the Constitution" and "not to abuse or exceed the Power given them." Accordingly, although "I am in Duty bound to support and maintain the just Prerogatives of the Crown; I am also bound to defend and protect all his Majesty's subjects in safe and free Enjoyment of their Lives, Liberties, Estates and Properties, so far as by Law I may."[23]

Chief Justice Wright concluded that judgment should be arrested. If the colonial law were valid, it would "Annul and Supersede the *Statute* of the 25 of Edw[ard] the 3d and *Magna Charta,*" which required proceedings to be "by legal processes." In short, "if this Law be valid and of Force, it oversets our whole Constitution." Wright was therefore "of Opinion that this Act exceeds the Power granted by the King's Commission, and is repugnant to the Laws of *Britain*" and "therefore by the King's Instructions ought not to operate to affect the Lives, Liberties, Estates and Properties of the People."

A sharp dissent came from the lay assistant justice who attended the proceedings, Thomas Lamboll, but merely because he thought English law allowed the colony to make laws that departed from those of England. South Carolinians were only required by their charter to follow British law "as near as conveniently as may be," and among the rights and privileges of Englishmen enjoyed by South Carolinians "in their Mother Country, and retain'd and brought over with them hither," was "that of giving their Consent by their legal Representatives to such good and wholesome Laws for the Government of the whole Community." Accordingly, Lamboll thought that "Justice and my Office oblige me to give my Judgment, that Sentence of Death be pronounced upon *Thomas Mellichamp.*"

[23] "Charlestown," *South-Carolina Gazette* (May 1–8, 1736).

At this point, the case was adjourned until *"a fuller Bench"* was present *"to decide the Cause by a Majority,"* and unfortunately the records of this reconsideration are lost.[24] As for Mellichamp, he was released on bail, allegedly to get married in Georgia, but more certainly to rejoin his family there in further criminal enterprises.[25]

Wright's willingness to do his duty in holding the South Carolina statute contrary to the English constitution suggests much about his fortitude, for his commission as chief justice had been carefully written to prevent him from holding colonial statutes unlawful. The Crown in 1730 had sent the governor of South Carolina a patent to appoint Wright as "Chief Justice . . . with full power & Authority to hold the Supreme Courts of Judicature," and the governor had necessarily repeated these words in his commission to Wright, but he added that Wright was "to hear & determine all Pleas, Civil & Criminal happening & arising within this Province according to the laws & Statutes of Great Britain and the several Acts of Assembly in this Province."[26] This dual limitation committed Wright to deciding as much in accord with local law as with British law, but as Wright understood, this sometimes was not possible, and he satisfied his conscience by interpreting his commission to require that he follow South Carolina law to the extent it was "agre[e]able to the Laws of *Great Britain.*"[27]

Chief Justice Wright's adherence to duty, however, became a thing of the past in 1742, when Benjamin Whitaker, a former attorney general, became the next chief justice. He initially hoped to avoid his predecessor's predicament, and he therefore in July 1742 insisted that he could not swear to the office on terms other than those directed by the Crown. As he later explained, "I entertained this Scruple from what I had observed in the time of the late Chief Justice, who often found the laws and Statutes of Great

24 Ibid.

25 His family, under his mother's leadership, specialized in receiving stolen goods, and Georgia responded to Mellichamp's return by indicting him again for forgery and expelling his family from the colony—after dispossessing them of their ill-gotten possessions. "Charlestown," ibid. (July 10–17, 1736); "Savannah, August 5," ibid. (Aug. 14–21, 1736). He was previously engaged to Sophia Hopkey, who also attracted the attention of John Wesley. While Mellichamp was in jail, she told Wesley, "I won't have Tommy for he is a bad man," but "I can have none else." Eventually her affections shifted to Wesley, but he was unwilling to marry her, whereupon she accepted an ill-matched suitor. Bufford W. Coe, *John Wesley and Marriage,* 73, 77 (Bethlehem: Lehigh University Press, 1996).

26 Letter from Benjamin Whitaker (Feb. 3, 1743), Transcripts of Records in the British Public Record Office, 21: 134–135, SCA, Mfm.

27 "Charlestown," *South-Carolina Gazette* (May 1–8, 1736). The ambiguities of Wright's commission made it particularly useful for him to add that the instructions to the governor required any judge to uphold the constitution. See below.

Britain incompatible with the Acts of this Province, which is a difficulty that still remains."[28]

By the autumn of that year, however, it was clear that Whitaker would not really be so bold. In the turbulence of the prior decade, Chief Justice Wright's decisions had provoked the Assembly to give the lay assistant judges, such as Thomas Lamboll, the power to outvote him—as presumably happened in *Mellichamp.*[29] Being a minority on his own court, Chief Justice Wright had not been able to resist the statutes that gave equal authority to the assistant justices, but the Privy Council recognized the threat to the royal prerogative and in 1736 disallowed these enactments.[30] The South Carolina legislature, however, subsequently adopted other statutes that again enhanced the authority of the assistant judges, and thus when Whitaker in 1742 became chief justice, he inherited assistants who were confident they could outvote him and even sit without him. Whitaker resented this, especially as the assistants were not even trained in the law, and because he could not remove them judicially, he sought a political solution. At the opening of the colony's General Assembly in September 1742, Whitaker was chosen as Speaker of the Commons, and when Lieutenant Governor William Bull made his opening speech, Whitaker not only gave the usual response on behalf of the Commons but also on the same day wrote a letter to Bull against the assistant judges.[31] Whitaker thus took advantage of his position as Speaker to attempt a demotion of his assistants, and as might be expected of a judge who aligned himself with the Commons, he now carefully disclaimed judicial authority over the lawfulness of legislation. Rather than suggest that he could hold the post-1736 statutes unlawful, he argued that because the earlier acts strengthening his assistants had been disallowed, the later ones could not be understood to have the ef-

[28] Letter from Benjamin Whitaker (Feb. 3, 1743), Transcripts of Records in the British Public Record Office, 21: 135–136, SCA, Mfm. For his success in getting his commission on such terms, see Royal Letters Patent (Oct. 21, 1741) and Commission (July 7, 1742), SCA, S213003, Vol. 5, Secretary of State, Misc. Records, Volume EE, pages 193–194.

[29] In addition, for at least three years, the Assembly denied him his salary. Petition of Robert Wright to the King (received May 1735), Transcripts of Records in the British Public Record Office, 17: 307, SCA, Mfm. According to his petition, the denial of salary was on account of his protests in the governor's council against legislation that infringed upon the king's prerogative, but his greatest affront to the House was his grant of a writ of habeas corpus to men committed by the House. Edward McCrady, *The History of South Carolina under the Royal Government 1719–1776,* at 152 (New York: Macmillan, 1899).

[30] W. L. Grant and James Munro, eds., *Acts of the Privy Council of England,* 3: 412 (Colonial Series) (Hereford: His Majesty's Stationery Office, 1910).

[31] Correspondence (Charles-Town, Sept. 20), *South-Carolina Gazette* (Sept. 13–20, 1742). Whitaker was chosen on September 13; Bull gave his speech to the General Assembly on Sept. 14; Whitaker responded on Sept. 16. Ibid.

fect of "expressly reenacting part of an Act, wc^{h} the King has repealed." He thus emphasized that he was merely interpreting in accord with the Crown's disallowance, and lest the implied deference to the South Carolina legislature go unnoticed, he introduced his argument for the confined effect of the later statutes by stipulating that because the king had a right of disallowance, colonial judges were precluded from holding colonial legislation unlawful:

> [T]he Judges in america are bound to Observe the laws that are pass'd by the General Assembly, till they are repealed by the King. [F]or though such Laws . . . may be repugnent to ye Laws of England, yet it is conceived Such laws, are not Ipso facto void, in themselves, but only voidable by his Majesty's disallowance or repeal, who tis humbly Apprehended has reserved to himself the sole power of Judging of Such Contriety, or repugnancy.[32]

This suggestion that the king, in his power of disallowance, had the exclusive power to judge the lawfulness of colonial acts was scarcely plausible in English law; but the Chief Justice was writing a memorial against his fellow judges, and for this worthy end, he needed to make his peace with the lower house of the legislature.

Like so many other American judges who gave way to local pressures, Whitaker could not have been entirely comfortable with his lack of fortitude, and within half a year he took a more equivocal position in an advisory opinion. The king's superintendent of quit rents, Henry McCulloch, asked Whitaker in 1743 for an opinion about the jurisdiction of the courts, and in giving his response, the Chief Justice observed that there was a question about acts "disagreeable or repugnant to the laws of England":

> The Question is whether these laws are void when they are first made, or only voidable by his Majesty's Disallowance & may be put in practice till his Majesty's Pleasure shall be signified that the same are repealed? and whether the Judges . . . ought to adjudge them ipso facto, void or only voidable, and so to be put in practice 'till they are repealed by his Majesty?[33]

[32] To the Honble William Bull Esqr Lieut Govr: and Commr in Chief in & over his Majesty's Province of So Carolina, Memorial of Benjamin Whitaker Esqr. his Majesty's Chief Justice of the said Province (Sept. 16, 1742), copied in Council Journal (March 15, 1743), 276, SCA, Mfm. Incidentally, Whitaker refers to the 1737 act in terms of the old-style calendar and so calls it the 1736 act. McGoveny notes Whitaker's views but assumes that "colonial minds" were "clouded" by confusion between disallowance and decisions holding acts void. McGovney, "The British Origin of Judicial Review of Legislation," 40. For some of the political background, see W. Roy Smith, *South Carolina as a Royal Province 1719–1776,* at 128–133 (New York: Macmillan, 1903).

[33] Letter from Benjamin Whitaker (Feb. 3, 1743), Transcripts of Records in the British Public Record Office, 21: 137, SCA, Mfm.

Whitaker probably took comfort in telling himself that this was an open question. It was, however, his more politic views that would have growing appeal among at least some South Carolina judges.

In 1759, for example, in *Williams Admin. de Bonis Non v. Watson's Executors,* a subsequent chief justice relied on Whitaker's argument to avoid overturning a local statute. The South Carolina Court of Common Pleas had to decide in this case whether a 1645 colonial act on administrators and executors was repugnant to English law and to the provision of the colony's charter requiring conformity to such law.[34] The question was potentially as disruptive as that which so troubled Connecticut three decades earlier, and Chief Justice James Michie simply evaded it. This former member of the governor's council held only a temporary appointment from the governor, and as might be expected, he held that his court lacked "a Power of Judging whether the Laws which the General Assembly make are Void or not," as this would give them "a Power Superior to the General Assembly," and although he was cautious enough to avoid saying that the Assembly was similar to Parliament, he hinted at this by noting that the "Judges in England" had not "Questioned the power of making Laws." More emphatically, he followed Whitaker in holding that the king's right of disallowance in the Privy Council precluded any other challenge to the laws, for "the King has reserved to himself & his Privy Council a Right of Judging of those [colonial] Laws and till the king thinks fit to repeal them they Continue their full Force and Obligation."[35] Michie probably feared the consequences of a decision that would unsettle South Carolina property rights,

[34] The defendant's counsel argued against the statute by observing of the charter that "by this Constitution, the Assembly could . . . by no means . . . make Law Contrary or repugnant to the Laws of England for that their power was expressly limited by the Charters." Plaintiff's counsel conceded this point about the charters or "Constitution" but responded that "the Act was not Contrary to the Laws of England or repugnant," but "was made Consonant to reason and as near as could be to the English Law." *Williams Admin. de Bonis Non v. Watson's Executors* (Court of Common Pleas, Nov. term, 1759), in *Cases and Materials on the Development of Legal Institutions,* 285–286, ed. Julius Goebel (Brattleboro: Vermont Printing, 1946), citing MS Journal of court. For Michie's appointment, which lasted but a term, see McCrady, *The History of South Carolina,* at 465.

[35] *Cases and Materials on the Development of Legal Institutions,* 288. With this notion that the Privy Council had an exclusive right to judge colonial laws, Michie worried:

> [I]f the Courts of America had a power to adjuge them Void 't'would Anticipate the Kings Judgment And would be two Powers of Repealing, which is Inconsistent with the Nature of our Constitution, this would be for the Courts *Jus dare* & not *dicere:* It is easy to see the Consequence of those Arguments, For if this Court has a Power to Adjudge our Laws to be Void, They have a power to dispense with them [and] such a Power will be Naturally inferr'd & every thing will be Left to precarious & Arbitrary Will and pleasure.

and he certainly managed to understand his duty in a way that posed no danger to local enactments.

The local pressure on colonial judges to uphold colonial legislation was never more graphically illustrated than by a litigious resident of Dedham, Massachusetts, Nathaniel Ames. He was a physician, a tavern-keeper, and the publisher of an almanac that he embellished with his own, execrable verse. He married his first wife, Mary, in 1735, and in October 1737 she bore him a son they named Fisher. Within a month, however, Mary died, and less than year afterward young Fisher followed her. Later, by his second wife, Nathaniel would father the other, longer-lived Fisher Ames.

The question for the Massachusetts courts was whether the property interest of the first Fisher Ames—in particular, his rights to the tavern—should go to his father, Nathaniel, or to the descendants of Fisher's aunts on his mother's side. The maternal relatives claimed under English law as collateral kinsmen of the whole blood.[36] Massachusetts, however, departed from English law, and Nathaniel claimed under a 1692 Massachusetts statute, which simply gave the child's intestate estate "to the next of Kin to the Intestate in equal degree."[37] This dispute became a matter of litigation only in the middle of the next decade on the death of Hannah, Fisher's grandmother and Mary's mother, who had enjoyed a life estate in the property under her late husband's will.[38] After repeated trials, the case finally was decided with a special verdict, on which the Superior Court of Judicature in 1749 upheld Nathaniel's claim under the Massachusetts statute.[39] Two of the judges, however—Chief Justice Paul Dudley and Justice Benjamin

It was one thing to distinguish between *jus dare* and *jus dicere,* but the Chief Justice was conflating the duty of the judges with the power of the king and his Privy Council: "So our Acts of Assembly if they are Contrary to the Kings Instructions or Repugnant to the Laws of England they are not void for the King may Confirm them But they Continue in force untill they are Repealed or made void." Ibid.

36 William Blackstone, *Commentaries on the Laws of England,* 1: 224 (London: 1765).

37 An Act for the Settling and Distribution of the Estates of Intestates, *Acts and Laws, Passed by the Great and General Court or Assembly of Their Majesties Province of the Massachusets-Bay, in New-England. Begun . . . the Eighth Day of June, 1692 . . . unto Wednesday the Twelfth Day of October following: Being the Second Session,* 7 (Boston: 1692).

38 Robert Brand Hanson, *Dedham, Massachusetts 1635–1890,* at 122 (Dedham: Dedham Historical Society, 1976); Winfred E. A. Bernhard, *Fisher Ames, Federalist and Statesman 1758–1808,* at 9–10 (Williamsburg: Institute for Early American History and Culture, 1965); Martha J. McNamera, "Nearest a Kin to Fisher," *Common-Place,* 2, no. 2 (Jan. 2002), at www.historycooperative.org. Further details are recorded in *Ames v. Gay,* in MSA, Superior Court of Judicature, Record Book, 1747–1750, at 268–269, Mfm.

39 For the verdict, see *Ames v. Gay,* Case No. 10 (Aug. 1748), MSA, Supreme Court of Judicature, Suffolk Docket Book No. 57, Reel 7. This verdict also appears in Case No. 40 (Feb. term 1749), in ibid. For the judgment, *Ames v. Gay,* MSA, Superior Court of Judicature, Record Book, 1747–1750, at 269.

Lynde—dissented on the ground that the colony's statute violated English law.

Nathaniel was appalled at this affront to local law and the merits of his cause, and he therefore displayed his resentment as few other men could do. He had the sign outside his tavern painted to show the judges sitting on the bench with the colony's statute book on the desk in front of them. The two dissenters were depicted facing backward, turning away from the local laws.[40]

According to an early nineteenth-century historian, the court ordered the sheriff to remove the sign and bring it before them, but "Dr. Ames heard the order given, being then in Boston, and by good luck and hard riding, had just time enough to pull down his sign before the sheriff arrived at Dedham."[41] Allegedly, he replaced it with a text for the benefit of the sheriff: "A wicked and adulterous generation seeketh after a sign, and there shall no sign be given unto it."[42] Ames celebrated his victory in less memorable lines:

> Four Times the *Sun* has in cold *Pisces* been,
> The rising *Pleiads* have four Autumns seen,
> Since I have stood th' opposing Lawyer's Tongue
> Who puzzl'd Right, and Justify'd the Wrong,
> An honest Cause by dint of Law, maintain'd,
> And *Virgil* like the *Mantuan* Lands have gain'd . . .[43]

Fortunately for Ames, he was a more able litigator than poet.

Although Privy Councillors could usually sidestep impolitic decisions by disallowing American statutes, colonial judges regularly had to strain against their duty if they were to avoid holding local statutes unlawful, and their practices were therefore a particularly feeble model for later judges who had to hold state statutes unconstitutional. Yet in squirming to avoid undesirable results, colonial judges often revealed their awareness of what

[40] Erastus Worthington, *History of Dedham,* 92, note (Boston: 1827); Sam[uel] Briggs, *The Essays, Humor, and Poems of Nathaniel Ames, Father and Son, of Dedham, Massachusetts, from their Almanacks 1726–1775, with Notes and Comments by Sam. Briggs,* 23–25 (Cleveland: 1891). For a nineteenth-century copy of the sketch for the sign, see ibid., 25. The original is preserved in the Ames Family Papers in the Dedham Historical Society. At the top of the sign was the heading, "Nearest a Kin to Fisher" and below "Aug 18 1749." Written on the drawing is the note: "Sir, I wish I could have some talk on ye above subject, being the bearer waits for an answer shal only observe Mr Greenwood thinks yt can not be done under £40, old tenor." Ibid., 25.

[41] Worthington, *The History of Dedham,* 92, note.

[42] Briggs, *The Essays, Humor, and Poems of Nathaniel Ames,* at 25; Robert Hanson, *Dedham, Massachusetts 1635–1890,* at 123.

[43] Briggs, *The Essays, Humor, and Poems of Nathaniel Ames,* at 215.

judicial duty ordinarily required, and their failure to do their duty provides a hint as to how much the common law ideal, more than their practices, would be the model for their successors.

Colonial Decisions about Acts of Parliament

Just how ready Americans were to embrace judicial duty when they found its implications convenient became apparent when they challenged what seemed to them oppressive acts of Parliament. Against these acts, Americans could take satisfaction in the consequences of judicial duty, but they once again departed from the common law ideal, for it required deference to the acts of the high court of Parliament, and Americans were not feeling very deferential. Whereas against colonial acts American judges often simply avoided their duty, against acts of Parliament they sometimes pursued their duty further than the law permitted.

The degree to which Americans strained the bounds of their duty in order to hold acts of Parliament unlawful is evident from their reliance on *Bonham's Case*. In this case of 1610, or at least in his report of the case, Chief Justice Coke had used words that might seem to suggest judges could hold statutes void:

> [I]n many cases, the common law will controul Acts of Parliament, and sometimes adjudge them to be utterly void: for when an Act of Parliament is against common right and reason, or repugnant, or impossible to be performed, the common law will controul it, and adjudge such Act to be void.[44]

This was not, however, an argument for holding statutes void, but rather for equitable interpretation. As has been seen, judges used arguments about what was void in conscience or against natural equity to establish the moral foundation for their equitable interpretation of statutes, and this is what Coke did in *Bonham's Case*.[45] Nonetheless, *Bonham's Case* was susceptible of being misunderstood, and many Americans took pleasure in a misinterpretation that allowed them to believe that judges could actually hold an act of Parliament unlawful.

[44] *Bonham's Case* (C.P. 1610), Coke, *Reports,* 8: 118a. In fact, he may not have used these words from the bench. Charles Gray, "Bonham's Case Reviewed," *Proceedings of the American Philosophical Society,* 116: 35 (1972). The phrase "common right" alluded to the shared liberty of the people, in contrast to the particular "liberty" or property right of an individual, and the phrase in Coke's report, "common right and reason," was thus parallel to "law and reason."

[45] S. E. Thorne, "Dr. Bonham's Case," in *Essays in English Legal History,* 275–276 (London: Hambledon, 1985); J. H. Baker, *The Law's Two Bodies: Some Evidential Problems in English Legal History,* 28 and note 96 (Oxford: Oxford University Press, 2001). For Coke's broad language and its significance, see Appendix I.

Even with the benefit of *Bonham's Case,* it required considerable dexterity to argue that judges could hold acts of Parliament unconstitutional, and although James Otis was not up to the task, he fortunately had John Adams to come to his aid. In 1761 James Otis argued in the *Writs of Assistance Case* against the statutory authority for the writs, and according to the rough notes taken in court by the young John Adams, Otis said that "[a]n Act [of Parliament] against the Constitution is void." The case arose on a petition that recited the relevant act of Parliament, and with words that harked back to cases of equitable interpretation, Otis argued that "an Act against natural Equity is void: and if an Act of Parliament should be made, in the very Words of this Petition, it would be void."[46] Thus far, this may have been only an argument for charitable interpretation of the statute, but two months later, when Adams used his notes to prepare a more elaborate account of Otis's speech, he shifted the argument more clearly toward holding the statute void under the constitution. Natural law and natural rights had long been considered suggestive as to what a people could be presumed to have consented to when forming a tacit, customary constitution, and Adams now had Otis say that "Reason & the Constitution are against this Writ" and that "No Acts of Parliament can establish such a writ; Though it should be made in the very words of the petition it would be void, AN ACT AGAINST THE CONSTITUTION IS VOID."[47] No longer only a moral supposition underlying charitable interpretation, this was a legal conclusion about the

[46] *Petition of Lechmere* (Feb. 1761), in *Legal Papers of John Adams,* 2: 127, eds. L. Kinvin Wroth and Hiller B. Zobel (Cambridge: Belknap, 1965).

[47] *Petition of Lechmere* (c. April 1761), ibid., 2: 143–144. For the change in emphasis from Adams's draft notes to his more formal report, see M. H. Smith, *The Writs of Assistance Case,* 364 (Berkeley: University of California Press, 1978).

When Otis returned to the argument in his 1764 pamphlet *The Rights of the British Colonies Asserted and Proved,* he sharpened his formulation to clarify that unconstitutional acts were void. He again echoed the reference to "natural equity" in Hobart and Bridgman, but now (following Adams) with greater emphasis on the constitutional implications: "The judges of England have declared . . . that *acts of parliament against natural equity are void.* That *acts against the fundamental principles of the British constitution are void.*" Not content with this, Otis printed an enormous explanatory footnote—by far the longest in his pamphlet—in which he recited the argument of Locke and Vattel that an assembly entrusted with the legislative power could not "change the constitution of the state." Even so, he remained concerned that Hobart's words about "natural equity" would be understood to refer to interpretation, for he recognized that English judges said they would "'strain hard rather than interpret an act void, ab initio.'" Otis therefore responded: *"This is granted, but still their authority"*—that is, Parliament's—*"is not boundless, if subject to the controul of the judges in any case."* Pursuing the point, he added: "Holt, Chief Justice, thought what Lord Coke says in Doctor Bonham's case a very reasonable and true saying," that an act of Parliament could be "void." James Otis, *The Rights of the British Colonies Asserted and Proved,* 72 and 73, note (Boston: 1764). This, however, missed Holt's point, which was that the remedy lay in the people. Philip Hamburger, "Revolution and Judicial Review: Chief Justice Holt's Opinion in *City of London v. Wood,*" *Columbia Law Review,* 94: 2130, 2133 (1994).

unconstitutionality of an act of Parliament.[48] It was a hint of things to come.

Five years later, some Virginia justices of the peace actually held an act of Parliament unconstitutional. Although the judges of colonial supreme courts had repeatedly hesitated to hold colonial statutes unconstitutional, the justices of the peace sitting on the Northampton County Court readily exceeded their duty when confronted with the Stamp Act. In response to patriotic resolutions urging the courts not to open—so they would not have to use stamped paper—the Northampton County Court declined to meet in January 1766. Yet by the end of the month, after "repeated complaints of the inhabitants, for want of a dew distribution of justice," the justices "resolved, from the extreme necessity of the case, to open the Courts, and proceed to business, as usual."[49] When the County Court reopened in February, the clerk and other court officers therefore found themselves in a predicament: Although they hesitated to use stamped paper, they also worried about their liability for failing to comply with the Stamp Act. To avoid this difficulty, they moved for an "Opinion" from the bench as to whether the Act "was binding on the inhabitants of this Colony" and whether "they the said Officers should incur any Penalties by not using Stamp Paper." The court responded by unanimously declaring their opinion:

> [T]hat the said Act did not bind, affect, or concern the Inhabitants of this Colony, inasmuch as they conceive the said Act to be unconstitutional, and that the said several Officers may proceed in the Execution of their respective Offices without incurring any Penalty by means thereof.[50]

[48] Later, Lieutenant Governor Hutchinson regretted that Americans were not content to understand *Bonham's Case* as a precedent for equitable interpretation: "Lord Coke's authority is often abused to serve particular purposes and when he says in Bonham's Case that the common law shall sometimes judge Acts of Parliament to be void, no notice is taken of what he says in the same case that they who make them would not put them into execution. When this shall be the sense of those who make Acts of Parliament for taxing the colonists, Lord Coke's authority may more properly, than at present, be adduced to justify courts of judicature and private subjects in the non observance of these Acts." Hutchinson Correspondence, Massachusetts Archives Collection, 25: fols. 129–130, as quoted in Smith, *Appeals to the Privy Council,* 521, note 227. Similarly, he complained that "our friends to liberty take the advantage of a maxim they find in Lord Coke that an Act of Parliament against Magna Charta or the peculiar rights of Englishmen is *ipso facto* void," and "[t]his, taken in the latitude the people are often enough disposed to take it, must be fatal to all government, and it seems to have determined great part of the colony to oppose the execution of the act with force." Lieutenant Governor Hutchinson (Sept. 12, 1765), Hutchinson Correspondence, Massachusetts Archives Collection, 26: fols. 153–154, 180, 183, as quoted by Theodore F. T. Plucknett, "Bonham's Case and Judicial Review," *Harvard Law Review,* 40: 63 (1938).

[49] "*Extract of a letter from* Northampton *county, in this province, January* 31, 1766," *Virginia Gazette* (March 7, 1766).

[50] Minute Book 1765–1771, at 31–32 (Feb. 11, 1766), LVA, Northampton County Court, Mfm 50. A copy with minor variants was printed in *Virginia Gazette* (Purdie & Dixon, Mar. 21, 1766). See also "Northamptoniensis" (Mar. 24, 1766), ibid. (Apr. 4, 1766).

In thinking about their duty, these judges might have paused to consider that they were reaching a constitutional decision that the law itself gave to Parliament; but just as colonial judges had often shied away from their duty when they faced colonial statutes, they were happy to do more than their duty as to an oppressive and unpopular act of Parliament.

Nor were the Northampton justices alone in going beyond their duty, for elsewhere in Virginia Edmund Pendleton reached the same conclusion. He was a justice of the peace and a magistrate of the Caroline County Court, and whether or not he was aware of the decision of the Northampton justices, he shared their distaste for the popular demands that courts should respond to the Stamp Act by shutting their doors. Only days after the Northampton resolution, this future president of the Virginia Court of Appeals wrote to James Madison, Sr., that "[w]e must resolve to admit the stamps or to proceed without them, for to stop all business must be a greater evil than either." He explained that "[f]or my own part I never have or will enter into noisy and riotous companys on the subjects," but "my sentiments I shall be always ready to communicate to serious men."

> As a majestrate, I thought it my duty to sit, and we have constantly opened court, and I shall not hesitate to determine what people will desire me and run the risque of themselves, and having taken an oath to determine according to law, [I] shall never consider that act as such for want of power (I mean constitutional authority) in the Parliament to pass it.

He had therefore hoped to take an approach in Caroline of a sort similar to that adopted in Northampton, and he asked his fellow justices "whether they would proceed in any business desired, notwithstanding that act." His colleagues cautiously "expressed their intention to proceed this spring, but thought it best to wait a little longer, as they had hitherto stop'd." Pendleton, in contrast, would not refrain from his duty. If Parliament lacked "constitutional authority" to pass the Stamp Act, he had to proceed with judicial business without the stamps, for he cared more about his oath than any penalty:

> Were I applied to for an attachment, or any other thing within my office out of court, I would grant it at the party's risque as to the validity of it, for I am not afraid of the penalty, at least so much as of breaking my Oath.

An English judge would have scoffed at the idea that it was within judicial office to hold an act of Parliament unconstitutional. This English deference to Parliament, however, had limited currency in Virginia in 1766, and in these circumstances, it is revealing that when a man such as Pendleton encountered an apparently unconstitutional English statute, he clearly understood the obligation of one who had taken "an oath to determine according to law."[51]

Yet the confidence of Americans that judges could hold acts of Parliament void did not last very long. The turning point was the publication of Blackstone's *Commentaries.* Blackstone explained that Parliament enjoyed "sovereign power" and therefore had "no superior upon earth." He acknowledged: "I know it is generally laid down . . . that acts of parliament contrary to reason are void. But if the parliament will positively enact a thing to be done which is unreasonable, I know of no power that can control it." Thus, when Parliament made its intent clear, "there is no court that has power to defeat the intent of the legislature."[52] This was a splash of cold water for those who dreamed of holding acts of Parliament unconstitutional. When the *Commentaries* were published in England, and especially after 1772, when they were published in America, "[t]he almost instant prestige that attached to the *Commentaries* led to the abandonment of *Dr. Bonham's Case* in the war of pamphlets, speeches, and resolves."[53] For example, Otis in 1765 gave up his position based on *Bonham's Case* and followed Blackstone in acknowledging the unchallengeable character of acts of Parliament.[54] Of course, *Bonham's Case* remained useful as a desperate last re-

[51] Letter from Edmund Pendleton to James Madison, Sr. (Feb. 15, 1766), in *The Letters and Papers of Edmund Pendleton 1734–1803,* at 1: 23, ed. David John Mays (Charlottesville: Virginia Historical Society, 1967). A rather different conclusion was reached on a similar underlying principle by the Westmoreland justices, who declined to act in their office because "the act for establishing Stamps in America . . . will impose on us a necessity, in consequence of the judicial oath we take, of acting in conformity to it's directions, and, by doing so, to become instrumental in the destruction of our country's most essential rights and liberties." To the Honorable the Governor and Council of Virginia (Sept. 24), *Newport Mercury* (Nov. 11, 1765).

[52] Blackstone, *Commentaries on the Laws of England,* 1: 90–91.

[53] Julius Goebel, Jr., ed., *The Law Practice of Alexander Hamilton,* 1: 284 (New York: Columbia University Press, 1964); Julius Goebel, Jr., *History of the Supreme Court of the United States: Antecedents and Beginnings to 1801,* at 1: 93–94 (New York: Macmillan, 1971). See also M. H. Smith, *The Writs of Assistance Case,* 192 (Berkeley: University of California Press, 1978). Tellingly, when "Candidus" in 1772 took a position similar to that once attributed to *Bonham's Case,* he argued that "whether Lord *Coke* has expressly asserted it or not . . . an act of parliament made against *Magna Charta* in violation of its essential parts, is void." Candidus, Letter to Messieurs Edes & Gill, *Boston Gazette* (Jan. 27, 1772), cited in ibid., 485. As might be expected, juries sometimes picked up where the judges left off, and thus the Chief Justice of Massachusetts in 1769 had to instruct a Suffolk County grand jury: "We, Gentlemen, who are to execute the Law, are not to enquire into the Reason and Policy of it, or whether it is constitutional or not." Josiah Quincy, Jr., *Reports of Cases Argued and adjudged in the Superior Court of Judicature of the Province of Massachusetts Bay, between 1761 and 1772,* 307 (Boston: 1865).

[54] James Otis, *A Vindication of the British Colonies* (Boston, 1765), in *Pamphlets of the American Revolution 1750–1776,* at 1: 545, ed. Bernard Bailyn (Cambridge: Belknap, 1956). For this point, see Bailyn's introductory comments at ibid., 547–548, 550.

sort—for example, when a lawyer represented slaves in a southern state.[55] The English case, moreover, still inspired law students to contemplate the

[55] For example, George Mason argued from *Bonham's Case* in a 1772 Virginia case, *Robin et al. v. Hardaway et al.* Mason represented descendants of Indian women who had been brought into Virginia by traders between 1682 and 1748 and then sold as slaves under a statute of 1682. Mason's strongest argument was that the 1682 statute had been repealed by subsequent legislation—most clearly by Virginia's 1705 codification of its slave laws. This statutory argument, however, was of no help to the descendants of Indian women enslaved before 1705, and therefore to help all of his clients Mason also needed to assert that the 1682 act was void from its inception. He could have argued that the 1682 Virginia act was a subordinate law and thus void if contrary to English law or reason, but in the aftermath of the *Parson's Cause* this argument was not likely to appeal to either Mason or the judges. He therefore relied on *Bonham's Case* to align the Indian claims with American claims and thus to bring American resentments against acts of Parliament to bear against an act of the Virginia legislature: "Now all acts of legislature apparently contrary to natural right and justice, are, in our laws, and must be in the nature of things, considered as void. The laws of nature are the laws of God; whose authority can be superseded by no power on earth. A legislature must not obstruct our obedience to him from whose punishments they cannot protect us. All human constitutions which contradict his laws, we are in conscience bound to disobey. And cited 8 Co. 118a Bonham's case. Hob. 87. 7. Co. 14. a. Calvin's case. And so he concluded the act of 1[6]82, originally void, because contrary to natural right and justice." Although improbable, this argument offered the best chance to free all of the plaintiffs. As might have been predicted, the Court did not rely on *Bonham's Case* and instead held that the 1682 act was "repealed by the act of 1705." *Robin et al. v. Hardaway et al.* (General Court, April 1772), Thomas Jefferson, *Reports of Cases Determined in the General Court of Virginia,* 114 (Charlottesville: 1829).

The practical consequences of this holding (at least for descendants of the women enslaved after 1705) can be observed in a related case decided the next month. Claiming trespass, assault and battery, and false imprisonment, the Indian Phillis won a jury verdict that she "is free and not a Slave." She recovered only one shilling damages and costs, but at least she established her freedom. *Phillis an Indian v. Stephen Dance* (General Court at Williamsburg, May 5, 1772), copy of record, College of William and Mary, Swem Library, Tucker-Coleman Papers, Reel M-39. For newspaper advertisements from 1772 and 1773 seeking the return of slaves of Indian ancestry who had left to seek their freedom in the General Court, see Peter Wallenstein, "Indian Foremothers: Race, Sex, Slavery, and Freedom in Early Virginia," in *The Devil's Lane: Sex and Race in the Early South,* 62, eds. Catherine Clinton and Michele Gillespie (New York: Oxford University Press, 1997).

Incidentally, the Court of Appeals considered the question afresh fifteen years later in *Hannah et al. v. Davis.* The jury found in a special verdict that Hannah and the other plaintiffs were descendants of Bess, an "Indian . . . brought from some Indian nation into the County of Richmond since the year 1705. viz. 1712." In the Court of Appeals, Thomas Nelson argued for the plaintiffs that the 1705 act "perhaps repealed" the prior statutes, "but if [the] act of 1682. be unrepealed yet it being contrary to the law of God & the law of nature to make Slaves of the subjects of foreign powers, which the Indians certainly were, this Act is null and void." Although this argument may have been based on *Bonham's Case,* it concerned a subordinate act and thus may have alluded to the common law test of law and reason. On behalf of the defendants, Taylor responded at length that "[t]he Argument against Slavery applied equally to African as Indian nations," thus suggesting that the plaintiff's argument proved too much. John Marshall then argued for the descendants of Bess that although she may have been "detained in slavery," she "could still transmit the right of freedom to her posterity," and after further arguments for the defendants, William Nelson pursued Marshall's point by pointing to a further statute of 1705—not the slave codificapossibility that acts of Parliament could be held void, and it thereby probably contributed to the willingness of later American judges to hold state statutes unconstitutional.[56] Nonetheless, to use the case to hold an act of Parliament void was a departure from judicial duty, and when Americans recognized this, they gave up their reliance on their judges and began to prepare an appeal to the people and ultimately to God.

Although the law barred judges from holding acts of Parliament void, the judges otherwise had to decide the lawfulness of statutes, including both municipal and colonial legislation. Such at least was the ideal of their duty, and although the Privy Council and the colonial judges rarely did their duty in holding colonial statutes void, they often in the back of their minds apparently understood what their duty required. Their erratic, wayward practices usually fell short of their duty for colonial statutes and once or twice exceeded it for acts of Parliament, and their conduct therefore did not offer the sort of consistent pattern that later American judges could have relied upon when holding state statutes unconstitutional. The very irregularity of colonial practice, however, is revealing. Far from showing the importance of colonial experience in developing a power of judicial review, it suggests that in cases concerning the constitutionality of legislation, American judges after Independence would be particularly dependent on the common law ideal of judicial duty.

---

tion, but an act that opened up trade with the Indians: "Could the people of Virginia make Slaves of a nation with whom they were at peace? [Y]et the act of 1705. makes such a peace, and authorizes a free trade with them. The *holding* & *claiming* Bess as Slave, can not be construed to destroy her freedom—The bare *holding* or *claiming* her, could have not such effect." Reaching the same conclusion as the earlier case, "[t]he court seemed unanimously of opinion that the Act of 1682. was absolutely repealed by the Acts of 1705 . . . Judgement for, plts." *Hannah & Others v. Davis* (Apr. 20, 1787), St. George Tucker, Notes of Cases, 1: 44–45, College of William and Mary, Swem Library, Tucker-Coleman Papers, Reel M-62. For details about the opinion of each judge, see Notes of Courts Opinion (Apr. 28, 1787), Tucker-Coleman Papers, Reel M-43. For the litigation of such issues, see Charles Hobson, "St. George Tucker's Law Papers," *William and Mary Law Review,* 47: 1270–1272 (2006).

56 Law students sometimes quoted *Bonham's Case* in their notebooks. See, for example, Notebook of Levi Lincoln, 135, 138, 160, American Antiquarian Society, Lincoln Family Papers, Octavo No. 1; Extracts from Law-Writers, 173 (entry dated Feb. 1, 1788), William Plumer Legal Papers, Reel 19.

IV

LAW AND JUDICIAL DUTY IN AMERICA

This book must now shift from England and her colonies to the early American states, where the ideals of law and judicial duty continued to thrive. There was no need for an American development of a new judicial power, let alone a revolutionary creation of such a power, for the ideals of law and judicial duty endured within the framework of the common law. As in England, therefore, judges often felt obliged to hold government acts unlawful.

The continuity of the ideals of law and judicial duty in America is a theme introduced in Chapter Ten, where it will be seen that constitutions made by the people were still considered to have the obligation of law and that judges were still thought to have a duty to decide in accord with the law. To be sure, many men were disappointed when the common law ideals required unreasonable or unjust results, but as shown in Chapter Eleven, American lawyers tended to assume that the ideals of law and judicial duty themselves were required by reason and justice and that they were the necessary foundation for laws against particular injustices. Chapter Twelve traces the practical implications of judicial duty in a wide range of constitutional decisions, and by observing the range of decisions, the chapter confirms that judges had a general duty, arising from their office, rather than a distinct power to review legislation. This was the duty of all judges, high and low; it reached all judicial decisions, whether cases or other determinations; and it required judges to reach conclusions about the lawfulness of all kinds of government acts. Such a duty was perhaps more mundane than a power of review, but it was therefore of far greater strength and significance.

10

Law and Judicial Duty

As IN England, so in each American state, a constitution made with the authority of the people was part of the law of the land, and the judges had a duty to decide in accord with the law of the land, including the constitution. Much was different after 1776, but these basics and what they required of judges remained largely the same.

The Legal Authority and Obligation of Constitutions, as Discussed by the Clergy

In the 1770s and 1780s, when Americans contemplated and then engaged in revolution, it continued to be a familiar assumption that constitutions made with the authority of the people had the obligation of law, and few Americans spoke about this with greater sophistication than the clergy. Political writers such as Thomas Jefferson understood that it was "the authority which renders an act obligatory."[1] The clergy, however, perhaps especially New England ministers, more regularly explored the problems of authority and obligation, and their sermons today offer a valuable window on such questions—at least, that is, from a learned Congregationalist perspective. The New England clergy, being academically trained, often acknowledged the moral obligation of reason or justice and sometimes even used such analysis to limit legal obligation, but they generally tended to assume that the obligation of human law was naturally based on its authority and that a constitution made with the authority of the people had the highest obligation among the laws of the land.

The ideals of authority that had seemed appealing amid European

[1] Thomas Jefferson, *Notes on the State of Virginia,* 222 (Query 13) (Paris: 1782).

fractures were particularly attractive in the disjointed circumstances of America, where colonists repeatedly had to rely on ideals of authority to establish their own societies. For example, already at the settling of Hartford and the neighboring towns in the late 1630s, the Rev. Thomas Hooker preached about "the foundation of authority" in "the free consent of the people." Along lines already familiar in Europe, he explained that "the choice of pubic magistrates belongs to the people by God's own allowance" and that they had it "in their power also to set the bounds and limitations of power and place" for their officers and magistrates.[2] The next year, the people to whom he made this suggestion acted upon it by adopting their Fundamental Orders. In these laws, they agreed to "assotiate and conjoyne our selves to be as one Publike State or Com[m]onwelth" and "enter[ed] into Combination and Confederation togather" not only for religious purposes but "also in o[u]r Civell Affaires to be guided and governed according to such Lawes, Rules, Orders and decrees as shall be made, ordered & decreed" in the manner they then specified.[3]

By the mid-eighteenth century, Americans were regularly relying on the ideals of authority not only to overcome their own divisions but also to justify their divergence from Britain. The Crown in the sixteenth century had employed the ideal of authority to achieve both unity within the realm and freedom from Rome, and Americans now also increasingly used this ideal, in the version that located authority in the people, to secure both cohesion and independence. As summarized by an American clergyman, "the same principles that oblige us to submit to civil government, do also equally oblige us, where we have power and ability, to resist and oppose tyranny. . . . For if magistrates have no authority but what they derive from the people . . . it will follow, that . . . the people, which gave them their authority, have a right to take it from them again."[4]

Mid-eighteenth-century American ministers tended to espouse ideals of authority in matters of law but with a lingering attachment to the older theory in which natural law was the measure of the obligation of particular laws. American ministers continued to wrestle with this older account of obligation in their academic study of morals, and as might be expected of learned clergymen, they frequently introduced elements of this traditional account into their discussions of the legal obligation derived from author-

[2] Thomas Hooker, Hartford Election Sermon (1638), in *The American Puritans, Their Prose and Poetry,* 89, ed. Perry Miller (Garden City: Doubleday, 1956).
[3] Fundamental Orders (1639).
[4] Samuel West, *A Sermon,* 23 (Boston: 1776).

ity—not typically to challenge the ideal that authority was the source of legal obligation, but to overlay some substantive moral limitations that at least were binding in conscience.

The ministers, however, had difficulty relying on their moral analysis to resolve the broad questions of law and politics that ever more frequently occupied Americans, and this became particularly clear during the Revolution. Most immediately, the clergy could not easily rest on their moral analysis to justify independence from Britain. The Rev. Simeon Howard, for example, briefly made use of the moral reasoning when in 1776 he preached against Parliament. According to Howard, if a legislature were to "make laws requiring the subjects to do things immoral, and which they knew to be so," then "the subjects would be at liberty to refuse obedience." From this, he concluded that "only such laws as are not plainly inconsistent with the end of society, or, in any other respect, inconsistent with the law of nature . . . can restrain and limit the natural liberty of those who belong to it."[5] This academic vision of natural law could enjoy some currency as a ground for disobeying particular statutes—whether the Stamp Act in 1766 or the various Intolerable Acts in 1774—but it was of limited value when Americans in 1776 needed to reject the entire authority of the English government. For this, as will be seen, Howard and other Americans needed arguments about authority, in which natural law was the measure of the people's allegiance and the source of their authority to make laws for their own society.[6]

Indeed, when ministers elevated moral obligation as an argument against the legal obligation of particular British laws, they took the risk of seeming to suggest that individuals could anarchically disobey any laws they considered unjust. Ideas about legal authority were so appealing precisely because they could overcome the discordant views that individuals were apt to take about reason and justice, and the American ministers who thought unjust laws might lack legal obligation were therefore usually at pains to limit the implications for individualistic departures from law. When the Rev. Samuel West in his 1776 Massachusetts election sermon defined the authority of the magistrate, he initially hinted at a moral qualifica-

[5] Simeon Howard, *A Sermon Preached to the Ancient and Honorable Artillery-Company, in Boston, New-England,* 11 (Boston: 1776).
[6] For natural law in late eighteenth-century America, see Philip Hamburger, "Natural Rights, Natural Law, and American Constitutions," *Yale Law Journal,* 102: 907 (1993); Helen K. Michael, "The Role of Natural Law in Early American Constitutionalism: Did the Founders Contemplate Judicial Enforcement of 'Unwritten' Individual Rights?" *North Carolina Law Review,* 69: 421 (1991).

tion to the obligation of law, for he said that "we ought chearfully to obey the magistrate and submit to all such regulations of government, as tend to promote the publick good." This was obviously in tension with ideals of authority, and West therefore quickly acknowledged that "this general definition may be liable to be misconstrued" in that "every man may think himself at liberty to disregard any laws that do not suit his interest, humor, or fancy." Anxious to stave off this risk of anarchy, West explained that in most instances, "it becomes us, as good members of society, peaceably and conscientiously to submit, tho' we cannot see the reasonableness of every law to which we submit."[7]

In fact, ministers tended to express their doubts about the obligation of unreasonable laws merely as moral qualifications in sermons that otherwise largely accepted the view, conventional in legal and political inquiry, that authority was the basis of legal obligation. West, for example, notwithstanding his brief academic caveat about obedience, more generally recognized in Calvinist manner the force of authority, and although he focused on the implications for allegiance and popular resistance, he did so in a manner suggestive about legal obligation. On the one hand, to oppose magistrates "when in the exercise of lawful authority, is an act of disobedience to the Deity," whose command was evident not only in scripture but also in natural law, for "reason, which is the voice of God plainly requires such an order of men to be appointed for the public good." On the other hand, "if magistrates have no authority but what they derive from the people . . . it will follow, that when they act contrary to the end and design of their creation, they cease being magistrates, and the people, which gave

[7] West, *A Sermon,* 17–18. As for religious objections to laws, he drew the line at what individuals considered sinful. Ibid., 18. In contrast to the academic view taken by West and many other ministers, a more secular commentator observed: "Should it be said law is the dictate of reason, I answer, it is more, it is the dictate of reason defined," and "[i]f every man's private judgment was to be the rule of right and wrong, there would be about as many rules as men; which would be just as well for society, as to have no rules at all." "Observator" No. 7, *Connecticut Journal* (Apr. 19, 1771).

A direct rejection of authority came from David Hoar—a mentally ill citizen of Massachusetts. In a strange document he sent to Chief Justice William Cushing, Hoar wrote: "So far from thinking a Supreme power can exist in, or be derived from the populace, we cannot but be sure it is the gift of God's all-creating goodness; and operates irresistibly, in such person and council as receive the same immediately from heaven." Pursuing such reasoning, Hoar concluded: "Your want of a moral person, to constitute legislative and executive office, is an entire vacancy of social and judiciary morality." He concluded: "If you convict me of error, I then submit to your direction; but if not, the emoluments of Government, must be inheritted by men, in such proportion as they attend to the dictates of reason." "In original Council, David Hoar president" (Concord May 22, 1787), Massachusetts Historical Society, William Cushing Papers. The Chief Justice saved the document, but not before docketing it "Hoar's Lett[e]r" and adding below "a Crazy man." Ibid.

them their authority, have a right to take it from them again."[8] Both allegiance and resistance rested on a divinely derived authority, and this left little room for moral limits on the obligation of law.

The way in which ministers increasingly accepted that legal obligation rested exclusively on authority can be observed at Princeton. Beginning in the late 1760s, John Witherspoon lectured that governmental authority and legal obligation were unchallengeable, except by revolution:

> It is frequently observed, that in every government there is a supreme irresistible power lodged somewhere, in king, senate, or people. To this power is the final appeal in all questions. Beyond this we cannot go. How far does this authority extend? We answer, as far as authority in a social state can extend; it is not accountable to any other tribunal, and it is supposed in the social compact that we have agreed to submit to its decision.

Having conveyed authority to their government, the people had to submit to it—the only "exception" being that "if the supreme power, wherever lodged, come to be exercised in a manifestly tyrannical manner," the people "may certainly if in their power, resist and overthrow" their government. Until this point, however, if a law was made with the authority conveyed by the people, it had legal obligation, and any resistance to it was a rejection of "the government altogether." The obligation of law came from the authority of the people, and recognizing that the obligation of law was therefore wholesale rather than retail, Witherspoon taught Americans to submit to their laws or, if their government was sufficiently "corrupt," to resist the government as a whole.[9]

The theory of authority not only justified revolution but also formed the basis of a response within the legal system, for it left unconstitutional laws without obligation. The Rev. John Tucker, for example, used his 1771 Massachusetts election sermon to trace the derivation of authority from God to individuals, to the people, and finally to government. In the ab-

[8] West, *A Sermon,* 16–17, 23.

[9] John Witherspoon, *An Annotated Edition of Lectures on Moral Philosophy,* 145, ed. Jack Scott (Newark: University of Delaware Press). He added: "If it be asked who must judge when the government may be resisted? I answer, the subjects in general, every one for himself. This may seem to be making them both judge and party, but there is no remedy. It would be denying the privilege altogether, to make the oppressive ruler the judge." Ibid. Manuscript notes by Princeton students show that Witherspoon adhered to these lectures almost word for word during most of his time at Princeton. See, for example, Andrew S. Hunter, *Lectures on Moral Philosophy, 1771–1772,* Princeton University, Rare Books and Special Collections, C0199, No. 538, and Robert G. Johnson, *Lectures on Moral Philosophy, 1786–1789,* ibid., C0199, No. 1445.

sence of government, when men were in their natural state or condition and thus were only subject to the superior authority of God, they had "an equal claim to liberty," and from this assumption about equal individual authority, Tucker drew the familiar conclusions about the authority of civil government:

> No one, by nature, nor by any special grant from the great Lord of all, has any authority over another. All right therefore in any to rule over others, must originate from those they rule over, and be granted by them. Hence, all government, consistent with that natural freedom, to which all have an equal claim, is founded in compact.

In the English manner, Tucker scarcely differentiated this compact, by which individuals gave their consent, from the act by which the people made their law:

> [T]he fundamental laws, which are the basis of government, and form the political constitution of the state;—which mark out, and fix the chief lines and boundaries between the authority of Rulers, and the liberties and privileges of the people, are, and can be no other, in a free state, than what are mutually agreed and consented to.

In sum, "[w]hatever authority" the government had "to make laws, appoint officers, &c." was "an authority derived from the community, and granted by them."[10]

Hence the absence of obligation in laws without constitutional authority. Although the Rev. Tucker gave a nod to the obligation of justice by saying that a man was "not to disobey a just law, calculated for the public good, because . . . it operates against his private interest," he immediately made clear that legal justice was to be understood in terms of constitutional authority. The "limits . . . marked out, and fixt, by the known, established, and fundamental laws of the state" were "the connecting band between authority and obedience." Being "the just measure and extent of submission," these fundamental laws were also the "boundaries, beyond which, submission cannot be justly required." As to obligation, "[t]he constitutional laws

[10] John Tucker, *A Sermon,* 13–14 (Boston: 1771). The underlying idea of consent was widely taught at colleges and universities. At Princeton, for example, Witherspoon taught undergraduates, "Dominion, it is plain . . . can be acquired justly only one way, viz. by consent." Witherspoon, *An Annotated Edition of Lectures on Moral Philosophy,* 146. Similarly at Harvard, William Vaughan, an M.A. student, discussed "whether the origin of a civil regime is founded in the consent of the people." Harvard, *Quæstiones* (Cambridge: 1775) ("An Regiminis civilis Origio, in Populi Consusu, fundetur?").

of the state, are, properly, the supreme power, being obligatory on the whole community,—on the highest officer, as well as the lowest subject"—and "all disobedience in subjects, to constitutional authority, is rebellion against government." As to the limits of obligation, the constitutional laws were those by which "the very law-making power itself is limited," and "all assumed power in Rulers, not granted them by the constitution, is without just authority, and so far forth, can claim no submission."[11]

The clergy were not alone in recognizing that legal obligation, including that of a constitution, came from the authority of the people. There were, in fact, numerous lawyers, judges, and political writers who pursued this point in a less academic manner, and it will soon be seen that many such men understood the implications for unconstitutional laws. As can be illustrated already here in the words of a North Carolina lawyer, his state had a "Constitution which existed before the Governm[ent] and which enacted and regulated it." This constitution was "in the Nature of a Charter not to be violated," and therefore "every Law, made contrary to or inconsistent with the Principles [set] down and marked by it, is considered absolutely void and not binding on the Citizens."[12]

[11] Tucker, *A Sermon,* 18, 29–31. Similarly, the Rev. Moses Mather preached to the assembled officialdom of Connecticut in 1775 that "[t]he obligation of obedience to a law, arises wholly from the authority of its makers, over those on whom it is enjoined." By this reasoning, if Americans had not given any constitutional authority to Parliament, it was difficult to conclude that they were bound by its acts: "[I]f the Americans are naturally independent of the power of parliament, and by no concessions and civil constitutions of their own have submitted thereto, and put themselves under it; no acts of parliament can make them dependant," and "the Americans are under no obligation of obedience to its laws." [Moses Mather], *America's Appeal to the Impartial World,* 5–6, 39 (Hartford: 1775). The earlier popularization of such ideas in America can be illustrated by Charles Chauncy's argument that rulers "must be just in the *use of their power;* confining it within the limits prescribed in the constitution they are under. Whatever power any are vested with, 'tis delegated to them according to some civil constitution. And this, so long as it remains the constitution, they are bound in justice to conform themselves to." Charles Chauncy, *Civil Magistrates Must Be Just, Ruling in the Fear of God. A Sermon,* 10–11, 14 (Boston: 1747). He emphasized: "To be sure they ought not to act in violation of any of its main and essential rights." Ibid., 14–15.

[12] Letter from Samuel Johnston to Alexander Scrysmoure (Edenton, July 11, 1784), in Hayes Collection, Johnston Family Series, Box 2, Folder 101, Southern Historical Collection, University of North Carolina at Chapel Hill, also quoted by John Charles Waldrup, "James Iredell and the Practice of Law in Revolutionary Era North Carolina," 270 (Ph.D. dissertation, University of North Carolina, Chapel Hill, 1985). A newspaper essayist wrote that "an 'unconstitutional law of the land' is an impossibility," for "nothing can be law, or has a right to be so called, that is contrary to the Constitution." Letter to Mr. Oswald from "Brutus," *Independent Gazetteer* (Phila.) (March 1, 1783). A New Jersey essayist similarly observed that "any bill enacted contrary to the constitution, I humbly conceive to be no law." A True Patriot, No. VII, *New Jersey Gazette* (May 12, 1779).

Divinely Derived Authority and Legislative Freedom

Human lawmakers, whether the people or their legislators, seemed to have an authority derived from God to choose the law they would enact. As in Europe, the hierarchy of law was understood to give lawmaking authority to the people and thereby also their legislators, and although in the process of adopting legislation these lawmakers might often have a moral obligation to consider the dictates of natural law, they were usually thought free to adopt laws, to the extent of their authority, as they pleased.

The lawmaking authority of men was widely understood to be at least loosely derived from God, thus giving human law its strength of obligation. Clergy of a roughly Calvinist persuasion often argued that human lawmaking will had legal obligation because this was God's will, but whereas traditional Calvinists simply said that civil government was ordained by God, many American Calvinists combined this observation with their reasoning from nature. The Rev. Tucker, as has been seen, preached the equal liberty of men and the consequent necessity of their establishing government through their consent, but while thus arguing from nature that any particular government "proceeds immediately from men," he also explained that "civil government" was in general "the ordinance of God," who raises men "to places of authority and rule." Their civil government appeared to be "agreeable to his will," for it was "founded in the very nature of man," and what was "the dictate of nature" and "the voice of reason" could "be said to be the voice of God."[13]

At the same time, many other Americans—not only political writers but also a substantial number of Calvinists—took a much less direct view of how legal obligation was derived from God. President Witherspoon of Princeton, for example, carefully avoided any hint of the conventional Calvinist position that government was "ordained." Instead, he traced the obli-

[13] Tucker, *A Sermon,* 12–13.

Of course, divine will had long been a potent model for human claims of absolute power, and therefore American ministers, like many of their European predecessors, sometimes cautioned that "[t]ho' God is an absolute, yet he is a holy and righteous sovereign," and "[s]uch is the perfection of his nature, that he never can do anything but what is fit and right." Samuel M'Clintock, *A Sermon Preached Before the Honorable The Council, and the Honorable the Senate and House of Representatives, of the State of New Hampshire, June 3, 1784. On Occasion of the Commencement of the New Constitution and Form of Government,* 28 (Portsmouth: 1784). Recognizing the significance of the point, Iredell rejected a claim that the North Carolina General Assembly enjoyed an absolute power similar to that of Parliament by pointing out that even the power of "the Supreme Being" was "not altogether absolute." On the contrary, "His *infinite power* is limited by his *infinite wisdom.*" James Iredell, "To the Public" (Aug. 1786), Duke University Rare Book, Manuscript, and Special Collections Library, Iredell Papers, Box 1.

gation of human law up to God by explaining the divine scheme in which "the principles of our nature lead to society." He recognized that "our nature as it is now, when free and independent, is prone to injury, and consequently to war," and that there were thus "inconveniences of the natural state," but he also believed that "in our nature, as it is the work of God, there is a real good-will and benevolence to others," and he therefore concluded that not only "necessity and interest" but also "nature prompts to society." Having been prompted by nature to form civil society, men established civil "dominion" through their consent, and their consent was the basis of legal "obligation" in their society.[14] From this point of view, human laws had obligation, not because government, as established by men through their consent, was divinely ordained, but rather, more obliquely, because it was the nature of men, as created by God, consensually to form human society and its laws.

However divine the source from which the authority of men was ultimately derived, men were all too human in their exercise of lawmaking will, and it was understood that the freedom achieved by the ideal of authority came at the cost of leaving room for injustice in particular laws. If individuals, the people, and their government were each free to reach their own decisions within their different spheres of authority, then erroneous exercises of will were unavoidable. The urbane president of Yale, Ezra Stiles, optimistically generalized that "[b]esides a happy policy as to civil government, it is necessary to institute a system of LAW and JURISPRUDENCE founded in *justice, equity,* and *public right.*"[15] At Princeton, in contrast, the more sober-minded Witherspoon warned that "no human constitution can be so formed, but that there must be exceptions to every law," and thus "in

[14] Witherspoon, *An Annotated Edition of Lectures on Moral Philosophy,* 122–123, 142, 146. Although the Rev. Moses Mather did not depart as much from traditional Calvinism, he somewhat similarly explained: "Free agency, or a rational existence, with its powers and faculties, and the freedom of enjoying and exercising them, is the gift of God to man," and because "[t]he right of the donor, and the authenticity of the donation, are both incontestable; hence man hath an absolute property in, and right of dominion over himself, his powers and faculties." Accordingly, "where a man enters into, and takes the benefits of a government, he implicitly consents to be subject to it's laws; so, when he transgresses the laws, there is an implied consent to submit to it's penalties." And "from this principle, all the civil . . . or rightful authorities, that are ordained of God, and exist in the world, are derived from their native source." Thus, "human authorities, dominions and powers" came "from God, the sovereign ruler, as the fountain, *through the voice and consent of the people.*" [Mather], *America's Appeal to the Impartial World,* 5–6.

[15] Ezra Stiles, *The United States Elevated to Glory and Honour. A Sermon,* 39 (2nd ed.; Worcester: 1785). In the terse phrasing of an academic exercise at Harvard in 1778, "[n]o civil law is equitable unless it agrees with the principles of natural law," Harvard, *Theses* (Cambridge: 1778) ("Nulla lex civilis æqua est nisi pricipiis juris naturalis congruit").

every nation," even under the best of human rulers, there might be "oppression under form of law"—an observation that seemed to confirm "the necessity of forming the manners of a people."[16]

As Witherspoon understood, however, the freedom enjoyed by legislators in a system of authority had some advantages. Not only rulers and their generalizations were imperfect, and to govern imperfect men—"[t]o limit and direct persons in the exercise of their own rights, and oblige them to show respect to the interfering rights of others"—legislators had to make laws that limited men in ways natural law did not. Witherspoon explained that "[a] number of things in this view may become illegal, which before were not immoral." Such restraints might be "arbitrary," but although "[w]e may sometimes do things in a way better than that appointed by law . . . yet that is not allowed."[17] Conversely, laws could permit what was immoral. The Rev. Elizur Goodrich noted that "in all well regulated civil communities, laws of natural, universal and unchangeable obligation hold the first rank." Nonetheless, "the force of civil society cannot extend to all laws of this kind; but only to such upon the observation of which the common quiet of mankind entirely depends." Thus, "[t]he principles and laws of justice are fixed and unchangeable—they depend not on human authority; but the particular regulations, by which they have force in society, as civil laws, not being determined by the law of nature, may be changed, when they are found inconvenient and hurtful to the community"—this being "the legislative authority of a state."[18]

Standing between the authority of God and that of a state's legislature was the authority of the people, who were free to judge for themselves what natural liberty they should retain under their constitutions. This was their authority, and although the Rev. Simeon Howard had briefly suggested that morality was a measure of legal obligation, he was unequivocal as to how, amid the diversity of human societies, each people had the authority to judge the extent of their own constitutional liberty:

> This liberty will be different in different communities. In every state, the members will, probably, give up so much of their natural liberty, as they think will be most for the good of the whole. But different states will judge differ-

[16] Witherspoon, *An Annotated Edition of Lectures on Moral Philosophy,* 162.
[17] Ibid., 163, 181.
[18] Elizur Goodrich, *The Principles of Civil Union and Happiness Considered and Recommended. A Sermon,* 13, 15 (Hartford: 1787). Natural law thus "must be admitted into every civil state; but, that it may have force in society, the public standard must be fixed" and "an awful penalty annexed to transgression," for "[t]hese are circumstances, which are not determined by the law of nature; but must be adjusted by civil regulations suited to the condition of particular commonwealths." Ibid., 15.

> ently upon this point; some will give up more, some less, though still with the same view, the publick good. And every society have doubtless a right to act according to their own judgement and discretion in this matter, this being only an exercise of that natural liberty in which all are born.[19]

As put by the Virginia Court of Appeals in the next decade, the state's "constitution or form of Government" was one that "the People in 1776 . . . established as the foundation of that government which they judged necessary for the preservation of their persons and property."[20]

The choice of the people in establishing a constitution could be used for good or for ill—as was clear enough in 1776 and would become even clearer over the course of American history. The choice, however, belonged to the people. Having an authority derived in one way or another from God, the people could judge for themselves what constitution they would enact and what liberty it would protect.

Express Constitutions

In adopting their constitutions, Americans paid new attention to some old issues. It was familiar that constitutions were laws, and the word "constitution" itself implied an enacted law, but whereas the English could only enjoy an express enacted constitution in their historical imagination, Americans actually enacted express constitutions. Americans therefore had to be more self-conscious than their predecessors about a series of questions, including enactment, formality, intent, clarity, and permanency.

A constitution made by the people, as in Europe, could be understood to be both a contract and an enacted law, and at common law it was the enactment that mattered. John Locke and many of his countrymen had assumed that an "original Constitution" was a mode of consent and yet was also the people's "positive voluntary Grant and Institution," and Americans

[19] Simeon Howard, *A Sermon Preached to the Ancient and Honorable Artillery-Company,* 9 (the printed word "bound" being corrected in manuscript in the American Antiquarian Society copy to read "born"). Earlier, Chauncy preached:

> [I]t cannot be affirmed, that this or that particular form of government is made necessary by the will of God and reason of things. . . . So that it seems left to the wisdom of particular communities to determine what form of government shall take place among them; and, so long as the general ends of society are provided for and secured, the determination may be various, according to the various circumstances, policies, tempers and interests of different communities."

Chauncy, *Civil Magistrates Must Be Just,* 10.

[20] Order and Remonstrance of the Judges (May 12, 1788), Supreme Court of Appeals, Order Book No. 1, 1779–1789, at 131, LVA.

similarly took for granted that a people both agreed to their constitution and enacted it as a law.[21]

Americans frequently spoke of their constitutions as contractual. Being an academic, Witherspoon echoed the three stages of consent that Pufendorf observed in the formation of civil society: "[t]he consent of every individual to live in, and be a member of that society"; a "consent to some particular plan of government"; and a "mutual agreement between the subjects and rulers" providing for "subjection on the one hand" and "protection on the other." The second of these—the plan of government—was usually said to be the enactment of the constitution as a law, but Witherspoon was content to consider it merely a matter of consent—perhaps because he was intrigued by the notion that "[e]very transaction almost may be considered as a contract, either more or less explicit."[22] Like the English, Americans who spoke in popular circumstances often collapsed Pufendorf's tripartite scheme into a single transaction, contractual or legislative. From the contractual angle, some said it was the contract between the people and their rulers, and some assimilated it to the initial act of consent, saying that it was "a solemn, explicit agreement of the people among themselves."[23]

Notwithstanding the appeal of reducing constitutions and, indeed, all transactions to contract, many Americans simultaneously assumed that constitutions were laws, and especially when they sat in constitutional conventions they tended to specify that although a constitution might be a contract, it was also an enactment by the people. State legislatures repeatedly said they did "ordain and establish" or otherwise enact their statutes, and some state constitutional conventions similarly took care to use words of enactment—whether by saying that the people did "ordain and declare" their constitutions, that they did "ordain, declare, and establish" them, or that they did "ordain, determine, and declare" them.[24] The Massachusetts

[21] John Locke, *Two Treatises of Government,* 381 (II.xi.141), 387 (II.xiii.153), ed. Peter Laslett (Cambridge: Cambridge University Press, 1960).

[22] Witherspoon, *An Annotated Edition of Lectures on Moral Philosophy,* 168. There were all sorts of obvious "objections," such as that every individual had "not given an actual consent," but these problems were "easily solved" with the notion of implied consent. His first example was that "[t]hough *every individual* has not given an *actual consent,* yet his determination to live with any society *implies it.*" Ibid.

[23] Joseph Lathrop, *A Sermon, Preached in the First Parish in West-Springfield, December 14, MDCCLXXXVI, Being the Day Appointed by Authority for a Publick Thanksgiving,* 8 (Springfield: 1787).

[24] For "ordain and declare," see the Virginia Constitution of 1776, and for the past tense, see the Georgia Constitution of 1777; for "ordain, declare, and establish," see Pennsylvania and Vermont; for "ordain, determine, and declare," see New York.

constitution was particularly explicit about its combination of contract and enacted law. It explained that under "the Great Legislator of the Universe," the people were both "entering into an original, explicit, and solemn compact with each other" and "forming a new Constitution of Civil Government, for ourselves and posterity," which the people simultaneously did "agree upon" as a contract and "ordain and establish" as a law.[25]

Recognizing the common law formality for an enacted law, some conventions even enrolled or otherwise recorded their constitutions. It will be recalled that, at common law, legislative bodies were legislative courts, and that the formality required for their legislative will to become binding was not publication, but the enrollment of their acts in their records. Thus, for example, the 1776 New Jersey Constitution was carefully recorded in the office of the Secretary of State.[26] In Massachusetts and New Hampshire, where the people were asked to ratify the work of the drafters, the constitutions themselves closed by providing that "[t]his form of government shall be enrolled on parchment, and deposited in the secretary's office."[27] Similar practices occurred in the formation of the federal government. The 1787 Philadelphia Convention completed its work by having the U.S. Constitution "enrolled," but because it was only a drafting convention, this was not the end of the matter.[28] Some of the state ratification conventions were sufficiently self-conscious about the formalities required for legislation that they sent engrossed copies of their ratification documents to the archives or secretaries of their states.[29] The Pennsylvania Ratification Convention spe-

[25] Massachusetts Constitution of 1780, Preamble.

[26] New Jersey Constitution of 1776, NJSA. On the last page, it is endorsed: "Recorded in Lib: AB of Commissions folio 187, in the Secretary of Office of the State of New Jersey at the City of Burlington." Ibid.

[27] Massachusetts Constitution of 1780, Chapter VI, Article XI; New Hampshire Constitution of 1784, last paragraph.

[28] Before the Constitution was signed, all the states assented upon "the question to agree to the Constitution enrolled in order to be signed." *The Records of the Federal Convention of 1787,* at 2: 644 (Madison's Notes, Sept. 17, 1787), ed. Max Farrand (New Haven: Yale University Press, 1937).

[29] The New Jersey Convention resolved that "the secretary be directed to deliver the duplicate of the Ratification of the Federal Constitution to the Governor of this state, for the purpose of being lodged among the archives of the state." *The Documentary History of the Ratification of the Constitution,* 3: 187 (Dec. 19, 1787), ed. Merrill Jensen (Madison: State Historical Society of Wisconsin, 1978). Similarly, at the end of the Virginia Ratification Convention, an "engrossed form of the ratification . . . containing the proposed Constitution of Government" was read and signed by the president of the Convention, Edmund Pendleton, and, on motion, was "deposited by the Secretary of this Convention in the archives of the General Assembly of this State." *The Documentary History of the Ratification of the Constitution,* 10: 1151–1552 (June 27, 1788), eds. John P. Kaminski et al. (Madison: State Historical Society of Wisconsin, 1993). In Connecticut, the "Ratification being engrossed, duplicates on parchments were subscribed and certified accordingly, the one to be

cifically resolved that "the secretary deliver to the master of the rolls (for the purpose of having it recorded) one of the scrolls, containing the Constitution, Ratification, and names subscribed."[30] In Georgia, even more elaborately, the Convention ordered a committee "to see the Great Seal affixed to the said Constitution and Ratification" and then to have them "recorded and deposited in the office of the secretary of the state."[31] These conventions could not have made it clearer that they were enacting a law.

Popular or at least populist committees and county conventions sometimes seemed to defy the authority of constitutions and the laws established under them, but these challenges to the enacted will of the people provoked sharp rejoinders about the necessarily formal character of the acts of the people.[32] English and American Whigs had long feared that the people might be said to have informally acquiesced in a loss of constitutional liberty, and although this sort of constitutional evolution might be justified with the civilian doctrine of desuetude or with an account of sociological development, these were notoriously Tory visions of constitutional law.[33] In contrast, Whigs were apt to cut through such arguments by observing that mere practice, custom, or informal acquiescence could not defeat the conclusive evidence provided by an act of record.[34] This was one reason seven-

---

transmitted to Congress and the other lodged in the office of the secretary of this state." Jensen, ed., *The Documentary History of the Ratification of the Constitution,* 3: 560 (Jan. 9, 1788).

30 Jensen, ed., *The Documentary History of the Ratification of the Constitution,* 2: 605 (Dec. 13, 1787). The proceedings only record that the motion was made and seconded, but the motion appears to have been adopted.

31 Ibid., 3: 276 (Jan. 2, 1788).

32 Such bodies flourished after the Revolution as mechanisms to mobilize at least the appearance of popular opinion against men who stood on the formalities of law—for example, against Tories who hoped to recover their land or debts under the Treaty of Peace, and against legislatures and courts that hesitated to release debtors from their legal obligations. When in 1783 some Americans formed committees to protest against complying with the article of the Treaty "respecting the Tories," the commissioners who had negotiated it wrote to Congress from Paris that "[p]opular committees are considered here, as with us, in the light of substitutes to constitutional government, and as being only necessary in the interval between the removal of the former and the establishment of the present." Letter to the President of Congress from Adams, Franklin, and Jay (Sept. 10, 1783), in *The Diplomatic Correspondence of the American Revolution,* 10: 218, ed. Jared Sparks (Boston: 1830).

33 As J. G. A. Pocock observes, it was no coincidence that the most remarkable seventeenth-century English writer on the sociological changes underlying the development of English law was a Tory, Robert Brady, whose *Introduction to the Old English History* (1685) was far more insightful about history and less acceptable as law than what was produced by Whigs. J. G. A. Pocock, *The Feudal Law and the Ancient Constitution,* 182–228 (Cambridge: University Press, 1987).

34 For example, when Moses Mather in 1775 argued against the authority of Parliament, he understood that "it may be objected, that several acts of parliament respecting America, have been acquiesced in," but he answered that "[n]either the parliament's making laws, nor the

teenth-century English Whigs had tended to insist that their constitution was an original act, even if only recorded in the memory of the people, and now that Americans possessed express constitutions that were understood to be acts of record, they could all the more decisively dismiss challenges arising from other forms of consent.

A formal enactment by the people seemed particularly important in America as an obstacle to the people's transient whims. Samuel Johnston wrote that the North Carolina Constitution "stands as a kind of Security for the Stability of our Government without which our Citizens would be in such a State of fluctuation as must eventually produce Anarchy."[35] His brother-in-law James Iredell, who often worked with Johnston to protect the rights of Tories, added that the Constitution "sprang from the deliberate voice of the People," and on this assumption Iredell hoped it would provide "for the security of every individual, as well as a fluctuating majority of the people," for "[w]e knew the value of liberty too well, to suffer it to depend on the capricious voice of popular favor, easily led astray by designing men, and courted for insidious purposes."[36] Tories were a particularly unpopular minority, and after the North Carolina judges in *Bayard v. Singleton* briefly protected them by holding a state statute unconstitutional, Iredell rejected complaints that the decision was an affront to the sentiments of the majority: Nothing could be more "ridiculous . . . than for the Representatives of a People solemnly Assembled to form a Constitution, to set down a number of political dogmas, which might or might not be regarded" according to shifts in either legislative or public opinion. On the contrary, the solemnity of the Constitution's adoption barred such departures:

American's acquiescing therein, can create an authority to make them on the one hand, nor an obligation to obey them on the other, though they may be considered as some evidence thereof." [Mather], *America's Appeal to the Impartial World,* 41. As for more general common law assumptions about the inapplicability of the doctrine of desuetude, Elisha Boudinot quoted conventional English sources in one of his notebooks during the first half of the 1770s: "*Non User* is a good Argument to shew how a Law is to be understood where the construction is doubtful, but NonUsers can not make an Act of Parliam! to be antiquated or loose its force." Elisha Boudinot, Notes of Cases in Practice, 33, Princeton University, Rare Books and Special Collections, Manuscript Division, Thorne Collection of Elias Boudinot, C0001, Box 3, Folder 2. See similarly *Paxton's Case* (Massachusetts Superior Court, 1761), Quincy, *Reports,* 52.

35 Letter from Samuel Johnston to Alexander Scrysmoure (Edenton, July 11, 1784), Southern Historical Collection, University of North Carolina at Chapel Hill, Hayes Collection, Johnston Family Series, Box 2, Folder 101.

36 "To the Public," Duke University Rare Book, Manuscript, and Special Collections Library, James Iredell Papers, Box 1.

> [I]t must have been intended as I conceive, that it should be a system of Authority, not depending on the casual whim or accidental ideas of a Majority either in or out of doors for the time being; but to remain in force until[,] by a similar appointment of Deputies specially appointed for the Same important purpose, an alteration should be with equal solemnity & deliberation made. And this, I apprehend, must be the necessary consequence since surely equal authority is required to repeal as to enact.

Considered as "a system of Authority" formally adopted by the people, the Constitution remained binding both against the informal opinion of the people and against the formal act of a body of lesser authority.[37]

On similar assumptions, Alexander Hamilton observed that the judges could not acquiesce in informal constitutional change—even if a legislative majority were supported by a popular majority. It was "the right of the people to alter or abolish the established Constitution, whenever they find it inconsistent with their happiness."

> [Y]et it is not to be inferred from this principle, that the representatives of the people, whenever a momentary inclination happens to lay hold of a majority of their constituents incompatible with the provisions in the existing constitution, would on that account be justifiable in a violation of those provisions; or that the courts would be under a greater obligation to connive at infractions in this shape, than when they had proceeded wholly from the cabals of the representative body.

The legislators and judges might have accurate knowledge of a shift in popular sentiment, but the formal enactment of the Constitution made it an act of record, which was impervious to any custom, practice, or opinion: "Until the people have by some solemn and authoritative act annulled or changed the established form, it is binding upon themselves collectively, as well as individually; and no presumption, or even knowledge of their sentiments, can warrant their representatives in a departure from it, prior to such an act."[38]

As with other legislative acts, constitutions created legal obligation through their intent. The modern literature on American law tends not to acknowledge that intent was a matter of lawmaking will—whether the intent of a people in their constitution or of their legislature in statutes—and the literature therefore tends to treat intent as an interpretative technique

[37] Letter from James Iredell to Richard Dobbs Spaight (Aug. 26, 1787), in *The Papers of James Iredell,* 3: 309, eds. Donna Kelly and Lang Baradell (Raleigh: North Carolina Department of Cultural Resources, 2003).

[38] Alexander Hamilton, Federalist Number 78, *The Federalist,* 527–528, ed. Jacob E. Cooke (Middletown: Wesleyan University Press, 1961).

rather than the source and measure of legal obligation.[39] American law, however, must be considered within the long-standing shift toward authority. Whether in religion or law, let alone the arts, the will of men had come to seem obligatory within the scope of their authority, and there is no reason to think that Americans in the decade after declaring Independence moved away from this modern concept of legal obligation. Of course, ideals of reason and justice could still be said to have primacy in that they established the ideal of authority, and certainly reason and justice had a role within ideals of authority and will as rough guides in matters of morals and legislation. In religious and academic discussions, moreover, it has been seen that the older ideals of reason and justice sometimes still seemed to qualify the obligation arising from authority. Authority and will, however, remained the standard measure of legal obligation—this being why reason and justice so often seemed in tension with the law. The underlying point was summed up by the drafters of the New Hampshire Constitution: "The will of the legislator" was "the law of the subject."[40] To this it was only necessary to add that "the intention of the people" had priority over "the intention of their agents."[41]

[39] The notable exceptions are Richard S. Kay, "Adherence to the Original Intentions in Constitutional Adjudication: Three Objections and Responses," *Northwestern University Law Review,* 82: 226 (1988); Keith Whittington, *Constitutional Interpretation: Textual Meaning, Original Intent, and Judicial Review,* 113–123 (Lawrence: University Press of Kansas, 1999).

H. Jefferson Powell argues that the intent of a document "referred to the meaning an interpreter was entitled to derive from the document using the common law's techniques of construction." H. Jefferson Powell, "The Modern Misunderstanding of Original Intent," *University of Chicago Law School,* 54: 1534 (1987). This, however, would seem to put the cart before the horse, for intent was significant as the will of the authoritative lawmaker in its act of record, and the common law techniques were understood to be mechanisms for discerning this intent.

Incidentally, Powell aptly notes that "[t]he 'intent of the act' and the 'intent of the legislature' were interchangeable terms," but his conclusion is that "the interpreter" could not look "at any evidence concerning that 'intent' other than the words of the text and the common law background of the statute." H. Jefferson Powell, "The Original Understanding of Original Intent," *Harvard Law Review,* 98: 897–898 (1985). In particular, he argues that interpreters could not look at the personal intent of the framers. There is evidence, however, that the personal intentions of the framers of a will, statute, or other act were often understood to be revealing about the intent of the act. Charles A. Lofgren, "The Original Understanding of Original Intent?" *Constitutional Commentary,* 5: 77 (1988). In addition to Lofgren's evidence, it might be noted that when Samuel Ashe of the North Carolina Superior Court defended his conduct in *Bayard,* he declared that "if my Opinion of our Constitution is an error, I fear it is an incurable one, for I had the honour to assist in the frameing it, and confess I so designed it, as I believe every other Gentlemen concerned did also." Letter from Samuel Ashe to the Hon'ble Speakers of the General Assembly (Dec. 14, 1786), NCSA, General Assembly, Session Records 1786–1787, Box 3, Joint Resolutions—Committee of the Whole of Two Houses on Administration of Justice Folder.

[40] *An Address of the Convention for Framing a Constitution of Government for the People of New Hampshire,* 5 (Portsmouth: 1783).

[41] Hamilton, Federalist Number 78, *The Federalist,* 525.

Although in theory the relevant intent was that of the lawmaker, this intent continued at common law to be associated with the lawmaker's act. It is common today to distinguish between the intent of individuals and the meaning of their words, but eighteenth-century lawyers—in America, as in England—took a more layered and less literal approach. They began with the words as the presumptive guide to intent, but when these seemed unclear, they referred more directly to the intent. Even at this point, however, they did not simply allude to the intent of the lawmaker, for a statute or constitution had to combine the obligation of the lawmaker's will with the force of an act of record, and therefore, rather than assume they should literally seek the intent of the lawmaker, lawyers often spoke ambidextrously of the intent of the lawmaker and the intent of its act. Obviously, one could not hope literally to discern the intent of an act, but by framing their inquiry in such terms, common lawyers could suggest how they were avoiding the difficulties they would have encountered if they had been more literal about words or intent.

These assumptions—about examining the words and then the intent, and about seeking the intent of the act—were general common law assumptions, and they thus applied equally to all sorts of acts, ranging from wills to statutes. For example, the words of a will were the initial measure of its intent, and they often had presumptive meanings at law, but occasionally the words or the law concerning them were obscure—as can be illustrated by a legal opinion given by Brockholst Livingston in 1783. Upon being asked about a will, he observed that "[t]he principal question" in the case "is one of those which the silence of the law has involved in some difficulty," but should "the law be doubtful, the intention of the Testator must govern, and what this is in the present case, no disinterested Person can be at a loss for."[42] In more Christian terms, one had to follow the spirit where the letter was weak. This metaphorical language might seem today to go beyond intent, and it is possible that lawyers understood it to suggest an especially open, expansive pursuit of intent, but whether as to wills or constitutions, they did not ordinarily, if ever, say as much, and judges do not appear to have used the analysis about letter and spirit any differently from the less metaphysical analysis about words and intent. When Edmund Pendleton—President of the Virginia Court of Appeals—gave his opinion in 1782 in *Commonwealth v. Caton,* he said that the constitutional question "should be decided according to the spirit, and not by the words of the con-

[42] Letter from Brockholst Livingston to Col. Henry Livingston (Oct. 8, 1783), New York Historical Society, James Duane Papers.

stitution," for "[t]he language of the clause is inaccurate, and admits of both the constructions mentioned by the *attorney general.*" Having laid this foundation, Pendleton concluded, "I prefer the first, as most congenial to the spirit, and not inconsistent with the letter, of the constitution."[43] Regardless of the type of act, where the words were unclear, what prevailed was the spirit or intent, and this was the spirit or intent not simply of the maker, but of the maker's act.

Many Americans were anxious for clarity in their constitutions, and ultimately this meant a clear intent. One reason to seek clarity was that the

[43] *Commonwealth v. Caton* (Virginia Court of Appeals 1782), Call, *Reports,* 4: 19.

Pendleton reached this conclusion after listening to Attorney General Randolph, who argued for equitable interpretation of both the statute and the Virginia Constitution—thus "reconciling" the statute with the "spirit" of the Constitution. Randolph laid the foundation for his conclusion by suggesting that the words of both enactments were unclear, and in the course of making this argument, he urged that the Constitution's "words must be free from ambiguity and decided, or cannot have the supremacy." Edmund Randolph, Notes of Argument in *Commonwealth v. Lamb &c.,* Library of Congress, James Madison Papers, 91: 104. William Treanor assumes that Randolph's argument "reflects a conception of judicial review involving a marked degree of deference to the legislature"—this being part of Treanor's argument that "an antiliteralist approach to judicial review . . . could support both judicial deference . . . and assertiveness." William Michael Treanor, "The Case of the Prisoners and the Origins of Judicial Review," *University of Pennsylvania Law Review,* 143: 517, 556 (1994). Randolph, however, was arguing that the words of the Constitution must be clear or cannot have supremacy over its spirit, and as seen above, Pendleton was persuaded to give his opinion along similar lines—although with at least one difference, as will become apparent in the next paragraph.

It was understood that the intent of different types of documents might have to be ascertained in slightly different ways, but judges on the whole do not appear to have adopted (let alone, agreed upon) any special convention about their interpretation. At one end of the range of opinion, some men argued that because constitutions protected liberty, they had to be understood as close to the letter as possible—as when a newspaper commentator on freedom of the press cautioned against "innovations" and quoted Montesquieu that "[i]n Republics, it has been observed, 'the very *nature* of the *Constitution* requires the Judges to keep to the *letter* of the law.'" "Wilkes," "On the Liberty of the Press," *Independent Gazetteer* (Phila.) (Dec. 28, 1782). At the same time, when Virginia Attorney General Edmund Randolph in *Commonwealth v. Caton* had to argue against the words of the state's constitution, he suggested that because of the generality of the constitution, this document could not be understood in accord with the letter, and further that it had to be interpreted "liberally"—in a open, generous manner—to discern its spirit. This was as much as to say that constitutions, by virtue of their generality, were necessarily imprecise or uncertain. He explained that his "object" was "to mark a difference of construction, which should prevail in interpreting the act of government, and an act of assembly," and the reason why "[i]n the former the liberality, necessary to catch its spirit, must be adopted," was that "the constitution describes general outlines only; whereas a law professes the detail." Edmund Randolph, Notes of Argument in *Commonwealth v. Lamb &c.,* Library of Congress, James Madison Papers, 91: 104. Pendleton, however, declined to accept so ambitious a proposition and, instead, merely focused on the ambiguity of the particular constitutional clause in front of him. As for Randolph, he soon expressed views very different from those he took in *Caton.* See note 48 and text below.

people's will could have obligation only to the extent it was clear enough to be known. Law might draw its obligation from the lawmaker's will, but it could not be binding if it could not be understood, and it therefore seemed essential for the lawmaker's intent to be at least clear enough to be discerned.

The underlying problem that seemed to require clarity was the old danger that men were not apt to agree about what was reasonable or just, and although this difficulty could be considered a result of the inadequacy of men, it could also be said to arise from the uncertain or intangible character of natural law. The "Law of Nature" was "unwritten, and so no where to be found but in the minds of Men," and therefore, as Locke explained, "it serves not, as it ought, to determine the Rights, and fence the Properties of those that live under it." Men avoided this threat to liberty and the other "[i]nconveniences" of the state of nature by forming civil society and its government, for only in this manner could they could obtain the certainty of "establish'd *standing Laws*"—not to mention judges "who are to decide Controversies by those Laws."[44]

At a more general level, men assumed that, whether in nature or in civil society, clarity was a necessary ingredient of perfect rights. Reciting conventional legal theory, Witherspoon told his students that what were "called perfect rights" were those "which can be clearly ascertained in their circumstances, and which we may make use of force to obtain." Thus, "[j]ustice consists in giving or permitting others to enjoy whatever they

[44] John Locke, *Two Treatises of Government,* 371 (II.ix.131), 376–377 (II.xi.136), ed. Peter Laslett (Cambridge: Cambridge University Press, 1960). Locke similarly wrote that in the state of nature, "[t]here wants an *establish'd,* settled, known *Law,* received and allowed by common consent to be the Standard of Right and Wrong, and the common measure to decide all Controversies between them. For though the Law of Nature be plain and intelligible to all rational Creatures; yet Men being biassed by their Interest, as well as ignorant from want of Study of it, are not apt to allow of it as a Law binding to them in the application of it to their particular Cases." Ibid., 369 (II.ix.124). For an even sharper critique of the "uncertain and unaccountable Principles" of the law of nature, see Samuel Parker, *A Demonstration of the Divine Authority of the Law of Nature and of the Christian Religion,* 5–6 (London: 1681).

The assimilation of Lockean views by ordinary Americans can be observed in the notebook of a Virginian, George Gilmer, who quoted Locke that the "[f]reedom of men under government, is to have a standing rule to live by common to every one of that society & made by the legislative power erected in it." This was "[a] liberty to follow my own will in all things where the rule prescribes not"—that is, "not to be subject to the inconstant uncertain unknown arbitrary will of another man, as freedom of nature is to be under no other restraint, but the law of nature." In this spirit, he also quoted: "Wheresoever law ends, tyranny begins." George Gilmer, Commonplace Book, 122–123, 132 (before May 1778), Virginia Historical Society, Mss 5:5, G4213:1 (quoting Locke, *Two Treatises of Government,* II.iv.22). (In the manuscript, there is a period following "legislative power" that Gilmer forgot to delete when he added the rest of the sentence.)

have a perfect right to—and making such an use of our own rights as not to encroach upon the rights of others."[45] From this perspective, anything that could not be "clearly ascertained" could not be part of the justice enforceable under law, whether natural or civil.

Clarity seemed important in law and especially constitutions not only to establish legal obligation and justice, but also to authorize and contain the power of government, including the discretion of judges. More will be said about discretion when this chapter turns to judicial duty, but judicial discretion is already significant here for understanding why Americans wanted clarity in law. Aristotle had thought that laws should leave judges as little discretion as possible, and Witherspoon now echoed this point, saying that "it seems to be the very spirit of a free constitution, to have every thing as strictly defined as possible, and to leave little in the power of the judge." He understood that a people would pay a price for curtailing judicial discretion, the most obvious cost being the need for "a multiplicity of laws," which "is so apt to lead to litigation and to end in ambiguity, that perhaps judges of equity, chosen by the district in which they live and are to act, and chosen but for a time, would be a more just and equitable method of ending differences." This, however, required judges to be not merely wise but dispassionate, and "the difficulty of settling a constitution so as always to secure the election of impartial judges, has made modern states, where there is liberty, prefer a multiplicity of written laws."[46]

Scholars were not alone in understanding the danger from judges—as can be illustrated by the former Massachusetts judge James Sullivan. In 1786 he made the familiar point that uncertain laws gave judges a legislative power:

> It is necessary in every free government to have the modes of doing justice at public tribunals, clear, precise and uniform, otherwise the judge and the officer would be the law makers and deciders, at the same time, and in their own manner; and the *legislative authority and judicial authority would be no longer* separate.

[45] Witherspoon, *An Annotated Edition of Lectures on Moral Philosophy,* 110–112. After elaborating "[t]he perfect rights in a state of natural liberty," Witherspoon noted:

> The imperfect natural rights are very numerous. But they are nearly the same in a state of nature as in a state of society, as gratitude, compassion, mutual good offices—if they will be no injury to the person performing them—Indeed, they must be the same in a natural and in a social state, because the very definition of an imperfect right is such, as you cannot use force to obtain.

Ibid., 123.

[46] Ibid., 162.

Sullivan acknowledged that human language bore all of the imperfection of human beings, but like so many of his contemporaries, he understood this to be a reason to preserve such clarity as could be obtained, and although his proposal for achieving this goal was more curious than conventional, it reveals the intensity of his desire for clarity. Sullivan was interested in land law, and he optimistically hoped that lawmakers would draft their statutes as technically as conveyances:

> [S]o vague are all the forms of expression ever yet hit upon, that the best we can do is to affix, as well as we can, appropriate meanings to certain expressions, and carefully to use these in all parts of our systems of jurisprudence, so that we may render the laws as intelligible and technically certain as may be; for it is of infinitely more consequence to have the laws, as a rule of conduct, fully known, than it is to have them right.

Of course, such an approach, "like other valuable attempts, must, in this imperfect state, bear many marks of imperfection, and fall vastly short of the patriots eager exertions." This, however, was true of all human endeavors, for "have we not the same difficulty in every other science as we have in that of the law?"[47]

In fact, Americans overwhelmingly said they wanted their constitutions to be drafted with clarity—even if not necessarily like either conveyances or statutes—and no document was more suggestive as to how clarity was compatible with the generality of a constitution than the only extant official document about drafting from the 1787 Constitutional Convention. The Convention's Committee of Detail self-consciously worked from the example of the state constitutions, and when Edmund Randolph prepared a draft of the U.S. Constitution for the Committee, he began by observing that "in the draught of a fundamental constitution" it was necessary:

> To use simple and precise language, and general propositions, according to the example of the constitutions of the several states. For the construction of a constitution necessarily differs from that of law.[48]

[47] Zenas [James Sullivan], For the Independent Chronicle, *Independent Chronicle* (April 27, 1786). For the attribution to Sullivan, see Massachusetts Historical Society, James Sullivan Transcripts.

[48] Edmund Randolph, Draft Sketch of Constitution, *The Records of the Federal Convention of 1787,* Supplementary Volume, 183, ed. James Hutson (New Haven: Yale University Press, 1987).

Randolph had earlier suggested that the generality of constitutions deprived them of clarity or precision, but if he ever really adhered to this position, he did not do so for long. When arguing for the state of Virginia in *Commonwealth v. Caton,* Randolph had suggested that because of the generality of the Virginia Constitution, this document had to be inter-

The second sentence got crossed out, and it is understandable both why it was written and why it was deleted. A constitution was a sort of law, but rather than spell out details in the manner of a statute, it had to state "general propositions." Thus, whether Randolph was suggesting how a constitution should be construed or, more probably, how it should be constructed, its construction would be like that of a statute but also slightly different. Having no need to theorize about these complexities, the Committee sim-

---

preted in accord with its spirit—as if generality necessarily created a sort of uncertainty. See note 43 above. Whether or not he fully believed this, he took a different view when more clearly expressing his own opinion little more than a year later. Again in his capacity as attorney general, he had to write an opinion on the duty of Virginia to turn over an offender to South Carolina under the Articles of Confederation, and now, rather than treat generality as a kind of uncertainty, he merely mentioned the generality of the Articles to introduce his detailed analysis of how this document should be interpreted: "So great a variety of matter does the confederation embrace, that of necessity it could not extend every subject in detail. It has therefore omitted to define whether any or what satisfaction, ought to be given to the state, from which a citizen is demanded, as an offender, of his commission of a high misdeameanor in the demanding state"—at which point he began his interpretation. Letter from Edmund Randolph to Governor Benjamin Harrison (Jan. 21, 1784), LVA, Executive Papers. This does not appear to have been an argument from ambiguity, and in 1787, as seen above, he expressly treated "general propositions" as compatible with "precise language." (Incidentally, in his letter about South Carolina's demand, Randolph explained that the full faith and credit clause of the Articles operated "to procure respect, not supremacy and infallibility" for the public acts of another state; that a citizen "ought not to be delivered up, without competent evidence of his guilt"; that a high misdemeanor was one involving "an unequivocal attack on the majesty of a state"; and that an assault—with the use of a fist and a switch—on a man who was a legislator and justice of the peace, even if during the meeting of the Court of General Sessions, was not a high misdemeanor. For South Carolina's request, see Governor Benjamin Guerard to Governor Benjamin Harrison [Dec. 16, 1783], LVA, Executive Papers, Letters Received.)

More generally, the framers understood the possibility of drafting in a vague, open-ended manner—leaving details to be filled in later. When the Convention considered the power of Congress, one general proposal was that "the Natl. Legislature ought to possess the Legislative Rights vested in Congs. by the Confederation." This was easy enough, but a second proposal was that Congress also have the power "to legislate in all cases to which the separate States are incompetent; or in which the harmony of the U.S. may be interrupted by the exercise of individual legislation." Pierce Butler of South Carolina called "for some explanation of the extent of this power; particularly of the word incompetent," as "[t]he vagueness of the terms rendered it impossible for any precise judgment to be formed." Nathaniel Ghorum of Massachusetts responded that "[t]he vagueness of the terms constitutes the propriety of them. We are now establishing general principles, to be extended hereafter into details which will be precise & explicit." Although the Convention was only establishing general principles that it would soon extend to precise and explicit details, John Rutledge joined his fellow South Carolinian by moving that there be "a specification of the powers." Madison's Notes (July 16, 1787), *The Records of the Constitutional Convention of 1787,* at 2: 16–17 (Madison's Notes, July 16, 1787). See also Charles Warren, *The Making of the Constitution,* 314 (Cambridge: Harvard University Press, 1947). In other words, the framers expected that they themselves, not the courts, would specify these general principles to make them precise and explicit, but even this mode of proceeding provoked objections.

ply removed the second sentence and contented itself with its point about "simple and precise language, and general propositions."

Even when Americans alluded to the "principles" of their constitutions, they tended to assume that these should be fixed and inflexible. The principles underlying their constitutions might be somewhat open-ended, but it was expected that the principles that amounted to particular limitations in a constitution would be unchanging and determinate barriers. Anti-Federalists tended to argue that "in laying down a political system it is safer to rely on principles than upon precedents [of government practice], because the former are fixed and immutable, while the latter vary with men, places, times and circumstances."[49] As put by James Monroe, "fundamental principles form a check, even when the spirit of the times hath changed, indeed they retard and controul it."[50] Federalists agreed that a bill of rights was "[a] declaration insisted upon by free people . . . that certain principles shall be the invariable rules of their administration," for Federalists recognized that "the preservation of these principles are necessary for the preservation of liberty." Federalists asked, however, "can there be a difference, whether these principles are established in a separate declaration, or are interwoven and made a part of the Constitution itself?"[51] This was a disagreement as to whether principles of this sort should be enumerated as powers or rights, not whether they should be anything but fixed.

The clarity of constitutions seemed particularly important for the preservation of liberty, and although it may be doubted how successfully Americans achieved this desired precision, many of them were proud of what they had done in their constitutions. At the commencement of the New Hampshire Constitution in 1784, the Rev. Samuel McClintock preached, "Were it necessary, I might shew with what precision the rights belonging to men in a state of society are defined in the *Declaration of Rights,* and the life, liberty and property of the subject guarded with a jealous care against oppressive power."[52] The confidence that many men felt about the clarity of their constitutions did not come so easily to those who suffered under state majorities or to Anti-Federalists when they contemplated the constitution

[49] "William Penn," To the Citizens of the United States (Jan. 3, 1788), in *The Complete Anti-Federalist,* 3: 175, ed. Herbert J. Storing (Chicago: University of Chicago Press, 1982).
[50] James Monroe, *Some Observations on the Constitution* (1788), ibid., 5: 292. For more on principles, see Philip Hamburger, "The Constitution's Accommodation of Social Change," *Michigan Law Review,* 88: 317–319 (1989).
[51] *Observations Upon the Proposed Plan of Federal Government,* 6 (Petersburg: 1788). See also Speech of Edmund Pendleton (June 12, 1788), in *The Documentary History of the Ratification of the Constitution,* 10: 1197.
[52] M'Clintock, *A Sermon Preached Before the Honorable The Council,* 23–24.

designed for the more distant, federal government. Yet in their bitter complaints about the vagueness of the U.S. Constitution, Anti-Federalists were especially insistent that precision was essential in a constitution—that it was the very nature of a constitution to be "formed on principles of equal right" and that "those principles should be precisely delineated and guarantied by the most solemn sanctions."[53] Rather than dispute the need for clarity or precision, Federalists tended to respond that the U.S. Constitution was clear or at least as clear as human language and circumstances permitted.[54] The adequacy of the result was disputed, but almost no one questioned that clarity was desirable.

In retrospect, these yearnings for clarity may seem to have been incompatible with the need for a later accommodation of social developments—the need for what is sometimes called a "living constitution"—but Americans tended to think that they could avoid such difficulties by adopting "permanent" constitutions, which omitted limitations that might have to evolve. From this perspective, men already at the time of drafting had to adapt their constitutions to future conditions. This anticipation of change was necessary not only as to governmental structures but also as to enumerations of rights. For example, just as the limited domain of the common law had left room for social change notwithstanding the relative rigidity of the law, so Americans in their constitutions tended to protect only very basic liberties and to exclude rights they thought might become obsolete, and they thus hoped for constitutions that would continue to secure their liberty amid social evolution. The framers of the U.S. Constitution even discussed how America would soon become a society of industrial employees—of "mechanics" who would "receive their bread from their employers"—and with this self-consciousness about the profound changes that lay ahead, the framers thought it important, as put by the Committee of Detail, "[t]o insert essential principles only; lest the operations of government should be clogged by rendering those provisions permanent and unalterable, which ought to be accommodated to times and events."[55] Ameri-

[53] Republicus, *Kentucky Gazette* (Feb. 16, 1788).

[54] Hamburger, "The Constitution's Accommodation of Social Change," 308–309. Echoing Locke, James Madison reminded Americans of the inevitable imprecision arising from human ideas, faculties, and language, thus making "a certain degree of obscurity" unavoidable, but even while discouraging expectations of "faultless" constitutional distinctions, Madison no less than Locke hoped for such clarity as could be obtained. Madison, Federalist Number 37, *The Federalist,* 237.

[55] Remarks of Gouverneur Morris (Aug. 7, 1787), in *The Records of the Federal Convention of 1787,* at 2: 202; Edmund Randolph, Draft Sketch of Constitution.

Some Anti-Federalists hoped for a constitution that would be permanent in another way—not by leaving room for social change, but rather by protecting liberty notwithstandcans thus drew a sharp distinction between constitutional and statutory change. As James Iredell explained in the North Carolina Ratifying Convention, "there is a material difference between an article fixed in the Constitution, and a regulation by law," for "[a]n article in the Constitution, however inconvenient it may prove by experience, can only be altered by altering the Constitution itself, which manifestly is a thing that ought not to be done often," but "[w]hen regulated by law, it can easily be occasionally altered so as best to suit the conveniences of the people."[56] Americans obviously could not hope to anticipate all future contingencies, and they therefore had to provide for amendments, but they frequently said that their goal was to achieve clarity while minimizing the necessity for change.[57] This was a daunting endeavor, and the drafters of the New Hampshire Constitution candidly told the people of the state: "The task of forming a Constitution, adapted not only to our present situation, but to the probable situation and circumstances of remote posterity, is an arduous one indeed!"[58]

The express constitutions of America thus required Americans to focus on questions of enactment, formality, intent, clarity, and permanency; and in all these matters the people were the final judge. These issues had already to some degree arisen in connection with statutes and charters, but they now were also becoming closely associated with constitutional law, for not only in historical imagination, but increasingly also in reality, the people had adopted express constitutions.

---

ing changes in society. "Cato" argued for a bill of rights on the ground that although "[i]t is alleged that the opinions and manners of the people of America are capable to resist and prevent an extension of prerogative or oppression . . . you must recollect that opinion and manners are mutable, and may not always be a permanent obstruction against the encroachments of government." "Cato" [George Clinton], *Essays on the Constitution of the United States,* 266, ed. Paul Leicester Ford (Brooklyn: Historical Printing Club, 1892).

56 Debate in North Carolina Convention (July 28, 1788), in *The Debates in the Several State Conventions on the Adoption of the Federal Constitution,* 144–145, ed. Jonathan Elliot (Washington, 1836).

57 Hamburger, "The Constitution's Accommodation of Social Change," 300–301. Even when early Americans occasionally said that constitutions would have to change with circumstances, they tended to assume that the people would make the necessary modifications. As put by the Rev. Jonas Clark, "the same societies or nations may require different constitutions, at distinct and distant periods and stages of their existence," and "[u]pon the whole, the propriety or impropriety of this or that constitution or mode of government, for this people or another, depends upon a variety of circumstances; such as character, situation, manners, customs, trade, connections, &c.—of which the people, are, or, most certainly, ought to be the best, if not the only competent judges." Jonas Clark, *A Sermon,* 16–17 (Boston: 1781).

58 *An Address of the Convention for Framing a New Constitution of Government for the State of New Hampshire to the Inhabitants of the State,* 3–4 (Portsmouth and Exeter: 1781). For further evidence of the desire for a "permanent" constitution, see Hamburger, "The Constitution's Accommodation of Social Change," 239.

Manifest Contradiction

Although the obligation of a statute adopted under a constitution depended in part on the constitution's particular requirements, it also more generally depended on the relationship among different laws, and as to this question, lawyers appear to have assumed that a law was binding unless manifestly contrary to a law of greater authority and obligation. Manifest contradiction has come to seem a mere "rule of administration" adopted by judges in response to their function of enforcing constitutions against other branches of government—in particular, an approach deferentially taken by judges when "dealing with the legislative action of a co-ordinate department."[59] Yet rather than be narrowly concerned with constitutions, manifest contradiction was the measure of the relation between any two conflicting laws, and rather than develop from ideas about judicial self-regulation it arose from the obligation of law in conscience.

The notion of manifest contradiction had developed during the Middle Ages. At its foundation, the obligation of law seemed to depend on understanding or judgment in conscience, and although there was considerable dispute in the Middle Ages about the degree of certainty that would bind the conscience, it came to be widely recognized that a determination or enactment could not have obligation in conscience if it was manifestly erroneous.[60] In one application of this analysis, if an individual's judgment was manifestly erroneous, he had to abandon it, and in this manner the king himself had to reconsider his judgments—as when English writs of error directed in the king's name that if "manifest error" had intervened in a case, then the error should be amended.[61] More generally, because a manifest error unbound the understanding or judgment in conscience, this sort of error became the measure of contradiction necessary for one law to displace the obligation of another.[62]

[59] James B. Thayer, "The Origin and Scope of the American Doctrine of Constitutional Law," *Harvard Law Review,* 7: 150, 152 (1893). In focusing on the administrative role of the judiciary, Thayer even went so far as to conclude that the manifest contradiction rule did not apply to advisory opinions, because this "in reality, is not the exercise of the judicial function at all," and accordingly in these opinions, "the scruples, cautions, and warnings . . . and the rule about a reasonable doubt . . . have no application. What is asked for here is the judge's own opinion." Ibid., 153–154.

[60] In what once had been the "prevalent" medieval theological tradition, manifest error was simply that which was apparent, as opposed to secret or hidden, but John of Paris "sets manifest error against a pronouncement on an elusive issue which has not been identified as an error." Takashi Shogimen, *Ockham and Political Disobedience in the Late Middle Ages,* 115 (Cambridge: Cambridge University Press, 2007).

[61] Later, jury verdicts would similarly be overturned for manifest error. Already in the Middle Ages, moreover, what was manifest might not need to be proved.

[62] For example, whereas "the champions of the Curia suggested or assumed that the official

Even as to a single act, when one understanding of its intent conflicted with another, it was often said that the manifest intent prevailed. The intent of an act—whether an individual's intent in his last will or a legislature's intent in a statute—could not be binding unless it could be discerned. Sometimes, however, although one intent could perhaps be discerned from the words, another intent seemed manifest or plain, and in these circumstances lawyers tended to assume that the manifest intent of the maker of the act was binding.[63] It was in this sense that the "plain" meaning of an enactment mattered—not as a semantic claim, but as an observation about the obligation of the intent that had been made manifest or plain. Notions of obligation, as has been suggested, were closely tied to epistemological questions about the evidence that could bind the understanding in conscience, and although this was why the intent of the lawmaker had to be discernible, it was also why the manifest intent of an act had greater obligation than any other possible intent of the act. An intent that was plain or manifest bound the conscience in a way that could not reasonably be resisted or escaped, and it thus was evident not merely in the

head of the Church was the best exponent of natural law . . . the Imperialists maintained that it was the safe course to follow the emperor's judgment in case of doubt, and rash to dispute it unless it were so contrary to settled principles as to be manifestly erroneous." Frederick Pollock, "The History of the Law of Nature: A Preliminary Study," *Columbia Law Review,* 1: 22 (1901).

63 The moralist Jeremy Taylor went so far as to say that "unlesse it be manifest that the words doe not represent the intention of the law-giver, the conscience of the subject is to obey the words of the law." Jeremy Taylor, *Ductor Dubitantium, or the Rule of Conscience In All Her General Measures,* 2: 400 (III.vi.Rule 1.6) (London: 1660). This, however, confused manifest intent with manifest obligation and probably was based on a civilian-influenced perception of interpretation as a threat to the obligation of the words. More conventionally, in response to the usual use of manifest intent, Blackstone argued about a will in *Perrin v. Blake* that "by the legal operation of the words, which are not in my opinion controlled by any manifest intent to the contrary, the heir could only take by descent." "An Argument in the Exchequer Chamber on Giving Judgment in the Case of Perrin and Another Against Blake, by the Hon. Mr. Justice Blackstone," in *A Collection of Tracts Relative to the Law of England,* 1: 510, ed. Francis Hargrave (London: 1787).

Americans sometimes flipped around the typical use of the notion of manifest or plain intent to buttress arguments against equitable interpretation. For example, when a slave sought her freedom by arguing from equitable interpretation of a New Jersey statute, it was said in response that the act was "plain, simple & easy to be understood." *Beulah a Negro v. Barber & Buxton* (New Jersey Supreme Court 1775), Elisha Boudinot, Notes of Cases in Practice, 56, Princeton University, Rare Books and Special Collections, Manuscript Division, Thorne Collection of Elias Boudinot, C0001, Box 3, Folder 2. Some details about the case appear in Appendix II. Similarly, in answer to an argument for equitable interpretation, Chancellor Wythe emphasized that his understanding of the Virginia Constitution "is, manifestly, the intention of the clause." *Commonwealth v. Caton, et al.* (Court of Appeals 1782), Call, *Reports,* 4: 11. In these cases, it would have been enough to say that the intent of the words was clear, but it was all the more emphatic to conclude that the intent was plain or manifest.

weak sense of being apparent, but in a stronger sense, such that it was beyond any reasonable challenge or doubt.[64]

What was manifest was especially significant between conflicting laws. When a law had an obligation in conscience, its obligation was assumed to remain in force until it was displaced by a contrary law of greater obligation, and as moral theorists had long understood, the error or contradiction "must be manifest: for if it be doubtfull, the law retains her power; for it is in possession, and the justice of it is presumed."[65] This presumption in favor of the obligation of a law, unless manifestly contrary to a law of greater obligation, flourished as to all sorts of law—natural, divine, and human—and in the traditional version of the hierarchy of law, it thus had the virtue

64 This sort of analysis of understanding or judgment underlay discussions of reasonable doubt. As shown by a number of scholars, ranging from Barbara Shapiro to James Whitman, seventeenth-century commentators tended to resolve questions concerning obligation in conscience by distinguishing between what was merely probable and what was beyond a reasonable doubt. Barbara J. Shapiro, *"Beyond Reasonable Doubt" and "Probable Cause": Historical Perspectives on the Anglo-American Law of Evidence,* 40 (Berkeley: University of California Press, 1991); James Whitman, *The Origins of Reasonable Doubt: The Theological Roots of the Criminal Trial,* 165–167 (New Haven: Yale University Press, 2008). The underlying problem was to understand what displaced the obligation of a determination or judgment in conscience, and this difficulty was not new, but whereas in the Middle Ages it had been analyzed in terms of manifest error or contradiction, it now came to be understood among writers on conscience as a matter of moral certainty, which was "such a certainty as excludes all reasonable doubt." E[dward] W[orsley], *Reason and Religion,* 35 (Antwerp: 1672). The way in which the one formulation evolved into the other can be illustrated from the work of Edward Stillingfleet, who was hardly unlearned in epistemological matters. Responding to a Catholic theological position on the Second Commandment, he asked: "But is this so plain and clear, that a Mans Conscience can never make any just and reasonable Doubt concerning it?" [Edward Stillingfleet], *The Doctrines and Practices of the Church of Rome Truly Represented,* 123 (London: 1686). Like what was manifest, what was beyond a reasonable doubt could deprive a judgment or understanding of its obligation in conscience, and it thus increasingly became explicit that what was manifest (be it a manifest intent or a manifest error or contradiction) stood beyond any reasonable doubt.

Lest there be any confusion, it should be noted that this was not the highest degree of certainty. As explained by John Wilkins, although "*Physical and Mathematical* Certainty may be stiled *Infallible,*" what was known as "*Moral* Certainty" was merely *"Indubitable."* This was the sort of certainty that "doth not admit of any reasonable cause of doubting, which is the only certainty of which most things are capable." John Wilkins, *Of the Principles and Duties of Natural Religion,* 9 (London: 1675). Later, Stillingfleet distinguished this sort of certainty from what was self-evident, observing how early philosophers came "to proceed upon such Evidence of Perception, and Sense, and Ratiocination, as might in things not Self-evident form an Assent which excludes all reasonable Doubt of the contrary." Edward Stillingfleet, *A Discourse Concerning the Nature and Grounds of the Certainty of Faith,* 35 (London: 1688).

65 Taylor, *Ductor Dubitantium,* 2: 411 (III.vi.Rule 3.1). Obligation in conscience could not be "lightly geaven over," as an earlier writer explained, "without evident and manifest reason." John Rastell, *A Replie against an Answer (falslie intitled) in Defence of the Truth,* fol. 8[r] (Antwerp: 1555).

of protecting human legislation from casual claims about higher laws.[66] The presumption acquired all the more strength with the shift in the hierarchy toward authority, for when a law was willed, its intent had an obligation in conscience on account of the maker's authority, and this obligation remained in place until the law was dislodged by a manifestly contrary law. Such was the obligation of law and the limit on such obligation for lawyers in America. For example, when Alexander Hamilton asked which law should prevail "where the will of the legislature declared in its statutes, stands in opposition to that of the people declared in the constitution," he predictably concluded that "wherever there is an evident opposition" (apparently meaning a manifest or strongly evident opposition) "the laws ought to give place to the constitution."[67]

Even prior to the question of whether an error or contradiction was manifest was the standard of contradiction. As a matter of logic, the necessary degree of opposition had long seemed to be an inconsistency or contradiction, which was often described as what was flatly or absolutely contrary. Legislation, however, could establish a looser measure of incompatibility, and Parliament's 1696 Act for Preventing Frauds and Regulating Abuses in the Plantation Trade rendered American laws void if they were in "[any] wayes repugnant" to relevant English law. The statute could have used the word "repugnant" simply to mean inconsistent, but it probably employed the word out of caution, to cover any possible broader meaning.[68] Americans, however, were familiar with the ideal of contradiction, and many of them insisted that their statutes remained lawful unless flatly inconsistent with English law. For example, in his interpretation of the 1696 act, the London agent for Massachusetts and Connecticut argued in 1721 that "*a Law in the Plantations may be said to be repugnant to a Law made in* Great-Britain, *when it flatly contradicts it.*"[69] A half-century later, another London agent for Connecticut similarly refused to concede more than that "if the General Assembly [of Connecticut] should make a law *repugnant* to a *stat-*

[66] For a sixteenth-century illustration from St. German, see Chapter Four at note 51.
[67] Hamilton, Federalist Numbers 78 and 81, *The Federalist,* 524–525, 543. For an earlier American example of a claim of "evident contradiction"—between a Pennsylvania statute and the practice of Pennsylvania courts and juries—see Governor's Answer (11th month, 20th day, 1738), *Votes and Proceedings of the House of Representatives of the Province of Pennsylvania. Beginning the Fourteenth Day of October, 1726,* at 3: 332 (Philadelphia: 1754). See also Chapter Four at note 51.
[68] 7 & 8 William III, c.22, §8 (1696). As already suggested, the word "repugnancy" could simply mean contradiction, but it could also have a slightly broader meaning, and Parliament therefore sometimes took the safe route of using the word "repugnant."
[69] Jeremiah Dummer, *A Defence of the New-England Charters,* 57 (London: 1721). To this he added: *"so far as the Law made here mentions and relates to the Plantations."* Ibid.

ute of Great Britain, (not in the sense of *diverse f[ro]m,* but *flatly,* and in *terms contradictory* to it,) such law, by the *saving [clause] in the charter, might* be void."[70] This insistence on a flat or direct contradiction was a rather strained interpretation of the 1696 act, but it drew upon the old notion that only a contradiction—indeed, only a manifest contradiction—would render a lesser act void.

When contemplating contradictions between their own constitutions and statutes, Americans sometimes explained that the contradiction had to be evident or manifest in the sense that it was unavoidable. In 1782, in *Commonwealth v. Caton,* one of the lawyers, St. George Tucker, argued to the Virginia Court of Appeals that "[i]f any Act" of the General Assembly "shall be found absolutely & *irreconcileably* contradictory to the Constitution, it can not admit of a Doubt that such act is absolutely null & void."[71] Hamilton similarly explained in the *Federalist* that "[i]f there should happen to be an irreconcileable variance" between two enactments, "that which has the superior obligation and validity ought of course to be preferred."[72] These lawyers were apparently alluding to a contradiction that could not reasonably be doubted or avoided, and they thereby were expounding the old ideal of manifest contradiction.

The notion of manifest contradiction, by the way, was a measure of

[70] Letter from William Samuel Johnson to Governor William Pitkin (Feb. 13, 1768), in Trumbull Papers, in *Collections of the Massachusetts Historical Society,* 9: 259–260 (fifth series) (Boston: 1885).

[71] "To. W.N.," Argument on Behalf of the Prisoners, Addressed to William Nelson, William and Mary College Library, Tucker-Coleman Papers, Legal Papers, Virginia Supreme Court of Appeals, Mfm Reel M-44.

[72] Hamilton, Federalist Number 78, *The Federalist,* 525.

The work of William Treanor questions whether "only clearly unconstitutional statutes" were to be held unconstitutional—his primary evidence being his assessment that in many cases "there were plausible arguments in favor of the statute." William Michael Treanor, "Judicial Review Before Marbury," *Stanford Law Review,* 58: 459 and note 11 (2005). There are obvious evidentiary risks, however, in relying so heavily on twenty-first-century second-guessing of eighteenth-century judges. There are also risks in systematically restating the question of manifest, plain, or evident contradiction in terms of what was "clearly unconstitutional." On the basis of this restatement of the question, Treanor observes that there were often plausible arguments for the constitutionality of statutes that were held unconstitutional, but the manifest contradiction standard did not imply the absence of plausible alternative arguments. On the contrary, it acknowledged otherwise plausible alternative conclusions and offered a measure of when they nonetheless lacked obligation, and it therefore cannot be evaluated on the basis of whether or not there were plausible arguments in favor of a statute. Last but not least, the requirement that a contradiction be manifest or plain was ancient and general, and as will be seen in Chapters Thirteen and Fourteen, there were allusions to it in states that ranged from New Hampshire to North Carolina. Accordingly, if any substantial number of American judges took the view that they should sometimes abandon the manifest contradiction requirement, it is puzzling that they did not say so.

statutory error or contradiction rather than of constitutional truth. At times, what was manifest came close to a measure of truth. For example, it has been seen that when judges sought to understand the intent of a statute, a manifest intent prevailed over a more weakly evident intent and thus became a measure of moral certainty or confidence. So too, the related notion of beyond a reasonable doubt served as a measure of certainty for jurors in criminal trials. These, however, were not instances in which there was a challenge to the obligation of an already binding determination or rule. In contrast, where was a challenge to the obligation of a lower court judgment or to the obligation of a statute enacted by a body with lawmaking authority, the question was whether the obligation of the existing determination could be displaced, and this was possible only if the judgment was manifestly erroneous or the statute was manifestly contrary to a law of greater obligation. Of course, to say that a statute was manifestly contrary to a constitution was to exhibit confidence in the truth of this conclusion, but the application of the measure was to discern whether the statute was contrary to the constitution, and this was a matter of contradiction or error.

Although a contradiction had to be manifest, it did not have to be based on a manifest intent. To be sure, when one possible intent of a constitution was discernible but another was plain or manifest, the manifest intent of the constitution would prevail, and this was therefore the stronger foundation for establishing a manifest contradiction with a statute. Such was the tack taken by the lawyers for the prisoners in *Commonwealth v. Caton* when they argued that "the act of assembly" at stake there "was contrary to the plain declaration of the constitution; and therefore void."[73] Often, however, there was no tension in a constitution between different possible intents, but rather merely a discernible intent that was less than manifest, and this absence of manifest intent did not preclude judges from finding a manifest contradiction. In these more typical circumstances, although the discernible intent of the constitution was not plain or manifest, it could be ascertained, and this meant it was binding and could deprive a manifestly contrary statute of its obligation.

Just as nothing about a manifest contradiction required it to arise from a manifest intent, so too nothing required it to come from an express intent. Still, the possibility that a manifest contradiction might be based on less than a constitution's express intent left open opportunities to undermine the requirement of a manifest contradiction, and this troubled at least

[73] *Commonwealth v. Caton* (Court of Appeals 1782), Call, *Reports,* 4: 7. The President of the Court, Edmund Pendleton, also alluded to the question as concerning what was "contrary to the plain terms of th[e] constitution." Ibid., 17.

one judge, Spencer Roane. This strong-tempered Virginian therefore insisted that a manifest contradiction had to be an express contradiction. He eventually came to realize, however, that his position was unsustainable. In 1793, in *Kamper v. Hawkins,* he observed that he "[h]ad formerly supposed" that the "Judiciary ought not to refuse to execute a law unless expressly repugnant to [the] Const[itution]," but he "has since changed his opinion." He did so with good reason, for although a manifest contradiction between a statute and a constitution rested on the intentions of these enactments, the intent of any enactment could be discerned from either its words or the intent that lay below their surface—in religious terms, from either the letter or the spirit. Even if discerned beneath the words, the intent of the constitution was the measure of its obligation and could render a manifestly contrary law of lesser authority devoid of obligation. Roane therefore backed down, and in words that echoed old discussions of what was binding in conscience, he explained that judges "should distrust their Judg^{ts} until Conviction on *clear grounds,* founded on fundamental principles, either within the Letter, or obviously within the Spirit of the Const[itution]."[74] Yet as apparent from his allusion to what was "obviously" within the spirit of the Constitution, he remained adamant that the spirit should not be used as an avenue for subverting the requirement of a manifest contradiction. The awkwardness was that in formulating an alternative to his express contradiction standard, he came close to suggesting that a manifest contradiction had to come from a manifest intent. As summarized in another report, he said that "I now think that the judiciary may and ought not only to refuse to execute a law expressly repugnant to the Constitution; but also one which is, by a plain and natural construction, in opposition to the fundamental principles thereof."[75] A natural construction was

[74] *Kamper v. Hawkins* (General Court 1793), St. George Tucker, Notes of Cases, 3: 28, College of William and Mary, Swem Library, Tucker-Coleman Papers, Reel M-62.

[75] *Kamper v. Hawkins* (General Court 1793), Brockenbrough and Holmes, *Reports,* 35–36. Roane added that "the judiciary may and ought to adjudge a law unconstitutional and void, if it be plainly repugnant to the letter of the Constitution, or the fundamental principles thereof"—the latter being "those great principles growing out of the Constitution, by the aid of which, in dubious cases, the Constitution may be explained and preserved inviolate." In this way, he again acknowledged that, in discerning whether a law contradicted a constitution, judges might in "dubious cases" have to interpret the constitution by looking beyond its "letter" to its "spirit." At the same time, he also once again made clear that this approach was not to be abused, for he emphasized "fundamental principles" and said that they were "land-marks"—a traditional common law metaphor for what was fixed and certain. Ibid., 40.

For rather different interpretations of Roane's opinion in *Kamper,* see Timothy S. Huebner, "The Consolidation of State Judicial Power: Spencer Roane, Virginia Legal Culture, and the Southern Judicial Tradition," *Virginia Magazine of History and Biography,* 102: 56 (Jan.

one thing; an obvious or plain construction, however, was as much as to say a manifest intent. Worried that the manifest contradiction requirement was not sufficiently confining, Roane had previously insisted that there also be express intent, and he now simply shifted to a demand for manifest intent. As in so many matters, Spencer Roane could not escape his passions, and thus in fear of one sort of distortion, he proposed others.

When considered out of context, the requirement of a manifest contradiction may seem to have been the response of Americans judges to their functional role in holding the acts of other branches of government unconstitutional—as if the judiciary had to defer to the legislature where its acts were not manifestly contrary to the constitution. Revealingly, however, when Spencer Roane assiduously distorted the manifest contradiction requirement, he was reacting to his fear that it would not sufficiently protect the will of the legislature from the judiciary. Rather than a judicial response to any such narrow, American problem, the manifest contradiction requirement was an ancient and general assumption about what was binding in conscience. For a law to have obligation, its intent had to be at least discernible; and for the obligation of one law to be displaced by the obligation of another, it had to be manifestly contrary to that other law.

Judicial Duty

Questions about the constitutionality of government acts came before the judges because of the duty of their office. Not only at Westminister, but also in America, judicial office most centrally included a duty to decide in accord with the law of the land.

Judicial commissions and occasionally judicial oaths rehearsed what was otherwise assumed. New York judges, for example, received commissions requiring them "to hear and determine" cases "according to the Law of our said State."[76] Similarly, the judges of the South Carolina Court of

---

1994); Treanor, "The Case of the Prisoners and the Origins of Judicial Review," 529, 555. Treanor aptly observes that a contradiction did not have to rest on an express intent, but he apparently understands this to mean that a judge could find a statute void even if it was not manifestly contrary to a constitution—or, as he puts it, "clearly unconstitutional." Treanor, "Judicial Review Before Marbury," 492.

[76] See, for example, Commission to Richard Morris, Robert Yates, and John Sloss Hobart, Justices of the New York Supreme Court of Judicature and others (May 6, 1786), New York Historical Society, Misc. Mss., Suffolk County NY; Commission to Richard Morris, Robert Yates, & John Sloss Hobart, Justices of the New York Supreme Court of Judicature and others (April 17, 1787), New York Historical Society, Queens County NY Collection. Justices of the peace in New Jersey received commissions that in traditional language required them to act "according to the Laws, Statutes and Ordinances." [Governor William Livingston], *The State of New-Jersey, To ____ Greeting* ([New Jersey: 1776]).

Chancery swore to "do equal right to all manner of people . . . according to equity and good conscience, and the laws and usages of South Carolina."[77] Judges also had to take the generic oaths that were established for men in government across different branches, but these oaths referred to law more generally than judicial oaths, requiring merely that government officers act "agreeably" to the constitution and laws of their state or that they "support" the constitution.[78] Only in Pennsylvania and Vermont did this sort of generic oath require each government officer, whether executive or judicial, to bind himself to "do equal right and justice to all men, to the best of my judgment and abilities, according to law."[79]

The way in which judicial oaths were understood to protect judicial duty and the law of the land can be observed just prior to the Revolution in the New York case of *Forsey v. Cunningham.* Waddel Cunningham had brutally beaten and stabbed Thomas Forsey, and in 1764 in an action for assault and battery, a jury in the New York Supreme Court awarded Forsey £1,500 damages. Recognizing that there was little ground for a writ of error, Cunningham's attorney in fact sought a civilian-style appeal or rehearing of the evidence in the governor's council, and although the Supreme Court denied this writ as contrary to law, Lieutenant Governor Cadwallader Colden seized upon the opportunity. Eager to challenge the jurisdiction of the judges, he issued a writ of his own barring the Supreme Court from further proceedings until the case had been reheard by the

[77] An Act for establishing a Court of Chancery (1784), in *The Statutes at Large of South Carolina,* 7: 208, ed. David J. McCord (Columbia: 1840).

[78] According to the Massachusetts Constitution, persons elected or appointed had to swear, "I . . . do solemnly swear and affirm, that I will faithfully and impartially discharge and perform all the duties incumbent upon me . . . agreeably to the rules and regulations of the Constitution, and the laws of this commonwealth." Massachusetts Constitution of 1780, Chapter VI, Article I. For the U.S. Constitution's oath to "support this Constitution," see U.S. Constitution, Article VI.

Academic classes on morals and theology often touched on the office of judgment, whether in the court of conscience or the courts of law, and sometimes such study leaned in the direction of the common law. Note, for example, the 1785 Harvard thesis that "[j]udges are bound to decide in accord with what is alleged and proved, not according to conscience." Harvard, *Theses* (Cambridge: 1785) ("Judex secundum acts allegata et probata, non secundum scientiam suam, sententiam ferre debet").

[79] Pennsylvania Constitution of 1776, Oath or Affirmation of Office; Vermont Constitution of 1777, chapter II, Article XXXVI.

Incidentally, justices of the peace whose commissions expired were sometimes appointed again under new commissions, and this could lead to an awkward situation when they "consider[ed] themselves as duly qualified to discharge the duties of said office without again taking the Oaths required by Law." The difficulty was that their unauthorized acts "unless made valid by the legislature will be liable to be made nul and void." They could not, however, rely on getting corrective legislation. See, for example, Resolve making valid the doings of Justices, MSA, House of Representatives, Miscellaneous 1790, No. 3356 ("Rejected"). Indeed, such legislation might have raised interesting constitutional questions.

Governor and his council. When Chief Justice David Horsmanden nonetheless signed the judgment against Cunningham, Colden issued another writ requiring the record to be brought before the Council. At stake was ultimately the right to a jury trial, but more immediately the question was one of judicial oaths.[80]

In the early 1760s, the judges and their political supporters had become embroiled in a bitter controversy with the Lieutenant Governor as to whether they would hold their office on good behavior, and when they eventually had to accept it only at the king's pleasure, the new governor, Robert Monckton, was at least politic enough to allow them to take the same oaths as the English judges.[81] It had been traditional for New York judges to swear in "general words" that "you will well and truly execute the Office of a Justice of the Supreme Court, according to the best of your Skill and Understanding," but Governor Monckton now told the judges that he "disliked that general form," and after the judges advised him "that there was a more extensive Oath" in the statute of 18 Edward III, they took this long version, which was the medieval statutory oath requiring the judges not to deny justice and to certify to the king if they received a letter from him or anyone else asking for a delay.[82]

When Lieutenant Governor Colden initially demanded that the judges stay their proceedings in *Forsey v. Cunningham,* the three men responded to Colden and the Council that they were barred by their medieval oath from delaying the proceedings. Chief Justice Horsmanden explained that he was writing "in compliance with my Oath of Office," under which he was "bound to certify to the King's Majesty" about Colden's writs, "which I consider as Letters in Delay of Justice." Under their oath, Horse-

[80] For accounts of the case, see Eben Moglen, *Settling the Law: Legal Development in Provincial New York,* 255–258 (New York: Columbia Law School, 1994); Julius Goebel, Jr., *Cases and Materials on the Development of Legal Institutions,* 289 (Brattleboro: Vermont Printing, 1949); Thomas E. Carney and Susan Kolb, "The Legacy of *Forsey v. Cunningham:* Safeguarding the Integrity of the Right to Trial by Jury," *The Historian,* 6: 663 (2007).

[81] For the dispute over tenure, see Milton M. Klein, "Prelude to Revolution in New York: Jury Trials and Judicial Tenure," *William and Mary Quarterly,* 17: 439 (third series) (1960).

[82] *The Report of an Action of Assault, Battery, and Wounding, Tried in the Supreme Court of Judicature for the Province of New-York, In the Term of October 1764, Between Thomas Forsey, Plaintiff, and Waddel Cunningham, Defendant,* 18–19 (New York: 1764). Although the English oath was actually associated with 20 Edward III, it had traditionally been printed as 18 Edward III. The judges spent several days reworking it into modern English and altering its invocation, which in its traditional form better suited "the Church of *Rome.*" Ibid. Just how seriously the New York judges understood their oath is suggested by Justice Smith, who noted that "lest thro' Surprise or Forgetfulness he might deviate from it, he found it necessary frequently to read it, especially before the holding [of] the Supreme Court, on the Circuits." Ibid., 20.

manden added, the judges had to "proceed to execute the Law notwithstanding the same Letters."[83] William Livingston similarly wrote that "the Course of the Law . . . must at all Times be free and uninterrupted; and this is so particularly provided for, that by the Oath we have taken, we are deny no Man['s] Right by the King's Letters, nor none other Man's, but to proceed notwithstanding such Letters."[84] Justice Smith more generally told the Council that "his Oath of Office, as well as his Commission, respected only the common Law and its Proceedings, and could not admit him, by any possible Construction, to decide or determine by any other Law."[85] These New York judges, like their seventeenth-century English predecessors, lacked tenure but were bound by their oaths, and modeling themselves on Coke and his contemporaries, they self-consciously took their place in the history of the common law and insisted on doing their duty.

After Independence, the judges in the American states could no longer easily be considered servants of the executive, and thus, although their duty still belonged to them as individuals, it now became more clearly associated with a separate branch or power in government. James Iredell, for example, explained about the "Judicial Power" that "[t]he duty of the Power . . . in all cases, is to decide according to the *Laws of the State*."[86] Nonetheless, the duty remained a part of the office of the individual judges. Repeatedly, state judges found themselves standing alone, not as a branch of government, nor even as a court, but as individual judges, who had to decide difficult cases or defend themselves against threats of impeachment, and in these painful moments they tended to speak about the office they held as individ-

83 Ibid., 8, 13.
84 Ibid., 22.
85 Ibid., 20–21. In the end, however, he hesitated to give an opinion, because "it was likely that the Validity or Legality of that Writ would come into Question in the Supreme Court," and he therefore wondered "whether it would be proper that at present he suspend his Judgment on that Point, as extrajudicial Opinions ought to be given very sparingly, and with great Caution, if at all"—a point to which the Council acceded. Ibid.
86 "To the Public," Duke University, Rare Book, Manuscript, and Special Collections Library, James Iredell Papers, Box 1. The essay was published in the *North Carolina Gazette* (Newbern) (Aug. 17, 1786). For the context of Iredell's statement, see Chapter Fourteen. Notwithstanding what he wrote in 1786, Iredell did not forget that the duty belonged to a judge as an individual, for less than a decade later, he began an opinion: "It is my misfortune to dissent from the opinion entertained by the rest of the court upon the present occasion; but I am bound to decide, according to the dictates of my own judgment." *Oswald, Adm. v. State of NY* (U.S. Supreme Court 1793), Dallas, *Reports,* 2: 45.

A self-consciousness about how one should refer to the judiciary is suggested by the allusion of the dissenting members of the Pennsylvania Council of Censors to "[t]he judicial branch, as it is called." Reasons of Dissent, *Journal of the Council of Censors,* 145 (Philadelphia: 1783).

uals and about the oaths by which they were personally obliged to God to do the duty of their office.

Attorneys general and solicitors general shared in the judges' duty. It will be recalled that in England, the king's serjeants took an oath to "Administer the *Kings* matters, after the course of the Law," and that attorneys and solicitors general thus acquired an administrative version of the duty to decide in accord with the law.[87] So too, in America. In 1786 in Virginia, the state auditor, John Pendleton, received an "urgent application" from Judge John Tyler for unpaid salary. Pendleton was uncertain whether he should pay the amount, and he therefore wrote to Attorney General Edmund Randolph for "the favour of his opinion, whether the salary annexed to an Office in the Judiciary Department should commence from the appointment or the qualification of the member"—that is, from the time the governor signed the commission or the time the judge took his oath under it. "At first Jn° P was inclined to take the latter period[,] but on second thought rather thinks the former most reasonable. A Gentleman elected into a public Office supposes himself engaged from the time of his appointment & declines all other business—the qualification is not deemed necessary until he is about to operate in his Office."[88] Randolph, however, took another view, for although he wanted to be gracious, he felt a higher obligation to decide in accord with the law, including the rules of interpretation:

> I have considered this matter with some attention, and wished from my friendship for the gentleman alluded to to carry his salary farther back than his qualification. But acting under oath, & bound to interpret the law according to fixed rules, I am afraid that I cannot declare my opinion from an earlier commencement of salary, than the qualification.[89]

[87] *The Book of Oaths and the Several Forms Thereof, both Ancient and Modern,* 138 (London: 1689).

[88] Opinion of Edmund Randolph respecting the Commencement of Tyler's Salary (on or after May 6, 1786), LVA, Auditor of Public Accounts, A.G.'s Opinions, RG 48, Box 138.

[89] Ibid. He added: "I have thus decided in a similar instance two or three years past." Ibid. (The word "under" in the text is only a guess.)

When St. George Tucker pressed John Pendleton on such a question in July 1788, Attorney General James Innes opined, that "the four additional Judges appointed under the district court law ought to receive their Salaries from the date of their respective commissions, provided they have signified their acceptance thereof to the Executive in due time." John Pendelton, Case for the Attorney General's opinion (July 2, 1788) together the opinion by James Innes, LVA, Edmund Randolph Executive Papers, Box 54. They apparently, however, did not get paid from the date of their commissions, and in the ensuing litigation in Chancery, Tyler and Tucker took their cases by adjournment to the Court of Appeals. Tucker persisted there and had his appeal dismissed. *St. George Tucker v. The Auditor* (June 23–24, 1789), Supreme Court of Appeals, Order Book No. 1, 1779–1789, at 146, LVA. Tyler, however, was more astute. Prior to the judgment against Tucker, Tyler's counsel "re-

This was a duty not unlike that of the judges.

Whether as to judges or government attorneys, this sort of duty confined discretion. Although today it is sometimes thought that the judicial function is relatively open-ended, the drafters of the New Hampshire Constitution worried instead that "the objects" of legislative power were so "various and numerous, and its limits so extensive, as to render it almost impracticable to ascertain them." In contrast, the drafters were confident that "the judicial and executive departments are so accurately defined, in every free State, that the least deviation may be detected and punished."[90] It may be doubted whether judicial power could really be so accurately defined, but lawyers had great confidence in the ideal that judges should decide in accord with the law of the land.[91] Blackstone had repeated Coke's conceit that the law rather than the judge decided cases, and in New Hampshire the young law student William Plumer industriously copied from Blackstone into his one of his notebooks that "Judgments are the sentence

---

quested the Court not to proceed to give an opinion in this case it being his intention to dismiss his appeal in the said Court of Chancery." *John Tyler v. The Auditor* (June 22, 1789), ibid., 144. Although Tyler thus retreated, he eventually prevailed, and he thereby obtained "ten pounds for payment of so much adjudged by the District Court to be due to John Tyler esquire as a Judge; being the difference between the time of his appointment and qualifications." Sandra Gioia Treadway, ed., *Journals of the Council of the State of Virginia,* 5: 209 (Sept. 21, 1790) (Richmond: Virginia State Library, 1982).

Doubts about the judges' salaries had included questions about payments in kind. In 1781, for example, when Attorney General Edmund Randolph was asked how payments in tobacco should be calculated, he concluded: "I am of opinion clearly, that the judges of the Supreme courts are intitled to the valuation of Tobacco immediately preceding the time of actual payment." Opinion of Edmund Randolph on Judges' Salaries (March 7, 1781), LVA, Auditor of Public Accounts, A.G.'s Opinions, RG 48, Box 138.

[90] *An Address of the Convention for Framing a Constitution of Government for the People of New Hampshire,* 5 (Portsmouth: 1783). On the question of administrative commissions that left discretion, Plumer assembled English quotations (which echoed Coke on commissions of sewers) showing that such discretion was presumably to be within reason and law. He quoted Coke, *Institutes,* 2: 56, 298; Holt as reported in Lord Raymond, *Reports,* 1: 500; Jacob's *Law Dictionary;* and Lord Mansfield in *Rex. v. John Wilkes* (K.B. 1770), Burrow, *Reports,* 4: 2539, to the effect that "Discretion, when applied to a court of Justice, means sound discretion guided by law. It must be governed by rule, not by humour: it must not be arbitrary, vague & fanciful; but legal & regular." Extracts from Law-Writers, 94 (entry dated Dec. 11, 1787), William Plumer Legal Papers, Reel 19.

[91] For the affinities Americans felt with the constitutional sensibilities they found in Coke, see Barbara Aronstein Black, "An Astonishing Political Innovation: The Origins of Judicial Review," *University of Pittsburgh Law Review,* 49: 696 (1988); Barbara A. Black, "The Constitution of Empire: The Case for the Colonies," *University of Pennsylvania Law Review,* 124: 1157 (1976). For a sense of how far Americans could go in imitating Coke, see Thomas Jefferson, "Whether Christianity is a part of the Common Law?" (c. 1774?), in Thomas Jefferson, *Reports of Cases Determined in the General Court of Virginia,* 137 (Charlottesville: 1829). For the date, see Merrill D. Peterson, *Thomas Jefferson and the New Nation,* 60 (New York: Oxford University Press, 1970).

of the *law,* pronounced by the Court." Thus, "[t]he judg^t tho' pronounced or awarded by the judges, is *not their* determination or sentence, but the determination & sentence of the *law.*"[92]

The expectation of Americans that constitutions should leave as little room as possible for judicial discretion was never more widely debated than in the controversy over ratification of the U.S. Constitution. As already hinted, both sides shared the ideal of clarity and limiting judicial discretion, but whereas Anti-Federalists complained that the Constitution was so vague as to leave discretion in federal judges, Federalists insisted that the Constitution was clear or at least as clear as human language permitted. Anti-Federalists protested that the Constitution could not limit discretion in general terms and that it should therefore have been more particular, especially in listing rights. Brutus, for example, thought that to prevent the "equivocal" and "ambiguous" provisions of the Constitution from "justify[ing] the courts" in adopting a "latitude of interpretation" about federal power, the Constitution's principles "ought to have been clearly and precisely stated," and the Constitution ought to have been supplemented with "the most express and full declaration of rights." Federalists, however, saw no need for a particularized enumeration of rights. In contrast to Brutus, who feared that the "general and indefinite terms" of the Constitution left room for discretion, the framers and then the Federalists thought the Constitution could be both "general" and "precise."[93] Even when Federalists candidly acknowledged, as did Madison, that there would inevitably be some uncertainty, they did not give up on eventually confining it, for although the "exposition of the Constitution" would be a "copious source" of difficulties, this would only persist "until its meaning on all great points shall have been settled by precedents"—"until their meaning be liquidated and ascertained by a series of particular decisions and adjudications."[94] Similarly, Hamilton suggested that the meaning of the Constitution would be

[92] Extracts from Law-Writers, 173 (entry dated Feb. 1, 1788), William Plumer Legal Papers, Reel 19, quoting William Blackstone, *Commentaries,* 3: 395–396. See also William E. Nelson, *The Americanization of the Common Law: The Impact of Legal Change on Massachusetts Society, 1760–1830,* at 96, 171–172 (Athens: University of Georgia Press, 1994).

[93] Brutus, Essay II (Nov. 1, 1787), in *The Documentary History of the Ratification of the Constitution,* 13: 525 (1981); Brutus, Essay XI (Jan. 31, 1788), ibid., 15: 515–516 (1984); Edmund Randolph, Draft Sketch of Constitution. For the extent of the Anti-Federalist demand for particularized guarantees and for the scathing Federalist response, see Philip Hamburger, "Trivial Rights," *Notre Dame Law Review,* 70: 1 (1994).

[94] Letter from James Madison to Samuel Johnston (June 21, 1789), in *Papers of James Madison,* 12: 250, eds. Charles F. Hobson et al. (Charlottesville: University Press of Virginia, 1979); James Madison, Federalist Number 37, *The Federalist,* 236.

"liquidate[d]" over time.[95] Rather than see this liquidation of meaning as an opportunity for judicial flexibility, Hamilton played upon the familiar common law ideals, arguing that an "inflexible and uniform adherence to the rights of the constitution, and of individuals" was "indispensable in the courts of justice"—as was "a reliance that nothing would be consulted but the constitution and the laws." Indeed, "[t]o avoid an arbitrary discretion in the courts, it is indispensable that they should be bound down by strict rules and precedents, which serve to define and point out their duty in every particular case that comes before them."[96]

It was understood that in doing their duty, the judges served broader constitutional functions, including the protection of constitutional liberties, but whereas English judges traditionally had to protect liberty from royal power, American judges mostly had to secure it from legislative power and the underlying force of popular sentiment. It was still possible for Calvinist clergymen to propound that "[c]ivil rulers and magistrates" in general

[95] Hamilton, Federalist Number 82, ibid., 553.

[96] Hamilton, Federalist Number 78, ibid., 529.

The sort of common law assumptions about discretion that underlay the debate over the U.S. Constitution can be illustrated by an opinion given by Justice Lyons of the Virginia Court of Appeals. He recalled that "in Scotland there existed in the days of Queen Mary a Court of discretion," and after he "animadverted sharply upon it," he added that "[b]y the opinion of Judges, Lawyers, divines & Historians, Judges should not exercise discretion." Lyons then came to the question in the case at hand, explaining that he was "not at liberty either in Cases of *Life* or *property* to exercise his own private Discretion in a Case such as this where the point had been so solemnly adjudged." *Commonwealth v. Percy* (Virginia Court of Appeals, Nov. 10, 1787), St. George Tucker, Notes of Cases, 1: 81, College of William and Mary, Swem Library, Tucker-Coleman Papers, Reel M-62. Of course, in alluding to his private discretion, Lyons probably meant merely his individual discernment of the law rather than an exercise of will.

American judges often adopted simplified versions of traditional pleading and practice, but rather than think they were altering English law with an exercise of discretionary will, they could understand themselves to be exercising discretion in the sense of discerning their state's law, which was the law that applied to their circumstances. This point arose, for example, in a Pennsylvania case in which a defendant had "not received such notice of trial, as made it reasonable for him to prepare." The state's Supreme Court recognized that the Pennsylvania rule had to depart from that of England, for although "[i]n *England* the proof of actual notice is required," this could not be the rule "with us" where "the Gentlemen of the law are not so numerous, as they live dispersed, and as there are no regular posts." Yet rather than simply say that they could exercise discretion to change the law, the judges apparently alluded to Coke's view that "discretion is discernment by law what is just," this being a discretion arising from "the circumstances of the matter." More specifically, they concluded that "a reasonable notice of trial must be given to the party, not merely to his attorney," for "after all, the rules for bringing on causes must be influenced by a legal discretion, applicable to the peculiar circumstances of every case." *Cecil's Lessee v. Lebenstone* (Supreme Court of Pennsylvania 1786), Dallas, *Reports,* 2: 96. For the passages in Coke, see Chapter Four. More generally, see Nelson, *The Americanization of the Common Law,* Chapter 5.

"are set up by the people to be the guardians of their rights."[97] Lawyers and many others, however, took this to be the distinctive function of the judges. Against the threat from the Crown in the seventeenth century, Englishmen had often given up on the judges and had eulogized Parliament for defending their constitutional liberties; but in the eighteenth century, especially in the wake of the Wilkes controversy, many Whigs came to feel the limits of this solution, and similarly, against state legislatures, Americans fell back on the judges. State legislatures and popular majorities repeatedly threatened the freedom of various racial, religious, political, and propertied minorities, and therefore many such groups—Africans and Indians, Baptists and Universalists, Tories and Englishmen, creditors and debtors—turned to the courts for protection. When Universalists in Massachusetts faced establishment criticism for being un-Christian in resorting to judicial remedies, they explained that they were acting "in defense of what we suppose to be our just, invaluable and constitutional rights," and that "should we fly to the law-makers instead of that great law made by the people to govern the legislature itself, we should . . . betray our country's freedom."[98] From a more structural perspective, after the New Hampshire courts rejected a statute that infringed the rights of debtors, William Plumer wrote to a friend: "If our elective government is long supported, it will owe its existence to the Judiciary. That is the only body of men who will have an effective check upon a numerous Assembly."[99] Similarly, in New York, where the rights of Tories and Englishmen were at stake, Hamilton declared that "the courts of justice are to be considered as the bulwarks of a limited Constitution against legislative encroachments."[100]

Judges faced enough populist opposition that they often had reason to contemplate the divine character of their office and their accountability to

[97] West, *A Sermon,* 15.

[98] *An Appeal to the Impartial Public by The Society of Christian Independents, Congregating in Glocester,* 3–4, 31 (Boston: 1785).

[99] Letter from William Plumer to William Coleman (May 31, 1786), *A Collection of Letters Written to and by Wm Plumer,* 1: 69, William Plumer Papers, Mfm Reel LC2, also quoted by Lynn W. Turner, *William Plumer of New Hampshire 1759–1850,* at 34–35 (Chapel Hill: University of North Carolina Press, 1962). He preceded this generalization by noting that although "our feeble government" was "unhing'd," still "[o]ur Courts of Law are fine, & in these degenerate days, dare to be honest." Ibid.

[100] Hamilton, Federalist Number 78, *The Federalist,* 527. When proposing what became the U.S. Bill of Rights, Madison said: "If they are incorporated into the constitution, independent tribunals of justice will consider themselves in a peculiar manner the guardians of those rights." Madison's Speech in the House of Representatives (June 8, 1789), in *Creating the Bill of Rights: The Documentary Record from the First Federal Congress,* 83, eds. Helen E. Veit, Kenneth R. Bowling, and Charlene Bangs Bickford (Baltimore: Johns Hopkins University Press, 1991).

God. Echoing the old, English admonitions to the common law judges, the colonial minister Samuel Dunbar reminded the Massachusetts judges in 1760 that their office was divine and that they too would be judged:

> [H]igh is your office, awful is your work: and in some cases attended with peculiar difficulties, perhaps temptations. You need not only the *Laws* of the land for your directory, but wisdom, fidelity and courage, to make a right and just application of them.—You are to hear the cause of your brethren and to judge righteously, between every man and his brother; not to respect persons in judgment, but to hear the small as well as the great; and not be afraid of the faces of men; for the judgment is the Lord's. You must take heed, therefore, what you do; for you judge not for man, but for the Lord, who is with you in the judgment.—Wherefore be you with God, and let the fear of the Lord be upon you.

He therefore admonished the judges to "[p]ut on righteousness, and let it cloath you, and your judgment will be as a robe, and a diadem: your greatest comfort, your brightest ornament." It was not enough, however, for judges to vest themselves in divine righteousness. In addition, worldly judges had to keep an eye on the next world:

> Remember, Sirs, that tho' *now* you sit upon the *Bench,* you must *one Day* stand at the *Bar.* If you have been with God in the judgment, and studied to do justice, to discountenance vice, and to encourage vertue, you will be acquitted in the great *Audit day;* and *Christ,* the Judge, will confer inexpressible honour upon you; will take you to be *Assessors* with him, and you shall *judge the World, yea Angels.*—But, if you have forsaken god, and been unjust Judges, wo[e] unto you, a more severe & tremendous sentence will be past upon you, than you ever past upon the most flagitious criminal.

He closed: *"Now therefore, be instructed, ye judges of the earth, and serve the Lord with fear."*[101]

The sacredness of these ideals lasted long after the sermons became a distant memory. By the late eighteenth century, the clergy no longer so forcefully warned the judges of their fate in a higher court, and if the judges

[101] Samuel Dunbar, *The Presence of God with His People, Their Only Safety and Happiness. A Discourse,* 30–31 (Boston: 1760). This was the Massachusetts election sermon for the year, and Dunbar acknowledged that he was departing from the usual form to "address the Honourable the *Judges* in our Courts of Judicature, and the Honoured the *Justices* in our Towns and Counties." Ibid. For less elaborate treatment of the religious themes, see John Hancock, *The Instability of Humane Greatness, Illustrated and Exemplified In a Funeral Discourse At Braintree April 23. 1738. Upon the Much Lamented Death of the Honourable Edmund Quincy,* 28 (Boston: 1738); Bunker Gay, *The Accomplished Judge; or, A Compleat Dress for Magistrates. A Sermon Preached at Keene, At the First Opening of the Inferior Court, in the County of Cheshire. October 8, 1771,* at 27–28 (Portsmouth: 1773).

heard such sermons, they probably thought them better suited for their seventeenth-century forebears. It was still familiar, however, that "judges are obliged to judge righteously, upon pain of damnation," and although they were usually spared stern warnings about the judgment awaiting them in heaven, they continued to understand that they held an office that was in some sense sacred.[102] Eventually there would be little remaining memory of the divine office of judgment and the obligation to adhere to it, thus leaving these ideals to survive only in a threadbare deference to the outward robes of office. In the eighteenth century, however, the divine ideals retained a force that was not yet merely cultural, and it will later be seen that when the judges were pressed by importunate legislators, they still often looked up to the highest of judges and spoke in sacred cadences about their office and their oaths.

It thus appears that the ideals of law and judicial duty generally remained familiar in late eighteenth-century America, at least among lawyers. Express constitutions gave greater prominence to some questions, and changing attitudes toward religion left men less attentive to the divine nature of judicial office, but the ideals of law and judicial duty continued to be largely taken for granted.

[102] Amicus Judicum Bonorum, "The Just Ruler" (Dec. 25, 1772), *Connecticut Courant* (Dec. 29–Jan. 5, 1773). This was a commentary on the Massachusetts judges, who were being "tempted to judge wrong by a pension." Ibid. See also [John Allen], *An Oration, Upon the Beauties of Liberty, Or the Essential Rights of the Americans,* 22 (Boston: 1773).

Even after Independence, ministers sometimes instructed judges to "keep in view the infinitely great and supreme Judge *by whom all the judges of the Earth do rule.*" Quoting what was said to Jehoshaphat, the Rev. Peter Powers told the judges present at the first session of the General Assembly: *"Take heed what ye do, for ye judge not for man, but for the Lord who is with you in the judgment. Wherefore now, let the fear of the Lord be upon you"*—to which he added, "We wish you much wisdom and fortitude." Peter Powers, *Jesus Christ the True King and Head of Government. A Sermon Preached Before the General Assembly of the State of Vermont, on the Day of Their First Election, March 12, 1778, at Windsor,* 35–36 (Newbury-Port: 1778).

11

Reason and Justice within the Law

Americans, no less than the English, were sometimes painfully aware that judicial duty and the law of the land might conflict with aspirations for reason and justice. The rigor of a hierarchy based on the obligation of reason and justice had given way to the rigor of a hierarchy that established human authority and the obligation of human will, and thus just as Aquinas and the men who followed him had to accommodate authority within their conception of reason and justice, so Americans now had to pursue reason and justice within their account of authority. This could be a frustrating task. Yet although it could be bitterly disappointing to seek what was just through the will of the people or their representatives, and although all sorts of Americans took distinctive religious and moral approaches to the problem, American lawyers and judges tended to assume that nature itself established the authority of the law of the land and that the judges had a duty to decide in accord with this law. Rather than be opposed to authority, reason seemed to reveal that human authority was the natural avenue for men to achieve such worldly justice as could be attained through law, and from this perspective, although the people could avoid the injustice of their laws by altering them or by overthrowing their entire system of law, their judges could avoid injustice only though the law itself.

Subordinate and Sovereign Acts

An initial illustration of how the ideals of lawmaking authority and will limited inquiries about a law's rationality or justice can be observed in the different treatment of subordinate and sovereign acts. As in England, the acts of corporations, colonies, and other subordinate bodies were generally subject to the common law test of law and reason, and although this test only applied a very stereotyped concept of reason, it suggests how the law itself could impose a test of rationality. In contrast—also as in England—sovereign acts were thought by their nature to be beyond reconsideration for their rationality or justice. Sovereignty was the discretionary power that a governing body necessarily had to exercise over the people, and it was therefore assumed that when the people in their constitution authorized and limited the sovereign power of their government, they needed to avoid subjecting this discretionary power to any judicial reconsideration for its reason or justice. Were they to do otherwise, they would deprive their government of the sovereign power it needed to protect them and their liberty.

Subordinate laws, such as the acts of municipal corporations, constrained individuals differently and usually more severely than the law of the land, and as already seen, the common law test of law and reason allowed judges to uphold some such subordinate laws as reasonable. In particular, although local and other subordinate laws typically added to the legal constraints on individuals, the test of reason enabled the judges to conclude that some local constraints—those that were reasonable—contradicted the law of the land without going so far as to be unlawful. The element of reason thus tended to permit subordinate regulation of matters the law of the land had left unregulated.

This common law test of law and reason continued in America to be applicable to subordinate laws—as can be illustrated by a Massachusetts case on local custom. It will be recalled that the common law left extra space for local custom by asking whether a custom had a reasonable commencement rather than simply whether it was reasonable, and this was the test applied in the Massachusetts case. After some inhabitants had cleared a place along the banks of the Connecticut River and put up a seine, the owners of the land had taken the accumulated fish for themselves. The men who had put up the net sued the owners in 1770, and the jury gave a special verdict about the "ancient custom" of the inhabitants along the Connecticut River—finding that when any of them cleared a place along the river for seine fishing, "he held it against every body during the fishing season." When the case in 1779 eventually reached the Massachusetts Supreme Judicial Court, the plaintiffs' lawyers admitted that the colony's charter had vested "the property of the River . . . in the inhabitants of the Province" but argued that the inhabitants had "modified this property by the custom stated in the verdict," such that "when any one cleared a place for fishing—he held it against everybody." From this perspective, the question was whether such a right of seine fishing could "exist to exclude the owner of the soil." The lawyers for the owners, however, denied that custom could create any private right in the river. Most basically, "[i]t is against common right that fishing in public navigable rivers should belong to the crown or any individual." Moreover, "[t]o support the verdict by the *custom* is impossible," because "it militates against the Charter which gives the right of fishing to the inhabitants of the Province generally, & therefore the custom could not have a reasonable commencement." The lawyers for the owners then added that "[i]t is an uncertain custom—[which] savors of arbitrary power—and is in derogation of the rights of the subject and therefore void." The judges agreed and held "the custom absolutely *void* from its uncertainty & unreasonableness."[1] This was the old common law test for subordinate acts, and even under the generous version of reason that was applied to local custom, a claim of custom was unreasonable against rights of the subject established by charter.[2]

In addition to local custom, colonial statutes were among the laws

[1] *Frary et al. v. Cook et al.* (Hampshire County Superior Court, April term 1779), in *Notes of Cases Decided in the Superior and Supreme Judicial Court of Massachusetts from 1772 to 1789—Taken by the Honble William Cushing*, fols. 14[r]–16[r], Harvard Law School, Ms. 4083. According to English law, "every Subject of Common Right may fish with lawful Nets, *&c.* in a Navigable River . . . and the King's Grant cannot bar them thereof." Matthew Bacon, *A New Abridgment of the Law*, 4: 156 (London: 1778).

In Virginia, Governor Beverley Randolph later gave this as his reason for refusing to sign patents conveying islands in the James River—and because "I am not certain, that the law will justify my refusal," he wrote to the attorney general for an opinion. He explained: "Grants have issued for a number of small rocky Islands in James River. . . . These Grants are inten[d]ed to secure to the Grantees the exclusive right of fishing, a right, which appears to me to belong to all the Citizens of the state in Common. Upon this principle I have refused My signature to all patents of this nature, which have been presented to me." Letter from Beverley Randolph to "Attorney General" (April 3, 1790), LVA, Tucker-Ewell Papers, Accession 22397, Item No. 44. James Innes replied: "I have no doubts, whether the property claimed by the grantees . . . be not commons belonging to- and subject to the free use of, all the Citizens of this Commonwealth and indeed of the united States? . . . But, that you as the Governor of the State- are at liberty judicially to enquire into the propriety and legallity of such grants, I am greatly doubtful." He then assured the governor that "should these patents Contravene prior rights- there can be no question but that they may legally set aside" and "upon these grounds, then, I must leave it to your better Judgment, and to the wisdom of the Executive, to determine—if it will—or will not be proper to affix yr official signature?" Letter from James Innes to Governor Beverley Randolph (April 4, 1790), LVA, Gvoernor Beverley Randolph Executive Papers, Misc. Reel 5030.

[2] By the early nineteenth century, Nathan Dane observed that whether "[a] by-law is not good or to be executed when against the public interest or public policy" was "a question often agitated." Nathan Dane, *A General Abridgment and Digest of American Law*, 1: 460 (XX.i.12–13) (Boston: 1823). At least in the colonial period, incidentally, corporations still occasionally presented their by-laws to courts for allowance or disallowance. For example, in 1746 in Boston, the Suffolk County General Sessions resolved that "a By Law made by the Town of Roxbury for preventing danger by Fire which was passed May 5th 1746 was approved & allowed by the Court." Resolution (May term 1746), MSA, Suffolk County General Session of the Peace, Record Book 1743–1749, Reel 4.

that, being subordinate, still had the potential to be judged against law and reason. In retrospect, the early state cases holding colonial statutes void under this test have sometimes been lumped together with decisions holding state statutes void under state constitutions, which would suggest that the judges could hold state statutes unconstitutional for not being in accord with reason or justice. There was, however, a sharp difference between decisions about colonial statutes and those about state statutes, for whereas state enactments were sovereign, colonial enactments were subordinate and thus were generally subject to the common law test of law and reason.

As it happens, though, the element of reason in this test often got dropped, for reasons that hint as to how sovereign law could cut off inquiry about reasonableness. One impediment was Parliament's 1696 statute, which barred any colonial act repugnant to relevant English law. Even more immediately, as already noted, when an act or custom was contrary to constitutional or fundamental law, it could hardly be said to be reasonable. The way in which a colonial statute contrary to the English constitution was void, without reference to reasonableness, can be observed in *Bowman and others, Devisees of Cattel v. Middleton* in 1792. After two men received grants of overlapping tracts of land, the colony's legislature in 1712 intervened with a statute, but rather than confirm the title of the first grantee, the statute sustained that of the second, and the plaintiffs now claimed title under this enactment. Grants of property belonging to another person had traditionally been held void by the English judges, and when done by the king they were unlawful. Although a grant from a subordinate government body, such as a municipality or a colony, might in theory be justified as reasonable, a grant from such a body of property belonging to someone else could not ordinarily be considered reasonable, for like such a grant from the king, it violated the fundamental or constitutional liberty of Englishmen, including that established in Magna Charta.[3] Accordingly, when the South Carolina Court of Common Pleas heard its case in 1792, it apparently evaluated the 1712 statute as one would expect it to assess any other subordinate government act that deprived an individual of his property rights—simply under the element of law, unqualified by the element of reason:

> [T]he plaintiffs could claim no title under the act in question, as it was against common right, as well as against *magna charta,* to take away the freehold of one man and vest it in another, and that, too, to the prejudice of third persons, without compensation, or even a trial by the jury of the country, to determine the right in question. That the act was, therefore, *ipso facto,* void.

[3] See Chapter Nine at note 3 for the irrelevance of the reason justification for infringements of fundamental rights.

Already in 1712, the act had been void under English law, even Magna Charta, and "no length of time could give it validity, being originally founded on erroneous principles."[4]

Another case that held an unconstitutional colonial grant unlawful, without considering whether it was reasonable, was the *Symsbury Case.* This 1785 Connecticut decision concerned a boundary dispute between the towns of Symsbury and Windsor. The defendant held land under a title derived from the proprietors of Hartford and Windsor, who had received their title from the General Assembly in 1686. The defendant's land, however, also lay within the boundaries of an earlier grant, in 1670, from the Assembly to the proprietors of Symsbury. The Assembly had attempted in 1727 to resolve the dispute between Symsbury and Windsor by commissioning a survey, which left title to the disputed border area in the town of Windsor and those who held from it. The next year, the Assembly even adopted this survey in an enactment. Windsor's legislative victory, however, was precarious, for it had been the second grantee, and decades later, in the early 1780s, Jonathan Humphrey and the other proprietors of Symsbury initiated litigation against the unfortunate Thomas Bidwell—questioning his title and thereby challenging the 1686 grant and the 1728 statute sustaining it.

Although scholars speculate that Symsbury's challenge was based on natural law or on Connecticut's post-1776 customary constitution, a government grant of another person's property was a familiar constitutional problem in England, and the records of the case confirm that the decision turned on the English constitution. The lawyers for Symsbury pleaded on behalf of the town that it had "Never . . . Had any Distinct Meeting Resting and Acquiescing in the Affixing of Said Lines" by the surveyors, which was as much as to say that Symsbury had not formally acquiesced in the redrawing of boundaries. When the defendant's lawyers answered "in Barr" that "the Proprietors of . . . Symsbury have Ever Acquiecsed in the Line," Symsbury's lawyers pressed their constitutional argument, now asserting that the town's acquiescence was irrelevant—in other words, that its consent could not alter the legislature's constitutional power. They explained that because of the Assembly's instructions to the surveyors, and because of the consequent survey, Symsbury's "Original Grant By the General Assembly" and "their Deed & pattent are Greatly Altered Infringed Reduced & Curtailed[,] Which was not in the power of the General Assembly

[4] *Bowman & Others, Devisees of Cattel, v. Middleton* (May term, 1792), Bay (S.C.), *Reports,* 1: 254–255. For the meaning of "common right," see note 44 in Chapter Nine.

Constitutionally to Do," and "therefore the Pla[i]ntiffs Say that they Ought not to be barred . . . Without that the Proprietors of . . . Symsbury have Ever Acquiecsed in the Line . . . as the Defendant in his plea in Barr has Alledged." On these pleadings, Oliver Ellsworth and his fellow members of the Superior Court held that the Assembly's act "could not legally operate to curtail the land before granted to the proprietors of the town of Symsbury being prior to the grant made to the towns of Hartford and Windsor."[5] The underlying legal issue was sufficiently straightforward that the opinion did not have to explain that the 1728 colonial statute had been contrary to English law, let alone its additional test of reason for subordinate acts. As in *Bowman v. Middleton,* the case concerned a colonial statute that granted property belonging to another, and what would have been unconstitutional even if done by the king could not be justified as reasonable under the law-and-reason test when done by a subordinate body.

Although subordinate acts and customs had at least the potential to be examined for their reasonableness (as in the seine case), the act of a sovereign body could never be tested for its reasonableness. In England, it will be recalled, the king's absolute prerogatives and more generally his acts in Parliament were sovereign acts, and questions about the reasonableness of such acts were therefore assumed to be within the final judgment of the relevant sovereign body, whether the king or Parliament. This sovereign or absolute power seemed essential within any government, and therefore even when this power eventually was said to be subject to the English constitution, it remained absolute in the sense of being absolutely discretionary and outside any judicial reconsideration of its reasonableness.[6]

[5] For the pleadings in the Superior Court, see the copy contained in the Supreme Court file on defendant's appeal, *Thomas Bidwell v. Jonathan Humphrey,* &c. (Supreme Court of Errors Oct. 1785; decided May 27, 1786), file, page 27, 43, CSA, Supreme Court of Errors, Files. The Supreme Court found "Nothing Erroneous." Ibid., cover sheet. For the Superior Court opinion, see *Symsbury Case,* Kirby, *Reports,* 444 (Superior Court, Aug. term, 1785). In his dissenting opinion in a companion case between the same parties, Governor Huntington only conceded, "I think it ought to be admitted in the case before us, that the proprietors of Symsbury could not have their grant taken from them, or curtailed, even by the General Assembly, without their consent." Ibid., 452. The act of the Assembly consisted of its approval of the surveyor's report. Report on Western Border of Symsbury (Oct. 1728), *Public Records of the Colony of Connecticut,* 214–215 (Hartford: 1873).

Unlike these cases concerning colonial statutes, *Marshall et al. v. Clark* was at least a case in which state court judges held that a *state* statute could not retroactively defeat prior interests in land. On the adjournment of questions from the Supreme Court for the District of Kentucky, the judges of the Virginia Court of Appeals responded that a 1779 Virginia statute "could not have a retroactive operation to defeat a prior entry and location made according to the existing laws at the time." *Marshall et al. v. Clark* (Virginia Court of Appeals 1791), Call, *Reports,* 4: 273. This decision was probably based on the Virginia Declaration of Rights, but it is difficult to reach any strong conclusion without further evidence.

[6] Questions of sovereignty sometime get misunderstood today because of ideas about popu-

American constitutions tightened the legal limits on the executive's sovereign discretion but continued to leave this power free from any judicial second-guessing about its conformity to reason. On the one hand, most state constitutions carefully enumerated executive powers; on the other hand, they left governors free to exercise their specified authority as they pleased. What seemed more worrisome than the unreasonableness of executive acts was the possibility that governors would attempt to argue from English law that they enjoyed a power beyond what they were granted by American constitutions, and the Virginia and Maryland constitutions therefore took the precaution of authorizing executive power only while barring their governors from exercising any royal prerogative—stating that their governors "shall not, under any presence, exercise any power or pre-

lar sovereignty. According to Gordon Wood, "American theorists" relocated the concept of "legal sovereignty" in "the people-at-large"—"a transference that was comprehensible only because of the peculiar experience of American politics" and that created "this vital principle of the sovereignty of the people." Gordon S. Wood, *The Creation of the American Republic 1776–1787,* at 599–600 (Williamsburg: Institute of Early American History and Culture, 1969). Such a notion has certainly flourished in recent legal theory, but both conceptually and historically, there is considerable danger of overstatement. Since the seventeenth century, it had been conventional to distinguish the "supreme" power of the people from the "sovereign" power of the government they established. Some Americans in the 1780s made populist claims about the sovereignty of the people, but this locution was so arresting precisely because it broke from convention to describe the authority of the people in terms more familiar from governmental authority, and the appealing metaphor could not erase the essential theoretical distinction between governmental and popular power—between the civil or political authority exercised by some men over others, which traditionally was said to be sovereignty, and the more general authority exercised by the people, whatever it might be called. As put by one commentator, "[t]here is a wide difference between power being derived from the people and being seated in the people." "Maxims for Republicans," *Kentucky Gazette* (June 5, 1788). Thus, even when Americans were tempted to use the word "sovereignty" to describe the power of the people, they still tended to recognize that the power exercised by the people was different from that exercised by government, and they therefore had to distinguish between different two types or phases of sovereign power. For example, when the New York Assembly prefaced a statute regulating elections by noting the sovereignty of the people, it carefully observed that although sovereignty had its source in the people, it had to be exercised by government: that "the Liberty, Independence and Sovereignty of the People of this State, must necessarily be exercised by the legislative and executive Representatives." An Act to regulate Elections within this State (March 17, 1778), *Laws of the State of New York,* 15 (Poughkeepsie: 1782). When John Dickinson wrote in favor of ratification of the U.S. Constitution, he alluded to "the *supreme sovereignty* of the people"—adding the word "supreme" to indicate that this was a higher sort of sovereignty than that of government. Fabius [John Dickinson], "Observations on the Constitution Proposed by the Federal Convention" (April 19, 1788), in *The Documentary History of the Ratification of the Constitution,* 17: 181, eds. John P. Kaminski et al. (Madison: State Historical Society of Wisconsin, 1981). Similarly, James Sullivan distinguished between the "natural sovereignty" of the people and the "political sovereignty" of government. James Sullivan, *Observations upon the Government of the United States,* 21–23 (Boston: 1791). See also Robert Green McCloskey, ed., *The Works of James Wilson,* 1: 317 (Cambridge: Belknap, 1967). A less qualified rhetoric of popular sovereignty became more widely familiar only in the 1790s, often from the direction of France.

rogative, by virtue of any law, statute or custom of England."[7] As the President of the Virginia Court of Appeals, Edmund Pendleton, observed in 1782 in *Commonwealth v. Caton,* the state's constitution first "restrained the Governor from exercising any Prerogatives of the Crown under the laws & customs of England" and then "proceeds to authorize him, with the advice of Council to grant reprieves or Pardons" and other executive powers.[8]

The U.S. Constitution also focused on the boundaries of executive power rather than the reasonableness with which it would be exercised. The Constitution vested the executive power in the president, and it restricted elements of this power that corresponded to some of the absolute prerogatives once held by the king by enumerating them with subtle adjustments. For example, the Constitution gave the president the power to "require the Opinion, in writing, of the principle Officer in each of the executive Departments" but pointedly did not say he could require such an opinion from the judges. Similarly, it gave the president the power of pardoning, but not in cases of impeachment.[9] The Constitution even reallocated some of the king's absolute prerogatives to Congress. Only Congress, for example, had the power to declare war. The president, moreover, had the power to make treaties and specified appointments only with the advice and consent of two thirds of the Senate.[10] The federal and state constitutions thus followed the English one in bringing all royal or executive powers under the law, and they even sharpened the constraints of the law, but these American constitutions did not add a reasonableness requirement or otherwise deny an executive its final judgment or absolute, sovereign discretion about its acts under law.

American constitutions similarly kept legislative power within constitutional bounds while allowing legislatures to exercise their sovereign discretion. English kings had once claimed a power of making law by proclamation and even a power of legislative interpretation, but the English

[7] Virginia Constitution of 1776; Maryland Constitution of 1776, Article XXXIII.
[8] Transcript of Edmund Pendleton's Notes of his Opinion in *Commonwealth v. Caton, et al.*, Library of Congress, Force Papers, 8710, Series 7E, James McGuire Collection, Correspondence Folders.
[9] This sort of abuse was notorious from *Danby's Case* in 1679.
[10] As noted by one observer, the treaty requirement, like the requirement of advice and consent for appointments, "lessened the authority of the President." *Observations Upon the Proposed Plan of Federal Government,* 43 (Petersburg: 1788). More precisely, the Constitution's treatment of making war and treaties built upon earlier English cautions that ran alongside the law: "The Power of making War or Peace . . . is lodged singly in the King; tho', as my Lord *Hale* says, it ever succeeds best when done by Parliamentary Advice." Bacon, *A New Abridgment of the Law,* 4: 176 ("Prerogative").

constitution had seemed to bar these intrusions on legislative power, and American constitutions even more emphatically placed legislative power in their legislatures. Most prominently, the U.S. Constitution declared that "[a]ll legislative Powers herein granted shall be vested in a Congress of the United States."[11] Although the English Parliament had sometimes claimed a power above the law, the existence in America of constitutions in which the people expressly granted and limited legislative power clarified that this power was only sovereign or absolute and, indeed, was only lawful within constitutional bounds.[12] In short, legislative power, like executive power,

[11] U.S. Constitution, Article I.

[12] The U.S. Constitution expressly brought necessity itself under the law. Necessity had long been understood as the foundation of claims for an authority above the law of the land, but although some Englishmen had spoken in such terms about the absolute royal prerogative and, later, about absolute parliamentary power, others had insisted that all government power was subject to the constitution and that there was thus no power in any part of government above the law of the land. This sort of debate soon repeated itself in America, for state legislatures during the War of Independence often violated their constitutions on grounds of necessity. Recognizing that the American states perhaps could not have won their freedom without at least some of these departures from law, critics acknowledged the necessity but protested the unlawful acts, "least they should be brought into precedent, when no such necessity exists." From this perspective, "[w]e leave them . . . to be justified by the extremity of the times, and hope for better, when such expedients shall be thought unnecessary." *The Proceedings of the Council of Censors of the State of Vermont,* 7, 11 (Windsor: 1786). See also *A Report of the Committee of the Council of Censors,* 6 (Philadelphia: 1784). This sort of compromise, however, was disturbing, for when Americans had rejected Parliament's claim of absolute power, many of them had hoped to establish their own governments entirely under law. The difficulty, however, was inescapable, for not only in a struggle for independence but also in quite ordinary circumstances, it might not be possible for a government to conduct itself in a completely lawful manner. The failures of human language and foresight often left individuals and government little choice but to make claims of necessity, and with a deep sense of these human limitations, the Rev. Witherspoon cautioned his students at Princeton that "[t]here will remain a great number of cases in which . . . rights of necessity are to be used, even in the best regulated civil society"—even "after the most mature deliberation and foresight of probable events, and provision for them by specific laws." John Witherspoon, *An Annotated Edition of Lectures on Moral Philosophy,* 179–180, ed. Jack Scott (Newark: University of Delaware Press). Perhaps, therefore, like individuals, government necessarily sometimes had to violate the laws.

Fortunately, there was a solution. As Witherspoon acknowledged, "[i]f the law described circumstantially what might be done, it would be no longer a right of necessity, but a legal right." Ibid. Such was the path taken by the U.S. Constitution when it enumerated that Congress had a power to make all laws "necessary and proper" for carrying into execution its other enumerated powers—indeed, for carrying out "all other powers vested by this Constitution in the government of the United States, or in any department or officer thereof." U.S. Constitution, Article I, section 8. The Constitution thereby tamed necessity—whether in the legislative, the executive, or the judiciary—by bringing it within the law. The result was that Congress, like Parliament, had absolute discretion as to what in particular was necessary, but it had to conduct itself under the Constitution, which required that its acts done of necessity had to be within the scope of what was "necessary and proper" for carrying out more grounded constitutional powers.

was absolutely within the discretion of its part of government but under the constitution.[13]

Thus, whereas the common law in America still sometimes applied the test of law and reason to corporate by-laws and other subordinate acts, American constitutions left the reasonableness of sovereign acts to be decided by the bodies with sovereign power. In particular, American constitutions left each type of sovereign act to its own branch of government. This allocation of sovereign discretionary power seemed inevitable, for as explained by the erstwhile judge James Sullivan, there could not "be any such thing as a sovereignty which is not absolute as to the subjects within its extension."[14] The obligation of an act of a sovereign rested on the authority it received from its people, and within the scope of its constitutional authority, the sovereign alone was judge of the reasonableness of its acts.

Justice and Utility

Judges were at times acutely conscious that the law of the land might depart from higher moral and practical ends, such as justice and utility, but within their familiar ideals of law and judicial duty, they could only seek justice and utility as permitted by the law of the land—the law that had authority. As a result, although they could sometimes avoid minor injustices and inconvenience through mechanisms such as equity and equitable interpretation, they could not hold a government act unlawful for being unjust, not useful, or otherwise unreasonable.

[13] One of the more specific limits was the habeas corpus clause, which the U.S. Constitution enumerated with the other limits on the power of Congress, specifying that "the Writ of Habeas Corpus shall not be suspended, unless when in Cases of Rebellion or Invasion the public Safety may require it." U.S. Constitution, Article I, section 9. Habeas corpus had been protected by acts of Parliament, and therefore after the Declaration of Rights in 1689 ended the king's suspending power the writ could only be suspended by Parliamentary legislation—as when in 1777 Parliament adopted the first of a series of suspension acts aimed at Americans.

It was well understood in England that Parliament might occasionally have to suspend habeas corpus, and when American legislatures also adopted such measures, it became clear that if suspension statutes were sometimes necessary, they needed to have constitutional authorization. Otherwise governments would face the sort of problem encountered by Pennsylvania. The Assembly had suspended the writ "to secure the persons, and restrain the traiterous practices of the disaffected, when legal evidence could not be obtained against them," but because the state lacked a constitutional power authorizing the legislature to suspend habeas corpus, the suspension was illegal. As put by a committee of the Council of Censors, *"the acts of Assembly, which restrained for a time, the full operation of the writ of* HABEAS CORPUS, *are infringements of the Constitution." A Report of the Committee of the Council of Censors* [*on the Legislative Branch*], 24 (Philadelphia: 1784).

[14] Sullivan, *Observations upon the Government of the United States,* 23.

The way in which young Americans struggled to reconcile their law with their sense of justice can be observed with unusual clarity in the opinions of the students who mooted practice cases in the society they called the Institutio Legalis. Meeting in Newark and Elizabethtown, the students took turns presenting arguments, giving judgments, and occasionally reconsidering judgments on appeal. These mock lawyers and judges took different perspectives on how law could avoid injustice, not least in cases involving slavery, but as will be seen in Appendix II, where their views are reproduced in detail, the students tended to recognize that judges had to decide cases in accord with the law of the land. Sometimes, indeed, the students seem to have deliberately set themselves cases that would require them to wrestle with the problem of the law's injustice.

In the meantime, the difficult demands of judicial duty can be more briefly illustrated by a case decided in 1787 by Edward Shippen—President of the Philadelphia Court of Common Pleas. The case concerned the ship *Anna,* which brought a cargo of wine to Philadelphia. The mate had secretly brought his own shipment of wine on board, and upon arrival he furtively unloaded it—with serious consequences for the owner. Pennsylvania's revenue law provided that a vessel was to be forfeited if its goods were unloaded before their entry with the revenue collector, and although this "had been repeatedly called a hard law," Shippen instructed the jury that "[t]he Legislature has thought that nothing else would answer, and the Judges and the jurors are equally bound to obedience." He feared the jurors might fail to do their duty, and he therefore explained that there was no escaping the harsh statute. "If indeed the law was doubtful or latitudinal, admitting one interpretation, which would be just, and another which would be unjust, it would become us to prefer the former," but the intent was all too clear. Thus, although "the policy of the Legislature seems to bear hard on the subject, we are not to judge, and determine on its propriety—that is a matter for the deliberation of those who made the law—and however unjust it seems, we must acquiesce, or there must be a dissolution of society."[15]

[15] *Phile qui tam v. The Ship Anna* (Court of Common Pleas, Philadelphia County, July 1787), Dallas, *Reports,* 1: 207. The case was complicated by the more direct failures of the owners and the master, who deliberately filed a false manifest, but these matters apparently arose as evidence rather than as the central legal issue in the case. The jury returned a verdict for the informants. Ibid., 208.

Another case involved a dispute among persons claiming land owned by the proprietors of Pennsylvania. Chief Justice M'Kean of Pennsylvania observed that in such circumstances the agent of the proprietors had a power to grant the land to whom he pleased. The proprietors and their agent had "always felt an equitable obligation" to resolve such disputes in favor of the person who had settled on the land and made improvements, but M'Kean emphasized that if the proprietors, being the owners, "should not chuse to do so, the Court cannot

Equity could relieve men in some limited circumstances, but since the seventeenth century it had been framed to avoid challenging the duty of judges to decide in accord with the law of the land. In England, it thereby came to be considered an additional set of rules, and this conception of equity also became familiar in America—as when a student in the Institutio Legalis argued a moot case on the basis of "a Rule in Equity."[16] It will be seen that some judges who lacked professional training took another point of view, but Americans who studied law apparently tended to learn (in the words William Plumer copied from Lord Mansfield) that a court of equity "is as much bound by positive rules & general maxims, concerning property, as a court of law."[17] This regularized character of modern equity could be pursued with different degrees of rigor, and Thomas Jefferson, having a Whig distaste for discretion, emphasized that equity "shall not interpose in any case which does not come within a general description and admit of redress by a general and practicable rule." Thus, when "a Chancellor pretends that a case is distinguished from all others, it is thought better that that singular case should go without remedy, than that he should be at liberty to cover partial decisions under pretense of singular circumstances, which ingenious men can always invent."[18]

---

interfere." He explained to the jury that the court could not intrude upon the decisions of the proprietors:

> An attempt of that kind, would shake the very foundations of property; and render a verdict, or judgment, not a solemn determination on evidence and law, but an instrument of favour to the party, for whom the Court or Jury should entertain a predilection. But we must remember, that we are bound by oath, to administer justice according to the laws, without partiality, or prejudice.

McCurdy v. Potts, et al. (Supreme Court of Pennsylvania 1788), Dallas, *Reports,* 2: 99.

16 "Chancellor" Nehemiah Wade in *James Sterling v. Henry Moreland* (Chancery, Dec. 1783), *Proceedings of The Institutio Legalis,* 53, New Jersey Historical Society, Ms Group 214.

17 Extracts from Law-Writers, 99 (entry dated Dec. 12, 1787), William Plumer Legal Papers, Reel 19 (citing *Doe, ex dismiss. Long v. Laming* [K.B. 1760], Burrow, *Reports,* 2: 1108). *Doe* was the occasion for Mansfield's interpretation of the Rule in *Shelley's Case,* but it is not clear that Plumer paid much attention to the case or the judge, for he copied what he wrote from the reporter's Table of Principal Matters. Burrow, *Reports,* 2: sig. Pp[v] (Dublin: 1785). In the first half of the 1770s, Elisha Boudinot jotted down from English sources: "There cannot be one Rule of Property in the Court of Chancery and another in a Court of Law." Elisha Boudinot, Notes of Cases in Practice, 37, Princeton University, Rare Books and Special Collections, Manuscript Division, Thorne Collection of Elias Boudinot, C0001, Box 3, Folder 2.

18 Letter from Thomas Jefferson to Philip Mazzei (Nov. 1785), in *Papers of Thomas Jefferson,* 9: 69, ed. Julian P. Boyd (Princeton: Princeton University Press, 1954). It almost went without saying, moreover, that a court of chancery "cannot interpose in any case against the ex-

Judges could discern the common law where it was unclear by looking up to natural law, and in states (such as Pennsylvania) that lacked courts of equity, common law judges had especially good reason to resolve uncertainties by considering the principles of equity, but all of this was understood to be done within the framework of what was already settled. As summarized by Chief Justice Thomas M'Kean of Pennsylvania, when "there is no positive Law, no adjudged case, nor established rule, or order, to direct the Court . . . we must be guided by the principles of the law; by conscience, that infallible monitor within every judge's breast, and the original and eternal rules of justice. For equity is part of the law of *Pennsylvania*."[19] This sort of reliance on natural law and equity was very appealing as a means of avoiding injustice within the bounds of authority, but it was not a roving commission to do justice beyond the law—whether beyond its particular rules or more generally beyond its domain.

Similar to this equitable discernment of common law was the equitable interpretation of statutes, whether done at law or in equity. On the old assumption that equitable reasoning could reveal what the lawmakers presumably intended, M'Kean recited that "[w]here the intention of the Legislature or the Law is doubtful, and not clear, the Judges ought to interpret the law to be, what is most consonant to *equity*, and least *inconvenient*"—meaning, in accord with long tradition, what was inconvenient in law

---

press letter and intention of the legislature. If the legislature means to enact an injustice, however palpable, the court of Chancery is not the body with whom a correcting power is lodged." More generally, when writing of "the equity of the law," Jefferson explained that judges did not "extend the operation of laws beyond those cases which are clearly within the intention of the legislators," and that "[t]his intention is to be collected principally from the words of the law: only where these are ambiguous they are permitted to gather further evidence from the history of the times when the law was made and the circumstances which produced it." Ibid., 68–69.

19 *Pollard v. Shaaffer* (Supreme Court of Pennsylvania, Sept. 1787), Dallas, *Reports,* 1: 211 (denying recovery for enemy destruction of leased premises where the destruction was not contemplated by the parties—notwithstanding an express provision in the lease that the lessee should keep the premises in good repair). Similarly, in actions of debt on obligation, it had long been the "constant practice" of the Pennsylvania Supreme Court to allow defendants to plead payment and then give evidence of certain defenses that in England were only possible in equity, for as the Court explained, "there being no Court of Chancery in this Province, there is a necessity, in order to prevent a failure of Justice, to let the Defendants . . . prove mistake or want of consideration." *Swift v. Hawkins and others* (Supreme Court of Pennsylvania, 1768), ibid., 1: 17. Even this sort of limited recognition of equitable claims provoked the young John Dickinson to complain that in Pennsylvania, "where there is no court of equity," there was a danger that "every court assumes the power of legislation," thus assuming an "extensive & arbitrary authority." H. Trevor Colbourn, "A Pennsylvania Farmer at the Court of King George: John Dickinson's London Letters, 1754–1756," *Pennsylvania Magazine of History and Biography,* 451 (1962).

rather than the particular case.[20] Yet the presumption about intent that required equitable interpretation also limited it. Even "Courts of Chancery, and the general principles of equity, can never be allowed to contradict or defeat the express provisions of a statute," for as M'Kean explained, "in the interpretation of laws, recourse must always be had to the meaning of the Legislature."[21] There was often a tension between the claims for justice and those for intent, and it will soon become apparent that judges sometimes strained to find uncertainty, pressing against a statute's expressed intent in order to establish space for its presumed, more just intent, but it is difficult to find judges who admitted they were defying a statute's expressed intent, let alone who held this out as desirable.

As for the example of Mansfield, his learning on commercial matters was widely admired, but not his equitable freedom with the law of the land. Americans read Junius's letters denouncing Mansfield for his assault on English liberty, and although they cited his decisions on commercial law when these elaborated what the common law left uncertain, they often shared the English Whig reaction to Mansfield's eager use of lacunae and exceptions to unravel long-settled common law doctrines. A glimpse of how these conflicting attitudes filtered down to students survives in a commercial case mooted by the Institutio Legalis on a hypothetical special verdict. "Judge" William Griffith began by acknowledging that if he had known "the principal question originally intended to be litigated on the verdict was so fully settled by Lord Mansfield," he "should have directed the council to confine themselves" to another "part of the verdict." Griffith explained, however, that "the council for the deft seemed to doubt the legality of Lord Mansfield's decision in the above case," and Griffith therefore proceeded to analyze the question.[22] Both Mansfield's Toryism and his distaste for the hard boundaries of the common law did much to stimulate Whig fears, and one American publication imagined that the devil himself had asked his "trusty servants Bute and Mansfield" to educate George III for diabolical service. Toward the end of this satire, the hellish Mansfield sycophantically asked George to "recollect my long and faithful services," including how "I have

[20] *Kerlin's Lessee v. Bull et al.* (Supreme Court of Pennsylvania 1786), Dallas, *Reports,* 1: 178, citing Vaughan, *Reports,* 38, 285.

[21] *Hollingsworth v. Ogle et al.* (Supreme Court of Pennsylvania, April 1788), Dallas, *Reports,* 1: 258–259. He also noted that "even where there is no Act of Assembly to direct us, the common law . . . often furnishes a guide to which we are bound to yield attention and obedience." Ibid.

[22] *John Carr, assignee of David Andrews v. Noah Jones* (March 1787), *Proceedings of The Institutio Legalis,* 122, New Jersey Historical Society, Ms Group 214.

twisted the law into all shapes and forms to answer royal purposes."[23] With scarcely less passion, Jefferson worried that Mansfield aimed to render English law "more incertain under pretence of rendering it more reasonable."[24]

In New Hampshire some of the untrained judges occasionally did justice at the expense of the rules of law, and it may be doubted whether they thereby did their duty. Looking back on such decisions, some lawyers said that these judges had pursued a rough "equity." For example, William Plumer recalled of one New Hampshire judge that he "was predisposed to sacrifice law to equity. But his views of equity were not those of definite and certain principles of equity, which do not infringe the principles of law." Instead, he adopted an equity that "relieves suitors from the obligation of express and implied contracts where neither statute or common law interferes."[25] Similarly, some of the untrained judges instructed juries to follow their "common sense"—as when Superior Court Judge John Dudley once told a jury "to do justice between the parties, not by any quirks of the law out of Coke or Blackstone, books that I never read and never will, but by common sense and common honesty as between man and man."[26] It is no surprise that when professional and mostly Federalist lawyers flaunted their superior technical knowledge, a lay judge might express resentment and restore himself before the jurors by summarizing the law in a populist manner—indeed, under a label that perhaps alluded to the work of Thomas Paine.[27] Yet such instructions and other instances of the "equity" done by lay judges were the object of ridicule among the bar and are known today almost entirely from later memoirs in which the lawyers had the last laugh. Inevitably, judicial practice often departed from expectations about law and judicial duty, and it is to be expected that untrained judges, being human, would sometimes elevate their ignorance to an ideal, but although they

[23] *A Dialogue Between the Devil and George III. Tyrant of Britain* (Boston: 1782), in *Political Sermons of the American Founding Era,* 691 and 705, ed. Ellis Sandoz (Indianapolis: Liberty Fund, 1991).

[24] Letter from Thomas Jefferson to Philip Mazzei (Nov. 1785), in *Papers of Thomas Jefferson,* 9: 71.

[25] Biography of Paine Wingate, "Biographical Sketches . . . from the Manuscript of William Plumer," in *Early State Papers of New Hampshire,* 21: 827, ed. Albert Stillman Batchellor (Concord: Ira C. Evans, 1892).

[26] William Plumer, Jr., *Life of William Plumer,* 154 (Boston: 1857), discussed by John Phillip Reid, *Controlling the Law: Legal Politics in Early National New Hampshire,* 25 (DeKalb: Northern Illinois Press, 2004). Although the younger Plumer was recounting what he heard from his father, it is consistent with the other evidence.

[27] For example, it was recounted that "the elder Judge Livermore . . . having no law learning himself . . . did not like to be pestered with it at his courts." *Memoir, Autobiography and Correspondence of Jeremiah Mason,* 28 (Boston: Boston Law Book, 1917).

thus contended with the lawyers, they could not displace the ideals of the common law. In fact, as will be seen, even the judges of the Inferior Courts of New Hampshire revealed technical sophistication in their constitutional decisions of the 1780s and 1790s. What is most remarkable about state courts, even near the frontiers, is the degree to which they carefully followed traditional legal forms, whether in their writs, their records, or their reasoning.[28]

Judges sometimes acknowledged utilitarian considerations, but for the most part only as evidence of intent, equity, or the common law. In the Institutio Legalis, Jonathan Rhea argued that "the Laws respecting trade, are of universal concern" and "that every thing, which respect trade must receive the most liberal Construction"—in particular, that "Policies of Assurance, being greatly for the Advantage of Trade, are favored in Law" and that "Courts have always expounded them liberally, for the benefit of the Insured, and as it were leaned against the Insurers."[29] Insurance, however, was a matter of commercial law, in which the common law was understood to adopt the subordinate custom of merchants to the extent it was consistent with law and reason or (as sometimes reformulated) the public interest.[30] A more broadly applicable assumption about utility was the familiar view that considerations of inconvenience could illuminate unsettled questions, whether issues of common law or legislative intent. For example, when lawyers in *Commonwealth v. Caton* argued that the Virginia Court of Appeals lacked jurisdiction in the case, they noted the potential for incon-

[28] As Gordon Wood observes, "colonial adjudication was not simply a matter of applying some kind of crude, untechnical law to achieve common-sense 'frontier' justice," and "even as early as the late seventeenth century in new back-country counties the quality of legal procedures was remarkably sophisticated; and by the middle of the eighteenth century, in Massachusetts and New York at least, colonial jurisprudence approached very closely that of the English." Wood, *The Creation of the American Republic,* at 297. American knowledge of common law, moreover, came not only from books but also more directly from the Inns of Court, where more than one hundred Americans studied in the quarter-century before Independence. Colbourn, "A Pennsylvania Farmer at the Court of King George," 244. In a 1786 New Hampshire case, it was argued by one of the lawyers that "Justices in general know not the difference between *Case* & *Trespass,*" but this was apparently said on the assumption that regular judges would know the difference. *Moulton v. Morey* (Rockingham County Superior Court, April 1786), [Reports of Cases], 3, *William Plumer Papers,* Mfm, Reel 19, Legal Papers.

[29] *Blair McClenegan v. John Nisbit & John Bayard Insurers* (Feb. 1784), *Proceedings of The Institutio Legalis,* 60, New Jersey Historical Society, Ms Group 214. Chief Justice Lee had said that insurance policies were to be "construed largely, for the benefit of trade, and for the insured." *Tierney v. Etherington* (Guildhall 1743), as quoted by Mansfield in *Pelly v. Royal Exchange Assurance* (K.B. 1757), Burrow, *Reports,* 1: 349.

[30] For the conventional treatment of insurance as part of the law merchant and its adoption as custom at common law, see Bacon, *A New Abridgment of the Law,* 3: 583–585.

veniences in future decisions, and although President Pendleton concluded that his court did have jurisdiction, he recognized that the Court of Appeals had to be especially careful to assess such considerations, because its decisions would be final: "Arguments of inconvenience are properly considered in determining a new case, especially in this Court, whose decisions will in a manner fix the law."[31]

Although inconvenience was relevant for discerning the law where it was uncertain, lawyers generally were unwilling to allow utility to rival the law of the land as the measure of judicial duty—as can be observed in North Carolina. In December 1786, when members of the North Carolina General Assembly proposed a bill that would have created a court of chancery, they ambitiously provided that in all matters brought before the court, the chancellor with the assistance of "any two or more of the Judges of the supreme Courts of law . . . shall finally decree According to equity and public utility." This was bold, and when the Committee on the Administration of Justice revised the bill, it dropped the words "and public utility."[32]

The extent to which Americans hoped to attain justice and the general welfare through their exercise of lawmaking authority was never more saliently enunciated than in the U.S. Constitution. This document began: "We the people of the United States, in order to . . . establish justice" and "promote the general Welfare . . . do ordain and establish this Constitution for the United States of America." The people thereby declared that they were seeking justice and utility through their exercise of lawmaking authority. Indeed, by ordaining their law, they established it as the measure of the justice and utility that would have the obligation of law and that would thus be within the duty of the judges.

Of course, the people could exercise their authority unjustly, but as to such problems the people were the judge. On account of the failings of human nature, human justice appeared to require a system of authority, and within such a system there was always a danger that the people, being merely human, would will what was unreasonable or unjust. The people, however, were the only earthly judge of how they should exert their law-

[31] Transcript of Edmund Pendleton's Notes of his Opinion in *Commonwealth v. Caton, et al.*, Library of Congress, Force Papers, 8702, Series 7E, James McGuire Collection, Correspondence Folders. In contrast, he noted that the General Court, when deciding whether or not to adjourn the case to the Court of Appeals, had the task of "weighing the difficulty & Importance of the case in one scale, and the delay & other inconveniences in the other," but this was a decision that was "left" to them by the legislature. "This direction the legislature have in my opinion given them, & I have neither power nor inclination to take it from them." Ibid., 8703–8704.

[32] A Bill to Amend and Alter the Court System, 21, NCA, General Assembly, Session Records 1786–1787, Box 5, folder House (Dec. 16, 1786) Bill to Amend the Court System.

making will. They had both the underlying coercive force in their society and the primary lawmaking authority, and therefore, against their unreason and injustice, the only recourse seemed to be an appeal to the people themselves and ultimately to God.

Equitable Interpretation: Rutgers v. Waddington

It is necessary to return to the doctrine of equitable interpretation and to linger in its vicinity for the remainder of this chapter, for no common law doctrine occasioned greater aspirations for the pursuit of justice through law. Some federally inclined Americans, it will be seen, hoped to develop the doctrine into a broader power to do justice—notably in *Rutgers v. Waddington.* Their approach, however, threatened the authority and intent of state legislatures, and therefore rather than expand the doctrine of equitable interpretation, their efforts served mostly to remind Americans why equitable interpretation had to be founded on intent.

The degree to which in America, as in England, equitable interpretation only avoided such injustice as was not intended can be observed in the 1789 South Carolina case of *Ham v. M'Claws.* A 1788 South Carolina statute barred the importation of slaves into the state, and the state's attorney general sought to enforce this act against two children, aged four and eight, who came to South Carolina from Honduras with their slaves. They could not have known about the passage of the act, because it was adopted while they were "on the high seas" on their way to America, and their counsel therefore argued that "it would be one of the hardest cases ever decided in a court of justice, were the negroes in question, taken from the children to whom they belonged." The lawyers for the children laid the foundation that "the act was obscurely penned," and they then suggested that in light of the injustice of the statute's general words, "the intention of the legislature, must have been to exempt those negroes from forfeiture, who were upon the way, or on the point of arriving in the State." In support of this equitable interpretation, the lawyers made the familiar claim that the injustice of the statute would otherwise render it "null and void."[33]

The judges agreed and thereby avoided the injustice of depriving the little children of their slaves. Echoing the lawyers, the judges began by reciting that "statutes passed against the plain and obvious principles of common right, and common reason, are absolutely null and void, *as far as they are calculated to operate against these principles.*" The judges then, in the ac-

[33] *Ham v. M'Claws & Wife* (South Carolina Superior Court 1789), Bay, *Reports,* 1: 91–94.

customed manner, used their claim about what was void in conscience to justify their equitable interpretation:

> [W]e would not do the legislature, who passed this act, so much injustice as to sit here, and say, that it was their intention to make a forfeiture of property brought in here, as this was. We are therefore bound to give such a construction to this enacting clause of the act of 1788, as will be consistent with justice, and the dictates of natural reason, though contrary to the strict letter of the law.[34]

Notoriously, slavery itself might be considered inconsistent with justice and natural law. The doctrine of equitable interpretation, however, merely avoided the injustice that the legislature did not intend. Thus, while the doctrine could preclude the forfeiture of slaves, it could not bar slavery, for this was an injustice about which the legislature's intent was all too clear. Nor was this merely a southern application of the doctrine. Northern judges troubled by slavery also recognized that equitable interpretation could only avoid unintended injustices, not the larger, deliberate one.[35]

What differed between North and South in such cases was that whereas northern judges usually worried about the injustice to slaves that equitable interpretation usually left in place, the southern judges in *Ham v. M'Claws* worried about the injustice to the owners that equitable interpretation could cure. Ironically, however, it is *Ham* that usually gets cited by scholars as an illustration of the power of judges to do justice.[36] As in later periods of American history, inequity was perceived differently by different judges, often depending on prevailing sentiments in their section of the country, and *Ham* thus offers a hint as to why equitable interpretation was only a very

[34] Bay, *Reports,* 1: 96. Although the lawyers said that statutes against the principles of common right and justice were "null and void," they merely used this to argue that "the judges were bound to give such a construction to acts, as would comport with the intention of the law makers," even if it were "*contrary* to the *letter* of the act." Ibid., 94. As in England, this sort of statement about what was void in the court of conscience could not be taken literally in a court of law. Instead, it supplied the moral basis for construing the statute in accord with the legislature's presumed intent. See Chapter Two and Appendix I.

[35] For a northern illustration, see Appendix II. A sort of charitable interpretation was also used to free slaves after their masters allowed them to join the fight against Britain. A judge in one of these cases explained that "as at the time of the enlistment, no person but a freeman could by the resolutions of Congress be enlisted into the Continental Army, the consent of his master to the enlistment, amounted in law to a compleat emancipation." Correspondence (New Haven), *Independent Journal* (NY) (Dec. 22, 1784). In other words, if the consent was ambiguous, it had to be charitably understood in accord with the congressional resolutions.

[36] For a critique of similar moral confusion about South Carolina contract law, see A. W. B. Simpson, "The Horwitz Thesis and the History of Contracts," *University of Chicago Law Review,* 46: 600 (1979).

contingent opportunity for the sort of justice that would stand the test of time.

Still, among those who resented statutory injustices, there was much to be said for equitable interpretation, for it left judges opportunities that they could not so easily find when they held a statute void. Judges could not simply declare a statute void of obligation because it was unjust, but they could sometimes conclude that because the statute was indeterminate, one had to rely on a charitable presumption about the intent in order to understand the duty to which the statute gave obligation. Some judges even thought they could rely on the generality of a statute's words to conclude that it was indeterminate and thus in need of charitable interpretation. With or without this sort of boot-strap argument, there was always a danger that when judges relied on equitable reasoning to avoid injustice, they might dexterously pursue a legislature's presumed intent to escape its expressed intent, and this had already led English lawyers to caution that the doctrine had to be used with care.[37] Yet far from regretting such risks, some ambitious Federalists in the 1780s contemplated the possibility that judges could use an expanded version of equitable interpretation to moderate illiberal state statutes. These Federalists understood that judges could not hold state laws void for being unjust, but they imagined that judges could instead avoid local injustice through equitable interpretation. What held out hopes for a judicial amelioration of illiberal state statutes, however, would also stimulate fears about a judicial invasion of legislative power.

Nothing did more to elicit these hopes and fears than *Rutgers v. Waddington,* and therefore to understand why equitable interpretation could not openly become an avenue for the sort of justice that reached beyond

[37] See Chapter Two. Like other presumptions about interpretation, equitable interpretation was a matter of law—as can be observed in an advisory opinion by Attorney General Edmund Randolph of Virginia. A Virginia statute on military personnel provided for payments to the "line," and in 1783 the state auditors needed to know who was qualified to receive such amounts. In particular, the auditors worried whether the "line" included military staff, and they therefore sought the Attorney General's opinion. Randolph responded that "altho' in the strictness of military language, the term *'line'* may not comprehend the staff; yet the equity of the construction does comprehend them." In adopting this equitable construction, moreover, he opined according to law:

> Whatever difficulties arise upon the laws, can be best determined by the legislature. I now go upon rules of legal construction only: and therefore if you conceive that the legislature did not intend to let in the staff, it would be proper to mention the matter to them. But upon the laws, I think the staff of the state intitled.

Opinion of Edmund Randolph to Auditors with respect to state military staff (April 18, 1783), LVA, Auditor of Public Accounts, A.G.'s Opinions, RG 48, Box 138.

legislative intent, it is necessary to examine *Rutgers* in detail.[38] The case had its beginnings in 1776, when British forces under General Howe took New York City. Among the many patriots who fled was Elizabeth Rutgers, a widow who owned a substantial brewing business on Maiden Lane. Although her brewhouse and malthouse were soon ransacked, a pair of British merchants subsequently occupied and repaired the buildings—at first with the permission of a civilian officer of the British Treasury, the Commissary General, and then under the authority of a military officer, the British Commander in Chief.[39]

The law of nations was understood to be a largely an elaboration of the law of nature as applied to nations rather than individuals, and therefore, not surprisingly, the Continental treatise writers on the subject disagreed on some important issues, including whether private individuals, acting with military sanction, could occupy private enemy property during wartime. On its own, the law of nations, like the law of nature, lacked authority and thus was not considered legally binding at common law, but if one took the view that the law of nations allowed militarily sanctioned occupation, and if this rule was understood to have been adopted as a justification at common law, Rutgers and other Americans whose property had been occupied would have difficulty recovering damages. This eventually became more than a theoretical question, for in the spring of 1783 the Americans and the British signed the Treaty of Peace, and by November the British evacuated New York City.

Seeking to clear away the possible impediments to claims against the British occupiers, the New York legislature in March 1783 passed the Trespass Act, which left the common law remedy untouched but created a parallel, statutory trespass action for occupied or injured property. For purposes of this statutory cause of action, the act expressly eliminated any

38 This case was elegantly documented by Henry B. Dawson in the nineteenth century and more thoroughly by Julius Goebel in the twentieth. Henry B. Dawson, ed., *The Case of Elizabeth Rutgers versus Joshua Waddington* (Morrisania, N.Y: 1866); Julius Goebel, Jr., ed., *The Law Practice of Alexander Hamilton; Documents and Commentary,* 1: 282 (New York: Columbia University Press, 1964).

On account of Hamilton's briefs, in which Hamilton urged that the Tresspass Act was unconstitutional, *Rutgers* is often understood as a precursor of judicial review, and it is even sometimes taken to suggest that judges were free to hold statutes void for violating natural law or at least the law of nations. Contributing to such views is the scholarship of Julius Goebel, who lays out many important details about *Rutgers* but who concludes that the case "stands out" as "a marker on the long road that led to the ultimate foundation of the American doctrine of judicial review." Goebel, ed., *The Law Practice of Alexander Hamilton,* 1: 282, 297–298.

39 Ibid., 1: 290.

justification based on military authority, stating that "no Defendant or Defendants shall be admitted to plead, in Justification, any military Order or Command whatever, of the Enemy, for such Occupancy, Injury, Destruction, Purchase or Receipt, nor to give the same in Evidence on the general issue."[40] To patriots eager to recoup their losses, no words were clearer or more welcome.

Elizabeth Rutgers took the opportunity to bring an action under the Trespass Act against Joshua Waddington—the agent for the merchants who had occupied her brewery. She brought her action in the Mayor's Court of New York City. Modeled on the Mayor's Court of London, its judges consisted of municipal officers—Mayor James Duane, various aldermen, and a professional judge, the City Recorder, Richard Varick.

One of the lawyers defending Waddington was the brilliant young Alexander Hamilton, who believed that retribution against Tories was illiberal and thus contrary to American interests. Hamilton hoped Americans would have the "liberality" to overcome their local and anti-British prejudices and would thereby reorient their society around a cosmopolitan federal government. Worried about ungenerous measures—of which the Trespass Act was only one—he urged New Yorkers to avoid falling into narrow animosities against their former enemies. To this end, he declared that "[t]he world has its eye upon America" and that "[t]he noble struggle we have made in the cause of liberty, has occasioned a kind of revolution in human sentiment."[41]

There will be occasion to see that Mayor James Duane was deeply sympathetic to such views, but it is enough for now to observe that he went to great lengths to reach his conclusion in *Rutgers v. Waddington.* He began by sidelining the other judges, and he then wrote an opinion that strained conventional assumptions about the law.[42] A range of questions were raised

[40] An Act for granting a more effectual Relief in Cases of certain Trespasses (March 17, 1783), *Laws of the State of New-York, Passed at Kingston, in the Second Meeting of the Sixth Session of the Legislature,* 283–284, chapter 31 ([1783]).

[41] [Alexander Hamilton], *A Second Letter from Phocion to the Considerate Citizens of New-York,* 21, 40–41 (New York: 1784). Although these statements were made in opposition to another antiloyalist proposal, they clearly also represented his views about the Trespass Act. For the role of liberal sentiments in the formation of the nation, see Philip Hamburger, "Liberality," *Texas Law Review,* 78: 1215 (2000).

[42] The lengths to which he would go were evident already in his efforts to ensure that he alone would write the Court's opinion. The aldermen who sat on the Court did not attend closely to their duties in the case, and Duane was all too pleased to take up the slack. The Recorder was suffering from ill heath, and Duane wrote to the aldermen that it was his "hope to be able to form an Opinion" the following week. He self-consciously emphasized that "I shall be in no Objection" if the other judges wanted to participate, but at the same time he carefully suggested to them the risk of delay and how much work they could spare

in the case, but Duane eventually rested on two: the military authorization under the law of nations and the Trespass Act's bar to any justification based on such authorization. It was in the course of giving his opinion on this pair of issues that Duane used equitable interpretation for liberal ends and thereby provoked all the more clarity about the doctrine's limitations.

Duane attempted, on the first question, to show that the justification based on military authority, although drawn from the law of nations, had legal obligation in New York. The law of nations was open to all the risks familiar from reasoning about the law of nature, but Duane eagerly sifted through the views of "distinguished philosophers"—ranging from Grotius and Pufendorf to Wolfius and Vattel—and explained, as if he were a scholar rather than a judge, that "it can be no more an objection or reproach to the law of nations, than it is to any other science (for all partake of imperfection)–that a difference of sentiments and opinions should be discovered among different authors." He candidly said that he hoped to "use" his review of their different perspectives "to justify the preference, which we shall give to Mr. Vattel, in points where we shall find him at variance with other writers"—Vattel being the critical choice because he had most clearly suggested that during an occupation, military permission could justify individuals in enjoying the benefit of enemy property. Quite apart from the various opinions about the law of nations, Rutgers' lawyers objected that "these states are not bound by the *customary and voluntary laws of nations,* any fur-

---

themselves. Letter of James Duane to the Aldermen of the City of New York (Aug. 14, 1784), New York Historical Society, James Duane Papers. In the event, Mayor Duane did not even wait to complete his opinion before giving judgment. Goebel, ed., *The Law Practice of Alexander Hamilton,* 1: 307, note 68.

After the Mayor held against Rutgers, a committee was appointed at Mrs. Vandewater's tavern to protest the decision, and recognizing what Duane had done, the committee interrogated the aldermen: "Had or had not the Mayor your consent that the subject should be deprived of any part of the remedy which the Trespass Law gives, by its literal construction?" The responses were rather defensive. Alderman Broome said he was not present for the case and, having his own "case depending on the Trespass Law," he "did not chuse to judge of it"; Neilson "did not conceive himself adequate to judge of the matter, and therefore submitted it wholly to the Mayor and Recorder"; Gilbert ambiguously said that Rutgers was "a proper plaintiff, and was entitled to damages"; Lott said he "did not attend the whole of the trial, but was asked his opinion by the Mayor or Recorder" and answered that "the plaintiff should have the full benefit of the law, agreeable to its literal construction"; Blag and Ivers not only took this position but also added that they "were much surprised to find that any distinction of time was held up in favor of the defendant; that they understood from the Mayor's information to them just before judgment was given, that full damages were to be allowed the plaintiff, for the whole time Waddington possessed the property of Rutgers, agreeable to the opinion of a jury." *Columbian Herald* (Charleston) (Nov. 23, 1784). Ivers, as it happens, was a plaintiff in another Trespass Act action, in which Hamilton was counsel for the defendant. Ibid., 1: 301.

ther than as either of them, has adopted or engrafted them." Duane, however, thought this "fully answered" by the clause of the New York Constitution in which "the common law is declared to be part of the law of the land"—his explanation being that "the *jus gentium* is a branch of the common law."[43] In fact, only some elements of the law of nations had been adopted in the common law, but this did not stop Duane.

The second step was to avoid the bar created by the Trespass Act, and this was where equitable interpretation entered Duane's argument. Hamilton had argued that the judges should hold the Trespass Act void because it

[43] *Arguments and Judgment of the Mayor's Court of the City of New-York in a Cause Between Elizabeth Rutgers and Joshua Waddington,* 23 (New York: 1784).

It had been widely understood that the civil law, the law of nations, and other "foreign" law enjoyed obligation in common law jurisdictions only to the extent it had been adopted within the law of the land. A colonial clergyman summarized the standard common law approach when he said that although "many of the rules of the Roman civil law, are received and adopted by universal consent in England, and are obligatory upon the people," the English accepted the obligation of such rules "not from the authority of the Roman Emperors that ordained them, but from their own act in receiving and adopting them." [Moses Mather], *America's Appeal to the Impartial World,* 42 (Hartford: 1775). Similarly, it was said that the authority of admiralty "is merely derivative, from the sufferance and permission of the Courts of common law," and "the Courts of common law maintain a constant controul over the Courts of civil law jurisdiction." *Taxier, et al. v. Sweet, et al.* (Supreme Court of Pennsylvania 1766), Dallas, *Reports,* 2: 83.

Mansfield had once claimed to recall Lord Talbot saying that "the law of nations, in its fullest extent was part of the law of England," and although Mansfield was dexterous enough merely to play upon this overstatement, Hamilton urged it without qualification, and Duane adopted it as if it could be taken literally. *Triquet & Others v. Bath* (K.B. 1764), Burrow, *Reports,* 3: 1481, recalling *Buvot v. Barbut.* Shortly after Duane gave his opinion, Chief Justice M'Kean of Pennsylvania followed his example and more completely echoed Mansfield's allusion to Talbot—saying that "the law of nations . . . in its full extent, is part of the law of this State, and is to be collected from the *practice* of different nations, and the *authority* of *writers.*" *Respublica v. De Longchamps* (Oyer and Terminer, Philadelphia, Oct. 1784), Dallas, *Reports,* 1: 116. If taken literally, it was a bold thought, for although neither Duane nor M'Kean disputed the logic of authority, they appeared to presume a complete incorporation of the law of nations, and they thus placed the burden on the legislature to exclude specific portions of it.

In contrast, the conventional presumption was that a legislature had to specify what offenses against the law of nations would be punishable at law. Prior to 1787, Congress and the states assumed that (as put in a congressional resolution) the states would have "to enact punishments against violators of the law of nations" or (as put in Congress's transmission) the states would have "to enact Laws for punishing infractions of the Law of Nations." Resolution (Nov. 23, 1781), *Journals of the Continental Congress 1774–1789,* at 21: 1136 (Washington: Government Printing Office, 1912); By the United States in Congress Assembled (Nov. 23, 1781), Robert Treat Paine Papers, Reel 18. In 1787, on account of the uncertainty of the law of nations, it was recognized that not only the punishments but also the very offenses would have to be spelled out, and the U.S. Constitution therefore carefully authorized Congress to "define and punish . . . Offences against the Law of Nations." U.S. Constitution, Article I, section 8.

violated the Treaty of Peace and thus also the Articles of Confederation, but he understood the difficulty of arguing that the Articles or the Treaty were really part of the law of the land, and he therefore presented a fallback argument about equitable interpretation, which Duane now adopted. Such interpretation was only possible where the intent of the statute was obscure, and Duane therefore suggested (rather improbably) that the act was so general it could not be presumed to have barred justification by military authority under the law of nations. Duane conceded that the legislature could impose an unjust law if it made its intent clear, but he held that when the legislature used general words with unjust consequences, it could be assumed to have intended exceptions:

> The supremacy of the Legislature need not be called into question; if they think fit *positively* to enact a law, there is no power which can controul them. When the main object of such a law is clearly expressed, and the intention manifest, the Judges are not at liberty, altho' it appears to them to be *unreasonable,* to reject it: for this were to set the *judicial* above the legislative, which would be subversive of all government.
>
> But when a law is expressed in *general words,* and some *collateral matter,* which happens to arise from those general words is *unreasonable,* there the Judges are in decency to conclude, that the consequences were not foreseen by the Legislature; and therefore they are at liberty to expound the statute by *equity,* and only *quoad hoc* [that is, only in this respect] to disregard it.

Other judges might have hesitated to say that they would "disregard" the statute, for they ordinarily used the doctrine of equitable interpretation merely to pursue a statute's intent beyond its words, but when Duane applied the doctrine to a law as clear as the Trespass Act, his suggestion that he was disregarding the statute came close to the truth. Evidently self-conscious about his conclusion, the Mayor repeated that "[w]hen the judicial make these distinctions, they do not controul the Legislature"—on the contrary, "they endeavor to give their *intention* it's proper effect."[44] Yet what made his use of equitable interpretation so appealing to some and so troubling to others was precisely that it defeated the legislature's intent.

Just how far Duane went afield was suggested afterward when he allegedly sent his opinion to Lord Mansfield. Duane had cited Mansfield to show that the law of nations was generally adopted by the common law,

[44] *Arguments and Judgment of the Mayor's Court of the City of New-York in a Cause Between Elizabeth Rutgers and Joshua Waddington,* 40–41 (New York: 1784). In September 1784 the jury gave Rutgers £791/13/4, plus sixpence in costs—a mere fraction of what she had sought. Goebel, ed., *The Law Practice of Alexander Hamilton,* 1: 310–311.

and to Duane's embarrassment, the English Chief Justice was said to have responded—"with the greatest politeness"—that "the law of nations could never be pleaded against a law of the land."[45]

Duane's equitable interpretation of the Trespass Act stimulated both an appeal and public protest. His interpretation left room for him to conclude that the plea in justification, derived from the law of nations, barred Elizabeth Rutgers from recovering damages for the period when there was military authorization for the occupation of her property, and after she received a disappointing sum from the jury, she appealed to the New York Supreme Court. So too apparently did Waddington, but in the end the parties reached a "compromise," because Waddington's counsel apprehended "an unfavorable issue in the supreme court."[46] This was prudent, for although Duane thought the Trespass Act too general to be "clearly expressed," and although he thus thought the law of the land left room for the law of nations, many lawyers were apt to think that the law of nations on occupation was far less clear than the Trespass Act. Among those who disagreed with Duane were probably some justices of the New York Supreme Court, and thus, notwithstanding Duane's opinion against Elizabeth Rutgers, other injured patriots still proceeded with their claims under the Trespass Act—both in the Mayor's Court and more expansively in the Supreme Court.[47] In the meantime, Rutgers and her allies called for a public meeting at Mrs. Vandewater's tavern, where they organized in protest against Duane's decision. According to these outraged patriots, the Mayor's Court had in effect assumed the legislature's power to repeal a statute.[48]

[45] American Intelligence, *Columbian Herald* (Charleston) (June 17, 1785). This story about the correspondence was soon denied as "wholly void of truth," but Duane's vanity was such that he may well have written to Mansfield, and either way, the report of the correspondence is revealing. Correspondence (New York, July 19), *Freeman's Journal* (Phila.) (July 27, 1785).

[46] The Defense No. IV, *The Courier* (Boston) (Aug. 15, 1795). The essayist also said that "according to the general opinion of our bar, a defense under a military order was desperate, and it was believed that a majority of our supreme court would over-rule the plea." Ibid. See also Letter of Alexander Hamilton to Thomas Jefferson (April 19, 1792), in Goebel, ed., *The Law Practice of Alexander Hamilton,* 1: 311.

[47] Ibid., 1: 49, 523; Mayor's Court Papers, Columbia University, Special Collections, Salzer Collection. Richard Morris observes that *Rutgers* "did not settle the issue." *Select Cases of the Mayor's Court of New York City 1684–1784,* at 315, ed. William H. Manz (Buffalo: Hein, 1998). Moreover, Hamilton's plea in *Rutgers* depended on the law of nations as to occupancy and could not therefore be used to bar claims for injury to property. Goebel, ed., *The Law Practice of Alexander Hamilton,* 1: 298, note 45. After the repeal of the Trespass Act, the Supreme Court apparently "sustained Actions even where it appeared that Property had been seised and sold by the Direction of of the Quarter Master General of the British Army." Ibid., 1: 525.

[48] In advertising the meeting, Rutgers and her allies argued: "If the Legislature . . . had abrogated the trespass law, or any part of it, none could have doubted *their* right. . . . But an en-

After hearing from these protesters, the popular branch of the legislature, the Assembly, declined to punish the judges, but it at least generally asserted the danger of judicial departures from law: "[I]f a court . . . may take upon them to dispense with an act in direct violation of a plain and known law of the State, all other courts, either superior or inferior may do the like; and therewith will end all our dear bought rights and privileges, and Legislatures become useless."[49] As put by a newspaper writer, "the *Court* has received 'a rap o' the knuckles,' for deviating from the known and established *law of the land*."[50]

Rutgers' supporters made the best of this merely moral victory by addressing their fellow citizens on the peril from the courts if they had both final judgment and an expansive view of equitable interpretation. A committee of Rutgers' allies (appointed at the meeting at Mrs. Vanderwater's tavern) observed that the court had judged "contrary to the plain and obvious meaning of a statute," and that "a great part of the citizens of this metropolis" considered the decision "an assumption of power . . . inconsistent with the nature and genius of our government." The reality, however, was that the courts had the final decision: "[T]he reasoning of the Court and the reasoning of the legislature may lead them to very different conclusions," and "the Court reason last upon the case." The judges could therefore abuse equitable interpretation to reject statutes they considered unreasonable—for example, "they may judge the law unreasonable, because not consonant to the law of nations, or to the opinions of ancient or modern civilians and philosophers, for whom they may have a greater veneration than for the solid statutes and supreme legislative power of the state."[51]

The way in which Duane and some other men of federal sympathies

---

lightened, jealous, and free people will surely never consent to a Bench's assuming such a power. For what can be more essential to the security of property, of personal privileges, of the purity of our government, and of the general welfare of the people, than to preserve a clear and insuperable line of distinctions between the legislative and judicial branches of government?" Reasons for a Meeting of Citizens, published by Committee of Meeting at Vandewaters (Sept. 11, 1784), *Independent Journal* (New York) (Sept. 11, 1784).

[49] Resolutions (Nov. 2, 1784), *Votes and Proceedings of the Assembly,* 32–34 (5th meeting, 1st session) ([1784]).

[50] Letter to Mr. Holt, *New-York Journal, & State Gazetteer* (Nov. 18, 1784).

[51] *An Address From the Committee Appointed at Mrs. Vandewater's,* 6, 9–12 (New York: 1784). Incidentally, the committee thought it "absurd" that "there should be a power vested in courts of judicature, whereby they might controul the supreme legislative power," for "[s]uch power in courts would be destructive of liberty, and remove all security of property. The design of courts of justice in our government, from the very nature of their institution, is to declare laws, not to alter them." Ibid., 10. Taken out of context, this might sound like a rejection of decisions holding statutes unconstitutional. The committee, however, was concerned with misinterpretation.

imagined that they could use an expansive equitable interpretation to counteract local illiberality suggests much about the passions that threatened the nation in the 1780s. Duane had been one of the delegates to the Continental Congress who in 1782 had joined Madison in proposing the use of military force against recalcitrant states, and in 1784 Duane sent his published opinion in *Rutgers* to George Washington, with a letter regretting the "vain prejudices in favor of the Independence and Sovereignty of the individual States." Duane wrote with evident vanity that he had endeavored in his opinion to "inculcate more enlarged and liberal principles," and although he had "lost credit with our Assembly," he hoped for a better reception from the world and from Washington, who wrote back to Duane that "my Judgment yields a hearty assent."[52]

Washington was self-consciously "liberal," and he probably assented to Duane's liberal political stance more than any particular legal point, but Duane was not alone in his broad vision of something like equitable interpretation.[53] Three years later, in North Carolina, James Iredell defended the authority of the judges to hold a North Carolina statute unconstitutional by observing that although in England "the Powers of the Legislature" were "absolute," the judges there "avowed" that an act of Parliament *"inconsistent with natural justice"* was not "binding on the people." As Iredell apparently understood, such statements were merely hypotheticals, which were "avowed" in justification of equitable interpretation, rather than what judges actually did, but in his effort at persuasion he was willing to exploit their suggestion of a judicial power to hold an unjust act of Parliament void.[54] Edmund Randolph of Virginia actually wanted at least some judges to exercise this sort of power. As attorney general of Virginia, he had conscientiously adhered to the legal limitations on equitable interpretation, but now that he was a delegate to the Constitutional Convention

[52] Letter from James Duane to George Washington (Dec. 16, 1784), and Letter from George Washington to James Duane (April 10, 1785), in Goebel, ed., *The Law Practice of Alexander Hamilton,* 1: 315. With expectations of judicial review, Goebel describes Duane's opinion and his reactions to the ensuing disputes as "ambiguous." Ibid., 312, 314. Yet in his strained application of equitable interpretation and his statement about local prejudice and liberal principles, Duane was clear enough.

[53] For Washington's liberal sentiments, see Hamburger, "Liberality," 1277.

[54] Letter from James Iredell to Richard Dobbs Spaight (Aug. 26, 1787), in *The Papers of James Iredell,* 3: 307, eds. Donna Kelly and Lang Baradell (Raleigh: North Carolina Department of Cultural Resources, 2003). His view of judges who talked too loosely about holding legislation contrary to natural justice may be observed a decade later in *Calder v. Bull* (1798), Dallas, *Reports,* 3: 386, and for his consistency on this, see Helen K. Michael, "The Role of Natural Law in Early American Constitutionalism: Did the Founders Contemplate Judicial Enforcement of 'Unwritten' Individual Rights," *North Carolina Law Review,* 69: 451–452 (1991).

in Philadelphia, he could openly pursue his broader desire for justice by suggesting that the U.S. Constitution should give federal judges a power, not merely of interpretation, but generally to hold inequitable or unjust state statutes void: "that any individual conceiving himself injured or oppressed by the partiality or injustice of a law of any particular State may resort to the National Judiciary, who may adjudge such law to be void, if found contrary to the principles of equity and justice."[55]

Although the Constitutional Convention rejected this proposal and said nothing about interpretation, there apparently were some men, including Alexander Hamilton, who still desired an open-ended version of equitable interpretation. Hamilton could not openly tinker with the conventional version of equitable interpretation, but he hinted at what he had in mind. He thought it necessary for the federal judiciary to have an expansive role in constraining local injustice, and having persuaded Duane to follow a purportedly equitable presumed intent rather than the fairly clear intent of the Trespass Act, Hamilton now wrote in the *Federalist:*

> But it is not with a view to infractions of the constitution only that the independence of the judges may be an essential safeguard against the effects of occasional ill humors in the society. These sometimes extend no farther than to the injury of the private rights of particular classes of citizens, by unjust and partial laws. Here also the firmness of the judicial magistracy is of vast importance in mitigating the severity, and confining the operation of such laws.[56]

Rather than conflate questions about the constitutionality of statutes with equitable interpretation, Hamilton understood that whereas the one type of decision denied the obligation of a statute, the other merely avoided an unjust understanding of its operation. The one held a statute to be without legal obligation under the constitution; the other held that the obligation of the statute lay beyond the surface of its unclear words. All of this was entirely conventional, but in saying nothing of the limitations on equitable interpretation, and in emphasizing how it could serve a liberalizing function, Hamilton quietly left room for the wishful imagination of some ardent Federalists that equitable interpretation might support a broader judicial role than this doctrine traditionally could bear.

Amid the willingness of some Federalist lawyers to apply an expansive version of equitable interpretation to state statutes, the Anti-Federalist es-

55 Edmund Randolph's Suggestion for Conciliating the Small States (July 10, 1787), in *The Records of the Federal Convention of 1787,* at 3: 56, ed. Max Farrand (New Haven: Yale University Press, 1937).

56 Alexander Hamilton, Federalist No. 78, *The Federalist,* 528, ed. Jacob E. Cooke (Middletown: Wesleyan University Press, 1961).

sayist Brutus feared for the U.S. Constitution. Robert Yates had sat on the New York Supreme Court for more than a decade, and although the settlement in *Rutgers v. Waddington* deprived him of a chance to hear the case on appeal, he could not have been unaware of the decision. Nor was his fellow Anti-Federalist Melancton Smith unfamiliar with the case, for he had been a member of the committee appointed at Vandewater's.[57] Yates represented New York at the Philadelphia Convention, but he soon walked out to join Smith in the fight against ratification, and even if neither of these men can be certainly identified as Brutus, the letters published under this pseudonym were written with all the sensitivities that might be expected of a New Yorker dismayed by *Rutgers v. Waddington.*[58]

Rutgers revealed how federally inclined men might abuse the equitable interpretation of statutes, and Brutus now feared that an "equitable mode of construction" would be "applied to . . . the constitution."[59] In particular, he worried that federal judges would be authorized "not only to carry into execution the powers expressly given, but where these are wanting or ambiguously expressed, to supply what is wanting by their own decisions." This concern seemed to be substantiated by the Constitution's allusion to cases in law and equity, which led Brutus to conclude that federal judges would use their equitable powers to interpret the Constitution so as to determine "the sense of every article of the constitution . . . according to what appears to them, the reason and spirit of the constitution." As if this strained version of equitable interpretation were not bad enough, the judges' decisions would be final. The committee appointed at Vandewater's had already been troubled by the finality of lawless court decisions in New York, and it was all the more sobering to consider the finality of decisions by the U.S. Supreme Court: "The opinions of the supreme court, whatever they may be, will have the force of law; because there is no power provided in the constitution, that can correct their errors, or controul their adjudications. From this court there is no appeal." Brutus concluded that "[t]he judicial power will operate to effect, in the most certain, but yet silent and imperceptible manner . . . an entire subversion of the legislative, executive and judicial powers of the individual states."[60]

The doctrine of equitable interpretation was thus burdened with un-

[57] He was one of eight men added to the committee at a meeting of September 13. Correspondence (Sept. 21), *Columbia Herald* (Charleston) (Nov. 23, 1784).
[58] For the various attributions, all of them rather elusive, see *The Documentary History of the Ratification of the Constitution,* 13: 411–412.
[59] Brutus, Essay XII (Feb. 7, 1788), ibid., 16: 75.
[60] Brutus, Essay XI (Jan. 31, 1788), ibid., 15: 512.

realistic hopes and anxious fears. Eager to suppress illiberal state legislation, some enthusiastic Federalists desired a version of equitable interpretation that stimulated the disquiet of Brutus and others, who worried for the authority of the people. Nor was their concern about the abuse of equitable interpretation unjustified. If under a theory of presumed intent, judges could ignore the legislature's expressed intent, might they not also ignore the expressed intent of the people? Such fears would eventually seem prescient. In the eighteenth century, however, it remained conventional that equitable interpretation was only a means of avoiding injustice within the scope of intent. Even the most prominent advocates of an expansive use of equitable interpretation understood that they could not afford to challenge the ideals of legislative authority and intent, and it will be recalled that when the judges in *Rutgers* seemed to "deviat[e] from the known and established *law of the land*," they received "'a rap o' the knuckles.'"[61]

By now it should be evident that the judges, at least ideally, had to pursue reason and justice within the narrow lines established by law and judicial duty. Amid discordant views of reason and justice, it seemed necessary for the obligation of law to rest on the authority of the people and their legislators and for the duty of judges to be delineated by the law that enjoyed this obligation, the law of the land. Almost all human law inflicted some injustice, and some human laws inflicted much injustice, but it was the duty of the judges to decide in accord with the law of the land, and if on the whole they seem to have done their duty, this was not because they were indifferent to questions of injustice in law, but rather because they tended to understand the deeper rationality and justice of having a system of law based on authority.

[61] Letter to Mr. Holt, *New-York Journal, & State Gazetteer* (Nov. 18, 1784).

12

The Range of Constitutional Decisions and the Character of Judicial Duty

A CONCEPT can be studied not only abstractly from above but also more concretely from below, and in this manner the practical applications of judicial duty disclose the character of the ideal. It will be seen in particular that judges held government acts unconstitutional in all sorts of decisions, and this range says much about the breadth, strength, and familiarity of the duty to decide in accord with the law of the land.

It is often imagined that judicial review was primarily a power over legislation, and from this perspective, the array of relevant decisions seems very narrow, for if judicial review centrally concerned legislation, then the decisions from before 1791 shrink down to the relatively small number that held statutes void. It is difficult to believe, moreover, that so extraordinary a power as judicial review could have existed before it was well established through precedents—indeed, those laid down by the highest of courts, federal or state—and this further curtails the evidence, reducing it to supreme court cases on legislation. Any such analysis of judicial review, however, must be viewed with skepticism, for it looks ahead to a world very different from that in which judges derived their power from their duty.

In that older world, the judges were bound by their duty in all aspects of their office, and they therefore could hardly limit their constitutional decisions to cases, supreme courts, or legislation. On the contrary, they had to judge the constitutionality of government acts not only in cases but also in resolutions and advisory opinions; not only while sitting on supreme courts but also while sitting on lower courts; not only as to legislative acts but also as to executive and judicial acts. Opinions about constitutionality can thus be found among the full range of their decisions, and nothing says more about the breadth of the ideal of judicial duty, about the strength of its obligation, or about the social depth at which it was understood.

Resolutions

The judges decided constitutional questions in resolutions as well as in cases because even in their resolutions they were bound by their duty. This may seem unexpected to Americans accustomed to the federal case or controversy requirement, and certainly the extent to which judges in their office should adopt resolutions was already an awkward question. Yet if judges were to adopt resolutions on matters of law, they had a duty to do so in accord with the law of the land, and the fact that in their resolutions they sometimes declared government acts unconstitutional is suggestive about the generality of their duty.

Judicial resolutions are vaguely familiar from some 1792 federal circuit court pronouncements about the Invalid Pension Act. In the history of judicial review, these determinations seem anomalous, for rather than cases, they were judicial resolutions and some associated letters prepared by the judges. They were, however, not really so incongruous, for they followed a tradition familiar from English and state courts.[1] State court resolutions

[1] The Invalid Pension Act required the circuit courts to hear applications for pensions from invalid soldiers, but the judges of three federal circuit courts in 1792 refused, and what is more to the point here, they did so in resolutions and letters that followed the usual protocol on resolutions, which was familiar from some state courts.

On the Circuit Court for the district of New York, the judges avoided giving their opinion in a hearing on a particular application—perhaps because they thought they could not hear it as a case—and instead gave a general "opinion" or resolution explaining their constitutional objection, which they had entered in their court's record. They concluded with an order that the clerk send the President a certified copy of the relevant "extracts" from their record. Of course, the judges' opinion was a repudiation of an act of Congress, and they therefore closed their letter to George Washington by asking him "the favor" that he would give the certified extracts to Congress, this being the most "respectful and proper manner" to "communicate them." Extract from Minutes (Apr. 5, 1792), in *The Documentary History of the Supreme Court of the United States, 1789–1800,* at 6: 370–371, ed. Maeva Marcus (New York: Columbia University Press, 1998).

When a disabled veteran, William Hayburn, applied to the U.S. Circuit Court for the district of Pennsylvania a week later, the judges opined from the bench that they could not constitutionally decide on his petition, and they entered in their record that the petition "be not proceeded upon." Copy of Docket Entry (Apr. 11, 1792), ibid., 6: 46. Hayburn immediately applied for relief to the House of Representatives, and upon receiving information from Congressman Elias Boudinot about what the judges had said, the House turned Hayburn's memorial over to a committee. Yet the judges' conduct did not escape commentary on the floor of the House, and William Vans Murray, who had studied law in London, urged "the necessity of passing a law to point out some more regular mode, in which the Judges . . . shall give official notice of their refusal to act under any law of Congress, on the ground of an unconstitutionality." Even he, however, made "[n]o regular motion" on this subject. Debates in House of Representatives (Apr. 13, 1792), as reported in *General Advertiser* (Apr. 16, 1792), in ibid., 6: 48.

Several days later, in fact, the judges gave something like "official notice," but not to Congress, and not as to their "refusal," which already was a matter of record. Instead, they wrote were not uncommon, and they point toward the conclusion, already familiar from England, that even outside of cases, and even as to structural questions, the judges were bound to decide in accord with the law of the land.

There was a particularly strong tradition of resolutions in the county courts of Virginia. Although county courts often decided cases, they sometimes had to act on their own behalf, and in these instances they might adopt resolutions. It will be recalled that during the Stamp Act controversy in 1766, the clerk and other officers of the Northampton County Court sought an opinion as to whether they could avoid using stamped paper without violating the Stamp Act, and the justices resolved that the act was "unconstitutional"—presumably under the English constitution.[2] After 1776, the Virginia county courts continued to adopt resolutions, but now under their state constitution.[3] The usual procedure was to adopt a resolution as a court and enter it in the court's records. When the resolution concerned another branch of government, the court would order the clerk to send a copy

---

to President George Washington and merely shared their sentiments. Pointedly, they began by explaining:

> To you it officially belongs "to take care that the laws" of the United States "be faithfully executed." Before you, therefore, we think it our duty to lay the sentiments, which, on a late painful occasion, governed us with regard to an act passed by the Legislature of the Union.

They then elaborated the constitutional arguments already made in New York, to which they added that if the Court proceeded, its opinions or judgments would have been subject to "revision and controul" by the legislature and executive, which "we deemed radically inconsistent with the Independence of that judicial power vested in the Courts." Letter of James Wilson, John Blair, and Richard Peters (Apr. 18, 1792), to George Washington, ibid., 6: 53–54. As in New York, this opinion about the constitutionality of a statute was significant for Congress, but if the judges were to convey a resolution or opinion to any other branch, they would only send it to the executive. Indeed, after the intrusive suggestion in Congress that they owed this body some official notice of their decision, they did not ask the President to share their letter with Congress.

Two months later, when John Sitgreaves and James Iredell served as judges in the North Carolina district, they echoed the Pennsylvania decision in a letter to the President—a letter being an act of the individual judges rather than their court and thus milder than a resolution. Iredell had also sat in Pennsylvania, but the judges in North Carolina no longer felt it necessary to remind Congress of their independence, and they therefore closed their letter to Washington by "tak[ing] the liberty to request, Sir, that you will be pleased to lay this letter before the Legislature of the United States." Letter from James Iredell and John Sitgreaves to George Washington (June 8, 1792), ibid., 6: 284, 287.

2 Minute Book 1765–1771, at 31–32 (Feb. 11, 1766), LVA, Northampton County Court, Mfm Reel 50.

3 For the cultural background to these county court resolutions, see A. G. Roeber, *Faithful Magistrates and Republican Lawyers: Creators of Virginia Legal Culture, 1680–1810,* Chapter 5 (Chapel Hill: University of North Carolina Press, 1981).

to the governor, and when it related to the legislature, the court might further request the governor to transmit it to that body.[4]

The Virginia county courts sometimes used resolutions to defend their constitutional rights—as when the Middlesex County Court in 1784 asserted what it considered its constitutional right to name its new members. The Virginia Constitution stipulated that "[t]he Governor, with the advice of the Privy Council, shall appoint Justices of the Peace for the counties" and "in case of vacancies, or a necessity of increasing the number hereafter," such appointments were "to be made upon the recommendation of the respective County Courts."[5] In accord with this provision, the Middlesex County Court in 1783 recommended four men for appointment as justices. Governor Benjamin Harrison and his Council, however, worried that most of the proposed men were Tories, and Harrison therefore only issued a commission for one of them, William Steptoe.[6] Rather than qualify Steptoe, the Court resolved in April 1784: "This Court thinking them-

[4] The justices also could simply write a letter to the governor, but this was a distinctly more cautious approach. A notable example occurred when the Essex County Court in Virginia recommended that Robert Beverley and Meriwether Smith be reinstated on their bench. This aroused the ire of Spencer Roane, who "from the solicitation of a number of respectable Citizens in this County" protested to the governor that Beverley was a Tory and that the justices of the Court who supported the nomination "consisted *almost entirely* of junior Magistrates." Letter from Spencer Roane to Governor Edmund Randolph (Sept. 3, 1787), LVA, Governor Edmund Randoph Executive Papers, Box 50. In these circumstances, when the governor rejected the two men, the justices who supported them could not be confident of getting a majority again in their favor. They therefore wrote a letter to the governor, "not to call in question your discretionary powers," but "with real concern" that "this is not the first time that our solemn recommendation hath been rejected by the Executive from misrepresentation," and they therefore asked him "to reconsider the matter, and return the commission agreeable to the recommendation." Letter from Six of the Essex County Justices to Governor Edmund Randolph (Mar. 27, 1788), LVA, Governor Edmund Randolph Executive Papers.

In response, as it happens, the Council gave an unusually explicit defense of its constitutional power in appointing justices of the peace. Its first argument was that "[t]he exercise of the power to reject . . . is warranted by the very nature of an appointing authority, and by the distinction, maintained throughout the constitution, between different gradations in the choosing of officers (to wit, an appointment, a mere recommendation, and the ministerial act of commissioning)." It also pointed to an early state statute as evidence of how the constitution was then understood, and to "a maxim of republicanizm, which forbids any standing body . . . to increase its number or elect its members at pleasure." *Journals of the Council of the State of Virginia,* 4: 225 (Apr. 7, 1788), ed. George H. Reese (Richmond: Virginia State Library, 1967).

[5] Virginia Constitution (1776). Similar concerns arose in connection with the appointment of militia officers.

[6] *Journals of the Council of the State of Virginia,* 3: 313 (Dec. 4, 1783), ed. Wilmer L. Hall (Richmond: Commonwealth of Virginia, 1952). Those not appointed were Ralph Wormley, Philip L. Grymes, and Robert Spratt.

selves under the Constitution competent to the recommendation of persons proper to act as Justices of the Peace in the said County," we "[d]o again recommend" all four men "as proper persons to serve as Justices of the Peace for this County."[7]

The standoff lasted for years. The Court was not adjudicating a case, and as each side therefore entered the dispute equally, almost as a party, neither had any special authority to expound the law or any reason to back down. Even after three years of deadlock, the Court only repeated its initial recommendation, and the Governor and his council reiterated their determination to stand firm.[8] In explaining why they were so adamant, the Governor and his council voted to assure the Court that their board would "on no occasion, without good cause," exercise its "constitutional right of refusing to appoint" recommended persons, but they thought it was "still unfit to call into an Office, instituted for the support of the Government, those, who during the War have been uniformly disaffected thereto." Accordingly, the County Court was "to be informed, that on these grounds" the three objectionable men "cannot be added to the Commission." Of course, the Governor and his council added that "the former appointment of Mr William Steptoe . . . is still open for his qualification," and that "if the number of acting Justices be too small," the board "will be at all times ready to remove the inconvenience, upon any recommendation which they may not be bound by duty to oppose."[9]

In 1788, the Court still was "adhearing to their former declaration that they under the Constitution, possess the right of pointing out to the Executive those qualified to Act as Magistrates," and it therefore "again recommend[ed]" the men it had formerly nominated "as proper persons to be added to the Commission of the Peace for the County of Middlesex."[10] At this point, after almost five years, Governor Edmund Randolph and the Council finally gave in. They issued the commission, but they carefully avoided acknowledging any concession of the constitutional point.[11]

One member of the Council was so outraged by this decision that he filed a long, impassioned dissent. William Heth was a "new member" of the Council and it therefore "was with much concern, and extreme diffidence"

[7] Resolution (Apr. 26, 1784), Middlesex County Court Order Book 1783–1784, at 36, LVA, Mfm Reel 6.
[8] Recommendation (Feb. 27, 1787), Middlesex County Court Order Book 1786–1787, at 42, LVA, Mfm Reel 42.
[9] Reese, ed., *Journals of the Council of the State of Virginia,* 4: 50–51 (Mar. 2, 1787).
[10] Recommendation (June 23, 1788), Middlesex County Court Order Book 1787–1789, at 138, LVA, Mfm Reel 41.
[11] Reese, ed., *Journals of the Council of the State of Virginia,* 4: 270 (Aug. 2, 1788).

that he felt "impelled to differ in opinion with the other members," who "have now given their assent, to the recommendation of the Court of Middlesex." Heth noted that the Council had already rejected the nominated men two or three times on account of their British loyalties during the war, and he insisted that their disaffection should remain a bar to office. More generally, he argued that the Council had "the unquestionable *right* under the constitution, to reject any recommendation," and he therefore "conceive[d] the dignity of this board, to be, in some degree insulted, by the said repeated recommendation of the Court of Middlesex." He thought "we ought now to have persevered in exercising that right; and the more especially, as no reasons have been now assigned, why we should *recede* from such opinions of former boards." The Middlesex County Court, however, was more persistent than the Council. Heth was not "altogether singular" in his "[s]entiments" on the Middlesex recommendation, but as he observed, "I find myself entirely alone, in the opinion which I have given thereon."[12]

The Middlesex County Court had no obligation to recommend its nominees, and yet having done so, and being of the view that it had a constitutional right to get its nominees appointed, it felt inclined and perhaps obliged to defend its position. It is an initial suggestion as to how in resolutions about their own constitutional rights or powers, judges began as parties and ended up trying to decide as judges. They could often avoid reaching a conclusion about a constitutional question if they were willing to exercise their power in a manner acceptable to the other branches; but having once entered into a controversy with another branch, they could feel a general duty as citizens and government officers to defend the Constitution's allocation powers and a specific duty as judges to decide in accord with the Constitution. To be sure, the resolution of the Middlesex County Court focused on the constitutionality of their own demand rather than the unconstitutionality of the executive's conduct, but their duty to decide in accord with law extended to determinations about their own acts as well as the Governor's, and both sides clearly understood that when the judges upheld their own constitutional power, they implicitly rejected the governor's claim to a "constitutional right of refusing to appoint."[13]

[12] Ibid., 270–272.

[13] The Executive had statutory authority to try to remove county magistrates, and it most notoriously used this power against Arthur Campbell, who was a justice of the peace for Washington County. As a child he had been captured by Wyandotte Indians, who held him for two years near what is now Detroit. As an adult, Campbell supported the idea that settlers in the western part of Virginia should consider joining the new state of Franklin, and it was for this disloyalty, which seemed to some almost treasonous, that he was tried. Under

A resolution of the Fairfax County Court more directly declared an executive act unconstitutional, and it is therefore an even better example of

---

"An act to extend the powers of the governor and council," the governor's council had the power to try and remove justices of the peace, and in 1786 the Council charged Campbell with misconduct. Hall, ed., *Journals of the Council of the State of Virginia,* 3: 497 (Dec. 13, 1785). One member of the Council, however, Beverley Randolph, already dissented on constitutional and other grounds. Ibid., 498. Campbell's lawyers made similar objections to the Council's jurisdiction, and although they were "overruled," there was again a dissent—this time from Spencer Roane. Ibid., 542–543 (Apr. 5, 1786). See also Proceedings in Council against Arthur Campbell (Apr. 3, 4, and 5, 1786), LVA, Governor Patrick Henry Executive Papers, Box 3, Folder 4, Apr. 2–10, 1786. Eventually, on August 31, 1786, the Council removed Campbell from his office. Ibid., 3: 577 (Aug. 31, 1786).

The Washington County Court protested in the form of a recommendation of appointment, thus hinting at its constitutional objections: "Ordered that it be earnestly recommended to his Excellency the Governor and the honorable the council of state that Arthur Campbell be and remain a Justice of the Peace in the County of Washington and that the order of the Executive bearing date the thirty first day of August last, be rescinded." Copy of Order of Feb. 4, 1787, Washington Recommendations (Mar. 20, 1787), LVA, Governor Edmund Randolph Executive Papers, Box 46. The Council, as might be expected, simply docketed it, "nothing done." Ibid.

By late 1787, the Executive had reconsidered its power. Writing to the Speaker of the House of Delegates, Governor Edmund Randolph noted:

> Within the last few days we had discussed and decided several charges against different justices of the peace. We were thereby naturally led to consider the principles of the law, under which we sat in judgment, and to trace the consequences of its execution. In its principles, it has been supposed not to be perfectly reconcileable with that canon of the constitution, which requires the judiciary to be seperate and distinct from the Executive, or with that declaration in the bill of rights, which demands on criminal accusations, a trial by jury. The Executive too have no power to enforce the attendance of Witnesses or to award costs in Vexatious prosecutions. In the consequences of the law we foresee the certainty of deterring many valuable men from accepting seats on the bench: We therefore request that we may no longer remain the tribunal on these impeachments, and that the generally Assembly will believe, that this abridgment of Authority is desired merely from a conviction of its necessity, not from any reluctance to discharge the duties of the Executive, howsoever laborious.

Letter from Edmund Randolph to the Speaker of the House of Delegates [Joseph Prentis] (In Council, Dec. 11, 1787), Randolph-Tucker Papers 1723–1901, Huntington Library, Brock Collection, Misc. Reel 4222, BR Box 6 (13). The General Assembly agreed with this assessment of the constitutional question and soon passed an act repealing as much of the prior statute as gave the governor and his council a power to try and remove justices of the peace, observing that this power "appears to the present assembly to be contrary to the true spirit of the constitution," in particular its separation-of-powers clause. An act respecting the appointment of county court clerks, recommendation of surveyors, and for other purposes (Jan. 8, 1788), in *Laws of Virginia,* 12: 507, ed. Waller Hening (Richmond: 1823).

Arthur Campbell subsequently resumed his role as justice of the peace, and William Edmiston brought a *qui tam* action against him, under a statute allowing a £300 penalty against anyone who presumed to exercise the office of justice of the peace without being qualified. As might be expected, when a special verdict left the facts with the General Court, the judges held that *"the law is for the defendant." Edmiston v. Campbell* (General Court 1792), Brockenbrough & Holmes, *Reports,* 1: 18.

how judicial duty required judges, even in their resolutions, to decide the constitutionality of government acts. The issue arose from the decision of Governor Benjamin Harrison and his council in July 1784 to regularize the appointments of justices of the peace. To this end, he asked the active magistrates of each county to have their clerk send the executive a certified list of the current magistrates, with information as to whether they were still active, present in the county, or even alive. Although it was not unreasonable to treat the dead or otherwise departed as having relinquished their positions, Governor Harrison and his advisers understood that the Constitution required another approach for judges who were merely inactive, and he therefore requested the active justices to inquire about the possibility of resignations—"to have enquiry made of those who have refused to act whether they mean to do it in future or not and if possible to procure their answers in open court or by letter." There had been demands in the legislature for district or circuit courts, which would have diminished the significance of the county courts, and Governor Harrison took advantage of this political threat to observe that "nothing is more desirable than a reformation of the Courts of Justice." In other words, the Governor's reformation of existing courts would be less painful than new courts, and lest this not be enough to induce cooperation with his request for information, he closed with the warning that "[n]o new Commissions will be issued until such returns are made."[14]

By October, after receiving information from many counties, the Governor began to issue new commissions, which omitted dead, departed, and otherwise inactive justices.[15] It was an admirable exercise in efficiency, but although the new commissions avoided one problem, they created another, for the new commission in each county listed justices already serving under earlier commissions and thus required existing justices to repeat their oaths under their new commission.

The Fairfax County Court had complied with the request for information, but when it received one of the new commissions in early 1785,

[14] Governors Office, Executive Letter Books, 356–357 (July 1, 1784), LVA, Mfm Reel 3. The circular letter actually was sent out on July 4. For the decision of the Council to send the letter, see Hall, ed., *Journals of the Council of the State of Virginia,* 3: 361–362 (July 1, 1784).

[15] The Council advised Harrison to "issue New Commissions of the peace & oyer & terminer" to such counties as had returned the requested information—thus sending each of them a single commission for all justices in each county, including "all those who are named in the former commissions except such as have been certified to be dead, to have resigned," "to have removed out of the County," or "to have refused to qualify & to have neglected to qualify for more than twelve months after being named in the Commissions." Ibid., 3: 385–386 (Oct. 25, 1784).

there were difficulties—initially because the commission did not include the men the Court had recently recommended. At its November meeting, the County Court did not yet know that the new commission had been issued, and being worried "that there is not a sufficient number of Magistrates in the County that will act to do the business thereof," it "recommended" eleven men to the governor.[16] Shortly afterward, on December 3, the new commission arrived, and having been prepared in October, it included none of the eleven recommended justices. As it happened, the clerk of the Fairfax County Court, Peter Wagener, had not yet forwarded the County Court's recommendation to the Council, and he therefore now sent it with a memorandum suggesting that the executive issue yet another commission for the entire bench—one that included the eleven additional justices. This would have the advantage, Wagener noted, of saving the existing members of the court "the trouble of twice swearing" to the new commission.[17] On December 1, Patrick Henry became governor, and he sent no new commission—neither an additional commission for the eleven recommended justices nor an expanded, replacement commission for the entire bench. The justices of the county were therefore left waiting, and as the winter months passed, they had ample time to worry about the fate of their recommendations and about the propriety of the new commission they had already received.

When the Fairfax County Court finally had the October commission "presented and read" in March 1785, the Court rejected it because it appointed the existing justices anew to a judicial office they already held. In a resolution transcribed in their records and transmitted to the governor, the justices protested that under the new commission, they were "constituted & appointed de novo" and consequently were "required to take the oaths of qualification over again, notwithstanding they had before taken them under the Commonwealth and several of the Justices have been for many years acting Majistrates by virtue of former commissions for the County." Among the Court's objections was that "constituting and appointing the former acting Justices de novo necessarily implies the power of vacating the

[16] Resolution (Nov. 17, 1784), Fairfax County Order Book, 96, Fairfax Circuit Court Archives; Certified resolution of Fairfax County Court (Nov. Court 1784), LVA, Governors Papers, Executive Papers: Letters Received, March–May 1785 (Box 38).

[17] The clerk wrote: "A commission bearing date 25º October 1784 . . . came to me the 3d December foll[owin]g and not yet presented in Court—If the Governor thinks proper to send up another to include those now recommended It will save the trouble of twice swearing—and You may bring it up agt the next Court." Memorandum from Peter Wagener (Mar. 29, 1785), LVA, Governors Papers, Executive Papers: Letters Received, March–May 1785 (Box 38).

former Commissions." The new commission thereby jeopardized a justice's seniority (which determined his right to the lucrative post of sheriff) and even threatened his office:

> [T]hat the Justices, derive their office entirely from the last [commission] and consequently that by issuing a new Commission and misplacing any man in it he would lose his rank and might be degraded from the first to the last Justice in the County or by leaving out any Justices name he would thence forward be deprived of his office both of which it is notorious were frequently practised under the former government.

Thus, a *de novo* commission could be used as a means of "turning any man out of his office of a civil Majistrate as prejudice, malice or caprice might dictate without a hearing or without cause of complaint against him." On such assumptions, together with the separation-of-powers provision in the state's Declaration of Rights, the Court concluded: "[I]t is conceived that the exercise of such a power is altogether illegal[,] giving to the Executive department of the State an undue and dangerous influence over the Courts of Justice directly contrary to the declaration of rights and to the fundamental principles of our free government."[18] This resolution was not an opinion in a case, but it unmistakably declared an executive act unconstitutional.

As in Middlesex, the executive refused to concede the constitutional issue but otherwise had to give way. Governor Henry initially declined to issue a further commission. For its part, the Court did not again consider the *de novo* commission and simply reiterated its recommendation.[19] After almost two years of this stalemate, Henry and his council in October 1786 probably recognized that they could not afford to stand in the way of new appointments to the Fairfax bench. The Council had attempted to reform the county courts by issuing new commissions that omitted the names of dead, absent, or inactive justices, but now rather than insist that its reforms be carried out through a new commission for the whole bench, it merely re-

[18] Fairfax County Court Order Book 1783–1788, at 114–116 (Mar. 22, 1785), Fairfax Circuit Court Archives. Although the threat to the tenure of judges was the more serious problem, the question of seniority also was significant. A few years later, when there were "[t]wo instances" in which "younger justices of the peace" were "recommended over the heads of older justices, for the office of sheriff, without the smallest imputation on the characters of the latter," Governor Edmund Randolph thought the matter "sufficiently important to be communicated to the general assembly" with a question as to "[w]hether it be expedient to provide against a repetition of such recommendations." Letter from Edmund Randolph to the Speaker of the House of Delegates (Oct. 25, 1788), LVA, General Assembly, House of Delegates, Office of Speaker, Executive Communications, Box 4, Folder 73.

[19] Recommendation (July 17, 1786), Fairfax County Order Book 1783–1788, at 250, Fairfax Circuit Court Archives.

solved that the justices who "have refused to act as Magistrates" and who "have left the County" were to "be removed from the office of Justices for the said County." Exactly how this resolution would accomplish their removal was unclear, but having saved the appearance of its policy, the Council issued a commission simply for the eleven recommended justices and "cancelled" the *de novo* commission.[20] The Fairfax justices probably had little doubt that they had done their duty as judges to decide in accord with the law, including the Virginia Constitution, but more immediately they

[20] Hall, ed., *Journals of the Council of the State of Virginia,* 3: 584 (Oct. 16, 1786).

Seven years later, the York County Court would go even further than the Fairfax Court: It would reject the underlying request of the governor for information. Ever since October 1784, governors had expected county recommendations to arrive with certified returns as to which judges were inactive, and governors soon further required that county courts make recommendations only when "a majority of the acting Justices . . . shall be present" and that county court clerks "specify in the certificate thereof, the names of the Magistrates present." Ibid., 3: 543 (Apr. 7, 1786). The York County Court regularly acquiesced to such demands in the 1780s. It even responded deferentially when the governor asked for further information before issuing a commission—this occurring when in April 1787 the clerk certified that "[a] majority of the Justices named in the last Commission" were "present" but failed to list who was inactive. Recommendation (Apr. 17, 1787), LVA, Executive Papers, Civil Appointments Prior to 1790, Box 4, York Folder; Letter from R. Waller, Clerk, to Governor Edmund Randolph (May 24, 1787), ibid.

The York County Court, however, changed its tune in early spring 1792 after making a recommendation for the appointment of three gentlemen. York County Order Book No. 6, 1788–1795, at 425 (Mar. 21, 1792), LVA, Mfm Reel 34. Governor Henry Lee declined to appoint the named men until he had received the certifications from the clerk that governors had regularly expected since 1784, and when the Court, apparently on constitutional grounds, refused to satisfy his request, he had to justify his position. He wrote that "I acknowledge the Constitution to be the only guide for the officers of the Commonwealth, and that it is the duty of all good citizens to resist the usurpation of power by any branch of the Government"—a hint that he understood the judges to have stood upon their duty as citizens rather than as judges. He then explained that he did not "consider the regulation of the Executive, on this point, repugnant to the Constitution," because the executive needed the requested information to exercise its power of appointment: "The department authorized to commission, and to judge of the necessity of the encrease of the number of magistrates, must also have the power to establish such regulations as tend to the acquirement of the information necessary to their right conduct." Copy of Letter from Governor Henry Lee to Clerk of York County Court (June 8, 1792), LVA, Executive Papers, Letters Received 1791–1794, Box 74.

After "some deliberation" at their next meeting, the York County Court resolved that "it is their opinion, that under the Constitution the Court alone have a right to judge of the necessity of an Increase of Magistrates and of persons proper to fill up vacancies," and that "it would be shrinking from a Duty the Constitution and their oath impose on them to do anything but to require the appointment conformable to their recommendation." They then ordered the clerk to "transmit a Copy of their Resolution to the Governor." York County Orderbook No. 6, 1788–1795, at 472 (July 16, 1792), LVA, Mfm Reel 34. These differences lasted until 1793, when the Court repeated its recommendation, and the then governor just gave in and issued a commission. York County Orderbook No. 6, 1788–1795, at 507 (Jan. 21, 1793), 512 (Mar. 19, 1793), LVA, Mfm Reel 34.

must have been satisfied that they had successfully asserted what they considered their own constitutional rights.

In a subsequent resolution, the Fairfax County Court declared it could not constitutionally adopt a motion that had been brought before it, and on this question, the justices had a combination of duties. In all of the resolutions mentioned here, the justices of the county courts seem at least to have understood that they had the specialized duty of judges to decide in *accord* with law. Yet whereas in the prior two resolutions they apparently combined their judicial duty with their assertion of their own rights, in the second Fairfax resolution they combined the duty of their office with an assertion of their more basic duty *under* law. The county courthouse in Alexandria had long been in disrepair, and traditionally the county courts had raised levies for the construction and repair of their buildings.[21] George Mason, however, and some other Anti-Federalists in Fairfax worried that Alexandrians exerted too much influence in the Fairfax court, and they felt this all the more strongly after Alexandrians largely supported ratification of the U.S. Constitution—a decision that would soon lead to the transfer of Alexandria to the new federal district.[22] Mason and his allies therefore refused to support any repair of the existing courthouse. This local controversy became a dramatic constitutional question in January 1789, when a motion was made in the County Court to raise a levy on tobacco for repair of the court building or construction of a new one. It was "one of the fullest courts ever remembered in the county; there being no less than one-and-twenty worshipfuls assembled."[23]

Although "the power of the court to lay levies . . . was never before questioned," Mason persuaded most of the gentlemen on the bench to reject the motion on the ground that "the Court had no legal authority to levy on the inhabitants of the County any money or Tobacco for any purpose whatever." In particular, they were "of opinion that power was taken from the County Courts by the bill of rights of this Commonwealth."[24] The version of the resolution sent to the governor emphasized that "the

[21] The statutes of Virginia had authorized county courts to levy on tobacco for various particular purposes (albeit not the repair of the Fairfax courthouse) and had recognized a general power of county courts to make levies but without specifically authorizing it.

[22] For the politics, see Nan Netherton et al., *Fairfax County, Virginia: A History*, 132–133 (Fairfax: Fairfax County Board of Supervisors, 1978).

[23] From a Correspondent (Alexandria, Jan. 22), *The Virginia Herald and Fredericksburg Advertizer* (Jan. 29, 1789), also printed in *Virginia Independent Chronicle* (Richmond) (Feb. 4, 1789).

[24] From a Correspondent (Alexandria, Jan. 22), *The Virginia Herald and Fredericksburg Advertizer* (Jan. 29, 1789); Fairfax Circuit Court Archives, Fairfax County Court Order Book 1788–1792, pt. 1, at 84–85 (Jan. 20, 1789).

power of levying by the Courts was destroyed by an express article in the bill of rights of this Commonwealth"—perhaps the separation-of-powers provision, but more probably the sixth, that men "cannot be taxed or deprived of their property for public uses, without their own consent."[25]

The Fairfax County Court decision stimulated fears for the constitutionality of the legislative acts that had authorized other county levies. One newspaper commentator observed that "in at least fifty instances since the revolution," a county levy "has been recognized by the legislature, and particular acts passed, prescribing it as a duty on the county magistrates." Admittedly, the court had only decided the unconstitutionality of its own power, but its conclusion seemed to reach the legislation: "The decision of the court was, that these laws being all contrary to an express article of the bill of rights, and constitution, [they] ought not to be acted on," and "if this decision be well founded, the evil cannot be remedied by the legislature." Instead, "the proper remedy cannot be applied but by a convention."[26]

George Mason, however, could sustain neither his reasoning in this decision nor his influence on the Court. The justices asked the clerk to send a copy of their resolution to the Governor, and probably at the request of some of the more skeptical magistrates, the clerk explained that "as the matter will be gone into at our next Court," the magistrates "wish to have the advice of the Council, and the Attorney General's Opinion concerning the power of the County Courts in levying upon the Titheables of their County sufficient to defray the Expences of their County."[27] The Governor and his council referred the Court's resolution to the attorney general, and after receiving his opinion, the Governor sent it to the clerk of Fairfax County. It was probably persuasive, for Mason made no effort to rally his supporters on the bench. A month after the initial decision, when Mason and most of his allies were notably absent, the Court "reconsidered their power in laying levies for the use of the County," and a majority now "were of opinion that they had a right to levy."[28]

These instances suggest that judges were bound by the duty of their

25 Copy of resolution sent to Clerk of the Council (Jan. 28, 1789), in LVA, Governor Beverley Randolph Papers, Box 58; Virginia Constitution of 1776, Declaration of Rights, §5.
26 From a Correspondent (Alexandria, Jan. 22), *The Virginia Herald and Fredericksburg Advertizer* (Jan. 29, 1789).
27 Letter from Peter Wagener to Governor Beverley Randolph, LVA, Governor Beverley Randolph Papers, Box 58 (Jan. 28, 1789).
28 Fairfax Circuit Court Archives, Fairfax County Order Book 1788–1792, pt. 1, at 88 (Feb. 17, 1789).

office not only in their cases but also in their resolutions. Of course, the justices in these resolutions actively pursued their own rights and duties under law, and it is therefore difficult to separate out what they did on their own behalf *under* law from their decisions as judges, who were obliged to decide in *accord* with law. This ambidextrous character of judicial resolutions was familiar in county courts, which exercised both administrative and judicial power, but it will be seen in a later chapter that the blurring of roles was already becoming more awkward in other courts.[29] Here, it is enough to observe that as in England, so too in America, the duty to decide in accord with the law of the land, including the constitution, apparently reached resolutions as well as cases—thus offering a preliminary hint about this duty's breadth.

Advisory Opinions

Another type of decision that was not a case, but in which the judges were bound to do their duty, occurred when the judges gave advice. Particularly in Massachusetts, advisory opinions were common, and in these opinions, as in their other decisions, the judges' duty required them to follow the Constitution.[30]

The Massachusetts Constitution required advisory opinions. On account of English abuses of such opinions, and more generally because of the principle of separation of powers, Americans tended to doubt whether judges should give advisory opinions. The Massachusetts Constitution of 1780, however, stated that "[e]ach branch of the legislature, as well as the governor and council, shall have the authority to require the opinions of

[29] See Chapter Seventeen. The mixing of administrative and judicial office in justices of the peace was carefully analyzed as early as the sixteenth century, when the civilian Richard Cosin pointed to the mixed role of justices of the peace in order to justify the inquisitorial procedure of the ecclesiastical courts. [Richard Cosin], *An Apologie for Sundrie Proceedings by Jurisdiction Ecclesiasticall,* 2: 82 ([1593]). His attempt, however, to analogize from what was increasingly viewed as an exception could not have lent credibility to his argument.

[30] Such opinions were also occasionally requested in some other states. See, for example, G. S. Rowe, *Embattled Bench: Pennsylvania Supreme Court and the Forging of a Democratic Society, 1684–1809,* at 155 (Newark: University of Delaware Press, 1994). For an illustration from the westward part of Virginia, see the opinion obtained by the field officers for the District of Kentucky from the judges and attorney general for the district about the delegation of executive powers to the officers under a Virginia militia statute and the sixth Article of Confederation. Opinion of George Muter, Caleb Wallace, & Harry Innes ([1786]), LVA, General Assembly, House of Delegates, Speaker, Executive Communications, RG 79, Box 4, Folder 38; printed in William Hayden English, *Conquest of the Country Northwest of the River Ohio 1778–1783 and Life of General George Rogers Clark,* 2: 1059 (Indianapolis: Bowen-Merrill, 1896).

the justices of the supreme judicial court, upon important questions of law, and upon solemn occasions."[31] Under this provision, the judges did not usually evaluate or review any actual act, but rather merely gave their opinions as to what the Constitution required on a stated question, which often arose from a particular proposal, but ordinarily was put to them in general terms. As in England, the judges gave these opinions in jointly signed letters rather than from the bench, and they thus did not act as a court. Predictably, they could not find any instruction in the Massachusetts Constitution as to how they should decide the proffered questions of law. Yet having taken their oaths as judges, they remained bound (like their English colleagues) to give their opinions, even their advisory opinions, in accord with the law of the land.

The judges in these advisory opinions regularly decided structural questions of a sort that only occasionally arose in cases.[32] For example, in early 1781, shortly after the adoption of the state's constitution, the houses of the legislature turned to the judges to resolve a dispute about taxation. The houses disagreed as to which house had the power to settle the proportionate value of taxable property in each of the state's towns. At a time of scarce cash and growing debts, this allocation of tax burdens weighed on the minds of constituents, and it is no surprise that in apportioning taxes, the two houses reached very different conclusions.

The Constitution stated that "[a]ll money bills shall originate in the House of Representatives," and the House of Representatives therefore thought that, "agreeable to the spirit of the clause . . . it is their exclusive right & duty to originate an inquiry into the returns made from the several Towns & plantations for the purpose of settling a valuation & *finally* to conclude on the proportion of rateable property within each town & plantation in this State." The Senate, in contrast, believed that "the above recited clause does not apply to the settlement of a Valuation, & therefore . . . by virtue of the equal rights & powers, which are given by . . . the frame of Government to the two branches of the Legislature, the Senate have an equal right & concern with the house of Representatives in originating & compleating, the Settlement of a Valuation." The two houses at least agreed that "it is essential to the public interest" that they should "unite in their

[31] Massachusetts Constitution of 1780, Chapter III, Article II. Another such provision appeared in the New Hampshire Constitution of 1784, Part II, Article 74.

[32] A structural question about the distribution of power between the General Assembly and one of its component houses arose in the first Virginia pardon case, *Commonwealth v. Caton* (1782). Moreover, the later Virginia pardon cases, *Commonwealth v. Minns* (1785) and *Commonwealth v. Fowler* (1785), concerned executive power.

construction of the Constitution without delay," and they therefore, on February 20, 1781, asked the judges to deliver in writing "on or before the Twenty second instant, their respective opinions on the above Questions in debate."[33]

This was, perhaps, the first occasion that the justices gave an advisory opinion under the Constitution, and although in response to later requests they would try to concur in joint opinions, the four judges came before the Senate on February 22, 1781, with separate written opinions. One reason may have been the constraint of time. Justice Nathaniel Peaslee Sargeant observed that "I have endeavored to consider the subject" as "fairly and fully as the very short time allowed me would permit," and "[p]erhaps if I had heard all the arguments that have been made use of, I might be of a different opinion."[34] Justice James Sullivan bluntly "wished that a longer space than two days had been allowed me."[35]

The judges opined that each house had an equal right to settle valuations. For example, Chief Justice Cushing observed that the two houses equally had to assent to legislation, including the legislation raising taxes, and from this he concluded that whether the settlement of a valuation "be considered as an act of legislation, or only as a necessary step to legislation," the Senate as well as the Representatives "must have a right to examine the lists of valuation returned, and adjust the same for themselves, or to concur in such adjustment."[36] The other justices largely agreed, although two of them explored what Cushing left aside—that because a settlement of valuation was not legislation, the two houses could act on it either separately or jointly, as they pleased. Justice James Sullivan, for example, wrote that whereas legislation was "by force of the Constitution . . . subject to the control of both Houses," a valuation "is merely a mode of acquiring light from and rectifying mistakes in the evidence" about property holdings, and "I can see no necessity, arising from any part of the Constitution, of its being an act of both Houses"—thus leaving them free to make "separate rules of proportion for themselves respectively, although it might be more conve-

33 Order of General Court for an Opinion Respecting the Power of the Senate to Examine the List of Valuation (Feb. 20, 1781), Massachusetts Historical Society, William Cushing Papers.

34 Opinion of Nathaniel Peaslee Sargeant (Feb. 22, 1781), *Massachusetts Reports,* 126: 550 (1880). Although the originals have not yet been located in the Massachusetts State Archives, the general accuracy of these transcriptions is apparent from a comparison with Cushing's draft. "Opinion upon a question referred to us by the General Court" ([Feb. 22, 1781]), Massachusetts Historical Society, William Cushing Papers, 1781–1782 File.

35 Opinion of James Sullivan (Feb. 22, 1781), *Massachusetts Reports,* 126: 554 (1880).

36 Opinion of William Cushing (Feb. 22, 1781), ibid., 126: 549.

nient to do it jointly."[37] In giving their opinions, the judges understood that they were bound to disappoint one house of the legislature or the other, and Justice Sargeant therefore concluded by telling the legislature that he trusted "your Honors will excuse my freedom in consideration that duty is of superior obligation to politeness."[38]

In contrast to this dispute within the General Assembly, some requests for advisory opinions concerned the relation of the legislature to other branches of the government, and here too the judges did their duty. The Governor's council consisted of nine men, and when in 1784 two vacancies occurred—one by death and the other by resignation—the question arose as to whether the two houses of the General Court had "a constitutional right" of electing men to fill the empty places. "The letter of the constitution provided" such a mechanism to replace a councillor only as part of the initial appointment process—if "the person elected did not accept of his appointment"—and this suggested to the Senate that the two houses had no power to appoint new members of the Council where, as in the current instance, the men had "in fact accepted" and had "officiated" for a while before their death and resignation removed them from the Council. Put succinctly, the Constitution did not specifically authorize the legislature to replace such councillors, and the Senate assumed that under the Constitution the legislature "had no right to act without the letter of it." The House of Representatives, however, analogized the current circumstances to what had been spelled out by the Constitution, and on this basis the lower house argued that it was "fully within the spirit and meaning of the frame of Government" for the legislature to appoint a councillor in place of one who had died or resigned.[39] After the two houses thus staked out their differences in a joint conference, the Senate asked the judges "[w]hether the two branches of the General Court have a Constitutional right to fill up Vacancies in the Council that happen by Death or Resignation of the members thereof."

[37] Opinion of James Sullivan (Feb. 22, 1781), ibid., 126: 556.

[38] Opinion of Nathaniel Peaslee Sargeant (Feb. 22, 1781), ibid., 126: 551. The two houses and the governor shortly afterward created a committee of both houses "to report the proportion that the several towns . . . shall pay toward the public taxes." Resolve (Mar. 9, 1781), *Acts and Laws of the Commonwealth of Massachusetts 1780–1781,* at 1: 359 Chapter 228 (np: Wright and Potter, 1890); *Massachusetts Reports,* 126: 556 (1880). To the extent this resolve ended the disputes between the houses over valuations, it may have stimulated challenges to valuations at an earlier stage in proceedings, at the time the valuations came from the counties. For a hint of this, see Resolve Relative to Aggrieved Persons on Valuation (Oct. 16 & 17, 1781), MSA, House Documents, 1781, No. 829, Box 15.

[39] "Proceedings of the General Court" (From the *Boston Magazine* for October 1784), *Salem Gazette* (Nov. 9, 1784).

The judges observed that this was only one of several questions about vacancies to which the Constitution did not give an express answer. For example, the Constitution did not state how to fill vacancies in the offices of secretary, treasurer, receiver general, and commissary general, and it obviously could not therefore be concluded that "[i]n case of a Vacancy by Death or Resignation" the government was "to be without those officers—it cannot be." Generalizing from this, the judges suggested that the Constitution's intent had to be pursued beyond its letter and, indeed, that the Constitution had to be construed like a remedial statute and thus beneficially: "We are certainly to construe the Constitution beneficially in favour of the People of the Government, for whose benefit it was made, and not in the Nature of a Penal Statute, which is to be Construed strictly." The judges concluded that the Constitution had been "designed" to ensure that notwithstanding the deaths or resignations of councillors, "those offices should be always filled, and that a Council of nine Persons, should exist," and as the Constitution "expressly provided" that vacancies occurring in the appointment process "shall be filled up," this "*implies* a Constitutional Power of filling up Seats *directly* and *positively vacated by Death* or *actual* Resignation." In short, "the two branches of the General Court have a Constitutional Right to fill up Vacancies in the Council that happen by Death or Resignation."[40]

Another advisory opinion focused on the effect of a recess on an unsigned bill. The Constitution required that no bill or resolve "shall become a law, and have force as such, until it shall have been laid before the Governour for his revisal," and "if he have any objection," he "shall return the same, together with his objections thereto, in writing," but it added that "to prevent unnecessary delays, if any bill or resolve shall not be returned by the Governour within five days after it shall have been presented, the same shall have the force of law." This provision might allow the legislature "to hurry" the governor by passing an act shortly before a recess—most egregiously, the evening before the recess, as happened at the end of a three-day meeting in September 1790. The effect (perhaps inevitable in so short a meeting) was to place the governor in the "embarrassing situation" of having to accept or reject the bill as presented to him, without any time to send it back with suggestions for revisions, and this might mean that he had to "waive the right he possessed by the Constitution" of "revising" the act or "be subjected to the disagreeable necessity of impeding the public busi-

[40] Opinion of the Justices on Right of Two Branches of Legislature to Fill Vacancies in the Council (Nov. 12, 1784), MSA, Senate Documents, Misc. 1784, No. 177, Box 6.

ness." When the legislature reconvened in late January 1791, the governor's allies complained about the tactic, and although they defended his review of legislation as a valuable part of the legislative process, a number also insisted that he had a constitutional right to review all proposed bills and even went so far as suggest that the unsigned bill had not acquired the force of law: "Some say it is now a law; —others say it is not; —because the five days which ought to be allowed, have not been."[41]

Amid these debates as to whether a late bill could confine the governor's legislative role, the Senate in February 1791 put the question to the judges. According to the Constitution, the last Wednesday in May was the annual commencement of a new General Court, and each year's General Court was to be dissolved the day before. The Senate therefore began by asking whether a bill or resolve "laid before the Governor for his approbation, less than five days before the Recess of the Gen[l] Court next preceding the last Wednesday in May . . . but not acted upon by him, has by the Constitution the force of Law."[42] The judges replied that "[i]f by *recess* in this question is meant a recess after a prorogation or a recess after an adjournment, where there is no subsequent meeting of y[e] same General court on that adjournment, we are clearly of Opinion that such bill or resolve by y[e] constitution *has not* y[e] *Force of Law*"—the underlying, common law principle being that legislation was the act of a court and that therefore a bill or resolve could not acquire the force of law "after y[e] session is ended." This, however, was just the prelude to the Senate's second and more central question, about bills and resolves "laid before the Governor for his approbation, less than five days before any Recess of the General Court" in "other" situations. The judges explained that "a recess upon an adjournment," after which the same General Court would meet, had a very different effect from a closing recess or adjournment, for "all ye days of ye courts sitting are but one session, althô an adjournment intervenes." In these circumstances, if a bill or resolve "lays more than five days before ye Governor for his approbation, (including ye days of ye courts sitting before ye adjournment, & so many days of ye courts sitting upon ye adjournment, as will make up ye full

[41] Massachusetts Constitution of 1780, Part II, Chapter I, Section I, Article II; Speeches of Gardiner and Davis, "Sketch of the Business in the House of Representatives" (Feb. 8, 1791), *Independent Chronicle* (Mar. 3, 1791).

[42] Massachusetts Constitution of 1780, Part II, Chapter I, Section I, Articles I and II; Order of Senate, Certified by Samuel Cooper, Clerk, sent to the Justices of the Supreme Judicial Court (Feb. 14, 1791), loosely inserted in Francis Dana's Letterbook of Supreme Judicial Court Advisory Opinions, at page [19], Massachusetts Historical Society, Dana Family Papers, Ms. N-1088, Vol. 39.

term of five days,) without ye Governors returning ye same with his reasons for not approving it, we conceive such bill or resolve has ye force of Law."[43]

These advisory opinions were not cases, and they concerned structural questions that might today be thought beyond the cognizance of the judges—or at least within their discretion to avoid. The judges, however, had an office of deciding cases, and under the Massachusetts Constitution they also had a duty to give advisory opinions, and once a constitutional question came before them in either manner, they had a duty to decide in accord with the law of the land. To repeat the words of Justice Sargeant, the justices had a "duty" that was "of superior obligation to politeness."[44]

[43] Opinion of the Justices (Mar. 9, 1791), MSA, Senate Documents, Misc. 1791, No. 1372, Box 36. In the second question, the Senate asked "[w]hether a Bill or Resolve having passed both Branches of the Legislature & being laid before the Governor for his approbation, less than five days before any Recess of the General Court, other than such as is stated in the preceding question, & not acted upon by him, has by the Constitution the force of Law." Order of Senate, Certified by Samuel Cooper (Feb. 14, 1791), loosely inserted in Francis Dana's Letterbook, at page [19], Massachusetts Historical Society, Dana Family Papers, Ms. N-1088, Volume 39. Incidentally, Dana sketched out a draft of the justices' opinion on this order.

[44] Opinion of Nathaniel Peaslee Sargeant (Feb. 22, 1781), *Massachusetts Reports,* 126: 551 (1880).

A further request for an advisory opinion concerned the contentious question of a committee on accounts. In the spring of 1785 and again in the summer, the two houses passed resolves appointing a committee "to receive, examine and pass upon all accounts" and even authorized the committee "to pay the accounts that shall be allowed by them"—this being a means of asserting control over government payments. Resolve (Mar. 15, 1783) and (June 27, 1785). Upon the passage of the second of these, Governor James Bowdoin refused to give his approval, complaining that the resolve violated the state's constitution, including its separation-of-powers clause. Governor Bowdoin's Message (July 1, 1785), Journal of the Senate, 157 (July 1, 1785), Records of the States of the United States, Mfm. The Senate responded by asking the judges for their opinion whether the resolve "is agreeable to the Constitution," but the summer session soon came to an end, and the judges apparently assumed the matter had been put to rest. Journal of the Senate, 167 (July 4, 1785), ibid. When the legislature met again in October, however, the House asked the Senate whether the Senate had taken the Governor's objections into consideration and importunately expressed its "earnest desire" that the Senate would act on these objections, and the Senate therefore ordered their President to write to justices of the Supreme Judicial Court "requesting their immediate answer" to the earlier order "requiring their opinion," which got translated by the President into a request that the justices "would, as soon as may be, give their Opinion on the Resolve of the two Houses." Journal of the Senate, 178 (Oct. 21, 1785), 207 (Oct. 27); Letter of Samuel Phillips to William Cushing & the Other Justices of the Supreme Judicial Court (Oct. 27, 1785), Francis Dana's Letterbook of Supreme Judicial Court Advisory Opinions, [14], Massachusetts Historical Society, Dana Family Papers, Ms. N-1088, Vol. 39. Not having heard from them a week later, the Senate voted that the judges be asked for an "immediate answer" because "part of the publick business is retarded for want of it"—all of which again was softened in the letter to a request for their opinion "as soon as may be" and an explanation that the "impatience of the public Creditors is the occasion of this repeated appli-

Lower Courts

Little is more revealing about judicial duty than the decisions of lower courts. On the assumption that the development of judicial review could only have been an exercise of judicial power, the history of judicial review centers on state supreme courts and ultimately the U.S. Supreme Court. The judges of lesser courts, however, also held the acts of other parts of government unconstitutional, and their lowly decisions turn out to be of the highest significance.

Lower courts frequently considered constitutional issues. It has been seen that the Virginia county courts decided such questions, and although they did not ordinarily go further than to assert the constitutionality of their own decisions in opposition to contrary executive decisions, the judges in at least one instance—the 1785 Fairfax resolution against a new commission for existing judges—more directly declared an act of the executive contrary to the state's bill of rights. In later chapters, it will be seen that inferior courts in Massachusetts also examined constitutional questions and that the inferior courts of New Hampshire repeatedly held a state statute unconstitutional.

The judges of county and inferior courts tended to be men of limited power and competence. They did not typically have more than local influence, they often were not lawyers, and they thus were not the sort of men who could have created a judicial power over the constitutionality of execu-

---

cation." Journal of the Senate, 207 (Nov. 3, 1785); Letter of Samuel Phillips to William Cushing, etc. (Nov. 3, 1785), Francis Dana's Letterbook, [14].

The judges (except Sewall, who was absent) wrote back eleven days later that the Senate's letter "was received by the Court this morning," and in their desire to answer promptly, the judges merely wrote that "[t]he Court after having carefully considered the Constitution of the Commonwealth, are of opinion that the Resolve of the Two Houses of the Legislature referred to them as above, is not in any respects repugnant to the same." They added that "[t]he present engagements of the Court will not admit of their going into the reasons or grounds of this opinion, but if it shou'd be thought expedient, they will do it, when they may have sufficient leisure for that purpose." Opinion of the Justices (Nov. 14, 1785), MSA, Senate Documents, Misc. 1785, No. 284, Box 9. Upon reading this opinion, the two houses again passed their resolve and sustained it with the necessary two thirds of each house—the lower house meeting the mark by only a fraction. Journal of the Senate, 235 (Nov. 16, 1785), 239 (Nov. 17, 1785), ibid.

An additional request for an opinion came when, two years later, the Senate asked the justices "to give their Opinion, upon the Bill, confirming Estates to foreigners, whether it is consistent with the treaty of peace, the practice of Nations, & the Constitution of this Commonwealth." Journal of the Senate, 384 (Feb. 22, 1787), Records of the States of the United States, Mfm. Neither this request nor any response to it appears in Francis Dana's Letterbook. Perhaps the judges hesitated to respond on account of the nature of the question. Unfortunately, the relevant legislative file no longer survives.

tive and legislative acts. Already in England, however, even justices of the peace had the same duty as higher judges to decide in accord with the law of the land, and American lower court judges actually held government acts unconstitutional. Their decisions are admittedly unhelpful as precedents for judicial review, but sometimes the evidence that seems most negligible is actually the most significant. Precisely because lower court judges were of such limited power and legal sophistication, their decisions reveal the strength of judicial duty and the depth at which it was familiar in American society.

Recognizing that judicial duty reached all judges, regardless of their status, James Iredell explained that lower courts shared the power of the highest judicial courts to hold acts unconstitutional. During the controversy over the North Carolina case of *Bayard v. Singleton,* some men challenged any "judicial power . . . to question the power of an Act of Assembly," and on behalf of this position, some made the arresting argument that if the Superior Court could hold statutes unconstitutional, mere county courts would also have this power. The full range of judges, however, had a duty to decide in accord with the law, and therefore when James Iredell defended the power of the Superior Court judges to hold statutes unconstitutional, he did not dispute the fears about county courts. The judges had a "duty . . . to decide according to the *Laws of the State,*" and after discussing this duty and its implications for judicial power, Iredell noted: "But it is said, if the Judges have this power, so have the County Courts. I admit it. The County Courts, in the exercise of equal judicial power, must have equal Authority."[45] All judges, even the most inferior, enjoyed a power to hold acts unconstitutional—not because they were competent to exer-

[45] "To the Public," Duke University Rare Book, Manuscript, and Special Collections Library, James Iredell Papers, Box 1, which was printed in *North Carolina Gazette* (Newbern) (Aug. 17, 1786). He added for the sake of reassurance that "the liberty of appeal . . . ultimately rests every thing almost with the Superior Courts." Ibid.

One of the lowest bodies to reach a constitutional decision was a court-martial. The presiding officer was a colonel of the Virginia militia, John Guerrant, Jr.

> This Court taking into Consideration the Authority Vested in them by the Federal Constitution, and [being] of opinion, 'that they have no Constitutional power to impose fines upon the delinquencies which have occurred since the last Court Martial.[']
>
> Ordered that all fines assess'd for delinquencies since the Adoption of the New Constitution be remitted.
>
> Howell Lewis, Captain of Calvary, dissenting from the above determination.

Copy of resolution of Court Martial held at the Court House (Goochland County? Apr. 6, 1790), LVA, Governor Beverley Randolph Executive Papers (Apr. 6, 1790), Misc. Reel 5031.

cise discretionary power over executive and legislative acts, but because all judges, high and low, had a duty to decide in accord with the law.

Executive Acts

The duty of judges extended to the acts of all parts of government, including the executive. In pursuit of their duty, English judges had regularly decided the constitutionality of royal acts, and similarly American judges now examined executive acts, as can be illustrated by a pair of Virginia cases on conditional pardons. It has already been seen how in 1785 the Fairfax magistracy resolved that their new commission from the governor was unconstitutional, and in the same year the Virginia Court of Appeals twice rejected the governor's attempt to grant conditional pardons.

Many eighteenth-century Englishmen and Americans regretted the severity of the criminal law. In an era in which felonies tended to be hanging offenses, it was commonplace to hope for legislation "rendering crimes and punishments more proportionate to each other," and this was one of Thomas Jefferson's goals when he and his law reform committee revised the laws of Virginia. Their bill "for Proportioning Crimes and Punishments," however, took a rather symmetrical view of what was proportionate—so much so that Jefferson worried it would need "reconsideration."[46] On the one hand, it imposed mere labor for horse stealing and thus was too mild for contemporary taste, at least among horse owners; on the other hand, it required castration for sexual offenses and mandated that noses, lips, and ears be sliced off for maiming. The bill concluded by abolishing pardons—on the theory that executive mercy would become unnecessary once criminal offenses were punished proportionately. Until the bill was passed, however, Jefferson and some contemporaries hoped to use conditional pardons as a substitute method of moderating punishments.[47] The Virginia Constitution stated that the governor "shall, with the advice of the Council of State, have the power of granting reprieves or pardons," and beginning in 1780 Jefferson and later governors spared felons from capital punishment

[46] Letter from Thomas Jefferson to George Wythe (Nov. 1, 1778), in *The Papers of Thomas Jefferson,* 2: 230, eds. Julian P. Boyd et al. (Princeton: Princeton University Press, 1950). Jefferson attributed the harsh "scale of punishments" to the rest of the committee, but he clearly was very attached to the bill. Ibid.

[47] A Bill for Proportioning Crimes and Punishments in Cases Heretofore Capital, ibid., 2: 492–493, 498, 500, 503. For Jefferson's bill and its relation to the use of conditional pardons, see Kathryn Preyer, "Crime, the Criminal Law and Reform in Post-Revolutionary Virginia," *Law and History Review,* 1: 68–69 (1983). Jefferson believed that once laws were "proportionate and mild," they should "never be dispensed with." Letter from Thomas Jefferson to Edmund Pendleton (Aug. 26, 1776), in *The Papers of Thomas Jefferson,* 1: 505.

on the condition that they undergo a lesser penalty.[48] Jefferson and his successors thus used conditional pardons to achieve part of what he planned to accomplish more systematically through his bill.

In the spring and summer of 1785, Governor Patrick Henry granted such pardons to John Fowler and John Minns—the one a laborer who had committed an unspecified felony, and the other a schoolmaster who had supplemented his income by turning to robbery.[49] Each was spared execution on the condition that he submit himself to be confined for three years of labor. Neither complied, and Attorney General Edmund Randolph therefore moved in October 1785 in the General Court that the felons be brought to the bar. After each was led there by the keeper of the public jail, the Court demanded "what he had to say for himself" as to "why the Court here should not again proceed to award execution against him." Each felon pleaded his pardon, and the Attorney General predictably replied that the prisoner "did break the condition of the said Letters of pardon." The prisoners did not dispute this, and "with the approbation of his counsel and with the consent of the Court," each of them agreed with the Attorney General on a statement of his case: "[I]f the Court shall be of opinion that the condition to the said Letters of pardon annexed are not sufficient and binding in Law," then "the said Letters of pardon are an absolute discharge," but "otherwise that execution shall be awarded de novo." It was, the General Court thought, "a case of Novelty and difficulty," and the Court therefore decided to "adjourn the same to the Court of Appeals."[50]

Exactly why a conditional pardon was legally vulnerable had already become clear six months earlier in the governor's council. At that time, when considering the fate of several other convicted prisoners, the Council recommended to Governor Henry that the men "be pardoned on condition that they labour bodily in such manner & on such works as a Majority of the Director of public buildings shall direct"—some for three years, the others for five.[51] One councillor, Joseph Jones, however, submitted a formal, written dissent. He understood that "many very respectable and enlightened Citizens" thought conditional pardons would not only "reform

[48] Virginia Constitution of 1776.

[49] For Jefferson's conditional pardons, see Preyer, "Crime, the Criminal Law and Reform in Post-Revolutionary Virginia," 68.

[50] *Commonwealth v. Fowler* (General Court, Oct. 27, 1785), Supreme Court of Appeals, Order Book No. 1, 1779–1789, at 56–59, LVA; *Commonwealth v. Minns* (General Court, Oct. 27, 1785), ibid., 62–65. For an illustration of earlier conditional pardons, see Letter from Edmund Randolph to Thomas Jefferson (Feb. 23, 1781), in *The Papers of Thomas Jefferson,* 4: 694.

[51] Hall, ed., *Journals of the Council of the State of Virginia,* 3: 420 (Mar. 10, 1785).

Offenders and . . . restore them in time to the Community as usefull Citizens, but also more effectually deter others from committing the like offences," and he sympathetically expressed "my wish to see the experiment fairly made." Yet "at the same time I think the experiment should be made under the express sanction of legislative authority." He acknowledged "the falibility of my own judgment" and therefore took care to "deliver this opinion with all imaginable deference and respect to the opinions of others," but "[d]oubting as I do the right of the Executive under the Constitution to grant conditional pardons, I dissent from the above advice." In his view, "the Power of the Executive by the constitution . . . is confined to suspending for such time as they think proper the execution of the sentence of the law, or, in mercy, wholely to forgive the offender," but "not to change or alter the nature of his punishment."[52]

The Court of Appeals almost certainly adopted this reasoning or something like it. In both cases, it "certified to the said General Court as the opinion of this Court that the Condition annexed to the letters of Pardon . . . is illegal & that thereby the said Letters of Pardon are absolute."[53] Considering the alternative, John Fowler and John Minns must have been grateful.

Of course, even if the executive could not lawfully place conditions on its pardons, there remained a possibility that legislative authorization could help. As it happened, on the very day that the two cases had been adjourned to the Court of Appeals, the House of Delegates had asked a committee to prepare and introduce the proposed revision of the laws, including Jefferson's bill for proportionate punishments. The House proceeded to adopt a series of his proposed bills for revising the laws but balked at the one on punishments.[54] Instead, following Jones's suggestion about an "experiment . . . under the express sanction of legislative authority," the House now joined with the Senate to enact that the governor have the power (ex-

[52] Joseph Jones' Protest (Mar. 10, 1785), LVA, Patrick Henry Executive Papers, Box 2, Folder 16.

[53] *Commonwealth v. Fowler* (Court of Appeals, Nov. 4, 1785), Supreme Court of Appeals, Order Book No. 1, 1779–1789, at 61, LVA. Similarly, see *Commonwealth v. Minns* (Court of Appeals, Nov. 4, 1785), ibid., 62–65. *Fowler* was heard on Oct. 31 and Nov. 1, and *Minns* only on Nov. 4, when both were decided. In reprinting the record in *Fowler,* the reporter Daniel Call assumed that the "counsel for the prisoner contended . . . [t]hat the constitution provided for pardons simply; and that, in the present case, the language of the letters patent was positive, and put the liberty of the prisoner beyond the control of the executive." Call, *Reports,* 4: 37.

[54] Letter from James Madison to Thomas Jefferson (Jan. 22, 1786), in *The Papers of Thomas Jefferson,* 9: 195, discussed by Preyer, "Crime, the Criminal Law and Reform in Post-Revolutionary Virginia," 69.

cept in cases of murder or treason) to grant conditional pardons.[55] This was, however, only a temporary statute, and when the yearlong experiment came to an end, the General Assembly allowed it to lapse—perhaps because at least seven pardoned felons, being unwilling to satisfy the condition of labor, had simply escaped.[56] Shortly after the Assembly thus abandoned its authorization of conditional pardons, the House again rejected Jefferson's bill. As explained by one opponent, the bill's "chimerical" attempt to establish an "exact Scale of punishments" would introduce "Barbarity," and its substitution of "this imaginary scale" for the traditional executive grant of mercy would deprive men of a mechanism that "extends forgiveness according to the Circumstances of each particular Case."[57] The attempt to establish proportionate punishments in Virginia thus came to a halt, but not before the judges had held it was "illegal" for the executive to place conditions on its pardons. Evidently executive acts were vulnerable to judicial duty.

Judicial Acts

Far more remarkable than these judicial decisions holding executive acts unconstitutional was a decision holding a judicial act unconstitutional. In pursuit of their duty, judges had no compunctions about concluding that a

[55] The statute authorized the governor, other than in the excepted cases, "to pardon or reprieve any person or persons adjudged or sentenced to suffer death for a felonious offence, upon such conditions of bodily labor to be performed by each person so pardoned or reprieved, as the governor, with the advice of council, shall seem proper." It added, however, that if any person who received such a pardon were to "escape during the term of his or her condemnation to such labour," the governor could "declare such person to be out-lawed," and then anyone could kill or capture him (and in the latter case he was to be executed). An act empowering the governor, with the advice of the privy council, to grant conditional pardons in certain cases (1785), in *Laws of Virginia,* 12: 45–46. See also *Journal of the House of Delegates of Virginia,* 70 (Dec. 3, 1785), 76 (Dec. 8, 1785) ([1786]).

[56] American Occurrences, Richmond (Aug. 23), *New-York Journal* (Sept. 7, 1786). One of these men was an Irishman, John Fowler—perhaps, ironically, the same laborer who, together with Minns, had escaped once before.

The conditional pardons apparently led to the introduction of chain gangs in Virginia. Using his power to grant conditional pardons, the governor "has exposed to public view a number of criminals in chains, to work on streets for a certain time proportioned to their crimes," leading one commentator to fear that the experience "will not reclaim them, because a continual view of their situation destroys all the feelings of social benevolence and humanity." Extract of a Letter from a Gentleman in Williamsburgh, to his Friend in Savannah (Sept. 8, 1786), *Independent Gazetteer* (Nov. 16, 1786).

[57] Speech of John Wickham on the Bill for Proportioning Crime & Punishments (1786?), University of Virginia Library, Alderman Library, Wickham Papers, Reel 1, Part V Miscellaneous Books, Vol. II. He thought the goal of an exact scale of punishments "has long been the favorite Topic of visionary Projectors," and he observed that the state's constitution vested the power to pardon "in the Governor of the State and the plain Consequence is we have no Right to pass this Bill." Ibid.

lower court judge had decided a constitutional question erroneously. It was another matter, however, to hold that a judge or his court had acted unconstitutionally or otherwise unlawfully. As in England, this conclusion could be justified only when a judge stepped beyond his court's jurisdiction, and no state decision reached such an opinion more emphatically than a 1778 case in North Carolina. It is an apt case to conclude this chapter on the range of constitutional decisions, for it provides further evidence, of a dramatic sort, that judicial duty was of general application—that it applied in constitutional decisions about all types of government acts.

During the early years of the Revolution, when Americans were beginning to free themselves from Britain, the Quakers of North Carolina initiated another struggle—one within their own consciences, to liberate themselves from the sin of slavery. Beginning in 1772, the North Carolina Yearly Meeting adopted ever stronger positions against slavery, until in 1776 it finally concluded that all members "who hold slaves be earnestly and affectionately advised to Cleanse their Hands of them as soon as they Possibly can."[58] As it happened, the Revolution gave the Quakers an opportunity to act upon these sentiments. Although a 1741 North Carolina statute had prohibited the manumission of slaves, it had given enforcement powers to local churchwardens, and after Independence this "could not be carried into Execution, because in the change of Government there remained no Church wardens to execute the same."[59] The Quakers of Pasquotank and Perquimans Counties took advantage of this lapse to manumit their human property, and they thereby began efforts that would last well into the nineteenth century.

Their sacrifice on behalf of freedom left other citizens fearful for their safety and property, and the General Assembly in late spring 1777 therefore reenacted its old prohibition on manumission but with enforcement in the hands of private individuals. Significantly, the substantive prohibition and the penalty remained largely unchanged. The substantive bar, like that of the 1741 statute, was that "no Negro or Mulatto Slave shall hereafter be set free" (the only exception being "for meritorious Services" as "adjudged . . . by the County Court"). The remedy clause also echoed the colonial enact-

[58] Minutes of the North Carolina Yearly Meeting, 148 (26, 10, 1776), in Guilford College, Hege Library, Friends Historical Collection. More generally, see *A Narrative of Some of the Proceedings of North Carolina Yearly Meeting on the Subject of Slavery within Its Limits* (Greensborough: 1848).

[59] Report of Joint Committee, Journal of the House of Commons (Jan. 26, 1779), in *State Records of North Carolina,* 13: 659–60 (1896; Wilmington: Broadfoot, 1993). For the colonial act, see An Act, concerning Servants and Slaves (1741), *A Collection of All the Public Acts of Assembly of the Province of North-Carolina: Now in Force and Use,* 173 (Newbern: 1752).

ment—providing that the local sheriff should hold any liberated slave and that the County Court should order all such slaves to be sold "to the highest Bidder." What changed was that now any freeholder could capture the slaves and initiate the proceedings, thus taking the role once served by churchwardens.[60] Emboldened by this statute, whites hauled the liberated slaves before the sheriffs, and the Pasquotank and Perquimans County Courts soon sold many men, women, and children, including those liberated prior to the passage of the statute.[61]

The North Carolina Bill of Rights did not guarantee freedom from servitude, but its Article 24 forbade retrospective laws, stating that "retrospective Laws, punishing Facts committed before the Existence of such Laws, and by them only declared criminal, are oppressive, unjust, and incompatible with Liberty, wherefore no Ex post Facto Law ought to be made."[62] Although this was of little help to most slaves, it at least offered hope for those who had been freed before the passage of the 1777 statute. It would also eventually provide the basis for the judges of the North Carolina Superior Court to hold that the Perquimans County Court had violated the Constitution.

Ever mindful of their obligation to the highest of judges, the Quakers hired lawyers to argue before the more worldly justices of Perquimans and Pasquotank Counties. These lawyers "employed by the Negroes" included Jasper Charlton, James Iredell, and the latter's brother-in-law Samuel Johnston, and in July 1777 they attempted to prevent the Perquimans County Court from selling some of the slaves manumitted before the passage of the reenslavement statute.[63] In these tense circumstances, in which

[60] As put by the 1777 act, "it shall and may be lawful for any Free holder in this State, to apprehend and take up such Slave, and deliver him or her to the Sheriff of the County." An Act to prevent domestic insurrections, and for other purposes," chapter 6, §§II & IV (1777), *State Records of North Carolina,* 24: 14–15. One fifth of the proceeds was to be "paid to the Takers up of such Negroes or Mulattoes." Ibid. The mode of apprehending liberated slaves was modified by "An Act to Amend an Act Entitled 'An Act to Prevent Domestic Insurrections,'" chapter 22 (1778), ibid., 24: 964.

[61] Order for sale of free negros (Sept. 11 or 12, 1777), Pasquotank County, County Court Minutes (1754–1777), NCSA, CR 075.301.2; Order for payment of Sheriff Thomas Reding (Sept. 12, 1777), ibid., 390; Return of accompts by Sheriff Thomas Reding (Sept. 1778), in Pasquotank County, County Court Minutes (1777–1781), fol. 62r, NCSA, CR 075.301.4; Orders of Perquimans County Court of Pleas and Quarter Sessions (July 22, 1777, Oct. 21, 1777, and Apr. 21, 1778), copy certified to Edenton District Superior Court (Nov. 6, 1778), Edenton District, Records of the Superior Court (1774–1779), NCSA, DCR 2.022.28, 1778 Folder.

[62] North Carolina Declaration of Rights, §XXIV (Dec. 17, 1776), *State Records of North Carolina,* 23: 978 (Goldsboro: Nash Brothers, 1904).

[63] "An account of the substance of the trial of several Negroes that had been manumitted by Friends subsequent to an Act of the General Assembly of the state of North-Carolina, passed

the lawyers were at odds with the court itself, a substantial crowd came to listen.

Although the lawyers began by arguing that the judges should interpret the reenslavement statute consistently with the Constitution, they soon had to argue more basically that the judges could not repudiate the Constitution.[64] Working from familiar doctrine on charitable interpretation to show that the statute was not retrospective, Iredell explained that the statute could "not be otherwise understood in the present case, without a reflection upon the assembly, that they had violated the constitution, which he could not suppose they would do." At this point, Justice Christopher Wright interjected "that the Assembly were to form the constitution," and he had at least a semblance of justification in saying this, for the state's Provincial Congress had served both as a temporary legislature and as a constitutional convention. Samuel Johnston answered, however, that the Provincial Congress had been elected for the purpose of adopting the Constitution and that the Constitution was therefore binding on the Assembly. As a consequence, "the Assembly had no more power to alter the constitution, than the court had to make the laws that they were to act by, in courts of justice." The court was threatening to ignore the Constitution, and the lawyers therefore now challenged the court's conduct as much as the legislature's. Johnston reminded the justices that "the Assembly" was "bound and limited by the constitution"—just "as the court was bound and limited by the law and oath that they had taken"—and that therefore "the court had no right by that law" to order the sale of "the Negroes that were manumitted before the passing [of] that act."[65]

Having heard this suggestion that the justices were breaking the bounds of the law and their oath, "the large number of persons who were present" remained "very quiet and attentive." They waited as the justices conferred,

---

at Newbern in the month of April or May last," *To the Senate and House of Representatives of the United States, In Congress Assembled. The Memorial and Address of the People Called Quakers, from their Yearly Meeting held in Philadelphia, by Adjournments, from the 25th of the 9th Month, to the 29th of the same inclusive, 1797,* at 5 ([Philadelphia]: 1797).

64 Jasper Charlton opened the twofold argument for the slaves—that the statute's application to any slave who "'is, or shall be set free,' cannot with any propriety of speech be construed to look back and include" the slaves manumitted prior to its enactment, and that in any case, "such a construction would contradict the twenty-fourth section in the Bill of Rights . . .—wherefore no ex post facto law ought to be made." Ibid. The statute's words about a slave who "is, or shall be set free" could be considered ambiguous, especially in contrast to an earlier passage in the statute that used only the word "shall," and the lawyers therefore had good reason to turn to the Constitution to discern how the statute should be interpreted. Ibid.

65 Ibid.

and "after some time" the Perquimans County Court decided—with "a small majority" of three out of five justices—"for the Negroes to be sold."[66] The Pasquotank County Court reached the same conclusion, and on the order of the two courts, the local sheriffs dispersed the slaves "to the highest bidders."[67]

It was no accident that the resulting case in the Superior Court was one of the rare instances in which judges held not an executive act, nor a legislative act, but a judicial act unconstitutional, for the lawyers knew the doctrine on *coram non judice,* and although they were not seeking damages, they sought a judgment against the court on the ground that it had egregiously overstepped its jurisdiction. This was what allowed the Superior Court to hold the act of the Perquimans County Court unconstitutional—thus making the case an illustration of how judicial duty reached all parts of government, including the judiciary.[68] At the May 1778 term of the

[66] Ibid. Another skirmish in the Perquimans County Court concerned Dinah and three other former slaves. The "Negroe Woman named Dinah" claimed "to be a free Woman in virtue of a manumission from Rachel Wilson," and subsequently indentured herself as a servant for life. Afterward, "certain Persons apprehended and took the said Negro Woman into Custody," and when "the Question, whether she should be sold or not, came on to be considered" at the Perquimans County Court in late October 1778—"together with a question of the same nature concerning three other Negroes . . . who had been manumitted and indented also"—the Court on motion, "without requiring any proof whatever of their manumission, declared that they thought it was their duty, by the words of the Act, to order the sale of them." However, "James Iredell, who acted as Attorney on behalf of those Negroes and their Masters, produced in Court, their Manumissions and Indentures, by which it appeared that their Manumissions were before the passing of the said act." Nonetheless, Dinah and the others "were ordered by the said Court to be sold during the sitting of the Court, and they were sold accordingly." Affidavit of Jesse Copeland (in the hand of James Iredell) (Nov. 7, 1778), NCSA, Edenton District Records of the Superior Court 1774–1779, DCR 2.022.28, 1778 Folder.

[67] Affirmation in Support of Motion for Order to Show Cause (May 5, 1778), University of North Carolina at Chapel Hill, Wilson Library, Southern Historical Collection, Collection 1294-z, Manumission Papers.

[68] Although at the time the sales began in 1777, there was "no Superior Court to Appeal to," the legislature at the end of the year instituted Superior Courts, and this created an opportunity to challenge the conduct of the county courts. The Quakers initially contemplated an appeal whenever "there should be any more of those Manumitted Negroes order'd to be sold," but the lawyers knew better. As in later cases in American history, there were risks in seeking an appeal from an errant court, and the lawyers therefore recommended a writ of certiorari from the Superior Court. The Committee of Twelve—the standing committee for the North Carolina Quakers—took "under weighty Consideration the case of an Absolute Refusal of an appeal from the Judgment of Pasquotank Court to the Superior," and "having Consulted several Attorneys on the Occasion, it was advis'd to apply for a Certiorari on behalf of the whole of the Negroes, that were sold by order of Perquimons & Pasquotank Courts." Report of Committee of Twelve (26, 10, 1778), North Carolina Yearly Meeting Standing Committee Minutes, 37–38, Guilford College, Hege Library, Friends Historical Collection. The lawyers "agreed to undertake the Cause for the Sum of Six Hundred pounds of the present Money in Circulation." Ibid. For the Yearly Meeting's discussion

Edenton Superior Court, one of the lawyers, William Hooper, moved for a writ of certiorari to the Perquimons County Court to remove all of its proceedings regarding "the Sale and enslaving" of thirty-three individuals, and his arguments included the claim that "there are manifest Errors, and Irregularities in the said Proceedings" because the 1777 statute permitting the sale of manumitted slaves was only prospective.[69] Yet rather than merely claim error, he also argued that the Perquimons County Court itself had violated the law.

According to one account, he said of the former slaves that "the said Persons, tho. Free Subjects of the State were Sold and enslaved by Order of the said Court. in express Violation of the Constitution of this State and contrary to Natural Justice."[70] What this might mean became clear from a Quaker version of an affidavit, an "affirmation," that Hooper and his colleagues used to present their arguments in writing. This affirmation emphasized that the judges had blatantly violated the bill of rights—that the "seizure detention & sale both in the County of Pasquotank & Perquimans" had been "an exercise of power without right & a gross infringement of the civil liberties of divers subjects of this state & in positive violation of the Bill of rights," which was "part of the constitution of this State." To be sure, even when judges engaged in a "positive violation" of law, they did not necessarily act unlawfully, and the lawyers therefore recited that these judicial acts were "unjust illegal & extrajudicial"—in other words, they were contrary to natural law, in violation of North Carolina law, and beyond the court's jurisdiction.[71] The judges of the Superior Court responded to these arguments by ordering that a writ of certiorari be issued to the Perquimans County Court.[72]

---

and approbation and its efforts to raise the £600, see North Carolina Yearly Meeting Minutes, 1: 167–168.

69 Copy of Order of Edenton District Superior Court for writ of certiorari (term beginning May 1, 1778), NCSA, Edenton District Records of the Superior Court 1774–1779, DCR 2.022.28, 1778 Folder. The thirty-three individuals were Glasgow, Tom, Susannah, Jack, Cudjoe, Patience, Hannah, Silla, James, Ned, Langa, Phoebe, Jacob, Will, Sibb, Peter, Cuff, Rose, Hannah, Rose, Dick, Jane, Richard, Jane, Pompey, David, Zelpha, Violet, Fanny, Dick, Abraham, Judy, and Rose. Affirmation in Support of Motion for Order to Show Cause (May 5, 1778), in Collection 1294, Manumission Papers, Southern Historical Collection, University of North Carolina at Chapel Hill.

70 Copy of Order of Edenton District Superior Court for writ of certiorari (term beginning May 1, 1778), NCSA, Edenton District Records of the Superior Court 1774–1779, DCR 2.022.28, 1778 Folder.

71 Affirmation in Support of Motion for Order to Show Cause (May 5, 1778), University of North Carolina at Chapel Hill, Wilson Library, Southern Historical Collection, Collection 1294, Manumission Papers.

72 They "[o]rdered that a Certiorari Issue accordingly unless Sufficient cause to the Contrary

Upon receiving the record and hearing arguments for the slaves, the Superior Court judges ordered the certified proceedings to be "Quashed and held as Null and Void," and more to the point here, they held the County Court to have acted contrary to the North Carolina Constitution:

> The Court [ordered the proceedings quashed and held null and void] for divers and Manifest Irregularities in the face of the Records Certified, and because it appears to them, that the said County Court, in such their Proceedings, have exceeded their Jurisdiction, Violated the Rights of the Subjects, and Acted in direct opposition to the Bill of Rights of this State considered Justly as part of the Constitution thereof, by giving a Law not intended to affect this Case a retrospective operation thereby to deprive Free Men of this State of their Liberty contrary to the Law of the Land.[73]

In reciting these points, the Superior Court evidently recognized that few judicial acts contrary to law deserved to be held unlawful, and it therefore explained, in a more grounded manner than the lawyers, what distinguished the conduct of the Perquimans County Court. The foundation for the Superior Court's holding was, of course, that the County Court had exceeded its jurisdiction. On this basis, the Superior Court held that the County Court had violated the rights of the subjects. There had to be a particularly serious violation, however, and not content to advert to natural justice to make this point, the Superior Court observed that the County Court had acted in direct opposition to the Bill of Rights. In these circumstances, the Superior Court held the proceedings of the County Court unconstitutional.

---

be shewen within the three first days of the next ensuing Term," and although the clerk of the Perquimans County Court was slow to respond, a second writ, "[r]eturnable immediately," eventually elicited a certified copy of the Perquimans proceedings. Order to Show Cause (May 5, 1778), NCSA, Edenton District Superior Court, Minute Docket, April 1768–Nov. 1781, DCR 2.001, at 99; Order of Edenton District Superior Court (Nov. 5, 1778) for writ of certiorari, NCSA, Edenton District Records of the Superior Court 1774–1779, DCR 2.022.28, 1778 Folder.

James Iredell had felt obliged to accept a place on the Superior Court, and at the May 1778 meeting of the Edenton Superior Court, he was one of the judges who granted the rule to show cause why a writ of certiorari should not issue, but he resigned in June to resume his law practice, and he soon rejoined his friend William Hooper as one of the lawyers for the slaves. In July he therefore was present in the Perquimans County Court, where he witnessed that the rule to show cause "was delivered to the said Court, and read openly." Affidavit of James Iredell (Nov. 5, 1778) on Copy of Order of Edenton District Superior Court for writ of certiorari (term beginning May 1, 1778), NCSA, Edenton District Records of the Superior Court 1774–1779, DCR 2.022.28, 1778 Folder.

73 *State v. Clerk of Perquimans County* (N.C. Superior. Ct., 1778), NCSA, Proceedings and Orders (Nov. 9, 1778), Edenton District Superior Court, Minute Docket April 1768–Nov. 1781, DCR 2.001, at 108–109.

No case more clearly illustrates how judicial duty reached decisions about the constitutionality of judicial acts, and no case ended more sadly. Although the lawyers immediately obtained two additional writs of certiorari to the Perquimans and Pasquotank courts, many purchasers promptly relocated their property. As reported two weeks after the Superior Court decision, "[s]ome of the purchasers Seem Inclinable to let their Negroes have their liberty," but "others are sending them away in a private Manner, So that it is not yet known fully how Matters will terminate."[74] The next year the General Assembly, having heard from inhabitants of Pasquotank, secured purchasers in their title to slaves sold during the two years before the 1777 act by enacting that "all such Sales made *bona fide,* and for valuable consideration, shall be deemed good and valid, to all Intents and Purposes." The Assembly also clarified that the procedures provided by the 1777 act for capturing and initiating sale could be used retrospectively—that "the same proceeding may be had against all such illegally liberated Slaves . . . in the same Manner as if such Negro Slaves had been set free after the passing of the same." Although this provision might at first glance seem to have departed from the Constitution and the Superior Court's holding, the Assembly apparently assumed that it was merely introducing a retrospective enforcement procedure for an offense that, as it emphasized, had already been "contrary to the Laws of this State."[75] The manumitted slaves thus "were again reduced to slavery."[76]

[74] Letter of Thomas Nicholson to Robert Pleasants (Little River, Perquimans County, 21st, 11th month, 1778), A Bundle Letters Addressed to Robert Pleasants, 3: 126–128 (typed transcript), Valentine Museum Library (originals on deposit at Haverford College). For the additional writs, see Proceedings and Orders (Nov. 9, 1778), NCSA, Edenton District Superior Court, Minute Docket April 1768–Nov. 1781, DCR 2.001, at 108–109.
[75] An Act for apprehending and selling certain Slaves set free contrary to Law, and for confirming the Sales of others, and for other Purposes, c.12 (1778), *Acts of Assembly of the State of North-Carolina . . . the 19th Day of January, at Halifax, in the Year of our Lord 1779, being the third Session of this Assembly,* 20–21 ([1779]). There is no evidence that the judges or the lawyers for the slaves distinguished between retrospective prohibitions and retrospective remedies, and nor should this be a surprise, as such an argument would not have been in the interests of the slaves, and the County Court apparently was unrepresented.
[76] *To the Senate and House of Representatives of the United States, In Congress Assembled. The Memorial and Address of the People Called Quakers, from their Yearly Meeting held in Philadelphia, by Adjournments, from the 25th of the 9th Month, to the 29th of the same inclusive, 1797,* at 3 ([Philadelphia]: 1797).

Two decades after the decision against the Perquimans County Court, the Quakers could only make the modest claim that "[i]n consequence of this decree several of the negroes were set at liberty." "Quaker's Memorial" (22nd of 1st Month, 1798), *Porcupine's Gazette* (Feb. 2, 1798). Most were not so fortunate, being enslaved under law or being taken beyond the reach of law. Such, for example, was the fate of Jenny, who was separated "from her children" and "carried into the back country." *To the Senate and House of Representatives of the United States, In Congress Assembled. The Memorial and Address of the People Called Quakers,* at 3–4.

Nonetheless, the Superior Court judges of North Carolina had decided in accord with the law—even to the point of holding the County Court proceedings unconstitutional—and on a question as delicate as slavery, this says much about the breadth and the force of judicial duty. Unfortunately for the slaves, the judges could only decide in accord with the law of the land, and the law was meager.

In sum, the variety of constitutional decisions shows the strength of obligation, the cultural depth, and above all the conceptual breadth of judicial duty. The judges evaluated the constitutionality of government acts in the full range of their decisions—not only in cases but also in resolutions and advisory opinions; not only while sitting on supreme courts but also while sitting on lower courts; not only as to legislative acts but also as to executive and judicial acts. Although their decisions about legislative acts will now be examined in Part V, it should already be apparent that the judges did not have a specific power regarding cases on legislation. Instead, they had a general, culturally familiar, and profoundly binding duty to decide in accord with the law of the land.

V

JUDICIAL DUTY IN AMERICA AS TO LEGISLATIVE ACTS

It has been seen that the ideals of law and judicial duty applied to all sorts of government acts in America—legislation being the one sort not yet considered. It is now therefore necessary in Part V to examine whether American judges were required by their duty to hold unconstitutional state statutes unlawful.

Chapter Thirteen observes that the English legal obstacles to holding acts of Parliament unlawful had never been applicable to American legislation and that American judges regularly (although of course imperfectly) did their duty as to unconstitutional state statutes. Decisions holding state statutes unconstitutional stirred up controversy, especially in the lower houses of state legislatures, but it will be seen in Chapter Fourteen that the debate tended to be rather lopsided, for it was much easier to rest on the ideals of law and judicial duty than to try to qualify them. Finally, Chapter Fifteen turns to some cases in which judges did *not* hold statutes unconstitutional, for even if these cases may initially seem irrelevant, they reveal the ease with which American judges could contemplate questions about the constitutionality of legislation.

At a more general level, it can be observed that judicial duty thus had a more complete reach as to American legislation than as to English legislation. Although the common law had barred judicial decisions holding acts of the high court of Parliament unlawful, it had not stood in the way of decisions holding colonial or state legislation unlawful, and thus, both before and after Independence, judges could hold American legislative acts void in the same way they could reach this conclusion about other sorts of government acts. This scope of judicial duty within the ideals of the common law acquired practical force when American judges in 1776 began to serve under American constitutions, for being unburdened of colonial fears and resentments, the judges became more willing to do their duty in holding legislative acts unlawful. Now even in practice, judicial duty gave Americans a formal mechanism for enforcing constitutional law against all parts of government, and this, it will be seen, was fortunate in a nation such as the United States.

13

Holding Legislative Acts Unconstitutional

BEING a general ideal, judicial duty reached not only executive and judicial acts but also legislative acts. One might assume that it was a momentous step for judges to hold state legislation unlawful and void, but it did not appear so substantial in the context of judicial duty. When considered within this duty—a duty so broad that it was binding on all types of judges in all sorts of decisions about all kinds of acts—the question was not whether the judges should experiment in developing a new sort of power for themselves, but rather why legislative acts should be excluded from the reach of their duty.

Sovereignty

In retrospect, it is often thought that Parliament's sovereign power protected its acts from being held unconstitutional, and from this perspective, it would seem that if the American states were sovereign, Americans judges had to invent a new power for themselves after Independence if they were to hold state statutes unconstitutional. It is true that judicial duty must have acquired heightened significance when American judges had to shift their attention from the subordinate legislation of colonies to the sovereign legislation of states. Yet this is not to say that on either side of the Atlantic sovereignty by itself was much of an obstacle to judicial decisions holding statutes unconstitutional. It could seem to be such an obstacle in England, where the common law already barred judicial decisions holding acts of Parliament unconstitutional. As will be seen, however, the common law obstacles continued to be inapplicable in most American jurisdictions, and when claims of sovereignty stood on their own, they were unlikely to protect any sort of government act from judicial evaluation about its constitutionality.

Although Parliament in the eighteenth century was said to have sovereign power, mere sovereignty was not what placed government acts, whether royal or parliamentary, beyond the reach of the judges. For example, acts of the Crown had regularly been held unlawful by the judges, and although the king's absolute prerogative was nothing less than his "sovereign" power, his acts within the absolute prerogative eventually came to be subject to the law of the land and its courts. Thus, at least by the last half of the seventeenth century, what distinguished sovereign acts was not that they could escape judicial scrutiny, but rather simply that they stood beyond reconsideration for their conformity to reason or justice—these being matters inherently within sovereign discretion. It was a point that Chief Justice Holt expounded when differentiating sovereign and subordinate acts; he explained that "an Act of parliament," which was an act of a body with "Sovereign power," binds "Absolutely without any dispute to be made of its Justice or Equity."[1] Sovereignty, in this analysis, was a barrier to judicial reevaluation of the reason or justice of an act of Parliament, not a general impediment to holding such an act unconstitutional.

A broader sort of sovereignty—essentially, the old theory of absolute power recast as sovereignty—increasingly appealed to some Whig politicians and Tory academics precisely because it suggested a power above the constitution, but this was not the sort of analysis with which the English judges had understood the Crown to be under law, and it was therefore more apt to flourish in political debates and academic commentaries than in the courts. Although in Parliament men increasingly said that their institution had a sovereign power above the law and its courts, in the courts, as Holt recognized, sovereignty was merely a bar to judicial reconsideration of acts for their justice or equity. What therefore more broadly protected acts of Parliament from being held void were the common law barriers: the customary character of the English constitution and the status of Parliament as the highest court in the realm. Of course, as has been seen, a high court could come to consider itself sovereign in the sense of absolute, and eventually this shift toward viewing Parliament as having a sovereign power above the law obscured the more modest, legal impediments to judicial decisions holding its acts unconstitutional. Yet even when the generalization about Parliament's absolute sovereignty acquired a force of its own, it was only plausible because it was layered on top of the preexisting legal assumptions that already barred judicial decisions holding acts of Parliament unconstitu-

[1] *City of London v. Wood* (1702), British Library, Add. Ms. 35980, fols. 2[v], 13[r].

tional. Considered more generally, not merely as applied to Parliament, but as an abstract ideal that was also applicable to the king or, later, to state legislatures in America, sovereignty could not very plausibly be a power above the law, which stood in the way of judicial decisions about lawfulness. Indeed, it has been seen that when considered as a generally applicable ideal at common law, it was apt to be merely the basis for a sovereign discretion about the reasonableness or justice of an act.

The two conceptions of sovereign power—the one a power above the law, and the other a discretionary power within the law—left some room for Americans after 1776 to take different views of judicial decisions holding state statutes unconstitutional. Men sitting in state legislatures could imagine that these bodies had an uncontrollable sovereign power like that claimed for Parliament. Men sitting on the bench, however, might well doubt whether the sovereignty of state legislation placed it above the reach of the law or the courts. Inasmuch as English judges had already decided the constitutional boundaries of sovereign acts of the Crown, it was difficult for American lawyers to conclude that the mere sovereignty of legislation placed it beyond the law or the courts. In fact, being keenly aware of the claims made by the Crown in the seventeenth century and by Parliament in their own century, American lawyers and judges tended to draw the lesson that even absolute, sovereign power, although discretionary, had to be kept subject to law, and this certainly seemed to be the approach taken by Americans in their constitutions. When claims of absolute or sovereign power were occasionally raised in American cases concerning legislation (for example, as will be seen, in Virginia and North Carolina), lawyers and judges had little difficulty pointing out that their countrymen had rejected Parliamentary notions of absolute or sovereign power and had only granted limited authority to their legislatures.

Undoubtedly, the newfound sovereignty of American legislation gave the duty of American judges after 1776 a profound importance. Yet it cannot be assumed that Americans adopted a lawless sovereignty, and even in England absolute sovereignty by itself did not prevent the judges from holding any government act unconstitutional—not even acts of Parliament, which were already beyond constitutional evaluation for other reasons. It therefore should be no surprise that sovereignty did not prevent American judges from doing their duty as to government acts. Rather than the abstract question of sovereignty, what more clearly mattered for the duty of American judges in holding state statutes unconstitutional was the absence of the common law obstacles to holding acts of Parliament unconstitutional.

The Absence of English Obstacles

The duty of American judges in deciding the constitutionality of American statutes was different from the duty of an English judge as to an act of Parliament. In English law, as already noted, a pair of legal obstacles prevented judges from holding acts of Parliament unconstitutional, but these traditional barriers had not ordinarily been applicable to other legislation, including the acts of American legislatures. Accordingly, whether before Independence or afterward, judges in the course of doing their duty had to evaluate the constitutionality of all sorts of American legislation.

The first of the English legal obstacles was the existence of a customary constitution, which could be declared and altered by the nation's legislative court. When Parliament adopted a statute, it in effect declared that the constitution permitted such an act. Corporations and colonies, however, had express charters or constitutions, and their legislative courts therefore could not claim a power to declare their constitutions as if they were customary laws. Nor, of course, did customary constitutions ordinarily become an obstacle after Independence, for when the colonies became states, they generally maintained express governing documents—now more often called "constitutions" than "charters," but still express rather than customary.

This was St. George Tucker's point when in 1782, in *Commonwealth v. Caton,* he argued that the Virginia Constitution and Declaration of Rights were express and that they could therefore not be declared or interpreted by the state's legislature. Ordinarily, it would be enough simply to observe that the Bill of Rights and Constitution were "the *Basis and Foundation of Government*" and that because "any Act of the Legislative" that was "absolutely contradictory, or repugnant to the Constitution" was "absolutely null and void . . . the Judges are not bound to consider such Act as a Law." Tucker recognized, however, that objections might be drawn from Britain's customary constitution—that "it may be urged" that in Britain "constitutional Acts, may, nay, have been altered by the British Parliament." He therefore pointed out that "no paral[l]el can possibly be drawn between the Constitution of G.B. & this Country." He explained that "the Constitution of G[reat] B[ritain] partakes of the nature of their Common Law" and that as Parliament therefore had "power not only to explain the common Law, but also the Constitution, it follows that they may by a subsequent Act explain certain points of the Constitution differently from what they were explained in a former Act." This was little more than a "Fiction in Law" by which "the British Constitution may be modelled agreeably to the will of Parliament, whose omnipotence in this Instance seems generally admitted." Not so, however, in Virginia: "But the Case is otherwise with our Constitution—the British is constructive—ours is express." Accordingly, although Britain's "traditional" constitution had been "explained at different Times, & by different Parliam.ts and in different modes," Virginia's "on the contrary w[a]s framed with all the solemnity of an original Compact between Citizens about to establish a Government most agreeable to themselves." To this he added that "it was committed to writing and made public to all the Citizens who became parties thereto" so "that it might not be misinterpreted."[2] It was enough for Tucker to observe that the Virginia Constitution was express, but he clinched his argument against any Parliamentary power in America by noting (in a manner that would soon become commonplace) that, unlike the English constitution, American constitutions were written.

James Iredell similarly noted that the people had consented to legislative power with express rather than customary limitations. When the North Carolina judges in 1786 were weighing the constitutionality of a state statute in *Bayard v. Singleton,* Iredell argued that "we have as much agreed to be governed by the Turkish Divan as by our own General Assembly, otherwise than on the express terms prescribed."[3] In contrast—as Iredell wrote in 1787, after the judges held the statute unconstitutional—if North Carolina had been "[w]ithout an express Constitution, the Powers of the Legislature would undoubtedly, have been absolute (as the Parliament in Great Britain is held to be); & any Act passed . . . would have been binding on the People."[4] Britain's customary constitution, like the rest of the common law, was subject to Parliament's power to declare or alter such law, but royal charters and now popular constitutions were express, and they thereby left American legislatures no power to declare or alter them.

[2] "To. W.N.," Argument on Behalf of the Prisoners, Addressed to William Nelson, William and Mary College Library, Tucker-Coleman Papers, Legal Papers, Virginia Supreme Court of Appeals, Mfm Reel M-44. Similarly, in response to desperate suggestions that the judges had a duty to decide in accord with the law of the land but not the Constitution, Tucker answered that the Constitution was the primary part of this law: "For altho' it be true that the Judges are sworn to decide in all matters brought before them agreeably to the Laws of the Land, yet is the Constitution the first Law by which they are bound, and any Decision contrary thereto is absolutely subversive of that Government of which it is undoubtedly the Basis & Foundation." Ibid.

[3] "To the Public," Duke University Rare Book, Manuscript, and Special Collections Library, James Iredell Papers, Box 1.

[4] Letter from James Iredell to Richard Dobbs Spaight (Aug. 26, 1787), in *The Papers of James Iredell,* 3: 307, eds. Donna Kelly and Lang Baradell (Raleigh: North Carolina Department of Cultural Resources, 2003). For a caveat to this statement, see Chapter Eleven at note 54.

The second obstacle to decisions holding acts of Parliament unlawful was Parliament's status as the high court, but this similarly was not a barrier to decisions about state enactments, for state legislatures were not ordinarily high courts. Although all bodies with legislative power were traditionally "courts"—ranging from a manor court to the high court of Parliament—the legislative courts of corporations and colonies had been subordinate courts, which were always subject to the decisions of the king's courts. A colonial legislature, such that of South Carolina, could attempt to intimidate local judges by claiming to be a high court, but in English law colonial legislatures were merely the legislative courts of local bodies, and royal judges therefore owed these bodies none of the deference due to the high court of Parliament.[5] From this perspective, judges had a duty to uphold English law against colonial legislatures as much as against municipal bodies in England.

It gradually even became clear in the colonies that American legislatures were not high courts, to which judges had to defer, and one way this became evident was through the differentiation of judicial and legislative courts. English lawyers had sometimes worried about their general courts, but they had traditionally thought of the problem in terms of the old ideal that no one should be judge in his own case, and from this perspective, they expected the king in Parliament or a local lord in his manorial court to avoid hearing a case in which he had a legal interest.[6] The principle that no one should be judge in his own case also came to be applied to the general courts of corporations and colonies, but this was not a sufficient response to the difficulties created by American general courts, which used their judicial power to prevent the judicial courts in the colonies from upholding the rights of the Crown. Accordingly, when Crown lawyers in the seven-

[5] Nor would Crown lawyers concede that the lower houses of American assemblies enjoyed the privileges of the House of Commons. After the Pennsylvania House of Representatives imprisoned a publisher in 1758 for his critical publications about a prior Assembly, the Privy Council ordered the Governor to preserve the laws "against all usurpations and encroachments whatsoever by the Assembly," for as the Attorney General and Solicitor General explained, whatever power to imprison lay in Parliament, "this extraordinary power ought never to be Suffered in these inferior Assemblys in America who must not be compared either in power or privileges to the Commons of Great Britain." Order of Privy Council, & Opinion of Attorney General & Solicitor General (June 26, 1759), *Acts of the Privy Council,* 4: 384 (London: His Majesty's Stationery Office, 1911).

[6] For the general approach to manorial courts and the numerous exceptions, see D. E. C. Yale, "*Judex in Propria Causa:* An Historical Excursus," *Cambridge Law Journal,* 33: 87–92 (1974). Regarding the king in Parliament, note the pronouncement that Britton attributed to Edward I: "[I]n cases where we are party, our pleasure is, that our Court, to wit, the earls and barons in time of parliament, shall be judges." Simeon E. Baldwin, ed., *Britton: An English Translation and Notes,* 85 (I.xxiii.8) (Washington: John Byrne, 1901).

teenth and eighteenth centuries found themselves struggling against the judicial ambitions of colonial general courts, they increasingly insisted that colonial charters establish separate judicial systems, including supreme judicial courts.[7]

The establishment of supreme judicial courts thus became part of a policy of preventing colonial legislatures from behaving as if they were little Parliaments. To be sure, some colonies carefully established judges in nothing higher than superior judicial courts, and even when there were supreme judicial courts, the Crown could not always preclude legislative appeals. Yet the Crown's efforts to establish supreme judicial courts in the colonies left little doubt about English policy and law: A legislature might be called the "General Court," but if there was a judicial court that was supreme, it had final judgment, and in theory there could be no appeal from its decisions, except to the superior legal system in England. Whereas in England there was no appeal from the high court of Parliament, in America there would eventually be no appeal beyond the highest judicial courts.

The tendency toward establishing supreme judicial courts continued after 1776, and it suggests the growing expectation in America that judges should not have to defer to the decisions of a legislative court. In colonies such as Pennsylvania and New York, the highest judicial court had already been the "Supreme Court," and it did not lose this status when the colony became a state.[8] In some other colonies, moreover, there was a shift toward having supreme judicial courts. Although the Massachusetts legislature remained the "General Court," the highest judicial court, which had been merely the "Superior Court of Judicature," now became the "Supreme Judicial Court." In North Carolina, where the charter had left the relation of the courts to the legislature somewhat murky, the state's constitution enjoined the Assembly to appoint "Judges of the Supreme Courts of Law and Equity," and although the General Assembly instead established Superior Courts, the Constitution's implications were clear enough.[9] Among judges and lawyers, this expectation that there would be a supreme judicial court

[7] Smith notes that royal instructions mostly limited only the lower houses of colonial legislatures. Joseph Henry Smith, *Appeals to the Privy Council from the American Plantations,* 638 (New York: Columbia University Press, 1950). The Privy Council, however, appears to have taken a broader approach, and in any case, as Osgood observes, "[b]efore the first century of colonial development had passed, the councils had ceased to regularly perform judicial functions, and supreme or superior courts had been organized." Herbert L. Osgood, *The American Colonies in the Seventeenth Century,* 2: 278 (Gloucester: Peter Smith, 1957).

[8] A supreme court also existed before and after Independence in New Jersey, except that there the 1776 Constitution allowed the governor and his council to hear appeals. New Jersey Constitution of 1776, Article IX.

[9] North Carolina Constitution of 1776, Article 13.

was so strong that even when judges only sat on a "Superior Court," they were apt to think that it was in effect a supreme court. A majority of the judges of the Rhode Island *Superior* Court, for example, protested to the lower house of the state Assembly that although they had not "the least power or authority . . . to contravene or controul the constitutional laws of the State," they "conceive that the entire power of construing and judging the same, in the last resort, is vested solely in the Supreme Judiciary of the State."[10]

This vision of judicial courts as not inferior to any Parliament-like legislative court acquired clarity and a forceful theoretical expression in the ideal of separation of powers. Ideals about the different faculties of the soul had long been developing into what would become the principle of separation of powers—it being noticed as early as the Middle Ages that if legal obligation came from the will of an authoritative lawmaker, this might imply a differentiation of legislative, judicial, and executive power.[11] The English, on account of the complexities of their government, did not usually discuss this tripartite division, but they were certainly capable of doing so—as when Chief Justice Holt observed that "the people" elected their representatives with "power and authority to act legislatively, not ministerially or judicially."[12] At the very least, the English were well educated in the view that if no one could be both judge and party, then the powers derived from the different faculties of the soul might have to be separate offices in government. Thus, even "school-boys," it will be recalled, knew "that *Legem f*[*a*]*cere* and *Legem dicere* were powers clearly distinguished from each other in the nature of things, and wisely separated by the wisdom of the English Constitution."[13] Put another way, the natural distinction between these powers seemed to require their institutional separation.

The English emphasis on distinguishing lawmaking and judging prominently came together with the old tripartite separation of powers in

[10] Memorial "To His Excellency the Governor, and this Honour the Speaker fo the Lower House of Assembly: To be Communicated to Both Houses," in James M. Varnum, *The Case, Trevett against Weeden,* 45 (Providence: 1786).

[11] Brian Tierney locates this tripartite division in the writing of the fourteenth-century Dominican Hervaeus Natalis. Brian Tierney, "Hierarchy, Consent, and the 'Western Tradition,'" *Political Theory,* 15: 649–650 (1987). See also Brian Tierney, *Religion, Law, and the Growth of Constitutional Thought 1150–1650,* at 45 (Cambridge: Cambridge University Press, 1982).

[12] *Case of Paty et al.* (Q.B. 1705), *The Judgements delivered by the Lord Chief Justice Holt in the Case of Ashby v. White and Others, and in the Case of John Paty and Others,* 60 (London: 1837).

[13] Speech in House of Lords (Jan. 9, 1770), *Anecdotes of the Life of the Right Hon. William Pitt, Earl of Chatham,* 2: 15–17 (London: 1792).

the writing of Montesquieu, who thus made it easier for Englishmen and Americans to talk about the separation of judicial and legislative power as part of the broader separation of three parts of government. Locke had adopted the notion of judge in one's own case as a metaphor for the state of nature and thus also for absolute power, and Montesquieu drew upon this reasoning to conclude that "there is no liberty, if the power of judging be not separated from the legislative and executive powers."[14] Americans repeatedly echoed such sentiments, as when the Virginia Constitution generalized that "[t]he legislative, executive, and judiciary departments, shall be separate and distinct, so that neither exercise the Powers properly belonging to the other."[15] Of course, the principle of separation was widely assumed to be based in nature, and rather than make an abstract declaration of it, most American constitutions more concretely allocated the three powers in one way or another to different branches of government.[16] Yet even with these constitutional allocations of the tripartite powers it was the sepa-

[14] Montesquieu, *The Spirit of the Laws,* 185–186 (XI.vi.) (Dublin: 1751). As to Locke's views, see John Locke, *Two Treatises of Government,* 293–294 (II.ii.13), ed. Peter Laslett (Cambridge: Cambridge University Press, 1960); Philip Hamburger, "Revolution and Judicial Review: Chief Justice Holt's Opinion in *City of London v. Wood,*" *Columbia Law Review,* 94: 2127 (1994). Locke's analysis of the state of nature was obviously of particular significance for the separation of judicial from legislative power. At a more concrete level, although Locke did not separate a judicial power from the executive, he held it was "necessary there should be a *Power always in being,* which should see to the *Execution* of the Laws that are made, and remain in force. And thus the *Legislative* and *Executive Power* come often to be separated." Locke, *Two Treatises of Government,* 383 (II.xii.144). See also ibid., 343 (II.viii.88).

[15] Virginia Constitution of 1776. The Virginia Bill of Rights emphasized that "the legislative and executive power of the State should be separate and distinct from the judicative." Virginia Bill of Rights, §5. For other separation provisions, see Maryland Constitution of 1776, Declaration of Rights, §6; North Carolina Constitution of 1776, Declaration of Rights, §4; Vermont Constitution of 1786, Chapter II, Plan or Frame of Government, Article VI.

For the separation of judicial and legislative power and its implications, see Saikrishna B. Prakash and John C. Yoo, "The Origins of Judicial Review," *University of Chicago Law Review,* 70: 931 (2003). In contrast, some earlier scholars largely question whether Americans really wanted to separate legislative from judicial power. "The Progress of Constitutional Theory Between the Declaration of Independence and the Meeting of the Philadelphia Convention," in *American Constitutional History: Essays by Edward S. Corwin,* 4, eds. Alpheus T. Mason and Gerald Garvey (New York: Harper Torchbooks, 1964); Gordon S. Wood, "Judicial Review in the Era of the Founding," in *Is the Supreme Court the Guardian of the Constitution,* 155, ed. Robert A. Licht (Washington, D.C: AEI Press, 1993).

[16] This approach that had the advantage of clarifying that it was not separation in general but a constitution's particular separation of powers that was binding as law.

Incidentally, although the natural foundation of the different powers tends to get lost in the scholarly literature, it once was quite familiar. With a Lockean understanding of the state of nature, the Rev. Moses Mather preached: "By nature, every man (under God) is his own legislator, judge, and avenger, and absolute lord of his property. In civil government, rightly constituted, every one retains a share in the legislative, taxative, judicial, and vindictive powration of judicial and legislative power that remained particularly satisfying and familiar to common lawyers. As Caleb Strong observed in the 1787 Constitutional Convention, "[n]o maxim was better established" than "that the power of making ought to be kept distinct from that of expounding, the laws."[17]

This separation of judicial and lawmaking power seemed in America to leave judgments about law, including constitutions, exclusively in the judicial courts, and separation thus confirmed that, at least as a matter of common law ideals, American legislatures were not little high courts of Parliament—a point that became evident in 1782 in *Commonwealth v. Caton.*

ers." [Moses Mather], *America's Appeal to the Impartial World,* 7 (Hartford: 1775). Edmund Randolph argued in *Commonwealth v. Caton* that persons "who have either never yet entered into a formal social compact, or having abolished an old one are about to conclude another . . . possess every power, legislative, executive and judiciary," and thus the people in their constitution "delineat[ed] the degree, to which they have parted with legislative, executive and judiciary power, as well as prescribing how far each of the simple forms of government is to be pursued in acts of legislation." Edmund Randolph, Notes of Argument in *Commonwealth v. Lamb &c.,* Library of Congress, James Madison Papers, 91: 104. A newspaper commentator recited: "All citizens are equal, and originally possessed of legislative, executive, judiciary and military powers." "A Few Plain Maxims of Common Sense," *Virginia Independent Journal* (Mar. 19, 1788).

Rather than generally provide for separation of powers in their constitutions, Americans typically took the principle for granted and attempted to agree on the practical allocation of powers that would give it effect. This specification of the principle could be difficult, for as was acknowledged in New Hampshire as to the executive and legislative powers, "although there is a considerable majority for keeping the executive power separate from the legislative; yet there is . . . a diversity of sentiment concerning the manner, and hands, in which the same should be deposited." *An Address of the Convention for Framing a Constitution of Government for the People of New Hampshire,* 2 (Portsmouth: 1783). Article XXXVII of the New Hampshire Constitution of 1784 ended up requiring that the branches of government "be kept as separate and independent . . . as is consistent with that chain of connection that binds the whole fabric of the constitution in one dissoluble bond of union and amity." Similarly, Madison later observed that constitutions could not simply adopt the theory of separation, because while "[n]o political truth is certainly of greater intrinsic value," the branches of government could not be "totally separate and distinct from each other." Instead, each branch needed some *"controul"* over the others. James Madison, Federalist Number 47, *The Federalist,* 324–325, ed. Jacob E. Cooke (Middletown, Conn.: Wesleyan University Press, 1961). These difficulties were sobering and were yet another reminder that American constitutions were carefully written to require separation of powers in the way and to the degree they provided for it.

Like so many ideas attributed to Madison, his point that the parts of government could not be so separate as to be without checks upon each other obviously was far from unfamiliar. See "On Opposition to Courts, and Independency of Parliaments" (review of essay by Osborne [James Pitt] in *London Journal,* April 24, 1731), *Gentleman's Magazine,* 1: 163 (1731); John Witherspoon, *An Annotated Edition of Lectures on Moral Philosophy,* 144, ed. Jack Scott (Newark: University of Delaware Press); New Hampshire Constitution of 1784 (as quoted above); Samuel M'Clintock, *A Sermon,* 24 (Portsmouth: 1784).

[17] Madison's Notes (July 21, 1787), in *The Records of the Federal Convention of 1787,* at 2: 75, ed. Max Farrand (New Haven: Yale University Press, 1937).

When arguing in this case that the Virginia General Assembly lacked the power of Parliament to declare constitutional law, St. George Tucker not only observed that the Virginia Constitution was express but also noted that it separated powers. Such an argument was especially easy for Tucker, because as already seen, the Virginia Constitution generalized that the judicial power should be "separate and distinct" from the others. It thus was clear that "the power of interpreting all the Laws of this Commonwealth in particular Cases, is vested in the Judiciary alone," and "it follows that they alone (if any of the Departments of Government can do it) can decide what is or is not Law," including "the validity or nullity of different Laws contradicting each other."[18]

Similarly, when the President of the Virginia Court of Appeals, Edmund Pendleton, gave his opinion in *Commonwealth v. Caton,* he emphasized that the state's constitution was noncustomary and that it separated powers. Some commentators in Virginia had made "an objection" that was "drawn against the permanency of a constitution from the changes, which laws have made in European governments, and especially in England."[19] In other words, if European constitutions evolved, as declared at different times by their legislatures, then perhaps a similar historical process could be observed in Virginia—the argument being if that the state's statutes were evolving legislative declarations of its constitution, they were, in the manner of acts of Parliament, beyond judicial decisions holding them unconstitutional. Pendleton, however, dismissed this research about customary constitutions, for even if it revealed the requirements of any such constitution, the research disclosed little about "the Obligation to adhere to it."[20] More

[18] "To. W.N.," Argument on Behalf of the Prisoners, Addressed to William Nelson, William and Mary College Library, Tucker-Coleman Papers, Legal Papers, Virginia Supreme Court of Appeals, Mfm Reel M-44.

[19] Edmund Randolph, Notes of Argument in *Commonwealth v. Lamb &c.,* Library of Congress, James Madison Papers, 91: 104. Randolph recorded this objection at the end of the extant portion of his notes, and his response therefore is not known. Pendleton, however, apparently responded to similar concerns.

[20] Transcript of Edmund Pendleton's Notes of his Opinion in *Commonwealth v. Caton, et al.,* Library of Congress, Force Papers, at 8705–8706, Series 7E, James McGuire Collection, Correspondence Folders. Pendleton even found a little help from Britain, where Coke in his *Institutes* seemed to contradict what he said in his report of *Bonham's Case:*

> Even in Britain, where we might most expect to get some Rule to assist us, We find the same author Ld Coke asserting at one time the omnipotence of Parliament, who may even change the Constitution, & another [time] exalting the Judiciary above them, giving Courts power of declaring Acts of Parliament void because they are impertinent or contrary to right and Reason, both of which are mere speculative opinions & neither of them worthy of adoption by the Legislature or Judiciary.

Ibid.

generally, like Tucker, Pendleton rejected the reasoning from customary constitutional law on the ground that the Virginia Constitution was an express act—indeed, an act of record declared by the people—which separated and limited judicial and legislative power:

> We however have happily in our hands the certain record of our Constitution containing the original Social compact, wherein the People have made their Government to consist of three great branches, the Legislative, Executive & Judiciary, allotting to each, its proper powers, & declaring that they shall be kept separate & distinct, neither exercising those which belong to another.

He concluded that each of these therefore had "its limits, the Legislative as well as the others, which if they Pass, it would seem their Act would be void, as well as that of an Attorney would be, which was not Warranted by his appointment."[21]

Thus, state statutes in almost all American jurisdictions were free from the pair of barriers that prevented judges from holding acts of Parliament unlawful. First, whether before or after 1776, American jurisdictions did not typically have customary constitutions. Second, their legislatures did not usually amount to high courts, for although colonial legislatures occasionally hankered after something like parliamentary power, such pretensions could not survive under the common law, the differentiation of judicial courts, or the separation of powers. Already in the colonies, therefore, judicial duty often required decisions about the constitutionality of legislative acts. Of course, prior to Independence, in the heat of colonial resentments, judges often refrained from holding American statutes unlawful, but even in their evasions such judges tended to recognize that their duty would otherwise extend to American legislation, and when judges after Independence had to decide in accord with constitutions made by their own peoples, they could not easily shut their eyes to what their duty required. Some of them still anxiously sought to evade their duty, but they had no need in 1776 to develop a power allowing them to hold legislative acts unconstitutional. Instead, as already observed, they soberly had reason to ask why, in decisions on legislation, they should not do their duty of deciding in accord with the law of the land.

Four Sets of Cases (with a Choice for the Reader)

If judicial duty in America had long extended to legislative acts, then it should be no surprise that state judges held state statutes unconstitutional, and this is what happened. Four groups of cases can illustrate how state

[21] Ibid., 8706.

judges in this way did their duty. Some of the judges resolutely stood up to popular pressures, and some gave way to their fears, but all of the judges, even in their weakness, clearly understood their duty and eventually held the statutes in these cases unconstitutional.

Although the cases are not entirely unfamiliar, they have been much distorted by being squeezed into the overarching narrative of judicial review. When cast within this stylized account, they get reduced to the usual trope that state judges in the 1780s creatively experimented with a judicial power as to legislation but did not yet always have the strength or independence to overcome legislative opposition. The evidence, however, reveals neither the assertion of a nascent judicial power nor any overwhelming legislative opposition. Instead, men could take judicial duty for granted, and far from facing uniform legislative resistance, the judges typically encountered problems only in the lower houses of state legislatures. Outside these populist venues, there was considerable recognition that freedom depended on the law of the land and the dedication of the judges in doing what their office required of them.

The four sets of cases examined here all held statutes unconstitutional for violating state guarantees of a jury trial. Trial by jury was the essential mechanism for deciding factual questions at common law, and state legislatures frequently considered juries inconvenient—thus giving the judges ample opportunity to uphold the right to a jury. Although it will later be seen that these jury cases were neither the only *decisions* nor even the only *cases* holding state statutes unconstitutional, they were the most prominent state cases in the decade and a half after Independence.

Rather than read the entire remainder of this chapter, the reader may wish to select a state—New Jersey, New Hampshire, Rhode Island, or North Carolina—and read about its case or cases. All four sets of cases are examined in considerable detail to show how they fit within the broader argument here about law and judicial duty. Any one of them, however, will suffice to illustrate how judges held statutes unconstitutional, and the reader should therefore feel free to read about any one state and then proceed to the next chapter.[22]

New Jersey: Holmes & Ketcham v. Walton

The first case holding state legislation unconstitutional was probably *Holmes & Ketcham v. Walton* in 1780, but this is not to say that the judges

[22] If uncertain how to choose, the reader might try the last, North Carolina case, as this most directly prepares the way for the following chapter.

or all of their contemporaries found the decision novel or unexpected. Sometimes celebrated as the earliest precedent for judicial review, it is also sometimes disparaged for the weakness of the evidence—the primary problem being that if the judges were creating a judicial power to declare statutes unconstitutional, it is puzzling that they did not say they were doing anything so momentous. It has therefore even been questioned whether the judges in the case actually held a statute unconstitutional.[23] In fact, the judges probably held two statutes unconstitutional, and rather than consider themselves to be establishing a new judicial power, they appear simply to have done their duty. The judges, as it happens, repeatedly put off their decision, but even this is revealing. Although it is commonly assumed that the judges delayed because they were fearful of the General Assembly, they evidently delayed because they were solicitous for the safety of the state during the conflict with Britain, and what stands out about the case is that

[23] In the primary study of the case, Austin Scott claims it as a precedent for judicial review, and this inevitably leaves the evidence looking meager. Austin Scott, "Holmes v. Walton: The New Jersey Precedent: A Chapter in the History of Judicial Power and Unconstitutional Legislation," *American Historical Review,* 4: 459 (1899). The additional evidence considered here includes the legal context of the small claims statutes, the Supreme Court's rule on writs of certiorari, Willcocks's later characterization of the holding in the pleadings at new trial, and Livingston's letter to Scudder.

Later historians seize upon the disparity between Scott's claim and his evidence to question whether the case was a precedent, and for good measure they add their own misunderstandings. For example, Louis Boudin assumes that earlier and later New Jersey statutes specifying six-person juries concerned courts within regular common law jurisdiction. Louis B. Boudin, "Precedents for the Judicial Power: Holmes v. Walton and Brattle v. Hinckley," *St. John's Law Review,* 3: 173 (1929). As will be seen, however, these statutory six-person juries in New Jersey were only for "small causes"—those below the jurisdiction of the common law courts. Most of the confiscation cases in New Jersey, including the claim of Elisha Walton for over £29,000, obviously could not be viewed as below the common law jurisdiction within which individuals were understood to have a right to a jury. Accordingly, Boudin's doubts concerning the case are entirely misplaced. Boudin even suggests that no opinion was even given. Ibid., 191. Had he simply looked at the records of the court, he would have read that "the Court having taken time to consider of the same, and being now ready to deliver their Opinions gave the Same, Seriatim for the plaintiffs in Certiorari." NJSA, Supreme Court Minutes, Book 60 (Burlington/Trenton) April 1775–May 1782, No. 15, at 343–344.

William Crosskey questions whether the confiscation statute actually authorized a six-person jury, and on this basis suggests that the Supreme Court merely rejected a mistaken interpretation and application of the statute by the justice of the peace. In support of this, Crosskey points out that the defendant argued that the trial with a six-man jury violated the constitution and said nothing about the statute. William Winslow Crosskey, *Politics and the Constitution in the History of the United States,* 2: 950 (Chicago: University of Chicago Press, 1953). The formal pleadings, however, had to focus on the implications for the case at hand rather than the underlying reasoning. In fact, the legislative response to the case reveals that the legislature assumed its statute had authorized six-man juries and that the court would hold it unconstitutional—a conclusion confirmed by Livingston's letter and by the pleadings at new trial.

so many contemporaries recognized that the judges would eventually do their duty notwithstanding the exigencies of war.

Through much of the War of Independence, New Jersey formed a front line not only against the British but also among Americans. The larger conflict often descended into a civil war among neighbors, and this was notoriously worrisome in Monmouth County, which was only a short boat ride away from British-controlled New York. The fate of the wider struggle seemed to rest on preventing the traffic in contraband across these blurred lines, for the trade compromised loyalties and offered temptations for more substantial cooperation with the enemy. Such was the seriousness of the problem that Governor William Livingston of New Jersey publically "enjoin[ed] the civil and military Officers of the counties of Monmouth and Bergen to use their utmost vigilance in preventing all commercial intercourse with the enemy," and he more privately worried that the illicit trade could not be suppressed "without having Recourse to measures which I could not be warranted in Commanding our Militia to adopt." He therefore repeatedly urged that the "total Suppression" of this "most pernicious and detestable Trade" was "one of the most important Objects that can engage the Attention of the Legislature."[24]

Against this threat, the New Jersey General Assembly enacted in 1778 that any individual could seize goods transported across enemy lines (together with the wagon or other vehicle) and secure title to them before a justice of the peace—this being the procedure that would give rise to the case of *Holmes & Ketcham v. Walton.* To be precise, the statute provided the same sort of hearing as was used for small claims: "[I]t shall and may be lawful for either of the Parties to the Trial to demand a Jury, and upon such Demand the said Justice is hereby required to grant the same, and to proceed in all other Respects as in the like Case in the Act, intituled, 'An Act to Erect and establish Courts . . . for the Trial of small Causes."[25] New Jersey's 1775 small causes statute required claimants to proceed before a justice of the peace and a jury of six men, and in adopting these proceedings, the

[24] Proclamation of Governor William Livingston (Aug. 22, 1778), *The Papers of William Livingston,* 2: 422 (New Brunswick: Rutgers University Press, 1980); Letter from Governor William Livingston to Henry Laurens (Aug. 22, 1778), ibid., 2: 423; Letter from William Livingston to the Assembly (June 7, 1782), Ibid., 4: 423 (1987).

[25] An Act to prevent the Subjects of this State from going into or coming out of the Enemy's Lines, without Permissions or Passports, and for other Purposes therein mentioned, Chap. 45, §6 (Oct. 8, 1778), Department of State, Secretary of State's Office, Enrolled Laws (1710–1999); printed in *Acts of the General Assembly of the State of New-Jersey. At a Session begun at Trenton on the 28th Day of October 1777, and continued by Adjournments until the 8th of October, 1778. Being the fourth Sitting of their Second Session,* 104–106 (Trenton: 1778).

1778 confiscation act allowed those who seized contraband to get title to the goods with only half a regular jury.

Individuals enjoyed the right to a jury only within the jurisdiction of the common law. In England, the jurisdiction of the common law courts in civil cases had long been for claims above forty shillings, which thus became the English division between claims that could not be denied a jury trial and claims that could be relegated to justices of the peace or to so-called courts of conscience, which proceeded without a jury.[26] Although some local courts used six-man juries, they had to do so within the confines of the common law, and therefore at least in cases above the jurisdictional boundary, the common law courts "frequently held that a Custom in an inferior Court to try by six Jurors is void."[27] The problem faced by many American colonies, including New Jersey, was how to adjust the right to a jury for inflation. Some colonies passed statutes that raised the jurisdictional barrier substantially above forty shillings and thus sent a broad swath of small claims to justices of the peace. This, however, led to serious questions of law and policy, which troubled the Privy Council.

New Jersey attempted to bridge the gap by having justices of the peace call truncated, six-man juries. Beginning in 1740, New Jersey allowed cases of up to five pounds to be brought before a justice of the peace—although where the debt or demand exceeded forty shillings, either party could ask the justice for a trial by six men.[28] The colonial legislature later increased

[26] That trial by jury soon became a general right, which extended beyond the central courts, can be illustrated by the observation in a late fifteenth-century reading that "where I recover a debt above 40s. in . . . a prescriptive court; it is not a court of record, and yet . . . it is triable by the country." Robert Constable's Second Reading (1494), in *John Spelman's Reading on Quo Warranto,* 59, Appendix 1 (E), ed. J. H. Baker (London: Selden Society, 1997). For the more complex earlier history, see John S. Beckerman, "The Forty-Shilling Jurisdictional Limit in Medieval English Personal Actions," *Legal History Studies,* 1972, at 110, ed. Dafydd Jenkins (Cardiff: University of Wales Press, 1975).

[27] Matthew Bacon, *A New Abridgment of the Law,* 3: 234 (London: 1778). See also *Ball & Knight* (K.B. 1732), Barnardiston (K.B.), *Reports,* 2: 164; *Hutchinson v. Gamble* (Ch. 1776), Brown, *Reports,* 2: 531. Revealingly, Rolle's *Abridgment* stated: "Un custom en un Inferior Court a trier issues per 6. Jurors nest bon, coment que Plusors Courts hont *ceo use,* & mults Judgments depend sur ceo. *Trin. 8 Car. B.R. enter Tredinwicke & Peryman adjudge* en brief derror sur un Judgment en *Bodmyn* en *Cornubia,* & le Judgment revers accordant, coment donque appiert al Court per plusors certificates que pluis que *20.* Courts en *Cornwall* hont mesme customes, & infinite trials la accordant." Henry Rolle, *Un Abridgment,* 1: 564 (London: 1668). For another report of the case, see Croke, *Reports,* 3(Car.): 259–260.

[28] An Act to erect and establish Courts, in the several Counties of this Province, for the Tryal of small Causes (1740), *Laws of the Royal Colony of New Jersey,* 2: 520–524 (New Jersey Archives, 3rd series) (Trenton: New Jersey State Library, 1977). Only if a six-man jury was not demanded could a party disappointed with the result seek an "Appeal" and in effect get a new trial, which if for an amount "above forty Shillings," was to be "by a Jury of the Country in the usual Manner"—that is, by twelve men. Ibid.

the small claims jurisdiction to six pounds and then in 1769 to ten pounds, but this last increase provoked the Privy Council to disallow the 1769 act—not because it thought that in America, unlike England, the constitution placed a fixed limit on small claims jurisdiction, but rather because New Jersey was raising the amount too quickly, which seemed dangerous.[29] New Jersey was therefore stuck with its six-pound jurisdictional limit, and in its last pre-Revolutionary small causes statute—that of 1775—it again provided that justices of the peace could hear cases up to six pounds and that in cases of more than forty shillings either party could demand a six-man jury.[30]

The 1778 confiscation act, however, adopted this summary procedure for all claims to seized contraband, regardless of their value. It was this

[29] An Act to erect and establish Courts in the several Counties in this Colony, for the Trial of Causes of small Causes (1760), *Laws of the Royal Colony of New Jersey,* 4: 28 (New Jersey Archives, 3rd series) (Trenton: New Jersey State Library, 1977); An Act to erect Courts in the several Counties in this Colony, for the Trial of Causes of Ten Pounds, and under (1769), ibid., 4: 564.

One of the objections mentioned to the Privy Council by the lawyer for the Board of Trade was that this sort of "Summary and Domestick Justice . . . necessarily encourages a litigious Spirit, and frequently the practice of perjury," and it "serves too often to favour the establishment of much petty Tyranny in men altogether unfit to be entrusted with such power"—considerations that "have weighed so far with the Legislature of Great Britain, that this kind of Jurisdiction has been always given with caution, sometimes with reluctance, and never hitherto to his knowledge, extended beyond the sum of forty Shillings Sterling." New Jersey's preceding, six-pound act had been adopted only recently, and therefore in light of the various objections to an expansion of small claims jurisdiction, "it is surely too early after the passing of that Act to make so wide a stride." The lawyer for the Board further explained that "he made no objection to the former Act, because other Colonies have extended these Laws as far, or nearly so, and this Colony has many years had one to five pounds extent, but this Subject is at least one, that requires great caution and slow progress." Decision on New Jersey Act of Nov. 1769 (June 7, 1771), *Acts of the Privy Council of England,* 5: 309–311 (Colonial Series) (London: Her Majesty's Stationery Office, 1912).

[30] An Act to erect and establish Courts in the several Counties in this Colony for the Trial of Causes of small Causes, and to repeal the former Act for that Purpose (1775), *Laws of the Royal Colony of New Jersey,* 5: 306 (New Jersey Archives, 3rd series) (Trenton: New Jersey State Library, 1977).

Incidentally, the 1775 small causes statute, which had allowed six-man juries for claims under six pounds, had appeared in Samuel Allinson's 1776 compilation of New Jersey statutes, and the next year, Article XXI of the state's new constitution explained that the existing colonial statutes of New Jersey, as published in Allinson's recent edition, would continue to be binding, unless altered by legislation or contrary to the Constitution:

> That all of the laws of this Province, contained in the edition lately published by Mr. Allinson, shall be and remain in full force, until altered by the Legislature of this Colony (such only excepted, as are incompatible with this Charter) and shall be, according as heretofore, regarded in all respects, by all civil officers, and others, the good people of this Province.

New Jersey Constitution of 1776, Article XXI, discussed by Austin Scott, "Holmes v. Walton: The New Jersey Precedent," 458.

small claims procedure, normally allowed only for claims up to six pounds, that Major Elisha Walton used to get a judgment for goods valued at more than £29,000.[31]

Elisha Walton was an American officer who would soon become a leader of the Monmouth County Association for Retaliation, and in May 1779 he and his men seized the textiles and other goods of two local business partners, John Holmes and Solomon Ketcham. This was not Walton's first seizure from these men, for almost exactly a year earlier he had relieved them of goods worth £20,000, which he had sold "at public vendue."[32] Walton, however, apparently never got the proceeds, and now that he and his allies in Monmouth had the authority of the 1778 confiscation act, they hoped for a more successful seizure.[33]

This second attempt against Holmes and Ketcham took place when military "orders were issued for those who lived near the Lines to remove their Goods."[34] This relocation conveniently forced the smugglers to transport their goods under close observation, and Major Walton promptly secured the spoils, both physically and legally. He took the defendants and their goods to his house and then, two days after the seizure, obtained a trial before a sympathetic justice of the peace, John Anderson, who rapidly called a six-man jury, heard the evidence, and gave judgment for Walton.

[31] Apparently the goods were remarkable. William Hilsey "was one of the Jury that tried the Goods in controversy" in 1779, and at the new trial, he testified that when "the Goods were produced," they "appeared to be imported Goods of the first Quality—Several whole Pieces of Silks & Linnens packed very close in bl^{s}—Buckles & buttons of the newest fashion . . . &c." Another man who later saw the goods, Col. Thomas Henderson, observed that "the assortment was extraordinary." He estimated, for example, that there were "between 7 & 800 y^{d} of silk of different hands" and "between 4 & 500 y^{d} of silk Gauze." *Walton v. Holmes & Ketcham,* State of Facts sur Trial (Sept. 1, 1781), 8, 9, NJSA, New Jersey Supreme Court, Case File 44928.

[32] These details appear in Wikoff's plea in *Wikoff Qui Tam v. Holmes & Ketcham* (Jan. 3, 1780), Monmouth County Archives, Monmouth County Court of Oyer and Terminer.

[33] Exactly what they desired was clear enough from a petition from Walton and others in Monmouth on behalf of those who had been "plundered, and deprived of their Property by some of the Fugitives that have joined the Enemy." Walton and his compatriots demanded that the legislature pass a law to "provide some way whereby those that have been robbed of their Property by such Fugitives as have left Estates . . . may have Restitution out of them." Petition from the Inhabitants of Monmouth Praying a Reimbursement for Losses out of the Fugitives Estates, NJSA, Department of Education, Ms. Collection, Box 4–1, Revolutionary War Documents, Folder 76 (first read May 25, 1779 and eventually "Negatived"). In stirring up Walton's neighbors to join him in seeking gain from Tories—whether fugitives or those dealing in contraband—the petition probably served its most immediate purpose, for even before the legislature read this petition on May 25, 1779, Walton took his "[r]estitution" into his own hands.

[34] Evidence of Andrew Bown, State of Facts sur Trial, 1 ([Sept. 1, 1781]), NJSA, New Jersey Supreme Court, Case File 44928. This was the evidence heard in the new trial.

Lest the summary procedure and friendly judge not be sufficient, Walton treated the jury "with strong Liquor . . . before they gave their verdict."[35] He left nothing to chance, for he understood there was risk as well as opportunity. If he failed to get the proceeds of the sale, his men might become resentful, and later, after William Willcocks, the lawyer for Holmes and Ketcham, prevented Walton from getting the money, Walton was among the inhabitants of Monmouth County who complained that "the withholding [of] the money from the men has almost Raised a mutiny."[36]

Willcocks obtained a writ of certiorari from Chief Justice Robert Morris requesting Anderson to certify a record of his proceedings to the New Jersey Supreme Court.[37] A brilliant litigator, Willcocks supplemented his request for a certiorari by filing a *qui tam* action for a friendly third party, William Wikoff, against his own clients—this being an attempt to preclude Walton's claim.[38]

The Supreme Court's uneasiness about the fact-finding process in the confiscation proceedings became apparent even before the Court heard the certiorari brought on behalf of Holmes and Walton. The Court noted in September 1779 that in "extend[ing] the Jurisdiction of Justices of the Peace without any limitation of the value of the Property seised," the confiscation act "occasions the frequent prosecuting of Certioraries for re-

35 "Reasons" why judgment should be reversed and annulled (Reason No. 6), *Walton v. Holmes & Ketcham* ([Nov. 1779]), NJSA, New Jersey Supreme Court, Case File No. 18354. For the role of these individuals in Monmouth County's highly charged political controversies, see Michael S. Adelberg, "'A Combination to Trample All Law Underfoot': The Association for Retaliation and the American Revolution in Monmouth County," in *New Jersey History,* 115: 3, 13 (1997).

36 Petition of the Subscriber[s] Inhabitants of the County of Monmouth (Dec. 23, 1779), NJSA, Department of Education, Ms. Collection, Legislative Records, Box 4–1, Folder 51. Elisha Walton was among the first subscribers.

37 Willcocks was a Princeton graduate and member of the New York bar who settled in New Jersey after the occupation of New York in 1776. "William Willcocks, Jr.," in *Princetonians, 1769–1775: A Biographical Dictionary,* 55–56 (Princeton: Princeton University Press, 1980). In the spring of 1777, he became aide-de-camp to General William Alexander—Lord Stirling—and in this capacity probably served in New Jersey, his assistant being James Monroe. After the British evacuation from New York, Willcocks returned in time to serve as co-counsel with Alexander Hamilton in *Rutgers v. Waddington,* which "made his name as a lawyer." Ibid., 56. He also, as it happens, was secretary of the Whig Society of Monmouth.

38 Writ of Capias Corpus in *Wikoff Qui Tam v. Holmes & Ketcham* (Monmouth County Common Pleas, July term 1779), Wikoff's Plea (Jan. 3, 1780), Walton's Plea in Abatement (July 25, 1780), Monmouth County Archives, Monmouth County Court of Oyer and Terminer. It was a technique Willcocks had already used with some success against Walton's first seizure of goods from Holmes and Ketcham. After losing on certiorari on the second seizure, Walton brought his own *qui tam* action in debt for £29,428/13/4½. Writ of Capias Corpus in *Walton v. Holmes & Ketcham* (Monmouth County Inferior Court of Common, April 25, 1781), ibid. In almost all these documents, the justice who signed for the Court was of course Anderson.

moving the Plaints brought before the said Justices to the Supreme Court," and this caused the Court anxiety about the factual record in these cases. It explained that because of the "want of some regular and established Practice" in the proceedings of the justices of the peace, "many difficulties" would "arise in ascertaining the facts" that had been "proved to the Justice and Jury." The Court clearly understood it might have to hold at least the juries unconstitutional, and although ordinarily a court in this situation would therefore have expected to overturn the judgments below, this court was apparently considering another possibility. If the Court had simply reversed the judgments it would have ended up requiring all of the plaintiffs, who were patriots and military officers, to return contraband to Tory defendants, and rather than reach such a sweeping decision, the Court evidently wanted to secure factual records of a sort that would allow it to decide at least some of the confiscation cases on the merits. To this end, the Supreme Court made a rule requiring attorneys who sought writs of certiorari in confiscation cases to create a record by settling upon "the State of Facts" and reducing these "to writing by way of Bills of Exception."[39] This rule was too late for the certiorari in *Holmes and Ketcham v. Walton.* Yet in revealing that the Supreme Court was worried about the facts that had been proved where a six-man jury was used "without any limitation of the value of the Property seised," the rule said much about the judges' basic political and constitutional concerns.

When the New Jersey Supreme Court in November heard arguments on the writ of certiorari brought by John Holmes and Solomon Ketcham, Willcocks filed various reasons for reversal, including the unconstitutionality of the trial with six jurors. He argued that "the judgment given by John Anderson . . . ought to be reversed and annulled" on evidentiary and procedural grounds, and because "the Jury . . . consisted of six men only when by the Laws of the Land, it should have consisted of twelve men." Willcocks concluded that "according to the Laws and Customs of the State of New Jersey," Justice Anderson "should have given Judgment for the said John and Solomon."

Willcocks subsequently realized that the constitutional point was the one on which he would prevail, and he therefore elaborated it in a set of

[39] NJSA, Supreme Court Minutes, Book 60 (Burlington/Trenton) April 1775–May 1782, No. 15, at 290–291. Where this ad hoc creation of a record was "neglected or refused," the attorney for a plaintiff on certiorari was to take "Affidavits of Witnesses for establishing the facts which appeared on the Hearing of the Plaint before the Justice" and was to give notice to the defendant or his attorney to cross-examine the witnesses and "examine any other he may think proper"—all of which statements and examinations were to be "part of the return of said Certiorari." Ibid.

"Additional reasons." The state constitution guaranteed that "the inestimable right of trial by jury shall remain confirmed as a part of the law of this Colony, without repeal, forever," and Willcocks therefore argued that the judgment had to be reversed:

> For that the said Justice had not Jurisdiction of the said cause or plaint but the same was *coram non Judice.*
>
> For that the Jury who tryed the said plaint before the said Justice consisted of six men only contrary to Law.
>
> For that the jury who tried the said plaint before the said Justice consisted of six men only contrary to the constitution of New Jersey.
>
> For that the proceedings and trial in the said plaint in the Court below, and the Judgment thereon *given* were had and given contrary to the Constitution, practices and Laws of the Land.[40]

Some scholars complain that the case was not a precedent for holding statutes unconstitutional because these lists of "reasons" did not explicitly claim that the statute was unconstitutional.[41] The lists, however, were only Willcocks's formal filings for a reversal. These filings stated the specific conclusions about the proceedings below that would justify reversal—that the jurisdiction, jury, and judgment were unconstitutional and otherwise unlawful. Having thus narrowly recited why the proceedings before Justice Anderson should be reversed, Willcocks would have discussed the more general, underlying point, about the unconstitutionality of the seizure statute, in his oral argument.

For almost a year the Supreme Court repeatedly delayed giving judgment. The court heard arguments in November "on both Sides, on the Reasons filed in this Cause" but then simply entered "Curia advisare vult."[42] Four days later, the Court recorded that it "will further advise on the Arguments . . . till the next Term," which was in April.[43] The Court in November apparently hoped it could resolve the question by its next term, for it "[a]dvised the Commanding Officer" in Monmouth County "Not to Suffer any Dividend to be made of Prize money, untill [the] Supream Court in

[40] "Reasons" and "Additional Reasons" on certiorari why judgment should be reversed, *Walton v. Holmes & Ketcham* (Nov. 1779), NJSA, New Jersey Supreme Court, Case File No. 18354; New Jersey Constitution of 1776, Articles XXII. At the September term, Willcocks had moved that the case be argued the following term, and the Supreme Court so ordered. NJSA, Supreme Court Minutes, Book 60 (Burlington/Trenton) April 1775–May 1782, No. 15, at 289–290.

[41] Crosskey, *Politics and the Constitution,* 2: 950; Boudin, "Precedents for the Judicial Power," 194–195.

[42] NJSA, Supreme Court Minutes, Book 60 (Burlington/Trenton) April 1775–May 1782, No. 15, at 303 (Nov. 11, 1779).

[43] Ibid., 309 (Nov. 15, 1779).

April Next."[44] In April 1780, however, the Court was "not . . . ready to give Judgm! on the Reasons filed and agreed in this Cause," and it therefore again "[o]rder'd that a Curia advisare vult until next Term be enter'd." Significantly, this was done on the motion of Willcocks's co-counsel, Elias Boudinot, which suggests that the two understood it was in their interest to let the Court take its time.[45] There was no entry for the case in the May term, and finally in September 1780—after almost a year's delay—the judges decided the case. Perhaps the judges delayed because they were afraid of the legislature, but perhaps they had something else on their minds.

Although the bare record of the judgment reveals nothing of the judges' reasoning, and although their opinions have not survived, they unanimously "deliver[ed] their Opinions . . . Seriatim for the plaintiffs in Certiorari." On the motion of Boudinot for Holmes and Ketcham, the Court then gave judgment for the plaintiffs and ordered that "the Judgment of the Justice in the Court below be revers'd and said Plaintiffs be restored to all Things."[46] It has been said that the judges in this case were unlikely to have held the legislation unconstitutional, for judicial review had yet to be established by precedents.[47] Contemporaries, however, who were closer to the evidence than any historian, evaluated the probabilities very differently.

Nine month prior to the decision, on December 24, 1779, Governor William Livingston heard a rumor from Congressman Nathaniel Scudder that one of the justices of the Supreme Court had privately revealed his opinion—apparently in favor of Holmes and Ketcham. Livingston was disturbed that the judges might disclose their opinions before deciding the case, but he recognized their duty:

> The Cause between Walton & Holmes is of the greatest Moment; & I hope none of the Judges have given their opinions, as you have heard respecting one before they have been judicially called upon. I should be sorry that the supposed Event of the Controversy should give the Tories any Cause of Triumph; but the Judges you know are bound to determine according to Law in whose favour soever that may appear to be, let the Consequences be what they may.[48]

[44] Petition of the Subscriber[s] Inhabitants of the County of Monmouth (Dec. 23, 1779), NJSA, Department of Education, Ms. Collection, Legislative Records, Box 4–1, Folder 51. Both Elisha Walton and Thomas Henderson were subscribers.
[45] Ibid., 321 (Apr. 7, 1780).
[46] Ibid., 343–344 (Sept. 7, 1780).
[47] See, for example, Crosskey, *Politics and the Constitution,* 2: 950.
[48] Letter from William Livingston to Nathaniel Scudder (Dec. 24, 1779), in *The Papers of*

Governor Livingston had earlier served on New York's Supreme Court—most notably in *Forsey v. Cunningham*—and he therefore had good reason to understand what the New Jersey judges might be bound to do. Less sympathetically, some residents of Monmouth County complained to the legislature after the decision in *Holmes* that the justices of the Supreme Court had "set aside some of the Laws as unconstitutional"—evidently the 1778 confiscation act and a December 1778 amendment to it, which allowed recovery of the value of the goods in addition to the goods themselves.[49] Indeed, when Walton obtained a new trial against Holmes and Ketcham in 1781, Willcocks protested to the Supreme Court that there was no law authorizing trial of the offense: The statute originally authorizing a six-man jury was unconstitutional, and although a subsequent statute authorized a jury of twelve, this was not retrospective. In Willcocks's summary, the subsequent law "authorizing a trial by twelve men" had no "retrospective clause," and "as a trial by six men is unconstitutional there is no law existing by which this cause could be tried."[50]

William Livingston, 3: 279–280 (New Brunswick: Rutgers University Press 1986). Unfortunately, the letter from Nathaniel Scudder has not been located. Ibid., 280, note 1.

[49] Petition from Sixty Inhabitants of the County of Monmouth, in *Votes and Proceedings of the General Assembly of the State of New Jersey,* 39 (Dec. 8, 1780) (Trenton: 1780). The amendment provided that "each and every Person in whose Possession any Provisions, Goods, Wares or Merchandize, may be seized as aforesaid, shall, besides such Provisions, Goods, Wares and Merchandize, forfeit to the Amount of the Value thereof, to be recovered in an Action of Debt by any Person who will sue for the same . . . one Half to the Use of the Prosecutor, and the other half to the Use of the State." An Act to explain and amend an Act, intitled, An Act to Prevent the Subjects of this State from going into, or coming out of, the Enemy's Lines, without Permissions or Passports, and for other Purposes therein mentioned," §§4 and 5 (Dec. 11, 1779), Peter Wilson, *Acts of the General Assembly of the State of New-Jersey,* 13, Appendix VI (Trenton: 1784).

[50] Willcocks argued: "That this Present Cause being commenced and undetermined at the time of the late law authorizing a trial by twelve men[,] it is not comprehended by the late Law[,] it not having in it any retrospective clause—and as a trial by six men is unconstitutional there is no law existing by which this cause could be tried." Certiorari with State of Facts, Exception No. 2 (Sept. 1781), NJSA, New Jersey Supreme Court, Case File No. 44928. In his reasons for reversal on certiorari, he observed that "this trial (which was called & intended for a non trial) Was had between Elisha Walton Plaintiff & John Holmes And Solomon Ketcham Defendants. Whereas in truth & in fact there never had before been a trial between these parties & so the said attorneys for the Defendants say. [Thus,] This trial could not be warranted by the order & Jud[t] of the Sup Court for a New Trial." He also argued that "There was not any Law of this State authorizing a New Trial in this cause." Reasons on certiorari for reversal of new trial, *Walton v. Holmes & Ketcham* (Sept. 1781), NJSA, New Jersey Supreme Court, Case File No. 18354.

Of course, Willcocks's conclusion that there should not have been a new trial probably went too far, for the subsequent statute merely provided for the constitutional trial of an offense already prohibited by prior law. The issue, however, troubled at least one other contemporary. In his letter to Scudder, Governor Livingston noted that "tho' the Legislature may apply a Remedy, yet those ex post facto Laws have always been considered as unfriendly

Even more revealing than the holding of unconstitutionality was the Supreme Court's delay. It has come to be assumed that the judges hesitated to reach a decision for fear of popular and legislative resentment. Yet they had less narrowly corrupt reasons. As Governor Livingston observed in December 1779, the case was "of the greatest Moment," and if the judges reached the conclusion already discussed by one judge, it would "give the Tories . . . Cause of Triumph." After three years of combat within the state, the judges could not have wanted to hold an essential wartime measure unconstitutional without giving the legislature time to adopt a replacement confiscation process that used lawful, twelve-man juries.

It thus probably was no coincidence that when the Governor responded to the rumor about the indiscreet judge, the legislature was wrestling over the language of the replacement law—in particular, over the statute's implications for the constitutionality of the prior, six-man proceedings. On November 12, the day after the arguments in court, Jonathan Deare of Middlesex obtained leave in the legislative council to introduce a bill that would "[s]upplement" the seizure acts by requiring a jury of twelve men.[51] When the House considered this bill in December 1779, some members took offense at the suggestion that the General Assembly had acted unconstitutionally, and they proposed to remove the bill's requirement of twelve men or at least to leave a choice of either six or twelve "at the option of the Defendant."[52] Although these members failed in their attempts to preserve a six-man jury, they briefly succeeded in adding a proviso preserving the outcome of the six-man proceedings that had already occurred under the confiscation act and the act amending it:

> Provided always, That Nothing herein contained shall be taken or construed to invalidate or make void any Trial or other Proceedings had by Virtue of the said recited Acts . . . because such Trial was had by a Jury of six Men only, if such Trial and other Proceedings have been in other Respects agreeable to Law.[53]

---

to Liberty." Letter from William Livingston to Nathaniel Scudder (Dec. 24, 1779), in *The Papers of William Livingston,* 3: 280.

[51] Motion of Jonathan Deare (Nov. 12, 1779, *A Journal of the Proceedings of the Legislative-Council of the State of New-Jersey, in General Assembly Convened at Trenton, on Tuesday the Twenty-Sixth Day of October, in the Year of our Lord One Thousand Seven Hundred and Seventy-Nine. Being the First Sitting of the Fourth Session,* 14 (Trenton: 1780).

[52] Motion of Hornblower (Dec. 18, 1779), in *Votes and Proceedings of the General Assembly of the State of New Jersey,* 86 (Trenton: 1780); Motion of Josiah Hornblower (Dec. 18, 1779), in ibid., 87.

[53] Motion of Peter Wilson (Dec. 18, 1779), in *Votes and Proceedings of the General Assembly of the State of New Jersey,* 86. Incidentally, former Chief Justice Robert Morris, who had since resigned from the Supreme Court, now sat in the House and asked to be "excused" from

The legislature evidently understood that the judges were going to hold the confiscation statute void for being unconstitutional, and this proviso merely aimed to prevent the judges from invalidating the six-man trials that already had occurred. Yet this attempt to preserve the validity of past proceedings was no less troubling than the effort to perpetuate trials with six men, and the Council therefore rejected the bill it had earlier supported in an untainted form.[54]

If the judges were going to hold the confiscation act unconstitutional, a compromise would be necessary, and the dispute between the House and the Council came to a head on the afternoon before Christmas—the same day that Livingston responded to the rumor about one of the judges and expressed his hope that none of them had already given an opinion. The two houses that afternoon agreed that the statute should have a new first section, which carefully avoided any reflection on the constitutional issue by reciting that whereas "it may be prudent to have the Judgment of a greater Number than six Jurors" in confiscation cases, "it shall and may be lawful for either of the Parties in such Suit to demand a Jury of twelve Men, which Jury such Justice is hereby empowered to grant, and to issue a *Venire* accordingly.[55] This compromise acknowledged the advisability of twelve, without conceding the unconstitutionality of six. The statute became law on Christmas Day 1779, and thereafter either party could demand a jury of twelve.[56]

Yet this legislation curing future proceedings was not enough for the Supreme Court. The law left no mechanism for the Court to award new trials before the justices of the peace, and therefore if the Court were to re-

---

voting on this proviso, perhaps because he had signed the writ of certiorari, and perhaps because the proviso justified the former proceedings brought by Walton and, at least by the next year, Morris was counsel for Walton. The House, however, refused Morris's request, and he voted for the proviso, which passed the House. Vote (Dec. 18, 1779), ibid., 88.

[54] Message from the Council (Dec. 22, 1779), in *Votes and Proceedings of the General Assembly of the State of New Jersey,* 96 (Dec. 23, 1779) (Trenton: 1780).

[55] Report of Committee appointed to join a Committee of the Council in a free Conference, in *Votes and Proceedings of the General Assembly of the State of New Jersey,* 101–102 (Dec. 24, 1779) (Trenton: 1780). For the compromise, see Scott, "Holmes v. Walton: The New Jersey Precedent," 462.

[56] A Supplement to the ACT, intitled, An Act to explain and amend and Act, intitled, An Act to prevent the Subjects of this State from going into, or coming out of, the Enemy's Lines, without Permissions or Passports, and for other Purposes therein mentioned, Chap. 21, §1 (Dec. 25, 1779), Wilson, *Acts of the General Assembly of the State of New-Jersey,* Appendix VII, 14, 15. The compromise character of this act is amply suggested by another section, which stipulated that in condemnation cases "the Burden of Proof on the Trial shall lie upon the Defendant; any Law, Usage or Custom, to the Contrary notwithstanding." Ibid., §5.

verse the decision in *Holmes & Ketcham v. Walton,* then Holmes, Ketcham, and many other Tories who had suffered under six-man juries would be able to recover the value of their contraband. At the very least, such a victory would be open to the defendants who had obtained certioraris before the September 1779 rule requiring the preservation of a factual record. Perhaps, even worse, some Tories would be able to collect the value of their goods from leading patriots, who probably no longer had the wherewithal to pay. This would have been devastating for the American cause in Monmouth and other front-line counties, and when Major Walton and other patriots in the spring of 1780 began to recognize all that might follow from reversals in *Holmes* and the other seizure cases, they anxiously petitioned the legislature to enact that in the event of any "Reversal of the Judgment" in such cases, the plaintiffs could "go to trial anew on the Merits."[57] There was a real danger that a judicial reversal would become a political and military reversal, and although the judges would not alter their decision to avoid a serious military setback, they were willing to defer their decision until the government had prepared itself for their judgment. Apparently with such thoughts in mind, the justices of the Supreme Court wrote in May 1780 to the Speaker of the House, "recommending that on Reversal of Judgment for Error in Cases of Seizures of Goods, supposed to have been brought from within the Enemy's Lines, the Defendant in Error, on Payment of Costs, may be allowed a Trial *de Novo* in the Court below upon the Merits of the Cause."[58] Having thus been importuned by various plaintiffs and their allies and even by the judges, the General Assembly promptly adopted the proposal, and it thereby finally left the judges free at their next meeting, in September, to decide *Holmes & Ketcham v. Walton.*[59]

[57] Petition of Sundry Freeholders and Inhabitants of the County of Middlesex (May 13, 1780), NJSA, Department of Education, Ms. Collection, Revolutionary War Documents, Box 4–1, Folder 90. Another petition noted the certioraris "under Pretence of Errors in the Proceedings of the Magistrate," and complained that "your Petitioners are informed that some of the Judgments are reversed by the Judges of the Supream Court upon that Principle & there remains no Redress for the Captor who ought fully to have been supported in every Case of a just Seizure." The petitioners therefore asked for a law "directing a rehearing in all such Cases as may be set aside in the Supream Court." Petition of the Subscribers Inhabitants of the County of Monmouth (undated), NJSA, Department of Education, BAH, Ms. Collection, Legislative Records, Box 1–19, Folder 30. Elisha Walton was one of the petitioners.

[58] *Votes and Proceedings of the General Assembly of the State of New Jersey,* 187 (May 13, 1780) (Trenton: 1780).

[59] An Act declaring the Effect of the Reversal of Judgments of Justices of the Peace in Prosecutions for the Forfeiture of Goods, Wares and Merchandize, as being brought from within the Enemy's Lines, for Error in the Proceedings, and to enable the Supreme Court to award new Trials in such Causes, Wilson, *Acts of the General Assembly of the State of New-Jersey,*

Notwithstanding these efforts to get legislative protection for patriots, the justices of the Supreme Court did not go far enough to satisfy the Monmouth County Retaliators. The radicals of the county (including Congressman Nathaniel Scudder, Major Elisha Walton, and Justice of the Peace John Anderson) had secretively formed this association earlier in 1780 with a recognition that their "distressing Mode" was "not agreeable to Law" but on the assumption that *"Necessity has No Law."*[60] Ten days after the Supreme Court overturned Anderson's decision in *Holmes & Ketcham v. Walton,* Scudder, Anderson, and many other Retaliators petitioned the Assembly against the disaffected citizens of Monmouth who "hold a constant Correspondence and Trade with the Enemy to the enriching [of] themselves & Ruin of the loyal Subjects of this and the other States in [the] Union."[61] Less than a week later, Scudder and Colonel Henderson—a witness in *Holmes & Ketcham v. Walton*—urged the Assembly to pass a law "authoriz[ing] the well-affected inhabitants to retaliate upon the property of the disaffected" of Monmouth County. The Assembly, however, took a very different view: Although the county needed a more "spirited" response from the government, the Retaliators were "an illegal and dangerous combination, utterly subversive to law" and "tending to the dissolution of the constitution and government."[62]

146–147, Chapter CCXVI. For the passage of the act, see *Votes and Proceedings of the General Assembly of the State of New Jersey,* 243 and 246 (June 17, 1780).

[60] Scudder wrote to the President of Congress, Henry Laurens, about the "Murder, Depredations and Kidnapings" in "this Part of the County" by "the Refugees and disaffected" and explained: "We have from the mere Necessity of our Case on the sole ground of Self-Preservation been compelled to enter into a general Association for the Purpose of Retaliation on the Persons and Property of the notoriously disaffected yet residing among us, for all Damages, Depredations, Burnings, Kidnapings &c: done or committed by any of the Refugees &c."—this approach being one of "[a]n Eye for an Eye & a Tooth for a Tooth." In justification, Scudder added: "We are well aware of the objections this distressing Mode is liable to, as being not agreeable to Law, but liable to abuse and likely sometimes to injure the innocent—But Alas! my dear Friend, *Necessity has No Law.* We could no longer consent to be murdered and plundered by Rule, while from the Laxness Timidity & Indecision of our Magistracy the Laws were rather a Screen for Tories, while they afforded little Security to the well-affected Citizen." Letter from Nathaniel Scudder to Henry Laurens (June 17, 1780), Pennsylvania Historical Society, Philadelphia, Dreer Collection, Members of Old Congress, Vol. 8:2, p. 111, discussed by Adelberg, "'A Combination to Trample All Law Underfoot.'" 11.

[61] Petition (Sept 17, 1780), Tilton, "New Jersey Petition of 1780 Concerning Retaliation," 75–76. A year later, the seventy-eight-year-old Anderson tendered his resignation, explaining, with more accuracy than he probably recognized, that "I think myself unfit now to attend the duty & office of a Majestrate." Letter from John Anderson to the Chairman of the Joint Meeting (Sept. 3, 1781), NJSA, Department of Education, Ms. Collection, Legislative Records, Box 1–14, Folder 71.

[62] Memorial (Sept. 23, 1780) and Committee Report (Sept. 29, 1780), as quoted by Adelberg, "'A Combination to Trample All Law Underfoot,'" 13–14.

Concerned about the danger both from Tories and from Retaliators, the judges of the Supreme Court had attempted to do their duty without stimulating either the confidence of the enemy or the anger of overzealous patriots. The judges had found themselves in a difficult position, for if they had upheld the right to a jury shortly after they first heard the case, they really would have given the Tories a "Cause of Triumph." The ideal of judicial duty, however, did not leave room for politic delay, and therefore, in the exigencies of wartime, the judges repeatedly took the case under advisement—thus preserving the ideal of their duty while actually giving the legislature time to prepare for the decision. The judges undoubtedly shared Livingston's view that "the Judges . . . are bound to determine according to Law . . . let the Consequences be what they may," but by delaying they gave the government an opportunity to avoid a Tory victory and all that would have followed from it.[63]

Rather than a precedent for judicial review, *Holmes & Ketcham v. Walton* was, at least when finally decided, a matter of judicial duty. Modern observers, expecting a precedent for judicial review, assume that the judges hesitated to claim so great a power as to hold a statute unconstitutional. Contemporaries, however, including the governor and the entire legislature, understood exactly what the judges' duty would probably require of them.

New Hampshire: The Ten Pound Cases

A series of cases holding a state statute unconstitutional occurred in New Hampshire in 1786, and although these cases never went beyond the Inferior Courts, this makes the decisions all the more interesting. These lower court cases from New England were recently documented by Richard Lambert, and in the history of judicial review, as he recognizes, they can only be understood as bold experimental efforts that contributed to the establishment of the judiciary's greatest power.[64] As already noted, however, it is improbable that Inferior Court judges—many of whom were not even lawyers—would have developed their own power to hold a state statute unconstitutional, let alone that they would have done so as resolutely as did the

[63] Letter from William Livingston to Nathaniel Scudder (Dec. 24, 1779), in *The Papers of William Livingston,* 3: 279–280.

[64] Richard M. Lambert, "The 'Ten Pound Act' Cases and the Origins of Judicial Review in New Hampshire," *New Hampshire Bar Journal,* 43: 37 (2002). He also discusses much of the political context.

judges of New Hampshire. Rather than make an experiment in judicial power, the judges would seem simply to have done their duty.

The Bill of Rights of the 1784 New Hampshire Constitution guaranteed a jury trial to the extent it had traditionally been enjoyed: "In all controversies concerning property, and in all suits between two or more persons, except in cases in which it has been heretofore otherwise used and practiced, the parties shall have a right to trial by jury; and this method of procedure shall be held sacred."[65] In New Jersey, this would have guaranteed a jury in actions above six pounds, but in New Hampshire, where the forty-shilling standard had been maintained, such a provision evidently did not allow for any deviation from the ancient measure of the right to a jury.

The next year, in November 1785, the New Hampshire General Court passed the so-called Ten Pound Act—a statute that allowed claims up to ten pounds to be determined without a jury. This statutory obstacle to jury trials in an inflated range of small claims cases was ostensibly a practical response to an economic crisis. Like so many of the states, New Hampshire was suffering from a shortage of specie, which left debtors unable to pay and creditors unable to collect. To escape this morass, the legislature needed to get money or at least goods back into circulation, and being attuned to popular discontent, it facilitated the enforcement of debts with a pair of statutes that appeared to offer something both to debtors and to creditors: One enactment allowed debtors to escape imprisonment for debt if they tendered payment in kind; the other created jurisdiction in justices of the peace to hear various small claims up to ten pounds.[66] This small claims statute, the Ten Pound Act, was ostensibly designed to ensure "the recovery of small debts in an expeditious way," but it might also be said to impose summary process on the collection of small debts.[67] It gave justices of the peace the power "to hear try and determine all pleas and actions of Debt and trespass where title of Land is not concerned" up "to the value of Ten pounds," and it deprived Inferior Courts of jurisdiction in such actions up through five pounds, except on appeal from a justice of the peace.[68] On an appeal to the Inferior Courts, parties could get a trial *de novo* with a jury—this being the conventional New England practice—but justices of the

[65] New Hampshire Constitution of 1784, Bill of Rights, Article 20.

[66] The first of these acts was An Act to prevent the bodies of Debtors from being taken or Execution when real or personal Estate can be found or is Tendered to Satisfy the demand (Nov. 8, 1785), *Laws of New Hampshire,* 5: 98 (Concord: Rumford, 1916).

[67] For some of the politics, see Lambert, "The 'Ten Pound Act,'" 37.

[68] An Act for the recovery of small debts in an expeditious way and manner, NHSA, Original Acts (Nov. 9, 1785).

peace did not proceed by jury trial, and the statute thus had the effect of eliminating juries in the initial round of a wide range of minor cases. Whereas in New Jersey the constitutional problem was the adoption of small claims procedures for claims of an unlimited size, in New Hampshire, under its more confining jury guarantee, the problem was the small claims statute itself—in particular, its barrier to jury trials in claims up to ten pounds.

Only one representative protested. Other legislators present apparently were satisfied about the constitutionality of the statute, and this should be no surprise, for its advocates presented it when "there was scarse[ly] a quorum of the House" and almost all of those attending were justices of the peace.[69] Already setting himself aside from such men, the young law student and legislator William Plumer self-consciously "acted from my own judgment of things," and when the House passed the act, "I entered my protest, singly and alone . . . principally on the ground that it was unconstitutional." Writing this later in life, he had the satisfaction of adding that "[t]he courts so pronounced it, and the succeeding legislature repealed the law."[70]

[69] William Plumer, Letter to William Coleman (May 31, 1786), *A Collection of Letters Written to and by Wm Plumer,* 1: 69, in *William Plumer Papers,* Mfm Reel LC2.

[70] William Plumer, *Life of William Plumer,* 59, ed. A. P. Peabody (Boston: 1857). Similarly, in May 1786, when "[t]he Inferior Court of Common Pleas . . . resolved that the Law authorizing Justices to try actions under £10 is unconstitutional," Plumer recalled that he, "[s]ingle & alone," had entered a "protest against the law." William Plumer, Letter to William Coleman (May 31, 1786), in *A Collection of Letters Written to and by Wm Plumer,* 1: 69, *William Plumer Papers,* Mfm Reel LC2. The journal of the House records: "Mr William Plummer entered his protest against the Act passed this day intitled an Act for the recovery of small debts in an expeditious way and manner—which protest is on file." Journal of the House 1785–1790, at 42 (Nov. 9, 1785), NHSA. Alas, the protest remains elusive.

A similar statute elicited a similar protest from William Hooper and others in the North Carolina House of Commons: "We hold it as the Constitutional Right of the Citizens of this State that they should not be deprived of their property but by the voice of a Jury of free Citizens of this state." Mr. Hooper's Protest ([Jan. 6, 1787]), NCSA, General Assembly, Session Records 1786–1787, Box 4, Folder Senate (Jan. 3, 1787), Bill to Amend Act (1785) for Increasing the Jurisdiction of the County Courts. Also in *Journal of the House of Commons. At a General Assembly begun and held at Fayetteville, on the eighteenth day of November, in the Year of Our Lord One Thousand Seven Hundred and Eighty-Six,* 79 (np: [1787]).

When this sort of issue arose earlier in Massachusetts, Rufus King attempted to bring it before the judges for an advisory opinion. After a committee of the House of Representatives considered the constitutional problem, it reported that, "consistent with the constitution, a Justice of the peace may be impowered to try actions exceeding the sum of forty shillings"—whereupon the House voted in favor of a four-pound bill. *Journal of the House,* 384 (Feb. 13, 1784), Records of the States of the United States, Mfm. Attempting to derail the bill, King later moved that:

> [T]he following question viz. "Whether a Law of this Commonwealth enacted since the establishment of the constitution, extending the jurisdiction of Justices of the

In the ensuing months, other men joined Plumer in protesting the Ten Pound Act. For example, a "Citizen" argued in the *New Hampshire Gazette* that "for almost ninety years preceding the constitution, every subject of this government was entitled to a trial by Jury, in all civil causes whatsoever, (those of the admiralty, probate, and matrimony excepted) where the demand exceeded forty shillings, in whatever court they originated and in the first stage of the action." He therefore demanded that the legislature explain "[b]y what mode of interpretation this law and the Constitution can be made to consist." Of course, "the law may answer the purposes of the legislative" in providing justice in an expeditious manner, but "[t]he question before us is that of *right* not of *utility*."[71]

The constitutional point, as shown by Lambert, apparently first arose in the case of *William Wallace Jr. v. Richard Tarlton*.[72] Wallace was from Deerfield and had apparently agreed to work twelve months for Tarlton, a cordwainer from Greenland, in exchange for a single fixed payment, but Wallace departed after five months and in January 1786 sought to recover nine pounds for the reasonable value of his work.[73] He brought an action of *quantum meruit* before Justice of the Peace Thomas Bartlet, who gave him judgment for the nine pounds "damage" plus costs.[74]

Tarlton, through his lawyer, Samuel Sherburne, immediately appealed to the Rockingham County Inferior Court in Portsmouth, where in February he initially took his chances on a *de novo* jury trial.[75] When the jury found for Wallace in the amount of £2/17/1 and costs, Sherburne attempted to dispose of this smaller judgment by turning to the Constitu-

---

> peace . . . to the trial of causes of property where the judgment in debt or damages may exceed the sum of forty shillings would be consistent with the spirit of the constitution?" should be proposed to the Hon. Justices of the Supreme Judicial Court for their opinion.

The motion, however, did not pass. Ibid., 416 (Feb. 25, 1784).

71 "A Citizen" (Dec. 8, 1785), *New Hampshire Gazette* (Dec. 16, 1785).

72 Lambert, "The 'Ten Pound Act,'" 40.

73 Wallace calculated what he was owed *pro rata* at thirty-six shillings per month or nine pounds, plus one pound in damages, apparently for failure to pay, thus adding up to the full ten pounds within the statutory jurisdiction of the justices of the peace. Account, NHSA, Rockingham County Superior Court Record No. 9279. The judgment for nine pounds suggests that the later case of *Britton v. Turner, New Hampshire Reports,* 6: 481 (Supreme Court of New Hampshire 1834), is not as innovative as is sometimes thought.

74 Certified Copy of Record of Trial before Justice of the Peace, NHSA, Rockingham County Superior Court Record No. 9279.

75 Ibid. Samuel Sherburne was a 1776 graduate of Dartmouth. To avoid being confused with a similarly named graduate of Harvard, he later adopted the name John S. Sherburne. *Sibley's Harvard Graduates,* 16: 233 (Boston: Massachusetts Historical Society, 1972).

tion.[76] According to the record of the Inferior Court, Sherburne moved for arrest of judgment on the grounds that:

> [A]t the Time of Forming the present Constitution for this State it was & for a Long time before even beyond the Memory of man it had been the Law & Custom of this State for Inferior Courts to Try all Matters of more than forty shillings Value & for Justices of the peace to Try only Civil Matters under that value[,] & by the Same Constitution it is Declared that all Trials of Property should be as had before that time been used & Accustomed[,] & this Action being brought Against the Express Letter & Spirit of said Constitution & Against the Law of the Land . . . Judgment Ought to be Arrested.

This was probably the first time such an argument came before the court, which therefore decided that the case should be continued "for Advisement."[77] At its May term, the Court had other such cases, and after reciting the plea it concluded "that Judgment in this Case ought to be Arrested."[78] At about the same time, in the similar case of *Bartlett v. French,* the Rockingham County Inferior Court again heard constitutional arguments on an appeal from a justice of the peace. This time, the defendant apparently raised the constitutional defense at the *de novo* trial, and to the deep annoyance of the plaintiff, Joseph Hall Bartlett, the court nonsuited him.[79] Just how irritated he was must wait to be seen.

Courts did not ordinarily state their opinions or reasons for their judgments in their record, and therefore the brevity of the judgments in these initial cases is to be expected.[80] The judges, however, had other Ten Pound Act actions on their docket, and perhaps because of the absence of much manuscript reporting in the state, they soon began to enter their reasoning about the Constitution in their record. It thus is clear that at least in these cases with relatively detailed records, the judges of the Rockingham

[76] Verdict, NHSA, Rockingham County Superior Court Record No. 9279.

[77] NHSA, Rockingham County Inferior Court, Minute Book, New Entries, Feb. term 1786, Case No. 13.

[78] NHSA, Rockingham County Inferior Court, Minute Book, Continued Cases, May term 1786, Case No. 143.

[79] NHSA, Rockingham County Inferior Court, Minute Book, New Entries, May term 1786, Case No. 56.

[80] A report of a Virginia case provides a rare comment on the practice of entering reasons on the record: "When about to enter the judgment, the judge presiding in court, upon being asked, said that when the court wished a reason for their judgment to be entered on record they would direct it to be done." In this instance, just after the record stated *"no error in the said judgment,"* the judge had the clerk interline the explanation: *"The court having properly refused the plea upon the second reason." Downman v. Downman's Exor.* (Virginia Court of Appeals 1791), Brown's Reports, *Miscellaneous Virginia Law Reports, 1784–1809: Being the Reports of Charles Lee, John Brown, David Watson & David Yancey,* 28–29, ed. William Hamilton Bryson (Dobbs Ferry: Oceana, 1992).

County Inferior Court, a mere lower court, were holding the legislation unconstitutional.

Macgregore v. Furber was one such case. James Macgregore of Londonderry was a merchant and the farmer and receiver of excise on wine, rum, brandy, and other distilled spirits for Rockingham County, and he charged Joshua Furber of Northwood with selling rum in retail quantities without a license. According to Macgregore, Furber had committed this offense five times, and there being a forfeiture of "forty shillings for each offence," Furber owed ten pounds. Macgregore therefore brought an action of debt for the use of the county as well as himself before Justice of the Peace John Neal.[81]

The trial took place in April in Londonderry, at the inn kept by Captain Jacob Martin, and in this homely setting the lawyers apparently debated not whether a justice of peace could hold a statute unconstitutional, but the merits of the constitutional claim. Furber's lawyer pled that the Justice of the Peace "ought not to take cognizance of this Action" because the plaintiff's claim was for more than forty shillings, and the Bill of Rights had "guaranteed a continuance of Tryal by Jury in all Cases where Tryals by Jury had been practised." Macgregore's attorney countered by pleading that the justice "has a right and ought to take cognizance of the said Writ and declaration," first because of the "late Law of this State" and, second, more specifically, because the Constitution did not "say that in Causes triable of more than forty shillings value, that the party shall have a right to trial by Jury in the first instance." Pursuing this point, he added: "[N]or does the Law restrain the party aggrieved from appealing to the Inferior Court where he may have the same Cause tried by a Jury in as full and ample a manner as if it had originated at an Inferior Court." Upon hearing these arguments, Justice Neal overuled Furber's plea to the jurisdiction, gave the parties a brief trial, and rendered judgment against Furber that he owed Macgregore ten pounds.[82]

Furber appealed to the Inferior Court, where the judges overturned the decision because, as they stated in their record, the statute was unconstitutional:

> [I]t Appearing to the Court that the Act of the Legislature impowering a Justice to hear & Determine Civil Actions of More than Forty Shillings is Manifestly Contrary to the Constitution of this State & this Action being Or-

[81] Writ of Attachment, NHSA, Rockingham County Superior Court Record No. 9320.
[82] Certified Record of Judgment, NHSA, Rockingham County Superior Court Record No. 9320. For a copy of the pleadings that more closely replicates the format of the originals, see Book of Pleadings, 34, *William Plumer Papers,* Mfm Reel 19, Legal Papers.

> iginally Commenced before a Justice for more than forty Shillings. It is Therefore Considered by the Court that the Original Pl^{t} James McGregore take nothing by his Writ.[83]

The court may have been inferior, but the judges understood their duty, even down to the standard of contradiction—that the statute was "Manifestly Contrary to the Constitution of this State."

The Rockingham County Inferior Court reached such decisions as often as they arose during its May term, and no lawyer did more to elaborate the constitutional arguments than Samuel Sherburne. When the case of *Treferrin v. Cate* came before Justice of the Peace Joseph Parsons, Sherburne pleaded for Samuel Cate that an unconstitutional statute was not law and echoed the seventeenth-century English arguments that the courts were the barrier between legislative power and the liberty of the people:

> 1st that the Constitution of this State is the source from whence all Legislative Power flows—
>
> 2^{d} That the Legislative of course cannot exercise a Power which is not deriv'd from the constitution—
>
> 3^{d} that every attempt of the Legislature to exercise a Power not deriv'd from the Constitution is A Tyranical usurpation of an Authority never delegated to them and an infringment of the Peoples Liberty A treasonable conspiracy against the Constitution and no Law—
>
> 4th That the Constitution has not vested the Legislature with Power to enable Justices to try causes of more than forty shillings Value[;] consequently the aforesaid Statute is an Arbitrary & unwarranted usurpation and cannot have the force of Law—
>
> 5th because the first buddings of Tyranny ought to be carefully watched by the Judicial Courts of this State which are the constitutional Barriers between the Power of the Legislature and the liberty of the People and ought early to be blasted before they increase to A size that may involve the People in the dark shades of slavery—[84]

Although the justice held for the plaintiff, the defendant appealed to the Rockingham County Inferior Court, which upheld his constitutional objections with the same entry in its records as in the *Macgregore Case:* that "the Act of the Legislature impowering a Justice to hear and Determine

[83] NHSA, Rockingham County Inferior Court, Minute Book, New Entries, May term 1786, Case No. 51.

[84] Record of Trial before Justice of the Peace Joseph Parsons (May 20, 1786), certified by Parsons to Rockingham County Inferior Court, NHSA, Rockingham County Superior Court Record No. 9347.

Civil Actions of more than Forty Shillings is Manifestly contrary to the Constitution of this State."[85]

Similarly, in *Furber v. Mason,* Samuel Bickford Mason appealed from a decision by a justice of the peace in favor of William Furber, and on Sherburne's motion for Mason in May 1786, the judges again recited what by now was the standard entry—that the act "is Manifestly contrary to the Constitution of this State."[86] Already in the May term, these decisions had become routine.

Numerous men—especially justices of the peace—raised an outcry against the Inferior Court judges. General Sullivan had sarcastically described the Ten Pound Act as "the Late Act for enlarging the powers, & furnishing the pockets of Justices of the peace," and when their scheme began to be questioned in the appeals from their courts to the Rockingham County Inferior Court, they responded by proposing that the Inferior Courts and their juries should be abolished.[87] Ratio confidently urged that "the Inferior Court should be altogether abolished" because it was "a very useless, burthensome and expensive tribunal" and because its juries, "without being of the least service to any one, are very expensive."[88] It was a refrain that only increased after the Rockingham County Inferior Court in May actually held the Ten Pound Act unconstitutional.[89] Tellingly, how-

[85] NHSA, Rockingham County Inferior Court, Minute Book, New Entries, May term 1786, Case No. 113.

[86] Ibid., May term 1786, Case No. 124.

[87] Letter of John Sullivan to Rev. Jeremy Belknap (Dec. 5, 1785), in *Letters and Papers of Major-General John Sullivan,* 440, ed. Otis G. Hammond (Concord: New Hampshire Historical Society, 1939).

[88] Ratio, Letter to Mr. Gerrish, *New Hampshire Mercury* (Apr. 19, 1786). He thought that "instead of the courts we now have, there should be a SUPREME JUDICIAL COURT . . . to which court all local actions should be instituted," and which would hear "all appeals from a Justice's Court in transitory actions." Ibid.

[89] In early June 1786, a newspaper correspondent asked "to be informed whether the institution of our Inferior Courts are intended as Sinecures for Judges, Clerks and Lawyers" and urged, "in the name of justice, and for the benefit of an already too heavily oppressed State, 'let them be abolished,' and all the people will HEARTILY SAY AMEN." Correspondence, *New Hampshire Gazette* (June 1, 1786). In August 1786, it was reported that "[t]he principal topics of politics, which circulated among our honest citizens" were "1. To reduce the Fees of Attorneys," "2. To raise the Jurisdiction of the Justices to hear and determine Actions of all kinds, and to any amount," and "3. to give the Justices power to grant an appeal immediately to the Supreme Court." Junius, "To the Inhabitants of the State of New-Hampshire," *New Hampshire Mercury* (Sept. 6, 1786). According to Junius, "the whole of the Senate, and more than one-third of the House of Representatives" were justices of the peace. Ibid. Such proposals continued to be made in 1787. See Instructions to Representatives from New Boston (Mar. 25, 1787), *Documents Relative to Towns in New Hampshire, Gilmanton to New Ipswich,* 12: 658 (Concord: 1883); An Act to abolish part of the Inferior Courts and Courts

ever, this public assault on the Inferior Courts is not known to have included complaints that their judges lacked the power to hold statutes unconstitutional.

The defenders of the Ten Pound Act in the House of Representatives took a stand against the judges during the summer of 1786, primarily on petitions from two unhappy plaintiffs, but as so often, the populist sentiments of a lower house did not get very far—not even, as here, against lower court judges. One petition came from James Macgregore, the farmer and receiver of the excise on spirituous liquors. Macgregore complained that because of the decision against him, he had been "put to great Cost . . . besides which he is greatly impeeded in the collection of the Excise," for "he knows not in what manner to inforce the payment of any sum . . . due to him where the ammount is between forty Shillings and five pounds." He therefore asked the House to "restore him in some way to his Law"—the New England locution for a legislative grant of a new trial—or in some "otherways" to give him "a restetution of the damages he has sustained when pursuing a plain Law of the State."[90] This petition roused the supporters of the Ten Pound Act to pass a resolution that "said Act is a constitutional Law of this state & ought to be observed as such" and that Macgregore should be restored to his law—in particular, that "the Judgment of the Inferior Court aforesaid be & hereby is rendered null & void" and that Macgregore "is hereby impowered to enter his said Action" at the Rockingham County Superior Court. The New Hampshire General Court was accustomed to restoring men to their law, but the first part of this resolution—that the Ten Pound Act was constitutional—went much further, and the Senate laconically left the resolution "to Lay over."[91]

The other petitioner, Joseph Hall Bartlett, vainly demanded an impeachment. He complained that upon the appeal against him to the Inferior Court, he found "to his great Supprise the Justices of Said Court by the assistence of the Bar were in there own opinion wiser than the whole Legislature," and rather than sustain his action, they "[d]ismised the Same and ordered your Petitioner Contrary to Law for to Pay a bill of Cost beside Loosing his Debt." He therefore prayed that the House would "Impeach Said Justices for Male Conduct" and that "if it Should appeare that they

---

of Sessions within this State and to prevent unnecessary expence to the good Subjects of the same, NHSA, Non-Engrossed Acts & Copies, RG III, Box 1, Acts-Copies 1787 Folder.

90 Petition of James Macgregore (June 6, 1786), NHSA, Petitions to the General Court. On Macgregore, see Lambert, "The 'Ten Pound Act,'" 41–42.

91 Resolve of House of Representatives (June 22, 1786), NHSA, General Court Records, RG III, Box 6; also in Journal of the House 1785–1790, at 159–160 (June 22, 1786), NHSA.

have acted Contrary to Law that they May be Dismised from there Said office and others May be appointed in there Stead that will Make the Laws there Rule of Conduct that there by your Petitioner May have Redress."[92]

By the time the House considered this petition, however, the Senate had made clear in response to Macgregore's petition that it would not countenance a direct condemnation of the Inferior Court's decisions, and the House therefore simply voted to bar any process in the offending cases from the May term—the goal being at least to stop execution on the May judgments.[93] This was also too much for the Senate. It understood that the legislature could not stay the proceedings of the courts, and it returned the petition with the dry comment that "the Vote of the hon[ble] House, on the within Petition does not constitutionally come before them for their consideration."[94] In short, the House in the summer of 1786 attempted to interfere with the judges, but the Senate refused to cooperate. It will become a familiar pattern, and it suggests that the opposition to judges who did their duty in holding statutes unconstitutional was not as widespread as may be imagined.

Rather than respond to the demands of the House, the Rockingham County Inferior Court continued to hear new appeals and even began to discipline recalcitrant justices of the peace. The Court in its May term had repeatedly held the Ten Pound Act unconstitutional, and it therefore in August (probably at the behest of the lawyers) focused on the next legal ques-

[92] Petition of Joseph Hall Barlett (June 12, 1786), NHSA, Petitions to the General Court.

[93] It resolved "that in all the Actions brought by appeal to the Inferior Court . . . in the County of Rockingham that exceeded the sum of Forty shillings, which the Court did not Sustain—there be no further process untill further order of the Gen! Court." Vote of House of Representatives (June 27, 1786), NHSA, General Court Records, RG III, Box 6; Journal of the House 1785–1790, at 177 (June 27, 1786), NHSA. The case files suggest that the Rockingham County Inferior Court simply ignored this resolution.

[94] Petition of Joseph Hall Barlett (June 12, 1786), with vote of Senate endorsed on the verso (June 27, 1786), NHSA, Petitions to the General Court.

In the midst of the ineffective petitions and House resolutions against the judges, the opponents of the Ten Pound Act made their own futile attempts. A member of the House of Representatives moved "for the repeal" of the act, but the House voted this down 64 to 16, and the two houses instead appointed a joint committee to "report such alterations and amendments as they may jud[g]e necessary." Journal of the House 1785–1790, at 138 (June 15, 1786), NHSA. This committee promptly reported a compromise proposal—that "for all Actions brought before a Justice of the peace for more than forty shillings the said Justice at the request of either party, shall call for a Jury, and that an Apeal at the request of either party shall be granted to the Inferior or Superior Court at the Option of the party." The House, however, accepted this proposal with the amendment that a party could only request an appeal to the Superior Court, and the Senate predictably left the resolution to lay over. Report of Committee (June 22, 1786), NHSA, General Court Records, RG III, Box 6; also in Journal of the House 1785–1790, at 158 (June 22, 1786), NHSA.

tion—the misconduct of justices of the peace who flouted the Court's rulings by continuing to hear cases above forty shillings without a jury.

Although when it initially met in August the Inferior Court simply quashed the judgments of justices of the peace in cases heard under the Ten Pound Act, it soon realized, as in the prior spring, that it had to recite its reasoning in its record.[95] Accordingly, in November 1786—in *John Davis v. Joseph Young*—it quashed the proceedings below with the explanation "that the sum Demanded Exceeds the Jurisdiction of the said Justice, and that no Justice of the peace can take cognizance thereof according to the Constitution of this State."[96] This focus on a justice's lack of jurisdiction was taken up the next summer by another Inferior Court, that of Strafford County, which twice in February 1787 dismissed Ten Pound Act cases on the ground that "the Justice could not by the Constitution of this State hold cognizance of the Original Plea."[97] When in June it again reached such a conclusion, it more elaborately recorded that "the Justice could not by the law of this State, nor the Constitution hold forth Cognizance of the original Plea."[98] If the Ten Pound Act was unconstitutional, the justice of the

[95] During the August term, in a pair of cases brought by William Duty, the defendants appealed from the judgments of a justice of the peace, and on the motions of their counsel, the Rockingham County Inferior Court decided simply to quash the actions—in the first case stating in the record that "this Action is quash^d for want of regularity in ye Proceedings." *William Duty v. Samuel Kelly and Elizabeth his Wife,* NHSA, Rockingham County Inferior Court, Minute Book, New Entries, Aug. term 1786, Case No. 50. Execution was issued in August 1786. Ibid. In the companion case, the record merely stated "this Action is quashed" without bothering to explain what was obvious from the prior case. *William Duty v. Samuel Kelly,* NHSA, Rockingham County Inferior Court, Minute Book, New Entries, Aug. term 1786, Case No. 51. It is not clear whether this William Duty was the one whom Plumer described as among the "infamous . . . Men noted for perjury, forgery, counterfeiting the current coin, horse stealing breaking goals, & such high handed offences." William Plumer, Letter to John Hale (Oct. 14, 1786), in *A Collection of Letters Written to and by Wm Plumer,* 1: 102, *William Plumer Papers,* Mfm Reel LC2.

[96] Rockingham County Inferior Court, Minute Book, Nov. term, 1786, New Entries, Case No. 9, NHSA.

[97] *Richard Perkins v. Solomon Lord* (Feb. term 1787), Strafford County Inferior Court, Book of Judgments & Levies 1786–1790, at 206, Strafford County Clerk's Office; *Ebenezer Horn v. Samuel Austin* (Feb. term 1787), ibid.

[98] *Benjamin Butler v. Jonathan Gilman* (June term, 1787), ibid., 303.

The Rockingham County Inferior Court focused on a more refined point shortly afterward in *Hills v. Wason.* This case was appealed from Justice Neal to the Inferior Court, which in its May term 1787 granted a continuance to take "Advisement" until its August term. Certified Copy of Record of Trial before Justice Neal, NHSA, Rockingham County Superior Court Record No. 9927; NHSA, Rockingham County Inferior Court, Minute Book, May term 1787, Continued Cases, Case No. 6. By that time the legislature had repealed the Ten Pound Act, but the constitutional issue in the case still required resolution. NHSA, Rockingham County Inferior Court, Minute Book, Aug. term 1787, Continued Cases, Case No. 133.

The issue was how to calculate whether a case exceeded the forty-shilling barrier, above peace had exercised jurisdiction beyond either constitutional or statutory authority.

It was a tumultuous period, when impoverished men were meeting in informal county conventions to demand relief, and their excesses reminded other citizens of the risks for both judicial and legislative authority. In mid-September, when the General Court met in Exeter, a self-created Rockingham County Convention encamped outside the town. Of the two hundred men who formed the "Convention," eighty had arms; the others, clubs and staves. At first these men simply addressed legislative demands to the General Court, and the House compliantly appointed a committee to consider their proposals. The Senate, however, refused to join any such committee. At this point the insurgents entered the town and, with drums beating, approached the legislature. They soon surrounded the meeting house, placed sentries to blockade legislators in the building, and fixed bayonets. The men shouted out their demands, including paper money, the cancelation of debts, freedom from taxes, and "the destruction of the Inferior Courts." Amid the chaos, William Plumer "went up to the mob" and "reasoned with several of them . . . but the answer I received was the bayonet pointed to my breast." The mob, however, was not resolute, and later that evening twenty men from the legislature, of whom Plumer was one, "agreed to raise a party, walk up immediately to the mob, & without weapons disarm them." The

---

which a defendant had a right to a jury and a justice of the peace lacked jurisdiction. As reported by William Plumer, "This cause was commenced before Justice Neal" as an "Indebitatus assumpsit for the ballance of [an] acc^{t} annexed to the writ. The whole acc^{t} was about 53/.- the ballance demanded 10/5^{d}." At trial before Neal, "[t]he def^{t} plead to the jurisdiction of the Justice, insisting that he was empowered to try actions only where they are under 40/.- & that the matter now in controversy is 53/.- the justice over-ruled the plea & gave judgment for the pla^{t} for 10/5^{d} & costs. Wason appealed, & now at this Court Pickering for the Appellant insisted that a Justice cannot take cognizance of an action brot on ballance of acc^{t}, if the whole acc^{t} exceeds 40/. altho' the ballance may be under that sum. He cited prov. law p. 5 Const. bill of Rights Art. 20." Then "Prentice [argued] for the App^{ee} contra," and the judges "*Per Curia* [said:] A Justice of the peace may legally take cognizance of an action bro't upon the ballance of an account, if that ballance is under 40/.- although the whole account may much exceed that sum. This has been the constant practice. Judgment for App^{ee} for 10/5 & Costs." *Isaac Hills v. John Wason* (Aug. term 1787), [Reports of Cases], 154–155, *William Plumer Papers,* Mfm Reel 19, Legal Papers.

Another question arose when a plaintiff in 1790 "declared upon a promissory note for ten bushels of rye, & averred it was of the value of £3," upon which the jury gave a "[v]erdict for 40/. damages & costs." Because he brought the action in Rockingham County Inferior Court, the defendant's counsel, Sullivan and Sherburne, moved that "the Court direct the Clerk to tax only as much costs as tho' it had been tried before a Justice of the peace, as it was within the jurisdiction of a Justice." The Court, however, held unanimously that "[t]he rye was of an uncertain value—the pla^{t} had a right to aver that it was worth £3—& to have that question determined in the first instance by a Jury." Anonymous (Rockingham County Common Pleas, Aug. 1790), ibid., 170–171.

sheer confidence of this maneuver confused the insurgents and led to their dispersal.[99]

After being assaulted, the legislature began to shift its position on the Ten Pound Act—the House becoming all the more lonely and strident, and the Senate all the more unwilling to criticize the judges, even mere Inferior Court judges, for doing their duty. Shortly before the siege, the two houses had cooperated by appointing a joint committee to consider revisions to the Ten Pound Act, and the committee had reported that "the said act stands in need of no alterations or amendments."[100] Following the challenge by the Rockingham Convention, however, the House had to act by itself, and it spoke out more bluntly. The House took the Ten Pound Act under consideration on Christmas Day 1786 and voted 44 to 14 that "it is a Constitutional Act."[101] Two days later, it requested that the clerk of the Rockingham County Inferior Court send the House a copy of the proceedings in each of the Ten Pound Act cases that had come up on appeal.[102] The House did not bother transmitting either resolution to the Senate.[103]

A winter of discontent further shifted sentiment against populist challenges and in favor of the judges—the center of attention being the uprising led by Daniel Shays against the government of Massachusetts and especially its courts. The rebellious debtors who joined Shays could not long prevent the Massachusetts courts from meeting, but they gave the people of New Hampshire cause to reflect on the fragility of republican government and the dangers of popular resentment against judges. The electors of New Hampshire brought a new array of representatives into the House in the spring of 1787, and when the legislators met at their summer session, Governor Sullivan urged them to consider that "[t]he forwarding [of] delegates to the convention at Philadelphia" was "an object worthy of your earliest attention."[104] The legislators eventually appointed delegates, but not before attending to a business that seemed more immediate.

This time, the House would defend the judges in the conduct of their

99 William Plumer, Letter to John Hale (Sept. 20, 1786), in *A Collection of Letters Written to and by Wm Plumer,* 1: 83–88, *William Plumer Papers,* Mfm Reel LC2.

100 Journal of the House of Representatives (Sept. 16, 1786), in *Early State Papers of New Hampshire,* 20: 704, ed. Albert Stillman Batchellor (Manchester: 1891). See also ibid., 20: 698.

101 Journal of the House 1785–1790, at 216 (Dec. 25, 1786), NHSA; Resolution, General Court Records, RG III, Box 3, Folder G5 House of Representatives 13–31 Dec. 1786 and Undated 1786.

102 Vote of House (Dec. 27, 1786), NHSA, General Court Records, RG III, Box 6. For slightly truncated wording, see Journal of the House 1785–1790, at 216 (Dec. 27, 1786), NHSA.

103 Vote of House (Dec. 27, 1786), NHSA, General Court Records, RG III, Box 6.

104 His Excellency's Address to both Houses of Assembly (June 12, 1787), *New Hampshire*

duty. A member of the House proposed an impeachment of the judges of the Rockingham Inferior Court, but by now there was less tolerance for this sort of attack—as apparent even from the clerk's sardonic record that a motion was made for "reading some papers . . . purporting to be an impeachment of the Honb[le] Justices of the Inferior Court."[105] The committee considering the papers reported that "the said Justices are not Impeachable for Mal-administration as their conduct is justified by the constitution of this State," and after the House voted 35 to 21 to accept the report, it immediately appointed members to a joint committee for drafting a repeal of the Ten Pound Act.[106] The next day, the General Court passed this repeal statute and adopted a new small claims act. Under this new act, justices of the peace could enter judgment on confession of any debt not exceeding ten pounds, or could refer such a debt for voluntary arbitration, but they could no longer hear cases over forty shillings without a jury.[107] The legislature's action was understood as a vindication of the judges. As several newspapers reported: "The General Court, during their late session, repealed the *Ten Pound* act—and thereby justified the conduct of the Justices of the Inferior Court, who have uniformly opposed it as *unconstitutional* and *unjust*."[108]

In the *Ten Pound Cases,* the judges of two lower courts repeatedly held a statute unconstitutional, and this is revealing. It suggests that far from acting on what they considered a power over legislation, they merely understood themselves to be doing their duty.

Rhode Island: Trevett v. Weeden

The judges in *Trevett v. Weeden* evidently struggled with their decision, but exactly why has not been fully understood. This 1786 Rhode Island case is

---

Gazette (June 30, 1787). The legislature had earlier voted to send delegates but with the proviso, insisted upon by the Senate, "[t]hat the said Delegates shall proceed to join the Convention aforesaid in case Congress shall signify to them that they approve of the said Convention as advantageous to the Union and not as an infringement of the Powers granted to Congress by the Confederation." Resolve (Jan. 17, 1787), in *Laws of New Hampshire,* 5: 247, ed. Henry Harrison Metcalf (Concord: Rumford Press, 1916). See also *Journals of the Continental Congress 1774–1789,* at 30: 116–117, ed. John C. Fitzpatrick (Washington: Government Printing Office, 1934).

105 Journal of the House 1785–1790, at 307 (June 26, 1787), NHSA.

106 Journal of the House 1785–1790, at 313–314 (June 27, 1787), ibid.

107 Journal of the House 1785–1790, at 318, 319 (June 28, 1787), NHSA; An Act to Repeal an Act Passed the Ninth Day of November . . . 1785, NHSA, Original Acts (June 28, 1787); An Act for the More Speedy Recovering of Small Debts and to Save the Costs Usually Attending the Recovery Thereof in the Present Course of Law. NHSA, Original Acts (June 28, 1787). See also "Bill [for] Confession of Debt &c 1787," General Court Records, Non-Engrossed Acts & Copies, RG III, Box 1, Acts-Copies 1787 Folder.

108 Correspondence (July 3), *New-Hampshire Spy* (July 3, 1787).

typically understood as part of the development of a judicial power to hold statutes unconstitutional. The judges, however, already had a duty to decide in accord with the law of the land, and their real difficulty was that the people of Rhode Island had not adopted an express constitution. To overcome this awkwardness, some of the judges persuaded themselves that there was a sort of express constitution in the colonial charter, and although these judges probably thereby ventured beyond their duty, their eagerness to do their duty in accord with an express constitution says much about the powerful attraction of their constitutional and judicial ideals.

Rhode Island was so fragmented it could not even adopt an express constitution. Whereas it will be seen shortly that Connecticut was sufficiently cohesive that it could afford a customary constitution, its eastern neighbor went to the other extreme. Deeply conscious of their religious and economic divisions, and lacking a communal sense of their identity, the people of Rhode Island could not easily think of themselves as a people united by a common constitutional custom. Nor even could they agree among themselves to write a constitution. Instead, the different political factions in the new state clung to their inherited charter for their own reasons, and the inability of the state to rise above these narrow interests was such that the state did not adopt a written constitution until 1842, when the aftermath of Dorr's Rebellion finally made this necessary.[109] The state's judges therefore could not be confident as to how they should treat a statute that in most other states would have been expressly forbidden. The judges did not have a tacit, customary constitution that would have required them to defer to the judgment of the legislature, but nor in their royal charter did they have an express constitution that was beyond declaration or alteration by their legislature.

The difficulties faced by the judges of Rhode Island became clear in *Trevett v. Weeden.*[110] When the War came to an end in 1783, the states had

[109] For hints of this, see David S. Lovejoy, *Rhode Island Politics and the American Revolution 1760–1776,* at 193–194 (Providence: Brown University Press, 1958). For statistics confirming that Rhode Island did not have "a popularly oriented democracy," see Joel A. Cohen, "Democracy in Revolutionary Rhode Island: A Statistical Analysis," *Rhode Island History,* 29: 7 (1970). It is conventionally said that Rhode Islanders retained their charter in 1776 because of their attachment to it, but to this must be added their divisions. Although some eighteenth-century commentators occasionally speculated that Rhode Island enjoyed a constitution like that of Connecticut, such arguments do not seem to have been very persuasive, for the people of Rhode Island lacked even the minimal cohesion necessary to adopt a written constitution.

[110] For detailed studies of the case, see Charles Warren, "Earliest Cases of Judicial Review of State Legislation by Federal Courts," *Yale Law Journal,* 32: 20 (1922); Forrest McDonald, *We the People: The Economic Origins of the Constitution,* 323–346 (Chicago: University of

to face in earnest the less glorious effort to pay off their debts—both their own and those of Congress. During the first half of the 1780s, Rhode Island relied on its import duties to make these payments, but it eventually had to increase its taxes on land, and amid a shortage of specie, this created a crisis for farmers, many of whom could not pay their taxes and other debts and therefore risked losing their property.[111]

The most popular solution in Rhode Island, as elsewhere, was paper money. A "Country" party formed around a proposal that the state print paper money and lend it to persons who offered land as security, and the party campaigned on this scheme in the spring 1786 elections, their ticket being printed under the heading "TO RELIEVE THE DISTRESSED."[112] After taking control of the governorship and the lower house of the legislature, they passed a statute in May 1786 authorizing paper money and making it legal tender.[113] Under the statute, if a creditor refused to accept this paper, a debtor could lodge his paper payment with any judge of the Superior or Inferior Court of his county—leaving the creditor to call upon the judge for the paper or forgo his claims.[114] It was only the first of a series of laws that would make Rhode Island notorious.

The very next month, the Assembly had to reinforce the May legal tender act with a penal statute. Creditors were apt to refuse the paper money, and on the ground that this was "subversive of those Laws and Principles upon which the Happiness, Welfare and Safety, of the People depend," the General Assembly imposed criminal penalties on anyone who refused to take the paper "in Exchange for any Article . . . expose[d] for Sale . . . for the Value mentioned on the Face of the said Bills." The penalty was £100, and lest the threat of a paper fine have little effect, the legislature added that for a second offense, the defendant also "shall be rendered inca-

---

Chicago Press, 1958); Irwin H. Polishook, "Trevett vs. Weeden and the Case of the Judges," *Newport History* 38: 45 (1965); Patrick T. Conley, "Rhode Island's Paper Money Issue and Trevett v. Weedon (1786)," *Rhode Island History,* 30: 95 (1971). The logical gymnastics required to hold a statute unconstitutional in a state that did not obviously have a constitution is noted in some histories of judicial review, even if in a somewhat different way than here. William Michael Treanor, "Judicial Review Before Marbury," *Stanford Law Review,* 58: 476–477 (2005), and Daniel J. Hulsebosch, "A Discrete and Cosmopolitan Minority: The Loyalists, The Atlantic World, and the Origins of Judicial Review," *Chicago-Kent Law Review,* 81: 855 (2006).

111 McDonald, *We the People,* 323–346; Conley, "Rhode Island's Paper Money Issue and Trevett v. Weedon (1786)," 96.

112 Conley, "Rhode Island's Paper Money Issue and Trevett v. Weedon (1786)," 96, 98, 108.

113 An Act for emitting One Hundred Thousand Pounds, *May 1786. At the General Assembly of the Governor and Company of the State of Rhode-Island and Providence Plantations,* 13 (Providence: [1786]).

114 Ibid., 16–17.

pable and unfit to elect, or to be elected, to any Office of Honour, Trust or Profit, within this State."[115] These penalties for refusing the paper only increased the flight to specie, and the paper money rapidly lost its value, reaching two thirds of its face value by July. It would go down to one third in October.[116]

The June penal law increasingly caused a food shortage, and therefore, in contrast to the scholars who write generally about the debt crisis and paper money, the citizens of Rhode Island's towns thought more essentially about food, particularly meat, and this will turn out to be significant. When farmers offered potatoes, meat, and other produce at prices calculated in specie, purchasers "flung" their paper money at them.[117] In Providence, a group of residents "went into the country" to find food for resale at market but found "no beef, veal or lamb, to be sold for paper." Similarly, a butcher who had "sold his meat for paper" complained that it was "out of his power to purchase any more meat for it."[118] The scarcity of food can be traced day to day in Providence in the diary of a Baptist preacher, John Pitman. Initially, on July 3, there was simply "much Confusion" about "the paper Money & the Laws to enforce it." By the thirteenth, however, it became clear that the law would be enforced, and Pitman jotted down in his diary: "Much disorder yesterday about Paper Money[,] one prosecuted for £100 fine for Refusing to take it, Shops shut, no meat in Markett[,] high threatenings, heard that Corn was taken away from one in Newport, &c." The next two days, it was "hard getting Provision," but thereafter this was hardly worth noting. On July 22 and later, Pitman found the "[m]arket yet Bad," and he attended some sobering "Town Meeting Debates Concerning Paper Money & some Method of Providing for the poor." It had been a bad month, and worse was to come. As August began, the Rev. Pitman noted that the town of Providence had "appointed a Comittee to meet the other towns in the state Concerning Paper Money." Attending to

115 An Act in Addition to and Amendment of an Act, . . . for emitting One Hundred Thousand Pounds, *June 1786. At the General Assembly of the Governor and Company of the State of Rhode-Island and Providence Plantations,* 8–9 (Providence: [1786]). The statute also penalized any seller who had "two Prices" for his goods—"a Silver-Money less than a Paper-Money Price"—or who otherwise in any way attempted to "depreciate" or "discourage" the paper. Ibid.

116 Warren, "Earliest Cases of Judicial Review of State Legislation by Federal Courts," 18; McDonald, *We the People,* 335–336; Conley, "Rhode Island's Paper Money Issue and Trevett v. Weedon (1786)," 101.

117 "A Lover of Justice and Peace," Letter to Mr. Carter (July 21, 1786), *Providence Gazette* (July 22, 1786).

118 John Brown, "To the Inhabitants of the State of Rhode-Island and Providence Plantations" (July 7, 1786), *Providence Gazette* (July 8, 1786).

his own needs—perhaps for safekeeping—Pitman "[b]egan to Pasture my Cow with Mrs. Young."[119]

The legislature responded to the collapse of the paper money and the economy by adopting a second penal statute, which further amended the May legal tender act and which would lead to the case of *Trevett v. Weeden.* Concerned that juries would not enforce the June penal act, the legislature in August authorized any purchaser whose paper was not accepted to bring a *qui tam* action against the recalcitrant seller in a special court—a court where the dispute would be tried "without any Jury, by a majority of the Judges present, according to the Laws of the Land." The judges' decision would be "final and conclusive," with "no Appeal."[120] Once again a state legislature deprived individuals of their right to a jury, and the Rhode Island judges therefore would have to consider how to do their duty when the people had not clearly adopted a constitution, customary or express.

Trevett v. Weeden had its beginnings in a butcher's shop. Although it has been speculated that *Trevett* was a test case arranged to challenge the tender law, John Trevett was more concerned with beef. He had served as a captain in the American navy since before Independence—often exhibiting remarkable courage and resourcefulness—but in June 1780, during a fateful skirmish off the coast of Bermuda, he suffered a serious foot injury, and his face and eyes "were badly blown."[121] Eventually returning to Newport, lame and without his right eye, he became a cabinetmaker, and like many other men of limited means, he struggled in the mid-1780s to avoid hunger. His brother Benjamin was among those in need, and when Benjamin in February 1786 wrote for assistance, John responded that he was in no position to help: "[Y]ou Complain of hard times and Wornt Me to Send you 30/ in Goods," but "I Cant Command itt att any Rate." With his mind on essentials, he explained that "My Farther and My self has not bene Abel to by a Pair of Shues this winter nor Lay in one Singel pound of Pork," and

119 Rev. John Pitman, Diaries (July 3, 13, 14 and 15, 22, and 24, Aug. 9 and 10, 1786), Rhode Island Historical Society, Mss 622, Box 1.

120 An Act, in addition to and in amendment of an Act, entitled, "An Act, in addition to and in amendment of an Act, made and passed by this Assembly, at their session holden in Newport, in May last, for emitting the Sum of One Hundred Thousand Pounds, in Bills of public Credit," *August 1786. At the General Assembly of the Governor and Company of the State of Rhode-Island and Providence Plantations,* 5–7 (Providence: [1786]). At least, however, the statute lowered the penalties to various amounts not exceeding fifty pounds, to be divided between the prosecutor and the state.

121 John Trevett, Ms Journal, Newport Historical Society, as quoted by Jacqueline M. Sinclair, ed., *Captain John Trevett: His Journal, Ancestry and Descent through Henry John Trevett,* 26 (Greenwich, Conn.: John C. and Jacqueline M. Sinclair, 1969). Trevett eventually also lost the use of his other eye. Ibid.

he proceeded to remind Benjamin that "My Farther and Mother Groes Ould and you must think of Luking out for your selfs." Of course, "[i]f itt was in My Power to Do [it] for you I would but Our Family Never Suferd So much as wi have Dune this winter." At times, "we was not Abel to by a Singel Peck of Meail."[122] Such food or other goods as Trevett obtained, he apparently tended to get by barter, and in the autumn of 1786 he worried he would once again be short of meat for the winter.[123]

In September, Trevett attempted to buy beef from at least three butchers, but when he offered paper money, they refused to accept it. He therefore sought redress under the August penal statute by bring *qui tam* actions against them, including John Weeden.[124] This butcher was almost as forlorn as his customer, for only two weeks earlier he had been "an object of charity in the streets of Newport," and now he would be "called upon to answer, criminally, for refusing beef at fourpence the pound, when it cost him sixpence upon the hoof."[125] Trevett complained that Weeden "Refuse[d] the paper currency of this State of the Emishion of May 1786 for Meait."[126] This crude complaint would soon get written up in more fulsome style as an information, in which Trevett—acting for the state and himself—prosecuted Weeden for "presumptuously daringly and contemptuously refus[ing] to take and receive" Trevett's paper money.[127]

Chief Justice Paul Mumford appointed a "Special Superior Court" in accord with the requirements of the August penal statute, but when it met, the clerk of the Superior Court, Robert Rogers, refused to serve as clerk of the special court. Clerks as well as judges had ideals of office, and Rogers "represented to the Justices present that he did not conceive it his Duty to act as Clerk of Special Courts"—although he "was ready to act as Clerk of the Term" of the regular Superior Court. The justices excused him, and when they met again the next day, they appointed another clerk. He did

122 Letter from John Trevett to Benjamin Trevett (Feb. 3. 1786), Newport Historical Society, Letters and Account Book of John Trevett 1783–1787, Vault A, No. 74.

123 In preparing to grow vegetables, he wrote: "Capt. Lowvin Peck Sir I want you to Inquir for Gardin Post I wornt 30 of them tha Must be Locost Post and I will pay in Desks or Tabels or any Joyners ware att Cash Prise or in Dry Goods and I Warnt you to send Me one pound of Good Oinyon Seed." Letter of John Trevett to Lowvin Peck (undated but after Feb. 3, 1786, and before May 10, 1786), ibid.

124 The others were Richard Bush and John Yeomans. See complaints, bonds to prosecute, and pleas, Newport Historical Society, Box 43, Folder 12.

125 James M. Varnum, *The Case, Trevett against Weeden,* 4 (Providence: 1786).

126 Complaint by Trevett against Weeden (Sept. 13, 1786), Newport Historical Society, Box 43, Folder 12.

127 Superior Court of Judicature, Court of Assize and General Goal Delivery, Newport County, Record Book F, at 281 (Sept. Term 1786), Judicial Archives, State Judicial Center, Pawtucket.

not have to serve for long, however, because as soon as the special court opened to hear complaints in *Trevett v. Weeden* and a companion case brought by Trevett against another butcher, the judges "adjourned" the Special Court "over into the Superior Court." They also ordered that these "proceedings of the Special Court" were "to be entered up on Record as the business of this Superior Term Court"—that is, in the record book of the Superior Court.[128]

In shifting the proceeding away from the special court, the judges, like their clerk, hesitated to act under a statute that seemed to require them to act unlawfully. They would have known that Coke and his brethren had refused to sit on an overly broad commission for ecclesiastical causes, and although the Rhode Island judges briefly sat on the special court, they did so only long enough to abandon it for a court of more lawful jurisdiction.

When *Trevett v. Weeden* came into the Superior Court, the leading lawyer for Weeden, the eloquent James Varnum, focused on what was "by far the most important" plea in Weeden's defense: that under the August penal act, the special courts were "not authorised or impower'd by said Act, to impannel a Jury" and that therefore the Act "is unconstitutional & void." Although Rhode Island's 1663 colonial charter had not mentioned trial by jury, and although in 1776 the people of the state had not adopted a constitution, customary or express, the drift of Varnum's argument had to be "[t]hat the trial by jury is a fundamental right, a part of our legal constitution: That the Legislature cannot deprive the citizens of this right: And that your Honours can, and we trust will, so determine." As for those who doubted whether the state had a constitution, Varnum denounced them:

> CONSTITUTION!——we have none:——Who dares to say that?—None but a British emissary, or a traitor to his country.——Are there any such amongst us? The language hath been heard, and God forbid that they should continue!

Reasoning from the existence of government, Varnum asked: "If we have not a constitution, by what authority doth our General Assembly convene to make laws, and levy taxes?" When they meet, "they make laws and levy taxes, and their constituents obey those laws, and pay their taxes," and "[c]onsequently they meet, deliberate and enact, in virtue of a constitution."[129]

128 Superior Court of Judicature, Court of Assize and General Goal Delivery, Newport County, Record Book F, at 280–281 (Sept. Term 1786), Judicial Archives, State Judicial Center, Pawtucket. See also Newport Supreme Court, Minute Book Aug. 1784–Aug. 1789, Judicial Archives.

129 James M. Varnum, *The Case, Trevett against Weeden,* 25 (Providence: 1786); Weedon's Plea, Newport Historical Society, Box 43, Folder 12.

Varnum suggested that the 1663 Charter memorialized an earlier, inexplicit compact of the people. "The powers of our Legislature are so clearly defined in the Charter, which is conclusive evidence of the compact of the people, as well as of the royal intention, that a recurrence to them will greatly assist us in the present question." Although the Charter said nothing about a right to a jury, it contained the familiar requirement that the colony's laws "be not contrary and repugnant unto, but, as near as may be, agreeable to the laws of this our realm of England, considering the nature and constitution of the place and people there." According to Varnum, the charter thus "expressly limits the legislative powers; and by invariable custom and usage they are still so confined, that they cannot make any laws repugnant to the general system of laws which governed the realm of England at the time of the grant." Varnum could not rely on custom so far as to suggest that Rhode Island had an inexplicit, customary constitution, for then, as in England, it could be declared and altered by the legislature, but he could suggest that there had been a compact that was at least partly recorded and rendered express in the Charter and that as a matter of custom this written constitution, including its incorporation of the essential elements of English law, remained binding even after the Revolution. In sum, the charter "was declaratory of, and fully confirmed to the people the Magna Charta, and other fundamental laws of England," and "[t]he revolution hath made no change in this respect, so as to abridge the people of the means of securing their lives, liberty and property."[130]

Having established the Charter as "a sacred stipulation" of "the most valuable part of their political constitution," Varnum easily showed that when the August penal act deprived defendants of a jury, it was "repugnant" to the laws of England and thus to the charter. He added that when the statute "authorizes the Judges to 'proceed to trial without any jury, according to the laws of the land,'" it was also repugnant to itself and therefore as a matter of interpretation was "impossible to be executed."[131]

Once Varnum had shown that the state had a constitution and that the penal act had violated it, he reminded the judges of their office and their oath: "The Judges are sworn 'truly and impartially to execute the laws that now are or shall hereafter be made, according to the best of their skill and understanding.'" They had to decide about the laws, moreover, independently of the legislature, this being a matter of their distinct office, which was a separate power of government:

130 Varnum, *The Case, Trevett against Weeden,* 15, 22–23.
131 Ibid., 15, 31.

> Have the Judges a power to repeal, to amend, to alter laws, or to make new laws?—God forbid!—In that case they would become Legislators.—Have the Legislators power to direct the Judges how they shall determine upon the laws already made?—God forbid!—In that case they would become Judges.—The true distinction lies in this, that the Legislative have the incontroulable power of making laws not repugnant to the constitution:—The Judiciary have the sole power of judging of those laws, and are bound to execute them; but cannot admit any act of the Legislative as law, which is against the constitution.

Yet even in thus relying on the familiar ideals of office and oaths, independence and separation, Varnum also played upon the gratifications of power. Toward the close of his oration, he declared: "Oh! ye Judges, what a godlike pleasure must you now feel in having the power, the legal power, of stopping the torrent of lawless sway, and securing to the people their inestimable rights!"[132] This was a far cry from the humility traditionally expected of those who were said to be gods on earth.

After listening to Varnum's breathless declamation, "the Counsel on the other side of the question" said "but little," and the judges the next day gave their opinions. The judges unanimously refused to take cognizance of the case, and as reported by a newspaper their reasons varied:

> Judge Howell . . . declared . . . the penal law to be repugnant and unconstitutional, and therefore gave it as his opinion that the Court could not take cognizance of the information.—Judge Devol was of the same opinion.—Judge Tillinghast took notice of the striking repugnancy in the expressions of the act, *"Without trial by jury, according to the laws of the land"*—and on that ground gave his judgment the same way.—Judge Hazard voted against taking cognizance.—The Chief Justice [Mumford] declared the judgment of the Court, without giving his own opinion.[133]

[132] Ibid., 27–28, 35–36.

[133] Correspondence (Oct. 2), *Providence Gazette* (Oct. 7, 1786). The record simply stated that "the said Complaint doe not come under the Cognizance of the Judges here present, and the same be and it is hereby dismissed." Superior Court of Judicature, Court of Assize and General Goal Delivery, Newport County, Record Book F, at 280 (Sept. Term 1786), Judicial Archives, State Judicial Center, Pawtucket.

The decision in *Trevett w. Weeden* narrowed the usefulness of the system of lodging paper money with judges, but men could still rely on the system to avoid their existing debts. After *Trevett,* there was no point in lodging paper money against a shopkeeper who refused to sell his goods for paper, because the purchaser could not bring proceedings against the shopkeeper in a special court. *Trevett,* however, did not eliminate the practice of lodging money by men who were indebted for goods, services, etc. they had already received, for they could still lodge paper money to hold off their creditors. Predictably, however, some judges refused to cooperate. Although debtors regularly resorted to Mumford, Hazard, and various other judges, it is difficult to find advertisements recording that anyone lodged paper money with Howell, Devol, or Tillinghast. Mumford reconsidered his role in these proceedings only af-

Thus two of the judges held the act unconstitutional—probably on Varnum's elaborate theory—and one held the act repugnant to itself, as if Varnum were clearly correct that the act's intent was so difficult to discern that the act could not be executed. The other two judges in varying degrees apparently kept their thoughts to themselves. Their relative silence, although hardly principled, may in a sense have been more honest, for the reality was that any explanation as to why the judges could not take jurisdiction was bound to seem somewhat strained.

The story did not end with the judges' decision, for the judges had to face the discontent of the lower house of the Assembly. The Country party attempted to hold the judges to account in the lower house, but even when summoning the judges, they ran into difficulty. The lower house feared that the judgment "may Tend directly to destroy and abolish the legislative authority In the State," and it therefore demanded that the judges of the Superior Court attend the Assembly to explain "the Reasons and Grounds of the afors^d. Judgment"—so that the Assembly could "adopt such measures as may establish the Supremacy of the legislative authority." The upper house concurred but only after expunging the words about establishing the supremacy of the legislature—an early indication that, as in other states, the upper house would not join an attack on the judges.[134]

Two of the judges, Devol and Mumford, claimed they were too ill to attend the Assembly.[135] Their affliction seems to have been of the sort that had already rendered Mumford almost speechless on the bench, and when

---

ter he became a victim of the law. A lessee of Mumford's, Israel Pearce, offered him paper money, and after Mumford refused to accept it, Pearce lodged the £60 with Justice Robert Stanton, this "being in full of the Principal and Interest of a Sum of Money, due to the Hon. Paul Mumford, Esquire, for fifteen Months and ten Days House-Rent." Advertisement, State of Rhode-Island, &c. (witnessed by Stanton Oct. 12, 1787), *Providence Gazette* (Nov. 3, 1787). It is unknown whether Mumford appreciated the irony of the situation, but he apparently no longer allowed men to lodge money with him.

Incidentally, it was said that "many of these tenders were afterwards ripped up w[h]ere the Evidence of the debt had not been surrendered, and the two witnesses could not be found to attest to the tender." John Howland, Autobiography, 118, Rhode Island Historical Society, John Howland Collection, Mss 499.

134 Resolve (Oct. 4, 1786), RISA, Acts and Resolves of the Rhode Island General Assembly, 1786–1787, Vol. 25, C-00210, at 61. On the same day, the lower house resolved and the upper house concurred "that no Sworn Attorney as such and while a Member of this House shall be admitted to speak or Plead out of his seat and at the Bar of the House on any private Petition when on trial before this Assembly." Ibid., at 62. The small scale of the legal and political community may be illustrated by the fact that this and all other lower house documents were signed by the clerk of the lower house, Benjamin Bourne, who represented Lippitt in *Seaver v. Lippitt.*

135 Resolution (Oct. 1786, 1st session), RISA, Rhode Island Colony Records, 1785–1791, at 309.

the Assembly asked for their attendance a month later, they remained indisposed. In the end, therefore, only three of the judges appeared to defend their decision.

The youngest justice, David Howell, spoke for over six hours against the legislative interference. He argued that the penal statute "was unconstitutional, had not the force of a law, and could not be executed." More generally, he defended the judges on the ground that "'they were not accountable to the Legislature for the reasons of their judgment.'" To dispel the accusation that the judges had undermined the legislative authority of the state by holding the statute unconstitutional, Howell emphasized that the "judgment of the Court" was that "'the information is not cognizable before them." Of course, he and at least one other judge had opined that the statute was unconstitutional, and Howell was not at his most persuasive when he disparaged the significance of their opinions in order to rest more safely on their judgment entered on record. Yet having done this, he could argue: "Whatever might have been the opinion of the Judges, they spoke by their records, which admitted of no addition or diminution." It was "out of the power, therefore, of the General Assembly to determine upon the propriety of the Court's judgment, without a particular explanation," and "[i]f this could be required in one instance, it might in all; and so the Legislative would become the Supreme Judiciary. A perversion of power totally subversive of civil liberty!" Howell added that "the Judiciary Power should be as independent as the Legislative. And consequently the Judges cannot be answerable for their opinion, unless charged with criminality."[136]

In a state without a constitution, the lower house might well be excused for its astonishment that some of the judges had held a statute unconstitutional, but even many in the Country party were apparently hesitant to seek impeachment. Although a motion was made to dismiss the judges, the three judges present threw the lower house on the defensive by submitting a memorial that they had not yet been charged with any crime. They insisted that they were accountable to give the reasons of their judgment "only to God (under the solemnities of their oath of office) and to their consciences," and they demanded that they be given "a hearing by counsel before some proper and *legal tribunal,* and an opportunity to answer to *certain and specific charges.*"[137] The House therefore contented itself

[136] Varnum, *The Case, Trevett against Weeden,* 38–39.
[137] Memorial "To His Excellency the Governor, and his Honour the Speaker of the Lower House of Assembly: To be Communicated to Both Houses," in Varnum, *The Case, Trevett against Weeden,* 45–46. This was drafted by Howell. Warren, "Earliest Cases of Judicial Review of State Legislation by Federal Courts," 21, note 12.

with voting that it had received "no satisfactory reasons . . . for their judgment" but that because they were "not charged with Criminality in giving Judgment" they were "discharged."[138] Underlying this capitulation were economic and political changes, for as a result of the judges' decision, food had reappeared in the markets, "shops and stores were generally opened, and business assumed a cheerful aspect."[139] The Country party was now in retreat, and in December the Assembly repealed the June and August penal laws.[140]

Country resentments, however, did not entirely dissipate, and the young David Howell, who had taken the lead in defending the judges' conduct, came to feel the burden of his resolute stand. The judges were annually appointed by the legislature, and anticipating that he would probably not be reappointed, Howell wrote to Governor John Collins in April 1787 to withdraw from consideration for renewal. He had first been appointed the year before, and after modestly reciting that he had accepted the position "with reluctance" on account of his "want of abilities & legal knowledge," he explained that his disinclination had only increased:

> My feelings became more sensibly affected when I found myself under the disagreeable necessity of, at least seeming to thwart the views of the Legislature: &, as, I feared, contravening the wishes & expectations of the bulk of the people relating to the penal law & the late . . . paper money.

He therefore "ever since heartily wished to be decently discharged from an office I could no longer fill to the satisfaction of the people." He had "actually written a Letter of resignation" already in the winter, but at the "solicitation" of his brethren, he had been prevailed upon to continue in his place until the end of his term. Now, as the anniversary of his appointment approached, he requested that "the place be filled by some other person."[141] Not surprisingly, when the legislature made its appointments, it only restored the politic Chief Justice Paul Mumford to the Superior Court.[142]

The two judges who had held the statute unconstitutional had strained to do their duty by deciding in accord with a constitution that arguably did

138 Resolve (Nov. 3, 1786), RISA, Acts and Resolves of the Rhode Island General Assembly, 1786–1787, Vol. 25: C-00210, at 77.
139 Varnum, *The Case, Trevett against Weeden,* 37.
140 RISA, Rhode Island Colony Records 1785–1791, at 345 (Dec. 1786).
141 Letter from David Howell to Governor John Collins (Apr. 30, 1787), Newport Historical Society, King Papers, Vault A, Box 134, Folder 3.
142 *At the General Assembly of the Governor and Company of the State of Rhode-Island, and Providence-Plantations,* 7 (1787]). Indeed, the Assembly appointed Gideon Wanton—probably one of Trevett's witnesses of that name—as a justice of the Inferior Court of Common Pleas for the County of Newport. Ibid., 4.

not exist, and there is no better commentary on the problematic character of the Newport decision, *Trevett v. Weeden,* than its long-forgotten companion case in Providence, *Seaver v. Lippett.* It was recalled more than a half-century later by John Howland, the son of the Kent County Inferior Court clerk, Benjamin Howland. The case began outside Elisha Brown's shop in Providence. At the time, all of the shops were closed on account of the penal laws. "Three or four of us neighbors were Standing in front of Elisha Browns Shop . . . when Judge Thompson who lived Opposite Came acrosst with a Jug and Box and asked Brown why he kept his Shop Shut." The judge "wanted to go in for Some necessary things," but Brown replied that "he dare not open it," for "as the Law Stood, it would not do for him to Sell for paper money," and "if he refused to take it he must pay a hundred pounds which he could not afford."

The judge, however, needed to fill his jug and imperiously demanded: "Neighbor Brown I tell you open your Shop. I will Insure you against any penalty." Brown "replyed quickly will you Judge"? The judge answered, "Yes, for Five dollers I will render you Safe from any penalty." At this, "Brown put his hand into his Breeches pocket and took out five dollars and handed them to the Judge who took the money and said open the Shop." The Judge then "[b]ought his Jug of Rum and Box of Suger." It was but the beginning of the lawlessness.

For several days, this "was only Shop opened in town," for "Brown would not tell others the reason of his Courage and Sold as much more as to place his five dollers." Then, however, Charles Lippitt opened his store, and others followed.

"[T]he only Complaint for violation of the penal Law was made by Obed Seaver," who went to Lippitt's shop to buy a jackknife. "Lippitt laid a bundle of Knives on the Counter, and Seaver Chose one and took out a pack of the paper bills and offered one of 25 Cents, the price of the Knife." Lippitt "told him he would not take the paper money." Seaver "put the bill into his pocket, and went to Judge Thompson and entered his Complaint against Lippitt according to the Law."

Judge Ebenezer Thompson was a justice of the Providence Inferior Court of Common Pleas, and he assigned the case to a special court, to meet in the courthouse, in the representatives' chamber. On the day of trial, it was "crowded with anxious people." In response to the complaint, Lippitt's lawyer spoke for about an hour and a half "chiefly against the Constitutionality of the Law" on the ground that "no man could be deprived of his property or life without a trial by a Jury of his peers, that every Bill of Rights in England as well as America Secured the Right of tryal by Jury," and "that the law in Question was therefore void and could not be enforced." Seaver's attorney then responded that Rhode Island was different from most other states—that "the power of the General Assembly was unlimited by the Charter or any decla[ra]tion of Rights established here."

When the lawyers finished, Judge Thompson stood up. He explained that "the Laws Should be obeyed," and after noting that "a great deal had been said about Constitutions and bill[s] of Rights and other things," he said that "the Court will take time to consider." The following week, the lawyers once more went through their arguments, and "when they had exausted themselves, the Judge again arose," and after reciting "nearly the same prologue" he had delivered before, he adjourned the court another week.

At the third session of the trial, "*we* were all there again Except the judge." After waiting an hour, "the paper money folks requested Martin Seamans the Sherif to go to the house of the Judge and ask him to come . . . as perhaps he had forgotten the time." About half an hour later, the sheriff returned to report:

> [H]e had been to the Judges House and Aske[d] the negro woman where her master was, and she Said our Cow ran away this morning and we dont know where she is[,] And Master has gown to Tockwotten to look for her[,] and if he finds her he will drive her home before dark to be milked.

At this point, John Howland, who was familiar with the duties often performed by his father, took matters into his own hands: "[A]s there was no Clerk to this Court, I ventured to proclaim, This Court is Adjourned without day, and we all departed."

It thus "was decided by Judge Thompsons White Faced Cow in her Session at Tockwotten that the penal Law was unconstitutional." This was "the only Tryal had under this penal Statute, in this county," and "the result was the Opening of the Shops and the market."[143] In fact, it may be doubted whether either Judge Thompson or his cow held the statute unconstitutional. Rather, Thompson ignored the statute and gave the people of Providence time to reach the same conclusion for themselves. With the assistance of his cow, he avoided any pretense of making a decision in accord with the law of Rhode Island, and his denial of jurisdiction at least had the virtue of being honestly beyond the law of the land.

[143] John Howland, Autobiography, 114–118, Rhode Island Historical Society, John Howland Collection, Mss 499. For a much sanitized version, see *The Life and Recollections of John Howland,* 101–104 (Providence: 1857). Howland began his memoir in 1840, at the age of seventy. There was no record because Thompson conveniently did not appoint a clerk for this special court.

After the readiness of the judges in Newport to accept Varnum's dextrous arguments, and after the more candid lawlessness of Judge Thompson in Providence, a last word should go to John Trevett, for whom neither the law nor a cow was a matter of humor. On a grim day in October, shortly after he lost his case against Weeden, Trevett wrote a series of letters in his continuing attempt to secure a cow, some beef, or least some pork. He had been "in hopes" that a plot of land he owned could be sold "for Beef," and when he learned otherwise, he "Was much Disapointed." He therefore wrote to friends to get their assistance "in Selling that Land . . . for the Most itt will fetch for Beef or Cows." Later that day, Trevett anxiously wrote to another friend: "I am in Warnt of Beef or Cows and Should not have sent to you now But my Necessity is such that I cant Do Without itt." In commissioning an acquaintance to sell his land, Trevett hoped he would "take his pay in Beef"—all on the assumption that his agent would learn "of Some Person that May have Beef to spair for the Land."[144]

To historians of judicial review, Trevett's case against Weeden has seemed to be about paper money and the development of a nascent judicial power to hold legislation unconstitutional. For the lame, half-blind Captain John Trevett, however, the case began and ended with his search for beef. Like Trevett, who sought beef he could not afford, some of the judges attempted to decide in accord with a constitution their state did not clearly have, and although it may be doubted whether the judges thereby did their duty, their hunger to do their duty in accord with an express constitution suggests much about their ideals.

North Carolina: Bayard v. Singleton

Few judges were less resolute in holding a statute unconstitutional than the judges of the North Carolina Superior Court, for in *Bayard & Wife v. Singleton* they delayed their decision out of respect for the legislature. Even they, however, eventually did their duty. Whereas *Bayard v. Singleton* is usu-

[144] Letter from John Trevett to Ezra (Oct. 20, 1786), Letter from John Trevett to Silas (Oct. 20, 1786); Letter from John Trevett to Colonel Smith (Oct. 20, 1786), Letter from John Trevett to William Burden (Oct. 20, 1786), Newport Historical Society, Letter and Account Book of John Trevett 1783–1787, Vault A, No. 74. In one letter, Trevett briefly alluded to the wider political events. He wrote, "I have no news to Rite you only ower Bank of Paper Money is like to be Made Good by a Test Ake." He then, however, crossed out all of this, other than the sullen statement that he had no news to write. Whether or not he recognized that his political prediction was wrong, he clearly had more personal concerns on his mind. Incidentally, in the passage Trevett crossed out, he had such difficulty spelling "Test Act" that he abandoned his first effort and then wrote the word as quoted above. Letter from John Trevett to unnamed recipient (Oct. 20, 1786), ibid.

ally taken to show how judges on the eve of the Constitutional Convention were exploring a new judicial power over legislation, it was actually an example of how judges with all too human foibles eventually rose to the level of their ideals.[145]

During the War, North Carolina systematically confiscated the property of British subjects, and the case of *Bayard v. Singleton* arose from the attempt of Elizabeth Bayard to recover part of her family's confiscated real estate. William Bayard's wife, Elizabeth, was one of five daughters of a wealthy New Bern merchant, Samuel Cornell. Whether because of his loyalty to Britain or his desire to hedge his bets, he departed for England in 1775, "leaving his Family in Newbern." Although Cornell was a British subject, his daughters claimed to be citizens of North Carolina, and therefore when Cornell realized that North Carolina would confiscate his properties there, he decided to convey these to Elizabeth and her sisters. He therefore returned in 1777 to New York, which was in British hands, and "from New York he came to Newbern in a flag of Truce," but the General Assembly "refused to let him come on shore unless he would take an Oath of Allegiance to the State." He refused, and "while on Board the Vessel in the harbour of Newbern he conveyed his Estate to his Children, by several Deeds of Gift which were duly proved and registered." He then "removed his Wife & Children to New York," but not before first getting "the permission of the Executive" and thus preserving their non-Tory status. He did this none too soon, for "[a]ll Mr Cornell's Estate was afterwards declared to be confiscated by Act of Assembly, and . . . sold by Commissioners appointed for the Sale of confiscated property."[146]

145 The usual source is *Bayard v. Singleton,* Martin, *Reports,* 1: 45. Like some other early state reporters, Martin wrote his reports of important early cases by weaving together other sources—in this instance, court records, Ashe's letter to the committee considering an impeachment, and the periodical and newspaper reports. A valuable account of the case appears in Chapter VII of John Charles Waldrup, "James Iredell and the Practice of Law in Revolutionary Era North Carolina," 259–260 (Ph.D. dissertation, University of North Carolina, Chapel Hill, 1985). See also C. Golumbic, "Who Shall Dictate the Law?: Political Wrangling between 'Whig' Lawyers and Backcountry Farmers in Revolutionary Era North Carolina," *North Carolina Historical Review,* 73: 79, 80 (1996).

146 Letter from Archibald Maclaine to Thomas Jefferson (c. Apr. 12, 1792), University of North Carolina at Chapel Hill, Wilson Library, Southern Historical Collection, No. 324 Hayes Collection, Box 2, Folder 119.

Cornell backdated his deed to Elizabeth. He arrived in Newbern on December 11, 1777, "under the protection of a British flag," and he executed the deed to Elizabeth on December 19, 1777. Apparently, "[t]his deed . . . had been handed to him without a date, and being asked what date he chose it should bear, he hesitated, and said he would look at the copy of a bill which was then in his possession, which bill he understood to be on its passage in the legislature, for confiscating the property of all persons of his description, who should not, within a limited time, come into the state, and be made citizens thereof, which bill after-

The property sold included Cornell's home, warehouses, and wharf in New Bern, which were purchased by Spyers Singleton, a prominent political figure in North Carolina. Singleton acted as an agent for Cornell while this Tory and his daughters were in New York, and when the Commissioners seized the Cornell properties, Singleton defended the interests of the daughters in the Craven County Court. Upon the Court's decision in favor of confiscation, however, Singleton more selfishly argued that he should be allowed to keep the New Bern properties for three years, as he had rented them from Elizabeth. Although the Court also denied this claim, Singleton waited until the Commissioners in 1782 sold the properties, at which point he simply purchased them for himself.[147] His prominence and his disloyalty to the Cornell family made his acquisition seem particularly odious, but other purchasers also took advantage of the Cornell family's misfortune.

The Cornell daughters hoped to recover their patrimony, and relying on Samuel Johnston as their lawyer, they brought a series of actions in 1784 in the New Bern District Superior Court—one action being by Elizabeth for the properties Singleton acquired in New Bern. She by now had married William Bayard, who by common law was the legal owner of her real estate, and they therefore pursued the claim together.[148]

Singleton countered through the Assembly, where he secured his new possessions in a manner so severe it immediately provoked constitutional objections. His lawyer, the former governor Abner Nash, conveniently happened to serve in the North Carolina House of Commons, where in December 1785 he obtained a statute securing purchasers in their possession

---

wards, in the same session, passed into a law. After looking at the aforesaid copy of that bill, he chose that the deed should bear date on the 11th of the same month, being the day he arrived in the harbour of Newbern." "Law case, tried and determined, at a supreme court of law and equity, for the district of Newbern, North Carolina, on the 30th of November, 1787," *American Museum; or Repository of Ancient and Modern Fugitive Pieces,* 371 (April 1788). See also Martin, *Reports,* 1: 50 (Newbern: 1797).

147 Waldrup, "James Iredell and the Practice of Law," 259–260. For the amount paid by Singleton, see Affidavit of Spyers Singleton (May 23, 1786), NCSA, New Bern District Superior Court, Miscellaneous Records, 1756–1807, DSCR 206.928.2, Confiscation—Bayard v. Singleton Folder.

148 Appearance Docket, recording Singleton's plea of not guilty, NCSA, New Bern District Superior Court, Appearance Docket Nov. Term 1784, Docket of new actions, DSCR 206.322.7, fol. 239; Declaration in Ejectment, NCSA, New Bern District, Superior Court Miscellaneous Records 1756–1807, DSCR 206.928.2, Confiscation—Bayard v. Singleton Folder. As an action of ejectment, it appeared in the records as an action by a fictional *Den on the Demise of William Bayard and his Wife Elizabeth v. Fen*—a fictional "Causal Ejector" who advised Singleton as the possessor of the property to appear in court "to cause your self to be made Defendant in my stead otherwise I shall suffer a Judgmint to be entered against me and you will be turned out of Possession." Ibid.

of forfeited estates. The act provided that purchasers of confiscated estates and those claiming under their title "shall be deemed not liable to answer any suit or suits in law or equity" commenced by anyone described in the confiscation statutes "as inimical to the states" or anyone "claiming by, from, or under them." In short, purchasers were not liable to persons whose property was taken—nor to their families—and the General Assembly made this effective by adding that the courts were "required, in all such cases upon the motion or affidavit of the defendant . . . to dismiss all such suitors, suits, action or actions."[149] When this act passed in the House of Commons, the passionate Archibald Maclaine and eight other members protested—the first reason being that "it is an *ex post facto* law . . . and therefore contrary to the constitution."[150] Apparently recognizing the immediate target of the statute, another North Carolinian forwarded Johnston "a Copy of this wonderful Law by which the Assembly have arrogated to themselves the judicial power."[151]

Five months later, in May 1786, these legal issues came before the New Bern Superior Court. When Samuel Johnston and the strong-willed William Davie opened the case for the Bayards against Singleton, the latter's counsel, Abner Nash and Alfred Moore, moved that the case be dismissed under the 1785 statute for quieting possession.[152] Johnston and Davie "warmly exclaimed" in response that it was "an article of our bill of rights, that *retrospective laws are oppressive, unjust and incompatible with liberty, wherefore no* ex post facto *law ought to be made.*" Accordingly,

[149] An Act to secure and quiet in their Possessions all such Persons their Heirs and Assigns who have purchased, or may hereafter purchase Lands and Tenements, Goods and Chattels, which have been sold, or may hereafter be sold by Commissioners of forfeited Estates, legally appointed for that Purpose (Dec. 29, 1785), *The Laws of the State of North-Carolina, Passed at Newbern, December 1785,* at 12–13 (Newbern: 1786). For Nash's participation, see Letter from Archibald Maclaine to Samuel Johnston (Dec. 24, 1785), Letter from James Hogg to James Iredell (Jan. 19, 1786), in *The Papers of James Iredell,* 3: 181; Waldrup, "James Iredell and the Practice of Law," 265.
[150] Protest (Dec. 28, 1785), *The Journals of the General Assembly of the State of North-Carolina,* 51 (second pagination series) (Newbern: 1786). They also protested that "a bill depriving all persons deriving their titles under obnoxious or incapacitated persons . . . is a violation even of the forms of justice, and as an unconstitutional law is nugatory." The final ground of protest was because "the laws of this state . . . must apply to all ranks of citizens; nor do we conceive it possible under the present bill to preclude any subject from the benefit of law by a denial of the known and established rules of justice, which protect the property of all citizens equally, nor to place any of them under the adjudication of the General Assembly, whose desire to redress the grievance may be fluctuating, uncertain and ineffectual." Ibid.
[151] Letter from James Hogg to James Iredell (Jan. 19, 1786), in *The Papers of James Iredell,* 3: 187.
[152] Correspondence (New Bern, June 7), *Pennsylvania Packet* (July 1, 1786).

> [T]he Assembly had clearly exceeded the limits of the power which the people. . . . delegated to their representatives in general assembly and . . . an act so illegally passed, was not to be looked upon as a law, nor were the people . . . obliged to obey an act, so diametrically opposite to the established form of government.

In defense of the statute, Singleton's lawyers "pleaded, that all acts of Assembly were laws, and their execution could not be prevented." The judges at this point could have decided dispute, but being "unwilling to approve of a law which seems unconstitutional, or of disapproving an act of the legislature without the most mature consideration," they "declined giving an immediate decision."[153]

One of the judges, Samuel Ashe, recited the principles that made it difficult for judges to avoid holding unconstitutional statutes void. Six months later, when a committee of both houses of the Assembly was contemplating impeachment proceedings against the judges, two of them—Samuel Spencer and John Williams—attended the committee, but Ashe was too ill to go and instead wrote a letter in his defense, including an account of what he had said the prior May in *Bayard v. Singleton.* He recalled that after "long arguments from the Council on each side, on constitutional points . . . the Court made a few observations on our constitution & System of Government." Ashe explained that "I on my part, (as far as I now recollect)," observed that Americans in each state had established a constitution that separated and limited the different branches of government:

> [T]hat at the time of our separation from Great Brittain, we were thrown into a similar situation with a Set of people Shipwrecked and cast on a Maroon'd Island—without laws, without majestrates, without Government or any legal authority—That being thus circumstanced, the People of this Country, with a general Union of Sentiment, by their delegates met in Congress, and formed that System, on those fundamental principles of Government comprised in the Constitution dividing the powers of Government into separate & distinct branches, to wit, the Legislative the Judicial, & Executive; and Assigning to each, several & distinct powers, and prescribing their several limits & boundaries.

Under a constitution that separated and limited these powers, judges would not be able to defer to the judgment of the legislature as to what was constitutional, but for now Ashe merely laid out his underlying assumptions

[153] Ibid. The record confirms that Nash's motion prompted "[o]pposition by M[r] Davie that the s[d] Act was unconstitutional and therefore no law." NCSA, New Bern District, Minutes of Superior Court 1768–1772 and 1778–1788, DSCR 206.301.1, fol. 416[v].

"without disclosing a Single Sentiment upon the cause, or the proceeding, or the law introduced in support of it."[154]

After Ashe thus talked around the issues, Judges Spencer and Williams "proposed to take an Advisare." Ashe "readily agreed—as the printer had never furnished me with the law, & I had then only read it cursorily—and as I had reason to believe the next Assembly meant to revise the law, & in respect to them, wished to decline an opinion."[155] When the judges met again at New Bern the following November, they again made no decision.[156]

This desire to delay out of respect for the Assembly, so that it could revise the law, became one of many charges of impeachment contemplated against the judges. The judges had already brought contempt upon themselves through their incompetence, their quarrels on the bench, their petulance toward lawyers, and their "[n]egligence of their duty, and delay of business," and therefore when a legislative committee at the end of the year considered demands for an impeachment, the judges' failure to reach a decision in *Bayard v. Singleton* was by no means the most serious accusation against them.[157]

154 Letter from Judge Samuel Ashe to the Speakers of the Houses of the General Assembly (Dec. 14, 1786), NCSA, General Assembly, Session Records 1786–1787, Box 3, Joint Resolutions—Committee of the Whole of Two Houses on Administration of Justice Folder.

155 Ibid.

156 New Bern District Superior Court, Minutes 1768–1772 and 1778–1788, NCSA, Mfm C.206.30001.

157 Spencer and Williams regularly "were engaged in the most bitter alteration," and at one meeting, "nothing was wanting but blows to complete the farce." According to an observer, "[t]hrice Williams furiously descended from the bench" and "fifty times Spencer interrupted him attempting to speak," saying "'Suffer me to do Justice[;] if you will not I wash my hands clean[;] I wish others could.'" Letter from William Hooper to James Iredell (Aug. 1, 1786), Duke University Rare Book, Manuscript, and Special Collections Library, James Iredell Papers, Box 1. Spencer was notoriously indifferent to public opinion, whether about his professional or his private life, and he famously was pecked to death by an agitated turkey.

The contempt of the bar for the bench ran deep. When a man asked the Superior Court to restore him to his rights under a judgment of the Court from several years earlier, the judges could not find the papers, but "[w]hen Mr. Ashe declared that he did not recollect any thing of it, Mr. Moore pertinently remarked that he was not surprised at it, for he remembered that his Honor had carried a recognizance to the Necessary." Letter from Archibald Maclaine to James Iredell (Aug. 3, 1786), in *The Papers of James Iredell,* 3: 225.

Ashe and Williams, moreover, did not even turn up for some court meetings, prompting the grand jury at a recent Morgan District Superior Court to thank Judge Spencer for his "faithful attendance" and to observe that "having but one Judge at the courts in this District is a grievance," which prevented the determination of several suits. Copy of Presentment by Grand Jurors of Morgan District Superior Court (Sept. term 1786), NCSA, General Assembly, Session Records 1786–1787, Box 3, Joint Resolutions—Committee of the Whole of Two Houses on Administration of Justice Folder. All of these "charges against the Judges" were "urged against their Honors with great violence." Letter from Alfred Moore to James Iredell (Dec. 14, 1786), in *The Papers of James Iredell,* 3: 245.

To the men arrayed on either side of *Bayard v. Singleton* and the related suits to recover confiscated property, the judges' delay seemed scandalous. On the one hand, Spyers Singleton and others who sought to defend their interests in confiscated land desired an impeachment because the judges had failed to decide in accord with the 1785 statute for quieting possession. As Singleton and his allies complained in a petition to the General Assembly, "the judges of the Court would not dismiss any of the Suits, tho expressly within the meaning & direction of the Law." The petitioners considered this "a denial of Justice to the Good Citizens of this state, and a misbehaviour in their Office," and Singleton and his fellow petitioners therefore asked the legislature to "take such measures . . . as may with Certainty announce to every individual of this State, that the Acts of the General Assembly are to be observed and Obeyed."[158] On the other hand, the leading advocates of the impeachment were lawyers whose complaints included the failure of the judges to hold the 1785 act unconstitutional. Archibald Maclaine, for example, angrily complained that the judges "delayed to decide thereon."[159] Thus, with respect to different levels of law, each side had reason to charge that the judges were guilty of "[d]ispenseing with laws" in "the Newbern case"—not because the judges had held the statute unconstitutional, but because they had declined to reach any decision.[160]

The pressure to avoid holding the statute unconstitutional weighed heavily on the judges, especially Samuel Ashe. No one threatened the judges, but in America a fear of opposing the popular sensibilities that underlay legislation could corrode the independence of judges from within. Ashe recalled that one reason he agreed with the other judges to take advisement was "a strange Malady with w[ch] I was then attacked, haveing not Slept 3 Hours in as many days & nights next preceding the trial, tho' I had taken repeated doses of laudanum." Not surprisingly, "I was afraid to give my Opinion in that Situation, in any matter especially in one of importance—I therefore immediately after the rising of the Court, fearing my malady would increase[,] left Newbern." He alone among the judges who met in May at New Bern had laid out the principles that would eventually require

158 Complaint of the Conduct of the Judges exhibited by the Inhabitants of Newbern (Dec. 22, 1786), NCSA, General Assembly, Session Records 1786–1787, Box 3, Joint Resolutions—Committee of the Whole of Two Houses on Administration of Justice Folder. Of course, the date of the petition is the date of its introduction rather than its drafting.

159 Archibald Maclaine, Protest Against the Resolution of the House of Commons, (Jan. 6, 1787), NCSA, General Assembly, Session Records 1786–1787, Box 3, Joint Resolutions—Committee of the Whole of Two Houses on Administration of Justice Folder. As will become apparent, Maclaine's views were complex, for he also thought that if the judges were in doubt, it was their duty "to state their doubts to the Legislature." Ibid.

160 Letter from Alfred Moore to James Iredell (Dec. 14, 1786), in *The Papers of James Iredell*, 3: 245.

a decision about the constitutionality of the statute, and later, under the cloud of a possible impeachment, he concluded his defense of his conduct in *Bayard* by telling the committee that "if my Opinion of our Constitution is an error, I fear it is an incurable one, for I had the honour to assist in the frameing [of] it, and confess I so designed it, as I believe every other Gentleman concerned did also."[161] These were not the words of a man who thought the judges could indefinitely avoid their duty—although under the mental pressure, he took his drugs, went home, and made clear during the impeachment discussions that he "stays at home."[162]

The strength of feeling on these questions at the May 1786 hearing had been such that Singleton and his lawyers did more than simply reason against William Davie's argument that the statute was unconstitutional. Singleton and his fellow purchasers of confiscated estates were disappointed that Davie's passionate speech against the constitutionality of the act "was by no means suppressed or discouraged by the Judges, or the States Attorney, who was then present in Court," and not getting a remedy from the bench, they persuaded the grand jury to present Davie on the ground that his "free investigation of the Assembly's conduct" was "a criminal step" that was "against the peace and dignity of the State."[163] Fortunately for Davie, the judges were "better acquainted with the rights of a lawyer defending his

161 Letter from Samuel Ashe to the Hon'ble Speakers of the General Assembly (Dec. 14, 1786), NCSA, General Assembly, Session Records 1786–1787, Box 3, Joint Resolutions—Committee of the Whole of Two Houses on Administration of Justice Folder.

162 Letter from Alfred Moore to James Iredell (Dec. 14, 1786), in *The Papers of James Iredell,* 3: 245.

163 Complaint of the Conduct of the Judges exhibited by the Inhabitants of Newbern (Dec. 22, 1786), NCSA, General Assembly, Session Records 1786–1787, Box 3, Joint Resolutions—Committee of the Whole of Two Houses on Administration of Justice Folder; Correspondence (New Bern, June 7), *Pennsylvania Packet* (July 1, 1786). See also Correspondence (New Bern, June 1), *Pennsylvania Packet* (Aug. 23, 1786). The grand jury heard testimony by Singleton, his lawyer Abner Nash, Richard Dobbs Spaight, and some men who had cases similar to Singleton's. The grand jury charged:

> William R. Davie Esquire . . . in the Course of his Pleadings did in open Court . . . Assent and say the Act of Assembly was in every respect unjust and expressly against the Constitution, that the said Act was the arbitrary edict of a leading party or faction of the Assembly that altho it was passed by the Assembly the said Act was Null and Void; and was not Law; and ought not to be Obeyed by the People; or words fully to those purposes; that he Considered the Assembly and Commissioners of Confiscation as one; and that they had Violently and unjustly Seized the property of the People, with many other Assertions, Saying the Commissioners ware Cr[e]atures of the Assembly.

NCSA, New Bern District Superior Court, Criminal Action Papers, DSCR 206.326.2, 1786 Folder. For the "decree that the prsentm^{t} be Quashed," see *State v. William R. Davie* (May 20, 1786), New Bern District Superior Court, Minutes 1768–1772 and 1778–1788, at fol. 321[r], NCSA, Mfm C.206.30001.

client" and "discharged him."[164] In thus sparing Davie, however, the judges must have wondered whether they themselves would soon become the object of populist resentment.

The judges in the end avoided impeachment for their misconduct in some cases, such as *Bayard,* by gratifying popular prejudice in other cases. Although the bar tended to be disgusted with the judges, most legislators actually approved of the judges' behavior on the key impeachment charge, which was that they had convicted two Tories, Francis Brice and Daniel McNeil, for returning to the state without permission and had sentenced them to banishment. These convictions and punishments had no apparent basis in law but were widely appreciated, and thus the most blatant wrongdoing of the judges actually preserved them from impeachment. After the joint committee considering an impeachment reported its charges to a committee of the whole house, the House and Senate voted in early January 1787 that the judges were not guilty of "Malpractice in Office"—a conclusion that provoked a vigorous dissent from lawyers such as Richard Dobbs Spaight, William Davie, William Hooper, and Archibald Maclaine.[165] Several days later, the Assembly even voted its "thanks" to the judges "for their long and faithful services."[166]

Following its exoneration of the judges, the General Assembly made a last attempt to protect purchasers of confiscated estates with a new, harsher

164 Correspondence (New Bern, June 7), *Pennsylvania Packet* (July 1, 1786).

165 Report by Committee Chairman Richard Dobbs Spaight (adopted Jan. 2 & 4, 1787), NCSA, General Assembly, Session Records 1786–1787, Box 3, Joint Resolutions—Committee of the Whole of Two Houses on Administration of Justice Folder; also in Vote (Jan. 2, 1787), *Journal of the House of Commons. At a General Assembly begun and held at Fayetteville, on the eighteenth day of November, in the Year of Our Lord One Thousand Seven Hundred and Eighty-Six,* 64 (np: [1787]). Already at the time of the trials, a year earlier, Maclaine observed that "[t]he Judges are in a fair way of becoming favorites with the Assembly; for they have had Frank Brice and a doctor MacNeill . . . indicted for misdemeanor, in returning to the State without permission." Letter from Archibald Maclain to Samuel Johnston or James Iredell (Dec. 24 1785), University of North Carolina at Chapel Hill, Wilson Library, Southern Historical Collection, No. 324 Hayes Collection, Box 2, Folder 106.

166 The Senate initially voted that the Assembly should present its thanks to the judges "for their faithful services and good conduct heretofore as Judges" and "especially" for their services in three cases, including those of Brice and McNeil, and the Senate explained that these men "were not citizens of this state nor of any of the United States" and that only "the banishment of our own citizens is unknown to the constitution and laws of the State." This was too much for the House, which countered with the resolution more simply thanking the judges for their services. Resolution (Jan. 5, 1786), *Journal of the Senate. At a General Assembly begun and held at Fayetteville, on the twentieth day of November, in the Year of Our Lord One Thousand Seven Hundred and Eighty-Six,* 71, 72 (np: [1787]); Resolution (Jan. 5, 1787), *Journal of the House of Commons. At a General Assembly begun and held at Fayetteville, on the eighteenth day of November, in the Year of Our Lord One Thousand Seven Hundred and Eighty-Six,* 74 (np: [1787]).

version of its December 1785 act for quieting possession. It observed that "doubts have arisen" under the 1785 act as to whether citizens claiming property seized and sold by the Commissioners of forfeited estates "were enabled to claim, or commence and prosecute a suit . . . for the aforesaid property." Accordingly, whereas the 1785 act merely stated that purchasers from the Commissioners (and those claiming under such purchasers) "shall be deemed not liable to answer" the suits against them, the 1787 act now simply denied that such suits could be brought.[167] This 1787 statute opened up the unsettling prospect that the legislature could completely bar a class of persons from the courts and, moreover, could impose this disability on their heirs and grantees.[168] The 1785 act, however, was already at issue in *Bayard,* and it remained the focus of the case—leaving the more severe 1787 statute to receive only cursory attention.

At the May 1787 term of the New Bern Superior Court, the judges finally faced up to the constitutional question, and they now understood it to concern not an *ex post facto* law but trial by jury. A newspaper explained that "the great constitutional point" was "whether a citizen can be deprived of the Right of a trial by jury, by an act of the general Assembly, made in opposition to the principles and express words of the constitution, the great fundamental law of the land."

After some initial sparring, Abner Nash moved under the 1785 act "to dismiss, without a trial by jury" not only *Bayard v. Singleton* but also "a considerable number" of other suits "brought for the recovery of property,

[167] An Act to amend an act, entitled, "And act to secure and quiet in their possessions all such persons . . ." (Jan. 6, 1787), *The Laws of North-Carolina At a General Assembly, Begun and Held at Fayetteville on the Eighteenth Day of November, in the Year of Our Lord One Thousand Seven Hundred and Eighty-six, and in the Eleventh Year of the Independence of the said State, Being the First Session of the Assembly,* 8 (Chapter VI) (Fayetteville: [1787]). It stated:

> That the citizens of this state are hereby declared to possess and enjoy the right and privilege to commence, prosecute and maintain any suit or suits . . . for any real or personal estate sold by any of the Commissioners of forfeited estates: *Provided* the said citizens do not hold or derive their titles, by, from or under any person or persons named or described by some one of the laws commonly called the Confiscation Laws.

Ibid., §1.

[168] The judges appear to have considered this statute largely beside the point. Nash's motion in May only required them to consider the 1785 act, and although Iredell, Davie, and Johnston apparently argued for the Bayards at the trial in November that the 1787 law was unconstitutional, the judges gave an opinion on other grounds. As they then explained, "the circumstances and limitted priviledges of persons who were sent out of this state under a particular act of our General Assembly, are not applicable to this case." *Bayard v. Singleton,* Martin, *Reports,* 1: 51.

which had been sold by the commissioners of confiscated estates." The judges took care to show that they were not eager to decide the constitutional question and therefore initially recommended that the parties in *Bayard* "consent to a fair decision of the property in question, by a Jury according to the common law of the land." Only "after every reasonable endeavour had been used in vain for avoiding a disagreeable difference between Legislature and the judicial powers of the State" did the judges "at length with much apparent reluctance, but with great deliberation and firmness," give "their opinions separately, but unanimously, for over ruling the aforesaid motions for the dismission of the said suits."[169]

The judges explained that "the obligations of their oaths, and the duty of their office, required them in this situation, to give their opinion on that important and momentous subject." Although they had delayed out of respect for the legislature, they now declared that "notwithstanding the great reluctance they might feel against involving themselves in a dispute with the Legislature of the State, yet no object of concern or respect could come in competition or authorize them to dispense with the duty they owed the public, in consequence of the trust they were invested with under the solemnity of their oaths."

They held the statute unconstitutional for violating the right to a jury trial. "[B]y the constitution every citizen had undoubtedly a right to a decision of his property by a trial by a jury." If "the Legislature could take away this right," it could do anything else prohibited by the Constitution: "[I]t might with as much authority require his life to be taken away without a trial by jury, and that he should stand condemned to die, without the formality of any trial at all."

> But . . . it was clear, that no act they could pass, could by any means repeal or alter the constitution, because if they could do this, they would at the same instant of time, destroy their own existence as a Legislature, and dissolve the government thereby established. Consequently the constitution (which the judicial power was bound to take notice of as much as of any other law whatever,) standing in full force as the fundamental law of the land, notwithstanding the act on which the present motion was grounded, the same act must of course in that instance stand as abrogated and without any effect.

The Court then "ordered, that the suits in question should stand for trial in the next term, according to the course of the common law of the land"—that is, with a jury—to determine "whether the plaintiffs have any legal title

[169] Correspondence (Newbern, June 7), *Virginia Independent Chronicle* (July 4, 1787).

to recover, or not." This question, the judges pointedly added, was one "which the court could not judicially undertake to know, till the causes should be thus tried."[170]

This result gave great satisfaction to William Davie, who "was agreeably surprised at the unexpected firmness and independence of Judge Williams." Recalling how the legislature at Fayetteville had considered impeaching the judges, Davie speculated that "this is the effect of the Fayetteville business."[171] It is often observed that there was legislative intimidation of state judges, but state legislatures could also stimulate the judges' sense of independence.

To members of the public unfamiliar with the delays in the decision, the judges appeared to have acted resolutely. A North Carolinian wrote to a newspaper to praise "the spirited and patriotic decision of our Judges" and to exclaim that "[a]s long as we shall have officers, who will not dread the frowns of power, our constitution, our liberties and our lives will be safe."[172] Men and women who were closer to the case, however, had less reason for confidence in the judges. The Bayards soon got their jury, but the judges instructed the jurors that land could "not be held by foreigners" and that Samuel Cornell had been a foreigner from the time of Independence. The jury accordingly gave its verdict against the Bayards, who thus won their constitutional right to a jury and lost their property. Immediately afterward, the remaining twenty-seven confiscation cases in the New Bern Superior Court "were all swept off the docket, by nonsuits voluntarily suffered."[173]

Thus, in New Jersey, New Hampshire, Rhode Island, and North Carolina, the judges did their duty by holding statutes unconstitutional. To be sure, many of them seem to have done so imperfectly, for in Rhode Island they were too eager to believe there was an express constitution, and

[170] Ibid.

[171] Letter from William R. Davie to James Iredell (June 19, 1787), Duke University Rare Book, Manuscript, and Special Collections Library, James Iredell Papers, Box 2. Revealingly, when reporting the decision to Davie, Samuel Johnston did not even bother to mention the substantive, constitutional question: "Mr Moore . . . i[n]sisted on the first motion that the Suits should be dismissed; the Judges on this occasion were very much embarrassed and would gladly have avoided giving any Opinion on that point but having no alternative they were reduced to the necessity of deciding one way or the other and were unanimous to return the Suits under a peremptory rule for Tryal the second day of next Court." Letter from Samuel Johnston to William Davie (June 7, 1787), Haverford College Library, Charles Roberts Autograph Collection, discussed by Waldrup, "James Iredell and the Practice of Law," 276.

[172] Horatius, Letter to Mr. Martin ("Long-Island, on Holston, June 20"), *Martin's North-Carolina Gazette* (July 11, 1787).

[173] "Law case, tried and determined, at a supreme court of law and equity, for the district of

in New Jersey and North Carolina they were too slow to decide in accord with their constitutions. The North Carolina judges, indeed, delayed not to ensure the survival of their state, but merely out of respect for the legislature. Even these judges, however, ultimately did what was required by "the obligations of their oaths, and the duty of their office."[174]

Newbern, North Carolina, on the 30th of November, 1787," *American Museum; or Repository of Ancient and Modern Fugitive Pieces,* 372 (April 1788).

[174] Correspondence (Newbern, June 7), *Virginia Independent Chronicle* (July 4, 1787).

14

A Lopsided Debate

Judicial decisions holding statutes unconstitutional often provoked local controversies, and these disputes are revealing. Rather than relatively even struggles between defenders and critics of the decisions, the controversies tended to be lopsided against the critics, who had to fight against widely assumed ideals.

This imbalance and its significance can be illustrated by the dispute in North Carolina about *Bayard v. Singleton.* This was the case, described in the previous chapter, in which the judges of the North Carolina Superior Court delayed a decision about a state statute out of respect for the legislature. Eventually in 1787 the judges held the statute unconstitutional for violating the defendants' right to a jury, but in the meantime the judges' unprincipled delay gave men on each side an opportunity to elaborate their views in unusual detail. Each side was angry, but their circumstances were very different, for the men who sought to limit judicial duty found themselves engaged in an uphill struggle. Whereas the advocates of holding statutes unconstitutional could simply ask the judges to adhere to their office, the opponents had to pressure the judges to carve out an exception from this ideal. The opponents thus not only had to formulate alternatives to the traditional understanding of judicial duty but also had to convince their legislature to adopt their proposals, and both the drafting and the persuasion turned out to be difficult. Judicial duty could be effortlessly assumed, and therefore those who sought to limit its application had their work cut out for them.

James Iredell

The ease with which men could rely on the ideals of law and judicial duty—together with hints as to how such ideals might become weak in

American circumstances—can be observed in an essay written by James Iredell. He published the piece to convince the judges in *Bayard v. Singleton* to hold the statute in the case unconstitutional, and his effort is well known as the first essay to argue that judges had to hold unconstitutional statutes unlawful. Iredell's essay, however, was not particularly innovative. Instead, it put in print what sometimes was said in court but ordinarily required little explanation, and it thus reveals the facility with which lawyers could make use of the ideals of law and judicial duty. At the same time, it is also suggestive in other ways, for it prompted sobering questions as to how long Americans would be able to take such ideals for granted.

Iredell wrote for the public, because he could not speak before the judges. He and his friends Archibald Maclaine and William Hooper had risked their reputations to help Tory families preserve their property from confiscation, and they would therefore have been natural choices to join Samuel Johnston in arguing for the Bayards that the statute impeding their claim was unconstitutional. The defendant, Spyers Singleton, however, arranged to have the three friends disqualified from participating in the suit against him—his method being to use some of his confederates to hire the three as counsel in a related matter. When Maclaine learned of how he and his friends had been *"silenced,"* he was furious and promptly wrote to Singleton, telling him "that though he had deprived me of a fee, he should not seal up my lips." Hooper, however, cautioned Maclaine that "we cannot appear against these scoundrels without injuring ourselves." The reality was that Singleton had gotten the better of them, and Maclaine concluded, "I suppose Johnston will laugh that we have been so damnably taken in."[1]

Although less impassioned than Maclaine, Iredell was even more determined not to be silenced, and as he could not argue in court, he made his appearance in print. His anonymous letter "To the Public" appeared in the New Bern *North Carolina Gazette* in August 1786—three months after the judges first delayed their decision in *Bayard v. Singleton* and nine months before they finally held the statute in the case unconstitutional.

Iredell began with North Carolina's rejection of absolute power. The people "were not ignorant of the theory, of *the necessity of the legislature being absolute in all cases,* because it was the great ground of the British Pretensions," but this absolute parliamentary power "was a mere speculative principle," and on their "own severe experience," the people of North

[1] Letter from Archibald Maclaine to James Iredell (Mar. 7, 1785), Duke University Rare Book, Manuscript, and Special Collections Library, James Iredell Papers, Box 1. This point about disqualification is recounted by John Charles Waldrup, "James Iredell and the Practice of Law in Revolutionary Era North Carolina," 267–268 (Ph.D. dissertation, University of North Carolina, Chapel Hill, 1985).

Carolina "decisively gave our sentiments against it." They had adopted their constitution as "the fundamental basis of our Government" so as "to impose restrictions on the Legislature that might still leave it free to all useful purposes, but at the same time guard against the abuses of unlimited power." Accordingly, there was "no doubt, but that the power of the assembly is limited and defined by the Constitution." The Assembly was merely "a *creature* of the Constitution"—to which Iredell wryly added, with his thoughts on William Davie, "I hope this is an expression not presentable."[2]

None of this, of course, was really in dispute, for the rejection of the absolute power of Parliament in favor of express limitations on an American legislature seemed "so natural, and indeed so irresistible, that I do not observe they have been much contested." Instead, "[t]he great argument is, that though the Assembly have not a *right* to violate the Constitution, yet if they *in fact* do so the only remedy is, either by our humble Petition that the Law may be repealed, or an universal resistance of the People." From this perspective, "the judicial power is not to presume to question the power of an Act of Assembly," and the people could only seek redress by meek petition or violent revolution. Neither of these extremes, however, was sufficient, for a petition "implies a supposition that the Electors hold their rights by the *favour of their Representatives,*" and revolution was an expedient of little use except in the face of *"universal oppression,"* which meant that "[a] thousand injuries may be suffered, and many hundreds ruined, before this can be brought about."[3]

Having shown the functional need for "the Judicial Power" to decide the constitutionality of legislation, Iredell easily relied on law and judicial duty—on the Constitution's obligation as law and on the duty associated with the judicial power. These were so familiar he only needed to allude to them briefly: "The duty of the Power I conceive, in all cases, is to decide according to the *Laws of the State,*" and "[i]t will not be denied, I suppose, that the Constitution is a *Law of the State,* as well as an Act of Assembly, with this difference only, that it is the *fundamental Law,* and unalterable by the Legislature which derives all its power from it." From these premises, Iredell concluded that "an Act of Assembly inconsistent with the Constitution is *void,* and cannot be obeyed without disobeying the superior Law to which we were previously and irrevocably bound." He then added: "The Judges therefore must take care at their peril that every Act of Assembly

[2] An Elector [James Iredell], "To the Public" (Aug. 1786), Duke University Rare Book, Manuscript, and Special Collections Library, James Iredell Papers, Box 1.
[3] Ibid.

they presume to enforce is warranted by the Constitution, since if it is not they act without lawful authority." With this hint that the judges otherwise risked a decision *coram non judice*—a risk not unfamiliar in North Carolina—Iredell summed up: "This is not an usurped or a discretionary Power, but one inevitably resulting from the constitution of their Office, they being Judges *for the benefit of the whole People* not *mere servants of the Assembly*."

Iredell recognized that there was "much alarm" lest the judges threaten legislative power, but he considered this the least of the dangers. Far more worrisome was the susceptibility of the judges to "the natural desire which must be entertained by every Man living in a popular Government of securing the favour of the People."[4]

When Archibald Maclaine read Iredell's essay in the newspaper, he feared that if judges in a place such as America were apt to defer to the people, then the people themselves might need to understand "true constitutional principles," and this particularly worried him because he thought it unlikely that this popular understanding could be accomplished by an occasional newspaper essay, whether by Iredell or anyone else. As Maclaine explained in a letter to his friend, it was "to be lamented, that those who may be esteemed tolerably qualified for giving information on subjects of so much importance to the people, are so widely scattered over an extensive country, and the greatest part of them so distant from the press, that it is extremely difficult to discuss such subjects so as to have the intended effect." Moreover, "[v]ery extraordinary exertions are necessary to arouse the people to a sense of their danger," for Americans were complacent. "[N]otwithstanding the plain principles of the constitution, they seem to think themselves safe from every species of internal tyranny," and this was, Maclaine thought, "a palpable proof of their ignorance, or want of virtue."[5] In a

[4] Ibid. When James Iredell later became a justice of the U.S. Supreme Court and heard cases on circuit, lawyers in the Rhode Island Circuit could cite *Trevett v. Weeden* to him as a precedent—as in *Robert Ferguson v. Ethan Clarke* (Newport, U.S. Circuit Court for the District of Rhode Island, June 26, 1795), Case Book, U.S. Circuit Court of Rhode Island, 53, University of North Carolina at Chapel Hill, Wilson Library, Southern Historical Collection, No. 365, James Iredell Papers, Box 1, Folder 11. Yet on the question of the judicial role, Iredell clearly preferred to think in terms of the underlying assumptions rather than mere precedents. For example, in another case from the first half of the 1790s he spoke generally: "The power of the Legislature is limited; of the State Legislatures by their own State Constitutions, and that of the United States; of the Legislature of the Union by the Constitution of the Union. Beyond these limitations, I have no doubt their acts, are void because they are not warranted by authority given." *John Tyndale Ware Adm. of William Jones . . . v. David Lawrence Hylton & Co. & Francis Eppes* (Richmond, U.S. Circuit Court for the District of Virginia, May term 1793), Case Book, U.S. Circuit for Virginia, 27–28, ibid., Folder 10.

[5] Letter from Archibald Maclaine to James Iredell (Aug. 24, 1786), in *The Papers of James*

popular government, freedom depended on the prevalence of accurate constitutional principles among the people as well as the judges, but even the best of essays could not adequately inculcate such principles among a people as dispersed and self-satisfied as Americans.

In other words, although Iredell could rely on the common law ideals of law and judicial duty and on Whig ideals of limited legislative power, these ideals might eventually become vulnerable in America. In England, where the people still largely deferred to the ideals inculcated by the courts and the Inns of Court, the common law ideals needed less public advocacy. In America, however, where the judges were more apt to be attuned to popular sentiments, the common law and other ideals underlying constitutional decisions would soon even be at risk among the judges, unless the people themselves were attached to these ideals. Thus, whereas in England at least the common law ideals could usually be left inexplicit, in America there was reason to worry they could never be made explicit enough.[6]

For the while, however, law and judicial duty did not need much explanation, and this was a great advantage for lawyers, such as Iredell, who asked judges to hold statutes unconstitutional. Because the ideals of law and judicial duty could be taken for granted, it was usually enough merely to mention them, and being able to rely with such confidence on these foundations of his argument, Iredell found his task relatively easy.

Archibald Maclaine and His Committee

Archibald Maclaine soon had his own opportunity to discuss the judicial role in deciding the constitutionality of statutes, for he was the chair of the joint committee that in December 1785 considered charges of impeachment against the North Carolina judges. This committee of the North Carolina General Assembly also included William Hooper, who like Maclaine had wanted to argue in *Bayard;* William Davie, who had actually argued the case and was indicted for his efforts; and Richard Dobbs Spaight, who had testified against Davie before the grand jury. These and the other members of the joint committee explored a wide range of limitations on the common law ideal of judicial duty, and they therefore carried the burden of explaining their positions and getting legislative support for them.

Iredell, 3: 231–232, eds. Donna Kelly and Lang Baradell (Raleigh: North Carolina Department of Cultural Resources, 2003).

[6] For the continuity and preservation of common law ideals in England, see J. H. Baker, "Personal Liberty under the Common Law, 1200–1600," in *The Common Law Tradition: Lawyers, Books and the Law,* 321 (London: Hambledon, 2000).

Even before the committee reported its conclusions, Richard Dobbs Spaight attempted to enact that the judges had no authority to decide the constitutionality of statutes. Spaight was popular enough to have been the speaker of the House the prior year, and he and another member of the House, John G. Blount, apparently were the advocates of A Bill Declaratory of the Powers of Courts and the Rights of Juries, which aimed, among other things, "to prevent those usurpation[s] in Judges of law of powers which are unknown to the Constitution and Laws of this State." To this end, it required that "when Matters Occur wherein the Operation of the Constitution and any particular Act of the legislature may interfere," the judges "are not to presume a dispensing or suspending power with the said Act but to Relate their opinion or doubt thereon to the next General Assembly that whatever doubts Arising between the construction of law and Constitution may be fully Resolved by the said Assembly."[7]

This was dangerous, and Archibald Maclaine therefore attempted to eviscerate Spaight's bill. Instead of being introduced directly in the House, the bill had come through the House's law reform committee, and it thus ended up as part of a more general Bill to Amend and Alter the Court System. When this general court reform package was discussed on the floor of the House, Maclaine offered an amendment to have the bill require that "when Matters Occur wherein the Operation of the Constitution and any particular Act of the legislature may interfere," the judges "are not to presume a dispensing or suspending power with the said Act *but shall decide according to the true spirit and meaning of the constitution and general laws of the land.*" This was more or less the traditional duty of judges, but the amendment lost, 24 to 58, with Maclaine, Hooper, and Davie among the minority and Spaight leading the list of the majority.[8]

Spaight thus briefly enjoyed support for barring judicial decisions about the constitutionality of statutes, but his proposal was soon altered and shelved. Seeking a compromise, the law reform committee (or perhaps

[7] A Bill to Amend and Alter the Court System, 18, NCSA, General Assembly, Session Records 1786–1787, Box 5, Folder House (Dec. 16, 1786) Bill to Amend the Court System. This was first read on December 18, 1786, and it already included Spaight's bill. Blount, incidentally, was also a member of the joint committee. The primary requirement of the jury provision was "that in all trials by Jury the office and duty of the s^{d} Judges shall be only to speak their opinion of the law and give their advice unless when Juries shall by special Verdict empower them to give the law on facts as particularly found or other matters of Law." Ibid., 16.

[8] Maclaine's Proposal & Vote (Dec. 22, 1786), *Journal of the House of Commons. At a General Assembly begun and held at Fayetteville, on the eighteenth day of November, in the Year of Our Lord One Thousand Seven Hundred and Eighty-Six,* 44 (np: [1787]). The italicized words are reproduced from Maclaine's proposal, where they appear in italics, and the others, to provide context, from the Bill to Amend and Alter the Court System.

a committee of the whole House) softened Spaight's proposal to ensure that judicial doubts about a statute would at least create a presumption against its lawfulness. As thus modified, the section required that "when Matters Occur wherein the Operation of the Constitution and any particular Act of the legislature may interfere," the judges "are not to determine on the same but to Relate their opinion or doubt thereon to the next General Assembly," and in these circumstances "the Act so objected to shall not have the force and operation of law unless two thirds of the members of the General Assembly . . . shall be of opinion that the said Act is constitutional."[9] Even this tamed version of Spaight's proposal met with little success, for on the day the Assembly exonerated the judges, the House laid over the Bill to Amend the Court System and simply published it for the consideration of the public.

Richard Dobbs Spaight was disappointed, and the next day he and Blount reintroduced their Bill Declaratory of the Powers of Courts and the Rights of Juries. They thereby revived a version of the proposal to prevent judicial "usurpation . . . of Powers which are unknown to the constitution and Laws of this State"—although exactly which version is unknown. Spaight's revived bill received the usual courtesy of being passed on its first reading, but after being passed a second time in the House, it was rejected by the Senate.[10]

A more moderate limitation on judicial duty might get more support, but it would be even more difficult to draft, and this was one of the challenges faced by Maclaine's committee, which was preparing impeachment charges against the judges. On this committee, men of rather different views had to agree about the standard from which the judges had departed, and they had to state it in a manner that would appeal to a broad array of representatives and senators. The committee thus had to take an ecumenical approach, and probably for this reason it attempted to formulate a mid-

[9] A Bill to Amend and Alter the Court System, 18b (rider number 22), NCSA, General Assembly, Session Records 1786–1787, Box 5, Folder House (Dec. 16, 1786) Bill to Amend the Court System. Compare Madison's proposal for a council of revision that could preclude decisions by the judges or the executive about the constitutionality of a statute. Madison's Observations on Jefferson's Draft of a Constitution for Virginia, in *The Papers of Thomas Jefferson,* 6: 315, eds. Julian P. Boyd et al. (Princeton: Princeton University Press, 1952).

[10] A Bill Declaratory of the Powers of Courts and the Rights of Juries, NCSA, General Assembly, Session Records 1786–1787, Box 5, Folder House (Jan. 3, 1787). The clerk noted "Mr. Blount and Mr. Spaight" on the docket, apparently as the sponsors of the bill. Unfortunately, only the first page of the bill's text survives, and although this portion reveals that the jury provision included the modifications introduced when the bill was part of the Bill to Amend and Alter the Court System, it is possible that Spaight returned to his original wording of the provision on the power of courts.

dle ground by relying on the old notion of a doubtful conscience. From this perspective, judges who had constitutional doubts that they could not resolve one way or another were in no position to hold a statute unconstitutional. Evidently with something like this in mind, Maclaine's committee reported that if the judges in *Bayard* had delayed on account of irresolvable doubts, they should have notified the legislature:

> [T]he Judges declined to decide either for or against the defendants, though another term has elapsed since the arguments were heard, whereas if any insuperable doubts arose on that Subject, your Committee submit whether they should not have stated them to the General Assembly, that the act in question might have undergone a revisal.[11]

This was not quite Spaight's position, nor the old point about manifest contradiction, but perhaps a muddle was all that could be expected from a committee that included men of such different principles as Spaight and Maclaine, let alone Davie.

Unlike Spaight, Maclaine thought the judges had a duty to decide in accord with the law of the land, if they could overcome their doubts. He was notoriously unable to repress his "ardour," and when the Assembly exonerated the judges, both Spaight and Maclaine dissented, each from his own point of view—Maclaine's being particularly clear because he wrote a scathing protest. Although only a small part of his protest concerned *Bayard* and the other confiscation cases, Maclaine repeated the committee's charge about the delay of the judges, and now that he was speaking for himself, he clarified his view that if the judges could get over their doubts, they had a duty to decide the constitutional question. The judges, Maclaine declared, should have been impeached:

> Because . . . the Judges Spencer and Williams without declaring their opinions even at this time, made an apology, that they delayed to decide thereon, out of respect to the General Assembly; whereas it was their duty to determine thereon if they were decided and uniform in their opinions, or if they doubted, to state their doubts to the Legislature.

Both Spaight and Maclaine had condemned the judges' delay, but whereas Spaight considered any judicial decision holding a statute unconstitutional to be a "usurpation" of legislative power, Maclaine thought the judges had no authority to delay holding an unconstitutional act void, unless they

[11] Report of Committee of Two Houses to whom was referred to the examination into the present mode of the administration of Justice in the Superior Courts of Law and Equity (c. Jan. 1, 1787), NCSA, General Assembly, Session Records 1786–1787, Box 3, Joint Resolutions—Committee of the Whole of Two Houses on Administration of Justice Folder.

were uncertain or divided. In other words, doubt as to whether or not a statute was unconstitutional was no basis for a judicial decision and thus had to be resolved by the legislature. Of course, if a law was not manifestly contrary to a law of higher authority and obligation, it was ordinarily considered lawful and obligatory, but Maclaine focused not so much on what was manifest as on the judges' doubts and divisions, and not so much on what had obligation as on what had to be referred to the legislature. At least, however, if the judges were decided and uniform, Maclaine thought "it was their duty to determine" the matter.[12]

Underlying Maclaine's fear that the judges were not doing their duty was his anxiety that the legislature was claiming judicial power. He and Spaight both regretted the legislature's confiscation of Tory property, but while Spaight thought the legislature was judge of its own acts, Maclaine was jotting down "Reasons . . . the Assembly cannot properly Act in a Judicial Capacity"—this being the title of a memorandum he drafted at roughly this time. He began by observing that "[t]he Assembly is the Sovereign of this Country[,] having all the powers of the people delegated to them under certain restrictions." Taking legislative power to be an extension of the people's power, Maclaine explained that "by the Constitution the people have restrained themselves within certain Limits"—to be precise, "in that Constitution the powers of the Assembly are defined beyond which they cannot go consistent with the safety of the State." This limited sovereignty of the Assembly was like the prerogative of the Crown, and thus "[t]he powers granted to the Assembly by the Constitution may very properly be called its prerogatives." The analogy was a reminder that the extent of such power could not be left to the judgment of the body exercising it: "[B]ut if a Citizen is injured by an undue exercise of this prerogative or by this Body's usurping powers which are not vested in it by the Constitution how is he to obtain redress? is he to seek it from the body who has done him the injury? that would be making it a Judge in its own case." With the obvious example in mind, Maclaine then asked: "[S]uppose for instance that the Assembly

[12] Archibald Maclaine, Protest Against the Resolution of the House of Commons, (Jan. 6, 1787), NCSA, General Assembly, Session Records 1786–1787, Box 3, Joint Resolutions—Committee of the Whole of Two Houses on Administration of Justice Folder. Maclaine expressed these views on *Bayard* in a protest that more generally complained about "the necessary consequences of suffering the judicial authority to usurp the rights of Juries, and to grasp at the Legislative and Executive powers of the State," and although his primary concern about *Bayard* was the failure of the judges to hold the statute there unconstitutional, he could loosely include his observations about *Bayard* within the broader theme of his protest on the assumption that if the judges had been in doubt, their failure "to state their doubts to the Legislature" would have usurped legislative power. Ibid.

should pass an Act to divest an individual of his property and apply it to some publick use without the consent of the proprietor"—"with what hopes of success would he make an Application to have it restored when this Application is to be made to the people or their representatives who are in possession of his property and consider it as their own. The Case would then stand thus. A.B. against the State of North Carolina, to be determined by the State."[13] Hence the necessity of the judges' "duty to determine" the constitutionality of statutes—at least, that is, according to Maclaine, "if they were decided and uniform in their opinions." Otherwise, the state would become judge in its own case.

Although Maclaine's understanding of the judicial role came closer to the common law ideal than the other limitations on judicial duty discussed in North Carolina, it shared their fate. Whereas the common law ideal of judicial duty could simply be assumed, the qualifications to this ideal had to be formally proposed and somehow enforced, and not even men as talented and prominent as Spaight and Maclaine were up to this task.

The Correspondence between James Iredell and Richard Dobbs Spaight

During the summer of 1787, shortly after the decision in *Bayard v. Singleton,* Spaight and Iredell corresponded about it. Each man had taken the lead in North Carolina in staking out the most sharply opposed positions about the role of the judges, and they now directly debated their views—the one with a deep sense of frustration and the other with an easy confidence in judicial duty.

Spaight and Davie were serving as delegates from North Carolina to the Constitutional Convention, and Spaight wrote to Iredell from Philadelphia in June 1787 after reading a report of the decision in *Bayard.* Spaight acknowledged that "the Assembly have passed laws unjust in themselves, and militating in their principles against the constitution," including not only the statute condemned in *Bayard* but also "the tender laws and the laws for increasing the Jurisdiction of the Justices of the peace"—the former making paper money legal tender for debts in specie, and the latter being roughly similar to the Ten Pound Act in New Hampshire.[14] What led

[13] Archibald Maclaine, Memorandum, University of North Carolina at Chapel Hill, Wilson Library, Southern Historical Collection, No. 324, Hayes Collection, Box 2, Folder 107.

[14] Letter from Richard Dobbs Spaight to James Iredell (Aug. 12, 1787), in *The Papers of James Iredell,* 3: 298.

In the same session in 1785 in which the General Assembly adopted the confiscation act that would lead to *Bayard v. Singleton,* it also passed a ten-pound small claims act that simi-

Spaight to complain, however, was not the particular statute the judges had "declared void," but rather "their usurpation of the Authority to do it." He protested: "I do most positively deny that [they] have any such power; nor can they find any thing in the constitution either directly or impliedly, that will support them, or give them any colour of right to exercise that authority."

Nor would a constitution ever give this power to the judges, he thought, for such a power was apt to become a discretionary exercise of will: "[I]t would have operated as an absolute negative on the proceedings of the legislature[,] which no Judicial ought ever to possess." There were three judges of the North Carolina Superior Court, and Spaight therefore thought that "the State, instead of being governed by the representatives in general Assembly would be subject to the will of three individuals, who united in their own persons, the legislative & Judiciary powers." Spaight thus feared the judges would exercise the combination of judicial and legislative power that Maclaine feared in the legislature. The "insufferable" judicial exercise of legislative will seemed all too probable because the judges were not subject to any control:

> If they possessed the power, what check or control would there be to their proceedings? or who is there to take the same liberty with them, that they

---

larly seemed to run up against the right a jury—a conjunction noticed by contemporaries. *The Independent Citizen, Or, The Majesty of the People Asserted against the Usurpations of the Legislature of North-Carolina, in Several Acts of Assembly, Passed in the Years 1783, 1785, 1786 and 1787,* at 5 ([Newbern: 1787]). Both the 1785 small claims statute and a January 1787 act increasing the jurisdiction to twenty pounds had their defenders: "[A]ltho' with great modesty, they are admitted on all hands, to be a small departure from the Constitution, yet, it is strongly alledged in defence of the bill, that Judges were remiss, that Lawyers have been guilty of abuses, that the Court dockets are too crouded, that the Justices are fully competent to the task, and it is a mean[s] of great easement to the people." Ibid., 6. Spaight, however, was among those who attempted to defeat the increase of jurisdiction to twenty pounds, both when this was included in the Bill to Amend the Court System and again when it was adopted in a separate statute. Maclaine's Motion & Vote (Dec. 22, 1786), *Journal of the House of Commons. At a General Assembly begun and held at Fayetteville, on the eighteenth day of November, in the Year of Our Lord One Thousand Seven Hundred and Eighty-Six,* 44 (np: [1787]); Hooper's Motion & Vote (Jan. 6, 1787), ibid., 76.

A bill of late 1786 (which was wrapped into the Bill to Amend the Court System) attempted to cure the worst features of the small claims act by allowing a party to appeal and thereby get a trial by jury. Although this provision did not remedy the absence of a jury in the first trial, before a justice of the peace, it stipulated that when justices "give a Judgment for any Sum exceeding five Pounds it shall be their duty to read the Law to the parties under which he give[s] said Judgment that the parties may know what steps they may take to secure to them the Justice they may think themselves entitled to." Bill to Amend and Alter the Court System, page 8(b), NCSA, General Assembly, Session Records 1786–1787, Box 5, House (Dec. 16, 1786) Bill to Amend the Court System Folder. It was passed by the Senate, but in the House on January 2, 1787, it was "read & laid over until the next Assembly." Ibid.

> have taken with the legislature, and declare there opinions to be erroneous? none that I know of. In consequence of which, whenever the Judges should become corrupt, they might at pleasure set aside any law, however just or consistant with the constitution, to answer their designs[,] and the persons and property of every individual would be compleatly at their disposal.

This showed "the absurdity and impropriety of such a power being lodged with the Judges."[15]

Spaight, it will later be seen, had the company of another delegate in Philadelphia that summer in thinking that judges exercised an illegitimate, discretionary power when holding statutes void, but Spaight at least recognized the need for some constraint on legislative power. In particular, he "acknowledged that our [North Carolina] constitution, unfortunately has not provided a sufficient check, to prevent the intemperate and unjust proceedings of our legislature." Like other Federalists, he thought "such a check would be very beneficial, & I think absolutely necessary to our well being," but "[t]he only one I know of, is the annual election, which by leaving out such members as have supported improper measures, will in some degree remedy, tho' it can not prevent such evils as may arise." Having thus shared his views, Spaight suggested to Iredell that the decision in *Bayard* "must clearly under go a public discussion," and he therefore "wish[ed] to know what is the general opinion on that transaction."[16]

In fact, there is little surviving evidence of public discussion, other than a few newspaper reports, which glowingly approved of the decision, and Iredell's response to Spaight suggests why the public debate expected by Spaight was unnecessary: Those who accepted that judicial duty extended to holding unconstitutional statutes unlawful could simply rely on the old common law ideals. Iredell bluntly began by observing that, "[i]n regard to the late decision at Newbern, I confess it has ever been my opinion, that any Act inconsistent with the Constitution was void; And that the Judges, consistently with their duties, could not carry it into effect."[17] Law and judicial duty were the essence of Iredell's views, and much of the rest of his letter merely explained why the judges could not escape their duty.

Under North Carolina's express constitution, the judges could not accept the legislature's judgment about the constitutionality of its statutes. As has been seen, Iredell understood that "[w]ithout an express Constitution, the Powers of the Legislature would undoubtedly, have been absolute (as the Parliament in Great Britain is held to be)." Americans, however, had

[15] Letter from Richard Dobbs Spaight to James Iredell (Aug. 12, 1787), in *The Papers of James Iredell,* 3: 298–299.
[16] Ibid.
[17] Letter from James Iredell to Richard Dobbs Spaight (Aug. 26, 1787), ibid., 3: 307.

ample "experience of the Evils . . . attending an absolute Power in a Legislative body," and this "suggested the propriety of a real, original, Contract between the People & their future Government, such perhaps as there has been no instance of in the world but in America."

An express constitution was particularly important as a means of protecting individual liberty. "In a Republican Government (as I conceive) *Individual Liberty* is a matter of the utmost moment," for "if there be no check upon the public passions, it is in the greatest danger. The majority having the rule in their own hands may take care of themselves; but in what condition are the Minority, if the power of the other is without limits?" Such considerations led North Carolinians to adopt "express provisions for the personal Liberty of each Citizen . . . when they formed the Constitution," and they thereby did not leave these rights "at the mercy of any Assembly whatever."[18]

Not merely express, the Constitution was a formal, written act of the people, of which the judges had to take notice. It will be recalled that when the judges decided *Bayard v. Singleton,* they recognized that the constitution was an act that they were "bound to take notice of as much as of any other law whatever," and Iredell similarly echoed the common law notion of an act of record, arguing that the North Carolina Constitution was "*a fundamental Law,* & a law *in writing*" of a "solemn nature," and that therefore "the Judicial power, in the exercise of their Authority, must take notice of it as the Ground work of that as well as of all other Authority." Far from being "a mere imaginary thing, about which ten thousand different opinions may be formed," the state's constitution was "a written document to which all may have recourse, & to which therefore the Judges cannot wilfully blind themselves."[19]

Iredell at the same time emphatically rejected Spaight's fears that "the Judges are appointed Arbiters, & [are] to determine as it were upon any application whether the Assembly have or have not violated the Constitution." Rather, Iredell pointed out, it was the necessity of giving judgment in a case that brought them to the point that they had to do their duty in deciding whether a statute was law. Like Justice Marshall a decade and a half later, Iredell explained that "when an Act is necessarily brought in Judgment before them, they must unavoidably, determine one way or another." The judges thus were "not at liberty to choose" whether to decide the constitutionality of a statute, "but must in all questionable instances de-

[18] Ibid.
[19] Ibid., 307–309.

cide." Whereas Maclaine and his committee, including Spaight, would have had the judges inform the legislature when they had doubts, Iredell recognized that once the matter was brought before a court in a case, the judges had no freedom to avoid a decision. Iredell conceded to Spaight that "[i]n all doubtful cases, to be sure, the Act ought to be supported," and that "it should be unconstitutional beyond dispute before it is pronounced such," but this was nothing more than a loose summary of the presumption in favor of a law unless it was manifestly contrary to a law of higher obligation—in this instance, the presumption in favor of a statute unless it was manifestly contrary to the constitution.[20]

Iredell closed his letter to Spaight on a conciliatory note, acknowledging that "I believe many think as you do upon this subject." He quickly added, however, that "I have not heard much said about it" and that "[m]ost of the Lawyers, I believe are of my opinion" on "the general question, independant of an application to any case."[21] There was, it has been seen, little debate about *Bayard* in North Carolina after the decision, and this is yet another reminder that some men had the advantage of relying on common law ideals. Men such as Spaight and even Maclaine struggled to explain and give legislative force to limitations on judicial duty. In contrast, men such as Iredell and the judges could rest on the obligation of the law of the land and the duty of the judges to decide in accord with it.

[20] Ibid., 308, 310.
[21] Ibid., 310.

15

Not Holding Legislative Acts Unconstitutional

Some cases did *not* hold statutes unconstitutional but nonetheless are suggestive. Such cases could not have been precedents for judicial review, and they may therefore initially seem—like the space surrounding a sculpture—almost the absence of that which deserves attention. These cases, however, were instances in which the judges did their duty, and even though the judges in these cases did not actually hold any statute unconstitutional, they revealed the comfort with which they usually decided constitutional questions relating to legislation.

Incidentally, some of the circumstances in which judges did not hold statutes unconstitutional offer further hints of the risks that lay ahead in a society so diffuse and fragmented that men might not feel much attachment to their law. The English remained sufficiently cohesive, hierarchical, and tradition-bound that they could continue to have much confidence in a customary constitution and their legislature's adherence to it. In contrast, Americans were so distant from Britain and in some ways from each other that they had particular reason to value express constitutional guarantees and judicial enforcement. This reliance of a more fractured society on more completely formalized law and enforcement should not come as a surprise, but the sort of circumstances that made such law and enforcement seem necessary could also undermine them, and although the full extent of the danger would become evident only later, there were already intimations in the eighteenth century.

Common Law Adjacent to Statutes: Slavery

At times, not statutes but common law in the vicinity of statutes came before the judges—as can be observed in the Massachusetts slavery cases, especially two of those concerning Quock Walker. These cases are familiar from the ample scholarship on slavery. They are also, however, revealing as constitutional decisions, not because they held any law unconstitutional, but rather because they decided the common law authority for slavery by reference to the Massachusetts Constitution. These cases on slavery thus suggest the frequency and unselfconscious ease with which judges handled constitutional law.

Scholars have made sweeping claims that the Quock Walker cases in the early 1780s finally abolished slavery, and other scholars have made equally broad claims that the cases did nothing of the sort.[1] Yet when these decisions are considered within a line of earlier cases, it becomes apparent that one and perhaps two of the Quock Walker cases relied on the Constitution to resolve the more complex question as to whether—somewhere amid the state's defunct statutes on slavery—there could be discerned a common law doctrine authorizing men to hold human property.

Quock's owner, Nathaniel Jennison, had acquired him by marriage. In 1754, when Quock was only a baby, he and his mother—together with the man who may have been his father—had been bought by James Caldwell of Barre in Worcester County. On James's death in 1763, when Quock was ten, he became the property of James's widow. She eventually married Nathaniel Jennison, and on her death, apparently about 1773, Jennison became Quock's sole owner.

[1] The Quock Walker cases have been explored with learned ardor by Chief Justice Horace Gray, Massachusetts Historical Society, *Proceedings,* 13: 292 (1st series) (1874), and Emily Blanck, "Seventeen Eighty-Three: The Turning Point in the Law of Slavery and Freedom in Massachusetts," *New England Quarterly,* 75: 24 (2002), and with skepticism by George Moore, *Notes on the History of Slavery in Massachusetts,* 211–222 (New York: 1866); William O'Brien, S.J., "Did the Jennison Cases Outlaw Slavery in Massachusetts?" *William and Mary Quarterly,* 17: 219 (3rd series) (1960); Robert M. Spector, "The Quock Walker Cases (1781–83)—Slavery, Its Abolition, and Negro Citizenship in Early Massachusetts," *Journal of Negro History,* 53: 12 (1968); Arthur Zilversmit, "Quok Walker, Mumbet, and the Abolition of Slavery in Massachusetts," *William and Mary Quarterly,* 25: 614 (1968); Elaine MacEacheren, "Emancipation of Slavery in Massachusetts: A Reexamination 1770–1790," *Journal of Negro History,* 55: 289, 303 (1970).

All of this scholarship has been skewed by a whiggish fascination with abolition. The oldest and the most recent articles cited above suggest that Chief Justice Cushing heroically "abolished" slavery in Massachusetts. Recognizing that the evidence does not really support this conclusion, most of the modern scholarship has suggested that the Quock Walker cases never really called slavery into doubt, and certainly if one examines the cases to determine whether they abolished slavery in the same sense as the Thirteenth Amendment, they are bound to seem a disappointment. Neither extreme, however, is justified once one examines the legal question that most clearly came before the judges, and it is for this purpose that this account brings to bear the additional evidence from *Cesar v. Greenleaf* and from Sargeant's notes of *Jennison v. Caldwell.* For the way in which Cushing and other men soon recast the question in terms of abolition, see note 15 below.

Quock recalled that his old master James Caldwell "said I should be free at 24 or 25," and his "Mistress told me I should be free at *21.*" Quock lived with Jennison more than seven years after coming of age, but in 1781 he finally decided to sell his labor as a free man.[2] The sons of James Caldwell—John and Seth—had probably grown up with Quock, and in April 1781, after consulting the lawyer Levi Lincoln, they hired Quock to work in their fields.[3]

Jennison was not pleased about Quock's departure and gathered some men to "bring him home." It was lawful in Massachusetts for a master to recover his indentured servant without recourse to a court, and Jennison applied this rough justice to the man he considered his slave. On May 1, 1781, when Quock was harrowing a field for the Caldwells, Jennison went with two other men into the field and "took hold of ye negro." At this point, one of the Caldwell brothers "came up & told Jennison he had no Business with Quacko," and as recounted by Joshua Winslow—one of the men assisting Jennison—"I took hold of Quackos Button hole & told him he must go home & he said he woud if they wou'd let him alone. I told him we cou'd not trust him," and the Jennison party therefore forcibly took him away. The Caldwell brother who was present later offered another perspective: "The Negro . . . was at work in my field with a team" when Caldwell "heard a screaming" and "got upon a Nole," and from a distance saw "Jennison & several others, who had got ye negro down." In particular, a "young fellow" was "upon ye negro." According to the hurried scribble of later trial notes, Caldwell recalled that "I took him off—[they had] bruised his fingers—carried him off—went to a saw mill—& told Jennison his Master had freed him—& Winslow let him go." Quock had "wounds in his hands & Arms."[4] As Jennison was allegedly injured in his property and Quock in his person, each brought a civil action in the Worcester County Inferior Court of Common Pleas, and in the resulting cases, the judges of Massachusetts examined whether the state had a common law of slavery—a customary law that was said to exist alongside colonial statutes and ultimately the state's constitution.

Slavery had an ambiguous place in Massachusetts law. Individuals in Massachusetts had long owned slaves, and the colony's statutes had ac-

[2] Trial on Indictment of Jennison, Massachusetts Historical Society, Chief Justice Charles Cushing, *Notes on Law Cases,* 89–90.
[3] Record of Pleadings in *Jennison v. Caldwell et al.* (June term 1781), Worcester County Court of Common Pleas, Record Book 1779–1782, at 10: 203, MSA, Mfm Reel 892261.
[4] Trial on Indictment of Jennison, Massachusetts Historical Society, Chief Justice Charles Cushing, *Notes on Law Cases,* 88–89.

knowledged this in the course of regulating slaves. No statute, however, directly authorized slavery, and English common law had tended to presume an absence of servitude, even if not in the colonies.[5] The bar and bench of Massachusetts had canvassed these contradictory considerations when slaves brought actions of replevin and trespass for their freedom—most prominently in a series of actions undertaken by the lawyer John Lowell. For example, in 1773 in *Cesar v. Greenleaf,* Cesar Hendrick—a mulatto laborer from Newburyport—brought an action of trespass against Greenleaf for false imprisonment, and already in this case both sides had to focus on the problem that the colonial statutes of Massachusetts acknowledged slavery without going so far as to authorize it. As no statute clearly authorized or forbade slavery, the lawyers had to dispute whether it was authorized by common law, and Greenleaf's lawyer therefore relied on the old colonial statutes and the pervasiveness of slavery across human history to suggest that in the absence of a direct prohibition, it could be taken for granted that there was authorization for slavery at common law. Lowell responded by drawing on the traditional English presumption against servitude: "Liberty is not be taken from him, or any man, by implication of law—There must be express law for it."[6] In these ways, the suits about slavery explored the common law authority for slavery in Massachusetts—a common law that was perhaps discernible in the vicinity of old statutes.

In the Quock cases, the parties similarly could not rely on statutes directly to authorize or forbid slavery, and they therefore in the same manner

[5] For a discussion of the statutes, see Spector, "The Quock Walker Cases (1781–83)," 17–23. For legal presumptions in England, see J. H. Baker, "Personal Liberty under the Common Law, 1200–1600," in *The Common Law Tradition: Lawyers, Books and the Law,* 328 (London: Hambledon, 2000).

[6] *Cesar v. Greenleaf* (Sept. 1773), [Reports of Cases], 3, *William Plumer Papers,* Mfm Reel 19, Legal Papers (copied from a report taken by Theophilus Parsons). This copy is more accurate than that printed in L. Kinvin Wroth and Hiller B. Zobel, eds., *The Legal Papers of John Adams,* 2: 64 (New York: Atheneum, 1968).

Judge Trowbridge summed up that the defendant "by the Prov[ince] law & by the custom of the Country seems to justify his doings," the implication being that "[t]he laws suppose slavery." On the other side, "[t]he master by admitting the baptism &c seems in a measure to have give the Pl^t his liberty." Trowbridge ended by asking: "shall this humanity be taken ag^t the def?" Although Cesar sought fifty pounds, the jury gave him eighteen pounds damages plus costs—not to mention his freedom. Ibid. See also George H. Moore, *Notes on the History of Slavery in Massachusetts,* 118 (New York: Negro Universities Press, 1968).

Arguments similar to Lowell's were made in Pennsylvania when it was said on behalf of a slave that "in *Pennsylvania,* there was no positive law for slavery" and that although "the acts of Assembly took notice of three sorts of slaves, *Negroes, Mulattoes,* and *Indians,*" the plaintiff, who was of a "pure" complexion, did not fall within any of the categories, and he "cannot be enslaved by mere implication." On instructions from Chief Justice M'Kean, the jury found for the defendants. *Pirate, alias Belt v. Dalby* (Supreme Court of Pennsylvania 1786), Dallas, *Reports,* 1: 167–168.

debated old statutes, the history of slavery, and now also the Bill of Rights in their efforts to clarify whether or not Massachusetts' common law authorized slavery. This is clearly evident from Jennison's action against the Caldwells for interfering with Quock's service to Jennison. When the case reached the Worcester County Supreme Judicial Court, Jennison's lawyers justified their client's conduct by suggesting that Quock had consented to serve Jennison and by arguing that the "custom of the country" authorized slavery.[7] At one point, Justice Nathaniel P. Sargeant jotted down notes about the colonial Massachusetts statutes on slavery—apparently because Jennison's lawyers were arguing that the statutes assumed the existence of slavery at common law.[8] The Caldwells' lawyer, Levi Lincoln, however, argued that slavery was not authorized by the common law of Massachusetts. He supported this position by observing that slavery was contrary to reason and by citing "Montesquieu's spirit of Laws" and the statute for "repeal of ye negro Laws"—that is, for the repeal of the statutes that regulated slavery but did not authorize it. Not least, he cited "Article 1st in bill of rights," which stated:

> All men are born free and equal, and have certain natural, essential and unalienable rights; among which may be reckoned the right of enjoying and de-

[7] Briefs by Levi Lincoln (June and Sept. 1781), Worcester County Court of Common Pleas and Supreme Judicial Court, fols. 146[r], 147[v], American Antiquarian Society, Lincoln Family Papers, Box 1, Folder 1. These have long been known as "the brief" used by Lincoln in making his argument in the Supreme Court. Emory Washburn, "Extinction of Slavery in Massachusetts," *Proceedings of the Massachusetts Historical Society,* 197–201 (May 1857). It is evident, however, that the two quires formed two distinct briefs, which were stored separately and were later bound separately in the papers of Levi Lincoln. Although it is not obvious which was used in Common Pleas in June and which in the Supreme Court in September, their basic arguments are very similar, and the words quoted here from the briefs appear in both, unless otherwise stated.

[8] Sargeant noted the following colonial statutes:

> Province Law 144. Act for indemnifying towns from charge for maintaining negros &c^{a}
>
> 145. Act respecting Indians negros & molatto Slaves making disorders in ye night time
>
> 151.2. act respecting Fornication & mixt & spurious Issue importation
>
> 157. act regulating free negros to work at Highways &c^{a} instead of training—& entertaining Negro Servants shall pay 5^{s}/—^{d}
>
> 174.5. act respecting Indians & other Slaves . . . forfeiture of all Indians brou't in to be sold unless Bo[n]d given for exportation.

Notes of Proceedings on Appeal by Judge Nathaniel P. Sargeant (Sept. 1781), Peabody Essex Museum, Phillips Library, Nathaniel P. Sargeant Papers, Box 1, Folder 12, Notebook beginning with Worcester Sessions, Sept. 1781, at 3. For these statutes, at the pages mentioned above, see *Acts and Laws, of His Majesty's Province of the Massachusetts-Bay in New-England* (Boston: 1761).

> fending their lives and liberties; that of acquiring, possessing, and protecting property; in fine, that of seeking and obtaining their safety and happiness.[9]

The point was not that Montesquieu was law or that the repeal statute or the Bill of Rights directly forbade slavery, but instead that from these sources it could be surmised that the state's common law did not authorize slavery. To buttress his legal arguments, Lincoln closed with an emotional appeal to the jury about the equality of all men before God. One of Jennison's lawyers then responded in kind with biblical and other examples to show that slavery was the "Universal Practice of all nations" and thus, presumably, was authorized by the common law of Massachusetts.[10] After the bench and the jury listened to this exchange, the judges instructed the jury. Their words have not survived, but the jury gave a verdict for the Caldwells.

That slavery lacked authority at common law, even though it was acknowledged by old statutes, was clearly determined on constitutional grounds in a final case concerning Jennison's assault on Quock Walker. In the autumn of 1781, a grand jury in Worcester indicted Jennison for assault and false imprisonment, reciting that he had used his "Fist & a large stick" to "beat bruise & evilly entreat" Quock and had held him captive for two

[9] Notes of Proceedings on Appeal by Judge Nathaniel P. Sargeant (Sept. 1781), Peabody Essex Institute, Phillips Library, Nathaniel P. Sargeant Papers, Box 1, Folder 12, Notebook beginning with Worcester Sessions, Sept. 1781, at 4.

The closest Lincoln came to arguing directly that laws authorizing slavery were void was when in one of his briefs (probably that for the trial in the Supreme Judicial Court), he argued: "The law of the state—any laws, against the laws of natu[re are] void—Laws that establish slavery [are] against the laws of nat[ure]." Briefs by Levi Lincoln (June and Sept. 1781), Worcester County Court of Common Pleas and Supreme Court, fol. 147[r], American Antiquarian Society, Lincoln Family Papers, Box 1, Folder 1. Although this sort of statement was partly for the benefit of the jury, it also had a place in Lincoln's argument to the judges, for it served to introduce his view that there was no authority for slavery at common law. He immediately afterward noted the argument made one of by Jennison's lawyers, that "the custom & usage of the country consider slavery as right." Having asserted that laws of the state against the law of nature were void, Lincoln now objected more narrowly that "Custom & usages against reason & right" were "void." Ibid., fol. 147[v]. The lawyers focused on custom and usage because Jennison's lawyers had to claim that slavery had been authorized by Massachusetts law both before and after Independence, and Lincoln responded for the Caldwells by denying that slavery had been authorized at either time, and therefore both sides talked in general terms that encompassed both the colonial past and the present—both the local, subordinate custom of the colony and the common law of the state. As law and reason was not only the old test for subordinate laws (including colonial laws) but also the means of discerning the common law where it was uncertain, Lincoln could almost effortlessly address the two sorts of analysis at the same time.

[10] Notes of Proceedings on Appeal by Judge Nathaniel P. Sargeant (Sept. 1781), Peabody Essex Museum, Phillips Library, Nathaniel P. Sargeant Papers, Box 1, Folder 12, Notebook beginning Worcester Sessions, Sept. 1781, at 4.

hours.[11] When the charge came to trial in April 1783, Jennison's counsel justified his conduct on the ground that "Quak is a slave" and the "former laws of ye province . . . give countenace to Slavery."[12] Chief Justice William Cushing, however, instructed the jury otherwise.

Speaking for the court, Cushing conceded that slavery had been countenanced in Massachusetts but denied any "doctrine" authorizing it:

> As to ye doctrine of Slavery & ye right of Christians to hold Africans in perpetual servititude, & selling & treating them as we do our horses & Cattle, that (it is true) has been heretofore countenanced by the province Laws formerly, but no where is it expressly enacted or established.

Instead, "[i]t has been a usage—a usage which took its origin, from ye practice of some of ye European nations, & the regulations of british Govmt respecting the then Colonies."[13] Cushing's allusion to usage was significant, for although common law traditionally recognized much local custom, usage was the local practice that the common law would not recognize or enforce.

This conclusion about slavery—that it was European usage rather than Massachusetts common law—seemed all the more clear from the changed sentiments of Americans and from the state's Declaration of Rights. Cushing explained:

> But whatever Sentiments have formerly prevailed . . . a different Idea has taken place with ye people of America more favorable to ye natural rights of Mankind, & to that natural innate desire of Liberty, with which Heaven (witht regard to color complexion or shape of *noses*) . . . has inspired all ye human Race. And upon this ground; our Constitution of Govmt, by wch ye people of this Commonwealth have solemnly bound themselves, Sets out with declaring that all men are born free & equal—& yt Every subject is intitled to Liberty, & to have it guarded by ye Laws, as well as Life & property—& in short is totally repugnant to ye Idea of being born Slaves.

Although the initial article of the Declaration of Rights was very general, Cushing could easily rely on it in the same way that he relied on the changed sentiments of Americans—not as a prohibition of slavery, let alone

[11] Indictment of Jennison, Worcester County Supreme Judicial Court (Sept. 1781), MSA, Supreme Judicial Court, Case No. 153693, Mfm Reel 644.

[12] Chief Justice Charles Cushing, *Notes on Law Cases,* 92–93 (Worcester County Supreme Judicial Court, April term 1783), Massachusetts Historical Society.

[13] Ibid., 94–95. At least according to his report of the case, Cushing spoke for the court. *Indictment of Nathaniel Jennison,* in *Notes of Cases Decided in the Superior and Supreme Judicial Court of Massachusetts from 1772 to 1789—Taken by the Honble William Cushing,* fol. 35[r], Harvard Law School, Ms. 4083.

a basis for holding slavery statutes void, but rather as further evidence that there was no common law doctrine in Massachusetts authorizing slavery: "I think ye Idea of Slavery is inconsistent with our own conduct & Constitution & there can be no such thing as perpetual servitude of a rational Creature, unless his Liberty is forfeited by Some criminal conduct or given up by personal Consent or Contract."[14] On this instruction denying a "doctrine of Slavery" in Massachusetts, the jury found Jennison guilty.[15]

[14] Cushing, *Notes on Law Cases,* 95–98, Massachusetts Historical Society.

[15] Ibid., 98. Although the scholarship on this case has tended to ask whether the case abolished slavery and, more generally, whether Massachusetts law in the late eighteenth century barred slavery, Cushing was responding to a narrower legal question, which was already familiar to the bar, and he and his brethren were therefore not unique in their view that the common law of Massachusetts did not authorize slavery—as can be illustrated by legislative developments two months before his decision. In February 1783, the House considered a bill to repeal the colonial "Act relating to Mulatto & Negro Slaves." Journal of House of Representatives, 3: 118 (Feb. 7, 1783), MSA. Yet it soon hesitated and instead created a committee "to bring in a Bill upon the following principles:

> 1st Declaring that there never were *legal* Slaves in this Government
> 2^{d} Indemnifying all Masters who have held Slaves *in fact*
> 3^{d} To make such provision for the support of such Negro's & Molattos as the Committee may find most expedient—

Ibid., 3: 444 (Feb. 8, 1783). In writing out the first principle, the clerk wrote "Slaves" but then crossed this out and wrote "*legal* Slaves"—thus by a felicitous accident recording the moment when either the clerk or the committee caught themselves using vocabulary that did not fully recognize the principles of the new bill. With this self-conscious sense of the importance of words, they drafted a new bill that was simply called "An Act respecting Negroes and Molattos." Ibid., 3: 529 (Feb. 28, 1783). The bill passed in the House but died after a first reading in the Senate. Ibid., 3: 537 (Mar. 4, 1783); Journal of Senate, 3: 413 (Mar. 7, 1783), MSA. The Assembly in any case was prorogued on March 26. Whether the prosecution of Jennison, which had lain dormant since 1781, was revived on account of the failure of the bill in the Assembly is unknown.

Although the bill, like the indictment of Jennison, merely concerned the lack of legal authority for slavery, another conception of the problem was already becoming popular and soon obscured the history. The clerk who (probably in the 1780s) prepared the index to the Journals of the House entered: "Slavery abolished . . . 8 Feb. 83." Index to Vol. 3 of Journals of House of Representatives, MSA. (For resolutions by the House seeking an index of its resolves, see ibid., 3: 529 (Feb. 28, 1783). Similarly, when Cushing in subsequent years prepared his reports, he rewrote his instructions about Jennison's indictment to reach a more dramatic conclusion: "In short, without resorting to implication in construing the Constitution, slavery is in my Judgment as effectually abolished as it can be by the granting of rights and privileges wholly incompatible and repugnant to its existence." *Indictment of Nathaniel Jennison,* in *Notes of Cases Decided in the Superior and Supreme Judicial Court of Massachusetts from 1772 to 1789—Taken by the Honble William Cushing,* fols. 34[v]–35[r], Harvard Law School, Ms. 4083. No longer merely an opinion about the common law that could be discerned from "our own conduct & Constitution," this was now an opinion about what the Constitution had "abolished." It was part of a broader rewriting of history that would gratify many nineteenth-century inhabitants of Massachusetts, that would annoy many twentieth-century historians, and that would in both ways distract attention from what actually happened.

Thus, in response to the claim that slavery enjoyed a common law authority evident from old statutes, the judges turned to the Constitution to show the absence of such authority. They did not thereby hold any enactment unconstitutional; but nor did they hesitate to rely on the Constitution to discern the common law that might otherwise be apparent from prior legislation.

Although cases on slavery have an inevitable fascination in America, they are included here merely to illustrate the confidence with which judges addressed constitutional questions in the interstices of legislative policy. The judges' lack of concern about pursuing constitutional issues in the neighborhood of statutes could be further illustrated with cases on religious taxes, but to spare the reader, these decisions are left to Appendix III. Here, it should suffice to note the contrast between the controversial substantive issues and the uncontroversial office of the judges. Slavery and religion were matters so sensitive and complicated that the Massachusetts legislature was slow to establish policy on these issues after the Revolution. Nonetheless, the judges regularly examined the legal authority that lingered in the vicinity of old statutes, and they did not waver when they therefore had to consult the Constitution.

Upholding Statutes as Constitutional: Whitney v. Peckham

In some of the cases in which judges did not hold a statute void, they candidly considered the lawfulness of a statute but did not conclude that it was unconstitutional. An initial illustration is *Whitney v. Peckham,* a long-forgotten Massachusetts case on legislative privilege. It was obviously not a precedent for holding a statute void, but it reveals how readily a judge could approach the constitutionality of a statute.

Robert Peckham was a deputy sheriff in Worcester County who had already attached Aaron Whitney's cattle, together with tons of hay and stalks, on "mesne process"—the intermediate process that occurred after the original writ starting a case and before the writ concluding the case, such as a writ of execution on judgment. Accordingly, when Sheriff Peckham received a writ of execution on a judgment against Whitney, Peckham sold the previously attached cattle and feed at auction. The proceeds, however, failed to cover the judgment (let alone the expense of keeping the cattle), and Peckham therefore twice arrested and detained Whitney—in September 1782 for three weeks and again in October for six hours—the purpose each time being to hold Whitney "until he paid . . . to obtain his discharge." Like the sale, these detentions were on final rather than mesne process.

Unfortunately for Peckham, Whitney was not only a shopkeeper but also a member of the Massachusetts House of Representatives. A representative for Northfield in Hampshire County, he was traveling to the General Court when he was first arrested and was returning from his legislative duties when he was arrested the second time. Whitney therefore brought an action of trespass *vi et armis* against Peckham on the ground that Whitney "was exempt from arrest as a Representative going to discharge his duty as such in the General Court." After Whitney prevailed in 1783 in the Hampshire County Court of Common Pleas, Peckham appealed to the Supreme Judicial Court, where in New England style he got a new jury trial.

Chief Justice Cushing explained to the jury that this issue—"whether the Sheriff could justify himself in arresting the debtor by the Execution"—was "the question of most difficulty." A late seventeenth-century colonial statute gave members of the General Assembly a very broad exemption from process: "[N]o member of the General Assembly, or his servant, during the time of the Sessions, or going to & from thence shall be arrested, sued, imprisoned or any way molested or troubled or compelled to make answer to any suit, bill &c. cases of high treason & felony excepted." Accordingly, "[i]f this stood alone—the Deft. undoubtedly must answer for a false imprisonment." Defendant's counsel, however, contended that "our constitution has limited this exemption to arrests on *mesne* process solely," and indeed the Massachusetts Constitution provided that "no member of the House of Representatives shall be arrested or held to bail on *mean process* during his going unto, returning from, or attending the General Assembly." The question was therefore whether "this article repeal[s] the old law." Whereas a question about the lawfulness of the colonial statute at the time it was passed would have rested on the old common law standard for subordinate acts—the test of law and reason—this question about the effect of the Constitution on a colonial statute was similar to any other inquiry about the constitutionality of a state statute.

Cushing concluded that the relevant article of the Constitution had not overturned the statute on exemption from arrest:

> There is no prohibition in this article to the Legislature that they shall not exempt their members on other processes than mesne—nor any restraining words like those found in other clauses where restrictions are imposed on the Legislature. It was undoubtedly the intention of the framers of the Constitu-

> tion to leave the General Court free to act on this subject provided they did not narrow the exemption contained in that instrument. We are therefore of opinion that the old law remains in full force notwithstanding this article & the Deft is answerable for the false imprisonment.

Upon being thus instructed that the old exemption law was not unconstitutional, the jury gave its verdict against the sheriff.[16] In *Whitney v. Peckham,* Cushing only had to consider the constitutionality of an old, colonial statute, but he thereby decided the constitutional right of a sitting member of the House of Representatives without any apparent anxiety or concern.[17]

[16] *Whitney v. Peckham* (Hampshire County Supreme Judicial Court, May term 1785), *Notes of Cases Decided in the Superior and Supreme Judicial Court of Massachusetts from 1772 to 1789—Taken by the Honble William Cushing,* fols. 51[r]–53[r], Harvard Law School, Ms. 4083. Cushing focused on the second arrest, perhaps because on that occasion Whitney had to turn over thirty-six pounds for his release. Ibid. For details about the first arrest and about the parties, see MSA, Supreme Judicial Court, Mfm Reel 20, Record Book Feb.–June 1785, fols. 184[v]–186[r].

Under the Massachusetts Constitution, members of the Council could also claim privilege, and in 1783 this was the subject of a request by a lawyer, Thomas Davies, for a private opinion. Understanding that a judge might not wish to have it known that he had given such an opinion, Davies wrote to Justice Sargeant that "[i]f your Honor shall see no inconvenience in answering my question . . . the most religious secrecy shall be observed." Of particular interest here, the letter spells out why creditors needed to get around constitutional privileges: "To arrest the member in his own county will be next to losing the debt" and "to attach what property of his can be found & to leave a summons would put the greatest part of the debt to hazard." Letter from Thomas Davies to Nathaniel Sargeant (June 7, 1783), Phillips Library, Peabody Essex Museum, Nathaniel Sargeant Mss.

[17] Incidentally, constitutional questions arose in Virginia as to judicial privilege. In November 1786 in the Virginia Court of Appeals, Chancellor Wythe "mentioned to the Court a Circumstance which he had accidentally heard which he considered as a high Breach of Privilege—The Chief Justice a few days had been served with a process from Henrico Court, the moment he stept off the Bench.—He therefore submitted to the Court the propriety of making a rule agt the Attorney who ordered the process, the clerk who issued it & the officer who served it, to appear before this court . . . to shew cause why an Attachment agt them should not issue for their contempt of this Court." Andrew Ronald was the attorney who obtained the writ, and being present in court, he "said he knew of no Law which privileged the Judges from arrest, sedenta Curia though he thought it highly proper such a Law should be made." Wythe responded that "no Law is necessary to be made," for "this privilege is a part of the common Law of England which we have adopted." Reasoning from the more familiar privilege of lawyers, Judge Lyons said, "parties attending their suits are privileged—so are their attorneys witnesses & so the Judges must be." Therefore the rule was awarded. *Ronald's Case* (Nov. 10, 1786), St. George Tucker, Notes of Cases, 1: 22, College of William and Mary, Swem Library, Tucker-Coleman Papers, Reel M-62.

After almost a year had passed, in October 1787, Ronald appeared before the Court, evidently seeking to return to practice there. According to the report, "it appeared he had acted with a good deal of delicacy to the Chief Justice," and he said that "he wished the Question of privilege to be considered." In particular, he argued from "the Bill of rights, which says no person shall be entituled to privileges but in consideration of services," and he noted that "the legislature have passed an Act wherein the Extent of privilege seems to be mentioned & expressio Unius est exclusio alterius." *Ronald's Case* (Oct. 29, 1787), ibid. Two weeks later,

Upholding Statutes as Constitutional: Commonwealth v. Caton, et al.

Unlike Chief Justice Cushing in *Whitney v. Peckham,* the judges in *Commonwealth v. Caton, Hopkins, & Lamb* publicly agonized over whether they could hold a statute unconstitutional. The judges eventually upheld the statute, and because they did so after much debate about their ability to do otherwise, the case is sometimes taken as evidence that the judges had not yet so far developed their power that they could establish a precedent for judicial review.[18] There is reason to think, however, that the power to hold statutes unconstitutional was merely an aspect of their duty and was not as uncertain as the case is sometimes taken to suggest.

The three defendants—John Caton, Joshua Hopkins, and James Lamb—had the mixed blessing of receiving pardons from the Virginia House of Delegates. Lamb was a wheelwright and the other two were planters. Each had at least briefly joined the enemy, and in June 1782 the General Court of Virginia convicted them of treason. At the end of its sitting, when the Court made its recommendations for mercy, the judges advised a pardon for James Lamb on the ground that, although guilty of treason, he had been "actuated in this Conduct rather from Resentment" than "a desire to assist the Enemy." (He had, according to the judges, joined an enemy raid against some errant Americans who "had committed . . . unwarrantable outrages on the persons & property of the Citizens of this state within the Enemies lines.") In contrast, "[n]othing particular appeared to the Court in favour of the two planters, Hopkins and Caton."[19]

The power to pardon for treason lay in the legislature, and Governor

---

after a full year had passed from the original ruling, the Court "declare[d], That the Judges are by Law privileged from service of all process in civil suits during the Time of their attendance at Court, and a reasonable time for traveling to and from the place of their Session. But as the Officers on the present occasion do not appear to have had any design to violate the privileges of the Court, rule discharged." *Ronald's Case* (Nov. 14, 1787), ibid., 2: 1.

[18] The standard sources are Daniel Call, *Reports,* 4: 5; David John Mays, *Edmund Pendleton 1721–1803, A Biography,* 2: 193–194 (Cambridge: Harvard University Press, 1952); Pendleton's Account of The Case of the Prisoners, in *The Letters and Papers of Edmund Pendleton 1734–1803,* at 2: 416, ed. David John Mays (Charlottesville: Virginia Historical Society, 1967). There are some discrepancies among the different accounts of the judges' opinions, but Crosskey goes beyond even his usual disparagement of the evidence when he accuses Daniel Call of having "fabricated" his report. William Winslow Crosskey, *Politics and the Constitution in the History of the United States,* 2: 959 (Chicago: University of Chicago Press, 1953). Most recently, William Treanor has drawn attention to the briefs of Randolph and Tucker. William Michael Treanor, "The Case of the Prisoners and the Origins of Judicial Review," *University of Pennsylvania Law Review,* 143: 491 (1994).

[19] Extract of a Letter from the Honble the Judges of the Genl. Court, LVA, House of Delegates, Office of Speaker, Executive Communications, Box 2, Folder 80.

Benjamin Harrison therefore sent the judges' recommendations concerning the three men to the Speaker of the House.[20] Lamb simultaneously petitioned the House that he was between sixty and seventy years old and had been "forced into the service of the enemy" for a nighttime raid by "a party of Men styled Refugees."[21] The next day, Patrick Henry moved in the House "to pardon Lamb & [the] others."[22] The House passed this resolution and sent it up to the Senate, but the upper house returned the pardon resolution later that day, "refusing to have any thing to do with it."[23]

The question that evidently disturbed the Senate was whether a pardon for treason rested in the House or whether it also needed the concurrence of the Senate. The Constitution of Virginia apparently placed the power in the House, for it stated of the governor:

> [H]e shall, with the advice of the Council of State, have the power of granting reprieves or pardons, except where the prosecution shall have been carried on by the House of Delegates, or the law shall otherwise particularly direct; in which cases, no reprieve or pardon shall be granted, but by resolve of the House of Delegates.[24]

A resolve of the House, however, may have been only a minimum requirement, and when the Assembly in 1776 enacted a definition of treason, it gave the power to pardon for this offense to the Assembly as a whole:

> [T]he governour . . . shall in no wise have or exercise a right of granting pardon to any person or persons convicted in manner aforesaid, but may suspend the execution until the meeting of the general assembly, who shall determine whether such person or persons are proper objects of mercy or not, and order accordingly.[25]

[20] Letter from Governor Benjamin Harrison to the Speaker of the House (June 17, 1782), ibid. See also *Journals of the Council of the State of Virginia,* 3: 110 (June 17, 1782), ed. Wilmer L. Hall (Richmond: Commonwealth of Virginia, 1952).

[21] Petition of James Lamb (June 17, 1782), LVA, Legislative Petitions, Princess Anne County, Box 209, Folder 7, Mfm Reel 163.

[22] House of Delegates, Minutes, 74 (June 18, 1782), LVA, RG 79. The resolve itself is reproduced in "A True Whig," Letter to Mess. Nicolson & Prentis, in *Virginia Gazette* (Richmond: Nicolson and Prentis, July 27, 1782); and in *Commonwealth v. Caton,* Supreme Court of Appeals, Order Book No. 1, 1779–1789, at 20–21, LVA.

[23] "A True Whig," *Virginia Gazette* (Richmond: Nicolson & Prentis, July 27, 1782).

[24] Virginia Constitution of 1776.

[25] An act declaring what shall be Treason, §III (1776), in *Laws of Virginia,* 9: 168, ed. William Waller Hening (Richmond: 1821). The effect of the Treason Act on the pardon power already had come up in June when Governor Harrison consulted Attorney General Randolph about a pardon for a man, Andrews, prior to his conviction for treason. According to Randolph, the Constitution gave the governor a "power to pardon . . . whether the pardon preceded or followed the conviction," and the Treason Act "cuts off your right of pardoning *only after conviction,* in treason." Randolph continued by explaining "why the legislature

If the Constitution only required a resolve of the House as a minimum, then this statute was constitutional and the prisoners, lacking a pardon from both houses, faced death. If, however, the requirement that there be a resolution of the House was exclusive, then the statutory requirement that the pardon come from both houses was unconstitutional. From this perspective, the House's pardon was sufficient to spare the prisoners, and the Senate had a constitutional reason to have nothing to do with it.

The high sheriff in Richmond thus found himself in a quandary. He had a rule of the General Court for execution of the prisoners, but on the day appointed for the execution, he was asked to liberate the prisoners after being handed "a copy of the [House of Delegate's] Resolution only, without any notice of its having been sent to the Senate, or their rejection of it." Not knowing what the law required of him, he "prudently respited the Execution, but kept the Prisoners in Goal, until the meeting of the General Court . . . when the Attorney General moved that the Prisoners might be brought up, & a new Rule made for their Execution."[26] The Court heard

---

should not lop off your otherwise constitutional power of pardoning, before conviction." For example, it being an era in which there were barriers to witnesses who were interested parties, Randolph observed that it might be necessary to pardon accomplices in order to obviate objections to their testimony. He closed, incidentally, by distinguishing questions of expediency from questions of law: "The matter being thus reduced to the question of expediency, and this being a political rather than a legal inquiry, I shall trouble your excellency no farther, than to assure you, that I am with great respect y.r mo. ob. Serv." Letter from Edward Randolph to Governor Benjamin Harrison (June 15, 1782), LVA, Benjamin Harrison Executive Papers, Letters Received.

[26] Transcript of Edmund Pendleton's Notes of his Opinion in *Commonwealth v. Caton, et al.,* Library of Congress, Force Papers, at 8695–8696, Series 7E, James McGuire Collection, Correspondence Folders.

If the sheriff misjudged the effect of the pardon, he himself risked violating the law. A newspaper essayist reported:

> [A]n affair which happened last week in the city of Richmond, has caused very considerable doubts to arise in the minds of many of the citizens of this state, in respect to the legality of a certain measure adopted there by the high sheriff, in regard to suspending the execution of a certain Hopkins, Lamb, and Caton, convicted of treason at the last General Court, and pursuant to their sentence, to have been executed on Friday last.

The essayist, however, thought that the sheriff had "acted strictly agreeable to law, while an opposite line of conduct, to wit: the execution of the criminals, might have subjected him to a trial for murder, notwithstanding his being in possession of their death warrant." "A True Whig," *Virginia Gazette* (Richmond: Nicolson and Prentis, July 27, 1782).

It was an old academic problem as to whether an executioner or other ministerial officer should refuse to execute a unjust sentence, and this was interesting precisely because it extended the standard questions about factual and moral knowledge from a judge to a person who was not authorized to judge. See, for example, Thomas Aquinas, *Summa Theologica,* 3: 1464–1465 (Q. 64, Art. 6), eds. Fathers of the English Dominican Province (Westminster, Md.: Christian Classics, 1981); Jeremy Taylor, *Ductor Dubitantium, or the Rule of Conscience* arguments when it met the following autumn, but it was "of the opinion that there is difficulty in rendering Judgment," and it therefore ordered that the matter "be Adjourned to the Court of Appeals," where Attorney General Edmund Randolph again moved for the prisoners' execution.[27]

The case was an irresistible occasion for the gentlemen of the Richmond bar to display their skills, and the Court of Appeals therefore became the arena for a sort of rhetorical competition. Although historians have taken the debate over the case as evidence that judicial review was still a nascent development, ambitious lawyers in Richmond saw the case as an opportunity to demonstrate their prowess before local society. The case was already a matter of controversy when the sheriff in the summer delayed execution, and commentators soon encouraged local lawyers to "exercise their talents in defence of [their] principles."[28] The Court of Appeals deliberately offered itself as a stage for this contest by announcing its hope that "the Gentlemen of the Bar, tho' not engaged as counsel, would generally deliver their sentiments" on the central questions, including "Whether the Act declaring what shall be Treason" was "contrary to . . . the Constitution" and "Whether a Court of Law could declare an act of the Legislature void because it was repugnant to the Act for the Constitution of Government."[29] In these circumstances, a debate about the judges' role was inevitable, but this is not to say that the judges' capacity to hold a statute unconstitutional was really in much doubt.

Attorney General Edmund Randolph introduced the proceedings in dramatic style. Although it has been suggested that the Attorney General was struggling to make up his mind about judicial review, his notes reveal, instead, a stylized rhetorical flourish, in which he initially gestured toward the mundane interests of the state but then stood firmly on the Constitution and his office. Randolph began, as might be expected of an ordinary lawyer, by methodically outlining his argument in the alternative:

> 1. that the association of the senate in the function of pardoning treason is justified by the constitution: and

---

In All Her General Measures, 1: 91–92 (I.ii.25) (London: 1660). At common law, however, the answers to such questions were very blunt, and in any case the problem faced by the Richmond sheriff was not that his judgment conflicted with the exercise of his authority, but rather that the law left him with a legal decision about the body that had authority to issue a pardon for treason, and this was a judgment he anxiously preferred to leave to the judges.

27 Supreme Court of Appeals, Order Book No. 1, 1779–1789, at 20–21, LVA.

28 "A True Whig," in *Virginia Gazette* (Richmond: Nicolson and Prentis, July 27, 1782).

29 Transcript of Edmund Pendleton's Notes of his Opinion in *Commonwealth v. Caton, et al.*, Library of Congress, Force Papers, at 8696–8697, Series 7E, James McGuire Collection, Correspondence Folders.

> 2. that, howsoever adverse the law, which vests this power in the general assembly may be, to the constitution, no court of judicature can pronounce its nullity.

In other words, the Treason Act was constitutional, and even if it were not, the court could not hold it void. Randolph, however, was no ordinary lawyer, and after completing his first argument, for the statute's constitutionality, he dramatically reversed his position on the second question and vindicated the power of the judges to hold a statute unconstitutional. It was a volte-face he carefully planned in his notes:

> 2. If my endeavors to reconcile the parent and her child (for such I call the constitution and the law) be the fruitless attempt of impotent benevolence, then indeed are we drawn to the two awful contemplations, which the second division of my discourse presents.
> 1. Is the treason law to be declared void, so far as it is repugnant to the constitution?
> 2. If it can be declared void, can any court of judicature pronounce its nullity?
>
> Here let me pause.
>
> But why pause?
>
> Do I tremble at the decision of my own mind, that a law against the constitution may be declared void? or . . . do I dread the resentment of the court, when I bear testimony against their competency to pronounce the invalidity of the law?
>
> No! the revolution has given me a coat of mail for my defense, while I adhere to its principles. That bench too is reared on the revolution, and will arrogate no undue power.
>
> I hold then, that every law against the constitution may be declared void.

The Attorney General himself thus supported the position of the prisoners that the Court could hold a statute unconstitutional and void. He differed from them only on the first question, in thinking the particular statute constitutional.

Randolph justified his conclusion that "every law against the constitution may be declared void" by observing that the Constitution was the measure of the law. The constitution made by the people was the "touchstone" of the powers they conveyed to their government, and only on the basis of the constitution could it "be decided how far the people, the fountain of power, have chosen to deposit it in the hands of their legislative servants." Thus, even before the other lawyers spoke, the Attorney General had already conceded that unconstitutional statutes could be held void, and he bluntly reminded the judges that at least on this question "you perceive that I argue in favor of the criminals." Randolph held an office that required him, like the judges, to decide in accord with the law of the land, and he therefore explained: "[M]y office does not extinguish that respect, which I shall owe to the constitution, as long as it remains such."[30]

After the Attorney General spoke, the prisoners' counsel argued—followed by three other gentlemen of the bar who served as *amici:* William Nelson, John Francis Mercer, and St. George Tucker. These "Voluntiers" differed "amongst themselves in sev! points, particularly as to the Power of the Court to declare an Act of Assembly void in any case."[31]

Tucker's notes have been located by William Treanor, and they show that however much the judicial role was disputed, the Attorney General was not alone among the bar in his confidence that the judges had to hold unconstitutional statutes void.[32] It has already been seen that Tucker relied on the express character of the Virginia Constitution and its separation of powers to show that legislative acts in Virginia were vulnerable to judicial decisions about their constitutionality, and more generally, like Randolph, Tucker considered the Constitution "the touchstone by which every Act of the Legislative is to be tried." Thus, "[i]f any Act thereof shall be found ab-

30 Edmund Randolph, Notes of Argument in *Commonwealth v. Lamb &c.,* Library of Congress, James Madison Papers, 91: 104. Edmund Randolph, Notes of Argument in *Commonwealth v. Lamb &c.,* Library of Congress, James Madison Papers, 91: 104. Randolph enclosed this initial draft of his argument in a letter to Madison of March 7, 1783, but it was filed separately and was not published in Madison's printed correspondence.

William Treanor is persuasive in arguing that this initial sketch can be relied upon as a rough indication of what Randolph said in court. His suggestion, however, that the draft is "evidence of Randolph's personal struggle to determine whether judicial review was valid" is improbable. Treanor, "The Case of the Prisoners and the Origins of Judicial Review," 507. Instead, it was surely a rhetorical gambit designed to present the state's position with dramatic effect.

According to Call's report, Randolph argued that "the court were not authorized to declare [the statute] void," and as Treanor suggests, Call's report may well be inaccurate in this regard. Call, *Reports,* 4: 7; Treanor, "The Case of the Prisoners and the Origins of Judicial Review," 507, note 55. Call explained that his reports were prepared "from the notes and memoranda of the judges and lawyers, who attended the courts, and examination of the records," and where Call was specific, he seemes to have relied on these primary sources with considerable fidelity. Call, *Reports,* 4: Reporter's Preface; Treanor, "The Case of the Prisoners and the Origins of Judicial Review," 532. Yet Call had to link the passages he drew from detailed primary sources, and he appears to have done this by creating transitional paragraphs that can still be distinguished by their generality and their occasionally mistaken surmises. His reports are thus a reminder as to why it is necessary in a volume such as this to rely as closely as possible on manuscript evidence.

31 Transcript of Edmund Pendleton's Notes of his Opinion in *Commonwealth v. Caton, et al.,* Library of Congress, Force Papers, at 8697, Series 7E, James McGuire Collection, Correspondence Folders.

32 Like Randolph's notes, Tucker's are discussed by Treanor, "The Case of the Prisoners and the Origins of Judicial Review," 491.

solutely & *irreconcileably* contradictory to the Constitution, it can not admit of a Doubt that such act is absolutely null & void." The Constitution was in this sense the place where "are explained those Fundamental Principles of our Government, of which the Judiciary Department is constituted the Guardian," and on these assumptions Tucker asked the judges to repudiate the requirement of the Treason Act that the Senate concur in the pardon.[33] In the end, however, the Court of Appeals upheld the statute, and it therefore certified to the General Court that "the pardon, by Resolution of the House of Delegates . . . is invalid."[34]

When the Court of Appeals reached its decision, each of the judges present spoke, and the opinion of the President of the Court, Edmund Pendleton, survives in particular detail. He thought that "the Treason Act, in fixing the Power of pardon for that offence in the General Assembly, does not counter the Constitution," and he therefore had no need to resolve whether the judges could determine the constitutionality of a statute. At the same time, he left no question about his sense of duty:

> But how far this Court in which it has been properly said the Judiciary Powers of the State are concentrated, can go in declaring an Act of the Legislature void, because it is repugnant to the Constitution, without exercising the Power of Legislation, from w[ch] they are restrained by the same Constitution is a deep, important, &, I will add, an awful question; from which, however, I will not shrink, if ever it shall become my duty to decide it. At present I am happy in having no occasion to make the decision; and still more happy in a sanguine hope that the wisdom and prudence of the Legislature, in making the Principles of the constitution direct the Spirit of their Laws, will render it unnecessary ever to determine it.[35]

Sixteen years earlier, after the Northampton County Court held the Stamp Act "unconstitutional," Pendleton had written that "having taken an oath to determine according to law," he would "never consider that act as such for want of power (I mean constitutional authority) in the Parliament to

[33] "To. W.N.," Argument on Behalf of the Prisoners, Addressed to William Nelson, William and Mary College Library, Tucker-Coleman Papers, Legal Papers, Virginia Supreme Court of Appeals, Mfm Reel M-44. Tucker wrote vertically along the inner margin here: "The Constitution forms the Barrier which the Judiciary can not transgress." Ibid.

[34] Supreme Court of Appeals, Order Book No. 1, 1779–1789, at 22, LVA.

[35] Transcript of Edmund Pendleton's Notes of his Opinion in *Commonwealth v. Caton, et al.*, Library of Congress, Force Papers, at 8706–8707, Series 7E, James McGuire Collection, Correspondence Folders. Pendleton had been Speaker when the Assembly adopted the Treason Act, and he now recalled that already at the time "the Question whether it was Anticonstitutional, was Warmly Agitated." Although as Speaker he "took no part in the debate," he had "settled" his opinion that the statute was constitutional, and he now "found no reason to alter" this view. Ibid., 8714.

pass it."[36] Now, when sitting as President of the Court of Appeals, he made it clear that he would not fail to decide the constitutionality of a Virginia statute "if ever it shall become my duty."[37]

Whereas Pendleton alluded to his duty but held back from saying what it obviously implied, Chancellor George Wythe was explicit. Wythe, like Pendleton, understood the Treason Act to be constitutional, and he therefore had no need to say more, but he spoke emphatically about judicial duty. He noted that one of the other Virginia judges, "imitating that great and good man lord *Hale,*" had said "he would sooner quit the bench" than hold a statute unconstitutional—this being an allusion to the belief of Matthew Hale when serving under Oliver Cromwell that he should resign rather than condemn a man to death.[38] Wythe, however, probably recognized that Hale's fastidiousness about sentencing while he served under a usurped regime was hardly an apt model for deciding a question of law in a constitutional regime, and Wythe therefore distinguished his own sentiments: "I feel no alarm; but will meet the crisis as I ought; and, in the language of my oath of office, will decide it, according to the best of my skill and judgment."[39]

Wythe understood, moreover, that judicial duty did not differentiate between questions of individual right and government structure:

[36] Letter from Edmund Pendleton to James Madison, Sr. (Feb. 15, 1766), in *The Letters and Papers of Edmund Pendleton 1734–1803,* at 1: 23.

[37] Transcript of Edmund Pendleton's Notes of his Opinion in *Commonwealth v. Caton, et al.,* Library of Congress, Force Papers, at 8707, Series 7E, James McGuire Collection, Correspondence Folders.

[38] *Commonweath v. Caton & al.,* Call, *Reports,* 4: 8. In fact, Hale had felt obliged to remain on the bench as long as he could. Hale accepted judicial office during the Interregnum, under Oliver Cromwell, because it was *"absolutely necessary, to have Justice and Property kept up at all times,"* and it therefore *"was no Sin to take up a Commission from Usurpers, if he made no Declaration of his acknowledging their Authority."* This service under a usurper, however, tore at Hale's conscience. He initially sat on both civil and criminal cases, as long as he could avoid hearing "offences against the State," but he soon worried about condemning men to death on behalf of a treasonous regime, and he only persuaded himself to stay on the bench by abstaining from further criminal decisions. Of course, a judge could not ordinarily refuse to hear cases, and having accepted a commission he had a duty to serve in it rather than resign, let alone threaten to resign, but such was Hale's reputation that Cromwell accepted the compromise. Hale thus "continued administering Justice" until his commission came to an end with Cromwell's death in 1657. At this point, although Richard Cromwell pressed Hale to accept another commission, Hale now felt *"he could act no longer under such Authority."* Gilbert Burnett, *The Life and Death of Sir Matthew Hale,* 36, 38–40, 49 (London: 1681). English judges, incidentally, had long before resolved that judicial acts under a usurper would remain valid upon the restoration of the king. *Swyrenden & Bagot v. Ive,* Y.B. Paschal, 9 Edward IV, pl. 2, Trinity, pl. 3 (1469), discussed by Paul Vinogradoff, "Constitutional History and the Year Books," *Law Quarterly Review,* 29: 279 (1913).

[39] *Commonweath v. Caton & al.,* Call, *Reports,* 4: 8.

> I have heard of an english chancellor who said, and it was nobly said, that it was his duty to protect the rights of the subject, against the encroachments of the crown; and that he would do it, at every hazard. But if it was his duty to protect a solitary individual against the rapacity of the sovereign, surely, it is equally mine, to protect one branch of the legislature, and, consequently, the whole community, against the usurpations of the other.

He therefore declared that "whenever the proper occasion occurs, I shall feel the duty; and, fearlessly, perform it." Even "if the whole legislature . . . should attempt to overleap the bounds, prescribed to them by the people, I, in administering the public justice of the country, will meet the united powers, at my seat in this tribunal; and pointing to the constitution, will say, to them, here is the limit of your authority; and, hither, shall you go, but no further."[40] He thus showed "that an Anti-constitutional Act of the Legislature would be void; and if so, that this court must in Judgment declare it so, or not decide according to the Law of the land."[41]

Most of the other judges agreed with Pendleton and Wythe that the statute was constitutional and therefore did not discuss whether they could hold an unconstitutional statute void, but at least two joined Wythe in addressing this larger question. On the one hand, Peter Lyons spoke "[a]gainst the Power of the Court to declare an Act of the Legislature void, because it was agt the Constitution"—although he did not rely upon this point, as he thought "this Act was not so." James Mercer, on the other hand, thought the Constitution reserved the power of pardoning to the House of Delegates and concluded that "[t]he Court must Declare the Constitution Superior to the Act."[42]

40 Ibid.

41 Transcript of Edmund Pendleton's Notes of his Opinion in *Commonwealth v. Caton, et al.*, Library of Congress, Force Papers, at 8716, Series 7E, James McGuire Collection, Correspondence Folders. Pendleton reported that Wythe defended this position with "several strong & sensible reasons of the nature of those used by Ld Abbington." Ibid.

42 Ibid. Call reported the opinions of Wythe and Pendleton in detail and then summarized: "Chancellor Blair and the rest of the judges, were of opinion, that the court had power to declare any resolution or act of the legislature, or of either branch of it, to be unconstitutional and void." Call, *Reports,* 4: 20. This appears, however, to be one of the generalities with which Call stitched together quotations, and it therefore cannot be relied upon.

Summarizing the opinions on the constitutionality of the statute, Pendleton wrote less than a week after the decision that the Court held "by 6 Judges against two, that the Treason Act was not at Variance with the Constitu[tio]n," which "it was thought . . . was the best Interpretation w[hi]ch the Inaccurate words of the Constitution would admit of." Letter from Edmund Pendleton to James Madison (Nov. 8, 1782), in *Papers of James Madison* 5: 261, eds. William T. Hutchinson and William M. E. Rachal (Chicago: University of Chicago Press, 1967). To another participant, it seemed that the judges had avoided the constitutional question by taking an optimistic view of the constitutionality of the statute. Putting aside the high-flown rhetoric of his argument in court, Attorney General Randolph now

At the time, Pendleton thought the case "was reduced" to a matter "of small moment, by the opinion of the Court that the Treason law was not contrary to the constitution."[43] Certainly many historians have agreed, for being a case that did not declare a statute void, it could not have been a precedent by which the judges established judicial review. Yet like so many other cases "of small moment," it is instructive. In no constitutional decision did lawyers and judges more elaborately display hesitancy about the judicial role than in *Commonwealth v. Caton.* The dispute over this question, however, was largely staged at the instigation of commentators and the Court of Appeals. In fact, the parties did not contest the judicial role, and the leading members of the bar and bench whose views are known in detail—the Attorney General, the Chief Justice, and one of the Chancellors—seem to have understood that law and judicial duty required the judges to hold unconstitutional statutes unlawful.

Connecticut's Customary Constitution

This chapter on the circumstances in which judges did not hold statutes unconstitutional must close with America's only customary constitution. In

---

bluntly observed: "The judges of the court of appeals avoided a determination, whether a law, opposing the constitution, may be declared void," and "[t]here surely was prudence in the path, which they took. But I doubt not, that to any but lawyers the construction, by which the two were reconcile[d,] would appear unintelligible." Letter from Edmund Randolph to James Madison (Nov. 8, 1782), ibid., 5: 263.

[43] Letter from Edmund Pendleton to James Madison (Dec. 9, 1782), ibid., 5: 382. The House of Delegates responded to the decision by questioning whether the judges were correct about the constitutionality of Treason Act's provision on pardons. The Senate obviously had already become skeptical of its power under the Treason Act, and now the House of Delegates—struck with a new concern that "so much of the Act . . . as vests the power of Pardon for such Offences in the General Assembly is unconstitutionable"—passed a bill restoring pardons for treason to the House. House of Delegates, Journals, 43–44 (Nov. 19, 1782), LVA; also in LVA, House of Delegates, Rough Bills, Resolutions, etc., Box 6 (Nov. 21, 1782). At this point, however, the Senate balked. With the benefit of a judicial ruling upholding its participation in the pardon power under the Treason Act, it was content to leave the statute on the books.

The two houses at least agreed on the fate of the prisoners. After the Court's decision, a newspaper speculated that "the unfortunate criminals, who have for a long time been suspended between hope and fear, will now probably be executed agreeably to their condemnation." Correspondence (Richmond, Nov. 9), *Virginia Gazette* (Nov. 9, 1782). The prisoners, however, petitioned for mercy, and the legislature pardoned them conditionally. House of Delegates, Journals, 32 (Nov. 15, 1782), LVA; An act granting a conditional pardon to certain offenders (1782), in *Laws of Virginia,* 11: 169. Pendleton wrote to James Madison in December that "the poor fellows are since pardon'd by the Assembly upon condition of the Banishment of two of them, & the third's [Caton's] becoming a Continental Soldier for the War." He added that "this method of recruiting has been used with several other Criminals, and if they prove good Soldiers they will make the state abundant amends for former offences." Letter from Edmund Pendleton to James Madison (Dec. 9, 1782), in *The Letters and Papers of Edmund Pendleton, 1734–1803,* at 433.

a nation of express constitutions, it often is forgotten that Connecticut took a less traveled path. The state self-consciously claimed to have a customary constitution, and its judges therefore found themselves in a very different relation to the legislature than was typical in America.

Connecticut purported to have an "ancient" constitution similar to that of England. In 1776, when other states began to exchange their charters for express constitutions, Connecticut's General Assembly declared that the state would keep the form of government it had inherited in its 1662 charter. The charter itself seemed to have confirmed an already existing constitution authorized by the people, and the Assembly now made explicit that the state's constitution was an ancestral inheritance, which secured freedom primarily by making the legislature annually dependent upon the people:

> THE *People of this State . . . having from their Ancestors derived a free and excellent Constitution of Government whereby the Legislature depends on the free and annual Election of the People, they have the best Security for the Preservation of their civil and religious Rights and Liberties.*

The General Court therefore *"Enacted and Declared"* that "the ancient Form of Civil Government, contained in the Charter from *Charles* the Second, King of *England,* and adopted by the People of this State, shall be and remain the Civil Constitution of this State, under the sole authority of the People thereof."[44] As the future Chief Justice Zephaniah Swift later explained, "[t]he constitution which originated from the people . . . continued in operation, after the declaration of independence, in the same manner as before, and was equally valid."[45]

Like Parliament, which in 1689 enacted the English Declaration of Rights as an enumeration of what it claimed were ancient constitutional rights, the Connecticut legislature in 1776 carefully listed the rights of the people of the state in a declaration of their ancient constitution. The Connecticut General Court was not the only legislative body in America

[44] An Act containing an Abstract and Declaration of the Rights and Privileges of the People of this State, and securing the same (1776), *Acts and Laws of the State of Connecticut, in America,* 1 (New London: 1784). Connecticut's almost unlimited legislative power had little appeal elsewhere in America, but it was not considered entirely implausible, even in a written constitution. In North Carolina, before Samuel Johnston had experience with state government, he wrote: "Some have proposed that we should take up the Plan of the Connecticut Constitution, for a Ground work but with some amendments. . . . After all it appears to me that there can be no check on the Representatives of the People in a Democracy but the people themselves." Letter of Samuel Johnston to James Iredell (Halifax, Apr. 20, 1776), in *The Papers of James Iredell,* 1; 350–351, ed. Don Higgenbotham (Raleigh, N.C.: Division of Archives and History, 1976).

[45] Zephaniah Swift, *A System of the Laws of the State of Connecticut,* 1: 57 (Windham: 1795).

to enumerate rights, but whereas, for example, the Virginia convention adopted the Virginia Declaration of Rights while acting as a "convention" of "the representatives of the good people of Virginia," the General Court of Connecticut merely acted as a legislature and claimed to declare what the people had already inherited *"from their Ancestors."*[46] It thereby made clear that the people enjoyed their rights under their ancient custom rather than through any express act of their own.

Even more than the customary constitution of England, the constitution of Connecticut concentrated almost all executive and judicial power within the legislature and, indeed, within its Council or upper house. The Council—consisting of the governor and lieutenant-governor, plus twelve assistants—was the effective power in the state, and the governor hardly constituted a separate branch of government, for he merely presided as an *ex officio* member of the Council and had no veto or much other independent power.[47] As in England, the legislature preserved its place above the judicial courts, and when it laid out the court system, it authorized a "Superior Court of Judicature" only after declaring that "the Supreme Power and Authority in this State" rested in the General Court.[48] In 1784, the legislature conceded that members of the Superior Court should not be members of the legislature, but at the same time it created a higher "Supreme Court of Errors"—formed by the lieutenant-governor and the Council—which amounted to little more than a judicial subcommittee of the General Court.[49]

In these circumstances, the judges of the judicial courts, like those in England, had to defer to the constitutional determinations of the legislative court. Zephaniah Swift defended this supremacy of the legislature by explaining that "[p]reviously to their passing any act," the legislators "must consider whether it be compatible with the constitution," and "[b]eing the supreme power, and bound to judge with respect to the question, in the

[46] Virginia Constitution of 1776, Preface; An Act containing an Abstract and Declaration of the Rights and Privileges of the People of this State, and securing the same (1776), *Acts and Laws of the State of Connecticut, in America,* 1 (New London: 1784).
[47] Richard J. Purcell, *Connecticut in Transition: 1775–1818,* at 117–18 (1918; Middletown: Wesleyan University Press, 1963). According to one historian, the governor held a position "compounded of dignity and shadow, scarcely having a separate, substantial existence." Henry Bronson, "Chapters on the Early Government of Connecticut," *Papers of the New Haven Colony Historical Society,* 3: 320 (New Haven: 1882).
[48] An Act for constituting and regulating Courts, and appointing the Times and Places for holding the same, *Acts and Laws of the State of Connecticut, in America,* 27, 29 (New London: 1784).
[49] An Act for regulating the Appointment of the Superior Court (1784), ibid., 267. Purcell writes that the Assembly "closely approximated the British Parliament." Purcell, *Connecticut in Transition: 1775–1818,* at 120.

first instance their decision must be final and conclusive." From this perspective, "[i]t involves the most manifest absurdity, and is degrading to the legislature, to admit the idea, that the judiciary may rejudge the same question which they have decided; and if they are of a different opinion, reverse the law, and pronounce it to be a nullity." Going even further, Swift declared:

> [W]here the judiciary are independent of the people and the legislature, and hold their offices by an appointment of the supreme executive, it is a total prostration of the government, to vest them with a power of deciding that legislative acts are null. The legislature will lose all regard and veneration in the eyes of the people, when the lowest tribunals of judicature are permitted to exercise the power of questioning the validity, and deciding on the constitutionality of acts.[50]

Of course, when a case turned on a *colonial* statute, the judges had to consider whether it was a lawful subordinate act under English law at the time of its adoption, and they thus could hold it void—this being what the judges of Connecticut's Superior Court apparently did in 1785 in the *Symsbury Case*.[51] The Connecticut courts, however, existed under a custom-

[50] Swift, *A System of the Laws of the State of Connecticut,* 1: 52–53. In an attempt to justify the Connecticut constitution in populist terms, Swift claimed that the legislature's "supreme power" was limited by the people themselves:

> The legislature are not under the controul or superintendence of the judiciary—if they pass laws which are unconstitutional, they are responsible to the people—who may in the course of elections dismiss them from office, and appoint such persons as will repeal such unconstitutional acts. On this power of the people over the legislature, depends their security against all encroachments, and not on the vigilance of the judiciary department.

Ibid., 53. As Timothy Dwight later observed: "The power of the legislature is considered as unlimited, except with respect to the rights of election, and the substance of the form of government." Timothy Dwight, *Travels in New England and New York,* 1: 196 (Cambridge: Belknap, 1969), also quoted by Purcell, *Connecticut in Transition: 1775–1818,* at 121. Although Swift and Dwight had political reasons to emphasize the elections, they might also have mentioned the social and cultural constraints, which were at least as significant, particularly in light of the election practices of Connecticut, which effectively gave life terms and even rendered many offices hereditary.

Corwin and Kramer quote Swift as evidence of opposition to judicial review in the United States. Edward S. Corwin, "The Establishment of Judicial Review," *Michigan Law Review,* 9: 283, 310–311 (1911); Larry Kramer, *The People Themselves: Popular Constitutionalism and Judicial Review,* 104–105 (Oxford: Oxford University Press, 2004). For example, Kramer relies on Swift to show that "any statement describing what judicial review 'was' should be treated with caution because a range of views existed as to both its propriety and its nature." Ibid., 104. Swift's views, however, were peculiarly adapted to Connecticut, where the legislature exercised even greater communal and judicial power than Parliament.

[51] See Chapter Eleven.

ary constitution, and indeed under a supreme legislative court, and they therefore could not hold a state statute unconstitutional.[52]

[52] Incidentally, the customary character of the Connecticut constitution is suggestive as to why Justice Samuel Chase turned to natural law in *Calder v. Bull.* In this case, the lawyers for Calder and his wife argued that a resolution of the Connecticut General Court granting a new trial in a probate proceeding was unconstitutional, and although they mostly insisted that the resolution violated the *ex post facto* clause of the U.S. Constitution, they also argued about the state's constitution. They suggested that the legislature had adopted "the charter as the Constitution" and that it had "[n]o power to act as a court but by enacting" that it would be a court, which it had not done. Bull's lawyers countered that the constitution was "made up of usages" and that the "[d]ecisions of the State courts," including apparently the General Court, should be considered "Precedents." Notes of Arguments in *Calder v. Bull,* James Iredell, Memorandum Book, 1798–1799, at 22, 43, Duke University Rare Book, Manuscript, and Special Collections Library, James Iredell Papers, M-5355. All of the judges other than Chase acknowledged the unlimited extent of legislative power under the Connecticut constitution, even though it "may, indeed, appear strange to some of us." Chase, however, protested in dicta that "I cannot subscribe to the *omnipotence* of a *State Legislature,* or that it is *absolute and without controul;* although its authority should not be *expressly* restrained by the *Constitution* . . . of the State." Drawing on familiar natural law modes of argument about tacit limitations on government in the absence of an express constitution, he explained that "[t]he purposes for which men enter into society will determine the *nature* and *terms* of the social compact," and without distinguishing between political and judicial remedies, he added that even without an express constitution, "[t]he *nature,* and *ends* of *legislative power* will limit the *exercise* of it." *Calder v. Bull* (U.S. Supreme Court 1798), Dallas, *Reports,* 3: 387–388, 398. To modern ears, this was a declaration of unwritten, natural law constraints, which operated alongside express constitutions. In fact, Chase was responding to the peculiar circumstances of Connecticut, and like many earlier, English writers, he used natural law to discern the powers to which the people under a customary constitution could be presumed to have refused their consent.

Notwithstanding his notion that under a customary constitution, judicially enforceable limits on government could be inferred from natural law, Chase recognized that under an express constitution, natural law was relevant to a court's constitutional reasoning mostly for purposes of interpretation. Thus, when he said that "[t]he obligation of a law in governments established on *express compact, and on republican principles,* must be determined by the *nature* of the *power,* on which it is founded," he understood that such reasoning simply created a presumption against dangerous or unjust powers that had not been expressly granted: "It is against all reason and justice, for a people to entrust a Legislature with such powers; and, therefore, it cannot be presumed that they have done it." This allowed Chase to contemplate judicially enforceable, natural limitations on the government of Connecticut while merely saying of the federal government that "All the powers delegated by the people of the United States to the Federal Government are defined, and NO CONSTRUCTIVE powers can be exercised by it." Ibid., 387–388.

Although Chase had attempted to distinguish the implication of his views for the Connecticut constitution and the U.S. Constitution, his reasoning still threatened the authority of both the people of the Union and the peoples of the states. Iredell therefore responded with the conventional understanding that when "the Legislature of the Union, or the Legislature of any member of the Union, shall pass a law, within the general scope of their constitutional power, the Court cannot pronounce it to be void, merely because it is, in their judgement, contrary to the principles of natural justice." He then added the traditional objection to treating natural law as if it were the measure of legal obligation: "The ideas of natural justice are regulated by no fixed standard: the ablest and the purest men have differed upon the subject." Ibid., 399.

Having only a customary constitution, the people of Connecticut had to rely on their legislators to protect their rights. This would not have seemed safe in most states, but the people of Connecticut understood themselves to enjoy a relatively homogenous society, largely undisturbed by immigration and other intrusions, and being united by their relative equality and their shared ancestry, many of them felt a strong, almost ethnic attachment to their traditional form of government. Their elected leaders, who exercised power through the state legislature, were bound to the constitution not merely by their annual election (really, their annual reelection) but also by their identification with their constitution and their sense of accountability—whether to their neighbors in their small towns, to their ministers, or to a more demanding judge in the world to come. Identity and accountability, both communal and religious, thus rendered the constitution so inflexible and strongly binding that judicial and even most structural restraints on government seemed largely unnecessary.[53] This was hardly a model for protecting rights that could have much appeal in the rest of the nation, especially when American life was becoming all the more mobile, diverse, and otherwise fragmented. Nonetheless, while this model flourished in a small corner of the continent, it reminded Americans of what it meant to have a customary constitution, and it still today suggests why the rest of the nation preferred express constitutions.

There were a range of reasons why Connecticut's type of constitutional custom—a custom that was strongly binding even though not judicially enforceable—could have little future in America. Even during the colonial period, as observed by a Massachusetts lawyer in 1773, there could

---

As it happens, shortly after *Calder* was argued, but before it was decided, the counsel for the plaintiff in a North Carolina case adopted the view (perhaps taken from the Connecticut arguments) that even if a statute was not an *ex post facto* law, it could be held "contrary to natural justice, and therefore void," and this gave Iredell a trial run in North Carolina for the opinion he would more famously deliver in the Connecticut decision. *Minge v. Gilmour* (C.C.D.N.C. 1798), Federal Cases, 17: 443, number 9631. Note also that the opinions in *Calder* printed by Dallas appear to have been solicited afterward from each of the judges. See, for example, Letter from A. J. Dallas to Judge Cushing (Nov. 8, 1798), Massachusetts Historical Society, William Cushing Papers, William Cushing 1798 File.

[53] For those, such as Noah Webster, who desired constitutional change, this customary or habitual conception of the constitution was stultifying. Webster had high hopes that men could create their own nation, their own language, and even themselves, and he therefore in Enlightenment fashion condemned legislative deference to custom as an irrational superstition or fear that barred legislative improvements, arguing that "[t]he Constitution of Connecticut is . . . a very bad one, not because the legislature *cannot* reform it, but because *they dare* not. An idea of some constitutional powers paramount to their own in the government, together with habit, prevents a reformation of the worst evils that can befall a government." Letter of Noah Webster to Thomas Jefferson (Dec. 12, 1790), in *Letters of Noah Webster*, 88, ed. Harry R. Warfel (New York: Library, 1953).

not be "in this country" the "[u]sage & custom" that was "from time whereof the memory of man is not to the contrary," for "the records shews the beginning."[54] The Revolution, moreover, was a rejection of much that was customary, including England's customary constitution. Most deeply, as already suggested, Americans lived in a sort of society in which they could not expect to be bound together by custom, let alone the social cohesion necessary to sustain it, and they therefore felt peculiarly dependent on express constitutions and judicial enforcement.

As the ideal of constitutional custom came under attack in Connecticut, some defended it as part of the people's "steady habits," but their habits might easily become all too unsteady.[55] Even rural Connecticut was becoming integrated with the economy and politics of the nation, and as individuals grew more self-conscious of their connections outside the state and their differences within it, they lost their attachment to their leaders and to their constitution as a shared inheritance. Republicans sought power by stimulating this shift in perceptions, most profoundly by encouraging the people of Connecticut to question whether they could rely on each other and especially their legislature to protect their rights: "If all men were perfectly wise and honest, we should want no constitution nor laws." In the world as it was, however, "legislators *stand as much in need of* constitutions, *to bind them and to limit their powers, as the* people *do of* laws, *to limit and control their conduct.*"[56] The people of the state thus came to believe they required more formal protection than mere steady habits; they had to ensure that their "rights" were "sure and stedfast, moored and grappled to our very soil, by the sheet anchor of a Constitution" rather than "still fluctuating on the wild waves of party politics."[57] The fractured character of Americans thus seemed to require a written constitution that protected liberty from the legislature rather than through it, and after an extended struggle over

[54] *Cesar v. Greenleaf* (Sept. 1773), [Reports of Cases], 3, *William Plumer Papers,* Mfm Reel 19, Legal Papers (copied from a report taken by Theophilus Parsons).

[55] Even the phrase "steady habits" was a retreat from the notion of ancient, inherited custom, for as David Daggett in particular understood, the state's system could no longer adequately be defended on entirely traditional terms. [David Daggett], *Steady Habits Vindicated* (Hartford: 1805).

[56] *William Judd's Address to the People of the State of Connecticut, on the Subject of the Removal of Himself and Four Other Justices from Office, by the General Assembly of Said State, at Their Late October Session, For Declaring and Publishing Their Opinion That the People of this State Are at Present Without a Constitution of Civil Government,* 13 ([New Haven]: 1804). Gaines suggests this was written by Abraham Bishop.

[57] "A Federal Republican," *The Politics of Connecticut: or, a Statement of Facts,* 11 (Hartford: 1817). Focusing on the party politics, Purcell observes that the Republicans thought "a constitution was invaluable, for whichever party was in control would use its position to hinder the opposition." Purcell, *Connecticut in Transition: 1775–1818,* at 164.

their constitution and ultimately over the character of their society, the people of Connecticut in 1818 finally joined the peoples of almost all other states in adopting an express constitution that could be enforced by the judges.

Connecticut's experience is suggestive of the broader tendency of American society and law. At the very least, it reveals how modernizing social developments left men peculiarly dependent upon formal law and enforcement, including written constitutions and judicial decisions holding statutes unconstitutional. The underlying social developments, however, did not end in 1818, and although they could erode communal attachment to a customary constitution and the legislature that declared it, they might also eventually undermine the attachment of individuals to written constitutions and conventional understandings of their provisions. Even formal constitutional law and enforcement rested on a depth of communal attachment and meaning, and as these foundations have become ever more dilapidated, it has been ever less clear how the formal structures can be sustained.

For now, it is enough to observe that the circumstances in which judges did *not* hold legislation unconstitutional are almost as revealing as the circumstances in which they did. In Connecticut's customary constitution, as in England's, judgments about the constitutionality of enactments belonged to the legislature rather than the judges. In states with express constitutions, however, even such cases as did not hold statutes unconstitutional can hint at the strength of judicial duty. In such states, the judges frequently handled constitutional questions concerning legislation with the confidence of men who understood what their office required.

VI

INDEPENDENCE AND AUTHORITY IN AMERICA

Judges had an office that at its most idealistic height was as narrow and elevated as a wire, and this taut path was particularly evident in matters of independence and authority. Judicial office required judges to exercise independent judgment in deciding cases, and it thereby gave them authority in expounding law, including constitutions. Their office thus placed them above the fray of politics and allowed them heightened authority, but it also left them at some risk if they stepped beyond their line of duty.

Chapter Sixteen observes how, as in England, the ideal of judicial office required and in a sense enabled judges to exercise judgment free from will—not least when they held government acts unconstitutional. Chapter Seventeen then explains how judges enjoyed authority in their exposition of law, including constitutions, while they remained within their office. In both ways—as to independence and authority—their office imbued them with much strength but sharply limited the circumstances in which they could enjoy it.

Although these implications of judicial office for independence and authority were already evident in England, they became especially pronounced in America, where fissiparous circumstances accentuated concerns about the boundaries of the different parts of government. In response to claims for lawmaking power, the English had become acutely aware of the different nature of judicial office and its independence and authority, and now, in a society in which ideals of lawmaking power were even more prominent, many Americans responded with particularly tight, clear-cut understandings of judicial office. The judges thus found themselves confined to a narrow space, but as long as they remained within their office, they could confidently enjoy the freedom and authority associated with it.

16

Independence

In America even more than England, judgment required independence from will. Judicial independence is sometimes taken to be a matter of power, which the judiciary exercises, as a branch of government, in response to the power of another branch, usually the legislature; and from this point of view, judicial independence almost gets reduced to an exertion of judicial will in opposition to legislative will. Yet far from considering their decisions in relation to legislative power an exercise of power or will, American judges apparently understood themselves to be acting on ideals of judgment. Their ideal of their office was one of judgment almost divinely unimpeded by will, and with this understanding of their identity and duty, judges could rise above a wide range of impediments, including legislative challenges.

The judges, however, were only human, and in a society in which the real power lay in the people, the legislature was hardly the most serious problem. In such a society, the question over the long term was not so much whether the judges could withstand external, institutional assertions of will as whether they could preserve their independence from the popular or at least populist sensibilities that would infiltrate their judgment from within. This internal subversion of judgment was not yet a persistent threat, but already there were hints of the danger that might lie ahead.

Internal Independence

Like their English predecessors, Americans worried about internal threats to the independence of judges—as became particularly clear when the Constitutional Convention in 1787 debated a council of revision. A judge's will, predisposition, or prejudice could simultaneously compromise his judgment and invade legislative power, and Americans, even more than the English, recognized the symmetry of this problem, which they succinctly captured under the rubric of "separation of powers."

The internal threat to judgment from human will remained a familiar theme in moral philosophy. Although the conventional distinction between the understanding and the will remained commonplace, a further faculty of the soul, the affections, had by now become a familiar explanation of what biased the judgment or swayed the will—thus partly secularizing the Augustinian or Protestant model of the soul by supplementing the grace of God with the mixed effects of worldly pain and pleasure. John Witherspoon taught generations of Princeton students that "[t]he faculties of the mind are commonly divided into these three kinds, the understanding, the will, and the affections," and that "[i]t is the soul or mind that understands, wills, or is affected with pleasure and pain." Even if an undisturbed judgment of the understanding could determine the will, the affections were apt to lead men away from dispassionate judgment. As Witherspoon explained, "[t]he affections are called also passions because often excited by external objects," and "[i]n as far as they differ from a calm deliberate decision of the judgment, or determination of the will, they may be called strong propensities, implanted in our nature, which of themselves contribute not a little to bias the judgment, or incline the will."[1]

Proposals for a federal council of revision invited questions about the judges' internal independence, because if a judge participated in making a statute, he might be predisposed toward the dictates of his will when later required to decide the enactment's lawfulness. Although English judges had stopped giving formal advisory opinions to the executive on particular cases that might come before them judicially, they continued in the House of Lords to give advice on legislation, not to mention opinions on writs of error and appeals.[2] In contrast, American judges ordinarily lacked any place in legislative proceedings, but they could be included on councils of revision, which exercised not only a sort of judgment but also a discretionary power over legislation not unlike the Privy Council's old power to disallow corporate and colonial laws. The danger was clearest in New York. For fear that "laws inconsistent with the spirit of this constitution, or with the pub-

[1] John Witherspoon, *An Annotated Edition of Lectures on Moral Philosophy,* 71–72, ed. Jack Scott (Newark: University of Delaware Press).

[2] Stewart Jay, *Most Humble Servants: The Advisory Role of Early Judges,* 7, 13, 21, 46 (New Haven: Yale University Press, 1997). The last of the former type of opinion was in 1760. Ibid., 20.

lic good, may be hastily and unadvisedly passed," the New York Constitution established a council of revision—consisting of the governor and at least two judges—"to revise all bills about to be passed into laws by the legislature." If the Council declared a bill "improper," the legislature could adopt the bill into law only by overriding the Council with a two-thirds vote of each house.[3]

When a proposal for a federal version of such a council came before the Constitutional Convention in Philadelphia, it stimulated a fierce debate, which remains revealing about how Americans viewed internal threats to independent judgment. The proposal came from James Madison and James Wilson, the most philosophically inclined of the framers. Fearing that the underlying danger in the new republic would be the force of popular and thus legislative power, they hoped to counteract the strength of Congress by joining the judicial to the executive power in a council of revision.

Although colleagues pointed out the risks to judicial office, Wilson and Madison persisted in their demands for a council of revision, for they considered this institution so "useful" that they thought the compromise of judgment a small price to pay.[4] Madison acknowledged that there was some "weight" to the "objection" that "the Judges ought not to be subject to the bias which a participation in the making of laws might give in the exposition of them," but he then observed "[h]ow much good on the other hand" would arise from this participation. Although he initially mentioned the benefit "the Code of laws w[oul]d receive from the Judiciary talents," his

[3] New York Constitution of 1777, Article III. In contrast, the Pennsylvania and Vermont Councils of Censors were elected and thus did not necessarily include judges.

[4] Madison's Notes (July 21, 1787), in *The Records of the Federal Convention of 1787,* at 2: 74, ed. Max Farrand (New Haven: Yale University Press, 1937). Madison went on at length about how "useful" the council would be. Ibid., 2: 73.

The controversy is revealing about the tensions that were possible between functional demands for a balance of power and more conventional expectations of a separation of powers. Madison and Wilson pursued so functional a view of a balance of power that they were relatively indifferent to what others considered the natural distinction among the different powers of government. Madison recognized, however, that he had to defend his council of revision from attacks based on the theory of separation of powers, and he therefore argued that the judiciary's participation in legislation was an addition to "the Theory in the Constitution"—explaining that the judiciary would acquire "a defensive power" with which it could "maintain the Theory in practice." Ibid. Most of Madison's colleagues also hoped to establish an effective balance of power within the government, but they wanted a balance that would preserve the natural boundaries of each government power. If the powers separated in government had foundations in nature, and if the separation of these powers was essential to preserve liberty, then a balance of power seemed politically plausible only to the extent it did not undermine the nature of the different powers—in this instance, the nature of judgment.

primary concern was "the utility of annexing the wisdom and weight of the Judiciary to the Executive" and thus securing a balance of power.[5]

The advocates of the scheme did not help matters when they argued that judges on the council of revision would be able to bar not only unconstitutional statutes but also those that were unjust. Wilson complained:

> Laws may be unjust, may be unwise, may be dangerous, may be destructive; and yet not be so unconstitutional as to justify the Judges in refusing to give them effect. Let them have a share in the Revisionary power, and they will have an opportunity of taking notice of these characters of a law, and of counteracting, by the weight of their opinions the improper views of the Legislature.

George Mason—who would soon display his own willful judgment on the Fairfax County Court—similarly worried that although the judges "could declare an unconstitutional law void," they "would be under the necessity as Judges to give . . . a free course" to "every law however unjust oppressive or pernicious, which did not come plainly under this description." Mason therefore joined Wilson in wanting "the further use to be made of the Judges, of giving aid in preventing every improper law."[6]

Men with greater attachment to the ideal of independent judgment reacted sharply to the proposed council. Elbridge Gerry of Massachusetts raised "doubts whether the Judiciary ought to form a part" of it, "as they will have a sufficient check agst. encroachments on their own department by their exposition of the laws, which involved a power of deciding on their Constitutionality." Gerry concluded that "[i]t was quite foreign from the nature of ye. office to make them judges of the policy of public measures."[7] Rufus King of Maryland seconded that "the Judges ought to be able to expound the law as it should come before them, free from the bias of having participated in its formation."[8]

At a higher level of generality, John Dickinson of Pennsylvania resisted the threat to independence by noting the maxim that "you must separate the Leg. Jud. & Ex." He conceded that it might therefore seem puzzling for

[5] Madison's Notes (June 6, 1787), ibid., 1: 138–140. In this second round, Wilson at least saw that each judge was accustomed to enjoying independent judgment in his office, and he therefore proposed that the "National Executive" be joined in the revisionary power by "a convenient number of the national Judiciary." Ibid.

[6] Madison's Notes (July 21, 1787), ibid., 2: 73, 78.

[7] Madison's Notes (June 4, 1787), ibid., 1: 97–98.

[8] Ibid., 98. According to another account, he said that "the Judicial ought not to join in the negative of a Law, because the Judges will have the expounding of those Laws when they come before them; and they will no doubt stop the operation of such as shall appear repugnant to the constitution." Pierce's Notes (June 4, 1787), ibid., 1: 109.

American constitutions "to give the Executive a share in Legislation," for if the executive was included, "why not the Judicial"? He explained that "[t]here is a Difference—the Judges must interpret the Laws," and thus "they ought not to be legislators."[9] Others pursued the separation of powers by observing that the Judges "are not to be presumed to possess any peculiar knowledge of the mere policy of public measures."[10]

Over the course of the summer, Wilson and Madison made four attempts to obtain versions of their council of revision, and consequently no proposal was so repeatedly rejected—the primary reason being that it created an internal threat to the independence expected in judicial office. Opponents again and again elaborated their views that the council of revision would establish "an improper coalition between the Executive & Judiciary departments."[11] Nathaniel Ghorum summarized the fears of his colleagues when he observed: "All agree that a check on the Legislature is necessary," but there were "objections agst. admitting the Judges to share in it which no observations on the other side seem to obviate"—the most substantial objection being that "the Judges ought to carry into the exposition of the laws no prepossessions with regard to them."[12]

[9] King's Notes (June 4, 1787), ibid., 1: 108. In another account, Dickinson said that "the one is the expounder, and the other the Executor of the Laws." Pierce's Notes (June 4, 1787), ibid., 1: 110.

[10] Madison's Notes (July 21, 1787), ibid., 73. For this reason, Nathaniel Ghorum of Massachusetts "did not see the advantage of employing the Judges in this way," to which he added: "Nor can it be necessary as a security for their constitutional rights." Ibid. Similarly, after condemning the proposal as a "dangerous innovation," Luther Martin of Maryland said that "[a] knowledge of mankind, and of Legislative affairs cannot be presumed to belong in a higher deg[ree] to the Judges than to the Legislature. And as to the Constitutionality of laws, that point will come before the Judges in their proper official character." Madison's Notes (July 21, 1787), ibid., 2: 75–76.

[11] Madison's Notes (July 21, 1787), ibid., 2: 75–76. Gerry observed that "[i]t was making Statesmen of the Judges; and setting them up as guardians of the Rights of the people." Of course, it had long been said in England and America that the judges were guardians of the people's liberties, but the judges were now being elevated as guardians outside their judicial role, and beyond this point Gerry "relied for his part on the Representatives of the people as guardians of their Rights & interests." Ibid. Gerry also observed that the proposal "was making the Expositors of the Laws, the Legislators," and this "ought never to be done." Upon hearing this, Caleb Strong of Massachusetts agreed, saying that "the power of making ought to be kept distinct from that of expounding, the laws," for "[t]he Judges in exercising their function of expositors might be influenced by the part they had taken, in framing the laws." Ibid., 75.

[12] Madison's Notes (June 6, 1787), ibid., 2: 79–80. The other objection was that the judges would "outnumber the Executive." Ibid. The more significant point was, as John Rutledge of South Carolina stated it, that "the Judges" were "of all men the most unfit to be concerned in the revisionary Council" and that they "ought never to give their opinion on a law till it come before them." Ibid. Later, Charles Pinckney "opposed the interference of the Judges in the Legislative business," for "it will involve them in parties, and give a previous

The framers of the Constitution could do little to guarantee this internal independence. They at least, however, had to avoid undermining it, and they therefore rejected an institutional structure that would have sapped the independence of the judges from within.

External Independence

The most immediate threat to independent judgment in America came from state legislatures, and although American judges usually lacked adequate constitutional protections against this external interference, they could fall back, like English judges, on the underlying ideal of independent judgment. It is customary to think about judicial independence in terms of constitutional guarantees of freedom from specific external dangers, and this institutional conception of the problem suggests that ideas of independence must have changed in America, where it was no longer the Crown but state legislatures that posed a threat. The ideal of independence, however, had never been centrally about external power; instead, the ideal had always essentially been about the office of independent judgment. In this office, the judges needed to overcome not only external impositions of will but also, more basically, their own mental failings, and this internally focused ideal could allow American judges to preserve their judgment against dangers from any direction, executive or legislative.

The external dangers to judicial office had shifted. Although seventeenth-century English judges regularly faced pressures from the Crown, eighteenth-century American judges encountered repeated intrusions from legislatures, especially their lower houses. Already in England, after the Revolution of 1688, the judges began to suffer at least as much from the House of Commons as from the king. Some colonial judges similarly experienced trouble from lower legislative houses in America—as when in 1693 the South Carolina House of Commons complained about courts that questioned the "[v]alidity" of acts of the Assembly.[13] It was but an early hint of how the dangers would increasingly be legislative.

A late but illuminating example of a moment of transition occurred during a Massachusetts controversy over salaries—a dispute in which the

---

tincture to the opinions." Only John Francis Mercer is known to have approved the motion on the ground that he "disapproved of the Doctrine that the Judges as expositors of the Constitution should have authority to declare a law void." Madison's Notes (Aug. 15, 1787), ibid., 2: 298.

[13] *Journals of the Commons House of Assembly of South Carolina for the Four Sessions of 1693,* at 17 (Jan. 18, 1693), ed. A. S. Salley (Columbia: Historical Commission of South Carolina, 1907).

Crown and a colonial legislature each feared the other as the threat to judicial independence. Traditionally, the General Court of Massachusetts had annually voted rather inadequate judicial salaries for the past year, and it could not always even be counted on for these amounts. This short leash had "kept the judges dependent," and the Crown therefore in 1772 considered offering the judges the security of regular payments. The Crown's approach, however, would have substituted royal grants for those of the legislature, and fearing that the Crown was bidding for the loyalty of the judges, the General Court increased the judges' annual salary and paid it "for the year to come." In addition, the House of Representatives demanded that each judge renounce any royal salary and accept only the annual grants from the Assembly. "Ten years before this time," as Governor Hutchinson observed, "the judges would have excused themselves from giving an answer to such a demand; but the house of representatives was become more powerful." Perhaps for this reason, but also because salaries had historically been paid by the legislature, three of the judges complied with the request of the House. A blunt refusal, however, came from the obstinate Chief Justice Peter Oliver, and for his independence from the legislature and his attachment to Britain, he soon found himself impeached. Anxious to protect both Oliver and the Crown, Governor Hutchinson barred a trial of the impeachment, but he could not prevent the dispute from falling into the hands of the people, some of whom "refuse[d] to appear and act" as grand jurors until the Chief Justice was tried.[14] The populace thus acted to protect

[14] Thomas Hutchinson, *The History of the Colony and Province of Massachusetts-Bay,* 3: 279, 317, 326, ed. Lawrence Shaw Mayo (Cambridge: Harvard University Press, 1936); Joseph H. Smith, "An Independent Judiciary: The Colonial Background," *University of Pennsylvania Law Review,* 124: 1150 (1976). For the articles of impeachment and Oliver's response, see *Essex Gazette* (March 1–8, 1774). The response of jurors can be illustrated by a 1774 Worcester protest to the justices, which began: "We the subscribers being returned by our Respective Towns to serve as Jurors of Inquest for this Court, beg Leave humbly to inform your Honours that it is agreeable to the sense of those whom we represent we should not impannel nor be sworn into this important Office provided Peter Oliver Esq[r] Sits as chief Justice of this Court." They explained that "as he Stands impeached by the Grant Inquest of the Province & that in the Name of the People of high Crimes & Misdemeanors it would be treating that respectable Body with great Contempt . . . to acknowledge him as suitable to fill this Office and act under him as Jurors till his Impeachment is passed upon & he is regularly acquitted of those Crimes laid to his Charge by the Supreme Court of the Province." To the Honourable his Majesty's Justices of the Superior Court of Judicature &c. Now Sitting at Worcester (1774), American Antiquarian Society, Worcester County Papers, Box 1, Court Petitions 1732–1819, Folder 12.

The way in which fears about Britain led some Americans to want their judges to be dependent on the people can be observed already in the writings of John Dickinson. He thought that "the judges ought, in a well regulated state, to be equally independent of the executive and legislative powers." He explained, however, that the danger in America was different from that in England: "The chief danger to the subject *there,* arose from the arbijudicial independence by boycotting a judge who had good reason to think that his freedom was thereby being threatened.[15] It is not clear whether the greatest danger came from the Crown, the legislature, or the people, but threats to judicial independence could evidently come from many different quarters.

The people would soon more formally and appropriately protect judicial independence in their constitutions, and therefore when challenges to judicial independence came from state legislatures, the judges could sometimes rely on constitutional guarantees of their freedom. Yet even the best of constitutions could not bar all external threats, and many states had only minimal or poorly drafted guarantees of independence, thus leaving the judges in such states particularly dependent upon their ideal of independent judgment.[16]

The Massachusetts Constitution illustrates how difficult it was to protect against all legislative pressures and how judges therefore still had to rest on their ideals. Although the Massachusetts Constitution followed the English Act of Settlement in protecting both tenure and salaries, it did not clearly enough bar the Commonwealth's traditional policy of annual grants. In its Declaration of Rights, the Constitution observed that "[i]t is essential to the preservation of the rights of every individual . . . that there be an impartial interpretation of the laws, and administration of justice," and to this end it secured judicial tenure and salaries. It even did so with an acknowledgment of the mere humanity of judges:

> It is the right of every citizen to be tried by judges as free, impartial and independent as the lot of humanity will admit. It is therefore not only the best

---

trary *designs of the crown;* but *here,* the time may come, when we may have to contend with the *designs of the crown, and of a mighty kingdom.*" The former was bad enough, "yet what innumerable acts of injustice may be committed, and how fatally may the principles of liberty be sapped, by a succession of judges *utterly independent of the people?*" "Letters of a Farmer in Pennsylvania," Letter IX (1768), in *The Writings of John Dickinson,* 1: 367, ed. Paul Leicester Ford (Philadelphia: Historical Society of Pennsylvania, 1895). The solution lay in salaries: "If the commission of the judges are *during the pleasure of the crown;* yet if their salaries are *during the pleasure of the people;* there will be *some check* upon their conduct." Moreover, "[f]ew men will consent to draw on themselves the hatred and contempt of those among whom they live, for the empty honor of being judges." Ibid., 370–371.

15 The ironies are discussed by Barbara Aronstein Black, "Massachusetts and the Judges: Judicial Independence in Perspective," *Law and History Review,* 3: 101 (Spring 1985).

16 Americans had not previously had much success in establishing satisfactory guarantees of independence, because the Privy Council had assiduously barred colonial attempts to establish American judges with tenure. As explained by the Board of Trade as to New York, tenure for judges would be "destructive to the Interests of Your Majesty's Subjects and tending to Lessen that just dependance which the Colonies ought to have upon the Government of the Mother Country." Report of Board of Trade on New York (Nov. 23, 1762), *Acts of the Privy Council,* 4: 499–500 (London: His Majesties Stationery Office, 1911).

> policy, but for the security of the rights of the people, and of every citizen, that the judges of the supreme judicial court should hold their offices as long as they behave themselves well; and that they should have honorable salaries ascertained and established by standing laws.[17]

Although this was elegantly stated, it did not bar the legislature from giving the judges inadequate permanent salaries and then usually supplementing these with variable additional amounts. The legislature was therefore able to continue its old policy of leaving the judges dependent on annual grants, and the judges therefore had to sustain their independence by rising above their concerns about their compensation. Unable to do this, several engaged in private practice on the side, thus preserving their independence from the legislature by risking their independence among private parties.[18]

The Pennsylvania Constitution was worse on tenure and better on pay, for it gave the judges of the Supreme Court terms of only seven years,

[17] Massachusetts Constitution of 1780, First Part, Declaration of Rights, Article XXIX.

[18] When the House in 1790 considered corrective legislation, its draft resolve noted that "several Justices of the Peace and several persons who hold and exercise Judicial Offices in this Commonwealth . . . continue to practise the Law, which may render them too liable to temptation & ought not any longer to be permitted among us." The bill, however, was not passed, probably because it would have had to be accompanied with an increase in salaries. An Act to prevent Judges of any of the Courts in this Commonwealth from practising the Law, Resolve making valid the doings of Justices, MSA, House of Representatives, Miscellaneous 1790, No. 3372.

Chief Justice Francis Dana drafted a memorandum in the very early nineteenth century arguing that the legislature should establish permanent salaries, and not surprisingly he emphasized that it was the role of the judges to hold unconstitutional legislation void and that they therefore should not be dependent on occasional legislative grants. The Question touching the Independence of the Justices of the Supreme Judicial Court, as well with respect to their Salaries, as to the Tenure of their Office, considered on legal and constitutional grounds (c. 1803–1806?), in Blue Notebook, Massachusetts Historical Society, Dana Family Papers, Ms. N-1088, Box 34, Folder: Francis Dana Notebooks.

The irregular method of paying salaries came to an end only when Theophilus Parsons in 1806 hesitated to accept the position of chief justice. He had helped to draft the Constitution, and he now explained in a long letter to the Governor that "by the Constitution of this Commonwealth, a permanent and honorable salary ought to be annexed to the office of a judge of the Supreme Judicial Court, and that all grants in part of this salary . . . which are not permanent, are against the provisions of the Constitution." He therefore accepted the office with the caveat that he could not "lawfully take what . . . the General Court cannot lawfully grant" and that therefore the fixed base salary was the "[t]he only salary . . . I can receive." *Memoir of Theophilus Parsons,* 228–229 (Boston: Ticknor and Fields, 1859). Shortly afterward, Joseph Story introduced the bill that fixed higher salaries. Simon Greenleaf, *A Discourse Commemorative of the Life and Character of Joseph Story,* 16–20 (Boston: 1845); William W. Story, ed., *Life and Letters of Joseph Story,* 1: 130 (Boston: Little & Brown, 1851).

For the difficulty of framing a provision against inappropriate increases in salary, see Madison's Notes (July 18, 1787), in *Records of the Constitutional Convention,* 2: 45; Speech of James Madison in Virginia Ratification Convention (June 20, 1788), in *The Documentary History of the Ratification of the Constitution,* 10: 1417, eds. John P. Kaminski et al. (Madison: State Historical Society of Wisconsin, 1990).

but it at least guaranteed them "fixed salaries."[19] Even this, however, did not constrain the Pennsylvania Assembly, which in 1781 blatantly reduced the judges' pay.[20] According to one commentator, "[t]he judicial branch of government" thus "becomes a creature of the legislative."[21] A committee of the Pennsylvania Council of Censors more moderately observed that "[j]udges should have nothing to hope or fear from any one." On this ground, it recommended that "[*p*]*ermanent salaries* should, without delay, be established by act of Assembly."[22]

[19] Pennsylvania Constitution of 1776, Chapter 2, Article 23.
[20] In 1778 the Assembly allowed the Chief Justice £1000 and the assistant judges £500 per annum, but in 1781 it reduced these amounts, giving the Chief Justice £900, the second justice £400, and the others only £300. An Act for the Support of Government, and the Administration of Justice (Dec. 27, 1781), *Laws Enacted in the Sixth General Assembly of the Representatives of the Freemen of the Commonwealth of Pennsylvania,* 2: 6 (Philadelphia: 1783) (volume 3 of the Laws of Pennsylvania). See also *A Report of the Committee of the Council of Censors* [on the legislative body], 22 (Philadelphia: 1784).
[21] Letter to Mr. Claypoole, *Pennsylvania Packet* (Apr. 23, 1782).
[22] *Journal of the Council of Censors,* 126 (Philadelphia: 1783). The executive of Pennsylvania also troubled the state's judges, but without much success. One case was that of Aaron Doan, in which the executive sought to diminish the punishment stipulated by law. Doan and his family had conducted raids against Americans, and upon indictment, he fled. He had therefore been outlawed and attainted by the judges in accord with procedures established by a Pennsylvania statute. Appalled at the thought of executing a man without trial, President John Dickinson and the Supreme Executive Council of the state refused to issue a warrant for Doan's execution and wrote to the judges with questions about the reasoning underlying their decision. The judges answered, but they carefully prefaced their response with caution that "the judges do not hold themselves bound to assign any reason for their judgments; and when they do give reasons, it is always *in public.*" They explained that "[t]his is mentioned, that the present proceedings may not be drawn into precedent." Their general answer was that "[i]f there be any thing improper in taking away the life of a man upon an attainder by a judicial outlawry, it belongs to the Legislature to alter the law in this particular; the judges cannot do it. But [the Executive] Council can interpose their mercy." *Respublica v. Doane* (1784–1785), Dallas, *Reports,* 1: 89–90. Rather than give way to the Court by simply pardoning Doan, Dickinson and the Council handed the matter to the Assembly, and when the legislature concluded that the judges had done their duty and that it could not interfere, Dickinson persisted so far as to leave Doane neither executed nor pardoned. The next president, Benjamin Franklin, finally pardoned Doan in 1787. G. S. Rowe, "Outlawry in Pennsylvania, 1782–1788 and the Achievement of an Independent State Judiciary," *American Journal of Legal History,* 20: 239–240 (1976).

In 1784, in the tumultuous case of the Chevalier de Longchamps, the executive again pressured the judges with questions—this time seeking greater punishment than the law allowed rather than less. Longchamps had assaulted Marbois, the aide to the French minister, and already before trial Dickinson asked the judges whether Longchamps could be delivered to the French, but the judges explained this was not possible. G. S. Rowe and A. W. Knott, "Power, Justice, and Foreign Relations in the Confederation Period: The Marbois-Longchamps Affair," *Pennsylvania Magazine of History and Biography,* 104: 286 (1980). After a jury found Longchamps guilty, Dickinson and the Supreme Executive Council responded to the demands of the French minister by asking the judges to postpone passing sentence until they had considered three questions: whether the defendant, a Frenchman, could be legally delivered to the French minister; whether he could be imprisoned until the French king declared that "the reparation is satisfactory"; whether, if he could be so impris-

This combination of a wayward legislature, an inadequate constitution, and the consequent need of judges to rely on their high-minded ideals was also evident in other states, and in North Carolina there is detailed evidence of one judge's response. The state's 1776 Constitution merely provided that judges and the attorney general were to "hold their offices during good behavior" and that together with the governor, they were to have "adequate salaries during their continuance in office."[23] Their salaries, however, were low, and several years after James Iredell quit the bench on this account, he argued that the legislature should protect the independence of the judges and the attorney general with better salaries:

> As nothing can be of more consequence than to have the judiciary department of Government well filled, and rendered absolutely independent, we think liberal Salaries should be provided for the Judges and Attorney General, and made equally permanent with their commissions, otherwise they cannot be truly independent, which is a point of the utmost moment in a Republic where the Law is superior to any or all the Individuals, and the Constitution superior even to the Legislature, and of which the Judges are the guardians and protectors.[24]

Three years later, during *Bayard v. Singleton,* when some feared that the judges would abuse their decisions about the constitutionality of statutes, Iredell answered (with more skill than satisfaction) that there was little reason to worry because the judges were "in fact dependent on the Assembly" for their salaries. The judges were only "nominally independent in point of station, when the Assembly may every session determine how much they shall have to subsist upon."[25]

---

oned, the Council could do anything to bring this about. The Court complied by hearing arguments and then bluntly sent the executive its opinion that Longchamps could not be delivered to the French, that he could not be imprisoned until the French king was satisfied because punishments must be "as the laws *expressly* prescribe," and that the third question was therefore "rendered unnecessary." The Court then proceeded to sentence Longchamps according to law. *Respublica v. De Longchamps* (Oyer and Terminer, Philadelphia, Oct. 1784), Dallas, *Reports,* 1: 115–116. In the Doan and Longchamp cases, the judges were polite, even accommodating, in considering the requests of the executive, but firm in their judgments.

[23] North Carolina Constitution of 1776, Articles XIII and XXI.

[24] "Instructions to Chowan County Representatives: To Charles Johnson Esqr Senator, and Thomas Benbury and Samuel Johnson Esqrs. Members of the House of Commons for the County of Chowan, and William Cumming Esqr. Member for the Town of Edenton (Sept. 1783), in *Papers of James Iredell,* 2: 449, ed. Don Higginbotham (Raleigh: Department of Cultural Resources, 1976).

[25] James Iredell, "To the Public" (Aug. 1786), Duke University Rare Book, Manuscript, and Special Collections Library, James Iredell Papers, Box 1.

Incidentally, the right of the judges to choose their clerks—familiar from English cases such as *Scroggs v. Coleshill*—was discussed in North Carolina in November 1784. The clerk of Washington County, William Cocke, had been elected in 1778 to the House of Com-

Notwithstanding that they had inadequate constitutional protection, the North Carolina judges could still rest on their ideal of independence, and when they faced the displeasure of an impeachment committee, in part for their delay in *Bayard v. Singleton,* even the irresolute Judge Samuel Ashe, who did not have the strength to attend the committee, defended his freedom from the legislature by looking inward. The outward point of law was that although judgments were reversible, a judge was not institutionally accountable for his errors:

> [F]ar be it from me to say, I have committed no Errors, it would be a presum[p]tion I am incapable of—for I do not pretend to infallibility—but my errors have been those of the head, unattended with any corruption or turpitude—the wisest men daily fall into such—look into the law books, where may be seen, a Judge giving an Opinion one day, and retracting it as error, at another;—where may be seen the Judge of one Court reversing for error, the Opinion of a Judge of another Court, and where may be seen, the House of Lords reversing the Opinion (as erroneous) of a whole Bench of Judges—and yet these errors have never been considered criminal, nor the Judges put to answer for them.[26]

Nonetheless, Ashe was being put to answer for his errors—at least, that is, what he took to be mere errors—and he therefore had to find independence

---

mons, only to be excluded because he held office as a clerk. Subsequently in 1782 and 1784, he was elected to the Senate without impediment from that house, until the Assembly in November 1784 forced him to choose between his two places by enacting that "from and after the present session . . . every person holding a public office of profit . . . shall be . . . incapable of being elected as members to serve in the general assembly, or to enjoy seats therein; and any member of the general assembly who shall accept any such office shall thereby vacate his seat"—all of which was said by the Assembly to be based on "the spirit of the constitution, and the principle of a genuine republic." An act to prevent persons holding offices of profit from enjoying seats in the general assembly, *Acts of Assembly of the State of North-Carolina, At a General Assembly begun and held at Newbern on the Twenty Second of October, in the Year of Our Lord One Thousand Seven Hundred and Eighty-Four,* 40 ([1784]). This prompted Thomas Iredell to report, not quite accurately, to his brother James: "The Assembly they say had dismissed Mr. Cock from the Office of Clerk[.] [P]ray is not that an Infringment on the Judges right." Letter from Thomas Iredell, Jr., to James Iredell (Nov. 19, 1784), in *The Papers of James Iredell,* 3: 105, eds. Donna Kelly and Lang Baradell (Raleigh: North Carolina Department of Cultural Resources, 2003).

[26] Letter from Judge Samuel Ashe to the Speakers of the Houses of the General Assembly (Dec. 14, 1786), in NCSA, General Assembly, Session Records 1786–1787, Box 3, Joint Resolutions—Committee of the Whole of Two Houses on Administration of Justice Folder. This did not satisfy some, such as Archibald Maclaine, who protested that "the plea of the Judges, that an error in judgement is no misdemeanor, cannot apply to most of the charges against them, and if admitted in the present instance, may be used hereafter to justify them in committing the greatest enormities." Archibald Maclaine, "Protest against the resolution of the House of Commons, declaring that the Judges ought not to be accused of any misdemeanors in office" (Jan. 1787), in NCSA, General Assembly, Session Records 1786–1787, Box 3, Joint Resolutions—Committee of the Whole of Two Houses on Administration of Justice Folder.

within. He was a decidedly mediocre judge, who had better reason than most to admit "humanum est errare," but he served in his office and defended his external freedom with an internal independence and integrity drawn from one who did not err:

> At my first appointment to the office, sensible of the importance of it, I entered upon it, not with levity, but awe; lifted up my heart to heaven, & implored its support, and determined that the wealth of empires should not allure, nor the Crush of worlds deter me from a religious & faithful discharge of it;—in this resolution I have persevered,—& I am now bold to challenge all the world, to fix one act of corruption or one single act of Turpitude upon me—no Sirs it can not be done, for my integrity is with me, My hands are clean & my heart is pure—pardon this vanity of boasting—the occasion has warmed & constrained me into it.[27]

Ashe's strong will, weak judgment, and poor health often got the better of him, particularly when he lacked the stomach for unpopular decisions. Yet even while succumbing to nervous fears and opiates, he understood how he had bound himself to his office, and with clarity about the height of his obligation, he defended his independence and ultimately did his duty.

Not merely in North Carolina but also elsewhere, this sort of religious devotion to the ideal of independent judgment could allow judges to rise above external assaults. The Rhode Island legislature annually appointed the judges for terms of a single year, and when the judges decided *Trevett v. Weeden,* Chief Justice Mumford preserved his position by remaining discreet. His colleague Thomas Tillinghast, however, was one of those who held the statute in the case void or at least ineffective. In so doing, he obviously sacrificed his reappointment, but notwithstanding the danger to his external independence, he found an internal freedom within his duty. He explained afterward that "he felt himself perfectly independent, while moving in the circle of his duty" and that "however he might be affected for the honour of the State, he was wholly indifferent about any consequences that might possibly respect himself." His opinion had "resulted from mature reflection, and the clearest conviction," and "he was happy in the persuasion that his conduct met the approbation of his God!"[28]

[27] Letter from Samuel Ashe to the Speakers of the Houses (Dec. 14, 1786), NCSA, General Assembly, Session Records 1786–1787, Box 3, Joint Resolutions—Committee of the Whole of Two Houses on Administration of Justice Folder.

[28] James M. Varnum, *The Case, Trevett against Weeden,* 43 (Providence: 1786). Similarly, his colleague Judge Hazard said that the judges' "obligations were of too sacred a nature for them to aim at pleasing but in the line of their duty." He added that it was "well known that my sentiments have fully accorded with the general system of the Legislature in emmiting the paper currency . . . but it was not possible to resist the force of conviction," and whether or not it was correct, "we derived our understanding from the Almighty, and to him only are

For American judges, the inward independence necessary to preserve their outward independence was already becoming singularly difficult, because "in a Democratical Government like ours," as Iredell had pointed out, "it is the interest of every Man ambitious of public distinction to make himself pleasing to the People." The most serious external threat to judicial independence in America therefore came not so much from the institutions of government as from the people, and under this inexorable pressure, which the judges felt as much within as without, the "great danger" was "of Men sacrificing their honour to their popularity, if their principles & firmness of mind are not of a texture to keep them steady in an honorable course."[29]

American judges thus required more fortitude than English judges of the prior century, for they more clearly stood alone. It had been difficult enough for judges to maintain their independence in England. There, when holding acts of the Crown unlawful, the judges could often be confident of popular support, and it is likely that this sense of popular sympathy gave some of the judges the courage to do their duty—although it also led Hale and others to caution themselves against desiring popular applause. In America, however, the underlying popular force of the society and the power of its government were typically aligned, and the judges therefore had to expect that the weight of popular sentiment would not be behind them if they held an act of government unlawful. In particular, as Hamilton observed, "it would require an uncommon portion of fortitude in the judges to do their duty as faithful guardians of the constitution, where legislative invasions of it had been instigated by the major voice of the community."[30] This was the lesson that judges such as Ashe in North Carolina and Tillinghast in Rhode Island learned so painfully. From the majority of their society, these men could at best hope for the restraint of a people who understood the necessity of leaving their judges unmolested, and in this sense, far more than in the past, the judges had a lonely task.

In sum, the threat from without ultimately had to be resisted within. No constitution was or could be drafted to forbid the full range of external dangers, and therefore even when judges under a well-drafted constitution attempted to fend off outward threats, they still had to look inward to the

we accountable for our judgment." Ibid. Like Ashe in North Carolina, Howell had observed that "error is the lot of humanity" and that judges could not be "accountable to the Legislature, in matters of opinion." Ibid., 39.

29 Letter from James Iredell to Richard Dobbs Spaight (Aug. 26, 1787), in *The Papers of James Iredell,* 3: 307–308.

30 Alexander Hamilton, Federalist Number 78, *The Federalist,* 528, ed. Jacob E. Cooke (Middletown: Wesleyan University Press, 1961).

ideal of independent judgment. This was a solitary endeavor, and it often required all the religious faith or at least intestinal fortitude a judge could muster.

Legislative Interference with Judicial Proceedings and Judgments: Massachusetts and New Hampshire

Among the legislative threats to judicial independence were challenges to the judgments and other proceedings of the courts. Rather than challenges to the independent judgment of the men who held judicial office, these were attacks on the institutional authority of their courts to proceed and give final judgments, but here too the judges could respond by adhering to their duty. It has sometimes been thought that when the judges faced this sort of legislative threat, they instrumentally held the offending acts void to protect their institutional interests—as if they were exercising will on behalf of their court or branch of government. They seem typically to have understood, however, that if they were to respond while remaining within their office, they had to exercise judgment in the pursuit of their duty without allowing any intrusion of will. Whether the legislative interference threatened their personal judgment or (as will now be seen) the institutional proceedings and judgments of their courts, their office and duty established but also limited their means of defense.

The understanding that legislatures should not interfere with judicial proceedings was hardly new. The most notorious case occurred in 1705 after John Paty and others sought damages from local officials who barred them from voting, and the House of Commons imprisoned the plaintiffs for a breach of privilege. In the subsequent habeas corpus proceedings, Chief Justice Holt opined in his dissent that "[w]hen the people qualified do elect their representatives, they give them power and authority to act legislatively, not ministerially or judicially," and on the basis of this separation of powers, he held that the Commons had unlawfully asserted a power "to restrain and diminish" the "liberty of the subject" to seek a judicial remedy—a liberty "secured to every one by the fundamental laws and constitution of the kingdom."[31] The narrow question about the privilege of the Commons in election cases went unresolved in 1705, and it did not even approach the larger question as to whether an act of Parliament could constitutionally prevent individuals from pursuing their otherwise rightful ju-

[31] *Case of Paty et al.* (Q.B. 1705), *The Judgements delivered by the Lord Chief Justice Holt in the Case of Ashby v. White and Others, and in the Case of John Paty and Others,* 60–61 (London: 1837).

dicial remedies. Nonetheless, if the resolution of cases generally belonged to the judges, then the legislature as well as the Crown had to avoid interfering in judicial proceedings, and although this ideal could not always be vindicated in the courts, it came to be widely venerated, not least in Parliament.[32] The ideal was less often respected by colonial legislatures, but it was very much on the mind of the Privy Council, which vigorously attempted to prevent colonial legislatures from hearing appeals or authorizing new trials.[33] After Independence, state legislatures generally conceded that judicial and legislative power had been granted to different branches of government, and most state legislatures therefore more or less abandoned their remaining attempts to alter the course of particular judicial proceedings. Yet there remained open questions about the constitutionality of some types of legislative intrusion—particularly in states such as Massachusetts and New Hampshire, where many legislators still assumed that in granting new trials after judgment, they were not interfering with judicial proceedings.

The Massachusetts legislature went so far as to consider staying judicial proceedings. English judges had taken a statutory oath to resist any royal request for a delay, and in America an executive or legislative stay in judicial proceedings was even more clearly a constitutional question. In Massachusetts at one point, perhaps in 1783, there apparently was a proposal for the legislature to stay an action in the Court of Common Pleas, and the Massachusetts Senate responded by seeking an advisory opinion from the judges as to whether such a resolve would be "consistent with the Constitution."[34] This was a version of the caution that might be hoped for

32 A hint as to how lawyers could take this view to heart can be observed in an early eighteenth-century treatise attributed to Hale, which interpreted a medieval precedent to show that "the Judges took no Regard to the Reversal [of the case] in Parliament, for that was not the Place where it ought to be revers'd." *The Original Institution, Power and Jurisdiction of Parliaments,* 53 (London: 1707). (The case was Y.B. Pascal 39 Edward III, pl. 28, fol. 14a (1365), and the treatise interpreted "Council" to mean "Parliament.") The ideal of noninterference, however, was sometimes qualified by the assumption that Parliament might in emergencies have to suspend habeas corpus.

33 As so often, English ideals collided with colonial practice. Whereas some colonial legislatures still heard appeals and otherwise decided matters ordinarily left to judicial proceedings, the Privy Council tended to disallow such decisions, at least when they took the form of statutes and so were vulnerable to disallowance. Joseph Henry Smith, *Appeals to the Privy Council from the American Plantations,* 637–645 (New York: Columbia University Press, 1950). The Council even objected to legislation that merely set aside prior judicial proceedings and authorized new trials, and in one instance, in 1770, it obtained the opinion of Chief Justice Wilmot that such a decision by the Rhode Island Assembly was an illegal and "usurped jurisdiction." Ibid., 650–651. There were also American protests against the legislative "practice of rejudging causes" that had been decided in the courts of law. See, for example, "Conservator" No. 7, *Connecticut Journal* (Apr. 19, 1771).

34 Draft Opinion of the Judges on the Question "Whether it be consistent with the Consti-

from an upper house, and what is known of at least one judge's opinion is very revealing about the limits on the judges' ability to defend their institution: The judges in their decisions could not defend themselves from legislative interference with the proceedings and judgments of their courts unless the interference collided with the law and thus came within their duty.

Only Chief Justice William Cushing's draft opinion has been located thus far, and he left blanks where he could later fill in whether "I" or "we" endorsed the opinion. Cushing began by observing that according to the thirtieth article of the Massachusetts Declaration of Rights, "[t]he Legislative shall never exercise the judicial power." But what did this mean for a legislative stay of judicial proceedings? Of course, the judicial branch by itself could not stay its proceedings:

> For the judicial to stay an action & all proceedings thereon,—would be to suspend the course of law and justice—& is not therefore within the judicial power. The business of the judicial, is to distribute justice to the Subject, according to fixt rules in the regular course of Law, & therefore it would be against their duty & trust, thus to Suspend an Action.

A legislative order staying an action, however, "tis not so properly an exercise of the judicial power, as the Suspending the exercise of the judicial power. And the question is, whether the Legislative are intrusted with this power by the Constitution."

On this issue, rather than exercise will to defend the judiciary, Cushing evidently confined himself to doing his duty, for he concluded that the Constitution gave the legislative a suspending power. King James II had claimed a power to suspend the laws and their execution, and against this abuse, the twentieth article of the Massachusetts Declaration of Rights stated that such powers "ought never to be exercised but by the Legislature, or by authority derived from it."[35] Article 20 further stated that the legislature was to exercise this power of suspending the laws or their execution "in such particular cases only as the Legislature shall expressly provide for." Accordingly, "[i]f this Art[icle] does not include the power in question," Cushing "kn[e]w not what Ideas to affix to the Article." He noted that James had abused his suspending power and that "[t]he like abuse or usur-

---

tution, for the Legislature to order an action depending in the Court of Common pleas, & all proceedings thereon to be stayed" (1783?), Massachusetts Historical Society, William Cushing Papers, 1783 File.

[35] Ibid. Article 20 stated: "The power of suspending the laws, or the execution of the laws, ought never to be exercised but by the legislature, or by authority derived from it, to be exercised in such particular cases only as the legislature shall expressly provide for." Massachusetts Constitution of 1780, First Part, Declaration of Rights, Article 20.

pation of power is guarded against" by an article that "seems aimed to restrain the Supreme Executive, by reserving such power solely to the Legislative." Cushing thus acknowledged that the Constitution in Article 20 merely shifted the danger from one branch to another, and he therefore could only hope that "the Wisdom of the Legislature will not make such extraordinary interposition to prevent the trial of private right in the standing Course of Law, but upon urgent & extraordinary reasons—of which, however, they are the Judge."[36]

It has been seen that against intrusions on the independence of their personal judgment, the judges could ultimately defend themselves and their office simply by exercising independent judgment in doing their duty. Similarly judges could hold off interference with the institutional judgments and proceedings of their courts by independently doing their duty. Yet as illustrated by the Massachusetts proposal to stay judicial proceedings, there was one difference: The institutional interference affected the power of the courts rather than merely the judges' own independent judgment, and therefore, as recognized by Cushing, the judges in the course of doing their duty could only hold off the institutional interference to the extent it was barred by the law itself.

[36] Draft Opinion of the Judges (1783?), Massachusetts Historical Society, William Cushing Papers, 1783 File. He noted that "[b]y the 11th Article, 'Every Subject—ought to find a certain remedy, by having recourse to the laws, for all injuries—to obtain right & justice freely—Compleatly—& promptly, conformably to the laws,'" but "[t]his Article seems merely directory to the judicial."

In notes that Cushing apparently prepared for this opinion, he experimented with a very different argument: that a legislative stay of an action would violate Article 10 of the Bill of Rights, which, as he noted, declared that individuals had a right to be protected in the enjoyment of their life, liberty, and property "according to *Standing Laws*." Although he initially emphasized these last words, Cushing soon drifted in another direction—toward the article's takings and compensation clause. According to Cushing, "it seems inconsistent with the Spirit of the Article, that the Legislative have power to take from an individual his property, except the public Exigence requires it, & even then, without giving him a Compensation therefor." Having ended up with this principle, Cushing then began his argument about the particular case: "Now in the Case stated for our opinion—A subject demands damages & Satisfaction for an injury or supposed injury done to his person & Liberty, by another." Cushing then gave up on this argument and apparently wrote his other draft, which recognized what the constitution explicitly allowed. Draft Opinion beginning "By the 10. Artc[l] of y[e] bill of rights" (1783?), in Massachusetts Historical Society, William Cushing Papers, 1783 File.

The advisory opinion on a suspending power was soon forgotten. Certainly it was not remembered when the dispute between William Vans and the executor of John Codman prompted renewed discussion of the question—for example, in *Power of the Legislature to Suspend a Law for the Benefit of an Individual in Massachusetts,* 13 (Boston: 1835). The author traced the drafting history of the clauses on suspension and reached a conclusion similar to that of the judges in the early 1780s. Ibid, 16–17. In contrast, see *Holden v. James* (Supreme Judicial Court, 1814), *Massachusetts Reports,* 11: 396, holding that the legislature could not repeal or suspend a law by relieving an individual of its operation.

Several years later, in 1787, the Massachusetts Senate asked the judges whether the General Court could at least intrude after criminal proceedings—in particular, whether the legislature could commute a punishment after sentencing—and on this question the law was such that the judges could defend their judgments by doing their duty. The request for their opinion was part of yet another attempt to moderate the criminal laws without altering them. It will be recalled that while Jefferson's bill for proportionate punishments languished, he and other governors of Virginia had attempted to soften the effect of their state's criminal laws by granting conditional pardons, and that when the judges of Virginia in 1785 held the conditions unconstitutional, the legislature temporarily authorized the governor to make such grants.[37] Although this experiment soon came to an end in Virginia, it was noticed by reform-minded legislators in other states, including Massachusetts. In 1787 some Massachusetts senators observed that "doubts have arisen whether a Pardon can with propriety be extended to an offender upon the express Condition, of his submitting to some other punishment," and they therefore proposed that the legislature authorize the governor to grant pardons "upon Condition."[38] The Senate, however, balked on the third reading. The reformers therefore instead suggested that the legislature itself could commute punishments. This threatened not only the executive's pardon power but also the judgments of the courts in criminal cases, and probably for at least one of these reasons, the Senate asked the judges "to give their Opinion, whether the General Court have a right, agreeably to the Constitution, in any case to commute a punishment, inflicted by Law, after sentence has been given."[39]

The judges were "all of opinion that the General court have not [such] a right." They depended on the legislature for annual supplements to their salary, but they did not hesitate to decide in accord with what they understood to be the law: "Our opinion is founded upon the VIIIth Art. of the 1st Sect. of the II^{d} chap. of the Frame of Government, which lodges the power of pardon, *after* conviction, solely in the Governor, by & with the advice of Council." The judges understood that when the Senate spoke of commuting punishment, it really "meant, a right of pardoning upon condition of the Convict voluntarily submitting to a less punishment," and this was "a necessary incident" to the governor's pardoning power. Although the judges

[37] See Chapter Twelve.

[38] An Act respecting Conditional Pardons, MSA, Senate Documents, Rejected Bills 1787, No. 802. Such authorization seemed necessary for any punishment "different in its kind, nature, or degree than that, by Law affixed to the particular Crime or offense for which he may stand Convicted." Ibid.

[39] Journal of the Senate, 185 (Oct. 31, 1787), Records of the States of the United States, microfilm.

thus rejected the legislative interference as an intrusion on the governor's power, they reminded the legislature in closing that there was a broader question, which they had not reached—a question that concerned not only the power of the executive branch but also perhaps that of the judicial: "And we need not cite the last article of the declaration of rights, which means to keep the Legislative, Executive & Judicial departments as Separate & distinct, as possible, in the exercise of the respective powers assigned them, by the Constitution."[40]

The sort of interference with the courts that the Massachusetts legislature most typically and vigorously pursued was its practice of granting new trials—what it called restoring men to their law—and it is this threat (initially considered in Massachusetts and then New Hampshire) that occupies the rest of this chapter. Although other threats to judicial proceedings and judgments had come before the judges of Massachusetts in requests for advisory opinions, legislators tended to be confident of their power to grant new trials, and this question therefore came to the Massachusetts judges in a case rather than an advisory opinion.

The case was *Giles Goddard v. Ebenezer Goddard and Hannah Metcalf,* and here again the personal independence of the judges in the course of doing their duty was the path by which they protected the institutional independence of their court. Hannah Metcalf and her husband had a homestead in Roxbury, and when Giles Goddard in 1786 claimed the property in the Suffolk County Inferior Court of Common Pleas, the sheriff served the summons on the current resident, who was Giles's nephew Ebenezer. This was Hannah's downfall, for as Ebenezer later admitted, "I never informed" Hannah or her husband about the summons "untill Judgment was recover'd" by Giles.[41] She and her husband thus suffered a default by non-

[40] Opinion of the Justices Respecting the Right of the Legislature to Commute a Punishment (Nov. 3, 1787), MSA, Senate Documents, Misc. 1787, No. 648, Box 18. In his later report of the opinion, Cushing altered some small details and after the word "incident" added a footnote justifying the opinion in the event that the Senate meant something other than a conditional pardon: "It might have been added at this mark of reference—'But if by such right—be meant a right of changing authoritatively the punishment of law—after sentence given—we are of opinion that it does not exist any where in the government.'" *Notes of Cases Decided in the Superior and Supreme Judicial Court of Massachusetts from 1772 to 1789—Taken by the Honble William Cushing,* fol. 61[r], Harvard Law School, Ms. 4083.

[41] Certificate of Ebenezer Goddard (Feb. 26, 1787), MSA, Resolves-1787, Chapter 32. This case is briefly noted by William E. Nelson, *The Americanization of the Common Law: The Impact of Legal Change on Massachusetts Society, 1760–1830,* at 230, note 228 (Athens: University of Georgia Press, 1994).

Giles Goddard was a housewright from Roxbury, and Ebenezer was his illiterate and apparently feckless nephew. Hannah Metcalf was the true defendant, who sought to retain an appearance, and they therefore petitioned the House of Representatives for a new trial. As their petition explained, Ebenezer "suffered the Action to be defaulted without giving the least notice therefore—in consequence of which your Petitioners have been injustly disseized . . . *under colour of Law.*"[42] It was a compelling claim, and the General Court in November 1787 adopted a resolve annulling the judgment against Hannah and her husband. The resolve allowed them to reenter their action at the Court of Common Pleas and "authorized & directed" this court "to proceed thereon according to law . . . in the same manner, as if the said action had been regularly continued."[43] By January 1788, however, Hannah's husband had died, and as the General Court had admitted her and her husband together to reenter their plea, she could not by herself take advantage of the existing resolve.[44] She therefore again petitioned the House of Representatives, which in March 1788 passed another resolve, "extend[ing] to her" and Ebenezer the "benefits" of the earlier one.[45] Giles therefore reiterated his claim for the land, and in July 1788 he again prevailed.[46]

The constitutional issue finally got resolved when Ebenezer and Hannah appealed to the Suffolk County Supreme Judicial Court. At the February term 1789, Giles demurred to any further proceedings in the case on the ground that the underlying legislation violated the Constitution's provision for separation of powers:

> [B]y the thirtieth article of the declaration of rights, it is declared, "That in the Government of this Commonwealth, the legislative department shall never exercise the executive and *Judicial* power, or either of them." That the Legislature of this Commonwealth cannot by act or resolve, nullify and re-

---

eight-acre property in Roxbury that earlier in the century had been the Goddard homestead. Her first, now deceased husband had purchased it in 1762 from Giles Goddard's uncle John. This troubled Giles, because his father and uncle inherited the property from their father in 1745, and John allegedly conveyed his interest to Giles's father in 1750—twelve years before John sold it to Hannah's first husband. Giles thus thought he had title from his father. He ended up having the sheriff serve the summons on Ebenezer because Hannah and her new husband, Jonathan, had leased the property to the town of Roxbury, which in turn had allowed Giles's nephew Ebenezer to live there. Petition of Jonathan and Hannah Metcalf (Feb. 1787), Extracts from the Records of Deed for the County of Suffolk, Summons to Ebenezer Goddard (May 1, 1786), Conveyance from John Goddard to John Newman [Hannah's first husband] (Dec. 1, 1762), MSA, Resolves-1787, Chapter 32.

42 Petition of Jonathan and Hannah Metcalf (Feb. 1787), MSA, Resolves-1787, Chapter 32.

43 Resolve of the General Court (Nov. 5, 1787), MSA, Resolves-1787, Chapter 32.

44 *Goddard v. Goddard* (Jan. 1788), MSA, fiche, Suffolk County Inferior Court of Common Pleas, Docket Jan. 1788, Docket No. 231.

45 Resolve of the General Court (March 28, 1788), MSA, Resolves-1787, Chapter 97.

46 *Goddard v. Goddard* (July 1788), MSA, fiche, Suffolk County Inferior Court of Common Pleas, Docket July 1788, Docket No. 222.

> voke a Judgment of Court, and the consequent proceedings thereon, without exercising the Judicial powers. That it plainly appears from the resolves of the General Court . . . that this suit is now pending here, on the *mere power and authority* of the same resolves.

Upon considering this plea, the judges decided that "they will take no further cognizance of this action, in consequence of the said Resolves."[47] If the power to overturn a judgment was judicial, it was exclusively within the constitutional power of the courts, and apparently on such reasoning the judges protected the power of their institution simply by doing their duty—by exercising independent judgment in accord with the law of the land.

Incidentally, during the course of the *Goddard Case,* the legislature began to recognize that it should at least share the power of restoring parties to their law, but although willing to share this power, it was not willing to abandon it. Just before the legislature first granted Hannah Metcalf a new trial, the House of Representatives proposed a joint committee to consider "the expediency of increasing the power of the Judicial Courts respecting new trials."[48] The House failed to persuade the Senate to concur, but by the next summer—perhaps because of Metcalf's return for second grant of new trial—both houses were ready to concede some authority to the courts, and they now enacted that the justices of the Supreme Judicial Court could review their own judgments as well as those of the Court of Common Pleas.[49] Even following *Goddard,* however, legislators continued to grant new trials. They were criticized for "their excentrick, extrajudicial decisions."[50] Yet most of them remained confident that their grants of new trial were entirely constitutional, for "[h]ow can this be called interfering in the judicial department; when they order the cause to be heard over again in a judicial court?"[51]

[47] *Goddard v. Goddard* (Suffolk County, Feb. 1789), MSA, Supreme Judicial Court, Mfm Reel 22, Record Book Sept. 1788–April 1789, fols. 129[v]–130[r].

[48] Journal of the Senate, 182 (Oct. 30, 1787), Records of the States of the United States, microfilm.

[49] An Act empowering the Justices of the Supreme Judicial Court, to grant Writs of Review in certain Cases (June 18, 1788), *Acts and Laws, Passed by the General Court of Massachusetts; Begun and held . . . the twenty-eighth Day of May, Anno Domini, 1788,* at 703 (Boston: 1788).

[50] Solon, Letter to Mr. Thomas (Apr. 2, 1790), *Massachusetts Spy* (Apr. 15, 1790). Solon generalized: "No judgment of a Court of law, be it ever so small, inconsiderable, or erroneous, should by the legislature be declared *null* and *void.* Because it is a direct exercise of the judicial power, and an express determination that the judgment, thus reversed, is wrong and erroneous; Which the Constitution plainly and clearly asserts, they shall not use or exercise." Ibid.

[51] Solon, Letter to Mr. Printer (from the *Gazetteer*), *New-Hampshire Gazette* (Dec. 11,

As it happens, the judges of the Massachusetts Supreme Judicial Court did not soon get another chance to hold legislative awards of new trial unconstitutional, for although disappointed litigants still obtained such grants, their lawyers understandably refrained from pressing the constitutional point in the Supreme Judicial Court. At least in the immediate aftermath of *Goddard,* lawyers practicing before Massachusetts' highest judicial tribunal apparently used legislative grants of new trial merely for bargaining, or for restarting litigation just long enough to reach a settlement, and they thus left the constitutional issue to linger in a sort of judicial limbo.[52]

1790). Solon replied that it was "an exercise of the judicial authority" and was "directly counter to the letter and spirit of the Constitution." Ibid.

52 The evidence is slight and much more research needs to be done, but it appears that the parties in these cases usually either agreed to limit the issues that could come before the judges or else did not even pursue their claims in court—presumably because they reached a settlement. Such at least is the pattern that can be discerned from the litigation on the five resolves that reopened proceedings in the Supreme Judicial Court during the five-year period from October 1788 through the end of 1793: (a) Resolve (Feb. 19, 1789) for the benefit of Noah Hall against Seth Williams, Admr., reopening case in Supreme Judicial Court, where the parties agreed to submit the case to referees. *Noah Hall v. Seth Williams* (Bristol County, Oct. term 1792), MSA, Supreme Judicial Court, Mfm Reel 22, Record Book 1792, at fol. 252[r]. (b) Resolve (June 3, 1790), for the benefit of Obed Hussey allowing him a new chancery of his bond (to account for payments he had made) against Nehemiah Rand, Admr. of estate of William Tufts in the Supreme Judicial Court, where Mary Hussey, administrator of Obed, "was allowed to enter this action in a manner and under circumstances specified in" an "agreement." *Mary Hussey, Extx. of will of Obed Hussey v. Nehemiah Rand, Admr. of estate of William Tufts* (Suffolk County, Feb. term 1791), MSA, Supreme Judicial Court, Mfm Reel 23, Record Book 1791, at fol. 38[r]. (c) Resolve (Feb. 14, 1791) for the benefit of Ann Marchant, Admr. of estate of John Marchant, against William M'Neil & Archibald M'Neil, allowing her to reenter her action in the Supreme Judicial Court, where the case does not appear to have been reheard. (d) Resolve (Jan. 1792) for the benefit of John Lucas and Edward Tuckerman, opining that it is expedient for them to have a writ of review of an action of covenant commenced by Thomas Beals against Joseph Barrell at the Supreme Judicial Court, where the case does not appear to have been reheard. (e) Resolve (March 13, 1793) for the benefit of Benjamin Edwards, who had won a judgment against William Oliver but had defaulted by failing to file a complaint upon Oliver's appeal, and who now was allowed to file a complaint against Oliver in the Supreme Judicial Court, where the case was filed, but neither party appeared. *Benjamin Edwards v. William Oliver* (Suffolk County, Aug. term 1795), MSA, Supreme Judicial Court, Mfm Reel 25, Record Book, at fol. 193.

In addition there were at least two resolves during this period that reversed decisions in the Supreme Judicial Court, but in a manner that apparently did not require further proceedings based on the resolve: (a) Resolve (March 1, 1790) for the benefit of Silas Fowler and his bail Abner Fowler voiding judgments against them on their recognizance in the Supreme Judicial Court. (b) Resolve (March 2, 1790) for benefit of Samuel Wells, reversing and rending null and void a sentence of outlawry against him in the Supreme Judicial Court.

It is possible that some judges or legislators drew a distinction among different types of legislative grants regarding judicial proceedings, and for these purposes they may have distinguished the decisions of the Courts of Common Pleas from those of the Supreme Judicial

In New Hampshire, litigants and their lawyers seem to have been more insistent about pursuing the constitutional question, and the judges therefore had greater opportunities to fend off the legislative meddling by doing their duty. New Hampshire's legislature had long been notably vigorous in restoring men to their law, and this tradition remained strong, especially in the House of Representatives.[53] This became clear when the Senate in 1786 made an attempt at reform by proposing that "all petitions for any . . . persons to be restored to their law" should be heard by the court in which the cause was "last pending" and that such court should decide "in as ample a manner as the General Court have usually done" whether to rehear the cause. The House predictably refused to concur.[54] It was not about

---

Court. This appears to have been the position that provoked Solon to argue that if the legislature "can legally declare the judgment of an inferior law court *null* and *void*," then "by the same rule they may make the like declaration upon a judgment of the highest law court of the State," which was little different from their "erecting themselves into a Judicial Court superior to the Supreme Judicial Court." Solon, Letter to Mr. Thomas (Apr. 2, 1790). Certainly, the Court of Common Pleas at about this time reopened its proceedings on a legislative grant in at least one case and probably others. *John Blanchard v. Samuel Blanchard* (Middlesex County Court of Common Pleas Nov. 1791), Massachusetts Supreme Judicial Court Archives, Middlesex County Court of Common Pleas Docket Book (Nov. 1791), & File Papers, Docket No. 63; Resolve (Feb. 19, 1791); Resolve (Feb. 24, 1791) (correcting prior resolve). Not much can be concluded from this case, however, as counsel do not appear to have raised any constitutional objection. Middlesex County Court of Common Pleas Record Book 1790–1792, at 462–464 (Nov. 1791), mfm. This books makes no systematic attempt to trace the fate of new trials in the Court of Common Pleas.

53 According to Smith, the colony of New Hampshire had already been "a particular offender in failure to distinguish between the proper fields of action of the respective governmental branches." Smith, *Appeals to the Privy Council,* 640.

54 "An Act to impower the Superior and Inferior Courts respectively to hear and determine upon all matters and causes for restoring persons to their law," MSA, General Court Records, Non-Engrossed Acts & Copies, RG III, Box 1, Acts-Copies 1786 Folder (passed third reading by the Senate Dec. 22, 1786). Recognizing how its bill was apt to be received, the Senate diplomatically explained that "the hearing of petitions before the General Court for restoring persons to their law . . . is very expensive to the State, as well as to parties concerned." Ibid. In the same year, the Vermont Council of Censors declared its opinion that "the General Assembly, in all of the instances where they have vacated judgments, recovered in due course of law, (except where the particular circumstances of the case evidently made it necessary to grant a new trial) have exercised a power not delegated, or intended to be delegated, to them by the Constitution. This mode of proceeding is an assumption of the judicial power in the last resort, and renders nugatory that important article in the Bill of Rights which provides, 'That in all suits between man and man, the parties have *a right to a trial by Jury, which ought to be held sacred.*' It supercedes the necessity of any other law than the pleasure of the Assembly, and of any other Court than themselves." *The Proceedings of the Council of Censors of the State of Vermont,* 14 (Windsor: 1786).

At some point in the prior years, incidentally, a motion had been made in the New Hampshire House for "an additional rule for the House, viz, No Member shall speak as an advocate to any petition or cause brought before this court, unless it appears to the House to sacrifice a venerable power it considered constitutional and that left its constituents so dependent and grateful.

The New Hampshire judges first rejected the legislature's grant of a new trial five years later, in a contract dispute between two merchants, Nathaniel Gilman of Newmarket and Elizabeth McClary—a widow from Epsom. The parties agreed to have the case decided by arbitrators, and the Rockingham Superior Court followed the arbitrators' decision in giving judgment to Gilman. Afterward, however, McClary petitioned the legislature that she had not been able to assemble some essential evidence until after the time of the arbitration, and on this complaint the legislature enacted in January 1791 that she "have liberty to re-enter her action at the Superior Court of Judicature"—in other words, that she be allowed an "appeal" or new trial.[55]

When the case came again before the Rockingham County Superior Court in September 1791, the judges, undeterred in their personal independence, did their duty and thereby protected the independence of their institution. Gilman's attorney, William Plumer, moved that the statute "could not entitle the original defendant to a trial by way of appeal," for if the statute reversed the court's judgment, "it was repugnant to the constitution of this State," and "if it did not reverse the judgment[,] the same might be pleaded in bar on the appeal." For the first point, Plumer probably relied on the Constitution's separation of powers clause in its Bill of Rights and, more concretely, on its allocation of judicial and legislative powers to different branches. After listening to counsel "and fully deliberating upon the constitution of the State and nature and operation of the act," the Court adopted Plumer's ambidextrous reasoning and unanimously refused to proceed:

---

that he is in such a manner interested that he cannot with propriety act as Judge." Predictably, this was "Rejected." NHSA, General Court Records, RG III, Minutes, June 1783–Dec. 1785, Box 6.

[55] Act to Restore Elisabeth McClary to her Law, NHSA, Original Acts (Jan. 25, 1791). See also NHSA, Rockingham County File No. 11056; NHSA, Rockingham County Inferior Court, Minute Book, Aug. term 1789, Continued Cases, Case No. 70; NHSA, Rockingham County Superior Court Minutes Sept 1789 term, New Entry Docket No. 35; Petition of Elizabeth McClary (June 1790), NHSA; Journal of the House of Representatives, 36–37 (June 14, 1790), NHSA. For some of the documents in this case, see Walter F. Dodd, "A New Hampshire Case of 1791," *American Historical Review,* 12: 348 (Jan. 1907). For brief discussions of the case, see Walter Dodd, "The Constitutional History of New Hampshire, 1775–1792," *New Hampshire Bar Association, Proceedings,* 2: 399–400 (1906); Lynn W. Turner, *William Plumer of New Hampshire 1759–1850,* at 33 (Chapel Hill: University of North Carolina Press, 1962); Lynn Warren Turner, *The Ninth State: New Hampshire's Formative Years,* 111 (Chapel Hill: University of North Carolina Press, 1983).

> [T]hat if the act virtually or really reverses the judgment of this Court it is repugnant to the bill of rights and constitution of this State[,] and that if the Act does not reverse the said judgment the court cannot render another judgment in the same case upon appeal while the first judgment remains in full force[.] It is therefore considered by the Court that the said Act is ineffectual and inadmissible and that the said action be dismissed.[56]

As in so many of the cases in which the legislature granted a new trial, there would have been much justice in a rehearing. The judges, however, had a duty to exercise independent judgment in accord with the law, and at least as to legislative grants of new trial, the independent judgment of the judges was enough to preserve the independence of their court and the judiciary.

It is unclear whether the *McClary* case was what largely ended the legislature's restoration of men to their "law" in New Hampshire, for at an unknown date, probably shortly afterward, another decision—the notorious *Pig Case*—may have had a greater effect. Jeremiah Mason was a young lawyer in Westmoreland, and a half-century later he recalled this "ludicrous instance" of the legislature's practice of granting new trials. A "poor man" took "two of his neighbors small pigs," worth about a dollar, whereupon the neighbor visited Mason's law office in hopes of "a prosecution for larceny." Mason was absent, and one of his students advised an action in trover, which was commenced. When the deputy sheriff served the writ, he found "nobody at Defendant's cottage" and so "left the summons safely placed between the door & the sill." The plaintiff, "living near," saw this and "[a]s soon as the Sheriff was out of sight . . . went & stole away the summons. [U]nluckily for him this was seen by a person at a distance." The defendant inevitably defaulted and learned about it only when he had a writ of execution served against him. When he further learned that the plaintiff had removed the summons, he angrily went to Mason's office. As Mason recalled: "He came to me with his complaint and I offered him to have the judgment & execution cancelled & to let him have a trial for the pigs." The defendant, however, rejected this "with contempt & forthwith applied to the Legislature" to get "a remedy for his grievance." The General Court "without notice to the opposite party immediately passed an act di-

[56] NHSA, Rockingham County Superior Court Record Book 1789–1792, at 303–304. After the Court "refused to allow Gilman any costs," Plumer "moved the Court to order their Clerk to issue an alias [or second] Ex[ecuti]on on the first judgt although more than a year had elapsed since the issuing of the first. The ground of my motion was that the special Act of the Legislature had prevented us from suing out an alias untill the full year & more had expired. The Court ordered the Clerk to issue the alias prayed for." *McClary v. Gilman* (Rockingham County Superior Court Sept. 1791), [Reports of Cases], 241, *William Plumer Papers,* Mfm Reel 19, Legal Papers.

recting the magistrate to cite the Plf before him[,] set aside the default & try the action & to allow to either party an appeal." Mason appeared for the plaintiff and "denied the power of the Legislature to pass the act & went into an argument on the constitutional restraints of the legislative power." In opposition, the defendant's counsel condemned "the audaciousness of the attempt of an inferior magistrate to question the power of the supreme Legislature." The justice, however, was not afraid. He had been "an officer in the revolutionary army," and "being desirous of sustaining his reputation for courage," he "promptly pronounced the act utterly void & refused to obey it." When plaintiff's lawyer sought an appeal, the justice disallowed it, "saying that as the whole proceeding was void he had no rightful power to record a judgment or grant an appeal."

The "farcical drama" had a second act, for the defendant obtained another statute, this one "directing the Court of Common Pleas to try the defaulted action." This court, however, also "determined they would do nothing with it." The small-minded neighbors in this case—together with their little pigs—"gained extensive notoriety" and tended to "bring special acts of the Legislature interfering with the regular course of the Courts . . . into ridicule and deserved contempt."[57]

After 1791, both the legislature and litigants in New Hampshire slowly abandoned their interference with judgments. The New Hampshire Assembly in 1792 followed the Massachusetts legislature in enacting that courts could grant actions of review or new trials, and afterward, as shown by Timothy Lawrie, the legislature only occasionally restored parties to their law.[58] Disappointed parties could still sometimes muster a legislative majority in favor of a new trial, but the judges regularly rejected these legislative commands—this being merely a matter of their independently deciding in accord with the law.

The process by which parties learned the futility of asking the legislature for new trials was perhaps never more painful than in the saga of the Jenness brothers, whose sad story has been noted by Lawrie. The brothers were the administrators of the estate of Richard Jenness, Jr., and they spent almost fifteen years attempting to overturn a judgment against them. After

[57] Jeremiah Mason, Autobiography, fols. 23–24 (ca.1844), New Hampshire Historical Society, Jeremiah Mason Papers, Box 2, Folder 17; also printed in *Memoirs of Jeremiah Mason,* 25–26 (1873; Boston: Boston Law Book, 1917). The statutes do not appear to have survived—a point also noted by Timothy A. Lawrie, "Interpretation and Authority: Separation of Powers and the Judiciary's Battle for Independence in New Hampshire, 1786–1818," *American Journal of Legal History,* 39: 324 (1995).

[58] Ibid., 323; An Act regulating process and trials in civil cases, §12 (Feb. 9, 1792), in *Laws of New Hampshire,* 5: 625, ed. Henry Harrison Metcalf (Concord: Rumford, 1916).

a creditor of the estate, James Seavey, won judgment in 1787 against the Jenness brothers in the Rockingham County Inferior Court, the brothers found new evidence that Seavey had already received payments on the debt. They therefore obtained a legislative act declaring the earlier proceedings "null and void" and allowing the defendants to re-enter the action, but the Inferior Court in 1792 merely "dismissed the action considering said act as unconstitutional."[59] In the next round, the Jenness brothers avoided another direct assault on the judgment of the Inferior Court and instead asked the legislature to grant them a writ of review in the Superior Court, but Seavey pled that a new judgment could not displace an existing final judgment, and on this ground the Superior Court in 1797 apparently also held the new statute unconstitutional or at least ineffective.[60] Not to be put off, the Jenness brothers asked the legislature for a third statute, which empowered the Superior Court "to grant a new trial or review if in their opinion Justice shall require it." Here at last was a mechanism that authorized rather than directed a new trial, and the Superior Court therefore gave the surviving two brothers "licence" to commence "a review or new trial" in the Inferior Court.[61] Yet it would soon become apparent that even this less forceful attempt to reopen a final judgment would not get past the familiar objections, for when the Inferior Court in 1799 allowed the case to be entered on a writ of review, it carefully preserved all exceptions and pleas to the writ and eventually dismissed the action.[62] In these disputes, the judges

[59] *Richard Jenness, Simon Jenness, & Thomas Jenness, Admrs. of Estate of Richard Jenness, Jr. v. James Seavey,* Rockingham County Superior Court, Minute Book, Feb. term 1797, at 7: 7, NHSA, summarizing case of same name, Rockingham County Inferior Court, Record Book, Aug. term 1792. For the statute, see An Act to restore Richard Jenness Simon Jenness and Thomas Jenness Administrators on the Estate of Richard Jenness . . . to their Law (Jan. 26, 1790), in Metcalf, ed., *Laws of New Hampshire,* 5: 504. More generally, see Lawrie, "Interpretation and Authority," 324–325.

[60] An Act to enable Richard Jenness, Simon Jenness and Thomas Jenness Administrators of the Estate of Richard Jenness deceased to review a certain action (June 20, 1793), *Laws of New Hampshire,* 6: 118 (Concord: Evans, 1917); *Richard Jenness, Simon Jenness, & Thomas Jenness, Admrs. of Estate of Richard Jenness, Jr. v. James Seavey,* Rockingham County Superior Court of Judicature, Record Book, Feb. term 1797, at 7: 10, NHSA.

[61] An Act authorizing the Superior Court of Judicature to grant the Administrators of the Estate of Richard Jenness a new trial or review in a certain action (Act of June 21, 1797); Rockingham County Superior Court of Judicature, Record Book, Feb. term 1799, at 8: 17–18, NHSA.

[62] In August 1799, the Court entered in the record "that all Advantages Exceptions & pleas as well to the writ as to the Action be saved and reserved to the Defendant and that the same shall be received and have the same force and Effect as if made at this Term." *Richard Jenness & al Admrs. v. James Seavey,* Rockingham County Inferior Court, Minute Book, Aug. term 1799, New Entries, Case No. 199. In January 1800, it initially made a similar entry, but subsequently added "dismist." Ibid., Rockingham County Inferior Court, Minute Book, Jan. term 1800, Continued Cases, Case No. 237.

did not act as the judiciary in defense of their power but rather merely exercised independent judgment in their cases, and once again, at least as to legislative grants of new trial, this was enough to hold off the legislative intrusions.

Much evidently rested on the ideal of independent judgment. State legislatures could threaten both the personal independence of the judges and the institutional independence of their courts, and although state constitutions barred some of these external assaults, the constitutional prohibitions tended to be inadequate and at any rate ineffective. Against the danger from legislatures, however, judges could usually take refuge in the office they held under their constitutions, for even against most external threats, the independence that ultimately mattered was internal. The judges could never be entirely secure in their tenure and their salaries, nor in the proceedings and judgments of their courts. With the ideal of independent judgment, however, they could sufficiently put aside their anxieties as to do their duty, and this was enough against almost all external threats to their independent judgment and even against many of the external threats to their institutional power. The judges and their courts thus depended for their independence not merely on constitutional protections, but more basically on their individual internal independence in doing their duty—on their interior capacity to exercise judgment free from their own will. The greatest risk to their independence would therefore one day come not so much from legislatures as from the judges themselves.

17

Authority

JUDICIAL office not only required independent judgment but also gave the judges authority to expound the law. In constitutional matters, this authority to expound law is often reduced to a question of power, and from this balance-of-power perspective (usually borrowed from the political theory of James Madison) it is sometimes suggested that although the judiciary has the final judgment in cases, the other branches of government can equally claim a final or absolute power in the decisions arising from their functions. Law, however, was not political theory, and the exposition of law by judges in resolving their cases had not merely the power of their courts but also the authority of their office. The authority of a court's judgment rested on the court's jurisdiction and record; but the authority of a judge's exposition of law arose from his office of judgment, and this was an authority that men in legislative and executive positions—in offices of will and force—could not enjoy. Thus, at least while judges remained within the bounds of their office, they enjoyed a distinctive authority to expound the law, including any relevant constitution. The difficulties would arise because judicial office was coming to be understood as almost exclusively centered on adjudication, and when judges failed to recognize this, they could easily stray beyond their office, thereby putting their authority and even their independence at risk.

Cases and Controversies

"Cases" and "controversies" are terms associated with jurisdiction, and it may therefore seem odd to begin a discussion of authority with such matters. Yet the office by which judges enjoyed their authority came to be understood more narrowly in eighteenth-century America than in the past, and this more focused vision of judicial office was both revealed and sharpened by the American statutes that tied jurisdiction to cases and controversies. To be sure, the Massachusetts Supreme Court judges still gave advisory opinions, and the Virginia county court magistrates still occasionally adopted resolutions, but Americans increasingly understood the ideal of judicial office as a matter of adjudication, and this became particularly clear through colonial and state enactments on jurisdiction. Whereas the jurisdiction of English courts was largely determined by common law (or statutes so ancient as to be considered common law), the jurisdiction of American courts typically had to be enunciated by modern statutes, and when these enactments defined jurisdiction in terms of a power to hear specified actions, suits, causes, cases, or controversies, they gave the already circumscribed judicial office a jurisdictional edge and thus clarified the outer boundary of judicial authority.

Each of the words regularly used to describe the jurisdiction of courts had its own, slightly different connotations. Whereas the words "actions" and "suits" could sometimes be used to distinguish actions at law and suits in equity, the words "cases" and "controversies" did not so clearly have legal meanings. Similarly, although "causes of action" had a specific, technical meaning, "causes" did not. Thus lawyers ordinarily spoke of an action as a cause defined and available at law, as when Sir Henry Finch explained that an "[a]ction is the handling of a cause in controversie before certaine Judges."[1] In addition, whereas in law a "cause," "case," or "controversy" ordinarily referred to a particular dispute, a "question" usually alluded to a more abstract disagreement, which rose above a particular legal dispute and thus might just as well be debated by a philosopher or a politician. From this perspective, when Parliament in 1640 impeached the judges who had given the advisory opinion upholding shipmoney, men complained about judges who "delivered an opinion, and judgment in an extra-judicial manner, that is, as came not within their cognizance, they being judges, and neither philosophers, nor politicians."[2] Questions that were not part of a particular legal dispute were in this sense philosophical or political questions. In this context, when American statutes defined jurisdiction in terms of "suits," "actions," "causes," "cases," or "controversies," they not only tightened the jurisdiction of courts but also sharpened conceptions of the sort of dispute that could come within judicial office.

A fortuitous glimpse of how American statutes on jurisdiction clar-

[1] Henry Finch, *Law, or, a Discourse Thereof,* 225 (London: 1627).
[2] Speech of Lord Falkland, in *State Trials,* 3: 1260, 1279.

ified the narrow boundaries of judicial office survives in *Commonwealth v. Caton, et al.* In 1782, the unhappy prisoners Caton, Hopkins, and Lamb were convicted of treason. Although they obtained a pardon from the House of Delegates, the Virginia Treason Statute required that they be pardoned by both houses, and although the state's constitution allowed the Assembly to transfer the pardon power from the Governor to the House of Delegates, it did not so obviously allow the Assembly to give this power to both houses. On the day set for their execution, the prisoners gave the sheriff the resolution of the House, and it will be recalled that because of the constitutional problem, he delayed their fate and thereby left the constitutional effect of their pardon to be decided in the courts of law.

The Court of Appeals eventually upheld the Treason Statute, but more immediately, it had to decide whether it had jurisdiction. The three prisoners initially were brought before the General Court, where they had been convicted four months earlier. Attorney General Edmund Randolph moved "for execution to be again awarded on the said Judgments," and the prisoners of course pleaded and produced the resolution of pardon passed by the House of Delegates. Yet rather than resolve anything, the General Court "adjourned" the proceedings to the Court of Appeals, which was composed of members of all the central courts, including the General Court, and by this means "the Judges of the General Court," who were "in doubts & difficulty," did not have to "plunge through & determine without the Assistance of the other Judges."[3]

The Court of Appeals thus faced the jurisdictional problem as to "[w]hether the General Court had power to adjourn a case capitally criminal into this court for difficulty."[4] Most awkwardly, the sheriff's quandary as to whether he should execute the prisoners was not obviously a "case," let alone the sort of case the General Court could adjourn to the Court of Appeals. St. George Tucker was among the lawyers who volunteered to defend the prisoners, and he began his argument that the Court of Appeals had jurisdiction by examining the two relevant state statutes—an initial act of 1778 and an amendment adopted a year later.

The 1778 act "establishing" the Court of Appeals confined the Court's jurisdiction to "suits" and "controversies" of specified sorts, and Tucker therefore did not understand this first statute to give the Court jurisdiction

[3] Supreme Court of Appeals, Order Book No. 1, 1779–1789, at 20–21, LVA; Transcript of Edmund Pendleton's Notes of his Opinion in *Commonwealth v. Caton, et al.*, Library of Congress, Force Papers, at 8702–8703, Series 7E, James McGuire Collection, Correspondence Folders.

[4] Ibid., 8696.

over more than civil litigation.[5] He recognized that "[t]he Jurisdiction of such Court is clearly confined to matters of Controversy"—in the sense of a controversy between two parties—"for the words, *suits, Controversies* & *Causes* are the only words therein, descriptive, of the subjects to be submitted to the Decision of the Court." Moreover, "after a *final judgement*" in another court, the act only allowed these "*suits, controversies,* or *Causes*" to be brought before the Court of Appeals by "Pet^{n}: appeal or Writ of Error." Speaking of this 1778 enactment, Tucker therefore conceded that because the original "Judgement of the General Court" in *Caton* was *"final"* and execution had been awarded, "it follows that *under this act* the present Case could not have been properly submitted to the Decision of the Court of Appeals." More broadly, "as the Law makes mention of no other subjects for the Decision of the Court but *suits, controversies,* and *Causes,* which I concieve to be mere Terms of *Litigation,* it seems equally to follow that *under this Act* the Court of appeals can have no rights to determine in *criminal Cases.*"[6]

In contrast, according to Tucker, the 1779 act "constituting" the Court of Appeals expanded its jurisdiction to include criminal cases.[7] This act gave the Court jurisdiction "*in such Cases* as shall be removed before them by adjournment from the other Courts . . . when *Questions* in their opinion, new & difficult occur." Tucker observed that this "sets the matter in a different Light," for "[i]n this last Sentence the word *Cases* is clearly a word of much larger & more extensive Import than the words *Suits, Controversies* & *Causes,* which are the words of the former statute." Whereas the 1778 statute's reference to suits, controversies, and causes seemed "to indicate matters merely of *Litigation,*" the provision in the 1779 act about cases removed by adjournment "applies equally to *criminal* as to *civil* Cases." Tellingly, Tucker added that "Cases" was "indeed the most comprehensive word that could have been made use of in defining the power & Jurisdiction of the Court."[8]

Yet even if the Court of Appeals had jurisdiction over criminal cases adjourned from the General Court, it was by no means clear whether there

[5] An act for establishing a Court of Appeals, in *Laws of Virginia,* 9: 522, ed. William Waller Hening (Richmond: 1821). Tucker was in error when he suggested that this act gave jurisdiction over "causes," probably because he was relying on memory.
[6] "Constitutional Question," William and Mary College Library, Tucker-Coleman Papers, Legal Papers, Virginia Supreme Court of Appeals, Mfm Reel M-44.
[7] An act constituting the Court of Appeals, in *Laws of Virginia,* 10: 39, ed. William Waller Hening (Richmond: 1822). This time Tucker quoted accurately.
[8] "Constitutional Question," William and Mary College Library, Tucker-Coleman Papers, Legal Papers, Virginia Supreme Court of Appeals, Mfm Reel M-44.

remained a case between the state and the prisoners, and Tucker therefore had to consider the possibility of a jurisdiction over political questions. Much was at stake—not least for the prisoners—but as there had already been a final judgment, the dispute might be considered a general, public disagreement rather than a case. The prisoners had no obvious mode of proceeding; the sheriff had sought guidance, but he too had no clear path to pursue at law; it was therefore the Attorney General who initiated matters in the General Court, and rather than suggest there was a new criminal case, he apparently sought a new writ of execution, thus reopening post-judgment proceedings in an earlier criminal case.

Worried that this was not a case of any sort and thus was not capable of being adjourned to the Court of Appeals, Tucker turned from the word "Cases" in the 1779 statute to the word "Questions." "The word *Questions* in the same sentence is likewise a word of comprehensive Sense & may apply to all subjects, *civil, criminal* or *political,* as arising in a Judiciary process." In fact, the statute did not permit the adjournment of questions independent of cases, but rather merely allowed the adjournment of "Cases" to the Court of Appeals when difficult questions arose within them, and Tucker therefore had to imply that political questions were one of the types of adjourned cases over which the Court of Appeals had jurisdiction. With this rather expansive understanding of "Cases," he concluded that "[t]hus the succeeding [1779] Statute clearly gives them the Jurisdiction in all *Cases*, removed to them by *adjournment* from any other Court."

Tucker understood that the issue before the Court in *Commonwealth v. Caton* arose after final judgment, and that "[a]n Objection may perhaps be made that where the Question is adjourned on account of Difficulty, from any other Court, it must be done *before Decision,* and the Judgement of the General Court having been final, such adjournment can not be made." Admittedly, the first, 1778 statute, "requires that the adjournment be made before Decision," but:

> [T]he subsequent Statute, by which the powers & Jurisdiction of the Court are evidently enlarged makes no mention of the time when the adjournment should be made, and of course leaves the court open at any time to hear & determine such *new & difficult Questions,* as the present, which clearly originated after Judgement, in its nature final, altho' the peculiarity of the Circumstances attending it have rendered it otherwise.

This was not exactly a persuasive way of dodging the final judgment problem, but it allowed Tucker to conclude that the jurisdiction of the Court of Appeals was "clearly established not only in criminal Cases, but I concieve in all cases which can possibly occur, whether civil, criminal, or political."[9] The reality was that Tucker faced a statute that gave the Court jurisdiction over "Cases," and he therefore had to understand cases to include not only civil and criminal cases but also political questions.

So strained an argument for jurisdiction over political questions probably did not satisfy most of the judges, particularly under a statute that confined their jurisdiction to "Cases." In the two opinions that survive in detail on this issue, President Pendleton and Chancellor Wythe agreed with Tucker that under the 1779 statute there was a "Case" that could be adjourned to the Court of Appeals.[10] Yet this was the extent of their agreement with Tucker about jurisdiction, for as Pendleton explained, "[t]he words" of the statute "are General & comprehensive enough to include criminal, as well as civil cases."[11] The prisoners came before the Court in a criminal case, in which the Attorney General had merely reopened post-judgment proceedings, and therefore neither Pendleton nor Wythe relied on Tucker's effort to recast political questions as cases. Nor is there evidence that any other judges agreed with Tucker on this.

Five years later, when the Constitutional Convention in Philadelphia drafted the U.S. Constitution, it enumerated the jurisdiction of the courts of the United States in categories of "Cases" and "Controversies." In particular, it listed "Cases" of specified subject matters and "Controversies" between specified parties. Some of the Virginians who voted on this provision (such as the erstwhile Attorney General John Randolph, Chancellor George Wythe, and his onetime fellow chancellor John Blair) had participated in *Caton,* but it need not be assumed that the Constitution's provision for the jurisdiction of federal courts followed the Virginia statutes or the decision in *Caton,* for it was only to be expected that courts were to have jurisdiction over actions and suits or, more generally, causes, cases, and controversies. The English had become cautious about resolutions and even advisory opinions, and Americans tended to go still further in narrowing judicial office, especially in their statutes defining jurisdiction.

The ideal of judicial office that underlay jurisdictional allusions to cases and controversies became explicit during the Constitutional Convention, as did the implications for the judicial authority to expound the law. In August 1787, the Convention's rough draft of the Constitution placed

[9] Ibid.

[10] *Commonwealth v. Caton, & al,* Call, *Reports,* 4: 9.

[11] Transcript of Edmund Pendleton's Notes of his Opinion in *Commonwealth v. Caton, et al.,* Library of Congress, Force Papers, at 8700, Series 7E, James McGuire Collection, Correspondence Folders.

the judicial power of the United States "in one Supreme Court, and in such inferior Courts as shall . . . be constituted by the Legislature of the United States," and it then gave the Supreme Court jurisdiction over cases arising under "laws passed by the Legislature." This last phrase was clearly too limited, and William Samuel Johnson therefore moved to insert a reference to the Constitution—so that the Court would have jurisdiction over cases arising under "this Constitution and the laws passed by the Legislature." This in turn, however, troubled James Madison, for it will be seen that he expected each branch of the government to enjoy the power of expounding the Constitution—the judiciary in their cases, and the other departments in their political decisions—and with this in mind, he worried that the Supreme Court was about to acquire jurisdiction not only over judicial cases but also over cases of a more abstract sort:

> Mr. Madison doubted whether it was not going too far to extend the jurisdiction of the Court generally to cases arising Under the Constitution, & whether it ought not to be limited to cases of a Judiciary Nature. The right of expounding the Constitution in cases not of this nature ought not to be given to that Department.

To protect a right of exposition for the other departments, Madison thus sought to confine the allusion to cases arising under the Constitution to "cases of a Judiciary Nature." Madison's colleagues, however, took this limitation for granted, and once this was explained, the Convention agreed to Johnson's motion without opposition, "it being generally supposed that the jurisdiction given was constructively limited to cases of a Judiciary nature."[12]

[12] Madison's Notes (Aug. 27, 1787), in *Records of the Constitutional Convention,* 2: 428, note 8, and 430, ed. Max Farrand (New Haven: Yale University Press, 1937). A portion of one of these quotations—"laws passed by the Legislature"—is reconstructed here from the debates. Ibid., 2: 430–431. For a different interpretation, see James E. Viator, "Marbury and History: What Do We Really Know About What Really Happened?" *Revue Juridique Thémis,* 37: 356 (2003).

It will be observed in the conclusion to this book that many assumptions about law have been lost to view, thus leaving Americans with constitutional texts largely denuded of the presuppositions that once gave them meaning, and the standing doctrine offers an undramatic but interesting illustration. Although what has come to be known as "standing" was once inherent in judicial office and could therefore be taken for granted in the Constitution's references to judges, it today must be derived from the Constitution's requirement about cases and controversies—a requirement that, by historical happenstance, hints at the confined character of judicial office. This link between standing and the Constitution's words may be fortunate, but the attempt to derive elements of something as fundamental as the boundaries of judicial office from the Constitution's allocation of jurisdiction leaves the authority of the standing requirement looking rather frail, and this is a reminder of how much can be lost even when basic substantive assumptions remain familiar.

Jurisdiction thus followed and accentuated the focus of judicial office on cases and controversies, and this had consequences for the authority of judicial expositions of law, including constitutions. Already in England the authority of the judges in expounding law had come to be centrally associated with their distinctive office of judging cases. Now, in conjunction with statutes establishing jurisdiction, judicial office had become even more tightly confined to cases and controversies, and this would further confine the circumstances in which the judges could expound the law with the authority of their office.

Authority to Expound Law

Within their office of deciding cases, judges could expound the law with authority. In order to act under law, the executive and legislative departments of government had to understand or "interpret" it, and to the extent they thereby (even if not as a matter of office) reached judgments about the law, their actions could be considered precedents within their own branches. The exposition of law by the judges, however, was more generally authoritative. The exposition of law traditionally belonged to the office of judgment rather than that of will or force, and such exposition seemed necessary for the judges in the exercise of their office if they not only had to understand or interpret the law but also had to explain what it was. At least therefore in their cases, the judges were understood to expound the law, including constitutions, with the authority of their office.

This authority in exposition, which belonged to the judges in their exercise of judgment, was different from the authority of a court in giving judgment, for the judgment given by a court was a matter of record, and a final judgment was almost beyond dispute. To be sure, much that was sacred in the ideals of law was not so clearly venerated on the ground, but it is nonetheless difficult to locate constitutional cases from the first fifteen years after Independence in which a party resisted the authority of a court to give judgment.[13] Final judgments were part of the record of a court, and by ancient law they were thus beyond challenge, except by superior courts of re-

[13] In the *Ten Pound Cases,* after the New Hampshire House of Representatives attempted without success to stay the Rockingham County Inferior Court from granting process on its judgments, a few of the defendants who prevailed and won costs on appeal had difficulty finding property on which they could execute their judgments. Yet the efforts of the House to stop execution and the mundane failure of a few parties to pay cannot be assumed to reveal a generalized objection to the authority of the courts to give judgment in constitutional cases, let alone an effective movement to resist the courts' authority.

cord. This had been the sanctity of acts of the high court of Parliament, and at lower levels it was the force of any judgment of a court of record.

Among those who accepted the force of judgments were the executive officers of the states. Nor should this be a surprise, for in addition to being subject to law in the same manner as other citizens, they had the duty of carrying out the law. It will be recalled that in 1785 the Virginia Court of Appeals held that the governor's conditions on his pardons for Fowler and Minn were unconstitutional, but it was never even contemplated that the governor or the attorney general might defy the judgment of the Court of Appeals. Similarly, James Iredell observed that "*if the power of judging rests with the Courts,* their decision is final as to the subject matter," which led him to ask: "Did ever a Sheriff refuse to hang a Man because he thought he was unjustly convicted of murder?"[14]

Even state legislatures ordinarily refrained from attempts to overturn judgments in the cases that held their statutes unconstitutional. When legislative acts or resolves were held unconstitutional in North Carolina, New Jersey, Rhode Island, and Massachusetts, no legislator is known ever to have proposed overturning the judgments of the courts. In New Hampshire, after the initial round of Ten Pound Act cases, the House voted "the Judgment of the Inferior Court" against James Macgregore "null & void," but the Senate refused to join this resolution, and only the House voted to stay process in the Ten Pound cases.[15] The only instances (at least among the cases examined here) in which a state legislature actually passed acts overturning judgments in constitutional cases occurred when the New Hampshire courts refused to accept legislative grants of new trials, and the legislature responded by again granting such trials. In these cases, legislators had a long tradition of assuming that they were not intruding on judicial power, and outside this narrow category of New Hampshire cases, legislators seem to have accepted the judgments in constitutional cases.

It was not in the judgments of their courts, however, but in their expositions of law that judges ordinarily held statutes and other governmental acts unconstitutional. In most cases holding government acts unlawful, courts gave judgment against a private party rather than a government or government officer, and even when a court gave judgment against a government or government officer, its judgment was not ordinarily the place in

14 "To the Public," Duke University, Rare Book, Manuscript, and Special Collections Library, James Iredell Papers, Box 1.

15 Resolve of House of Representatives (June 22, 1786), NHSA, General Court Records, RG III, Box 6; Vote of House of Representatives (June 27, 1786), ibid. See Chapter Thirteen.

which it explained that the act was unconstitutional.[16] In contrast, when defending their judgments in their opinions, the judges might have to expound their state's constitution and how it deprived a government act of its obligation, and because this reasoning was necessary in the course of their office, it had the authority of their office. It was an authority that ideally went no further than the exposition of law, and this allowed men such as Jefferson to say that "we take no judge's word for what the law is further than he is warranted by the authorities he appeals to." This was only a partial account of traditional common law ideas about judicial authority, but it was the sort of statement that appealed to radical Whigs and their American heirs when they faced constitutional threats. From this perspective, a judge's "decision may bind the unfortunate individual who happens to be the particular subject of it; but it cannot alter the law."[17] Even in the Whig ideals, however, it might be added that within the scope of the "authorities," a judicial opinion required by a case was an authoritative statement of "what the law is."

The executive did not share in this authority to expound law. An executive officer, like any other citizen, had a duty to obey the law, and he might feel particularly obliged to obey the law on account of his oath of office—if it required him to obey or support his state's constitution or other law. He therefore regularly had to reach his own conclusions about his duty under law, including his state's constitution. Yet he did not do so in an office of judgment, and he did not, as a part of his office, have to explain what the law was. For example, when the governor of Virginia insisted on his understanding of his constitutional power in his disagreements with the state's county courts, he had to exercise judgment in determining what the law was and had to argue for his conclusions, but he did not thereby either

16 Even when a relatively isolated court (for example, in North Carolina in 1778 or New Hampshire in 1786 or 1787) preserved the constitutional reasoning of its judges within its order in its recordbook, only the court's judgment—for example, to award damages or to quash or void a lower court judgment, etc.—had the force of a judgment.

17 "Whether Christianity is a part of the Common Law?" (c. 1774?), Thomas Jefferson, *Reports of Cases Determined in the General Court of Virginia,* 139 (Charlottesville: 1829). Chief Justice M'Kean of Pennsylvania acknowledged the maxim "that it is better the law should be determinate and fixed, although it were originally erroneous, than that it should be precarious and fluctuating, according to the different talents and dispositions of the Judges," but he also thought that a court was not bound by its own errors: "A Court is not bound to give the like judgment, which had been given by a former Court, unless they are of opinion that the first judgment was according to law; for any Court may err; and if a judge conceives, that a judgment given by a former Court is erroneous, he ought not in conscience to give the like judgment, he being sworn to judge according to law." *Hollingsworth v. Ogle et al.* (Supreme Court of Pennsylvania, Apr. 1788), Dallas, *Reports,* 1: 258; *Kerlin's Lessee v. Bull et al.* (Supreme Court of Pennsylvania 1786), ibid., 1: 178.

exercise an office of judgment or expound the law in circumstances in which this was required by such an office.[18] As might therefore be expected, Virginia's executive is not known to have claimed any distinctive authority to expound the constitution or any other law; nor are the county court magistrates or any other Virginia judges known to have conceded such an authority. Instead, the authority of the executive's exposition of law appears to have rested solely on the strength of the executive's reasoning.

Although some individual legislators and lower houses opposed particular judicial expositions of constitutional law, they seem consistently to have failed in their attempts to challenge the judges who held statutes unconstitutional. When the New Jersey judges in *Holmes v. Walton* were preparing to hold at least the jury provision of the state's seizure act unconstitutional, the legislature justified the provision, but it did so in the course of modifying the statute to satisfy the expected objections of the judges. In *Trevett v. Weeden, Bayard v. Singleton,* and the *Ten Pound Cases,* some men demanded proceedings against the judges, but they never managed to secure an impeachment, let alone a trial or a conviction.[19] After *Trevett v.*

[18] See Chapter Twelve. Not even the county courts claimed to speak with authority in these disputes, for even though they apparently thought themselves within the scope of their duty, they were not exercising their judgment in a case and at any rate were not required to give an opinion. This last point was succinctly noted by a majority of the justices of the Goochland Court when the executive refused to accept their recommendation of William Radford to serve as a militia colonel. The justices protested and toward the end of their Remonstrance, they added: "nor is it requir'd by the duties of their Office to mark the Grounds upon which they proceeded to recommend." Remonstrance of Nine Justices of the Goochland County Court to the Governor and Council of Virginia (Jan. 1, 1789), LVA, Beverly Randolph Executive Papers, Box 58.

[19] James Wilson thus had some justification for his confidence that federal judges would not be impeached for holding acts of Congress void. When John Smilie argued against ratification of the U.S. Constitution by raising the fear that Congress would impeach the judges "if they dare to decide against the law," James Wilson expostulated: "[T]he judges are to be impeached because they decide an act null and void that was made in defiance of the Constitution! What House of Representatives would dare to impeach, or Senate to commit judges for the performance of their duty?" Speech of James Wilson (Dec. 1, 1787), in *The Documentary History of the Ratification of the Constitution,* 2: 492, ed. Merrill Jensen (Madison: State Historical Society of Wisconsin, 1976).

A successful legislative challenge to a judicial exposition of a constitution might seem to have occurred when the North Carolina Superior Court judges held that the Perquimans County Court had acted unconstitutionally in giving a retrospective effect to the state's statute for capturing and selling manumitted slaves. The General Assembly responded by enacting a retrospective remedy against manumission, but it did not thereby directly challenge either the judgment of the Superior Court or even the holding of its judges, for the legislature assumed that the old colonial bar against manumission remained in effect. The legislature thus merely enacted a retrospective penalty for an offense that was already contrary to law. See Chapter Thirteen.

Weeden, the Rhode Island legislature did not reappoint four of the five judges, but this was fully within the legislature's power, as the judges held only annual commissions. Even in New Hampshire, as has been seen, the Senate blocked the agitation against the judges about the *Ten Pound Act* cases. Only on the issue of restoring men to their law did the Massachusetts and New Hampshire legislatures clearly repudiate the judges' expositions of their constitutions. Yet even on this question of legislative grants of new trial, neither legislature asserted that it generally had a power to expound its constitution; instead, it simply refused or perhaps more accurately was just slow to accept the authority of a judicial exposition that it evidently considered a departure from a clear constitutional allocation of power. Thus, in no state—other than Connecticut, of course—did a legislature generally question the authority of judges to hold statutes or other government acts unconstitutional.

In their anger about cases holding statutes unconstitutional, members of a lower house could propose legislation that would have broadly shifted the exposition of their state's constitution away from the judges, but they never persuaded enough of their fellow legislators to join these attacks. When *Commonwealth v. Caton* was adjourned to the Virginia Court of Appeals, "some of the members of the assembly" proposed "to convene a committee from the legislative, and judiciary departments who shal[l] enter into a discussion of the subject, and defin[e] the powers of each." This prompted Edmund Randolph to think "[a]t first sight" that "the measure appears eligible," for "without an accommodation fou[n]ded upon a reasonable construction of the constitution the appeal must be made to the people." In addition, some hoped, "as part of the scheme, that a council of revis[ion] shall be established, to keep the legislature in futur[e] cases within its just limits."[20] The General Assembly, however, apparently never pursued these proposals. Several years later, while the North Carolina Superior Court was considering in *Bayard v. Singleton* whether to hold a state statute unconstitutional, the House of Commons contemplated a proposal to prevent judicial "usurpation[s] . . . of powers . . . unknown to the Constitution and Laws of this State." The proposed bill, as has been seen, would have required that when "the Operation of the Constitution and any particular Act of the legislature may interfere," the judges "are not to determine on the same but [are] to Relate their opinion or doubt thereon to the

20 Letter from Edmund Randolph to James Madison (Oct. 26, 1782), in *Papers of James Madison,* 5: 218, eds. William T. Hutchinson and William M. E. Rachal (Chicago: University of Chicago Press, 1967).

next General Assembly." In retrospect, it may be thought that such a plan would appeal to the Assembly. The Senate, however, rejected it.[21]

In short, judges had authority to expound the law, including constitutions, within their office of deciding cases, and their authority to expound was not generally challenged by any legislature. Certainly, many representatives in the lower houses of American legislatures continued for a while in the colonial mode of opposing judicial decisions holding their statutes void. Yet as these men rapidly digested the implications of American Independence and popular constitutions, they tended to acquiesce in the decisions they disliked. The passions against decisions holding state statutes unconstitutional were more clearly populist than popular, and at least in the period considered here, they were so fleeting as to enjoy little support in the press. It is therefore no wonder that even when they did not burn out in lower legislative houses, they almost invariably were extinguished in the upper houses. A sense of respect for judicial authority ran deep in American society—even if not always so far down as to include all members of the lower house of a legislature.

Theorizing about Judicial Authority

Americans occasionally offered theoretical explanations for judicial authority, and their theories could cut in different directions. At common law, judges had a general authority to expound the law, including constitutions. From the perspective of a balance of power, however, James Madison and some others came to believe that, at least in constitutional matters, the judges shared their authority to expound with the other branches of government. This alternative theory had considerable appeal, especially among Madison's friends in Virginia, but in placing some constitutional questions beyond the traditional authority of the judges, and in thus treating constitutions more as a matter of power than of law, the balance-of-power theory ran into difficulties. As might be expected, this theory did not dislodge the common law ideal that the judges alone could give authoritative expositions of law, and although fortunately some theoretical justifications of the common law perspective have survived, it remained a point of view that usually could just be taken for granted.

The common law ideal of judicial authority was elaborated in theoretical terms by St. George Tucker in 1782 in *Commonwealth v. Caton.*

[21] A Bill to Amend and Alter the Court System, 16–18, NCSA, General Assembly, Session Records 1786–1787, Box 5, Folder House (Dec. 16, 1786) Bill to Amend the Court System.

Tucker, it will be recalled, defended the prisoners by arguing that their pardon from the House of Delegates was effective notwithstanding the Treason Act, which required that pardons for treason have the approval of both houses of the legislature. The Treason Act, he argued, conflicted with the Virginia Constitution. To this, he added that the statute could not be considered an authoritative interpretation of the Constitution, for there was a difference between legislative and judicial authority.

According to Tucker, Virginia's General Assembly could not expound the constitution because the authority to expound law rested exclusively in the judiciary as part of its power to decide cases. In Virginia, Tucker explained, "[o]ur Bill of Rights says 'the Executive and Legislative powers of the state should be separate and distinct from the Judiciary.'" Indeed, "[o]ur Constitution repeats, that, The Legislative, executive and Judiciary Departments shall be separate and distinct, so *that neither exercise the powers properly belonging to the other.*" It followed that the judiciary had the exclusive power of interpreting law in cases—that "the power properly belonging to the Judiciary Department, is, to explain the Laws of the Land as they apply to particular Cases, [and] consequently, that where such cases arise, the Interpretation of the Laws of the Land is in the *Judiciary alone.*"

Of course, the legislature could adopt interpretations of the constitution, but only generally, through its enactments. Each legislative act was a sort of interpretation, and "if the Legislative shall find that mischiefs have, or may arise from such Interpretation it is undoubtedly their province to explain their own Acts, so that no further Doubt may occur in the future Construction of them in such particular Cases as shall be brought before the Judiciary for their Explanation or Interpretation." This legislative interpretation, however, was different from judicial interpretation. It was "the undoubted province of the Judiciary to interpret all Laws whatsoever," and "altho' the legislative may by a future Act explain any point not sufficiently clear in a former Act," nonetheless "every Interpretation of a Law by the G[eneral] A[ssembly] in reality amounts to enacting a new Law, which is their undoubted province."

Tucker then returned to the theme of separation of powers to conclude that although the legislature had the power to explain its law or policy in *general* in statutes, only a separate body, the judiciary, could expound the law as it applied to *particular* persons. Aristotle had distinguished between the legislation of general rules and the adjudication of particular cases, and according to Montesquieu, "[t]he same Man or body of Men should not enact Laws, & afterwards carry them into Execution, for in this Case . . . arbitrary Laws may first be made & then tyrannically executed, or interpreted." This, Tucker observed, "is also the Spirit of our Constitution, which will not permit the Legislative to expound or interpret a Law as applying to *particular* persons, or Cases, altho' they have undoubtedly the right to explain their General Pollicy." Tucker thus blended Aristotle's distinction between lawmaking and adjudication with Montesquieu's separation of powers to prove that although the legislature could amend and in this sense explain its general policy, only the judiciary could decide the law as it applied in particular cases involving particular persons: "For if the Legislative have a right to determine or explain the Laws judicially, that is to decide in *Particular Cases*[,] the Judiciary, who are by the Constitution appointed as a counterpoise to it, is entirely annulled, & one of the Pillars on which our Government is established is totally destroyed." In sum, "as this right of Interpretation does not exist in the Legislative, nor yet in the Executive, it is consequently vested in the Judiciary alone, for neither Departm[t] according to the *Constitution shall exercise the powers properly belonging to the other.*"

This was an elaborate attempt to prove what was ordinarily taken for granted, and Tucker in the end "presumed" it was "admitted that the power of interpreting all the Laws of this Commonwealth in particular Cases, is vested in the Judiciary alone." From this, "it follows that they alone (if any of the Departments of Government can do it) can decide what is or is not Law, and consequently (I should presume) on the validity or nullity of different Laws contradicting each other."[22]

As already suggested, some men took a very different point of view—one drawn as much from political theory as from law—and no one more vigorously espoused this challenge to traditional ideals of judicial authority than James Madison. In the debates over a council of revision, he looked beyond the attributes of judicial office to secure what he considered the more realistic limitations of a balance of power among the branches of government, and from this perspective, elevated far above legal ideals rather than situated within them, he sometimes spoke about the equal authority of the legislature to interpret the U.S. Constitution. It would have been one thing to inquire about the somewhat puzzling nature of judicial authority—to ask about the character of the obligation of judicial expositions of law outside the walls of the courthouses in which they were enunciated. It was quite another, however, to say that the men who held an office of independent judgment, and who in the exercise of their office had to explain

[22] "To. W.N.," Argument on Behalf of the Prisoners, Addressed to William Nelson, William and Mary College Library, Tucker-Coleman Papers, Legal Papers, Virginia Supreme Court of Appeals, Mfm Reel M-44.

their judgments, had no greater authority in expounding law than the men who exercised offices of will and force, and who had no equivalent need in the exercise of their offices to explain what they did.

Madison's vision of the equal authority of the different branches of government in expounding their constitutional powers drew upon more conventional ideas, widely familiar in Virginia, that the judges could sometimes, as in their resolutions, go beyond their office of deciding cases to become parties in an appeal to the people. In these circumstances, it was assumed, the judges and the other branches of government enjoyed equal authority as contestants, including an equal authority to assert their understanding of the law. It may be questioned whether the judges enjoyed any advantage when they thus discarded the authority of their office for the dubious privilege of asserting their will as a party against another branch of government, but Madison was not deeply attached to the distinctive authority of judges, and therefore, as will be seen, although he understood the risks, he did not allow them to weigh on his mind.

Madison did not deny the authority of judges in expounding the law, but he understood the constitutional balance of power among the different branches of government to be an exception. Notwithstanding that "in the ordinary course of government . . . the exposition of the laws and constitution devolves upon the judicial" department, "the limits of the powers of the several departments" were another matter, and if the departments were equal and "independent," then they did not have any "more right than another to declare their sentiment on that point."[23] Madison explained this by observing that "[i]n the State Constitutions & indeed in the Fedl. one also, no provision is made for the case of a disagreement in expounding them."[24] These constitutions, however, omitted to explain many things, including the authority of the judges on non-constitutional questions, and if constitutions were law, it was unclear why their exposition did not lie exclusively within the office of the judges. As Madison once came close to recognizing, he was attributing an aspect of the office of judgment to men who held offices of will and force—to men almost inevitably "led by passion" and "dis-

[23] Madison in House of Representatives (June 17, 1789) (from *Congressional Register*), in *Debates in the House of Representatives,* 11: 926–927, eds. Charlene Bangs Bickford, Kenneth R. Bowling, et al. (Baltimore: Johns Hopkins University Press, 1992).

[24] Observations on the "Draught of a Constitution for Virginia" (c. Oct. 15, 1788), in *The Papers of James Madison,* 11: 293, eds. Robert A. Rutland and Charles F. Hobson (Charlottesville: University Press of Virginia, 1977). Madison added that "as the Courts are generally the last in making their decision, it results to them, by refusing or not refusing to execute a law, to stamp it with its final character. This makes the Judiciary Dept paramount in fact to the Legislature, which was never intended, and can never be proper." Ibid.

turbed by faction."[25] He did not have a plausible solution for this problem, and he therefore emphasized his balance-of-power justification and minimized the degree to which it detracted from the distinctive authority of the judges in expounding law.

Where this sort of analysis could lead would soon became apparent. In 1798 in the crisis over the Alien and Sedition Acts, Madison asserted the right of the states, as parties to the constitutional contract, to declare acts of Congress unconstitutional. It was a position with ominous implications, and it departed from the notion that the U.S. Constitution had been enacted by the people of the United States. Yet Madison's hopes for a complex balance of power extended to the states as well as the branches of the federal government, and he and his fellow Virginians now had reason to pursue this theory, even if it meant reducing the Constitution to a mere compact.

In the end, the calculations of utility that animated Madison's theory of a balance of power could not displace the authority of judges to expound law in their cases. A balance of power was essential for preserving liberty, but as already evident from the debates over the council of revision, Madison's contemporaries would not go so far as to abandon the common law ideals of judicial office and authority. Judicial authority arose from the office of judgment, which belonged to individual judges, and although Madison attributed the exposition of the Constitution to all of the departments of government, even if they did not exercise an office of judgment, most lawyers continued to adhere to their common law ideals.

Alexander Hamilton's *Federalist* Number 78 provides an unusually elegant illustration of how lawyers tended to perceive the authority of the judges to expound the law, including the U.S. Constitution. Both sides in the debates over the ratification of the Constitution tended to assume that judges would have this authority. Yet whereas Anti-Federalists such as Brutus acknowledged federal judicial authority and accordingly feared the Constitution was too vague, Federalists such as Hamilton considered the Constitution clear enough and came to its defense by pointing to the authority of the judges. Recognizing that the Constitution simply assumed a

[25] When Madison argued in the House of Representatives that a constitutional decision about the president's power of removal "may be made with the most advantage by the legislature itself," he immediately realized that this was implausible unless the legislature would decide the matter with the dispassion of the judges, and he therefore quickly added the qualification: "at least while the government is not led by passion, disturbed by faction, or deceived by any discoloured medium of light." This condition was improbable, but Madison did not let it disturb his hopes for a shared authority to expound the Constitution. Madison in House of Representatives (June 17, 1789), in *Debates in the House of Representatives,* 11: 926–927.

judicial authority to expound the law, Hamilton understood the necessity of reasoning about it from "the nature and reason of the thing," and he therefore marshaled the old philosophical and common law ideals about judgment and will, but now with an edge honed on the separation of powers.

He began with the distinctive character of judgment and judicial office. Drawing on familiar assumptions, he observed that the judiciary "can take no active resolution whatever" and "may truly be said to have neither Force nor Will, but merely judgment." Consequently, "the general liberty of the people can never be endangered from that quarter"—at least "so long as the judicial remains truly distinct from both the legislative and executive powers."

Some who opposed ratification of the federal constitution worried about "the right of the courts to pronounce legislative acts void, because contrary to the constitution," it being their "imagination that the doctrine would imply a superiority of the judiciary to the legislative power." In particular, they reasoned that "the authority which can declare the acts of another void, must necessarily be superior to the one whose acts may be declared void." To this centuries-old objection, Hamilton replied with the no less ancient answer that "every act of a delegated authority, contrary to the tenor of the commission under which it is exercised, is void." In other words, "the intention of the people" ought to be preferred "to the intention of their agents," and rather than "suppose a superiority of the judicial to the legislative power," it "only supposes that the power of the people is superior to both."[26]

Nonetheless, the legislature might claim authority to judge. If "the legislative body," in the manner of Parliament, were "themselves the constitutional judges of their own powers," then their "construction" was "conclusive upon the other departments." Hamilton answered that it could hardly be supposed that "the constitution could intend to enable the representatives of the people to substitute their *will* to that of their constituents." Instead, it was "far more rational to suppose that the courts were designed" to stand "between the people and the legislature," so as "to keep the latter within the limits assigned to their authority."

In the end, Hamilton understood that "[t]he interpretation of the laws is the proper and peculiar province of the courts," and he therefore concluded that the exposition of the Constitution belonged to the judges.

[26] Alexander Hamilton, Federalist Number 78, *The Federalist,* 523–525, ed. Jacob E. Cooke (Middletown: Wesleyan University Press, 1961). For an earlier illustration of both views, see Buchanan's dialogue in Chapter Three.

Whereas Madison suggested that some constitutional questions were to be resolved more like matters of power than of law, Hamilton accepted that if the constitution was a law, it was the province of the judges to expound it: "A constitution is in fact, and must be, regarded by the judges as a fundamental law," and "[i]t therefore belongs to them to ascertain its meaning as well as the meaning of any particular act proceeding from the legislative body." Obviously, the judges might "be disposed to exercise WILL instead of JUDGMENT," and if so "the consequence would . . . be the substitution of their pleasure to that of the legislative body." Yet the possibility that "the courts on the pretence of a repugnancy, may substitute their own pleasure to the constitutional intentions of the legislature" was an inescapable risk of having "judges distinct from that body." There had to be courts apart from the legislature, and in the course of their adjudications, "[t]he courts must declare the sense of the law."[27]

Judicial Resolutions: The Wilmington Declaration

The greatest danger to the authority of the judges in expounding law lay not in the executive or the legislature, but in the judges themselves. Their expositions of law enjoyed the authority of their office, but being men, they were apt to stray beyond their office, and they thereby put their authority and even their independence at risk. Over the centuries, the ideal of judicial office had come to be centered ever more narrowly around the adjudication of cases, and therefore one of the most dramatic ways that judges could overstep the limits of their authority was by expounding law in resolutions—this being what happened in 1785 in Wilmington, North Carolina.

It has been seen that Americans had sharpened their understanding of judicial office. Early seventeenth-century English judges still sometimes adopted resolutions, and Coke considered these declarations of law to have the highest possible authority outside of Parliament. Yet this ran counter to other developments that already were narrowing the authority of the judges, and by the seventeenth century, judicial authority in expounding law was becoming all the more confined to cases and even holdings in cases. Further, in America, the need for statutes specifying the jurisdiction of courts increasingly limited judges to deciding cases and controversies, and this restriction had great appeal in America because it seemed a manifestation of the natural distinction between judicial and legislative office, which was more abstractly idealized in terms of separation of powers. Amid these

[27] Ibid., 524–526.

tightened boundaries of judicial office, judges had to worry about their resolutions, not least their resolutions in which they asserted their own rights against the other branches of government, for they thereby went beyond the office in which they could expound the law with expectations of deference to their authority.

Hints of the danger have already been observed in the resolutions of the county courts of Virginia, for when the justices of these courts stood up for their rights, they abandoned their posture of sitting in judgment. The judges of these courts were justices of the peace, who exercised an office that was both judicial and administrative, and they could therefore be excused for departing from an exclusively judicial role. In their resolutions, indeed, they asserted constitutional interpretations on their own behalf, typically against the executive, and they therefore could not claim to be adopting these resolutions with the authority they enjoyed when judging cases and controversies among others. Accordingly, in the disputes over their resolutions, neither side—executive or judicial—deferred to the authority of the other, and each interpreted the Virginia Constitution for itself. The Virginia county court magistrates were sufficiently grounded in their local communities that they could hope to prevail in these political contests simply by exhausting the governor and his council, but because the justices in these circumstances did not stand on the distinctive authority of their office, they sometimes encountered opposition that they could not resist—as when George Mason and his allies on the Fairfax County Court initially rejected a county levy on constitutional grounds and then found, after a response from the executive, that they could not even sustain their position within their own court.[28] The risk that a resolution might provoke opposition from the other branches was much greater for higher court judges, who could not usually expound law with the political strength of their local community and who were therefore particularly dependent upon the authority and independence they derived from their office. Even more than local magistrates, higher court judges thus had reason to pause before adopting resolutions.

The initial example here of a judicial resolution against legislative power comes from the Wilmington District Superior Court in North Carolina. It is a story that must begin with a woman who brought the men of Fayetteville both much pleasure and much sorrow. Mary Brown became "infamous" by "Corrupting the morals of Youth" and "leading into Adultery the Masters of Families and seducing them from Domestic attentions,

[28] See Chapter Twelve.

living with them in shameful prostitution." To make matters worse, her business had the effect of "Countinancing and supporting the servants and slaves of the Inhabitants of this Town in all the Embezzlement of their owners property." She allegedly "escaped the punishments of the Laws" through "the address of her friends or the power of her money," and this, according to her opponents, "induced" them "to have recourse" to measures for her "expulsion." Like so many vigilantes, they took the view that "altho the laws d[id] not vindicate" their conduct, "yet the necessity of the case may Justifiy." Necessity, however, was no justification at law—as they found out when Mary Brown and her confederate Thomas Cabeen prosecuted them for a riot in December 1785 at the Wilmington District Superior Court.[29]

This might have been the end of the lawlessness, but some of the convicted vigilantes petitioned the General Assembly for relief from their fines, and the legislature and judiciary thus also went astray. When the General Assembly received complaints in late December from five vigilantes that their fines were "excessive," it hesitated to reach a decision without further information, and the Senate and the House therefore resolved that the convicted men "shall stand discharged from the payment of such fines" until the end of the next session of the Assembly, "when the premises may have been more fully enquired into."[30]

Nor was this the legislature's only experiment in suspending fines, for shortly afterward the legislature took a similar approach to several men who petitioned that they had forfeited their recognizances through no fault of their own. Simon Terrell and Joseph Kirk bound themselves by a recognizance for the delivery of a defendant, William Rains, before the Hills-

[29] Petition from Alexander McIver to His Excellency Governor Caswell (Nov. 27, 1786), NCSA, General Assembly, Session Records 1786–1787, Box 3, Joint Resolutions—Committee of the Whole of Two Houses on Administration of Justice Folder; Receipt of Petition of Inhabitants of Fayetteville (Nov. 28, 1786), *Journal of the Senate,* 6 (np: 1787). McIver was a butcher who traversed the charges against him, for being one of the rioters, but then defaulted by failing to appear.

[30] Resolve of Senate (Dec. 27, 1785) & Resolve of House (Dec. 27, 1785), *The Journals of the General Assembly of the State of North-Carolina,* 37–38 (first pagination series), 49 (second pagination series) (Newbern: 1786). The vigilantes who petitioned were Nathan Stedman the elder and Duncan Ochiltree, who had been fined £50 each, Nathan Stedman the younger and James Dick, who had been fined £25 each, and a Mr. Rouse, who had been fined £10. Ibid., 37. Another of the vigilantes, who sought similar treatment, observed that the Assembly "discharge[d] them from the payment of said fines, untill the further pleasure of that Honorable body should be known." Petition from Alexander McIver to His Excellency Governor Caswell (Nov. 27, 1786), NCSA, General Assembly, Session Records 1786–1787, Box 3, Joint Resolutions—Committee of the Whole of Two Houses on Administration of Justice Folder.

borough District Superior Court, but when they delivered Rains, the clerk of the court recorded neither their delivery nor his discharge, thus leaving Terrell and Kirk to suffer judgment on their forfeited recognizance. Equally deserving was John Jones, who gave a recognizance for another man who "was rendered unable by the loss of his eyes . . . to produce the body of the principal" in the Morgan District Superior Court. When these three complainants petitioned for relief, the General Assembly enacted that they be "released" from the judgments against them. More generally, in the same act, the Assembly authorized the judges to suspend executions on judgments on forfeited recognizances.[31] Nonetheless, when the Assembly the day before received yet another petition complaining about a forfeiture of a recognizance, the two houses bluntly passed a resolve for "suspending" the judgment given on the forfeiture.[32] Both as to the Fayetteville fiasco and as to the forfeited recognizances, the legislature evidently considered itself competent to release and suspend fines imposed by the judges.

The Wilmington District Superior Court was meeting in Wilmington in December 1785, and it responded with a resolution. According to the North Carolina Declaration of Rights, "all powers of suspending laws, or the execution of laws, by any authority, without consent of the Representatives of the people, is injurious to their rights, and ought not to be exercised." This legislative suspending power was probably only prospective, and it thus apparently did not leave room for any legislative remission or suspension of unpaid fines after a court had given judgment. As if to confirm this conclusion, the Declaration of Rights stated that "the legislative, executive, and supreme judicial powers of government, ought to be forever separate and distinct from each other."[33] Of course, the state could refrain from seeking writs of execution, and once the state's treasury had received the fines the state could remit them to the defendants, but could the Assembly suspend or remit fines prior to payment and thereby deprive a

[31] An Act to release certain Persons therein mentioned, from Judgments on forfeited Recognizances, and to impower the Judges to suspend Judgments hereafter to be given in all Cases (Dec. 29, 1785), Chapter XLIII, *The Laws of the State of North-Carolina, Passed at Newbern, December, 1785,* at 31 (Newbern: 1786). The statute provided: "That whenever it may appear to any Judge or Judges of the superior courts of law and equity, on any recognizance in their court adjudicated as forfeited, that there is much hardship in the case, then it may be lawful for such Judge to suspend executions thereon; and when the same shall have been so suspended, a state of the case shall be sent by the Judge or Judges to the next General Assembly, who thereupon are finally to determine." Ibid.

[32] Resolve of House of Commons (Dec. 28., 1785), *The Journals of the General Assembly of the State of North-Carolina,* 50 (Newbern: 1786). This was for William Walker, who suffered a judgment on a recognizance he gave in the March term 1785 in the Morgan District Superior Court.

[33] North Carolina Constitution of 1776, Declaration of Rights, Articles IV and V.

court's judgment of its obligation? Precisely because this sort of legislative interference concerned what happened after judgment, it was not likely to get resolved in a case, and the judges could have simply resigned themselves to this result. The judges, however, were not content with so passive a role, and at the December 1785 term in Wilmington "all the judges . . . did declare that the General Assembly had no power to remit or suspend the payment of fines until they should be paid into the Treasury."[34]

The men of Fayetteville who had hounded Mary Brown out of town were now unhappier than ever, and the next year they complained to the General Assembly. A committee of the House of Commons reported that Mary Brown and Thomas Cabeen had "rendered themselves obnoxious to the inhabitants of Fayetteville by many immoralities" and recommended that the condemned Fayetteville men "should be relieved from" their "fines" because it was "a case of peculiar hardship." The judges had spoken in their resolution against the legislative remission of fines, but the legislature apparently understood that such a resolution was of no authority. Upon hearing the report, the House and Senate "discharged and fully acquitted" the men of "the payment of the said fines" and pointedly declared that "all public officers are required to take notice and govern themselves accordingly."[35]

The joint committee that was considering an impeachment of the judges contemplated a charge against them on account of their resolution, but neither house was inclined to impeach, for the judges had made themselves popular.[36] Just as the vigilantes had acted on the "necessity" of casting

[34] Report of Committee of Two Houses to whom was referred to the examination into the present mode of the administration of Justice in the Superior Courts of Law and Equity (c. Jan. 1, 1787), NCSA, General Assembly, Session Records 1786–1787, Box 3, Joint Resolutions—Committee of the Whole of Two Houses on Administration of Justice Folder. The description of the resolution here is taken from the committee report reciting the allegations against the judges, which explained that "for the declaration of the Judges as to the power of the General Assembly," the committee "refer to the information of the practisers of the law on the Committee, who attend Wilmington Court." Ibid.

The judges apparently did not object to the statute authorizing the judges to suspend execution, and the next year at least one of the three judges, Samuel Spencer, certified that "the forfeiture" of a recognizance by James Blair and others "ought not of right and in justice to take place, because the same hath been occasioned by an omission of the . . . clerk." *The Journal of the Senate At a General Assembly begun and Held at Fayetteville,* 6 (Nov. 24, 1786) (np: [1787]). Of course, the inhabitants of Fayetteville were still petitioning for the relief of the men who attacked Mary Brown. Ibid., 10 (Nov. 28, 1786). Both houses resolved that McIver be refunded his money. Ibid., 14 (Dec. 4, 1786).

[35] Resolution (Dec. 29, 1786), *Journal of the House of Commons. At a General Assembly begun and held at Fayetteville, on the eighteenth day of November, in the Year of Our Lord One Thousand Seven Hundred and Eighty-Six,* 58 (np: [1787]); concurrence of Senate received (Dec. 30, 1786), ibid., 59.

[36] The committee associated the accusation about the judges' declaration with the further charge that "the Judges Spencer and Williams did in some instance receive monies levied for

out Mary Brown, so the judges had banished the Tories Brice and McNeil because this was "necessary" for "the peace of the community."[37] The judges had thereby acquired a reputation for being patriots, and the Assembly therefore dropped all charges against them, including the one concerning their declaration at Wilmington.

This whitewashing of the judges nauseated Archibald Maclaine. As has been seen, he protested that in *Bayard v. Singleton* Judges Spencer and Williams "delayed to decide thereon, out of respect to the General Assembly; whereas it was their duty to determine thereon if they were decided and uniform in their opinions." At the same time that he thus condemned the judges for failing to hold a statute unlawful, he also denounced their declaration at Wilmington because it was outside judicial office: It was "an extrajudicial interference with the power of the legislature, & tends to weaken the confidence of the people in their representa[tives]."[38] The judges' resolution was beyond their office, and it thus not merely lacked authority but also, in Maclaine's view, deserved impeachment.

Judicial Resolutions: The Cases of the Judges

No resolutions more dramatically revealed the danger of judicial adventures beyond judicial office than the so-called *Cases of the Judges,* which were, in fact, two resolutions by the Virginia Court of Appeals. They must be examined in detail here at the close of this chapter on authority because no other decisions so dramatically reveal the effect of the tightened conception of judicial office. In expounding law in resolutions rather than cases, and in so

---

forfeited recognizances and fines imposed by themselves." Report of Committee of Two Houses to whom was referred to the examination into the present mode of the administration of Justice in the Superior Courts of Law and Equity (c. Jan. 1, 1787), NCSA, General Assembly, Session Records 1786–1787, Box 3, Joint Resolutions—Committee of the Whole of Two Houses on Administration of Justice Folder. John Hay observed about these cases: "[S]ome observations having passed as to usual appropriations of fines hence naturally resulted [in] an inquiry into this matter that Judges might have such a provision for the discharge of their salaries as would not tempt to a conduct so highly indelicate to give it the mildest term." Letter from John Hay to William Hooper (Dec. 24, 1786), NCSA, General Assembly, Session Records 1786–1787, Box 3, Joint Resolutions—Committee of the Whole of Two Houses on Administration of Justice Folder. The two judges "endeavored to excuse it from the plea of necessity," to the disgust of Maclaine. Archibald Maclaine, "Protest against the resolution of the House of Commons, declaring that the Judges ought not to be accused of any misdemeanors in office" (Jan. 1787), ibid.

[37] As Ashe explained to the committee considering the impeachment, "the Court thought, the peace of the community made the measure necessary, & that the law & Treaty Justified it." Letter from Samuel Ashe to the Speakers of the Houses (Dec. 14, 1786), ibid.

[38] Archibald Maclaine, "Protest against the resolution of the House of Commons, declaring that the Judges ought not to be accused of any misdemeanors in office" (Jan. 6, 1787), ibid.

clearly misexpounding the Virginia Constitution, the judges of the Court of Appeals stepped outside the realm in which they could expect authority or even independence, and the governor and legislature responded by depriving the Court of Appeals of its jurisdiction and forcing the entire bench to resign.

In January 1788, the General Assembly adopted an act establishing a system of district courts. For years Virginians had worried about the difficulty of obtaining justice from their central courts in Richmond. The county courts could handle simple matters, but an additional system of district, circuit, or assize courts seemed necessary if parties were to enjoy the benefit of professional judges without having to travel long distances to the central courts in Richmond. Judges and lawyers had their own, complicated interests in these reforms, but more generally the state was suffering a severe economic crisis that left cash short and debt high, and in these circumstances a judicial reform that would ease the collection of debts was one of the few measures the legislature could take to restore financial confidence.[39]

The General Assembly, in its January 1788 District Court Act, attempted to create district courts at the lowest possible cost, and it therefore required existing central court judges to sit on the new courts without additional pay. The state was almost as short of specie as its citizens, and it therefore had had difficulty paying its judges. To adapt to this situation, the legislature created new courts with old judges.

The District Court Act thus gave the judges of the Court of Appeals an entirely new layer of burdens, and this seemed especially disturbing after the judges had already accepted diminished compensation. Their salaries had originally been five hundred pounds.[40] They had soon, however, been subjected to "various substitutions of Paper Money and Tobacco for Specie," which "the Judges considered as temporary expedients," and which seemed a public necessity rather than something "designed to affect their independence." They therefore "acquiesced, content to share in the public calamities, in hopes of a recurrence to the Constitutional principle in better times." Indeed, "they considered in the same light the Act of 1781, stating the Salary at £300, as dictated by necessity, and not proceeding from de-

[39] Act establishing District Courts (Jan. 2, 1788), in William Waller Hening, ed., *Laws of Virginia,* 12: 532 (Richmond: 1823). The district courts largely displaced the power of the county courts and thus were part of a shift in power away from local justices of the peace. See A. G. Roeber, *Faithful Magistrates and Republican Lawyers: Creators of Virginia Legal Culture, 1680–1810,* Chapter 6 (Chapel Hill: University of North Carolina Press, 1981).

[40] Such at least was the original salary set for the judges of the General Court and the Court of Chancery, who sat on the Court of Appeals.

sign, and therefore did not conceive it to be their Official duty to interpose."[41]

The judges' new task of manning the district courts, however, substantially expanded their work, and although it did not literally diminish their salaries, it seemed to the judges to have this effect. The judges sat on the Court of Appeals by virtue of their commissions for the other central courts—the General Court, the Court of Chancery, and the Court of Admiralty—all of which were courts of original jurisdiction, but only one of which, the General Court, was a court of common law. Accordingly, when the District Court Act required the judges of all these courts to sit on district courts, the chancery and admiralty judges acquired "jurisdiction in common Law cases, which . . . may be considered as a new Office, the labour of which would greatly exceed that of the former, without a correspondent reward." The judges of the General Court, moreover, would have duties that were "not changed as to their subjects" but that would be "more than doubled, without any increase of Salary." This "appeared so evident an attack upon the independency of the Judges, that they thought it inconsistent with a consciencious discharge of their duty to pass it over."[42] Exactly what sort of duty thus required them to resist they did not make clear, and if it was a general political duty to preserve their rights under the constitution rather than the distinctive duty of their office, they might be in trouble.

The judges defended themselves by adopting a resolution, and like some of the county courts, they thus assumed a stance rather different from that of men sitting in judgment on a case. It cannot be known whether a case would have ever arisen in which the judges could have decided the constitutional question judicially, but by taking up the issue in a resolution, the judges abandoned the confines of their office. Perhaps if they had waited until they themselves were asked to take oaths under their commissions for the district courts, they could have claimed to be in the same position as Edward Coke and his brethren when they were asked to take oaths under a commission for ecclesiastical causes. Worried that the commission was unlawful, Coke and the other judges refused to take their oaths or even

[41] Order and Remonstrance of the Judges (May 12, 1788), Supreme Court of Appeals, Order Book No. 1, 1779–1789, at 133, LVA. When the ephemeral frontier state of Franklin broke away from North Carolina, Virginians could entertain themselves by reading that it paid its judges in deer skins, its county clerks in beaver pelts, and its justices in muskrats. *Virginia Independent Chronicle* (Mar. 11, 1789). It was less amusing, however, that Virginia paid in tobacco.

[42] Order and Remonstrance of the Judges (May 12, 1788), Supreme Court of Appeals, Order Book No. 1, 1779–1789, at 133, LVA.

to sit down.[43] The Virginia judges, however, took the first opportunity to protest rather than the last—the occasion being the appointment of clerks under the District Court Act. Although the judges of the Court of Appeals were not to sit on the district courts until the summer of 1788, they were required by the act at their April 1788 session to appoint clerks for these new courts, and the judges took this as the occasion to protest. Obviously, there could be no question about the constitutionality of appointing the clerks, unless the act's inadequate compensation for the judges rendered the entire statute void, but the judges (being consumed with their sense of injured dignity) did not focus on this problem.[44] Thus, rather than confront the constitutional question for pressing reasons—because they had to decide it in a case, because they had to avoid acting unlawfully themselves, or at least because they felt it wrong to take an oath under an unlawful statute—they chose to adopt a resolution at the end of the April term, because they believed they "ought not to do any thing officially in execution of an Act which appeared to be contrary to the spirit of the Constitution." With this sense of fastidiousness about a statute that had not yet required them to do anything unlawful, the judges entered in their records that "the Court do Adjudge that Clerks of the said Courts ought not now to be appointed"—for reasons they explained "in a remonstrance to the General Assembly."[45]

Rather than act in their office of deciding cases, the judges explained that it was more generally as a branch of government—the judiciary—that they felt obliged to reach the constitutional issues. Their only "alternatives," they claimed, were "either to decide those questions, or resign their Offices." Although "[t]he latter would have been their choice, if they could have considered the questions as affecting their individual interests only," they had to consider "their Office." They found themselves "called by their Country to sustain an important post as one of the three pillars on which the great fabric of government was erected," and "they judged that a resignation would subject them to the reproach of deserting their station, and betraying the sacred interests of Society entrusted with them." With this sense of their duty to sustain their pillar of government, they "found themselves obliged to decide, however their delicacy might be wounded, or whatever temporary inconveniencies might ensue, and in that decision to declare, that the Constitution and the Act are in opposition and cannot ex-

43 See Chapter Six.
44 Instead, it was Governor Edmund Randolph and the Council that noticed this. See below.
45 Order and Remonstrance of the Judges (May 12, 1788), Supreme Court of Appeals, Order Book No. 1, 1779–1789, at 130, 134, LVA.

ist together, and that the former must controul the operation of the latter." It would have been one thing to give this opinion as judges in a case and thus within their office; it was quite another, however, to do so merely in defense of their office and thus as one of the "three pillars" of government in a contest with one of the others.[46]

This abandonment of the sphere in which they enjoyed judicial authority was risky enough, for it left their opinions with no greater authority than could be discerned from their reasoning. The judges, however, now compounded the risk through their mode of reasoning. Going beyond the Constitution or the principles it contained, they relied on the more general principle of independence that lay behind the Constitution so as to interpret the Constitution's limited guarantee of salaries to mean much more than had plausibly been intended.

The judges established the principle of independence by observing that "[t]he propriety and necessity of the independence of the Judges is evident in reason and the nature of their Office." To this they added the political function of the judges—that "they are to decide between government and the People as well as between contending Citizens," and "if they be dependent on either corrupt influence may be apprehended." Of course, having thus reasonably "supposed" a principle of judicial independence, the judges still had to inquire "whether the People have secured, or departed from, it in their Constitution or form of government." At a very general level, the people had "secured" judicial independence by "distributing" the governmental power "into three great branches, Legislative, Executive, and Judiciary" and declaring that these powers "be kept separate and distinct from each other." More specifically, "from the influence of the principle before observed upon," the people had "declared, that the Judges should hold their Offices during good behaviour."[47]

Yet the people's application of the principle of independence to the question of salaries had not been so satisfactory. On compensation for the judges, the Constitution merely stated that the judges of the various central courts "shall have fixed and adequate salaries," and the judges now admitted that this was incomplete but suggested that the word "adequate" provided a principle of proportionate compensation:

> Their independence would have been rendered compleat, by fixing the quantum of their Salaries, which perhaps would have been done, if the duties of

[46] Ibid., 131.
[47] Ibid., 131–132. For these separation and tenure provisions, see Virginia Constitution of 1776, Declaration of Rights, §5.

> Office had been at that time ascertained. But altho' it was not then done, yet in respect to this, the Constitution gives a principle, not to be departed from, declaring that the Salaries shall be adequate and fixed, leaving it to the Legislature to judge what would be adequate when they should appoint the duties.[48]

From this, the judges concluded that once the legislature had established their compensation, "their "[s]alary was thenceforth to be considered as fixed, while the duties should continue the same." Put another way, "when public utility should require an increase or diminution of duty, there should be an analogous alteration of Salary."[49] The judges thus decided that the constitution's guarantee of "fixed and adequate salaries" required the legislature to adjust their salaries—even if sometimes to diminish them. This position had its logic, but in pursuit of the principle of independence, the judges took so expansive a view of what was "adequate" as to require that their salaries be *unfixed,* and this might seem to confirm that in putting aside their robes to advocate their own rights, the judges sacrificed not only the authority of their office but also their capacity for carefully reasoned independent judgment.

Their interpretation rested not so much on the Constitution as on a functional conception of the principle of independence. Rather than recognize that the Constitution barred only the most dangerous threats to independence, the judges assumed it should be understood fully to preserve what the judges conceived to be the political function of judicial independence: "[T]he precaution of the founders of our government to secure liberty" would be in "vain" if the legislature, "tho restrained from changing the tenure of Judicial Offices, are at liberty to compel a resignation by reducing salaries to a Copper, or by making it a part of the Official duty to become hewers of wood and Drawers of water." It would also be in vain "if, in case of a contrary disposition, they can make Salaries exorbitant, or by lessening the duties render Offices almost Sinecures." In all of these instances, "the independence of the judiciary is . . . equally annihilated." Actually, independence had not always been thought to be annihilated in such circumstances, for judges could preserve their independent judgment even in the face of external threats as long as they could resist their desires and fears. Such had probably been the understanding of the Virginia judges when

48 Virginia Constitution of 1776; Order and Remonstrance of the Judges (May 12, 1788), Supreme Court of Appeals, Order Book No. 1, 1779–1789, at 132, LVA. Being judges rather than drafters, the members of the Court did not pause to consider whether a constitution could remain permanent if it were to fix the particular amount of their salaries.
49 Ibid.

they had accepted diminished salaries earlier in the decade. The judges of the Court of Appeals, however, now discounted the possibility of independent judgment under external pressures, and they thereby turned the ideal of independence inside out—making the external independence central—this being the basis of their claim that the Constitution had to be understood to protect a flexible, functional independence rather than the limited "fixed" protection it more clearly offered.[50] In short, the judges of the Court of Appeals not only abandoned their office of deciding cases but also, in the course of interpreting, stretched the principle of independence beyond the Constitution, and thus went even further into territory in which they could not expect to have any authority.[51]

The judges were engaged as disputants rather than as judges in a case, and with a deep sense of being aggrieved, they miscalculated the dangers of acting beyond the limited sphere in which they might enjoy authority. They paused to ask "whether they had power, and it was their duty, to declare that the Act must yield to the Constitution," and recognizing the "possible objection" that they were "assuming a right to controul the Legislature," they responded that "when they decide between an Act of the People and an Act of the Legislature they are within the line of their duty, declaring what the law is, and not making a new Law."[52] Such a decision was certainly within their duty, and if they were reaching a holding in a case, their decision might be authoritative, but was this true when they were adopting a resolution or relying on reasoning that went beyond the Constitution? Fifteen years later, in *Marbury v. Madison,* Chief Justice Marshall similarly observed that "[i]t is emphatically the province and duty of the judicial department to say what the law is," but he did so in a case, and he hastened to explain that "[t]hose who apply the rule to particular cases, must of necessity expound and interpret that rule."[53] There was no such necessity for the Virginia judges.

These judges understood that when they used a resolution to enter a contest with the legislature, they sacrificed much of their judicial authority, and in their view they thereby gave the decision to the legislature and then

[50] Ibid., 133–134.

[51] Four years later, when Timothy Ford argued about the jurisdiction of the U.S. Supreme Court "by a reference . . . to the *principles* of the constitution," he conceded that "objections to this mode of resolving constitutional points, have been insisted on by many." [Timothy Ford], *An Enquiry into the Constitutional Authority of the Supreme Federal Court, Over the Several States, in their Political Capacity,* 6 (Charleston: 1792).

[52] Order and Remonstrance of the Judges (May 12, 1788), Supreme Court of Appeals, Order Book No. 1, 1779–1789, at 131, 134, LVA.

[53] *Marbury v. Madison* (1803), Cranch, *Reports,* 1: 177.

the people. Rather than deciding a case, they were taking a position as a co-ordinate branch of government, and from this it followed that the only peaceful means of resolving the fate of the District Court Act rested with the acquiescence of the legislature. If the legislature did not comply, the judges could appeal only to the people, who were the highest worldly judge:

> [E]ver disposed to maintain harmony with the other members of government, so necessary to promote the happiness of Society, the Court most sincerely wish, that the present infraction of the Constitution may be remedied by the Legislature themselves, and thereby all further uneasiness on the occasion be prevented. But should their wishes be disappointed by the event they see no other alternative for a decision between the Legislature and judiciary than an Appeal to the People, whose Servants both are, and for whose sakes both were created, and who may exercise their Original and supreme power, whenever they think proper. To that tribunal, therefore, the Court, in that Case, commit themselves, conscious of perfect integrity in their intentions, however they may have been mistaken in their Judgment.[54]

Only three months earlier, in *Federalist* Number 49, James Madison had paraphrased Thomas Jefferson's argument, in his *Notes on the State of Virginia:*

> The several departments being perfectly co-ordinate by the terms of their common commission, none of them, it is evident, can pretend to an exclusive or superior right of settling the boundaries between their respective powers; and how are the encroachments of the stronger to be prevented, or the wrongs of the weaker to be redressed, without an appeal to the people themselves; who, as the grantors of the commission, can alone declare its true meaning and enforce its observance?

Madison conceded that "[t]here is certainly great force in this reasoning"—particularly "for certain great and extraordinary occasions"—but "there appear to be insuperable objections against the proposed recurrence to the people, as a provision in all cases for keeping the several departments of power within their constitutional limits." The greatest objection was that appeals to the people "would usually be made by the executive and judiciary departments," who would not "enjoy equal advantages" with the legislative—most profoundly because they were "too far removed from the people to share much in their prepossessions."[55] This objection, although raised

[54] Order and Remonstrance of the Judges (May 12, 1788), Supreme Court of Appeals, Order Book No. 1, 1779–1789, at 134, LVA.

[55] James Madison, Federalist Number 49, *The Federalist,* 339, 341. According to Madison, this appeal to the people would involve calling a constitutional convention. Jefferson, how-

by Madison against regular appeals to the people, might also, almost as forcefully, apply to judicial participation in a Madisonian balance of power among the departments of government. Madison, however, thought that a balance of power contrived through a government's "interior structure" would suffice to keep the departments within their limits—as if judges really had power rather than mere authority—and the judges of the Court of Appeals similarly hoped their resolution would induce the legislature's cooperation and thus render an appeal to the people unnecessary.[56]

Of course, most American judges defended themselves in a more cautious manner. Rather than exercise either will or judgment in resolutions, most judges merely exercised judgment in their cases. This was clearly within their office, and this allowed them to claim an authority that could prevail against the other branches of government. The judges of the Virginia Court of Appeals, however, followed the sort of path laid out by Madison and ultimately even the sort envisioned by Jefferson. They demanded that the legislature remedy its infraction of the constitution and, failing this, invited "an Appeal to the People."

The character of the judges' resolution was summed up several years later by Judge James Henry. In *Kamper v. Hawkins,* he had to decide whether the legislature could constitutionally place common law and equitable jurisdiction within a single court. It was suggested by counsel that this question had been resolved by the 1788 resolution of the judges of the Court of Appeals, but Henry could not rely on the resolution "as a binding precedent," for "I cannot view it as an adjudged case." He carefully avoided "saying any thing about the propriety or impropriety of that business," for it was "sufficient" to observe that the constitutional question "did not then come before the court in a judicial manner," but rather "was taken up as a general proposition, and when published, contained an appeal to the people," which "looked like a dissolution of government."[57]

---

ever, went further. He thought that in the Virginia constitution there was "no barrier between the legislative, executive and judiciary departments," and that therefore "the legislature may seize the whole" and reduce their quorum to one, whom they might "call a chairman, speaker, dictator, or by any other name they please." Getting rather carried away, Jefferson concluded that "[o]ur situation is indeed perilous" and that his fellow Virginians should call a convention "to fix the constitution"—in particular "to bind up the several branches of government by certain laws, which when they transgress their acts shall become nullities." By this means, the people would "render unnecessary an appeal to the people"—that is, a rebellion—"on every infraction of their rights, on the peril that their acquiescence shall be construed into an intention to surrender those rights." Thomas Jefferson, *Notes on the State of Virginia,* 234–235 (Query 13) (Paris: 1782).

56 James Madison, Federalist Number 51, *The Federalist,* 347.

57 *Kamper v. Hawkins* (General Court 1793), Brockenbrough & Holmes, *Reports,* 50. Judge

In May 1788, Governor Edmund Randolph could not afford to be so candid. He was a former attorney general who well understood the awkwardness of the situation, and although, upon receiving the judges' resolution, he evidently recognized that the judges had cast off the authority they ordinarily enjoyed in their office, he maintained a tone of formal respect. The judges had adopted their resolution when called upon to appoint clerks under the District Court Act, and Randolph and his council therefore concluded that "it is presumable, that in the opinion of the court of appeals the said act is a nullity in the whole."[58] It was not clear, however, that the judges thought their resolution settled the status of the statute, for as has been seen, they hoped "that the present infraction of the Constitution may be remedied by the Legislature themselves," and to this end they sent their resolution to the Governor with a request that he convey it to the General Assembly.[59] Randolph therefore issued a proclamation calling a special meeting of the legislature so it could "revise the said Act and examine the proceedings of the . . . Court, according to the standard of Constitutional right."[60] This was as far as Randolph would go in public to question the Court's standard of constitutional right, let alone its authority, and even in his letter transmitting the judges' remonstrance to the General Assembly, he merely noted that "[i]t is not our purpose to go into any opinion concerning it." He had to acknowledge, however, that the remonstrance left the constitutional questions to be resolved by the Assembly—that he and his council "have been induced to call the legislature at this inconvenient season from our anxiety for an uninterrupted course of justice, and

---

Nelson kept his thoughts within a parenthetical, saying that it "had been decided by the judges of the court of appeals, (whether judicially or not in another question,) that a law contrary to the constitution is *void.*" Ibid., 23. Judge Roane observed that "although a judge is interested privately in preserving his independence, yet it is the right of the people which should govern him," and far from actively pursuing their own interests, "[t]he only effect on the judges in such case should be, to distrust their own judgment if the matter is doubtful, or in other words to require clear evidence before they decide in cases where interest may possibly warp the judgment." Ibid., 39.

[58] *Journals of the Council of the State of Virginia,* 4: 239 (May 14, 1788), ed. George H. Reese (Richmond: Virginia State Library, 1967).

[59] Order and Remonstrance of the Judges (May 12, 1788), Supreme Court of Appeals, Order Book No. 1, 1779–1789, at 134, LVA.

[60] Governor Edmund Randolph, Proclamation (May 14, 1788), LVA, Governor Edmund Randolph Executive Papers, Box 53 (May 14, 1788). On the same day Charles Lee wrote to Washington that "the Governor does not seem to like the idea" of calling the General Assembly, "and this aversion is attributed to the circumstance, that the district bill was drawn by him." Letter from Charles Lee to George Washington (May 14, 1788), in *The Documentary History of the Ratification of the Constitution,* 9: 797, eds. John P. Kaminski et al. (Madison: State Historical Society of Wisconsin, 1990).

the necessity of having the constitutional questions, which are the subject of the remonstrance, settled as soon as possible."[61]

The special session of the General Assembly that met in June 1788 "declin'd entering into" the constitutional questions raised by the judges' resolution, for the members had more pressing concerns: They were "anxious to get home about their harvest."[62] They therefore simply passed a statute temporarily suspending the operation of the District Court Act until the General Assembly's next regular meeting.[63]

When the General Assembly met again, in late 1788, "[t]he arrangement of the Judiciary" was "the principal subject" before the House of Delegates, and some members wanted to take a vote condemning the judges. The "late conduct of our Judges" troubled men who did not believe the state's constitution was really "paramount [to] the Ordinary Legislature," and some such men now sought a vote on "'whether the Judiciary may declare a law, in their opinion ag[ai]nst the constitution, void.'" Cooler heads prevailed, and it was agreed to "pass by" this broad question, lest it "create heats & animosities that will produce harm."[64] Even so, the lesser question—as to whether the judges by adopting a resolution had gone beyond their office—must have remained on the minds of many delegates.

Some delegates sympathetically proposed a method for judicial participation in legislation that would be less disruptive than the method adopted by the judges the previous spring. The judges in their resolution had in effect merely disagreed with the legislature about the constitutionality of a statute, and the House of Delegates therefore passed a bill requiring the judges to share their concerns earlier and in a less dramatic fashion. The House thought "it would greatly tend to clear our Code of Laws from de-

[61] Letter from Edmund Pendleton to the General Assembly (June 23, 1788), Edmund Pendleton Executive Papers (June 23, 1788). Also printed in *The Letters and Papers of Edmund Pendleton, 1734–1803,* at 2: 509, ed. David J. Mays (Charlottesville, Virginia Historical Society, 1967).

[62] Letter from James Monroe to Thomas Jefferson (July 12, 1788), in *The Papers of Thomas Jefferson,* 13: 353, eds. Julian P. Boyd and Mina R. Bryan (Princeton: Princeton University Press, 1956). See also Letter from William Nelson, Jr. to William Short (July 12, 1788), in Kaminski et al., eds., *The Documentary History of the Ratification of the Constitution,* 10: 1703.

[63] An act to suspend the operation of the act, entituled An act establishing district courts, in *Laws of Virginia,* 12: 644 (1823).

[64] Letter from Alexander White to James Madison (Aug. 16, 1788), in *The Papers of James Madison,* 11: 233; Letter from James Monroe to James Madison (Nov. 22, 1788), ibid., 361. Madison's response to the Remonstrance of the judges can be discerned from his comments on the judiciary and a council of revision in his Observations on the 'Draught of a Constitution for Virginia" (Oct. 15, 1788), ibid., 11: 290–291, 293.

fects which the most perfect theory cannot foresee, and experience only can cure, where the earliest knowledge of these, from the operation of the Laws" was "communicated to the representatives of the people in General Assembly." The House bill accordingly proposed to make "the Executive, the chancellors and the Judges of the superior Courts" a sort of law-reform committee "to report to each Session of Assembly, the defects they find in the Laws, when reduced to practice, and carried into full execution, in order that the same may have the speediest and most efficacious remedy, that the Legislature in their wisdom, can apply."[65] Rather than prohibit the judges from holding statutes unlawful, whether in cases or resolutions, this bill offered the judges an earlier, interbranch mechanism for communicating their concerns about legislation. The Senate, however, rejected the bill—at the very least because the General Assembly was already pursuing another proposal, which was less tolerant of judicial departures from office.[66]

The General Assembly simultaneously reconstituted the courts and put the judges in their place. It did so, moreover, in at least one way that went further in protecting the judges than was sought by the Court of Appeals, for it separated the trial and appellate judges. It will be recalled that the judges of the Court of Appeals had consisted of the judges of the central trial courts—the General Court, the Court of Chancery, and the Court of Admiralty. Now this would change. At the trial court level, the Assembly persisted in its plan to create district courts, and it still hoped to save money by manning the district courts with central court judges, but this time it omitted Court of Appeals judges, requiring only that "the judges of the general court" were "to attend the district courts"—a plan it made feasible by doubling the number of judges on the General Court.[67] At the appellate level, although the Assembly left the old Court of Appeals undisturbed, it established a new Court of Appeals, with jurisdiction to hear the cases depending in the old Court of Appeals and all future appeals. This new Court of Appeals would begin to meet the following summer, and its judges would not have the burden of sitting on any trial courts, whether the General Court, the Chancery, or the district courts.[68] As for the Court of Admi-

[65] House of Delegates Journal, 310–311 (Dec. 10, 1788), LVA, RG 79.

[66] *Journal of the Senate of the Commonwealth of Virginia,* 60 (Dec. 13, 1788) (Richmond: 1828).

[67] An act establishing district courts, and for regulating the general court (Dec. 22, 1788), in *Laws of Virginia,* 12: 733 (1823).

[68] An act for amending the act, intituled an act constituting the court of appeals (Dec. 22, 1788), ibid., 12: 764. The House had proposed this act on the principle "[t]hat the Court of Appeals ought to be composed of judges not being members of any of the other Supreme

ralty, which was about to lose most of its jurisdiction to the new federal courts, it was abolished, and its judges were appointed to the General Court. The General Assembly thus created separate trial and appellate benches, and it did so without abolishing the old Court of Appeals and without depriving the judges of that court of their primary judicial offices on the central trial courts (other than, for good reason, the Court of Admiralty). The Assembly even elected the five judges of the new Court of Appeals from the ranks of the General Court and the Court of Chancery, which meant in effect that the Assembly persuaded five members of the old Court of Appeals to resign and transfer to the new Court of Appeals. Yet notwithstanding the outward respect shown by these measures, the legislature had simply bypassed the old Court of Appeals by stripping it of all its jurisdiction.

The General Assembly understood that its new statutes conformed to the resolution of the judges only in the most formal manner, for although it freed the appellate court judges of any trial work, it deliberately added to the burdens of the General Court judges without increasing their salaries. When the House of Delegates outlined the new court reforms, the House agreed that "such of the Judges, as will incur additional trouble and expense under the act establishing District Courts" should receive "an adequate but moderate allowance" on top of their General Court salaries "for every day of actual duty." Perhaps not surprisingly, this was the only feature of the original proposal that was not adopted. Rather than recognize that new duties required increased salaries, the Assembly merely gave the judges traveling expenses: It enacted that "in consideration of the additional services, to be performed by the judges of the general court as judges of the district courts, they shall receive . . . each, the sum of six pence per mile for travelling to and from the courts of their respective circuits."[69]

Courts." Resolution of the House of Delegates (Nov. 20, 1788), *Journal of the House of Delegates of the Commonwealth of Virginia,* 54 (Richmond: 1828).

[69] House of Delegates, Journal, 151–152 (Nov. 20, 1788), LVA, RG 79. See also Resolutions of the House of Delegates (Nov. 20, 1788), *Journal of the House of Delegates of the Commonwealth of Virginia,* 54–55 (Richmond: 1828); An act allowing travelling expences to the judges of the general court (Dec. 23, 1788), §1, in *Laws of Virginia,* 12: 768 (1823).

Another proposal, which was put in diplomatically nonconstitutional terms, was to restore the judges of the Court of Chancery and the General Court to their original salaries of five hundred pounds. The entire section, however, was rejected and crossed out. "A Bill to amend two acts of the general assembly intituled: an act for establishing a general court, and an act for establishing district courts," LVA, House of Delegates, Rough Bills, Resolutions, etc., Box 11, Rough Bills Nov. 1788 Folder.

Ironically, although the General Assembly had been meticulous in denying salary increases for additional duties, it carelessly omitted any salary for the judges of the new Court of Appeals, and it thereby almost derailed its own plans. In early February, Edmund

When the judges of the old Court of Appeals met again in March 1789, they understood that their court had been replaced, but even in their final act as a court, they protested. They complained that the "direct operation" of the new law "is the amotion from office of the whole bench of Judges of Appeals, & the appointment of new Judges to the same Court." At the same time, they emphasized that they were "willing to make any voluntary sacrifice" for the desirable goal of establishing the district courts. They therefore all resigned, but only after declaring that the act establishing a new Court of Appeals was "incompatible with their independence."[70]

In their swan song, the judges repeated the departures from office that had got them in such straits. Once again they insisted on a "duty to guard against encroachment" and adopted a resolution "solemnly protesting against every invasion of the judiciary establishments." Once again they relied on the general principle of "independence" beyond the degree it had

---

Pendleton—President of the old Court of Appeals and the senior judge appointed to the new Court of Appeals—wrote to Governor Beverly Randolph observe that in the new legislation, "no provision had been made for the payment of salaries to the Judges of the Court of appeals." This was awkward for the Governor, because if the judges stood by their avowed principle of independence or even just the plain words of the Constitution, they perhaps could not sit on the new Court of Appeals, and even more seriously, they might refuse to vacate their old positions, thus disrupting the entire court reform. It is not evident that anyone in any branch of government wanted such a result, and when Beverly Randolph consulted with the Council, they agreed that as the legislature had gone home, the Governor only could have the Auditor issue "the usual Warrants for seventy five pounds" to "each of the Judges of the new Court of appeals who may qualify to their appointments." They added that "a letter be written to each of the said Judges respectively informing them of this Order and assuring them that the matter will be represented to the general assembly at their next Session." *Journals of the Council of the State of Virginia,* 5: 44, ed. Sandra Gioia Treadway (Feb. 3, 1789) (Richmond: Virginia State Library, 1982). For the letters, see Copy of Letter from Governor Beverley Randolph to Edmund Pendleton (Feb. 3, 1789), LVA, Governor's Office, Executive Letterbooks, 9, Reel 4; Copy of Letter from Governor Beverly Randolph to the Judges of the Court of Appeals (Feb. 4, 1789), LVA, Governor's Office, Executive Letterbooks, 9–10, Reel 4. The omission being inadvertent and the circumstances being difficult, the judges did not protest. Letter from Peter Lyons to Governor Beverley Randolph (Feb. 10, 1789), LVA, Governor Beverley Randolph Executive Papers, Box 58; Letter from William Fleming to Governor Beverley Randolph (Feb. 10, 1789), ibid; Letter of Paul Carrington to Governor Beverley Randolph (Feb. 20, 1789), ibid; Letter from John Blair to Governor Beverley Randolph (Feb. 23, 1789), ibid.

The hurried legislation was so poorly drafted that it also caused serious administrative problems for judges, clerks, and sheriffs. See, for example, Memo (Northumberland Court, Apr. 2, 1789), St. George Tucker, Notes of Cases, 2: 16, College of William and Mary, Swem Library, Tucker-Coleman Papers, Reel M-62. The clerk of the General Court was so concerned that he presented an elaborate set of queries to the judges of the General Court in February and again in June 1789. Ibid., 2: 36–41.

[70] Resolution (Mar. 5, 1789), Supreme Court of Appeals, Order Book No. 1, 1779–1789, at 139–140, LVA. Pendleton had already resigned from the Court of Chancery only three days beforehand, as apparent from his memorandum to George Wythe (Mar. 3, 1789), in *The Letters and Papers of Edmund Pendleton,* 2: 553.

been protected by the Constitution, for although they objected to "any deprivation of Office . . . in any other mode than as pointed out in the Constitution," the reality was that they had not been deprived of their office, and they therefore had to conclude more abstractly that the recent statute creating a new Court of Appeals was "incompatible with their independence."[71] The General Assembly had played rough with the Court of Appeals, but only after the judges had actively entered a political contest as one of the three pillars of government—thus abandoning the authority they would have enjoyed by sitting passively in judgment of cases. Even in its severe response, the legislature avoided any public criticism of the judges, and it carefully preserved the tenure and salaries of the judges in accord with the Constitution. Nonetheless, it obliterated the jurisdiction of the judges who had gone beyond their office.[72]

The fate of the Virginia Court of Appeals illustrates how Americans had sharpened their ideal of judicial office and how judges who adhered to a broader vision of their office could easily step beyond their sphere of authority and independence without fully appreciating the consequences. Acting as the judiciary, the judges of the Court of Appeals took the posture of a party engaged in its own dispute rather than of judges deciding a controversy among others, and they thereby adopted a stance in which they

[71] Resolution (Mar. 5, 1789), Supreme Court of Appeals, Order Book No. 1, 1779–1789, at 139–140, LVA. Unlike other entries for sessions of this court, which ended with the signature of the presiding judge (usually Pendleton and otherwise Wythe), this entry for the final session of the Court was signed by all of the judges present.

[72] The implications weighed on St. George Tucker. Several years later, he observed that "if the Legislature might at any time discontinue or annihilate either of their Courts," then "a Judge without *any breach of good behaviour,* might in effect be removed from office, by annihilating or discontinuing the office itself." Indeed, in response to the 1788 resolution of the judges of the Court of Appeals, "the legislature *without any charge* of a *breach of good behavior* by any one of that Court, *removed a majority of the Judges from their Office,* as Judges of *that Court,* by new modelling the Court altogether." Tucker, however, was "far from considering this act of the legislature as unconstitutional . . . though perhaps in the Case of some of the Judges that might have been a Question." Instead, he thought "it proves, that the Judiciary can never be independent, so long as the *existence* of *the Office* depends upon the will of the ordinary legislature, and not upon a constitutional foundation," and from this he drew "a most important distinction between *Constitutional,* & *legislative,* Courts." *Kamper v. Hawkins* (General Court 1793), St. George Tucker, Notes of Cases, 3: 18–19, College of William and Mary, Swem Library, Tucker-Coleman Papers, Reel M-62. Having taken to heart the fate of the judges of the Court of Appeals, Tucker ended up following their example when he himself later sat on the new Court of Appeals. The Assembly in 1811 almost doubled the number of days the court was to meet, and as this both inconvenienced Tucker and intruded on his principles, he felt obliged to resign—although not before writing a protest in which he now quoted the 1788 Remonstrance of the judges to show that the additional burden imposed by the 1811 statute was unconstitutional. Letter from St. George Tucker to the Governor (Apr. 2, 1811), Mumford, *Reports,* 2: xvii–xix.

had difficulty exercising dispassionate, independent judgment in matters of law. They also revealed themselves to be poor judges of politics, for when they asserted themselves as an equal branch of government, they abandoned the authority of their office, only to find themselves utterly unequal to the contest they had invited. Judges could expound the law with authority and could enjoy independence, but only while they remained within their office.

VII

INEXPLICIT IDEALS

Part VII completes this inquiry by considering why constitutions typically remained inexplicit about the ideals of law and judicial duty. There has been more than a century of debate about why American constitutions did not usually declare themselves legally binding and about why they did not generally authorize judges to exercise a power of review. If American constitutions were meant to be binding as law, and if judges were meant to enforce them by holding unconstitutional acts void, then surely the constitutions would have said as much.

This inexplicitness, however, should not be a surprise, for the ideals of law and judicial duty lay at a logical and cultural depth below the surface of the law. It was on this account, as will be seen in Chapter Eighteen, that constitutions were often inexplicit. Although they frequently alluded to laws and judges, they did not ordinarily have to explain the underlying assumptions about the obligation of law or the office of judges. Only where the application of such ideals had the potential to be misunderstood did constitutions have to become explicit, and this is why, as will be observed in Chapter Nineteen, the U.S. Constitution clarified some applications of the common law ideals but did not otherwise have much to say about them.

The U.S. Constitution thus illustrates—what by now should be obvious—that even though the ideals of law and judicial duty were never a matter of consensus, they were sufficiently conventional that they did not ordinarily have to be explained. There had always been a range of challenges to the common law ideals—challenges that prompted common lawyers to explain and sharpen their views. Nonetheless, much of importance in any society can be left inexplicit, and in eighteenth-century America it was still usually possible, even if not always, to take the ideals of law and judicial duty in stride.

18

The Inexplicitness of Constitutions

In an era in which so little is left inexplicit, commentators have had difficulty understanding why their predecessors did not generally assert in their constitutions that these were legally binding laws and that judges had a power to enforce them. If constitutions had really authorized judicial review, it seems puzzling that they never made any general declaration to this effect. The ideals of law and judicial duty, however, were presuppositions *about* law rather than doctrines *of* law, and Americans could therefore usually take these ideals for granted in thinking about their constitutions and judges.[1]

Logical and Cultural Assumptions

The ideals of law and judicial duty rested on logical and cultural assumptions that lay below the surface of the law. The ideals were not without legal authority, for they were at least implicit in what was made explicit in constitutions. At the same time, the ideals rested on foundations much deeper than the law, and it was therefore unnecessary and even inappropriate for

[1] Corwin argues that "judicial review was rested by the framers of the Constitution upon certain general principles which in their estimation made specific provision unnecessary." Edward S. Corwin, *The Doctrine of Judicial Review: Its Legal and Historical Basis and Other Essays,* 2, 17 (Gloucester: Peter Smith, 1963). See also Edward S. Corwin, "The 'Higher Law' Background of American Constitutional Law," 42 *Harvard Law Review* 149 (1928), and the work of the scholars, including Wechsler, who examine the U.S. Constitution or *Marbury* for hints of the underlying logic of judicial review. Such scholarship observes that much could be taken for granted, but it does not focus on the ideals that actually were taken for granted, let alone on how they came be so widely assumed. For an earlier version of the argument here that the ideals of law and judicial duty could be taken for granted, see Philip Hamburger, "Law and Judicial Duty," *George Washington Law Review,* 72: 38 (2003).

Americans to explain in their constitutions that these laws had obligation or that judges had a duty to decide in accord with them.

Logically, a law could not establish its own obligation, and there thus was usually no reason for a constitution to assert that it was legally binding. Instead, constitutions were assumed to depend on natural law for their legal obligation. This higher law established the equal freedom of individuals in a society, and through their consent it also lent authority to the people and obligation to their law. The people might have reason to clarify in their constitution that it was made with their authority and even perhaps that it was their law, but they could not ordinarily accomplish anything by asserting in their law that it had the obligation of law.

Similarly, judges enjoyed an office, independence, and authority that could not adequately be sustained by human law and that did not typically need to be specified by it. The duty of English and American judges had never been so much a requirement of law as an office to which they bound themselves by their oaths. It was, moreover, an office that, like men themselves, seemed to have been created on a divine model and that required a specialized, almost divine exercise of one faculty of the soul—the faculty of intellect or understanding—which had to be employed in judgment uncorrupted by the faculty of will. Thus, although a common law judge had to decide in accord with the law of the land, he did so with a divine obligation and in imitation of divine judgment, and he thus had to reach far above earthly things in his pursuit of terrestrial law. This elevated obligation and model of judgment was the ultimate source of the judge's office, independence, and authority, and men could therefore add little to the strength of this duty, freedom, and power by specifying them. Indeed, were a human law to restate the duty or to give it human obligation, this law might simultaneously raise mere judicial error to a violation of law and might subvert the understanding that judges were responsible to a higher authority. Particularly when they sat in judgment on the rights of the people against their civil government, the silence of human law became valuable, for it left space for the view that the judges acted in imitation of the judgment of a higher judge, with accountability to him rather than one of the parties.

Culturally, the ideals of legal obligation and judicial duty were so deeply ingrained that they did not need to be stated, and in this sense, although they were thought to be derived from above, they also came from below. In decision after decision, judges said that acts were unconstitutional, and they reached this conclusion at approximately the same time, in decisions across America, from north to south, while sitting on courts that ranged from supreme courts to mere county courts. They did so almost entirely without the benefit of treatises, pamphlets, or newspapers expounding the utility of such a duty, and sometimes without any professional experience or education. Evidently the judges acted on assumptions that were widespread, easily accessible, and almost irresistible—assumptions so commonplace, clear, and binding that even the humblest types of judges could feel obliged to hold acts of governors and legislatures unconstitutional. Of course, such conclusions often provoked populist exasperation. Yet the ease with which all sorts of judges across America could act on their assumptions about law and judicial duty suggests how profoundly these ideals were a part of the logic and culture of Anglo-American law.

Constitutions: Ideals and Realities

Even when men challenged judicial decisions holding statutes unconstitutional, they apparently did not generally reject the underlying ideals. Instead, they tended to question the application of these ideals. For example, as seen in Chapter Fourteen, the men who protested against judicial decisions holding statutes unconstitutional did not repudiate the ideal of judicial duty, but instead argued more narrowly that questions about the constitutionality of state statutes, like questions about acts of Parliament, lay beyond the reach of the judges. In addition, as will now become apparent, it was sometimes objected that the people of a state had not really adopted their constitution. Rather than a challenge to the notion that constitutions had the obligation of law, this was a complaint that the people had not rigorously lived up to the ideal, and the limited character of this charge confirms how much the men who opposed judicial decisions holding statutes unconstitutional were hemmed in by their attachment to the very ideals that required judges to reach such decisions.

The gap between the ideal and the reality of a constitution was all too likely in the early American states. A constitution adopted by the people was the fundamental part of the law of the land and thus was even binding on the legislature, but what if the people had not clearly adopted their constitution? In particular, what if the people of a state responded hurriedly to the exigencies of the Revolution by leaving the adoption of their constitution to an interim representative body that also doubled as their legislature?[2] In these circumstances, skeptical men could simultaneously accept

[2] It was not a novelty that a convention, acting on behalf of the people, could constitute a new government, and drawing upon the events of 1688 and 1689, Daniel Defoe explained that a convention could be presumed to act for people: "The People assembled in a Universal Mob to take the Right of Government upon themselves, are not to be supposed to give

the ideal that a constitution made by the people was legally binding and yet could doubt whether their state had such a law.

The problem arose, for example, in North Carolina. When the state's "Congress" adopted the state's constitution in 1776, it noted that "the Representatives of the freemen of North Carolina" had been "chosen and assembled in Congress, for the express purpose of framing a Constitution." The Congress, however, also acted as a legislature, and this left room for dispute—even as soon as two years later, when the Perquimans County Court imprisoned and sold manumitted slaves. On the assumption that the state's constitution had been adopted by the legislature and thus remained within the legislature's control, one of the county court justices suggested that "the Assembly had a right to form the constitution" and thus could alter or depart from it in legislation. This elicited from Samuel Johnston the forceful answer that "the constitution was already settled by the members chosen for that purpose" and that therefore the General Assembly "had no . . . power to alter the constitution."[3] Such views probably resonated among the people of North Carolina, and certainly by the time of *Bayard v. Singleton,* Iredell could observe that his conclusions about the supreme obligation

---

their personal Suffrages to every Article, but they may agree to a Convention of such Persons as they think fit to Intrust, to Constitute *de Novo,* and may Delegate their Power, or part of it to such a Convention; and in such a Case general Concurrence is to be suppos'd, unless there be a publick Dissent." [Daniel Defoe], *The Original of the Collective Body of the People of England,* 17 (London: 1702).

The English convention Parliaments had served dual constitutional and legislative functions, and this was plausible because they claimed merely to restore the constitution, because they did so with statutes under a constitution that was customary, and because they relied on subsequent Parliaments to ratify their legislation. Americans, however, tended to adopt new, express constitutions, and they therefore had reason to worry that if state conventions served as interim legislatures, then perhaps they could not adopt constitutions without returning to the people to be chosen for this purpose. For example, in Delaware the Constitution was "agreed to and resolved upon by the Representatives in full Convention of the Delaware State . . . the said Representatives being chosen by the Freemen of the said State for that express Purpose." Delaware Constitution of 1776.

3 He said that "the Assembly had no more power to alter the constitution, than the court had to make the laws that they were to act by, in courts of justice." "An account of the substance of the trial of several Negroes that had been manumitted by Friends subsequent to an Act of the General Assembly of the state of North-Carolina, passed at Newbern in the month of April or May last," *To the Senate and House of Representatives of the United States, In Congress Assembled. The Memorial and Address of the People Called Quakers, from their Yearly Meeting held in Philadelphia, by Adjournments, from the 25th of the 9th Month, to the 29th of the same inclusive, 1797,* at 5 ([Philadelphia]: 1797).

In Rhode Island, it was not even obvious that there was a constitution, and thus, as has been seen, the central question in *Trevett v. Weeden* was not the verity of general principles about constitutions and judicial duty, but whether the people of this particular state had adopted a constitution.

of the state's constitution were "so natural, and indeed so irresistible, that I do not observe they have been much contested."[4]

The concern as to whether the local constitution had actually been adopted by the people was more substantial in Virginia. The state's constitution had been devised by a body that served both legislative and constitutional functions. This body called itself a "convention" in imitation of the convention Parliament that met in 1688, and like Parliament during the Interregnum it merely passed "ordinances." It thus apparently considered itself a transitional body, which both legislated as an interim government and acted for the people in adopting the state's Constitution and Declaration of Rights.[5] Prior to enacting the Constitution, the Virginia convention tended to state that its legislation was ordained by *"the delegates of the people"* or, more typically, by *"the delegates and representatives of the several counties and corporations within this colony"* meeting *"in general convention."* When it adopted the state's Constitution and Declaration of Rights, however, it said these were "*made by the representatives of the good people of* Virginia, *assembled in full and free Convention.*"[6] Virginians could therefore reasonably believe that their convention acted in different capacities when adopting legislative acts and when adopting constitutional acts. Nonetheless, the Virginia convention had not been specially elected with a view toward enacting a constitution, and some men therefore argued that only the Virginia legislature had made the state's constitution. The implication was that the legislature that thus enacted the constitution remained free to judge the constitutionality of its acts, as if it were a sort of Parliament—this being an argument that was made in *Commonwealth v. Caton.* The 1776 convention, however, had distinguished its different roles, and St. George Tucker could therefore respond by differentiating an act of "the civil Legislature" and "the Act of the political Legislature," which was done on behalf of the people.[7]

[4] James Iredell, "To the Public" (Aug. 1786), Duke University Rare Book, Manuscript, and Special Collections Library, James Iredell Papers, Box 1.

[5] When the judges of the Court of Chancery in 1785 published the state's statutes, it collected those made between 1775 and the establishment of the new government in 1776 under the running title "INTERREGNO." *A Collection of All Such Public Acts of the General Assembly and Ordinances of the Conventions of Virginia,* 30–38 (Richmond: 1785).

[6] *Laws of Virginia,* 9: 94, 109, ed. William Waller Hening (Richmond: 1821). Afterward, statutes came to be *"enacted by the General Assembly."* Ibid., 113.

[7] "To. W.N.," Argument on Behalf of the Prisoners, Addressed to William Nelson, William and Mary College Library, Tucker-Coleman Papers, Legal Papers, Virginia Supreme Court of Appeals, Mfm Reel M-44. The act of the political legislature was "in [the] nature of an original Compact between the Citizens of the Commonwealth." Ibid. For the conventions that had special elections in contemplation of adopting a constitution and those that did

No one did more to keep alive the questions about the Virginia Constitution than Thomas Jefferson. Already when his fellow Virginians were drafting the state constitution in 1776, he had asked them to delay matters until they had "a commission of greater latitude, and one more specific . . . by the people."[8] This was not an entirely public-minded suggestion, for he hoped he could attend a subsequent convention and could have the honor of doing the drafting. Whether or not he stirred up some of the objections raised in the Court of Appeals in 1782, he argued shortly afterward in his *Notes on the State of Virginia* that the convention's delegates "received in their creation no powers but what were given to every legislature before and since" and that they "could not therefore pass an act transcendant to the powers of other legislatures."[9] This objection never enjoyed many adherents among the people of Virginia, but Jefferson's publication ensured that it would remain on the minds of the judges. Probably to fend off such concerns, the judges of the Court of Appeals in their 1788 resolution against the District Court Act stated that they had written an opinion "declaring the Supremacy of the Constitution."[10] Even as late as the 1793, in *Kamper v. Hawkins,* some of the lawyers still relied on Jefferson's *Notes* to question the state's constitution, and all the judges therefore had to respond.[11]

---

not, see Allan Nevins, *The American States During and After the Revolution,* 129 (New York: Augustus M. Kelly, 1969).

[8] Randolph's Reminiscences, as quoted by Moncure Daniel Conway, *Omitted Chapters of History Disclosed in the Life and Papers of Edmund Randolph,* 28 (New York: Da Capo, 1971). When Jefferson urged Randolph to press these objections at the convention, Edmund Pendleton, Patrick Henry, and George Mason "saw no distinction between the conceded power to declare independence, and its necessary consequence, the fencing of society by the institution of government." Ibid.

[9] Thomas Jefferson, *Notes on the State of Virginia,* 219 (Query 13) ([Paris]: 1782 [actually 1784]). The *Notes* were "written in the year 1781" and "somewhat corrected and enlarged in the winter of 1782." Ibid., title page.

[10] Order and Remonstrance of the Judges (May 12, 1788), Supreme Court of Appeals, Order Book No. 1, 1779–1789, at 131, LVA.

[11] In *Kamper v. Hawkins* an objection was raised that the "Convention [was] not specially appointed to form a Constitution." *Kamper v. Hawkins* or *The Case of Injunctions* (General Court of Virginia, 1793), St. George Tucker, Notes of Cases, 3: 27, College of William and Mary, Swem Library, Tucker-Coleman Papers, Reel M-62. Although St. George Tucker, now sitting on the General Court, understood that the question had been decided by the judges of the Court of Appeals in their 1788 resolution, he again felt obliged to argue at length that "[t]he Convention then was not the *ordinary Legislature* of Virginia," but rather "was the Body of the *people,*" one reason being that it "had not the shadow of a *legal* or *constitutional* form above it." Instead, "[i]t derived its existence from a higher source; a power which can supersede all law, & annul the Constitution itself—namely the *people,* in their *sovereign, unlimited,* and *unlimitable authority* & *Capacity.*" Ibid., 3: 6, 9. William Nelson held that the "power to make Consts. must be derived from the people" and that it was "no arg[umen]t ag[ain]st this position that some Acts contrary to [the] Const. have passed," for "[t]hey may never have been questioned." Ibid., 27. Roane observed that the Constitution

These disputes as to whether particular state constitutions had been adopted by the people are a reminder that the challenges to judicial decisions holding legislation unconstitutional tended not to be direct protests against the ideal that constitutions had the obligation of law or otherwise against the ideals of law and judicial duty. The possibility that judges could hold statutes unconstitutional provoked a range of objections, including the point examined here, that the people of some states had not actually adopted their constitution. Yet far from showing that the common law ideals could not be taken for granted, this sort of objection reveals how men could try to avoid the implications of their ideals by taking the attitude of realists—or, from another angle, rigorists. The realities of human conduct rarely conform entirely to the rigors of ideals, and by taking a caustic view of the realities or a highly rigorous view of the ideals, men could adhere to the ideals while questioning their application. The common law ideals, including the notion that a constitution was law, were almost beyond dispute, and the challenges to judicial decisions therefore typically contested the application of the ideals rather than the ideals themselves.

The Explicit and the Inexplicit in State Constitutions

As a result of the strength of the ideals of law and judicial duty, they could be left largely inexplicit in most state constitutions. Only when their application was susceptible of doubt, as when they were applied to novel or complex circumstances, did their operation have to be explained.

One such instance was when a state constitution gave continued force to colonial law. The problem was that if colonial laws were given continued force by a state constitution, they might seem to enjoy constitutional obligation, and a state constitution that expressly preserved the force of colonial laws therefore had to bar any such implication. This, for example, is what the New Jersey Constitution did when it declared that preexisting common law and statute law "shall still remain in force." Having thus constitutionally attributed legal obligation to the laws that were in effect under the prior government, the Constitution prudently added, "until they shall be

---

had been "[s]anctioned for 17. years." Ibid., 28. Henry said that "[w]hether [the] Const: [was] properly form'd or not the fact is we have one—sanctioned by the people." Ibid., 29. Tyler relied on precedent to say: "Much trouble saved by former Judges. [The] validity of [the] Const: can not be disputed. . . . If a doubt of the original obligation of the Constitution the subsequent conduct of the people must shew it clearly." Ibid., 29–30. For further details, see Brockenbrough and Holmes, *Reports,* 21. Incidentally, rather than suggest that Virginia had a customary constitution, Roane, Henry, and Tyler were arguing that acquiescence cured the defects in the adoption of the express constitution.

altered by a future law of the Legislature," and it explained that "such parts" were "excepted, as are repugnant to the rights and privileges contained in this Charter."[12]

Another point at which the application of the common law ideals had to become explicit concerned the status of bills of rights. The English had viewed power and liberty as the two sides of a single line drawn by law and had treated their enumerations of rights as parts of their constitution. On the Continent, however, where constitutional theory often went untempered by experience, the generalization that a constitution decreed the form of government seemed to suggest that guarantees of individual liberty lay outside the constitution. Such was the reasoning adopted by Montesquieu. As noted by one Virginian, Montesquieu "makes a distinction between the laws that form Political liberty with regard to the constitution, & those by which it is formed in respect to the Citizen."[13] This was a disturbing thought for men who hoped in their bills of rights to establish binding constitutional limitations on government, and some Americans therefore thought they had to expressly incorporate their bills of rights into their constitutions—as when the Pennsylvania, North Carolina, and Vermont constitutions stated: "The declaration of rights is hereby declared to be to be a part of the constitution of this commonwealth, and ought never to be violated on any pretence whatever."[14]

Yet even when constitutions thus attempted to counteract Montesquieu's assumption about bills of rights, they did not bother to say more. These constitutions did not generally declare that unconstitutional laws were unlawful or void, for this was not in doubt.[15] Nor did they authorize

[12] New Jersey Constitution of 1776, Article XXII.

[13] George Gilmer, Commonplace Book, 121 (before May 1778), Virginia Historical Society, Mss 5:5, G4213:1, quoting Montesquieu, *The Spirit of the Laws* (XI.i).

[14] Pennsylvania Constitution of 1776, §46. Similarly, see North Carolina Constitution of 1776, Article XLIV; Vermont Constitution of 1777, §XLIII. In some states the solution was to include the bill of rights within the constitution. Not content with this, the Massachusetts Constitution began with a preface in which the people established "the following *Declaration of Rights, and Frame of Government,* as the Constitution of the Commonwealth of Massachusetts." Massachusetts Constitution of 1780, Preface.

[15] Some constitutions attempted to preclude amendment of various provisions, but this question was different. For example, the Delaware Constitution stated that "[n]o article of the declaration of rights and fundamental rules of this State," nor specified articles of the Constitution, "ought ever to be violated on any pretence whatever," and what this meant became clear when the Constitution added: "No other part of this constitution shall be altered, changed, or diminished without the consent of five parts in seven of the assembly, an seven members of the legislative council." Delaware Constitution of 1776, Article 30. Similarly, the New Jersey Constitution required legislators to swear not to annul or repeal the provisions of the constitution on annual elections, trial by jury, and religious liberty. New Jersey Constitution of 1776, Article XXIII. These were precautions against amendments.

the judges to decide the constitutionality of laws. None of this required mention.

The inexplicitness of American constitutions became the subject of explicit comment in the *Federalist.* Opponents of the proposed U.S. Constitution feared it would enable federal judges expansively to interpret and even "mould" federal laws in accord with "the *spirit* of the constitution." Hamilton responded in the *Federalist* that the U.S. Constitution was silent about this and that the Constitution did not give federal judges any greater power of this sort than was enjoyed by state court judges. Nonetheless, the Constitution was the supreme law of the land, and it would therefore suggest the intent of statutes (at least, presumably, where they were otherwise obscure) and would render them void where there was an evident contradiction:

> [T]here is not a syllable in the plan under consideration, which *directly* empowers the national courts to construe the laws according to the spirit of the constitution, or which gives them any greater latitude in this respect, than may be claimed by the courts of every state. I admit however, that the constitution ought to be the standard of construction for the laws, and that wherever there is an evident opposition, the laws ought to give place to the constitution.

More generally, Hamilton noted as to the latter point that "this doctrine is not deductible from any circumstance peculiar to the plan of the convention." Instead, it came "from the general theory of a limited constitution; and as far as it is true, is equally applicable to most, if not to all the state governments"—all state governments, that is, other than those of Connecticut and perhaps Rhode Island.[16]

Americans rarely even debated whether a constitution should contain a clause declaring it superior to other human law. One place where Americans are known to have entertained such a suggestion was Kentucky. In 1788, during the drawn-out process of adopting a constitution, a "Farmer" wrote to the *Kentucky Gazette* inviting gentlemen to share their opinions on the question: "Ought not the Constitution to have a clause declaring itself superior and permanent to any Law or act of Assembly that shall be made contrary to it."[17] It is suggestive of how little interest the idea aroused that a

[16] Alexander Hamilton, Federalist Number 81, *The Federalist,* 542–543, ed. Jacob E. Cooke (Middletown: Wesleyan University Press, 1961).

[17] "A Farmer" (Jan. 16, 1788), *Kentucky Gazette* (Feb. 2, 1788). Shortly afterward, the Political Club of Danville debated a similar proposal about the U.S. Constitution—that it should have a Declaration of Rights, specifying that "all laws, contrary to the true spirit, intent and meaning" of the Constitution "shall be void." Loose Papers (Feb. 23, 1788), in *The Docu-*

response came only five months later—from a "Cornplanter." All too happy to adopt a patronizing tone, the Cornplanter noted that the Farmer presumably meant to ask whether the constitution should declare itself superior and *paramount.* The Cornplanter then responded:

> To this I answer, in the affirmative else whence the use of a Constitution which is or ought to be, not only superior to, But the basis of both law and Government. The Constitution of a State is not only the guide of its Legislature but the sacred immutable compact between the people and those whom, for their greater security and happiness, they appoint to legislate and govern. It is the touchstone of Law, a barrier against innovation and tyranny; nor can law be binding that is repugnant to it.[18]

The Cornplanter eventually had his way, for when Kentucky at last adopted a constitution, the article that included the Bill of Rights declared not only that "everything in this article . . . shall remain inviolate" but also that "all laws contrary thereto, or contrary to this constitution, shall be void."[19]

Although men in many states considered it necessary to spell out the effect of their bills of rights on contrary laws, it was only in Kentucky that men bothered to specify the effect of their constitution. Elsewhere, the legal obligation of a constitution, let alone the duty of judges, was too obvious for words.

---

mentary History of the Ratification of the Constitution, 1: 411, eds. John P. Kaminski et al. (Madison: State Historical Society of Wisconsin, 1988).

[18] "Cornplanter," Letter to Mr. Printer, *Kentucky Gazette* (July 12, 1788). The Farmer's phrasing did not deserve so much contempt, for it echoed an old-fashioned argument for the same basic position as taken by the Cornplanter.

[19] Kentucky Constitution of 1792, Article XII. In contrast, when a constitution, such as that of Massachusetts, gave the General Court a power to make laws "so as the same be not repugnant or contrary to this Constitution," it was merely clarifying that the broad power to make laws, which appeared in the Frame of Government, was not independent of the limitations elsewhere in the Constitution—for example, in the Declaration of Rights.

19

Federal Clarifications

What could ordinarily remain beyond words in a single system of law might have to become explicit in a federal system. The common law ideals were familiar enough and usually required no explanation, but the Articles of Confederation raised questions about their application in America's federal system, and it therefore increasingly seemed necessary to have these uncertainties resolved in a new U.S. Constitution.

Clarifying What Was the Law of the Land

In a single state there was typically no reason to explain what was the law of the land or what sort of law was of superior obligation to another, but in the government established by the Articles of Confederation it was not obvious that the Articles or congressional enactments could be considered laws, let alone laws superior to state law. Accordingly, when delegates met in 1787 to place the United States on a firmer footing, they had to clarify not only that the Constitution and other federal law was supreme but also, more basically, that it was the law of the land.

It is well known that the Articles of Confederation left Congress without some essential powers. Of particular concern, Congress lacked power to raise money from the people, and it therefore had to importune the states for support—all too often with disappointing results.

The problem, however, was not merely one of inadequate powers but more basically a question of whether the Articles of Confederation or any congressional enactment amounted to the law of the land. Rather than a constitution with authority from the people of the American states, the Articles were a "league of friendship" among the states, and although the states "delegated" some of their power to Congress through the Articles, it was far from obvious that they thereby made the Articles a law.[1] Nor was it apparent that the states gave Congress a lawmaking power. Congress had no authority from the people, and from the states it only had authority to make "determinations." This was less than a lawmaking power, and Congress therefore promulgated its law-like determinations under the rubric of "ordinances"—the traditional label for acts without the legitimacy of the law of the land.[2]

In fact, instead of imposing any legal obligation, Article XIII of the Articles of Confederation only required a contractual commitment from the states: "Every state shall abide by the determinations of the united states in congress assembled, on all questions which by this confederation are submitted to them. And the Articles of this confederation shall be inviolably observed by every state." Just how different this was from the obligation of law became evident when the delegates to Congress closed the Articles with the fulsome declaration that "we do further solemnly plight and engage the faith of our respective constituents" that "they shall abide by the determinations of the United States in Congress assembled, on all questions, which by the said Confederation are submitted to them," and that "the Articles thereof shall be inviolably observed by the States we respectively represent."[3] The Articles and the determinations of the United States in Congress had to be plighted as a matter of faith precisely because they lacked the obligation of law.[4]

Although the absence of binding law in the Articles of Confederation would become painfully apparent with experience, it was already recognized at the outset—for example, by Chief Justice William Henry Drayton of South Carolina. When the General Assembly of South Carolina in 1778 considered whether to approve the Articles, Drayton argued against their ratification, primarily because they lacked the obligation of law and did not

[1] Articles of Confederation, Article II.

[2] Most famously, Parliament during the Interregnum called its acts "ordinances." Although Pelatiah Webster hoped in 1783 for the appointment of federal "judges of law, and chancery," he sarcastically added: "but I fear they will not be very soon appointed," for "the one supposes the existence of law, and the other of equity." A Citizen of Philadelphia [Pelatiah Webster], *A Dissertation on the Political Union and Constitution of the Thirteen United States of North-America,* 25 (Philadelphia: 1783).

[3] Articles of Confederation, Article XIII.

[4] John Trumbull put the difficulty in verse:

> For what's your Congress, or its end?
> A power t'advise and recommend;
> To call for troops, adjust your quotas,
> And yet no soul is bound to notice.

[John Trumbull], *M'Fingal. A Modern Epic Poem,* 54 (Hartford: 1782).

give Congress the power to make law, and he proposed overcoming these failures by adopting a revised confederation—not merely a confederation among the states but a "Confederation *of the* United States," expressly "uniting them together under one general superintending government." To clarify that acts of Congress would have the obligation of law, his improved confederation went beyond a mere congress of delegates from the states and systematically *"constituted"* a *"legislative"* and an *"executive"* and expressly *"described and limited"* their *"powers."* To ensure that the Confederation itself would have the obligation of law, it included a *"declaration of the obligatory nature of the confederation,"* which stated: "The articles of this confederation shall be strictly binding upon, and inviolably observed by the parties interested therein."[5]

Notwithstanding that the Articles went without these improvements, many lawyers recognized that they needed to understand the Articles and congressional ordinances as laws—the awkwardness being that this was often a self-conscious choice rather than something that could simply be assumed. The effort required to maintain the notion that the Articles were a law can be observed in an opinion given by Attorney General Edmund Randolph in 1784. The question was whether Virginia could arrest a malefactor wanted by South Carolina. Randolph hoped to argue from the Articles of Confederation, but a recent Virginia statute could be viewed as having repudiated the relevant provision of the Articles, and he therefore had to explain that this "did not hinder me from viewing the confederation, as a law, howsoever clothed in the garb of a contract."[6] Functionally, it was of-

[5] *The Speech of the Hon. William Henry Drayton, Esquire, Chief Justice of South-Carolina. Delivered on the Twentieth January, 1778. In the General Assembly Resolved into the Committee of the Whole; Upon the Articles of the Confederation of the United States of America,* 15, 20–21, 31 (Charlestown: 1778). These concerns about law included his "torturing apprehensions" about Congress's inability to raise money except through the states, for rather than contain "a clause, at least obliging the parties to furnish their respective quotas," the Articles had a clause that "is only directory." Ibid., 15–16.

Drayton, however, did not rest his confederation on the authority of the people, and he therefore assumed that Congress would ultimately have to enforce its acts with military force against the states. Recognizing one of the many problems with this, he promptly added: "To avoid, as far as may be, the dangers that may arise from an erroneous construction of the articles of this confederation; and to prevent a contrariety of opinion upon them, they shall be understood according to the expression and not otherwise. And all acts of the Congress, and of the committee of the United States, shall be taken, only in the same manner." Ibid., 31–32.

[6] Letter from Edmund Randolph to Thomas Jefferson (Jan. 30, 1784), in *Papers of Thomas Jefferson,* 6: 514, eds. Julian P. Boyd et al. (Princeton: Princeton University Press, 1952). As he explained in his formal opinion, "[t]he confederation is a law of the land." Letter from Edmund Randolph to Governor Benjamin Harrison (Jan. 21, 1784), LVA, Executive Papers.

ten desirable to consider the Articles a law, but the very fact that this required such careful explanation did not bode well.

The states so regularly ignored the Articles and congressional ordinances that some men turned from ideals of law to thoughts of force. Congressmen James Madison, James Varnum, and James Duane proposed that Congress secure an amendment to the Articles of Confederation that would allow Congress to use the military to obtain compliance with its determinations: "[I]n case any one or more of the Confederated States shall refuse or neglect to abide by the determinations of the United States in Congress assembled or to observe all the Articles of Confederation," Congress would be "fully authorized to employ the force of the United States as well by sea as by land to compel such State or States to fulfill their federal engagements."[7] This sort of solution, as Hamilton later observed, "would amount to a war between different parts of the confederacy," and it was therefore fortunate that most men, including Madison, would eventually seek a solution in the force of law rather than of arms.[8]

The Confederation's failure to establish congressional determinations as law became most disturbingly apparent from treaties. At common law, nothing had legal obligation except the law of the land and what it authorized, and because English monarchs could not introduce new legal obligations except through acts of Parliament, their treaties with foreign princes were without the force of the law of the land, other than to the extent Parliament gave them effect.[9] Treaties thus had contractual obligation under the law of nations but not legal obligation as part of the law of the land. Unlike Parliament, however, Congress did not even have the option of using statutes to give effect to its treaties, because like its treaties, its ordinances were mere "determinations," which lacked legal obligation. Congress was therefore in a bind. It could enter treaties, but it could not rely on

[7] Amendment to Give Congress Coercive Power Over the States and Their Citizens (Mar. 16, 1781), in *The Documentary History of the Ratification of the Constitution,* 1: 142, ed. Merrill Jensen (Madison: State Historical Society of Wisconsin, 1976).

[8] Alexander Hamilton, Federalist Number 16, *The Federalist,* 100, ed. Jacob E. Cooke (Middletown: Wesleyan University Press, 1961).

[9] Lieutenant-Governor Spotswood of Virginia wrote of "the common opinion here that the treatys of sovereigns do not bind the subjects unless confirmed by Act of Parliament." This was also the conventional view on the other side of the Atlantic, where the Crown's law officers gave an opinion in the late 1720s that a treaty "could not have had its effect with respect to His Majesty's subjects, unless the said articles had been confirmed either by Act of Parliament of Great Britain or by Acts of Assembly within the respective plantations." Joseph Henry Smith, *Appeals to the Privy Council from the American Plantations,* 531, notes 34 and 35 (New York: Columbia University Press, 1950).

its ordinances to make these commitments legally binding on the states, let alone the people of the United States.

When the Americans and British in 1783 brought the war to an end by signing the Treaty of Paris, they produced a treaty that in effect imposed legal burdens on the states, for although they could not declare in the Treaty that it was law, they appeared to have used it as if it were. The Treaty only recited that Congress shall "earnestly recommend" to the legislatures of the states that they "provide for the restitution" of property confiscated from British subjects; but it more forcefully asserted that creditors and persons with interests in confiscated lands "shall meet with no lawful impediment" in securing their rights—words that might seem to place a legal obligation on the states.[10]

Many of the states took offense at the suggestion that the Treaty was binding as law. Southerners recalled that treaties had not previously been binding as law; they also generally opposed any return of Tory lands and any suggestion that Americans had to repay British perfidy with cash.[11] Southern states therefore typically barred British subjects from recovering their property or collecting their debts, and although the most dramatic southern departures from the Treaty were legislative, the most persistent were judicial. The North Carolina judges, for example, regularly denied that the Treaty was part of the law of the land. The sole exception was when they banished the Tories Brice and McNeil and to this end "declared that the treaty of peace was the law of the land."[12] Otherwise, the North

[10] Treaty of Paris, Articles IV and V.

[11] Wythe Holt, "'To Establish Justice': Politics, the Judiciary Act of 1789, and the Invention of Federal Courts," *Duke Law Journal,* 1440–1449 (1989).

[12] Archibald Maclaine, Protest against the resolution of the House of Commons, declaring that the Judges ought not to be accused of any misdemeanors in office (Jan. 1787), NCSA, General Assembly, Session Records 1786–1787, Box 3, Joint Resolutions—Committee of the Whole of Two Houses on Administration of Justice Folder. Of course, the legislature did its part too. When the Senate received a bill "declaring that the late treaty of peace . . . is and hath been in full force in this state, as a part of the law of the land," it ordered the bill read and then "laid over till the next Assembly." Vote (Jan. 2, 1786), *Journal of the Senate. At a General Assembly begun and held at Fayetteville, on the twentieth day of November, in the Year of Our Lord One Thousand Seven Hundred and Eighty-Six,* 62 (np: [1787]).

On behalf of Brice and Macneil, their lawyer quoted Blackstone to argue that "if Judgements were to be the private Opinions of the Judges 'men would then be Slaves to their Magistrates, without knowing the obligations & conditions which they lye under.'" He then argued:

> In applying this Quotation to the present case, it may be confidently asserted that the Sentence is without precedent in England or this Country—it is the mere private Opinion of the Judges, not ordained by any Law, and is of dangerous consequences

Carolina judges, like many other southern judges, refused to acknowledge that the Treaty was legally binding. The British responded to such discrimination by refusing to relinquish the posts they held along the Canadian border, thus hinting that America might lose the territories it had secured through the Treaty of Paris.[13]

Congress understood that it could not, in the manner of Parliament, enforce its treaty commitments by making laws, and it therefore vainly declared in March 1787 that its treaties were part of the law of the land, which could not be contravened by state laws:

> That the Legislatures of the several States cannot of right pass any Act or Acts for interpreting, explaining or construing a national treaty or any part or clause of it, nor for restraining, limiting or in any manner impeding, retarding, or counteracting the operation and execution of the same; for that on being constitutionally made, ratified and published they become in virtue of the confederation part of the Law of the Land, and are not only independent of the will and power of such Legislatures, but also binding and obligatory on them.

This mere assertion that treaties were "part of the Law of the Land" was not likely to be persuasive in the South, and Congress therefore transmitted its

---

> to freedom; for, whatever palliation this Conduct may derive from the zeal of the Judges in guarding against the admission of disaffected persons, it must yet be acknowledged that such a discretionary power, in Judges who are liable to no controuling Authority, may in some future time, with less virtuous judges, be the means of subjugating the best friends of the Country, to arbitrary Banishm^t—and consequently render the people "Slaves to their Magistrates."

Argument against Indictment of Brice [mistakenly labeled, Indictment of McNeil], NCSA, General Assembly, Session Records 1786–1787, Box 3, Joint Resolutions—Committee of the Whole of Two Houses on Administration of Justice Folder. The argument against the indictment of McNeil was very similar. Ibid.

Anti-British prejudices ran so high that even in the next decade Thomas Jefferson, in his capacity as secretary of state, had to send a circular letter to the legislatures of the southern states, requesting information about enforcement of the treaty: "It is alleged that in some of the Southern States, there does not exist a single instance of the recovery of a British debt in their Courts, though many years have expired since the establishment of Peace between the two Countries." He therefore requested representatives and senators in each such state "to furnish him with such information, general or particular, as they can give with certainty." Letter from Thomas Jefferson to the Senators and Representatives of North Carolina (Apr. 11, 1792), University of North Carolina at Chapel Hill, Southern Historical Collection, No. 324 Hayes Collection, Box 2, Folder 119. On behalf of North Carolina, Maclaine responded: "I have heard of but few Suits brought by British Creditors for the Recovery of Debts in the State of North Carolina since the Peace," and he then gave some details, including information about *Bayard v. Singleton.* Letter from Archibald Maclaine to Thomas Jefferson (c. April 1792), ibid.

13 Julius Goebel, Jr., ed., *The Law Practice of Alexander Hamilton: Documents and Commentary,* 1: 521 (New York: Columbia University Press, 1964).

resolution to the states with an letter explaining how, when "a treaty is constitutionally made ratified and published by us, it immediately becomes binding on the whole nation and superadded to the laws of the land, without the intervention of State Legislatures."

The Articles of Confederation, however, had not clearly made treaties or anything else binding as part of the law of the land, and Congress therefore found itself in the peculiar position of having to ask the states to repeal their acts that were contrary to the Treaty:

> [W]e think it best that every State without exception should pass a law . . . declaring in general terms, that all Acts and parts of Acts repugnant to the treaty of peace . . . are repealed and that the Courts of Law and Equity in all causes and Questions cognizable by them . . . touching the said Treaty, shall decide and adjudge according to the true intent and meaning of the same, any thing in the said Acts or parts of Acts to the contrary thereof in any wise notwithstanding.

Congress had to make this request that the states repeal their laws repugnant to the Treaty precisely because the Treaty did not clearly amount to the law of the land and because Congress did not even clearly have the power to make laws carrying it out. In contrast, once the states passed the requisite legislation, it was obvious that the matter would get resolved by state courts: "By repealing in general terms all Acts and clauses repugnant to the treaty, the business will be turned over to its proper Department, viz, the Judicial, and the Courts of Law will find no difficulty in deciding whether any particular Act or clause is or is not contrary to the treaty."[14]

[14] Letter from Congress to the States (Apr. 13, 1787), in *Journals of the Continental Congress,* 32: 178, 181–183, ed. Roscoe R. Hill (Washington: Government Printing Office, 1936). The resolutions were based on Jay's proposals of October 1786, adopted on March 21, and are printed here from the letter of April 13 drafted by Jay. For the context of Congress's resolutions, see Allan Nevins, *The American States During and After the Revolution,* 652–654 (New York: Macmillan, 1924). For the compliance by most states, see Letter from Thomas Jefferson to George Hammond (May 29, 1792), in *Papers of Thomas Jefferson,* 23: 578–579, eds. Charles T. Cullen et al. (Princeton: Princeton University Press, 1990). Madison would soon observe: "The treaties of the United States to have any force at all, must be considered as part of the law of the land," and "[l]aws are a dead letter without courts to expound and define their true meaning and operation." James Madison, Federalist Number 22, *The Federalist,* 143. For the anxiety of British creditors, see a collection of rather doubtful opinions by English lawyers on claims under the Treaty, particularly as to whether such claims could be enforced in Maryland, where no statute established rights in accord with the Treaty. NCSA, Charles E. Johnson Collection, P.C. 67.26, Folder 21.

Lawyers who took the position that the Treaty had the force of the law of the land often had to hedge their bets—as apparent from Hamilton's arguments in *Rutgers v. Waddington.* In his briefs, Hamilton suggested that the Treaty had this strong obligation, but in his pleadings, he more realistically analyzed the Treaty in terms of contract—a view that Hamilton revealed in his formula that "any injury or damage" had been "virtually and effectually relin-

The problem evidently was not the role of the courts but the reality that neither a treaty nor any other congressional determination was a law.

Although it was painful for Congress to have to beg the states to repeal acts contrary to a treaty that Congress liked to consider part of the law of the land, this was merely the most salient example of how the Articles of Confederation created ambiguity about federal law. As has been seen, it was not obvious that the Articles themselves, which were merely a compact among the states, could amount to the law of the land; nor was it evident that any congressional "determinations"—whether treaties or ordinances—were part of the law of the land; nor was it entirely certain that any purported law of the Confederation was supreme over state law. This legal quagmire and the associated political crisis eventually made it apparent that the United States needed to be constituted anew—not merely with greater power, but also in a way that resolved the underlying uncertainties that had been generated by the Articles of Confederation.[15] The drafters of the U.S. Constitution thus had to do more than place legislative authority in Congress and specify the broadened extent of Congress's lawmaking power. More basically, they had to resolve three questions about authority and obligation: Would the Constitution have the popular authority that would make it a law? Would congressional enactments and in particular treaties be part of the law of the land? And would this law, like the law of the land in England, be supreme over all other law in the land?

The first step was to establish the popular authority of the Constitution, for this was the essential foundation of its obligation. The U.S. Constitution therefore began by declaring: "We the People of the United States . . . do ordain and establish this Constitution for the United States of America." Using conventional words of enactment, this opening phrase made clear that upon ratification, the Constitution was an act of law by the people of the United States for their entire land. Being made with the authority of the people, it had the advantage of being legally binding on

---

quished renounced and released" by the Treaty. Goebel, ed., *The Law Practice of Alexander Hamilton,* 1: 327–328.

[15] Even an Anti-Federalist such as Monroe could ask of Congress: "[H]ow are its treaties, laws, or ordinances to be carried into effect? Are they of authority and in force immediately within the states as soon as they are passed? Or does it require the intervention of a state law to give them validity? And if the law is necessary may not the state refuse to pass it, and if she does how shall she be compelled? It is well known . . . that no act of Congress, of what nature soever it may be, of force within them, until it is recognized by their own legislatures, prior to that even it is a nullity, and to that only does it owe its authority. . . . These are the defects or the principal defects of the present government, and they are inseparable from a league of independent states." [James Monroe], *Some Observations on the Constitution,* 6–7 ([Petersburg: 1788]).

them. As Hamilton put it, the new constitution extended "the authority of the union to the persons of the citizens," and thus rather than have to act "by military force" against the states, the government could exert itself "by the agency of the Courts" on individuals. This was the "COERTION of the magistracy" instead of the "COERTION of arms."[16] Law had its own sort of force—the obligation derived from the people and given coercive effect through the courts—and by ordaining and establishing the Constitution, the people made this sort of force the basis of their government's power.

A second step was to specify that the Constitution, congressional enactments, and treaties were all part of the law of the land. Traditionally, there was no need to explain that a constitution and the legislation under it were part of the law of the land or that treaties were not part of this law. Yet after so much confusion about the Articles of Confederation, about the congressional determinations made under them, and about the Treaty of Peace, it now was necessary to be explicit: "This Constitution, and the Laws of the United States which shall be made in Pursuance thereof; and all Treaties made, or which shall be made, under the Authority of the United States, shall be the . . . Law of the Land."[17]

[16] Hamilton, Federalist Number 15, *The Federalist,* 95. See also Hamilton, Federalist Number 22, ibid., 146.

Although Madison went along with the Convention's proposed constitution, he lacked much confidence in the efficacy of law and therefore continued to believe that balances of social and political power, even if not ordinarily military force, were necessary to constrain abuses of power, especially in the states. In the fall of 1787, he wrote to Jefferson:

> It may be said that the Judicial authority under our new system will keep the States within their proper limits, and supply the place of a negative on their laws. The answer is, that it is more convenient to prevent the passage of a law, than to declare it void after it is passed; that this will be particularly the case, where the law aggrieves individuals, who may be unable to support an appeal agst. a State to the supreme Judiciary; that a State which would violate the Legislative rights of the Union, would not be very ready to obey a Judicial decree in support of them, and that a recurrence to force, which in the event of disobedience would be necessary, is an evil which the new Constitution meant to exclude as far as possible.

Letter of James Madison to Thomas Jefferson (Oct. 24, 1787), in *The Papers of James Madison,* 10: 221, eds. Robert A. Rutland, Charles F. Hobson, and William M. E. Rachal et al. (Chicago: University of Chicago Press, 1977).

[17] U.S. Constitution, Article VI. The requirement of advice and consent also revealed that treaties were law. Some scholars assume that advice and consent must have meant more than ratification. Jack N. Rakove, "Solving a Constitutional Puzzle: The Treatymaking Clause as a Case Study," *Perspectives in American History,* 1: 275 (new series) (1984); Arthur Bestor, "Separation of Powers in the Domain of Foreign Affairs: The Intent of the Constitution Historically Examined," *Seton Hall Law Review,* 5: 540 (1974). "Advice and consent," however, was the language of lawmaking—as when acts of Parliament, especially after the Restoration, began by reciting that they were adopted by the king with the advice and consent of Parliament and by the authority of the same.

Indeed, all of these were to be "the supreme Law of the Land," and this was the third necessary clarification. English law was supreme over all other law in England, and the law of each state was supreme in that state. Yet it did not necessarily follow that the law of the United States was supreme over the laws of the particular states, and after the experience of Americans under the Articles of Confederation, it was only prudent to put the supremacy of the law of the land beyond any doubt.

The U.S. Constitution thus had to say much that in other constitutions required no explanation. Even so, the U.S. Constitution could also leave much unsaid. Although it specified its authority, the law of the land, and the supremacy of this law, it did not assert that the law of the land was obligatory. Nor did it stipulate the relative supremacy of the Constitution over federal statutes and treaties, let alone the relation of statutes to treaties.[18] As in a state constitution, the obligation of law and the hierarchy of law within a single system of law could be taken for granted.

Clarifying the Duty of State Judges

It has seemed odd that constitutions said so little about judicial review. The state constitutions said nothing, and the U.S. Constitution merely stated that "the Judges in every State shall be bound" by "the supreme Law of the Land"—thus remaining curiously silent about federal judges. The mystery, however, is not very deep. Americans could simply assume that state judges had a duty to decide in accord with their state's law and that federal judges would have a duty to decide in accord with federal law, and therefore the only substantial question concerned the duty of state judges as to federal law. As it happens, even this application of judicial duty was already taken for granted by at least some state judges, and therefore rather than have to

[18] While the Constitution, acts of Congress, and treaties were all part of the supreme law of the land, this was not to say that the legal obligation of an act of Congress was equal to that of an act of the people; nor, by the same token, was this to say that the legal obligation of a treaty was equal to that of an act of Congress. See, for example, Vasan Kesavan, "The Three Tiers of Federal Law," *Northwestern University Law Review,* 100: 1479, 1489 (2006).

Although many commentators analyze the status of treaties by asking what is necessary for their "execution," the determinative questions are those concerning legal and contractual obligation. The Constitution made treaties part of the supreme law of the land, and thus to the extent a treaty was intended by the president and the Senate to create legal duties, it had legal obligation; but a treaty could not have legal obligation to the extent it was contrary to an act of greater legal obligation—whether an act of higher legal authority or an act of equal but subsequent legal authority. Indeed, because a treaty was part of the law of the land, it could be deprived of its legal obligation only by these acts of greater legal obligation. At the same time, of course, as to the contractual obligation created by a treaty, the president could cancel for breach or otherwise assert the nation's contractual remedies.

create the role of state judges in the federal system, the Constitution only had to put to rest remaining doubts.

The degree to which the U.S. Constitution merely clarified rather than created the federal role of state judges can be illustrated by two earlier state court opinions on the privileges-and-immunities clause of the Articles of Confederation.[19] These opinions reveal that even before the drafting of the U.S. Constitution, the judges in some states evidently understood that they might have a duty to decide in accord with the law of the whole land.

One such opinion arose in Massachusetts. In January 1785 the Senate began to consider "An act for declaring & describing who are aliens to this Commonwealth and who are citizens of the same." Like similar enactments in other states, the Massachusetts bill attempted to deny rights to former Tories, and one way it did this was through an artificially narrow understanding of the privileges and immunities clause of the Articles of Confederation. The Articles guaranteed that "the free inhabitants of each of these States . . . shall be entitled to all privileges and immunities of free citizens in the several States," and with specified exceptions, this clause apparently protected any free inhabitant of a state.[20] The Massachusetts bill, however, seemed to deny the benefit of this provision to some returning Tories. The bill began by declaring that Massachusetts inhabitants who had fled before July 4, 1776, and had not returned to one of the states and obtained its protection before mid-April 1779 were "aliens to the Commonwealth." It then defined free citizens of the state as Massachusetts inhabitants who had not left, those who had left but had returned by mid-April 1779, and those had been naturalized. Finally, the bill guaranteed all the privileges and immunities of free citizens of Massachusetts to the free inhabitants of the other states while they were within the Commonwealth, but only if they had been free inhabitants of one of the other states on March 2, 1781 ("the time when the confederation of the united States was compleated") or had subsequently been born in such a state. Lest the implications be unclear, the bill barred aliens from various rights, including not only political rights, such as voting and holding office, which clearly were confined to citizens of the state, but also rights that might be considered among the privileges and immunities guaranteed to visitors from other states, such as the right to

[19] Other cases concerning the Articles included those regarding the full-faith-and-credit clause—although these tended merely to determine whether individuals could enjoy the benefit of state statutes or decisions. See, for example, *James et al. v. Allen* (Court of Common Pleas, Philadelphia County 1787), Dallas, *Reports,* 1: 188, which was mimicked by students in *Amos Standfast v. Nathan Poorman* (Aug. 1787), *Proceedings of The Institutio Legalis,* 138–139, New Jersey Historical Society, Ms Group 214.

[20] Articles of Confederation, Article IV.

hold, purchase, or inherit freehold and the right to maintain any action or suit.[21] In short, the bill denied privileges and immunities to various late-returning Massachusetts Tories, and when the bill came out of committee with revisions in June 1785, the Senate voted to consult the judges on the constitutional question of greatest local concern: whether inhabitants of Massachusetts who fled before July 4, 1776, "and who did not before the completing of the Confederation of the United States of America, return to one of the said United States, and obtain the protection therefore, but have been since the completing of the Confederation, or shall hereafter be admitted as free Inhabitants of any of the States in the Union, are, or will be, *by the Confederation,* while within this Commonwealth, entituled to all the privileges and Immunities of free Citizens of the same."[22]

The judges at first desired to be spared the necessity of answering the question, "it appearing that the subject matter thereof, is of a political nature, and not merely a question of Law." To this they added that it concerned "the Rights of all the States of the Union, and that the opinion or decision of the Justices of the Sup^{m} Judicial Court of this, or any other of the State, cannot determine the matter in question, but that the same is proper for the Consideration of the Congress of the United States." They therefore "would humbly propose that the honble Senate wou'd excuse us from giving our opinion in Law thereupon." In pointing out that the issue was "of a political nature," the judges did not deny that it was also "a question of Law," and in asking to be excused, they seem to have assumed that if the Senate insisted on an answer, neither the political subject matter nor the desirability of a uniform, federal determination would deprive them of their duty to reach a decision in accord with the law. In fact, the judges closed with a postscript: "Notwithstanding the foregoing, we would inform the honble Senate that the Court have settled their opinion . . . and are ready to deliver in the same, if it should be still judged expedient to require it of them."[23] The Senate promptly ordered that the justices "be acquainted, that the Senate do not excuse them from giving their opinion," and it will

[21] Act of Alienage (June 1785), MSA, Senate Documents, Rejected Bills, 1785, No. 344, Box 11.

[22] Letter from President S. Phillips to the Judges (June 2, 1785), Francis Dana's Letterbook of Supreme Judicial Court Advisory Opinions, 1, Massachusetts Historical Society, Dana Family Papers, Ms. N-1088, Vol. 39. See also Journal of the Senate, 42 (June 2, 1785), Records of the States of the United States, microfilm. The question was drafted by Ebenezer Bridge and Richard Cranch, the father of William. Ibid., 40 (June 2, 1785).

[23] Letter from Nathaniel Peaseley Sargeant, David Sewall, Francis Dana, and Increase Sumner to Samuel Phillips, President of the Senate (June 15, 1785), Francis Dana's Letterbook of Supreme Judicial Court Advisory Opinions, 2, Massachusetts Historical Society, Dana Family Papers, Ms. N-1088, Vol. 39. (In the quotation above, a wayward comma after the words "if it" is omitted.)

be seen that in doing their duty, the judges left the political and uniformity considerations behind. Apparently the judges thought these concerns were relevant for the Senate's decision but not their own.[24]

The judges in their opinion quoted the privileges-and-immunities clause of the Articles of Confederation and made two preliminary observations about naturalized citizens.[25] First, in answer to suggestions that the Tories naturalized by other states were impliedly subject to disabilities, the judges observed that naturalized aliens were presumptively equal to other citizens. Aliens therefore could not be subject to any conditions that had not been expressly imposed at the time of their naturalization:

> [A]n Act of Naturalization, may admit an Alien to certain priviledges, and exclude him from others; he may be naturalized under some particular disabilities: But if no such proviso is made, no Condition expressly annexed to the priviledge granted: *ex vi termini* [by force of the term] a Person naturalized, is a free Citizen to all intents Constructions & purposes whatever.

Second, in response to hints that the states lacked the power to make Tories free citizens, the judges added that an independent state could admit any class or type of alien as a citizen:

> A free sovereign & Independent State, must have a power of admitting, such Aliens to the right of Citizenship, as it shall judge expedient: unless some Compact or agreement appears to the Contrary.—And there is no clause in the several Articles of Confederation, that expressly, or by implication restrains any one of the States in the Union from admitting Citizens, from any class or denomination of Aliens.

[24] Journal of the Senate, 96 (June 17, 1785), Records of the States of the United States, microfilm.

[25] Before drawing these two conclusions, the judges established some initial premises. They observed that "all mankind are either Subjects or Aliens," there being "no medium" between these categories. The judges then rejected the bill's assumption that the phrases "Free Citizens" and "Free Inhabitants" in the Articles of Confederation only meant those who had been such in March 1781. These phrases were merely "different modes of expression used in the Confederation, to convey precisely the same Idea, with natural born Subjects, not held in Vassalage." Moreover, although "strictly speaking, there can be no natural born Subject of any of the United States, who has attained the age of *nine years;* yet the individuals of the several States on the 4th day of July, 1776, when they declared themselves Independent Sovereign States, are and must in contemplation of Law, be deemed and taken, as *natural born subjects.*" Last but not least, "[t]he phrase *Free Inhabitants* in the Confederation" had to be "construed to mean the Free Inhabitants of the respective States that were then, or should be existing at any subsequent period of time, during the Continuance of the Union," for "[t]o restrain the phrase, to the Identical persons *only*" who were inhabitants "at the time the Confederation was acceded to; would be making the Confederation limited and finite, against plain and express language, which declares that it shall be *perpetual.*" Opinion of Justices of the Supreme Judicial Court on an Article of the Confederation (June 22, 1785) (docketed Oct. 19, 1785), MSA, Senate Documents, Rejected Bills, 1785, No. 344, Box 11.

The judges concluded:

> [T]hat all persons, who are or shall be naturalized, by any State in the Union, from any Class or denomination of Aliens, are by the Confederation, *Considered* as Intitled to all the priviledges, and immunities of *free Citizens* in the several States; and of Course in this Commonwealth whenever they shall come to reside within the same.[26]

As this was only an advisory opinion on a question arising from what was not yet an act, the judges had no occasion to hold the act unconstitutional. Yet they clearly opined that under the Articles of Confederation, Massachusetts could not ordinarily deny the benefit of the privileges-and-immunities clause to naturalized aliens. Of greater significance, it is evident that in the course of doing their duty, state judges could decide in accord with the federal constitution even before the federal constitution stipulated that the judges in every state would be bound thereby.

An actual holding against a state statute under the Articles of Confederation can be observed in *Bayard v. Singleton.* It is familiar that in May 1787 the judges in the case held a North Carolina statute unlawful under the state's constitution, but this was not all they did. The state had confiscated Tory properties and then had sold the land to acquisitive patriots. Elizabeth Bayard was the daughter of the loyalist Samuel Cornell, whose confiscated home and other properties in New Bern were purchased by the unscrupulous Spyers Singleton. It will be recalled that Elizabeth and her husband, William, sued to recover her patrimony and that Singleton therefore obtained two statutes from the General Assembly—the first allowing him and others defending their interests in confiscated land to bar a trial by jury against them, and the second more generally forbidding any legal challenges.[27] These statutes applied not only to suits brought by persons such as Cornell, whose property had been confiscated, but also to suits brought by anyone claiming under them, such as Cornell's daughters. Samuel Cornell was a British subject, and the judges recognized that he could therefore perhaps be prevented from "maintaining or prosecuting any suit in the Courts of Justice in this State." The plaintiffs in the case, however, Elizabeth and

26 Ibid. As the judges did not reach their opinion until June 22, they waited until the next meeting of the legislature, in October, to send their opinion. Letter from Francis Dana to President of Senate (Oct. 15, 1785), MSA, Senate Documents, Misc. 1785, No. 283, Box 9. The opinion was "Read & ordered to lie" on October 19, 1785, and the bill apparently also rested, until it was revived in 1789, only to be tabled once again—this time, according to the docket, "till the determ[inatio]n of federal Congress shall be known on ye Subject." Act of Alienage (June 1785), MSA, Senate Documents, Rejected Bills, 1785, No. 344, Box 11.
27 See Chapter Thirteen.

William Bayard, were not British, and whatever disabilities could be applied to Elizabeth's father, "such disabilities in their nature were merely personal, and not by any means capable of being transferred to the present plaintiffs, either by descent or purchase." On this reasoning, the statutes obtained by Singleton had violated the plaintiffs' right to a jury trial under the North Carolina Constitution. Put simply, even if North Carolina statutes could impose disabilities on a British subject, they could not deprive Americans, such as the Bayards, of their constitutional rights.[28]

The Bayards, however, were from New York, and they therefore faced the additional question as to whether they had any claim to a jury under the North Carolina Constitution. The North Carolina judges responded by holding that under the Articles of Confederation, the Bayards had the privileges and immunities of citizens of North Carolina. In the compressed phrasing of the newspaper report, "[t]hese plaintiffs being citizens of one of the United States, are citizens of this State, by the confederation of all the States; which is to be taken as a part of the law of the land, unrepealable by any act of the General Assembly."[29] The judges of North Carolina apparently did not need a federal constitution to direct them to do their duty in accord with the Articles of Confederation.

It is evident that at least some state judges were willing to do their duty in holding state acts contrary to federal law, but would state judges do this predictably? The immediate problem was not that they would fail to understand their duty, but rather that they might quite reasonably question whether the Articles of Confederation or any congressional determination was binding as law, and far from being primarily a concern as to the Articles of Confederation, this was especially a risk as to treaties. For example, although the North Carolina judges in *Bayard* decided in accord with the Articles of Confederation, they almost always denied that the Treaty of Peace was part of the law of the land. The U.S. Constitution took care of such judges merely by stating that the Constitution, acts of Congress, and treaties constituted the "Law of the Land." Other state judges, however, might believe that they were sworn to decide in accord with the law of their particular land rather than the land as a whole, and against this danger the U.S. Constitution defined the Constitution, federal statutes, and treaties as "the supreme Law of the Land" and required that "the Judges in every State shall be bound thereby, any Thing in the Constitution or Laws of any State

28 Correspondence (Newbern, June 7), *Virginia Independent Chronicle* (July 4, 1787).

29 Ibid. It obviously cannot be determined from this newspaper report whether it was the judges or the correspondent who oversimplified the reasoning about the privileges-and-immunities clause by saying that the plaintiffs were citizens of North Carolina.

to the Contrary notwithstanding.[30] Although the high court of Massachusetts and even more clearly that of North Carolina already understood that it was the duty of state judges to decide in accord with federal law, including any federal constitution, there was good reason to remove any doubts.

What the U.S. Constitution said about the supreme law of the land and about state judges was revealing, but no less revealing is what the Constitution did not say. Although it defined the supreme law of the land, it did not explain the superior obligation of any part of this law over the rest; nor did it even explain that the supreme law of the land was binding. As for the judges, although it bound state judges to decide in accord with federal law, it said nothing of the duty of federal judges. As to these and most other matters of law and judicial duty, the U.S. Constitution, like the state constitutions, could remain largely inexplicit.

The Framers and Ratifiers

Part of what remained submerged beneath the words of the U.S. Constitution briefly came to the surface during the debates among its framers and ratifiers. The confidence with which such men discussed how judges would hold statutes unconstitutional has usually seemed to scholars to reveal "the intention of the framers" as to "judicial control" at an early stage of its development.[31] It is doubtful, however, whether the evidence really discloses much concerning the framers' intentions about a nascent power of judicial review. Instead, the evidence is suggestive as to what Americans could assume about the application of a long-familiar judicial duty.

A few of the delegates at the convention in Philadelphia regretted that judges would be able to hold statutes unlawful. It has been seen that Richard Dobbs Spaight took this view—both in North Carolina and again in Philadelphia, where he was a delegate—and it is telling that he complained of "such a power," which he apparently distinguished from the underlying ideals of judicial office and duty.[32] In the debates in Philadelphia, John Francis Mercer similarly complained that he "disapproved of the Doctrine that the Judges as expositors of the Constitution should have authority to declare a law void." John Dickinson "was strongly impressed with the re-

[30] U.S. Constitution, Article VI (1787). The use of the word "bound" was perhaps inexact, but overall the phrase was a clarification.
[31] Charles A. Beard, *The Supreme Court and the Constitution,* 15–16 (New York: Paisley, 1938).
[32] See Chapter Fourteen.

mark of Mr. Mercer as to the power of the Judges to set aside the law" and "thought no such power ought to exist," but "at the same time" he was "at a loss what expedient to substitute."[33] Rather than concede that constitutional decisions arose from judicial office, these men consistently emphasized their doubts about a distinct power or doctrine.

Other framers discussed this implication of judicial office with greater understanding and without opprobrium. Elbridge Gerry, for example, observed that "[i]n some States the Judges had actually set aside laws as being agst. the Constitution" and that this "was done too with general approbation."[34] Rufus King thought that "the Judges will have the expounding" of acts of Congress "when they come before them; and they will no doubt stop the operation of such as shall appear repugnant to the constitution."[35] Luther Martin argued that "as to the constitutionality of laws, that point will come before the judges in their proper official character."[36] George Mason also assumed that the judges "could declare an unconstitutional law void."[37]

Shortly afterward, such assumptions were aired in the ratification debates. In Connecticut, Oliver Ellsworth argued that "[i]f the general legislature should at any time overleap their limits, the judicial department is a constitutional check," and that "[i]f the United States . . . make a law which the Constitution does not authorize, it is void; and . . . the national judges . . . will declare it to be void."[38] In Pennsylvania, James Wilson defended the Constitution by noting that if the judges find an act "to be incompatible with the superior power of the Constitution, it is their duty to pronounce it void."[39] Writing in Maryland under the name Aristides, Alexander Contee Hanson noted that "every judge in the union, whether of federal or state appointment, (and some persons would say every jury) will have a right to reject any act, handed to him as a law, which he may conceive repugnant to the constitution."[40] Further south, John Marshall said

33 Madison's Notes (Aug. 15, 1787), in *The Records of the Federal Convention of 1787,* at 2: 298–299, ed. Max Farrand (New Haven: Yale University Press, 1937). By the same token, it was probably not a coincidence that when Hamilton said "this doctrine" arose "from the general theory of a limited constitution," he was anticipating possible objections. Hamilton, Federalist Number 81, *The Federalist,* 543.

34 Madison's Notes (June 4, 1787), *The Records of the Federal Convention of 1787,* 1: 97–98.

35 Pierce's Notes (June 4, 1787), ibid., 1: 109.

36 Madison's Notes (July 21, 1787), ibid., 2: 75–76.

37 Ibid., 2: 78.

38 Speech of Oliver Ellsworth (Jan. 7, 1788), in *The Documentary History of the Ratification of the Constitution,* 3: 553, eds. Merrill Jensen and John P. Kaminski (Madison: State Historical Society of Wisconsin, 1978–). So too "if the states go beyond their limits . . . the law is void" and "judges will declare it to be so." Ibid.

39 Speech of James Wilson (Dec. 1, 1787), ibid., 2: 451. See also ibid., 517.

40 Aristides, Remarks on the Proposed Plan of a Federal Government (Jan. 31, 1788), ibid., 15: 531.

that if the government of the United States "were to make a law not warranted by any of the powers enumerated, it would be considered by the Judges as an infringement of the Constitution which they are to guard." Put simply, "[t]hey would declare it void."[41]

Anti-Federalists did not disagree. For example, Brutus observed that "if the legislature pass laws, which, in the judgment of the [supreme] court, they are not authorized to do by the constitution, the court will not take notice of them."[42] What the Anti-Federalists feared was the danger that federal judges would go too far in holding state laws void and would not go far enough in reaching this conclusion about federal laws. After Edmund Pendleton remarked upon how his "brethren" in Virginia had "prevented the operation of some unconstitutional acts," Patrick Henry acknowledged that "the Honorable Gentleman did our Judiciary honour in saying, that they had firmness to counteract the Legislature in some cases," but he worried that the federal judges would not be so firm:

> Yes, Sir, our Judges opposed the acts of the Legislature. We have this land mark to guide us.—They had fortitude to declare that they were the Judiciary and would oppose unconstitutional acts. Are you sure that your Federal Judiciary will act thus? Is that Judiciary so well constructed and so independent of the other branches, as our State Judiciary? Where are your land-marks in this Government?

He doubted the clarity of the federal constitution and the independence of the federal judges, but he did so on the assumption that it was "the highest encomium on this country, that the acts of the Legislature, if unconstitutional, are liable to be opposed by the Judiciary."[43]

In the years that followed, judges repeatedly did their duty. State judges continued to hold state statutes unconstitutional under their constitutions, and by 1792 both state and federal judges held state enactments

---

[41] Speech of John Marshall (June 20, 1788), ibid., 10: 1431. Another Virginia Federalist, George Nicholas, asked "who is to determine the extent" of congressional powers? "I say, the same power which in all well regulated communities determines the extent of Legislative powers—If they exceed these powers, the Judiciary will declare it void." Speech of George Nicholas (June 16, 1788), ibid., 10: 1327.

[42] Brutus, Essay XII (Feb. 7, 1788), ibid., 16: 73.

[43] Speech of Patrick Henry (June 12, 1788), ibid., 10: 1219. One of Henry's fellow Anti-Federalists said about the *ex post facto* clause that "[w]hen this matter comes before the Federal Judiciary, they must determine according to this Constitution." Speech of George Mason (June 17, 1788), ibid., 10: 1361. See also Mason's speech (June 20, 1788), ibid., 1420–1421, and the speech of William Grayson (June 21, 1788), ibid., 1448.

unconstitutional under the U.S. Constitution.[44] In the same year, federal judges refused to proceed as directed by the federal Invalid Pension Act, and little more than a decade later, the justices of the U.S. Supreme Court in *Marbury v. Madison* held an act of Congress unconstitutional. These decisions are traditionally considered the beginnings of a new judicial power. They are, however, but further evidence of how the judges could do their duty.

[44] Two Rhode Island cases, in Bristol and Washington Counties in 1791, held Rhode Island's Substitute Act unconstitutional, and a federal case, *Champion & Dickason v. Casey,* (U.S. Circuit Court for the District of Rhode Island 1792), held a resolve of the Rhode Island General Assembly unconstitutional. Charles Warren, "Earliest Cases of Judicial Review of State Legislation by Federal Courts," *Yale Law Journal,* 32: 25, note 23, 27–28 (1922).

Conclusion

The history of judicial review is one of America's latter-day creation stories. According to the usual version of this story, what the people of America did not have the foresight to authorize in their constitutions, the judges subsequently established through their cases. This history of judicial self-authorization is only plausible, however, in the absence of much evidence from the 1780s or earlier, and by now it should be clear that there is ample evidence, even if not precisely of judicial review. The evidence reveals that judges could take the ideals of law and judicial duty for granted and that with these ideals, they felt obliged to decide in accord with the law of the land, including the portion of this law that was of highest authority and obligation.

Law

Were constitutions binding as law? The question matters for many reasons, but most prominently here because the legal obligation of constitutions had consequences for judges.

Constitutions are often said in retrospect to have been mere arrangements of political power, and they have therefore tended to escape questions about their place in the broader evolution of ideas about authority, will, and legal obligation. Since the Middle Ages, however, it has been familiar that the people could make a law establishing and limiting their government, and at least since the sixteenth century, if not earlier, their law has sometimes been known as their "constitution." Whatever else this reveals, it suggests that the notion of a constitution cannot adequately be understood merely within the political circumstances of Revolutionary America or any other particular time and nation, but more generally needs to be examined as a response to the tendencies of modern society.

Law seemed to medieval and early modern Europeans to derive its obligation from above—from its place within a divinely established hierarchy. Rather than merely a theological matter, this source of obligation had practical significance, for if not divinely derived, the obligation of human law might seem contingent on fluctuating opinions about the law's utility. If, however, human law derived its obligation from above, it could avoid this weakness.

The difficulty was that even if God in some sense gave obligation to human law, mere men had difficulty agreeing upon what law had this profound force of obligation, and in contemplating this problem, Europeans found themselves looking down into fissures that reached all the way to the very bottom of human society and human nature. Even in the best of circumstances, human reason rarely provided clear moral answers, and in the modernizing circumstances of medieval Europe, where men quarreled over law while confidently arguing from reason, many observers came to doubt whether men had sufficient intellect or dispassion to recognize God's eternal reason in their law. Accordingly, while some men still sought to ascertain how human law partook of eternal verities, others increasingly explored the possibility that law was obligatory because it was willed by those with lawmaking authority—perhaps at the highest level by God and certainly at a lower level by the men to whom his laws gave authority. It might be presumed that God would always exercise his will in accord with his reason, but if men were fallen creatures, who lacked the intellect to perceive what was reasonable or just, or who were too willful to discern or follow it, then the nature of men seemed to suggest that God had designed them to be governed. The natural law discerned from human nature thus seemed to subject men to the lawmaking will of their earthly rulers, and in this way much of the legal and political study of natural law shifted focus from questions about the substantive reason or justice of laws to questions about authority—most immediately, to questions about the authority of rulers to make law through their will. Sociologically, it is not surprising that men in a modernizing society would seek to overcome their divisions by looking to authority; theologically, the fractured character of men seemed to suggest that it was in God's scheme that they were naturally in need of human governance. Human failings thereby disclosed the high authority of human rulers, and in hammering out this theory, Europeans forged a divinely strong legal obligation on the crooked anvil of humanity.

The study of law thus acquired a focus on authority. Countless rulers, Roman and barbarian, had long asserted their authority to impose their will as law, but in response to growing fears about discordant human reasoning, questions of lawmaking authority became central and were pursued systematically. Human rulers were still expected to take the substantive moral injunctions of reason into account when legislating. The ideal of authority, however, left them a freedom within their authority to make law as they saw fit, and they thus could exercise their will in a manner that a philosopher, theologian, or academic might consider unreasonable or unjust.

Although the initial problem—human disagreement about what was reasonable and just—had a solution in ideals of authority and will, this remedy opened up a secondary problem of excessive authority. The risk was that if a ruler had lawmaking authority, then even his arbitrary and oppressive will was law. As it happened, the theory of legal obligation that created this danger could also resolve it by locating human authority and will deeper in the community. Rulers as a class might have divine authority to make law, but any particular ruler, according to this theory, received his authority from the people, who in turn enjoyed their lawmaking authority from God, as revealed through natural law and perhaps scripture. The people thus had authority to make law—their constitution—and whether they did so expressly in an enactment or tacitly in custom, they thereby established and confined the lawmaking authority of their rulers. On these assumptions, the Europeans who saw a remedy for human divisions in the lawmaking authority of their rulers could also limit the risks of this approach by finding a higher lawmaking authority in the people.

Much of modern politics and law, including constitutions, thus followed from a cautious assessment of humanity and the consequent elevation of authority and will as the source of legal obligation. Different men pursued authority along different paths across Europe's uneven social and political terrain, but they almost all did so in response to their perceptions of human division and discord. From these perceptions followed their conclusions about the divinely derived authority of human lawmakers and the divinely derived obligation of their will or intent. From these perceptions also followed the division of political and moral theory—in particular, the bifurcation of the study of natural law into a preliminary inquiry about authority and another inquiry about morals and legislation. From the same grim perceptions of a splintered humanity, moreover, followed the specialization of authority: among different individuals, among different peoples, between a people and their government, and within the branches of their government. The authority men enjoyed in these different spheres was nothing less than their freedom—whether their freedom as individuals, as a people, or in government—and although these different realms of authority would increasingly be pursued to the point of conflicting with each other, they flourished simultaneously, for they were all part of the systematic segregation and specialization of authority that was Europe's most distinctive response to the divided character of men in modern society.

Judicial Duty

English judges had a duty to decide in accord with the law of the land, including their constitution. This duty was part of the office of a judge, to which judges were bound by their oaths, and with their high ideal of this office and a sworn obligation to adhere to it, judges could find the strength to do their duty, even when it required them to hold unconstitutional acts void.

Judgment stood in sharp contrast to will. A judge's office required him to exclude will from his judgment—not merely to resist the will imposed from without, but more essentially that which arose within. Today, the sharp distinction between will and judgment may seem naive. Yet just as sharply drawn boundaries can make good law, so strongly stated philosophy can delineate valuable ideals, and in this manner the distinction between judgment and will helped to preserve judges from their fears and passions, to segregate judicial duty from lawmaking power, to protect parties from injustice, and to keep judges within their sphere of independence and authority.

The duty of common law judges to exercise judgment in accord with the law of the land long went without elaborate theoretical justification. Certainly, while Europeans tended to assume that the obligation of human law rested on its reason or justice, the English had to fear that this moralizing vision of legal obligation might threaten the obligation of their more grounded law. Eventually, however, in response to fears that men could not agree on what was reasonable or just, Europeans increasingly located the obligation of law in the authority of the lawmaker rather than the reason or justice of his laws, and when the hierarchy of law thus shifted toward authority, the English could finally discuss the natural foundations of their law without worrying that they might thereby undermine its obligation or the duty of their judges to decide in accord with it. English lawyers thus at last found support for their narrowly English ideals in an abstract theory, and they thereby simultaneously defended their distinctive law and more systematically aligned it with a general conception of law—one with which it already had strong, though understated, affinities.

The duty of judges complemented the obligation of the law of the land, for both the duty and the law rested on a worldly skepticism as to whether men could reliably agree about reason and justice. Especially in modernizing circumstances, if judges, like other men, could not be expected to understand what was reasonable and just without entering into dispute, then an ideal of judging in accord with considerations more elevated than the law of the land could seem to reintroduce the very disagreement and conflict that men had avoided by recognizing the authority of their legislature and the obligation of its will. The divided character of men thus not only suggested that lawmaking will had legal obligation, but also that judges had to decide in accord with such law—in accord with the law willed by their legislature and ultimately, the people.

On account of their duty to decide in accord with the law of the land, the common law judges had to evaluate the constitutionality of government acts. For centuries they therefore determined the lawfulness of government acts, ranging from local legislation to acts of the Crown, and when they came to view the constitution adopted by the people as the most fundamental part of the law of the land, they even had to examine whether the king's exercise of his absolute prerogative exceeded lawful bounds. They could not hold acts of Parliament unlawful, for Parliament was the highest court in the land, but they otherwise could do what is often said to have been first done by Americans.

The duty of the judges when holding government acts unconstitutional had the functional benefit of allowing them to enforce the constitution and thus preserve constitutional liberty. These functional considerations would eventually become so prominent as to obscure the ideal of judicial duty on which they depended, but this was a very late development, which occurred mostly in the twentieth century. During the period examined here, judges ordinarily assumed that they served the functions of enforcing the constitution and protecting liberty by doing their duty—by deciding in accord with the law of the land—and it appears that they were able to serve their utilitarian, political functions because their duty combined human law with a divine office and obligation. Without the human measure established by the law of the land, the judges would have borne so heavy a burden of discretion that they could not have regularly held acts of the king unlawful. Without the divine model of their office and their divine obligation to adhere to it, the judges surely could not have done their duty in the face of the king's will or even their own. With this divine model and obligation, however, their duty to decide in accord with human law enjoyed an authority that stood far above what could ordinarily be attributed to intellectual mechanisms of candidly human manufacture. Judges thus could find in their duty a combination of the human and the divine that allowed them to do what would otherwise seem improbable—not least when they held government acts unlawful.

The Academic Challenge

Men with relatively academic perceptions of law and judicial duty often challenged the common law ideals. They assimilated what they learned at university so wholeheartedly as to hope that judges would bring an academic-style rationality and justice to bear on English law, and at least in this sense they expected judges to decide in accord with a broader range of law than that of the land. The common law judges, however, held their ground. They were not blind to the realities of incompleteness and discretion, but they hoped to limit these realities. Although many of them found it satisfying to observe the relationship of the law of the land to the broader universe of laws, they generally refused to allow academic analysis to undermine their duty or the authority of English law. Their stance can easily be caricatured as a sort of anti-intellectualism—an obstinate blindness to both reality and justice. In fact, the common law posture was a highly effective defense against the threat from academic law, and this defense was essential for limiting government power and preserving liberty.

It has been observed that the common law ideals were open and capacious enough to include a wide range of academic learning—whether civilian or, increasingly, empirical—but only as long as the common law ideals were not thereby threatened. Even when many judges in the eighteenth century abandoned their fears of the learned law and openly integrated its lessons within the common law, they almost always took care not to do so at the cost of their common law ideals. It was one thing to use academic distinctions to understand the law of the land; it was quite another to take an expansive view of what was uncertain or otherwise to subvert the ideals of law and judicial duty.

Few tensions have more profoundly affected Anglo-American law than that between the common law ideals and academic ideals, and although the conflict diminished in the eighteenth century, it has subsequently intensified. The academic ideals have surfaced at different times in different ways (traditionally through the learned law and later through a range of other approaches), but they have consistently tended to rest on a potent combination of "realism" and idealism—on a dismissive realism about the law of the land and the capacity of judges to decide in accord with it and on a high idealism about rational, academic models of human law and how judges should follow such models. In particular, a "realistic" appraisal of the indeterminacy and mutability of the law of the land has seemed to suggest that judges unavoidably enjoy a substantial freedom to decide in accord with reasoning that reaches above the law of the land, and in the space left by this academic realism, the idealism about rational models could flourish. It must be added (though it is outside the scope of this book) that the skeptical, academic realism has been accentuated by a theologically inspired antiformalism; it must also be added (more clearly within the realm of this book) that the rational, academic idealism has been bolstered by Protestant and derivative ideas about the egotistical nature of men, who even in conscience must inevitably give way to their will. On these academic and theological assumptions, many Americans have responded to their modern, individuated circumstances by supposing that judges necessarily exercise discretion or will—indeed that they have an obligation in conscience to exercise such discretion in accord with their passion for justice, freedom, efficiency, or other higher ends.

The ideal, however, that judges had to decide in accord with the law of the land rested on its own realism—not an academic skepticism about the law of the land, but a deeper realism about the inadequate intellect and dispassion of men. No less than other individuals, judges were apt, as already observed, to disagree about what was reasonable and just, and it therefore seemed only realistic to view the authority of the people and their legislatures as the measure of judicial duty. The judges could not always manage to put aside their will and exercise judgment in accord with the law of the land, but they were nonetheless expected to live up to such ideals, which thereby have provided a very realistic foundation for the extensive liberty, including the constitutional liberty, enjoyed in common law systems.

America

Americans inherited the common law ideals of law and judicial duty. If constitutions willed by the people were part of the law of the land, and if judges had a duty to decide in accord with the law of the land, American judges, like their English predecessors, had no choice but to decide the constitutionality of government acts. As put by the judges in *Bayard v. Single-*

ton, this was required by "the obligations of their oaths, and the duty of their office."[1]

What was distinctive about America was not the legal obligation of constitutions, nor the duty of judges, but rather the circumstances that left judges free to decide the lawfulness of legislative acts. In America, judges acted under express rather than customary charters or constitutions and as to legislatures that, at least in the ideals of the common law, were not typically little versions of the high court of Parliament. Even before Independence, therefore, the legal obstacles to holding acts of Parliament unlawful did not ordinarily stand in the way of decisions holding acts of American legislatures unlawful. Thus, while working on the same principles as judges in England, the judges in most colonies ideally were free to decide the constitutionality of any American governmental act—executive, judicial, or legislative. Nor did this change when the colonies became states. Thus, the question faced by American judges after 1776 was not whether to create or otherwise develop a power of enforcing constitutions against statutes. Instead, the question was whether, now that judges could make decisions without colonial resentments, they had any plausible reason not to do what had long been their duty as to unlawful American legislative acts.

It has been tempting in retrospect to attribute great significance to the developments that brought sovereign legislative acts within judicial enforcement, but sovereignty by itself was not the essential legal issue. Already in the seventeenth century, the constitutionality of sovereign royal acts was decided by English judges. Already then, moreover, American legislative acts were within judicial reach, and they remained so when Independence elevated them from subordinate laws to sovereign laws. Evidently, on both sides of the Atlantic, what made government acts susceptible of judicial evaluation had little to do with sovereignty. Rather, what mattered all along was the absence of the English legal obstacles that had barred decisions holding acts of Parliament void. Such impediments—a customary constitution and Parliament's status as the high court—could not very plausibly apply to royal or executive acts or to legislative acts adopted in a place where there were express charters or constitutions and where England's common law had long denied a Parliament-like power to legislative bodies.

Americans were fortunate in their express constitutions and the unimpeded applicability of judicial duty to their legislation, for in their disjointed circumstances, they required a more completely formalized system of constitutional law and its enforcement than the English. A customary

[1] Correspondence (Newbern June 7), *Virginia Independent Chronicle* (July 4, 1787).

constitution and the need to accept the judgment of a high legislative court about the constitutionality of its own acts did not necessarily create a problem in England, for cultural, social, and political mechanisms gave substantial force to at least some English constitutional limitations, and Parliament could usually be expected to protect the most basic constitutional rights. Americans, however, lived in a nation of egalitarian ideals and stark physical and psychological distances, and therefore even in a place such as Connecticut, which had a customary constitution, they were unable to depend as much upon custom and informal enforcement.

Express constitutions were already the means of protecting individual liberty, and the judges in doing their duty often preserved the rights of minorities whom they might view with distaste. When the Rev. John Murray sued to recover the religious taxes paid by his Universalist parishioners, he obtained an instruction from Chief Justice Cushing that the Massachusetts Constitution protected even Murray's religious society.[2] When the manumitted slaves of Perquimans County sought to regain the liberty they had lost under a retrospective law, they won a judgment under the North Carolina Constitution from judges who probably owned slaves and who revealed no inclination to challenge slavery. Of course, the Massachusetts Universalists and especially the North Carolina slaves had only very limited legal rights, but they at least prevailed as to these rights, notwithstanding the overwhelming weight of public sentiment against them.

By virtue of their office, judges had a distinctive authority in their cases not only to give judgment but also to expound law. The exposition of law had traditionally been recognized as part of the office of judgment, and although the resolution of cases had always been the core of judicial office, this focus of judicial authority became more pronounced already in England under the pressure of ideals of lawmaking authority. After American statutes spelled out the jurisdiction of courts in terms of various actions, suits, causes, cases, or controversies, Americans grew especially accustomed to thinking about judicial office in such terms, and this tight conception of judicial office was all the more appealing when it came to seem a concrete manifestation of the separation of powers. Recognizing the implications, judges largely understood that their independence and authority belonged to them individually within their office rather than jointly as a court or a department of government. Some, however, without disputing the limits of their authority nonetheless adopted resolutions on constitutional questions, and they thereby could find themselves at the mercy of the other branches of government. When judges acted as the judiciary, and thus as a party in

[2] See Appendix III.

a contest with supposedly equal powers, they cast off their robes of office and exposed themselves to political elements they might not be able to withstand.

Lost Assumptions

Like much of what was left inexplicit in American constitutions, the ideals of law and judicial duty have almost been lost to view. They were assumptions about law rather than requirements of law, and they were thus more often alluded to than described. By the eighteenth century, the ideals were rarely challenged, and therefore only when novel or complex circumstances rendered their application unclear did it become necessary to make their implications explicit. This is why the supremacy clause of the U.S. Constitution recited what it did and nothing more, and this is why what once seemed obvious is now at risk of being forgotten.

What remained inexplicit in American constitutions is particularly at risk because of the diffuse and fragmented character of American society. Not having been made explicit in the law itself, the common law ideals of law and judicial duty were apt to be remembered only as long as the society and its lawyers preserved them, and this was difficult enough in England and its Inns of Court. In America's less cohesive society, and especially in its cosmopolitan, academic law schools, the old assumptions about law and judicial duty have lost their strength and clarity and today are scarcely understood, let alone inculcated. It thus would seem that even express constitutions have not been adequate for American society. It is a society that has left individuals all the more dependent on formal judicial enforcement of formal guarantees of constitutional rights but that has simultaneously undermined the inexplicit assumptions underlying such rights and enforcement, including not only assumptions about particular provisions of American constitutions but also, more basically, about the authority of the people, the obligation of their intent, and the duty of the judges.

The result is that Americans are increasingly apt to see only the express surface and to lose sight of the depths below. Herbert Wechsler, for example, thought it necessary to find the authority for judicial review somehow "grounded in the language of the Constitution," and although he understood he could not insist on explicit authority, he was sufficiently anxious about the text that he failed to perceive the judicial duty that lay just below its surface.[3] It is a common problem. Studying the U.S. Constitution as if it

[3] Herbert Wechsler, "Toward Neutral Principles of Constitutional Law," *Harvard Law Review*, 73: 3 (1959).

were a disembodied text rather than the act of a people, lawyers often miss the presuppositions underlying its words, including its words about judges and the law of the land. Such words once not merely referred to various judges and laws, but did so in the context of profound ideals of law and judicial office. Now, however, these words often seem little more than verbal snippets, endowed with little useful intent and divorced from any particular meaning.

By the same token, explicit constitutional authority has come to seem necessary for what once was so clearly evident it could be left implicit. In the 1780s, the ideals of law and judicial duty could be taken for granted across America by the lowest of judges, many of whom were not even lawyers. Similarly when James Iredell in 1787 and John Marshall in 1803 explained the role of the judges in holding statutes unconstitutional, they could still conjure up the common law ideals simply by mentioning them. Since then, however, express constitutional authority has come to seem essential, and such authority, inevitably, has proved elusive. It is difficult to discern express authority for what the Constitution largely took for granted, and the task becomes decidedly quixotic when modern scholars seek the Constitution's authorization not for judicial duty, but for "judicial review."

Perhaps unavoidably, the ideals discussed here flourished during a long but nonetheless transient period when European and American society was sufficiently fractured that men turned to ideals of authority and will, but not yet so fractured that they were unable to take them for granted. The loss of social cohesion, which in its early stages made common law ideals of law and judicial duty so valuable, continued unabated and eventually placed a greater burden on these ideals than they could sustain. These ideals were part of broader tendencies toward authority and will that seemed appealing amid modern divisions, but the broader tendencies gradually legitimized and stimulated further divisions, and it may be doubted how well the ideals of law and judicial duty that once thrived in England and America can survive when the fissures extend so far as to leave individuals with little attachment to any authority, other than perhaps their own. The flourishing of the common law ideals may therefore be considered a response to a stage in the individuation of men and the legitimization of their will—developments that would eventually go so far as to undermine the common law ideals. It is sobering to contemplate what will ensue when a society, being unable to cohere around substantive ideals of reason, adds a preliminary emphasis on ideals of authority, and then evolves so far as to be unable even to cohere around these thinner ideals. In eighteenth-century America, however, such threats to the ideals of law and judicial duty still remained mostly in the future.

The Significance of the History

The history of the ideals of law and judicial duty remains essential for understanding the authority and extent of judicial power. Too often, judicial review is said to be a development largely created or at least established by the judges—as if in the absence of any clear constitutional authorization, the judiciary lifted itself up by its own bootstraps and gave itself its own preeminent power. Welcoming the implications of this history, many scholars and judges candidly consider the scope and exercise of judicial review to be within judicial control. The historical evidence, however, points to other conclusions.

At a minimum, the evidence calls into question any reliance on the history of "judicial review." The speculation about how judges developed judicial review has always rested on the paucity of evidence—in particular, the shortage of evidence from the 1780s and earlier—but in light of the evidence about law and judicial duty presented in this book, the history of judicial review looks rather dubious. Of course, the sort of judicial power that draws authority from the history of judicial review may nonetheless remain appealing to some observers, but it should stand on its own legs rather than rest on the crutches provided by an imaginative historicizing of modern preconceptions.

More substantially, the evidence reveals both the authority and the nature of law and judicial office as traditionally understood by common lawyers. The point is not simply that judicial review was different and older than traditionally imagined, but rather that there was a more general judicial duty. Instead of having a power specifically relating to constitutional decisions—a power developed through their own exertions and thus of indeterminate authority and scope—the judges had a broader power that was neither more nor less than their duty. This duty was but an aspect of their office, and it required them to decide in accord with the law of the land, including any relevant constitution. The generality of the duty was what gave strength and balance to their constitutional decisions, for it authorized and bound the judges with the same ideals that elevated and confined them in their more mundane decisions. Their duty thus anchored an otherwise extraordinary power within the quotidian exercise of their office, and the result was a judicial power both more authoritative and less dangerous than that which prevails today.

The ideals of law and judicial duty had authority from both above and below. It has been seen that the authority for law and judicial duty was understood to come from far above the law of the land, and these ideals therefore did not need authorization even in the highest part of such law. At the same time, the ideals of law and judicial duty were so deeply ingrained that they could simply be taken for granted, and they therefore were implicit in what little the people made explicit in their constitutions. When, for example, the U.S. Constitution mentioned the law of the land and the judges, it did not need to spell out the nature of legal obligation or the office and duty of judges, for such things were obvious.

None of this is to say that it was easy for a judge to do his duty. On the contrary, in all sorts of cases, whether or not constitutional, judges could have difficulty deciding in accord with the law, especially when they had to discern the law at its edges. Even there, however, the judges were to do their best to exercise judgment rather than will and were to decide in accord with the law of the land. Their task, moreover, was not quite as difficult as may be supposed, for in England and America the law of the land had a relatively limited domain, and its obligation was confined by almost epistemological limitations. For example, where the intent of a statute or a constitution could not be discerned, it could not be obligatory, and where a statute was not manifestly contrary to the constitution, the statute simply retained its obligation.

At a more fundamental level, the ideals of law and judicial duty remain suggestive about the task of overcoming the fragmentation inherent in modern society, and this points beyond the conventional authority for the common law ideals to their deeper, moral authority. Far from being simply ideas about government, the common law notions of law and judicial duty developed in response to problems arising from human nature, especially as it came to be understood in an increasingly disjointed society. To be sure, the authority of the people and the obligation of the law of the land do not form the only possible solution to the problems arising from discordant reasoning about justice, and a judicial duty to decide in accord with the law of the land is not the only way of minimizing the reappearance of such discord among judges. Nonetheless, the ideals that formed the common law solution were not merely the arbitrary preferences of a local culture, but were the common law version of a familiar response to one of the most basic features of modernity—the use of legal authority to redress the peculiarly fractured character of humanity in modern circumstances.

It may well be objected that the common law ideals have nonetheless been profoundly disappointing—a conclusion that seems to be borne out by the range of injustices and oppression, including slavery, that were possible in common law systems. All systems of law, however, have been used for injustice and oppression, and common law systems at least offered a means of overcoming such failings. Indeed, the common law ideals and the freedom they secured did much to establish justice. It was not the sort of justice that might be imagined possible in a cohesive, homogenous society, but it was the sort of justice that can be achieved even in a much divided society—the sort of justice that consists of legal rights or that can be attained through such liberty. Although this modern kind of justice can sometimes seems rather thin, it has been invaluable against oppression, as evident from the various legal guarantees against slavery and other inequalities. On the whole, notwithstanding that the common law ideals could become an instrument of oppression, they more saliently have been the means of overcoming it.

Put in more positive terms, the common law ideals enjoy authority as the foundation of a strikingly successful combination of order and freedom in divided circumstances. The truth may be whole, but it is apt to be variously perceived in the modern world, and one reason the common law ideals have flourished is that they have avoided the danger of asking discordant individuals, including judges, to decide what is reasonable and just. In this sense, the ideals of authority were not merely a response to fears of division and disorder but were also more generally a manifestation of the epistemological sophistication necessary when men must cohere in uncohesive circumstances. In a world in which men could not expect to agree about reason and justice, the common law vision of authority allowed them to enjoy order amid their divisions, and by preserving and limiting different spheres of authority, this vision also preserved a substantial degree of freedom. Culturally, the common law ideals acknowledged the freedom of different lands to take their divergent paths in law; individually, they left room for the freedom of individuals as well as of government; and at least as pursued in England and America the cultural and individual freedom enjoyed under these ideals has been unparalleled.

The common law ideals thus acquired their most profound context in modernity rather than tradition. The difficulty of getting agreement, including agreement on what is reasonable and just in law, is the centrifugal reality of modern life, and although this has prompted men to turn toward authority, it has also led to a division of authority—a division among individuals, among peoples, among states, among the branches of government, and not least, between any two of these different bodies, such as between an individual and the state. In these circumstances, an artfully divided system of authority could take advantage of the fractious character of humanity in order to overcome it, and when such a system distributed authority through law and required it to be exercised through or at least under law, the system could transcend the divided character of modern life without simultaneously creating an even greater danger from the concentration of authority. The Anglo-American version of such a system, accomplished most saliently by means of a constitution, became the primary alternative to the consolidated and almost unlimited state authority that flourished in much of the rest of the world. This was a remarkable achievement, and at least thus far it has proved singularly well adapted to the modern world.

In the end, the common law ideals of law and judicial duty can be considered attempts to secure a firm footing at the edge of a chasm of lawlessness. A body that was the final judge might come to view itself as above the law of the land and thus absolute, and after the king in this way took advantage of his claim to be the final judge of his prerogative, Parliament responded by expanding upon its own claim of absolute power, which it based on its status as the highest court in the realm. Even in Parliament, however, a power above law was dangerous, and this gave particular significance to the constitutional solution, which could be understood to deny a power above law to any part of government. From such a perspective, any human power above human law resided exclusively in the people, whose constitution established a government entirely under law.

The power above human law, however, has not remained entirely in the people. The attribution of this absolute power to the people avoided some of the dangers of its being concentrated in government, but the people have been no more divine in their exercise of will than their kings and legislatures, and many Americans, in their desire to prevent the people from abusing the power above law, have invited their judges to exercise it. Thus, after the power above the law of the land finally shifted from government to the people, it has come to be at least partly relocated in the judges. In taking up this power, the judges have found sophisticated support in the old academic sensibilities, and not unlike some kings and Parliament when they claimed to be the final arbiter, American judges have acquired a taste for power above the law. Perhaps every society needs this sort of power, but in denying absolute power to Parliament, Americans did not give it to the judges, and although it is questionable whether the people, being merely human, will always act wisely and justly in exercising their power above the law of the land, it is even more doubtful whether the judges or any other persons in government can be trusted with such a power. Men will ever be discontent with law and ambitious for power, and judges will ever be vain enough to aspire to a justice above human law, but it is therefore all the more important for judges to recall the common law ideals of law and judicial duty.

Appendix I

Bonham's Case

Bonham's *Case* scarcely deserves mention in a history of judicial duty, except for reasons that have been largely forgotten. In his report of *Bonham's Case,* Coke spoke in bold tones about the *control* of acts of Parliament and about holding them *void,* and such language has led many scholars to assume that Coke was really declaring the power of judges to hold acts of Parliament void under common law—perhaps even under natural law. The exuberance of this interpretation has been tempered by the observations of Samuel Thorne and J. H. Baker that Coke was merely discussing equitable interpretation.[1] Nonetheless, the breadth of Coke's words remain suggestive, and it is therefore necessary take a further look—in particular, at his use of the words "void" and "control." The case occurred at a time when some judges of the non-common-law courts were claiming an Imperial, almost legislative discretion over statutory interpretation, free from any supervisory jurisdiction by the common law courts, and with this context in mind, one can begin to discern what worried Coke. Far from elevating judicial power, Coke explained equitable interpretation in a manner calculated to remind his readers that interpretation was not a matter of discretion, but of law.

It is necessary to begin with the word "void." Although common law-

[1] S. E. Thorne, "Dr. Bonham's Case," in *Essays in English Legal History,* 275–276 (London: Hambledon, 1985); J. H. Baker, *The Law's Two Bodies: Some Evidential Problems in English Legal History,* 28 and note 96 (Oxford: Oxford University Press, 2001). Gray shows that the discussion of control arose more clearly in Coke's report than in court, and I am grateful to him for sharing his transcription of *Darcy v. Allen,* which has been so useful here. Charles Gray, "Bonham's Case Reviewed," in *Proceedings of the American Philosophical Society,* 116: 44–48 (Feb. 1972). For a bold version of the thesis that Coke proposed a sort of judicial review, see Theodore F. T. Plucknett, "Bonham's Case and Judicial Review," *Harvard Law Review,* 40: 30–70 (1938), and a wide array of works by other scholars.

yers could refer to the possibility that an act of Parliament might be void, there has been some controversy as to what this meant. As a practical matter, no medieval common law judge is known to have held an act of Parliament void, and it therefore is conventionally assumed that although in theory a judge could hold an act of Parliament void, in practice he could not. For example, Chrimes observes that "judges in the fifteenth century were *theoretically* justified in nullifying statute law" if it was "contrary to the law of nature (or reason) or law of God," but he concludes that there is no instance in which they actually held a statute void."[2]

The judges, however, do not appear to have understood the matter as a mere inconsistency between theory and practice; instead, by the sixteenth century, they appear sometimes to have understood the discrepancy as a difference between two jurisdictions. In debating judgments in the interior court, the court of conscience, men often talked generally about laws being void, even though they did not necessarily mean that any such laws would therefore be held void in an exterior court of law. For example, when St. German discussed the possibility that an act of Parliament might be void, he usually seems to have meant that it might be void in conscience. The distinction between the interior court of conscience and the exterior court of law would have been familiar from moral discussions, and it was useful to St. German because he could still imagine that the chancellor was acting on his conscience—as if the chancellor's court were but a physical manifestation of the interior court. Although common lawyers might hesitate to accept the full extent of St. German's view of the chancellor's power, most of them would have understood the general distinction between the interior and the exterior court, and when reading about equity in St. German, they apparently understood that one could say that a statute was void, without implying that the common law judges in one of their exterior courts would hold it void.[3]

Even without requiring so direct a result in an exterior court, however, the severe judgment of the interior court could still be significant for common lawyers. St. German apparently assumed that where a statute was void in conscience, the chancellor in his putatively interior court could some-

[2] S. B. Chrimes, *English Constitutional Ideas in the Fifteenth Century*, 290–293 (Cambridge: Cambridge University Press, 1936).

[3] The underlying assumptions remained familiar in the following centuries. For example, Archbishop Bramhall flattered Parliament by drawing an analogy between the interior court and the exterior: "For as there lieth no appeal from God in the interior court, so there lieth no appeal from Parliament in the exterior court." A Speech made in the House of Peers (May 11, 1661), *The Works of the Most Reverend Father in God, John Bramhall*, 5: 141 (Oxford: 1845).

times give an equitable remedy. The common law judges in their unapologetically exterior courts could not follow the interior conclusion of conscience in the same way, but they could rely on it to give a milder sort of equitable remedy where this was compatible with the law of the land and their duty. Put more concretely, they could not give a remedy against the obligation of a statute, but by observing that the statute would otherwise be void in the interior court, they could lay the moral foundation for an equitable interpretation in their exterior court.

In *Bonham's Case,* Coke almost certainly used the word "void" in this sense. Dr. Thomas Bonham had practiced medicine in London without permission from the Royal College of Physicians, and its governing board or court, known as its "censors," therefore sentenced him to pay a fine and be incarcerated in the Fleet prison. After securing his release, Bonham brought an action for wrongful imprisonment, and in this action (as Ellesmere summarized more succinctly than Coke) the question was "what power the Colledge of phisicians had"—by their 1518 charter and by a later act of Parliament that confirmed the charter—"to imprison any other physicion that practised here in London without the licence of the Colledge."[4] A majority of the Court of Common Pleas, including Coke, held that the College could not lawfully imprison Bonham because the censors had acted as judge in their own case. To be both judge and party had long been considered contrary to natural law. According to many old precedents, moreover, a charter that made a man judge in his own case was to be construed, where possible, to avoid this injustice, and a majority of the judges in *Bonham's Case* appear to have adopted this sort of equitable interpretation, both as to the charter and as to the statute confirming it.[5]

The next year, in his report of the case, Coke elaborated the reasoning underlying the judges' interpretation:

> The censors cannot be judges, ministers, and parties. . . . And it appears in our books, that in many cases, the common law will controul Acts of Parliament, and sometimes adjudge them to be utterly void: for when an Act of Parliament is against common right and reason, or repugnant, or impossible

[4] "Observations on Ye Lord Cookes Reportes" (1615), in Louis A. Knafla, *Law and Politics in Jacobean England: The Tracts of Lord Chancellor Ellesmere,* 306 (Cambridge: Cambridge University Press, 1977). In fact, there was more than one statute. For details of the litigation, see Harold J. Cook, "Against Common Right and Reason: *The College of Physicians v. Dr. Thomas Bonham,*" in *Law, Liberty, and Parliament: Selected Essays on the Writings of Sir Edward Coke,* 127, ed. Allen D. Boyer (Indianapolis: Liberty Fund, 2004).

[5] D. E. C. Yale, "*Judex in Propria Causa:* An Historical Excursus," *Cambridge Law Journal,* 33: 87–92 (1974); Cook, "Against Common Right and Reason," 143, 146.

> to be performed, the common law will controul it, and adjudge such Act to be void.[6]

This suggestion that acts of Parliament could be adjudged "void" has intrigued commentators for centuries, but the immediate explanation is that Coke was laying out the moral basis for his equitable interpretation of a statute that would otherwise have made men judges in their own case. A statute that was repugnant to itself might be void in the sense that if its intent could not be discerned, it would have no legal obligation.[7] A statute, however, that made men both judges and a party could also be repugnant to itself or impossible in a more profound sense, such that it was contrary to the notion of law and reason. On this basis, when Coke said that an act of Parliament would be void if it was repugnant, impossible, or contrary to common right and reason, he was drawing upon a familiar mode of moral analysis to hint that the act of Parliament in *Bonham's Case* would be void—not at law, but in conscience—unless equitably interpreted to avoid the injustice.

Yet if Coke was merely dealing with equitable interpretation, why did he state that the common law would "control" acts of Parliament? Although this word in Coke's report is usually taken to suggest an expansive judicial power to hold statutes void, Coke appears to have had something very different in mind. He was explaining equitable interpretation, and in this context, his emphasis on the common law's "control" of acts of Parliament was no accident.

The significance of the word can be glimpsed in an exchange involving Nicholas Fuller several years earlier. In *Darcy v. Allen*—the *Case of Monopolies*—Edward Darcy had letters patent from Queen Elizabeth granting

[6] *Bonham's Case* (C.P. 1610), Coke's *Reports,* 8: 118a.

[7] Common lawyers could colloquially say that a statute was "void" in the sense that it was of no effect, and it has recently been suggested that this was Coke's meaning in *Bonham's Case.* Ian Williams, "Dr Bonham's Case and 'Void' Statutes," *Journal of Legal History,* 27: 111 (2006). The word "void" could certainly be used in the sixteenth century to refer to statutes that were ineffective because they did not make their meaning clear—the standard example being misrecital, as when Plowden observed that "statutes which misrecite things . . . shall be void, and none shall be concluded by them." *Heydon's Case* (K.B. 1571), Plowden, *Reports,* 400 (Dublin: 1792). See also *A Discourse upon the Exposicion & Understanding of Statutes,* 86–87, ed. Samuel L. Thorne (San Marino: Huntington Library, 1942); Christopher Hatton, *A Treatise Concerning Statutes, or Acts of Parliament: And the Exposition Thereof,* 18–19, 20–21 (London: 1677). Yet this cannot explain more than a minor aspect of what Coke was doing in his report of *Bonham's Case.* It can explain Coke's conclusion about acts of Parliament that were "repugnant," but not about those that were "impossible to be performed" and especially not about those that were "against common right and reason." More generally, in the context of equitable interpretation, it is difficult to avoid the conclusion that Coke was employing the mode of reasoning associated with equity.

him an exclusive right to make, import, and sell playing cards, and he brought an action in 1602 against Thomas Allen for making cards in violation of this grant. Nicholas Fuller was one of Allen's lawyers, and he argued in King's Bench that the letters patent were void. Fuller began by quoting Bracton on the monarch to the effect that "the law makes him King, whence it appears that the King must be subject to the law." To this, Fuller added: "That is not to be taken to mean only written law, but he must be subject 'legi Lonquenti', viz. to the interpretation of the law."[8]

Fuller, however, was not confident that the law by itself would be enough for his client, and he therefore hinted that interpretation amounted to judicial "control"—apparently to suggest that the judges had, if not quite discretion, at least much power to hold letters patent void. In justifying such discretion, he blurred together two different types of decisions, explaining that judicial "interpretation" or "control" included both a charitable interpretation of a patent to preserve the rights of the king and a decision that the patent was void under law for violating the liberties of the subject. Each was "control" of the patent:

> [T]he same reason that requires that the judges of the law may control the King's patent against the express letter thereof for the King's own benefit also requires that the judges may control the King's patent for the benefit of the subject, when it goes too far to the people's prejudice.

To illustrate the king's benefit from such control—a control that seemed to Fuller to include judicial exertions for the king in expounding letters patent—Fuller gave an example of charitable interpretation:

> Therefore, if the King grants to a man certain land with all manner of mines whatsoever, they have passed to the grantee. So, no doubt, a scholar or philosopher who judges according to the letter would hold. Nevertheless, the judges of the law will judge that no gold or silver mine will pass thereby. Thus to the King's advantage the judges will control the patent.

At this moment, Justice Fenner muttered "*sotto voce* that that is not controlling but expounding letters patent." Fuller had attempted to ingratiate himself with the judges by taking a sideswipe at "a scholar or philosopher," but he could not thereby reconcile the judges to his strained suggestion that judges did more than expound. Fuller felt obliged to continue so far as to complete his point about the power of judges over royal charters, saying "as they may control them for the King's own benefit, so they may also do for

[8] King's Bench Reports, British Library, Add. Ms. 25203, fol. 580[r], as translated by Charles Gray in his mimeographed teaching materials.

the benefit of the subject." He recognized, however, that he had been rebuked from the bench, and he therefore edged away from his suggestion about "control," now making clear he understood that "the King's grants" were "controled by the rule of the law."[9]

Among the lawyers who argued *Darcy v. Allen* was Attorney General Coke, who well understood the connotations of power in the word "control." After listening to Fuller, Coke in his response emphasized the rule of law, and whether or not Coke in later years remembered the *sotto voce* reprimand from the bench, he evidently shared Justice Fenner's view that judges did not control acts, whether charters or acts of Parliament. In his report of *Bonham's Case,* Coke wrote that sometimes "the common law will controul Acts of Parliament" and "adjudge" them "utterly void," and then after listing circumstances associated with equitable and other ameliorative interpretation of a statute, he repeated that "the common law will controul it, and adjudge such Act to be void."[10] Although Coke thus laid a foundation for his equitable interpretation by suggesting that the act of Parliament would otherwise be void in conscience, he also clearly indicated that the common law rather than judges exercised control.

Of course, it was not just any judges that worried Coke. In recent years, the non-common-law judges had been claiming a power to interpret acts of Parliament without accountability to the common law courts, and some men had even suggested (as seen in Chapter Seven) that such judges enjoyed a delegated Imperial-style power of legislative interpretation in the interstices of statutes. James I defended these pretensions of independent jurisdiction and delegated discretion, and thus what began as a relatively minor dispute (over writs of prohibition to ecclesiastical courts in cases of tithes) soon became a broad controversy as to whether "the Exposition of Statutes concerning Ecclesiasticall causes . . . belong[ed] to the Judges of the Realme or to th' interpretation of the Civilians and Canonists." When Coke attempted to defend the jurisdiction of the common law courts, James became furious and complained that the common law judges "alleadge statutes and reserve the exposition thereof to themselves."

[9] Ibid., fols. 580[v], 581[r], as translated by Charles Gray in his mimeographed teaching materials. In the original, Fenner's remarks appear within parentheses: "(a q. Fenner dit tacite q ceo nest un controllinge mes un expoundinge del tres patents)." Noy's printed report does not include Fenner's interjection, and it sufficiently sanitizes Fuller's argument as to leave the impression it was never more provocative than to suggest that "the Judges shall controll Patents contrary to the Letters, because they have the rules of Law to do so." Noy, *Reports,* 175.
[10] *Bonham's Case* (C.P. 1610), 5 Coke's *Reports,* 118a.

They presumed to "interprete the lawes themselves and suffer none else to interprete."[11] Coke, however, was not easily silenced, and he wrote a treatise showing that "Acts of Parliament made by [the] Kinge, the Lords and Com[m]ons, are parte of the Lawes of England" and "are to be interpreted by the judges of the laws of England . . . not by any Cannonist or ecclesiastical judge."[12] In short, James and his advisers had claimed an independent and almost legislative power of interpretation for the non-common-law courts wherever it could be claimed that statutes were uncertain, and because uncertainty was also the basis of equitable interpretation, Coke evidently worried that this conventional kind of interpretation would provide an opening for the more ambitious sort, one in which judges candidly exercised discretion or control. Coke therefore took care when using equitable interpretation in *Bonham's Case* to specify that not the judges but "the common law will controul Acts of Parliament."[13]

Indeed, because non-common-law judges were apt to rely on non-common-law sources to conclude that a statute was void in conscience, Coke went out of his way to suggest that even in the interior court, it was the common law rather than any other that determined when a statute was void. It will be recalled that when St. German had relied upon natural and divine law to show that English statutes could be void in conscience, his opponent, the serjeant at law, had protested that "the lawe of the realme is a sufficiente rule to ordre . . . your conscience," and now in the same spirit as the serjeant, Coke suggested that the common law would adjudge whether

[11] Roland G. Usher, *Reconstruction of the English Church,* 2: 242, note 1 (New York: D. Appleton, 1910); Julius Caesar's Notes, as printed in Roland G. Usher, "James I and Sir Edward Coke," *English Historical Review,* 18: 669 (1903).

[12] Usher, *Reconstruction of the English Church,* 2: 242. For example, where "an act of Parliament do authorize the ecclesiasticall judge that which before he could not doe, the judges of the Common Lawe shall judge and determine whether the ecclesiasticall Judge have pursued his aucthoritie given by the statute, or by Color of that statute hath done wrong to any of the Kinges subjects or no." Ibid.

[13] *Bonham's Case* (C.P. 1610), 5 Coke's *Reports,* 118a.

Significantly, the word "control" sometimes came up in disputes about jurisdiction. Shortly after *Bonham's Case,* Ellesmere complained about "the desire of the Reporter [Coke] to intrude upon other mens profession and to weaken the power of the Ecclesiasticall Court, as if they were not absolute in themselves in Jurisdiccions naturally belonging to them, but Subordinate [to] the Judges of the Common Law to be Controlled in thinges that fall not within ye Levall of the Common Lawe. "Observations on Ye Lord Cookes Reportes" (1615), in Knafla, *Law and Politics in Jacobean England,* 300–301. Doddridge wrote: "Law without equity were rigour. And yet again, of the other side, if all Lawes should change and be controlled as often in every case as equity would require, then should there be . . . no Law certaine." John Doddridge, *The English Lawyer,* 211 (London: 1631).

an act of Parliament was void in conscience.[14] The notion that an act of Parliament could be void was drawn from discussions of conscience—discussions that apparently took place in the non-common-law courts and that sometimes failed to accommodate the concerns of the common law. In this context, Coke recited the language of conscience precisely in order to emphasize that when the moral analysis of the interior court was used to set up equitable interpretation of an act of Parliament in an exterior court, it was ultimately the common law rather than any other that would determine the statute's obligation in conscience—that would "adjudge such Act to be void."

It hardly requires to be added that Coke's report of *Bonham's Case* invited difficulties. In the past, lawyers could talk unequivocally about acts of Parliament being void because they and their contemporaries took for granted that they only meant void in conscience. In the seventeenth century, however, men were anxious about authority, and some even lay in wait to seize upon Coke's words. Coke was engaging in a controversy with the non-common-law courts, and although he used old-fashioned words to refer to a familiar mode of interpretation, his open-ended locution allowed his enemies to allege that he meant much more. Chancellor Ellesmere, for example, took the opportunity to suggest that Coke's report "derogateth much from the . . . power of the parliament," thus throwing back an accusation that Coke had only recently, in the *Case of Proclamations,* aimed at Ellesmere.[15] Coke's critics also played with his words to undermine his critique of discretionary interpretation in the non-common-law courts—as when Ellesmere mockingly relied on *Bonham's Case* to justify an unusually broad conception of equitable interpretation in Chancery. On the one hand, Ellesmere chastised Coke for suggesting that "the Common Law hath such a Prerogative, as that it can controul Acts of Parliament, and adjudge them void," for such acts "ought to be revers'd by Parliament (only), and not otherwise." On the other hand, with malicious irony, the Chancellor cited *Bonham's Case* to defend his claim that he had a power, "an abso-

14 "The Replication of a Serjeant at the Laws of England," *Christopher St. German on Chancery and Statute,* 102–103, ed. J. A. Guy (London: Selden Society, 1985).

15 "Observations on Ye Lord Cookes Reportes" (1615), in Knafla, *Law and Politics in Jacobean England,* 306–307. Ellesmere asked, "when the three estates—the King, the Lords and the Commons—have spent their Labours in makeing a Law, then shall 3 Judges on the bench distroy and frustrate all their points because the Act advanceth the reason of a particular Court above the Judgement of all the Realme"? It was better "that Acts of parliament should be corrected by the same penn that drew theym, thayn to be dasht in peeces by the, opinion of a few Judges." Ibid., 307.

lute and uncontrolable Power," to interpret statutes against both "the Letter and Intent of the makers."[16] The misinterpretation of *Bonham's Case,* however, is another story, which can be told in another place.

Here it should suffice to observe that Coke in his report of *Bonham's Case* did not mean to suggest that judges could hold statutes void, let alone in accord with natural law. On the contrary, he aimed to make clear that control belonged to the common law rather than any judges. Even when judges merely laid the foundation for equitable interpretation by discussing whether a statute was void in conscience, it was, according to Coke, the common law that ultimately was determinative. Not only in the exterior court, but also sometimes in the interior, the common law was controlling.

[16] *Earl of Oxford's Case* (Ch. 1615), *Chancery Reports,* 1: 12. It surely was no coincidence that Chief Justice Hobart in the same year spoke of "that liberty and authority that Judges have over Laws, especially over Statute Laws, according to reason and best convenience, to mould them to the truest and best use." *Lord Sheffield v. Ratcliffe* (Ex. Ch. 1615), Hobart, *Reports,* 346. Of course, as Chancellor Nottingham later noted, this "was a very bold opinion." D. E. C. Yale, ed., *Lord Nottingham's 'Manual of Chancery Practice' and 'Prolegomena of Chancery and Equity',* 355 (Cambridge: Cambridge University Press, 1965).

Ellesmere made his claims in the *Earl of Oxford's Case* in the course of barring proceedings on a judgment at law, and as this was related to the larger dispute in which Coke sought indictments for *præmunire,* both *Bonham's Case* and Ellesmere's misuse of it can be understood as among the events that eventually led to Coke's dismissal.

Appendix II

The Institutio Legalis: Law and Justice in New Jersey

In 1783, some law students in New Jersey formed a society they called the Institutio Legalis. These young men, including some who would later become prominent, met regularly in Newark and nearby Elizabethtown to state and argue cases before a student judge, who would hear the arguments and later deliver a written opinion. Although only the product of students, who took turns serving as judge, the proceedings of the Institutio Legalis offer the earliest surviving complete set of written opinions from any state, and they offer a microcosm of different perspectives on law in the 1780s. The students often focused on technical questions, but they also worried about the demands of reason and justice, and they evidently understood that the tension between these demands and the law was one of the costs of a system of authority. Some of them pressed against the law to reach decisions in accord with reason and justice. The students considered as a group, however, appear to have been dissatisfied with such an approach, and their opinions thus reveal how morally serious young men, even when distressed by the injustice of the law, could struggle sincerely to decide in accord with it.

Judge Jacob de Hart, Jr., the son of a prominent New Jersey lawyer, self-consciously adopted the language of Coke to resist claims of natural reason.[1] In the summer of 1783, in an action of debt on obligation (an action of debt on a sealed deed), the defendant pleaded that he did not actually owe anything in the underlying transaction—this being the basis for claiming that it would be unjust for him to be held to his deed. Judge de Hart conceded that this objection could be pleaded to an action of debt on an informal or "simple contract," but he observed that it was of no avail

[1] His father had served in the Continental Congress and had helped draft the New Jersey Constitution.

against an action on a sealed deed, for "[t]he law requires order & form which the defendant ought to follow" and "[t]he Rules of law must be adhered to." De Hart explained: "I must not decide by the Rules of natural reason, but as my Lord Coke says by the Artificial Reason & Judgment of law which as he expresses it is the golden mete wand and measure to try the cause of the Subject."[2] De Hart took a similar approach when a defendant charged with high treason complained that "there is a former Indictment pending against the prisoner at the bar for the same crime." De Hart held that "[t]he finding [of] a new Indictment under these Circumstances, was certainly irregular and illegal," and he explained that "I cannot determine otherwise than the practice of former presidents will allow; if I determine otherwise it will be subverting the law[,] for the practice of the Court is the law of the court and I am to govern myself according to the right line of law and not by the crooked cord of private opinion." To this he added, "Ex facto Jus oritur"—the law arises from the fact, meaning in this case the deed.[3]

These echoes of Coke prompted Judge Richard Stockton the following autumn to assert the precedence of natural reason, albeit within the authority of the law. The case concerned the priority of claims against an estate. Stockton, whose father really was a judge, held that the executor was "Justifiable in paying off Simple Contract Debts before Debts by Specialty" when he had "no Notice of the latter either in Law or in fact." (In other words, if the executor lacked actual or presumptive notice of a debt evidenced in sealed deed, he was justified in paying off less formal debts, even if this left insufficient funds to pay the debt that had priority.) Explaining his decision, Stockton observed that "I am supported in this Opinion by many Books of unquestionable Authority—but what is more I am also supported by what ought to be of more weight in a Court of Justice than any Authority—the Light of Reason—for surely there could be no reason in punishing a man for what he could not help." Stockton thus raised the light of reason in opposition to de Hart, but he did not have to rely on it, for "the Law" itself to secure "the Advancement of Justice[,] has Garded against this inconvenience."[4]

Although some student judges occasionally took this sort of candid appeal to reason beyond the bounds of authority, other students reined in such efforts, as can be illustrated by a 1786 case concerning a release of

[2] *John Coxe v. Robert Smith* (July 1783), *Proceedings of The Institutio Legalis,* 14–15, New Jersey Historical Society, Ms Group 214.
[3] *State v. John Styles* (July 1783), ibid., 17–19.
[4] *John Coxe v. John Jackson Executor of John Coxe* (Nov. 1783), ibid., 45–46.

dower. Prior to marriage, Mary Williams released her claim to dower in consideration of one thousand pounds, but after her husband died she brought a writ of dower, her theory being that she still had a claim to her common law share of his estate because if she had no right of dower until her marriage, she could not have released it beforehand. Certainly, as Judge Alexander Macwhorter acknowledged, "[s]ome authorities . . . tell us that strictly at the common law a mere possibility or a right that had no present existance could not be released."

This old doctrine, however, had changed, and Macwhorter took the occasion to expound and even expand upon the liberal development of the law. The old doctrine "is owing to the literal & strict manner in which all legal acts were construed," which "looked not to the intentions of the parties but closely to the letter and word of the law." Tracing the development of the doctrine, Macwhorter noted that "sometime after as the courts became more liberal in their constructions and began to shew greater respect to the intentions of the parties—we find that this maxim was in some degree changed," and "it was generally held that a mere possibility might be released but could not be assigned at law." Indeed, "now by all the late adjudications it hath become an established maxim that a right merely possible may be released, and in equity may be also assigned." Accordingly,

> I am fully of opinion that at this day the trifeling distinction just mentioned is in our law courts also struck out, and that a possibility may here likewise be released and assigned—Both because it is agreeable to the intentions of the parties . . . And also because it is a favorite principle of the law that there shall be no incumbrance upon lands which may not be removed.

Observing that "some of the books expressly say that a settlement in personal chattels in certain cases will be a sufficient bar of dower," Macwhorter concluded: "And I am clearly of opinion that it will in all cases w[h]ere the intentions of the parties appear sufficiently evident, for the courts have now become so liberal in their adjudications that they will seldom if ever depart from the true intent of the parties where it appears, in order to comport with the strict letter of the law." Such was what "appear to me to be the sense of the authorities."[5]

The other students, however, seem to have had some doubts, for they met again to reargue the case on error. At this hearing, Chief Justice William Griffith upheld the decision, but on narrower grounds. He emphasized the conceded authorities in "[o]ur Modern Lawyers & Law Books," and he decided the matter on such authorities without reference to

[5] *Mary Williams, Widow v. William Digby* (Jan. 1786), ibid., 70–73.

Macwhorter's ideas about the "liberal" trajectory of adjudication. At the same time, though, he carefully balanced this approach by rejecting the artificial application of narrow, technical common law arguments, "which perhaps might be thought to savour rather more of the *summum Jus* than would be consistant with the true and solid reason of the Case."[6] It had long been said, *summum ius, summa injuria*—meaning, that the rigor of law is the height of oppression, and Griffith hoped to avoid this extreme as much as the other.

Recognizing the difficulty of altering the law directly on grounds of reason, Judge Josiah Ogden Hoffman used reasoning about the injustice of a particular case to escape the general authority of statutes and precedents, but not successfully. In the summer of 1787, in *John Denn ex dem John Young v. James Young,* Hoffman faced two questions that would long remain a source of annoyance in the law of wills:

> 1st Whether a will is duly executed according to the Stat[ute] of frauds & perjuries, where the witnesses attest at different times, and not in the presence of each other. 2d Whether the words "I acknowledge this to be my will,["] are sufficient, without signing in the presence of the witnesses?

Hoffman confessed he "never could see what the doubt was upon either of these questions." Yet "[t]hey have already received an adjudication. If they had not I should not hesitate in declaring that it is not requisite" to meet what ordinarily were considered the formalities of the Statute of Frauds, and he added that "[t]he words of the statute by this construction are complied with."

Although he could not generally overturn the precedents on the Statute of Frauds, Hoffman undermined them by arguing from the intent of the statute. The Statute of Frauds was conventionally understood to require that the testator had to sign in the presence of three witnesses and that the witnesses had to attest to the will in each other's presence, and an English precedent justified this interpretation by suggesting that "one witness is sufficient to prove the will, and that he swears not only to the subscription of the testator; but to the attestation of the other two witnesses." Hoffman answered, however, that "surely the man, that would perjure himself in swearing, he saw the testator subscribe, would not hesitate in perjuring himself in swearing that he saw the witnesses attest," and "[t]his too would be far from answering the intent of the statute," for whereas the precedent assumed that only one witness was necessary to prove the will, "the Statute clearly means, that not less than the oath of three witnesses should prove it,

[6] Ibid., 80–81 (Apr. 1786).

supposing that one man might frequently be found to commit perjury, but seldom three men."

In the end, Hoffman held that the facts of the case essentially satisfied the statute. The testator had signed, but not in the presence of the witnesses, who had attested, moreover, at different times. The testator, however, had acknowledged in front of them that the will was his, and Hoffman thought:

> The acknowledgment of the testator is a signing within the statute, [for] by the acknowledgment, he adopts the signing. The testator has gone farther, he has declared it to be his will, which is not necessary, nor is it necessary that the witnesses should know that it was his will, or that they should know the contents thereof—The intention of the testator is manifest and clear in the present case. It is the duty of the court to carry it into effect, as far as they can consistent with the rules of law[.] To disappoint it in this instance would be extending the construction of the statute against the meaning and words thereof, when on the contrary the court should incline to expound it, to effect, rather than prevent the intention of the testator.[7]

Hoffman thus relied on the testator's evident intention to exempt the case from the traditional understanding of the statute.

The result was almost inevitable. On appeal, Chief Justice David Ogden—probably a relation of the New Jersey Supreme Court justice of that name—"[c]ompared the Judgment of the Inferior Court . . . with the law" and decided that the "Judgment be reversed." The witnesses did not see the testator sign the will, and "all that they can say is he 'acknowledged it to be his will.'" Of course, "[t]his might be deemed a sufficient answer to common understanding: but instead of acknowledgments the Legislature saw fit to require an Actual signing," and "[t]he Court cannot substitute any other thing in the room and stead of what is made a requisite by the Statute." To this he added: "But if I doubted on the Laws of England[,] an act of the Legislature of this State[,] requiring the three witnesses to attest in the presence of each other[,] would bring me to a conclusion" in deciding to reverse.[8]

Even though not able to use reason against the authority of statute or precedent, judges still had to rely on reason to sort out the authorities and generalize from them—as Judge William Halsey explained in a case on a bill of exchange. The question was whether the endorsee had to make demand on the drawer before bringing an action against the endorser. After considering "the authorities adduced by the Gentlemen on both sides of the

[7] *John Denn ex dem John Young v. James Young* (July 1787), ibid., 127–129.
[8] Ibid., 133.

Question," Halsey decided that "a Demand is necessary on the original Drawer in Order to charge the Indorser," this conclusion being drawn "[f]rom these [authorities], from the Nature of the Question itself considered upon plain principles of Reason[,] from the greater advantage to Trade," and from "the opinion of Lord Mansfield upon a like Question." The confusion of the precedents required Halsey to resort to reason:

> Many Authorities are extant on this long litigated point, and were I to Judge merely from the number of Authorities in the Books, a decision would be attended with perplexity, but from a critical examination of the reason of former decisions, and the reasonableness of some more Modern it is less difficult, and the Grounds, in support of the demands appear more plausible, when set in competition with those on the contrary side of the Question.

Considering that "[t]he Reasonableness and Equity of the Question seem to be in favor of such a Demand—As well as the advantages that would result therefrom," Halsey followed Mansfield in adopting the precedents that appeared to make most sense.[9]

The students of the Institutio Legalis clearly felt the edge of legal authority most painfully in their cases on slavery, and where a statute left room for charitable interpretation, the judges could avoid the sort of injustice that the legislature presumably did not intend to sanction. Such were the circumstances in *Beulah, a Negroe v. John Bairbarice & William Buxton, Exrs. of Caleb Haines,* for Beulah suffered not only from slavery but also from the sharp practices of her master's executors.

Beulah's parents were David and Dinah, who had belonged to Caleb Haines. During his lifetime, he "gave his Negroes David & Dinah their freedom," and "by his last Will he recites his having given them their freedom." Subsequently, while free, "David and Dinah have several Children and among others Beulah now seventeen Years of Age." After David's death, Dinah is "unable to maintain herself with a Young Child," and "falls on the Ex[ecuto]r[s] for a maintenance."[10] This was the point at which the legally significant injustice occurred. There was an old colonial statute requiring that when anyone manumitted a slave, the master or his executors had to give bond to the queen that they would support the freed slave and thus prevent him from becoming a charge to the community. If they failed to give such security, the manumission was "to be void, and of none Effect."[11] Both Haines and his executors had earlier "neglected" to give such a bond,

[9] *Timothy Stone v. James Land* (July 1790), ibid., 172–173.
[10] *Beulah, a Negroe v. John Bairbarice & William Buxton, Exrs. of Caleb Haines* (July 1786), ibid., 93.
[11] An Act for Regulating of Slaves, *The Laws and Acts of the General Assembly of His Majesties Province of Nova Cæsarea or New-Jersey,* 24 (New Jersey: 1717).

and the executors therefore took advantage of their own failure to "reclaim all the children by virtue of the words in Act." Considering herself to have been born free, Beulah responded by obtaining a writ of habeas corpus.[12]

Far from being merely an abstract sufferer in a student exercise, Beulah was a real person. In 1775 she had gained her freedom in the New Jersey Supreme Court, and now in 1786 she became a hypothetical slave who made her claim in the student court. Nor was this shift from real court to moot court a coincidence. Her lawyers had included Elias Boudinot, and at least one of his students, William Griffith, belonged to the Institutio Legalis.[13]

The student Chief Justice, Alexander Macwhorter, ordered Beulah discharged. He acknowledged that he hoped to do justice, but he at first felt stymied by the lack of uncertainty in the statute: "The words in themselves are plain and simple, and I must confess from the many and ingenious Arguments of the Council for the Defendents, I was almost led to determine that no other Construction could be given to the Act . . . than that the Manumission was intirely void."

> But such a construction is wanting both of Benevolence & Humanity; and every Judge will be *astutus* to construe Statutes in such a Manner as will work

[12] *Beulah, a Negroe v. John Bairbarice & William Buxton, Exrs. of Caleb Haines* (July 1786), *Proceedings of The Institutio Legalis,* 93 New Jersey Historical Society, Ms Group 214.

[13] A report of the 1775 case survives in a notebook of Elias's brother Elisha. Justice Richard Stockton signed the writ of habeas corpus in May term 1775, and the case was argued in the November term. Beulah's lawyers took advantage of the ambiguity in the statute to suggest that the court had to follow the old common law presumption in favor of liberty, which they recited in the traditional terms, "That Life, Liberty and Dower are rightly favor'd in the Law." Speaking for the Court, Stockton explained that "[t]he Design of the Act was not to prevent a Negroe being made free but barely to Indemnify the Parish when a man frees his Negroe" and that "all statutes [are] to be construed according to their spirit & true Intent." Thus, "that manumission is good as to these Negroes, tho' void as to the Publick," and Beulah was "discharged accordingly." *Beulah a Negro v. Barber & Buxton* (New Jersey Supreme Court 1775), Elisha Boudinot, Notes of Cases in Practice, 52, 57–59, Princeton University, Rare Books and Special Collections, Manuscript Division, Thorne Collection of Elias Boudinot, C0001, Box 3, Folder 2. The record recited that the manumission "was good in Law against the said Caleb Haines and those claiming under him." *King v. Esther Barber and others* (Nov. term 1775), *Cases Adjudged in the Supreme Court of New-Jersey; Relative to the Manumission of Negroes and Others Holden in Bondage,* 7–8 (Burlington: 1794) (quoting the Court's Minute Book, 44, 142).

This was not, incidentally, the only time that the students drew on actual cases. For example, a 1787 moot case on the effect of the full-faith-and-credit clause of the Articles of Confederation mimicked a similar case in Pennsylvania, and the student judge, Alexander Macwhorter, recalled that "[a]fter hearing the Judgment delivered by *Judge Shippen of Philadelphia* I had little doubt remaining respecting the above Cause." *Amos Standfast v. Nathan Poorman* (Aug. 1787), *Proceedings of The Institutio Legalis,* 138–139, New Jersey Historical Society, Ms Group 214, alluding to *James et al. v. Allen* (Court of Common Pleas, Philadelphia County 1787), Dallas, *Reports,* 1: 188.

> Advantage to the Public and Injury to no one. And if such a Construction may be given in the present Case, consistently with the Words of the Act, we will give it in preference to any other. 4 Bac[on's *Abridgment*]. 648.

This was a more active vision of equitable interpretation than the citation really supported, but it aptly captured the place of equitable interpretation within the words of a statute. Here, the colonial statute failed to state whether the manumission was to be void as to both parties or only one of them, and this left room for Macwhorter to achieve justice by pursuing legislative intent. Whereas the defendants argued that it was the intent of the legislature "to prohibit manumission altogether," Macwhorter opined that "[t]he Intention of the Legislature is to be collected from the cause of making the Statute," and "[t]he cause of making this Statute was to prevent free Negroes from becoming a burthen on the Public." Macwhorter therefore thought he could discern justice within the parameters set by the words: "[S]hould we determine that the manumission was void as to one of the parties and good as to the other, which construction is often given to Statutes, we should at the same time come within the wording and Spirit of the Act, and surely Equity & Benevolence calls loudly for" this construction "in preference to the former." The executors had taken sharp advantage of a statute designed to benefit the public, and "it is absurd to suppose any Statute sh[d] be construed in a manner that would support fraud & injustice of this nature." Accordingly, "the manumission is void only as to the Public and not as to the Negroe."[14]

Another result, however, seemed necessary where the injustice was slavery itself, for it hardly could be presumed that the legislature had not intended this injustice. In the case of "James, a Negroe," James's mother, Dinah, was devised to John Stagg for twenty-one years, after which she was to be freed. James had been born, however, within those twenty-one years, and thus although the mother was to be free, her son apparently was not. When James sought his freedom on a habeas corpus, his lawyer began with a familiar analogy from villeinage. English courts had adopted a presumption of liberty in cases of villeinage, and James's lawyer argued that American slavery was "regulated by the same rules." Thus, if a villein in the situation of James's mother would have been considered "so far enfranchised . . . as to impart freedom to her issue," then she and her son similarly had to be deemed free "by implication." Recognizing the strained character of this argument, James's lawyer fell back on a second point: "[S]hall he not be dis-

[14] *Beulah, a Negroe v. John Bairbarice & William Buxton, Exrs. of Caleb Haines* (July 1786), *Proceedings of The Institutio Legalis,* 93–95 New Jersey Historical Society, Ms Group 214.

charged upon the principles of Natural Justice? What right has John Stagg to the issue of Dinah? By the bequest he is entitled only to the service of Dinah for 21 Years, & it would exceed the intention of the Testator that he should make her Issue perpetual slaves." This argument was carefully couched in terms of intent, but Chief Justice William Griffith understood that it was designed to introduce the broader claim that underlay much American opposition to slavery. As put in Griffith's summary of the second question, "is not James to be liberated by this Court on the principles of natural Justice?"

Griffith observed that the habeas brought by James "is one of those cases in which humanity & tenderness must give way to the more rigid, but more steady rule of Law & Policy."

> Among all Nations slavery has existed in some shape or other. Mankind ever ambitious of power & grasping at Wealth have agrandized the one & increased the other by means of slavery. As slavery then is recognized and regulated by the Common and positive Laws of our Country we must be guided by them—an innovation might be dangerous. It is to be hoped that the Legislature will one day or other view Slavery in a proper point of light, & legally invest the Court of Justice with a power of deciding on slavery more consistent with humanity and natural Justice.[15]

In the meantime, Griffith felt obliged to follow "the more rigid, but more steady rule of Law & Policy," which was anything but "consistent with humanity and natural Justice."

The students examined a final slave case in the fall of 1787 on a habeas corpus to John Dixon, "commanding him to bring up the Body of Caesar a Negroe in his Custody." Upon the appearance of Caesar in court, William Griffith, now playing the role of attorney general, made "application to the Court . . . for the Deft. to give security against transporting a Negroe Slave out of the State it appearing on bringing the Body up, he is making ready to send him away." Two questions were raised at argument:

> 1st. If there be a Law to prohibit the transportation of Negroes out of the State? If there be, then
>
> 2. Whether the Defendant is now before the Court in such manner that any thing can be done in the Prohibition—

Judge Gabriel H. Ford observed on the first question, about transportation, that "no written, positive or Statute Law makes it unlawful, and if there

[15] *James, a Negroe v. John Stagg* (Nov. 1786), ibid., 108–111. As in all of these cases, the arguments of counsel must be reconstructed from the judge's opinion.

be a Prohibition it is at the Common Law." After surveying the English law on slaves and distinguishing it from the law on villeinage, Ford noted that there was common law in America on slavery and that it was not encouraging:

> It appears to me with respect to Negroes, that a Common Law of our own has arisen and fixed itself in the Land. It is a fact that they have been constantly sold here like horses from hand to hand, and Transported to the West Indies; nor doth the memory of Man run to the contrary—if it does—when was it otherwise? The custom was known and in use among our Fore Fathers from the earliest settlement of the Country, & by them handed down to us their Posterity; and tho' it is said to be unjust and against reason, it is not more so than Villeinage in Gross, which however was established in England. The Importation of them has ever been allowed by the common Law, until a late restrictive statute; and it is not more possible to the freedom of our soil to force them away, than it was to force them to come here, and abandon the natural connexions of their own Country.—The Legislature began to restrain the common Law, and take measures to banish Slavery out of the State. They have already forbid, the Importation of more, and the exercise of this Right [of exportation], will further their wishes and still lessen the numbers among us.

Nonetheless, Ford gave "no opinion" on this first question about the right to export the slave, for this was "improperly and extra-judicially before the Court" on account of Ford's determination of the second question.

In considering the second issue, whether the defendant was in court "in such manner that anything can be done," Ford concluded that the "Cases in the Books incline me to think he is not"—to which Ford added, "and this Court must be bound by Precedent." The writ of habeas corpus "is meant for a summary relief in Cases of unlawful restraint, where the matter cannot admit of the slow progress of the Ordinary Forms of Justice." Under this writ "the sole tendency and command" was for the defendant "to bring the party restrained of Liberty into Court," and "having done that, he is at Liberty to depart." The Court therefore could not decide his property rights on the habeas:

> [T]o decide on a Question of his Property in his absence to the amount of £90- or £100- without Notice of the Motion and before he or his Counsel had time to advise or deliberate, would be a sudden and unprecedented extention of the Limits of their summary Enquiries and Work surprise & injustice. I am of opinion on the whole, that the proceedings on Habeas Corpus are too summary, to try Questions of extensive Property.

Perhaps an indictment would be more proper, "and then, he could probably be bound, not indeed to give the ultimate security, never to transport him; but only not to send him away, till the right of Transportation was determined." On the writ of habeas corpus, however, a decision that he must give security "will amount to a Declaration that he has no Right of Exportation at all,—which ought to be settled on better Notice to the party, and more formal and solemn proceedings." Ford therefore dismissed the motion for Dixon to give security and left the fictional Caesar to his fate.[16]

The students were painfully aware of the disparity between the law and their hopes for reason and justice, but they tended to understand that judges had to follow the law even when it was deeply disappointing. This was a severe burden. It was, however, the duty of judges and the students who served as judges. After weighing precedents in a case, Tobias Boudinot concluded: "I therefore have founded my Judgm[t] on th[e] . . . Authorities & given it with an unbiased Conscience agreeable to Law as I at present think."[17] Like a real judge, he felt the difficulty of reaching a judgment "agreeable to law," but he did the best he could.

[16] *State v. John Dixon* (Nov. 1787), ibid., 146–150. This appears to be the last slavery case discussed by the society during the eighteenth century. Among earlier cases in which the comparison with villeinage had been discussed was *Pirate, alias Belt v. Dalby* (Supreme Court of Pennsylvania 1786), Dallas, *Reports,* 1: 167–168.

[17] *Samuel Henry v. David Martin* (Feb. 1789), *Proceedings of The Institutio Legalis,* 169, New Jersey Historical Society, Ms Group 214.

Appendix III

Common Law Adjacent to Statutes: Religious Taxes in Massachusetts

It has been seen in Chapter Fifteen that even cases that did not hold statutes unconstitutional can be revealing, for they can illustrate the ease and comfort with which judges handled constitutional questions, and to pursue this point further, this appendix examines some Massachusetts cases on religious taxes. When questions of slavery came before the Massachusetts judges, they had no occasion to hold statutes unconstitutional, because the colonial statutes on the subject had been repealed, and the judges therefore had to consider whether there was any authority for holding human property under such common law as could be discerned from the old statutory scheme. As seen in Chapter Fifteen, they resolved this controversial question by looking to the Massachusetts Constitution, which seemed to suggest that notwithstanding what could be discerned from the old statutes, the state's common law no longer authorized slavery. Here it will become apparent that a similar approach can be discerned in a series of cases concerning the conduct of Massachusetts town officers in collecting religious taxes. Several of the cases are known from the scholarship on religious liberty, especially the detailed work of William G. McLoughlin, but it is also necessary to consider the cases for their treatment of official behavior in the vicinity of old statutes.[1] Although the judges in these cases did not clearly hold any statute or official act unconstitutional, they at least had to inquire whether, in light of the Constitution, the town officers acted with legal authority, and it will be seen that, as in the slavery cases, so in these religion cases, the judges showed notable unconcern when making constitutional decisions about controversial matters that came close to legislative policy.

[1] In discussing *Balkcom* and *Cutter,* this section relies heavily on William G. McLoughlin, *New England Dissent, 1630–1833,* at 1: 638–647 (Cambridge: Harvard University Press, 1971), who discusses the cases, the sources, and the religious context.

In Massachusetts, the Congregationalist church in each town had traditionally collected taxes for support of its building and minister. The legislature, however, early recognized the awkwardness, even if not the injustice, of requiring Baptists, Anglicans, and Quakers to pay for the support of a religious society they did not attend, and it therefore enacted that members of these dissenting societies could escape paying religious taxes to their town's majority church if they submitted certificates from their own congregations testifying that they were members in good standing.[2]

The Massachusetts Constitution of 1780 preserved much of this scheme but with a slightly different compromise on taxes—an arrangement that simultaneously acknowledged the realities of religious diversity and fortified the establishment. Article II of the Declaration of Rights asserted the right and duty of all men to worship God, and it thereby laid the foundation for making all persons pay taxes. In particular, to avoid the danger that men would become dissenters to avoid paying religious taxes, Article III of the Declaration of Rights assumed that all taxable men would pay for the support of religion. Having thus ended the exemption of specified groups of religious dissenters from having to pay religious taxes, it assured each individual that "[a]ll monies paid by the subject to the support of the publick worship, and of the publick teachers . . . shall, if he require it, be uniformly applied to the support of the publick teacher or teachers of his own religious sect or denomination."[3] Dissenters thus were in a sense treated more equally, but they were dragged within a system for funding all churches in each town, and they therefore now needed certificates not to avoid paying religious taxes, but to ensure that their taxes went to their own church.

The need for certificates, however, was not the dissenters' only worry, for there was a widespread expectation that only incorporated religious societies could receive the proceeds of religious taxes. Traditionally in Massachusetts incorporated societies had received such funds, and of course dissenting societies had not been incorporated. Many Congregationalists therefore thought it significant that Article III of the Declaration of Rights referred to "bodies-politic":

> [T]he legislature shall, from time to time, authorize and require, the several towns, parishes, precincts, and other bodies-politic, or religious societies, to make suitable provision, at their own expense, for the institution of the public worship of GOD . . . and for the support and maintenance of public protestant

[2] William G. McLoughlin, "The Balkcom Case (1782) and the Pietistic Theory of Separation of Church and State," *William and Mary Quarterly*, 24: 268 (third series) (1967).
[3] Massachusetts Constitution, Declaration of Rights, Article III.

> teachers of piety, religion and morality, in all cases where such provision shall not be made voluntarily.[4]

To the ears of Congregationalists, "bodies-politic" meant incorporated societies, and Article III thus seemed to confirm that for a dissenter to get his tax payments directed to his own society, he not only needed to give the tax collector a certificate of his membership in his society but also had to belong to a society with a charter of incorporation from the legislature.[5] The unfortunate religious dissenter who did not meet these requirements had to pay religious taxes for the support of the majority church in his town—or, if it was unusually large, for the majority church in one of its smaller parishes or "precincts." Baptists in particular tended to find themselves in this unhappy situation, for many of them had religious objections to giving certificates or obtaining incorporation.

Article III of the Declaration of Rights closed with two seemingly bold clauses: "[E]very denomination of christians . . . shall be equally under the protection of the law: And no subordination of any one sect or denomination to another shall ever be established by law."[6] Neither of these clauses, however, was as generous as may be thought. Rather than secure the antiestablishment principle of equal rights, the first clause merely promised equal protection of the law—that is, the equal protection of the law for the natural liberty enjoyed under law. This was a partial equality that Bishop Warburton had already popularized in England as a means of assuring a tolerant establishment, and the Massachusetts equal protection clause drew on this approach to offer dissenters a freedom from discriminatory penalties while still leaving room for the state to establish religion by granting special privileges.[7] The second, no-subordination clause similarly left space for an establishment, for the state established the majority in each town, not any particular sect or denomination, and the state could therefore claim that it did not subordinate any one sect or denomination. In short, the Declaration of Rights only offered limited guarantees of equality, which used appealingly egalitarian language to provide for equal natural liberty and unequal privileges.

The immediate problem under the religion provisions of the Massachusetts Declaration of Rights was that the colonial statutes on religious taxes had expired and in any case were no longer entirely applicable to the

[4] Ibid.
[5] McLoughlin, *New England Dissent,* 1: 644.
[6] Massachusetts Constitution, Declaration of Rights, Article III.
[7] Philip Hamburger, "Equality and Diversity: The Eighteenth-Century Debate About Equal Protection and Equal Civil Rights," *Supreme Court Review,* 295 (1992).

new situation, thus leaving towns to collect the taxes with such common law authority as could be discerned from defunct and obsolete statutes. The colonial enactments on religious taxes had been temporary acts, which had eventually expired, and religious taxes were sufficiently controversial that the legislature had not ventured to pass a new statute explaining how Article III was to be put into effect. To make matters worse, the old statutes had exempted specified dissenters from paying taxes if they could provide acceptable certificates, and consequently, although the 1780 Constitution assumed that money was to be collected from all taxable men and then distributed to various churches, the old statutes provided no mechanism for this collection and distribution across officially recognized religious lines. To be precise, under the old statutory system that collected taxes for the majority church and exempted qualified dissenters, certificates were given to an officer of the majority church in each town, but when Article III of the Declaration of Rights assumed that towns (or at least parishes or precincts) would collect taxes from all men for distribution to a range of different churches within their jurisdiction, the assessment of taxes could no longer be left to the officer of a single church. Instead, it had to be in the hands of a secular officer. The towns therefore followed their traditional practices, largely as stipulated in the old, expired statutes, but now with town rather than church officers deciding who had to pay the taxes and allocating proportionate amounts of the proceeds among dissenting churches—to the extent they were incorporated and their members submitted certificates. Religious taxes thus continued in a manner roughly instituted but not actually authorized by the old statutes, and these taxes therefore needed such common law authority as could be discerned in the shadow of the defunct legislation.

An early case that apparently relied on the Constitution to discern whether a town could tax dissenters was *Balkcom v. Wilkinson, et al.*—a 1783 case that has been carefully documented by William McLoughlin. Elijah Balkcom was a resident of the east parish or second precinct of Attleborough, Massachusetts. Shortly after the adoption of the 1780 Constitution, the townsmen of the parish, mostly Congregationalists, met to assess taxes, and in December 1780 "they voted to raise £23000"—in paper money—"for inlarging and repar[in]g their meeting house."[8] Balkcom, however, had earlier in the year "left the parish meeting" to become a Bap-

[8] Isaac Backus, Attleborough Sufferings and Deliverance (Feb. 26, 1782), Franklin Trask Library, Andover Newton Theological School, Isaac Backus Papers, Box 12 (Jan.–March 1782). Backus noted at the bottom of the page: "The above minutes I took at Balkcom's

tist, and having now joined the First Baptist Church, he refused to pay the parish taxes. Predictably, this Baptist church was not incorporated; nor apparently did Balkcom file a certificate.

In late December 1780, Balkcom refused to pay his taxes, and the assessors issued a warrant for his arrest. For almost a year the matter rested in abeyance, but toward the end of 1781, the constable for 1780, Eliphelet Wilmarth ("aided" by the constable for 1781, Colonel Stephen Richardson), seized Balkcom and "carried him out of the house into the road," where they led him "toward Taunton goal."[9] As he was forcibly taken down the road, Balkcom remained obstinate, until he reminded himself that he was "obliged to take care of his aged father."[10] He then paid the money and walked back home. Two months later he brought an action on the case before a justice of the peace against the three assessors—John Wilkerson, Elikanah Willmarth, and Daniel Richardson—for damages of forty shillings.

At a hearing held by the justice, Balkcom's lawyer, Colonel George Leonard, argued that Balkcom was a Baptist "and so by Law and the Constitution of said Commonwealth exempted and entirely excused from paying any Rates or taxes towards the support of any Minister of any other Denomination of Christians, or repairing any Meeting-House belonging to said Different Denomination and not liable by Law to be assessed therefor." It was a rather optimistic argument, and the justice of the peace gave judgment for the assessors—prompting the Baptist leader, Isaac Backus, to observe with bitterness that "the judge turned the case ag[a]inst the bap[tist]s without hesitation." Balkcom, however, appealed in 1782 to the Bristol County Inferior Court, and "[b]oth Parties" agreed that the determination of this court would be final.[11]

Feb. 26. 1782. from the papers laid before said court." See McLoughlin, *New England Dissent,* 1: 637–640; John D. Cushing, "Notes on Disestablishment in Massachusetts, 1780–1833," *William and Mary Quarterly,* 26: 169 (Third Series) (1969).

9 Isaac Backus, Attleborough Sufferings and Deliverance (Feb. 26, 1782), Franklin Trask Library, Andover Newton Theological School, Issac Backus Papers, Box 12. Constables often left dissenters' taxes until the end of year but then apparently felt obliged to take action, lest they become liable for the uncollected amounts. A tax collector would ordinarily distrain a cow, but as William G. McLoughlin observes, "evidently Elijah Balkcom had no cow, or else the tax collector wished to make an example of him, for he was told that if he did not pay his tax of £0.17.6.3 (in silver) he would go to jail." McLoughlin, "The Balkcom Case (1782)," 271.

10 Isaac Backus, Letter to Mr. Carter, *The Providence Gazette and Country Journal* (Mar. 2, 1782).

11 Isaac Backus, Attleborough Sufferings and Deliverance (Feb. 26, 1782), Franklin Trask Library, Andover Newton Theological School, Isaac Backus Papers, Box 12 (Jan.–Mar. 1782); Record (Mar. 16, 1782), Bristol County Inferior Court of Common Pleas, Docket Book 1773–1782, at 410, Case No. 39 (March Term), MSA.

The decision rested on the legal authority for, and perhaps the constitutionality of, a local executive act done within an expired statutory scheme. By now each side had some of the finest legal talent available—Balkcom being represented by William Bradford and James Mitchell Varnum, and the assessors by Robert Treat Paine. Balkcom's lawyers argued from religious principles and the Baptist interpretation of the Constitution to suggest that the old tax statutes—and now the practices they had put into place—were unconstitutional:

> The chief pleas for the appellant were, that RELIGION was prior to all states and kingdoms in the world, and therefore could not in its nature be subject to human laws . . . and as our constitution says, "No subordination of any one sect or denomination to another, shall ever be established by law," those laws are repealed thereby. And as the constitution was established by the people, it is stronger than any law the assembly can make, it being the foundation whereon they stand.[12]

Focusing on the unconstitutionality of the town's conduct, Balkcom's lawyers asked: "[A]re not certificates contrary to equality"? To prove this point, they further asked, "can a Baptist call on a Congregationalist for a Certificate"? And "would the Congregation[alist] wish it if the Baptists were most numerous"? Balkcom's lawyers thus apparently argued that both the old tax statutes and the town's conduct in line with those statutes were contrary to the equality clauses of the Massachusetts Constitution.[13]

Balkcom's lawyers also more specifically questioned whether there was any legal authority for the assessors. In response to the suggestion that the old tax statutes "continue in force," these lawyers argued that the judge could assume "no Law in force but what is introduced" and that therefore the assessors "must prove it."[14] Moreover, even if the old tax system survived at common law with an authority equivalent to that which it had enjoyed under the colonial statutes, these statutes had left only religious officers to assess and collect the taxes—in the words of Balkcom's lawyers, "the certificates heretofore required, were given to parish officers, officers of one particular sect, and not to officers of government."[15]

The judges obviously had no reason to rule on the constitutionality of

[12] Isaac Backus, *A Door Opened for Equal Christian Liberty, And No Man Can Shut It,* 5 (Boston: 1783).

[13] Robert Treat Paine, Minutes and Trials of Law Cases 1777–1782, Folder 21, Bristol Session, March Term, 1782, Massachusetts Historical Society. They similarly argued: "[I]f no Subordination, then no Certificate." Ibid.

[14] Ibid.

[15] Backus, *A Door Opened for Equal Christian Liberty,* 5.

the old statutes, as they had not authorized town officers and in any case had expired. Nor is it likely that the judges held the conduct of the town assessors unconstitutional, for this was unnecessary. Instead, the judges probably held the conduct of the town assessors to be without such legal authority as could be discerned in the vicinity of the old statutes—an authority that looked rather frail when considered in light of the Constitution. Certainly after the legal points were "learnedly discussed," the judges "retired a little by themselves, and then returned, and declared, 'that they were unanimously agreed in giving the appellant damages and costs.'" Backus was delighted and later observed that the case "not only settled the controversy in Attleborough, but has been extensively beneficial elsewhere."[16]

Sadly for religious dissenters, the success in *Balkcom* was transient. A hint of a different opinion came the next year in *Commonwealth v. Bradish.* Billings Bradish lived in a parish with a Congregational church belonging to the Rev. Holt, but Bradish himself was an Episcopalian, who "attended & paid taxes" at St. Peter's, the Episcopal church in Salem. Nonetheless, Bradish "was taxed to Mr Holt," and when "[t]he collector went to distrain for s[ai]d tax & attempted to drive away a cow," Bradish "waved a stick above his head, & threatened him" that "if he drove away the cow he would lay him flat with the ground." Bradish "finally obliged the collector to desist" but was then "indicted & found guilty" at the General Sessions of the Peace for Essex County. At trial, Bradish's lawyer argued that "the assessment was illegal & therefore Bradish had a right to defend his property." The Court, however, instructed the jury that "the Collector cannot take notice of an illegal assessment or the legality of it," and that in any case "the assessment on Bradish was legal & that every man ought to be taxed in the parish where he lives & the money paid over on order to the society where he attends." The Court explained that there was still authority to tax because "the *Constitution* makes no alteration in the laws in this respect."[17]

[16] When celebrating this victory, Backus observed that "some in Attleborough accused the baptists of great inconsistency, in [previously] protesting against the third article in our bill of rights, and yet now making use of it." He therefore pointed out that he had earlier "declared, that I 'fully concurred' with that part of it which we have now made use of." Ibid., 5–6.

[17] *Commonwealth v. Bradish* (Essex County General Sessions of the Peace, July 1783), [Reports of Cases], 123–124, William Plumer Papers, Mfm Reel 19, Legal Papers. The Court explained that the tax system "does not subject one order of christians to another—but it is only a local circumstance that every christian is liable to where the majority differ from him." Ibid. The accusation against Bradish was that he beat and struck the collector and threatened to split his brains open. Essex County Court of General Sessions of the Peace, Record Book 1776–1792, at 128 (July term 1783), MSA.

In 1783, incidentally, the judges of the Supreme Judicial Court relied on Article III of the

The authority to tax dissenters under something like the old statutory scheme and the constitutionality of such taxation became all the more clear in 1785 in *Cutter v. Frost, et al.* On December 30, 1784, two Cambridge tax collectors, Ephraim Frost, Jr., and Amos Warren, paid a visit to a local Baptist, Gershom Cutter, to collect a tax for Cambridge's northwest precinct or parish. They forcibly carried him four miles to the common jail in Cambridge and kept him there for two days "until they Compelled him to pay the sum of two pounds one shilling & six pence two farthings to regain his liberty." Cutter brought an action of false imprisonment and prevailed before a jury at the County Court at Concord, but he lost on appeal before another jury at the Supreme Judicial Court sitting in Cambridge.[18]

Constitution to understand the contractual relations between a congregation and a settled minister in the important case of *Inhabitants of Princetown v. Timothy Fuller.* When a congregation hired a minister, there were expectations that he would remain for life as a "settled" minister, but on rare occasions he might leave or his congregation might dismiss him, and whether they could dismiss him and in what circumstances was the question in this case. In 1767, Fuller became the minister of Princetown, but by 1775 "many disputes arose" between him and his congregants, and the church eventually "called an *ex parte Council,*" which "*advised* his dismission." When he nonetheless still "attempted to preach in the meeting house," they "hindered" him, and "he preached for some time in his own house, where a few attended." He now sued in assumpsit for his salary since his dismissal, and the case eventually came before the Supreme Judicial Court. *Inhabitants of Princetown v. Timothy Fuller* (Essex County Supreme Judicial Court, Nov. 1783), [Reports of Cases], 123–124, William Plumer Papers, Mfm Reel 19, Legal Papers.

On demurrer, the lawyers relied in part on the Constitution. For example, Sullivan argued that the decision belonged to the parish rather than a church council: "A religious equality & freedom is a favorite idea in the Constitution, but if a Council of churches must try this question it sets the church virtually to determine quod the rights of & contracts of the parish agst the 3^{d} articles of the Constitution which declares there shall be no religious *subordination.*" Ibid., 124–125. To this, Theophilus Parsons responded that "[t]he articles respecting subordination &c referred to in the Constitution can only respect persecution & the rights of conscience" rather than "matters of contract & property." Ibid., 126. In concluding, Sullivan added that "[t]he priviledge of removing from one [parish] to another is established by law & the constitution, on the broad basis of religious freedom & even to be of *no church* by the platform &c." Ibid., 135.

The judges instructed the jury that a minister took his office for life, subject to being dismissed upon charges and proof brought before a council. Sargeant and Cushing, moreover, suggested that far from being a denial of the parish's religious liberty, the church's right to dismiss was fully in accord the traditions of Massachusetts, which always had secured religious liberty. With the self-righteousness that has always flourished in Massachusetts, Sargeant confidently explained: "The people have enjoyed civil & religious liberty for 100 years without interruption & beyond any other country, & it never was more secure to em than it is now by the constitution." Ibid., 143. On these instructions, the jury gave a verdict for the inhabitants of Princeton with costs. For another, less detailed report, see *Notes of Cases Decided in the Superior and Supreme Judicial Court of Massachusetts from 1772 to 1789—Taken by the Honble William Cushing . . . ,* fol. 40[v], Harvard Law School, Ms 4083.

[18] Supreme Judicial Court, Record Book, June–Nov. 1785, fols. 260[v]–261[r]. The session began October 25, and Backus records the date of the decision as October 26. See McLoughlin, *New England Dissent,* 1: 642–645.

At this second trial, Justice Sargeant told the jurors that Cutter could not have any claim because under Article III, "no Society that is not under corporate Power, is known in Law in this Commonwealth." Sargeant then more centrally said that the old tax laws (or at least the scheme established by them) were in force and consistent with Article III: "that ye Temporary Acts for the Quakers & Baptists Churchmen are still in full forse & that the Third Article is perfectly conformable to said Laws." Lest his instructions fall on unreceptive ears, the judge reminded "the Jewrors" that they "were obliged to determine our Cause upon such Principals." After the jurors found for the tax collectors, Cutter's pastor, Thomas Green, reported these details to Isaac Backus with dismay, complaining that "[t]he judges gave a most shocking arbitrary Exposition upon ye Third Article of ye Bill of Rights."[19] Regardless which of these various tax cases was arbitrary and which was correct, they all reveal the ease with which the judges examined the Constitution in the course of determining what legal taxing authority still survived from the defunct statutory scheme.

If dissenters could not avoid paying religious taxes under the Constitution, the next question was whether they could at least get their share of the proceeds under the state's purportedly ecumenical establishment. As already noted, many towns still followed the old statutory scheme in declining to distribute tax proceeds to churches that were not incorporated, and this remained an impediment even for religious dissenters who were willing to cooperate with the tax system. Baptists often rejected the incorporation of churches as a form of dependence on civil power, complaining that Christ's kingdom did not need to be chartered by the Commonwealth of Massachusetts, and notwithstanding that Baptist churches increasingly sought to escape their financial straits by petitioning the legislature for a corporate charter, they could not count on a receptive hearing.[20] Inevitably, therefore, the refusal of towns to distribute tax funds to unincorporated churches became the next constitutional question.

[19] Letter of Thomas Green to Isaac Backus (Oct. 28, 1784), Franklin Trask Library, Andover Newton Theological School, Isaac Backus Papers, Box 13. Cutter was represented by Sullivan and Lincoln. Backus recorded: "Judge Sargeant declared their old laws to be in force, and that they knew no society in this Commonwealth but corporate bodies, with whom Judge Sewal concurred, and the jury turned the case against the baptists the next day. The other judges said little upon the case." William G. McLoughlin, ed., *Diary of Isaac Backus,* 2: 1172–1173 (Oct. 30–Nov. 2, 1785) (Providence: Brown University, 1979). After this defeat, Backus and other Baptists met to discuss litigation strategy, and they decided that Green should bring an action to recover the money for the Baptists, so that the Baptists at least would not be paying for the Congregationalists. McLoughlin, *New England Dissent,* 1: 646. Murray's action, however, did more to clarify this issue.

[20] For incorporation, see McLoughlin, *New England Dissent,* 1: 644–651.

In 1786, in *Murray v. the Inhabitants of Gloucester,* the Supreme Judicial Court decided that the Constitution barred this sort of refusal to distribute tax proceeds, and the judges therefore once again looked to the Constitution to decide upon the authority of town actions in the vicinity of statutes. Unlike the lowly Baptist complainants, the Rev. John Murray enjoyed notoriety. Born in England, he became a Unitarian and even a Universalist at a time when this was scandalous, and to escape religious opposition he departed for America. He served for a while as a military chaplain and eventually became the head of a congregation in Gloucester that called itself the Independent Church of Christ. When the town in 1782 seized the goods of some of his congregants to satisfy religious taxes, Murray brought an *indebitatus assumpsit* to obtain the money collected from them. The case of *Murray v. Inhabitants of the First Parish in Gloucester* wound its way through the courts until in 1786 Murray finally prevailed at the Essex County Supreme Judicial Court. After trial on the general issue, and after hearing extensive arguments of law, the judges summed up the law for the jury. According to one of Murray's supporters, "[t]he first [judge] was ambiguous, the second so trammelled, and inarticulate, as to be scarcely understood; but the remaining three, have acquired a glory which will be as lasting as time."[21]

The last three presumably included Chief Justice William Cushing, whose instructions fortunately survive in his own report. Cushing began his opinion by explaining the constitutional positions taken by each side. In Murray's view, although he was the minister of an unincorporated or "voluntary" religious society, he was "entitled by the Constitution" to recover the money paid by his congregants. The inhabitants of Gloucester, in contrast, argued "that the 3d. article of the Bill of Rights relates throughout to bodies corporate and their religious teachers solely and not to voluntary societies." The old statutes had provided for a distribution of tax funds to incorporated religious societies, and according to the inhabitants of Gloucester, the Constitution's allusion to "bodies-politic" preserved this assumption. Having thus summarized the dispute, Cushing concluded that "with

[21] *Records of the Life of the Rev. John Murray,* 206–207, 210 (Boston: 1816). For a brief sketch of this complex case, see Cushing, "Notes on Disestablishment in Massachusetts," 175–180. Murray's supporters were especially pleased with Judge Dana, who said that "Mr. Murray comes within the description of the constitution, and has a right to require the money." Ibid., 211. The constitutional issue also arose in earlier incarnations of the case. For example, when the case came before the Supreme Judicial Court sitting in Salem in 1785, "the Judges delivered their respective opinions of the case as founded upon the third article of the Bill of Rights, and committed it to the Jury," but when "the next day, they came into Court . . . the Foreman declared, that they could not agree upon a verdict . . . the Court referred the decision of the cause to the next term." Salem (Nov. 8), *Salem Gazette* (Nov. 8, 1785).

the arguments of the pltffs' counsel I feel much more satisfied than with those of the Defts—as they correspond nearer to my belief of the views of the framers of the constitution."

Incidentally, Cushing acknowledged that "[s]ome inconvenience may possibly arise from either construction of this article of the Declaration of Rights." Yet "particular or extreme inconveniences are not so much to be regarded as the general principles on which the Constitution is founded." These "great objects" were "to secure to every subject toleration in matters of religion; to prevent any subordination among the different sects of protestants; and any unequal burthens in consequence of a difference in religious professions or sentiments." Even these principles, however, were not determinative, for "[t]o effect these objects express provisions are made in our declaration of rights—leaving little room for construction."[22]

Cushing therefore completed his analysis by relying on Articles II and III of the Constitution:

> We are therefore led to this conclusion that the 2d & 3d articles of the declaration of rights do allow every protestant christian to require his taxes to be paid over to the teacher on whose instructions he attends—with this limitation only that the teacher be of a different sect or denomination from the teacher of the town, precinct or parish in which he resides.[23]

[22] *John Murray v. The Inhabitants of the First Parish in Gloucester* (Essex County Supreme Judicial Court, June term 1786), *Notes of Cases decided in the Superiour and Supreme Judicial Courts of Massachusetts from 1772 to 1789—taken by the Honorable William Cushing,* fols. 54[v]–56[r], Harvard Law School, Ms 4083. In particular, Article III allowed each dissenter to have his money allocated to his own society, and this barred towns from adhering to the old statutory assumption that they were only to give tax proceeds to incorporated societies. Cushing recited the Constitution's words that "'all monies paid by the subject to the support of publick worship & of the publick teachers—shall, if he require it, be uniformly applied to the support of the publick teacher or teachers of his own religious sect or denomination.'" He then observed:

> Certainly there is nothing in this clause which limits the payment of monies assessed for the support of the publick teachers—to the teachers of religious bodies corporate only. If such had been the intention of the framers of this article—here would have been the natural place to have inserted the limitation.

He was therefore "of opinion that the words used in this clause . . . clearly allude to a separation from the regular establishment—if it may be so termed—; for the monies paid by the subject are to be uniformly applied to the support of the teacher of his own religious *sect* or denomination." Pursuing this point, he added: "Sect does not mean a corporate body—but rather a division from some corporate body." Ibid., fols. 57[r]–57[v]. (Cushing was knowledgeable about Article III from his participation in framing the Massachusetts Constitution and from his work in attempting to draft legislation for "[s]upport of public worship." A Division of the Laws ([1781]), Robert Treat Paine Papers, Reel 18.)

[23] Ibid., fol. 57[r].

Murray and his parishioners were very self-conscious of their role in defending constitutional freedom. Their critics thought the litigation un-Christian. *An Answer to a Piece Entitled, "An Appeal to the Impartial Publick, by an Association,"* 14 (Salem: 1785). Murray's

This was a jury instruction on a minister's claim for tax proceeds rather than a congregant's claim for damages, and Cushing therefore had no need to hold any act of the town of Gloucester (or any of its officers) unconstitutional. Instead, he held that the Constitution now required towns to distribute tax proceeds without regard to whether a church was incorporated, and what is of particular interest here, he did so notwithstanding any common law authority to withhold taxes from unincorporated churches that may have survived in the proximity of the old statutes. The jury deliberated for hours and in the evening returned to tell the Court they could not agree. Chief Justice Cushing, however, "with some asperity" sent them back, and they remained in deliberation through the night, until they came into Court the next morning and unanimously gave their verdict for Murray.[24]

This would not be the end of John Murray's encounters with the courts of Massachusetts. Nor would it settle the constitutional issues about religious taxes, incorporation, and establishment. On the contrary, few men and few issues would be more contentious.

Judicial office, however, was not controversial. There typically was no need in the Massachusetts religion cases to hold any legislative or executive act unconstitutional. Nonetheless, the cases are revealing, for the judges in these cases decided highly fraught constitutional questions in the vicinity of statutes without any hesitation.

---

religious society, however, declared: "We have been told that we ought to apply to the legislature for an act of Incorporation, as the only remedy against the oppression we complain of; but could we be assured that our petition would be most readily granted, yet we should feel ourselves highly criminal in making the application. Providence has so ordered it, that we should in the first instance be called upon to contend for those religious liberties preserved by our excellent Constitution." Rather than "fly to the law-makers," they therefore turned to "that great law made by the people to govern the legislature itself." [Eppes Sargent], *An Appeal to the Impartial Public by The Society of Christian Independents, Congregating in Glocester,* 31 (Boston: 1785).

[24] *Records of the Life of the Rev. John Murray,* 211.

Chronological Table of State Decisions

This table lists the primary state determinations examined in this volume. The table makes no pretense of enumerating all early state decisions on constitutional questions. Indeed, some of the decisions listed here obviously did not hold government acts unconstitutional, and some did not even resolve constitutional questions. It should be noted that the dates of the cases, in contrast to the resolutions and advisory opinions, refer to the term rather than the actual date.

State of North Carolina v. The Clerk of Perquimans County
North Carolina, Edenton District Superior Court, Nov. 1778

State of North Carolina v. The Clerk of Pasquotank County
North Carolina, Edenton District Superior Court, Nov. 1778

Holmes & Ketcham v. Walton
New Jersey, Supreme Court, Sept. 1780

Advisory opinion on Senate's power to examine county valuations
Massachusetts, Feb. 1781

Jennison v. Caldwell, et al.
Massachusetts, Supreme Judicial Court, Sept. 1781

Balkcom v. Wilkinson et al.
Massachusetts, Bristol County Inferior Court of Common Pleas, Mar. 1782

Walker v. Jennison
Massachusetts, Supreme Judicial Court, Sept. 1782

Commonwealth v. Caton et al.—a.k.a. The Case of the Prisoners
Virginia, Court of Appeals, Nov. 1782

Commonwealth v. Jennison
Massachusetts, Supreme Judicial Court, Apr. 1783

Commonwealth v. Bradish
Massachusetts, Essex County General Sessions of the Peace, July 1783

Advisory opinion on legislature's power to stay judicial proceedings
Massachusetts, c. 1783?

Resolution on county court's power to recommend appointments
Virginia, Middlesex County Court, Apr. 1784 and June 1788

Rutgers v. Waddington
New York City, Mayor's Court, Aug. 1784

Advisory opinion on legislature's power to fill vacancies in the Council
Massachusetts, Nov. 1784

Fairfax County Court Resolution on new commissions
Virginia, Fairfax County Court, Mar. 1785

Advisory opinion on privileges and immunities under Articles of Confederation
Massachusetts, June 1785

Jonathan Humphrey et al. v. Thomas Bidwell—a.k.a. The Symsbury Case
Connecticut, Superior Court, Aug. 1785

Cutter v. Frost et al.
Massachusetts, Supreme Judicial Court, Oct. 1785

Commonwealth v. Fowler
Virginia, Court of Appeals, Nov. 1785

Commonwealth v. Minns
Virginia, Court of Appeals, Nov. 1785

Resolution on legislature's power to remit and suspend fines
North Carolina, Wilmington District Superior Court, Dec. 1785

Wallace v. Tarlton
New Hampshire, Rockingham County Inferior Court, May 1786

Bartlett v. French
New Hampshire, Rockingham County Inferior Court, May 1786

MacGregore v. Furber
New Hampshire, Rockingham County Inferior Court, May 1786

Treferrin v. Cate
New Hampshire, Rockingham County Inferior Court, May 1786

Furber v. Mason
New Hampshire, Rockingham County Inferior Court, May 1786

Murray v. Inhabitants of the First Parish in Gloucester
Massachusetts, Supreme Judicial Court, June 1786

Duty v. Kelly & Wife
New Hampshire, Rockingham County Inferior Court, Aug. 1786

Duty v. Kelly
New Hampshire, Rockingham County Inferior Court, Aug. 1786

Trevett v. Weeden
Rhode Island, Newport County Superior Court, Sept. 1786

Seaver v. Lippett
Rhode Island, Providence Special Court, autumn 1786

Davis v. Young
New Hampshire, Rockingham County Inferior Court, Nov. 1786

Perkins v. Lord
New Hampshire, Strafford County Inferior Court, Feb. 1787

Horn v. Austin
New Hampshire, Strafford County Inferior Court, Feb. 1787

Bayard & Wife v. Singleton
North Carolina, New Bern District Superior Court, May 1787

Butler v. Gilman
New Hampshire, Strafford County Inferior Court, June 1787

Hills v. Mason
New Hampshire, Rockingham County Inferior Court, Aug. 1787

Advisory opinion on legislature's power to commute a punishment
Massachusetts, Nov. 1787

Resolution on District Court Act
Virginia, Court of Appeals, Apr. 1788

Resolution on county levy
Virginia, Fairfax County Court, Jan. 1789

Goddard v. Goddard & Metcalf
Massachusetts, Supreme Judicial Court, Feb. 1789

Resolution on act establishing the new Court of Appeals
Virginia, Court of Appeals, Mar. 1789

Ham, qui tam v. M'Claws & Wife
South Carolina, Superior Court, Oct. 1789

Resolution on court martial's power to impose fines for delinquencies
Virginia, Goochland County (?) Court Martial, Apr. 1790

Anonymous
New Hampshire, Rockingham County Inferior Court, Aug. 1790

Advisory opinion on the effect of a recess on an unsigned bill
Massachusetts, Mar. 1791

Gilman v. McClary
New Hampshire, Rockingham County Superior Court, Sept. 1791

The Pig Case
New Hampshire, Westmoreland County justice of the peace, early 1790s

Bowman & Others, Devisees of Cattel, v. Middleton
South Carolina, Court of Common Pleas, May 1792

Resolution on county court's power to recommend appointments
Virginia, York County Court, July 1792

Index